Microsoft® Exchange Server V5.0

Planning, Design, and Implementation

Microsoft® Exchange Server V5.0

Planning, Design, and Implementation

Tony Redmond

Digital Press
Boston • Oxford • Johannesburg • Melbourne • New Delhi • Singapore

Library of Congress Cataloging-in-Publication Data

Redmond, Tony, 1959–
    Microsoft exchange server V5.0 : planning, design, and implementation / Tony Redmond.
         p.   cm.
    Includes index.
    ISBN 1–55558–189–7 (alk. paper)
    1. Microsoft Exchange server. 2. Client/server computing.
  I. Title.
  QA76.9.C55R424 1997
  005.7'13769—dc21   97–19416
                                          CIP

British Library Cataloguing-in-Publication Data

A catalogue record for this book is available from the British Library.

The publisher offers special discounts on bulk orders of this book. For information, please contact:

Manager of Special Sales
Butterworth–Heinemann
313 Washington Street
Newton, MA 02158–1626
Tel: 617-928-2500
Fax: 617-928-2620

For information on all Digital Press publications available, contact our World Wide Web home page at: **http://www.bh.com/digitalpress**

Order number: EY-W085E-DP

10 9 8 7 6 5 4 3 2 1

Design and composition by ReadyText, Bath, UK
Printed in the United States of America

Contents

Foreword

There is a group of people for whom the years 1990 to 1996 will be remembered as their version of the Second World War. For those were the years when the Exchange development team and a group of incredibly loyal customers worked to deliver on the vision of what we promised our customers and our colleagues.

I wrote a set of slides in July 1990 detailing the Microsoft messaging strategy and the functionality that we committed to deliver to our customers. We are all very proud of the fact that we delivered on every word on those slides. Yes, it took us a lot longer than we thought it would, but nobody did it any better, any faster. It was just a really complicated thing to do. It was our Second World War because we did not know what we were letting ourselves in for at the beginning. And because while we were in it we always thought that the end was just around the corner.

And because with the exception of some who bailed out when it got bad we all knew we would go onto the end, because it was just that important. We lived all those years with the burden of knowing that thousands of customers all over the world had put their careers on the line for us. And what a terrible burden that was. Knowing that all those customers were trusting us to come through for them. As the Worldwide Product Manager, I was responsible for every single customer worldwide who was prepared to wait. That responsibility was far worse than the derision of our colleagues in Microsoft. And that was pretty bad.

In 1995 Bill Gates was asked what the biggest disappointment of his year was and his reply was "The failure of the Exchange team to ship their product." We were booed at Company meetings. "How hard can it be?" was the comment of many of our colleagues. Well, really really hard; that is why it took so long.

For many of us the day we shipped Exchange Server 4.0 was the happiest day of our career because we were "free at last." But a week later many of us signed up for another round and Exchange Server 5.0 shipped three weeks before Exchange's first birthday, containing another 300 man years of development. DIGITAL was one of the customers who helped us design and deliver on the technology both then and now. DIGITAL was one of the "Bravehearts," the forty official customers who ran mission critical messaging on beta versions of Exchange server, starting over one year before we shipped. (Of course we know there were many more unofficial customers doing it too.)

And when we finally shipped they were one of the three customers who deployed over thirty thousand users of Exchange Server before we reached our one year anniversary. They validated Exchange by immediately embarking on a global deployment which is now over 50% completed and already running across five continents and 24 countries.

I maintain a global customer deployment document and have done for the last two years. DIGITAL started reporting deployment figures to me in July of 1995. Shortly after we shipped in March of 1996 their deployment rate took them to the number one slot in that document and they have maintained that position for over a year now. Of course certain other larger companies who have more employees (John, you know who you are!) constantly taunt DIGITAL with the fact that it is only a matter of time before they run out of employees to deploy Exchange to and so are overtaken by companies who have more of them!

DIGITAL's Exchange deployment has now overtaken Microsoft's in number of seats (though probably not in traffic—we send more than 2.5 million messages a day on Exchange including over 150,000 messages to the Internet). Yes, we ran out of employees to give mailboxes to! We actually finished our Exchange Server deployment within Microsoft before Exchange shipped. The whole deployment was done on beta code.

DIGITAL runs a production environment of over 40,000 seats of Exchange Server. This is currently the largest operational Exchange Server implementation in the world. So they bring to the table not only their years of experience selling and maintaining their own enterprise messaging systems but their experience gained through installing and maintaining the largest Exchange deployment in the world. There is no other organization in the world that has more employees involved today in designing and deploying customer implementations of Exchange Server. And DIGITAL continues to participate in the design process of Exchange Server. DIGITAL provided more feedback on the LDAP implementation in Exchange Server 5.0 than all other customers put together. Tony brings this wealth of expertise gained by DIGI-

TAL over the years with their messaging products and over the past two years with Exchange to you in this book. Here you will find the practical and in depth information that you need to design a successful implementation of Exchange Server in your company. Plan carefully. Exchange Server is a huge product.

Shortly before ship some of us were reviewing the documentation together. We ground to a halt on some point that nobody in the room was sure of. "Most of the experts on the project are in this room." I said: "Surely somebody must be able to resolve this." The development lead for Admin turned to me and said: "Elaine, I can't know any more, Exchange Server is bigger than my head." This became the catchphrase of the project. Exchange got too broad for one human brain. We all learned to specialize and accept that we would always be learning about Exchange. So carry on reading books, join the list server, attend Microsoft Tech-Ed and the annual Exchange Deployment conference. You will never be able to know enough, there will always be more to learn. I learn more every day. In Exchange Server 5.0 we bring you our current thinking driven by our customers on the functionality you need to deploy Enterprise messaging in your organizations.

Keep telling us what you think of our technology, where it works, where it does not. We plan to keep on improving it based on your feedback. In a year's time Tony will be writing another book around the new functionality we shipped as a result of you telling us what we need to do better. But if we can leave you one message it is this. We did what we told you we would do. Many of you helped, we thanked you at the time and will always be grateful. You know who you are. If you are interested in who "we" are you will find us on the Exchange Concepts and Planning Video that was part of the documentation kit for Exchange Server 4.0. As the credits roll there is footage of the weekly Exchange "let's carry on until we get it done" meeting that took place 3pm every Friday in the atrium of the development building. There you will see the people who designed, wrote, tested, and documented the code that was running on two million desktops within one year of ship.

Took years, really works.

Elaine K. Sharp

Worldwide Messaging Server Product Manager
Microsoft Corporation, March 1992 to October 1996

Preface

A practical approach

Microsoft, along with many other attributes, is probably the world's best marketing company when it comes to PC software. It is very easy to fall into the habit of believing everything that comes out of Microsoft HQ in Redmond, Washington (I think the name of the town is so appropriate...), and sometimes I feel that the books written about Microsoft products occasionally (or even a lot) fall into the trap of wearing rose-tinted glasses.

This is not a book lauding the virtues and benefits of the Microsoft Exchange Server, covering the V4.0 and V5.0 releases. It is, I hope, a hard-nosed and practical look at what the server is good at along with some views on the places where the server, in my view, falls down. All furnished with a pragmatic approach to the business of implementing Exchange and its clients within corporate messaging infrastructures.

Life doesn't give you many opportunities to go over old ground, but authors get the chance to rethink as they write books about new versions of products or technology in general. This book covers some of the material from my Exchange V4.0 book, but the text has been reviewed from top to bottom to emphasize points that have become clearer in the last year, to reshape opinions, or merely to add new details. The Exchange V4.0 book was completed and sent to the printers in May 1996, shortly after Exchange V4.0 was released. This isn't an excuse for the errors that are in that book (the challenge for the reader is to find those errors) as the fault for their inclusion is all mine. I hope that the errors have been corrected the second time round, although there's always room for new errors! Getting things right on the second attempt is not a trait specific to authors. Politicians are also prone to clarification, given the opportunity. One famous Irish politician under pressure from journalists to explain some error he had made in the past, changed his story and referred to the changes as being due to "mature reflection." My views on Exchange, how to best deploy it in different situations, and where its capabilities are leading us to have all changed in the last year. Maybe the changes made in this book are also due to mature reflection.

I have deliberately neglected the opportunity to write in detail about the various clients that can be connected to an Exchange server. Clients are mentioned whenever appropriate and a brief overview of their functionality is included. Overall, I believe the server is much more interesting than the clients, and the successful implementation of multiple Exchange servers distributed across a networked landscape presents enough issues to challenge even experienced electronic messaging specialists. The temptation to recycle the contents of the Exchange documentation has also been avoided. I should note that the documentation provided with Exchange is comprehensive and often illuminating. Much good advice is contained therein, and anyone who wants to work with Exchange should invest the necessary time to carefully peruse the documentation.

I work for Digital Equipment Corporation (referred to as DIGITAL from here on). There have certainly been a wide variety of views within different parts of DIGITAL over the last year or so. As a long-standing DIGITAL employee I'd very much like to see Exchange being implemented on Windows NT systems powered by the high-speed Alpha (sometimes called AXP) CPU. We also have our own messaging products on OpenVMS and UNIX and the competition between the different messaging factions is interesting to observe. I like to think that I'm a practical kind of person and I believe customers come to DIGITAL looking for clear and unbiased advice about all sorts of products including Exchange, and expect our consulting staff to deliver. A lot of the content in this book comes from that background and the aim is to help customers evaluate how well Exchange fits into their plans, with or without an existing messaging system in place, and then proceeding from that point to implement solutions working with Exchange in one way or another. The fact that DIGITAL now has one of the largest, if not the largest, Exchange operational organizations outside Microsoft, has added a great deal of experience and knowledge contained in this book. When I starting writing about Exchange, DIGITAL, like so many of the early adapters, was still struggling with issues like its network and the Windows NT domain infrastructure. Since mid 1996 the rollout of Exchange has progressed smoothly within DIGITAL, albeit with some hiccups. Knowledge of those problems and my personal observations gained from being a consumer of the Exchange implementation inside DIGITAL have flavored or changed my opinions!

I strongly believe that the experience gained through working with many other messaging systems in the last fifteen years will prove valuable during enterprise-scale implementations of Exchange. The longer I work with Exchange the more apparent it is that the majority of the lessons learned from the deployments of other corporate messaging system can be taken over and applied to Exchange. There are obvious differences, such as the interaction between Windows NT and Exchange, but establishing a good base for the deployment of any system is a good initial step to take, and using experience to avoid the pot-holes waiting along the road to trap the unwary is only sensible. I imagine that some of the views expressed in this book will conflict with those held by others. I'm not always positive about Exchange, but then again, I'm not always positive about any product (software and others) that I use. You've just got to make the best of what you've got.

The aim of this book

Writing a book about new computer software poses questions about the shape and content of the book to authors. I think it is impossible to attempt to write the definitive book about any software until that software has stood the test of time in the hands of normal users and system administrators. Exchange has a couple of years to go before that stage is reached. Above all else, it is the experience of working with software in production environments that generates the interesting parts of many books.

Even as Exchange enters its second year in production use it is still a relatively new e-mail server. I have attempted to document my impressions of the software and the issues and challenges involved in its implementation in product messaging environments. As such, this book is full of ideas and opinions, filled in with background information such as the SMTP versus X.400 debate that I hope will help you decide whether Exchange fits into your messaging plans. The target audience is, I think, composed of system administrators and planners, consultants, and anyone else who's interested in making their own assessment of Exchange, rather than people who want a set of detailed "how do I do that" lists covering every aspect of the operation and deployment of Exchange.

The sub-title for the book emphasizes corporate messaging environments. This gives you a good guide to my own experience and background which is heavily biased towards large-scale messaging projects involving thousands of clients and tens or even hundreds of servers. I think some very interesting challenges exist in the implementation of client/server based messaging systems in the corporate sector. A lot of this book focuses on those challenges rather than the somewhat easier, in my opinion, task of upgrading a Microsoft Mail Post Office to an Exchange server. Maybe this attitude reflects certain arrogance on my part, but thinking about the issues involved in corporate implementations has been a major and compelling reason for me to write this book. This book is based firmly on the experience I have gained in helping customers around the world think about all aspects involved in the implementation of Exchange. I've enjoyed the opportunity to engage my brain in discussing, reviewing, and hopefully solving some of the difficulties encountered along the way. As I've learned I have tried to capture the essence of the solution (many solutions are specific and even particular to an individual customer) so that others can learn too. By its very nature any book represents a fixed point in the evolution of an author's thinking and opinions on a subject, and the changes made between the Exchange V4.0 book and now demonstrate that learning is a never-ending process, especially in such a dynamic industry. Many topics are covered in a paragraph or two and I cannot and will not pretend that this is always enough information, especially if you are up to your neck in a large implementation project. For example, I have not been able to do the necessary research into the new Lotus cc:Mail connector to be able to discuss it at the level of detail that I would be happy to include here. Treat these topics as placeholders, items to be checked out and included in a project plan, or even calling for more extensive research through the formal documentation and white papers written by Microsoft. The Exchange Server administration guide, concepts and planning guide, and white paper on Windows NT domains are all essential reading for people involved in implementations. The "concepts" video included in the documentation set is also useful. Microsoft's TechNet CDs are another rich source of information and contain a wide range of articles and tools for Exchange Server. A TechNet subscription is a very useful tool for anyone dealing with Windows NT, Windows 95, Exchange or the other Back-Office products. If you're looking for a book that details the behind-the-scenes stories of how Exchange was developed don't read on. You won't find grand explanations about the philosophy surrounding Exchange, or even the reasons why some design decisions were made. I simply don't know these things. In the same vein this book does not attempt to provide step by step instructions for performing system management or other operations with the server. That type of information is best left to the formal documentation provided with Exchange, and does not need to be duplicated here.

Reading books from different authors will generate a wide spectrum of opinion about any topic and Exchange is no different. I like reading books to occasionally stop, think, and reflect on the issues presented by the people who've taken the time to sit down and analyze the product they describe. I suggest that you read the book with an open mind. Feel free to disagree with my views and insert your own. Books covering software topics are static sources of information. The content is frozen approximately six to ten weeks before publication date, and for this reason information contained in books can age rapidly once they're published. It is inevitable that new versions of the server, add-ons for Exchange (server or clients), and service packs will appear over time, so keep this point in mind as you read. Use the advice, opinions, and conclusions presented here in conjunction with your own experience and knowledge of the systems, hardware and software, in use in your company as inputs to the creation of your own implementation plan. Those who write in books or magazines know little about what you or your organization actually does, so never accept the written word as final. Make your own mind up.

My own Exchange environment

It's difficult to write a book in a pure vacuum. Day to day experience with any system or product is a great trainer. I work within a DIGITAL consulting group that's focused on large-scale messaging deployments for major corporate customers. The majority of our projects involve Exchange and DIGITAL's own messaging technologies, including ALL-IN-1, MailWorks for UNIX, TeamLinks, MAILbus 400, and AltaVista Directory Services as well as systems such as PROFS, Lotus Notes, HP Open Mail, and many others. To back up our consultants we have our own operational environment maintained separately from the "official" DIGITAL Exchange implementation. Our operational system is heterogeneous, distributed in an organization that spans multiple sites (13 at last count) across the world, and accommodates all of the technology we implement for customers. The screen shots used for illustrations throughout this book come from our production Exchange servers and connectors to X.400, the Internet, and Microsoft Mail. There are no pilot, test, or prototype servers in use and everything is based on the experience gained of putting Exchange to work as a production messaging system. If you look carefully at the screen shots you'll realize that our production systems are imperfect. In other words, they don't fully reflect the way that we might have liked to bring the systems into production had we the time and luxury of a fully planned and designed implementation. The names given to our Windows NT servers, for instance, follow no naming convention. In acknowledging such imperfections I suspect that our systems are not too far removed from many others in use throughout the world. The important thing is that we have learned from the mistakes we made putting Exchange into production, and most of the mistakes are noted here so that you can avoid the same pitfalls.

Building towards success

There's little doubt in my mind that Exchange is and will continue to be a successful product. Microsoft estimates that there are between seven and nine million users of Microsoft Mail and three million users of the original Schedule+ product. Using these figures, albeit in the knowledge that creating an accurate count of the users of any product is nearly impossible once sales go past the million mark, a quick calculation reveals that if there is an average of 25 clients connected to each Microsoft Mail Post Office there are some 28,000 post offices ready to be upgraded to Exchange, and this represents the major initial market. With these numbers in mind it is clear that while server upgrades will produce a nice revenue stream the really lucrative income will pour into Microsoft's coffers through client upgrades.

Apart from Microsoft Mail, the other initial markets for Exchange include migrations of other PC LAN-based e-mail systems such as Lotus cc:Mail as well as the direct replacement of obsolete mainframe mail systems like IBM PROFS. With such a wide set of targets to aim for Exchange will be successful. Growing into such well-established and lucrative markets is enough to quickly achieve success and establish a healthy installed base, certainly enough to give Microsoft the time to iron out the bugs that inevitably appear in the first releases of any complex and feature-rich product (even though Microsoft referred to the first release of Exchange as version 4.0, from a factual perspective it was a version one product). New versions of Exchange should continue to exhibit increased stability and throughput and keep the server on the short list for anyone looking for a solid base to build distributed corporate messaging infrastructures. The whole world of electronic mail is going through a boom period right now, and the success generated by Exchange in the corporate sphere is shared by other messaging systems. The technical community has nearly always been comfortable with electronic mail and the benefits it could bring to businesses. People within the technical community have been using electronic mail to overcome the barriers imposed by distance or time since the late 1970s, and a whole sub-culture built up around e-mail, but it's taken time for the concept to spread. Prompted by the explosive success of the Internet, everyone outside the IT community now has a basic understanding of electronic mail and are willing to try it out for themselves. Many millions of new mailboxes are added to the Internet every year, and counts of between 32 million and 60 million have been reported in 1995. Of course, no-one can physically count all the mailboxes in active use, so numbers like these have to be treated as estimates that have been arrived at with a great deal of deduction and a fair amount of "finger in the air" calculation.

Apart from making electronic mail more available to ordinary people, the Internet has also greatly driven down the investment required to go on-line with the Web or access other Internet resources. In most cases a simple low monthly payment is sufficient to enable connectivity into the big bad world of electronic communications. All of this makes electronic mail an exciting area to work in right now, and I hope that some of the excitement filters through the pages of this book.

Acknowledgments

All my previous books were much easier to write than this one. From one perspective it is easier to write about a new product, possibly because the level of knowledge available within the general computing community is lower than after the product has been available for some time. However, because I have tried to discover the potential pitfalls involved in implementation, the task of discovery and documentation has been harder, albeit more satisfying and generally a more elucidating experience. I have been greatly helped by many people, all of whom deserve my thanks.

Many people within DIGITAL and Microsoft who helped in one way or another as I struggled to come to grips with Exchange and assemble the information contained in the book. There's a long list of people to acknowledge and I'm sure that I will miss someone along the line. With this in mind I'd like to thank Frank Clonan, Pierre Bijaoui, Geoff Robb, Bill Rafferty, Kieran McCorry, Kevin Gallagher, John B. Horan, Eric Purcell, Peter McQuillan, and Pat Baxter. In particular I would like to acknowledge the special contribution made by Stan Foster. Stan is one of the internal messaging architects for DIGITAL and has been up to his neck in the ins and outs of the implementation of Exchange within DIGITAL. As such he has accumulated a wide range of practical knowledge about the good and bad in Exchange and has been very willing to share his experience with me. Stan also corrected many of the mistakes I made as the book was written.

I'd also like to acknowledge the contributions of my external reviewers, people who are either responsible for the deployment of Exchange in large corporate sites or those who advise on electronic mail technology in general. In this category I'd like to thank Chris Blandford, Sohrab Mansourian, and Don Vickers.

Elaine Sharp was the voice of Exchange for many people in the 1993–96 period when she managed the Exchange early adapters program. Elaine and I didn't get on so well at first, and certainly clashed over the content of my Exchange V4.0 book. Since then our relationship is much improved and I'd like to thank her for her efforts to "inform" me and improve the book's contents. We may not still agree on everything, but at least the arguments are good humored now. Brian Valentine, the General Manager of the Exchange development group, handled my queries with patience and made sure that most were answered. There are still a few outstanding! Mike Cash, International Publisher of Digital Press, hounded me to write the book and eventually succeeded. Once the decision was made to proceed Mike provided as much encouragement as an author would hope for from a publisher. Elizabeth McCarthy, the editor who handled the production process, made me meet my deadlines and coordinated everything in a most efficient manner. Finally, Graham Douglas of ReadyText handled all the complexities of taking the book from Word for Windows files into print. He also made sure that all the changes I wanted to make while the book was in production were inserted in the right place.

In closing let me note that all the errors in the book are mine. No-one else can claim responsibility. All I can offer in defense of any error is the simple fact that they are honest mistakes generated during my own experience gained working with Exchange. Exchange is a big product with lots of interesting (and some not so interesting) challenges for people interested in deploying it into a networked, heterogeneous messaging environment. I hope you have as much fun meeting that challenge as I've had. Whatever you do, keep the thought in mind that Exchange is only a software product and life is much more interesting than any one product can be. Let's go forward on that note.

Tony Redmond

The author invites comments on the content of the book. Please send e-mail to:

```
Tredmond@mail.dec.com
```

Introducing Microsoft Exchange Server

1.1　The Exchange program

Microsoft Exchange Server represents a new departure for Microsoft messaging products. Instead of a situation where it is enough to be able to send electronic messages to other users connected to a common system, the promise is held out of "Information Exchange," defined by Microsoft as the ability for people to share and manage information they need with anyone, anywhere, anytime. Of course, you need to be connected into the program before you can do all this, and, in one way, that's what this book is all about.

"Exchange" is often applied as a general catch-all title for the integrated suite of client and server electronic mail products released by Microsoft. It's important to differentiate between the clients and server because each stands on its own, linked by a common application programming interface (MAPI, Microsoft's Messaging Application Programming Interface). You don't have to use clients created by Microsoft with Exchange server, and you can connect Microsoft clients to other servers.

Exchange is viewed as a very strategic product within Microsoft. Developing a high-capacity robust mail server with client and gateway connections is not an easy task. Providing good migration facilities to accommodate the needs of an installed base (in this case, Microsoft Mail) adds complexity to the task, as does the requirement to build for an international market. To the end of 1995 some 800 man-years[1] had been used to develop the many millions of lines of code necessary to build Exchange Server and its clients. A massive development effort continues to keep Exchange ahead of its competitors. Sometimes, as we'll discuss later on, the rate of change enforced by the rapid pace of development poses a unique challenge for deployment teams.

---

[1]　Statistic supplied by Microsoft at the Fall DECUS conference in December 1995.

As large as it is, the massive Exchange code base does not represent the work done in associated development groups within Microsoft, such as that to develop the MAPI architecture and to make some necessary changes to the Windows NT operating system itself. All in all, the whole effort to bring Exchange to market has been enormous.

It's fair to say that Exchange was just about to ship for quite a long time. Never has a messaging product gone through quite such a long gestation, although I think it fair to say that the delay in the release date allowed both Windows NT and Exchange to mature to a point where both exhibit the qualities necessary for deployment in heavy-duty sites. Microsoft first started to reveal its plans for a high-end messaging and information server to the industry in 1993, but the complexities encountered during the development process contributed to the delayed release. Exchange was in beta test for 2.5 years and through seven different beta versions released to an ever-growing set of customers willing to undergo the trials and tribulations of working with beta software. To complete the trivial pursuit section I'll note in passing that during development Exchange Server had an array of code names including Spitfire, Touchdown, Firefox, and Mercury. The first version of Exchange eventually shipped in March 1996.

Exchange is designed to compete in corporate electronic mail markets. By their very nature corporate implementations tend to be international, so the fact that Exchange can run in English, French, German, and Japanese, and support clients running in 24 different languages is important. Any Exchange server can support any Exchange client no matter what language the client operates in, so a single Exchange server running English could, for instance, support the requirements of a Swiss installation where clients might run in English, French, German, and Italian. The internationalization of Exchange is based on the UNICODE base established by Windows NT itself.

1.1.1   The Exchange value proposition

New products coming to market for the first time must create a value proposition before customers will consider a purchase. This fact is as true about software applications as it is in respect of any other product. If it weren't, then any new product which appeared would instantly gain market share and acceptability. As we all know, while marketing executives might hope that their products would succeed, not all products do.

The value proposition put forward by Exchange can be broken down into a small number of succinct points:

- A strong set of electronic mail functionality for users, system administrators, and programmers
- Good security
- Highly integrated system administration
- A wide range of easily installed and configured connectors (gateways) to other messaging systems
- A building block approach to messaging infrastructures beginning with individual servers and growing right up to distributed networks of servers accommodating many thousands of users
- A distributed and largely self-managing directory
- A distributed document repository (public folders)
- Exploitation of the electronic mail infrastructure through mail-enabled applications and electronic forms

All provided in a reasonably priced, easy to install package.

The growing influence of Windows NT as a major operating system provides one of the major reasons why the value proposition put forward by Exchange is attractive to customers. Windows NT has developed rapidly over the last few years to a stage where it can provide a single-login, location-independent infrastructure onto which enterprises can layer and deploy distributed applications such as Exchange.

The evolution of TCP/IP to become the de facto protocol for networking is also an important point because much of the fundamental building blocks for TCP/IP-based distributed computing are included in the base Windows NT operating system. Off-site access for users is also facilitated by in-built standard remote access services (RAS). Microsoft's obvious dedication to the task of making Windows NT the operating system of choice for corporate computing is evident by the speed with which new and important technologies are built into Windows NT.

Apart from the growing feature list incorporated into the operating system, a number of trends have emerged in the recent past to support Windows NT. Among the most important of these are:

- The level of technical difficulty experienced in the migration of Novell NetWare V3.11 LANs to NetWare V4.0 (or above) has caused many companies to review their methods of providing shared file and print services to PC users. Windows NT provides excellent file and print services and quite a number of NetWare V3.11 installations have moved over to Windows NT, figuring that the move to NT is easier than an upgrade to NetWare V4.

- The opportunity exists to replace some large database applications running on mainframe and mini-computers with equivalent applications built around high-end Windows NT servers. Because of the huge disparity in hardware purchase and maintenance costs the financial equation is usually if not always highly favorable, even when the cost of migrating the application is factored in.

- Applications designed around the client/server model mean that the power of PC desktops can be leveraged in a much more powerful and cost-effective manner than the situation where PCs act as expensive terminal emulators for monolithic centralized application systems.

- Generally PCs (using the broadest possible definition of the term) have become all pervasive on the desktop. Video terminals and workstations still exist and there's a good population of low-end older PCs to deal with as well, but steadily dropping hardware costs and escalating performance levels mean that users receive much more "bang for their buck" than ever before. System management and administration must follow the dispersed PCs to regain control over applications and user environments before they disappear from sight.

The combination of Windows NT, which provides a common software platform for clients and servers, and highly functional applications, such as Exchange and the other components of the Microsoft BackOffice program, offers the potential to achieve great benefits for companies. Achieving those benefits and realizing the real potential of Windows NT is the challenge for those charged with the planning, design, and implementation of Windows NT and Exchange deployments.

1.2   A quick overview of Exchange

Microsoft Exchange Server is tightly integrated into the Windows NT operating system, taking full advantage of the multitasking and multithreaded attributes of the operating system. System management and administration is integrated directly into base system components to make life easier all round. You can, for example, create a mailbox for a new or existing user directly from the Windows NT account administration tool. Possibly more important are the facts that Exchange is layered directly on top of the Windows NT network and security models, so clearly if you haven't managed to get these items sorted out you won't be in a position to even think about implementing Exchange anytime soon.

We're just a couple of pages into the book but already the most fundamental and important point about any Exchange implementation has been made. That is, of course, the complete and total reliance on the Windows NT operating system. Anyone intending to do anything serious with Exchange must understand that Windows NT is the foundation stone the messaging infrastructure is built upon. A quickly put together or ill-considered implementation of Windows NT will result in a structure like a house built of cards—pretty to look at, but liable to complete, sudden, and catastrophic collapse. Microsoft cannot be blamed for not telling people to create a solid Windows NT infrastructure before attempting to implement Exchange. The message is repeated time and time again in very clear terms in all the technical white papers on the subject issued by Microsoft since 1994[2].

The close working relationship between Windows NT and Exchange implies that a certain degree of competence with Windows NT is required from anyone associated with the design or implementation of Exchange. This experience is not acquired by running SETUP.EXE, the ubiquitous Windows installation program to perform the 30-minute installation of Exchange, followed by a quick client upgrade for a Windows 95 PC. These activities will result in an operational server and client pair, but that's hardly the same as a corporate-standard messaging system. Ideally in-house staff or external consultants should be certified as Windows NT system engineers through the Microsoft Certified Professional[3] program.

While this book introduces many Windows NT operational concepts, and discusses some of those concepts to a certain degree, more knowledge than is contained here is needed before a full-scale implementation of Exchange can be approached with confidence. The Windows NT Resource Kit (an optional extra available from Microsoft) is particularly useful in this respect.

Of course, tight integration into the Windows NT operating system is a double-edged sword. The advantages gained (great system management) can only be achieved if Windows NT is going to be your preferred platform. If you want to use anything else like OpenVMS or any variant of UNIX then Exchange is not going to be very interesting at all.

---

[2]   Copies of the white papers are available from http://www.microsoft.com/exchange/ or from the Microsoft Technet (Technical Information Network) CD-ROM. Technet CD-ROMs are issued monthly to subscribers. The subscription fee is not high and the information gained is well worthwhile.

[3]   Classes covering Exchange are available from Microsoft ATECs (Authorized Training and Education Centers). A certification exam covering Exchange is included in the Microsoft Certified Professional curriculum and exam schedule.

The major pieces or services that collectively make up Exchange are:

- *The Message Transfer Agent (MTA)* used to route messages to other MTAs, either another Exchange server or what Microsoft charmingly terms "foreign" X.400 (1984 or 1988) MTAs. While its basic role is to interchange messages with other Exchange servers, the MTA also serves as a connectivity engine, which can be used to link Exchange to other different types of mail systems. The connectivity engine uses a series of "connectors" that understand the interconnectivity and formatting requirements of other mail systems to bridge between the raw database format used internally by Exchange. Out-of-the-box connectors are available for X.400, SMTP, and Microsoft Mail systems, and all are packaged in the Exchange "Enterprise Edition."

- *The Directory Store*, a collection of all the data (names and connection information) relating to the Exchange organization (a collection of sites and servers, or individual computers running Exchange) together with user account information and shared resources such as distribution lists and "custom recipients." All Exchange servers in the same organization share a single replicated directory. There is no chaining or referral as would be found in the more traditional model of a distributed directory. All queries are resolved against a local copy of the distributed directory.

- *The Information Store*, a structured repository broken down into two distinct sections. The first stores personal data for users, grouped into folders, while the second holds all the information available in public folders. The repositories are implemented as relational databases, optimized to store the type of non-structured data classically found in messaging or electronic file cabinet systems. The Information Store is not a passive repository. It takes care of public folder replication and delivers any messages addressed to users located on the same server. The database technology used by the Information Store is similar in many respects to that applied to transaction processing applications and provides advanced features such as the capability to automatically recover transactions (messages) from logs should problems occur with the database. On-line backup is also incorporated, allowing users to work while system administrators take care of daily housekeeping. To my knowledge, these features are not found in the file system or database used by any other high-end messaging system, and are, in effect, a significant competitive advantage for Exchange. See the discussion about the database technology used by Exchange beginning on page 239 for more detailed information.

■ *The Exchange Administrator and System Attendant* programs provide system management facilities for an Exchange server. These can be broadly defined in activities such as creating new user accounts (mailboxes) that require manual intervention, and those that are carried out in the background; for instance, the monitoring of connections between different servers. Manual tasks are performed with the Administrator program, but one of Exchange's most impressive features is the level of automated management carried out by the System Administrator.

All of these components run as multi-threaded Windows NT services executing their functions independently of each other. All of the services used by Exchange are managed using standard Windows NT utilities, such as the "Services" option that can be invoked from the Control Panel applet. Other aspects of Exchange, such as the management of the contents of the directory and information stores, are managed through the Exchange administration program.

In addition to the base services, Exchange can make use of a number of optional components, not all of which will be operational on every server. These include the Directory Synchronizer, a connector to handle messages going out into the Internet, the Key Management server (to control message encryption and decryption), the Microsoft Mail connector, and the Schedule+ Free/Busy connector. Third party gateways (called connectors in Exchange-speak), such as those that link into older IBM mainframe-based e-mail systems like PROFS, SNADS, MEMO, and OfficeVision complete the comprehensive functionality line-up.

Figure 1.1 *The basic structure of the Microsoft Exchange Server*

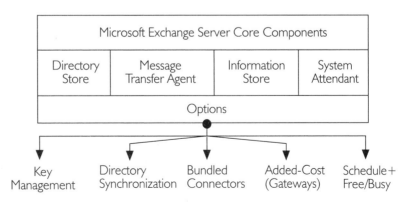

Clearly, sites running existing mail systems will have to pay special attention to directory synchronization. Microsoft provides synchronization tools for Microsoft Mail systems, but, as we'll discuss later on, synchronizing with other sources of directory data is not accomplished as easily.

1.2.1   Packaging

Microsoft has adopted a building block approach for Exchange packaging to allow people to purchase only the parts of the server that they really need. The different packages available for Exchange are described in Table 1.1. Microsoft is a global company and local market conditions may dictate different packaging. Pricing also differs from country to country and special offers may be made available from time to time. Contact your local Microsoft office or reseller for up-to-date information.

Table 1.1   *The different packages available for Microsoft Exchange Server*

Package	Functionality
Microsoft Exchange Server V5.0 (standard edition)	Basic server package including all the components necessary to install a single server—public and private information stores, Schedule+, directory service, the MTA, Microsoft Mail connector, Internet Mail Server, Lotus cc:Mail connector, Active Server components, Internet News Service, Electronic Forms Designer, the administration program, and the migration wizard. Software for the Exchange (Windows and Macintosh) and Outlook clients is also included. This edition includes 5 client access licenses.
Microsoft Exchange Connector	Required to link multiple Exchange servers together to form an integrated messaging system. The connector allows an Exchange server to join an existing Exchange site and/or to connect with other sites. Functionality added with this connector includes public folder and directory replication, encryption control through the Key Management server and digital signatures, and the Remote Access Server connector.
Microsoft Exchange Internet Mail Service (previously called the Internet Mail Service)	Required to connect an Exchange server to the Internet, using the Internet Simple Mail Transport Protocol (SMTP) to send and receive messages from other Exchange servers or other SMTP-compliant messaging systems. The connector includes support for the MIME protocol for exchanging multi-format files. This component was separate in V4.0, but bundled in all editions of Exchange V5.0.

Table 1.1   *The different packages available for Microsoft Exchange Server (continued)*

Package	Functionality
Microsoft Exchange X.400 connector	Required to allow an Exchange server to connect to other X.400-compliant messaging systems, or to use an X.400 backbone to link Exchange servers together, including the ability to connect servers within a single site.
Microsoft Exchange Server, Enterprise Edition	All of the functionality included in the standard edition and all the connectors that are separately available (site connector and X.400 connector) bundled into one package designed for corporate messaging deployments. This edition includes 25 client access licenses.

The choice presented by the different packages allows people to start small with a single server and then grow through additional servers, or by adding the different connectors to meet their messaging requirements. Those charged with corporate deployments will probably select the enterprise edition straightaway, if only because the enterprise edition is a very convenient way of getting all the base functionality required by large-scale deployments in a single package. Corporate deployments always seem to require some special items, so the enterprise edition doesn't hold the solution to all problems, but it's a great start.

Remember that client access licenses are required before any client can connect to an Exchange server. Some of the packages include a number of client access licenses, but it's unlikely that there'll be enough for all the clients you want to operate.

Generally speaking, installations running Microsoft Mail post offices (DOS) covered by the Microsoft Select maintenance program will receive upgrades to Exchange on a one to one basis. Client licenses maintained under the same program will also be upgraded. Select maintenance was never offered for Microsoft Mail for Macintosh, so Apple fans will have to pay for a new server. Various contractual limitations and different business conditions apply from country to country, so it's wise to check with Microsoft locally to determine exactly what will be upgraded and what additional components you'll need to buy in order to move to Exchange.

1.2.2   New versions of Exchange on the horizon

The development of Exchange continues at a frantic pace. New versions of the server can be expected to appear at frequent intervals and the complete versions issued at these times are supplemented by the release of service packs (patch kits) every 90 days or so. Some people get worried about service packs appearing at such a frequent interval, looking at this fact as evidence that the software is bug-ridden and unstable, and also worrying about how they can deploy updates to all the server computers that may be operating across their enterprises.

Such worries are understandable. The issue of how to plan for frequent software updates for servers is not something that can be swept underneath a carpet without some thought, and a plan to allow for cross-organization upgrades should be included in any plan for corporate implementations of Exchange. You don't have to install every service pack, but it may be necessary to install a specific service pack in order to move to a new version of Exchange in the future. For example, service pack 2 (or later) for Exchange V4.0 must be installed before you can upgrade a server to Exchange V5.0. Why? Some changes were made in the service pack to Exchange's internal structures.

You may agree or disagree with Microsoft's policy that requires you to install a service pack before upgrading to a new version, but I suggest that you accept this as a fact of life, part of the cost of doing business in this space, and move on. The more important thing to remember is to always carefully review the full list of bug fixes in each service pack to allow for an intelligent, informed decision as to whether it is good and wise to deploy an optional service pack to all servers. Remember that all the bug fixes have reference numbers that can be used to check against the Microsoft Knowledge Base (via the Web or TechNet CDs). The Knowledge Base includes a full description of each problem and the fix that was made. Reviewing a selection of the relevant articles will give you a flavor of the contents of the service pack.

I don't worry about the number of bug fixes that appear in service packs. All software has bugs. Anyone who tells you otherwise is either lying or has never engineered any large and complex software project. The fact that service packs (a collection of bug fixes that can be applied to a software product such as Exchange or Windows NT) appear at regular intervals tells you that Microsoft is serious about developing a quality product. At the end of the day Microsoft doesn't want to delay the availability of bug fixes to customers. A cynical view asks the question why didn't they test for or otherwise find these bugs in the first place, but some bugs just don't appear until they're put under the spotlight of production use within customer messaging environments. Some of the bugs found in the Internet Mail Service (largely fixed in service pack 2 for Exchange V4.0) are classic examples of how a component used across a wide variety of different production environments suddenly exhibits problems that need to be fixed. The fixes were made, the service pack issued, the product's quality improved.

Because of the intensely competitive nature of the e-mail market Microsoft needs to come up with new product releases at regular intervals. Full product releases typically concentrate on a theme or central focus that addresses a particular segment of the overall e-mail market. Based on product delivery and plans announced to date I believe that three distinct themes can be seen in Exchange development.

- *Achieve market share* (Exchange V4.0): This version of Exchange focused on how to migrate the vast population of Microsoft Mail clients and post offices over to Exchange. The reason is simple—achieve market share and presence.

- *Embrace the Internet* (Exchange V5.0): The advent of Active Messaging, HTML and HTTP support, NNTP Connector, and POP3 support for client access all enabled better links with the growing mass of Internet-enabled browsers and e-mail clients. Exchange also joined the common trend for all Microsoft products to leverage off the Internet.

- *Performance and Scaleability* (Exchange V.next): Technical advances such as clustering for Windows NT, lifting the 16GB limit for the information store up to 16 TB, and better support for multi-processor systems allow very large Exchange servers to be built. The theoretical vision of a 20,000+ user system demonstrated at trade shows becomes closer, especially as high-end processors such as the Pentium Pro and Alpha continue to crank out ever-increasing chip speeds. At the same time a close eye must be kept on developments in Windows NT. The move towards the unified Active Directory is especially important to Exchange.

These themes represent my view of Microsoft's development strategy for Exchange. When Microsoft is asked to outline their strategy they break things down slightly differently. Brian Valentine, general manager of the Exchange development group, broke the development strategy for Exchange into four main areas as follows (1996 Exchange Deployment Conference):

1. Architectural-level improvements
   - Continual enhancement of the level of reliability, scaleability, and security provided by Exchange
   - Easing the load placed on system administrators for day to day operations, especially in small offices

2. Compliance with standards
   - Build around native Internet protocols
   - Deliver native-format content to Internet systems

3. Integrated groupware

   o Develop and deliver groupware and workflow based on native Internet standards

4. Common development

   o Build and deploy e-forms and other applications based on Internet standards

These statements deserve some comment. Microsoft believes that one of Exchange's major strengths is its solid architecture, mostly because the architecture allows Exchange to expand and accommodate new protocols and standards as they become important within the messaging market. Over the past few years we've seen fluctuations in protocol popularity as X.400, SMTP/MIME and other standards find new supporters and detractors, and the situation is complicated by the appearance of new protocols such as POP3, IMAP4, SSL, HTML, and so on. Exchange has been designed and built from scratch to be a multi-standard server, beginning with dual messaging protocols in V4.0 (the server is equally happy to talk to other messaging systems via either SMTP or X.400) and expanding in V5.0 to bring in POP3, HTML, HTTP, and so on. The desire to incorporate new standards can be expected to continue, and Exchange is well poised to move forward precisely because of its solid architectural base.

Through its sheer burgeoning mass, the Internet exerts the most important current influence on messaging today. In essence, Exchange is Microsoft's Internet mail server. Look at the Microsoft statements about building on "native Internet protocols" or delivering "native Internet content" in Exchange and you'll get a good idea of how Microsoft views the future. The Internet is great, but a lot of the information presented or available within the Internet is relatively unstructured and difficult to find. Through the absorption and integration of Internet protocols Exchange is well positioned to become a provider of structured and well organized information for Internet users. The ability to use a Web client to browse through the data held and managed on an Exchange server is a compelling example of how structured data can be provided to Internet users; the fact that the same data is available to many other clients just adds value.

1.2.3   Planning for change

In such a turbulent and fast changing world it's important that you should plan for change. As explained above, Exchange will evolve, but you also need to include Windows NT in the equation. Exchange and Windows NT should really be viewed as a single unit that will become more tightly coupled as the years go by. It is safe to say that developments like NT V5.0 (often spoken of as the elusive "Cairo" release) will impact Exchange; it's just hard to be exact as to where and how the impact will fall. However, at the end of the day the wise system planner factors in server software upgrades at least once a year and sets aside time, money, and personnel to review developments as they are delivered by Microsoft. Failure to do so could result in an organization not getting the advantages they seek from the Windows NT/Exchange combination. On the other hand, being too focused on upgrading may lead to problems that you definitely don't want to get into, such as the premature deployment of immature (even beta) software into the production environment. Look for a comfortable compromise between rushing in to install the latest and greatest code and getting behind the development curve.

1.3   Building an implementation plan for Exchange

Implementing a computer system is not always easy. Good implementations require a structure to build on, and Exchange is no different. Successful projects are built on a foundation established by a well-thought-out implementation plan that breaks the essential tasks required to complete the implementation down into a number of important stages. An implementation plan is not a project plan because there's much more focus on design, making decisions that have a huge effect on the overall shape the project will take. Eventually the implementation plan serves as an input into the project plan. At this stage the design decisions have been made and documented and the project plan can break the individual sections of the implementation plan into the tasks and schedule that will lead to the deployment of Exchange servers and clients.

The essential elements of an implementation plan vary from company to company and installation to installation. For example, the choice made about the Windows NT domain model to use or the server hardware to install Exchange on may already have been set down and can't be changed, even if you know that things would flow a little more smoothly if just a little change could be made. In all cases it's good to review the items that could feature in an implementation plan, just to make sure that everything is covered in your deployment.

Table 1.2 lists the major headings that I use within the implementation plans I write for Exchange.

As stated above, you don't have to use all of these headings. Use whatever makes sense in your situation, adding or subtracting headings as you see fit. Remember, you know more about your own requirements than anyone else!

Table 1.2   *Elements of an Exchange implementation plan*

Major heading	Minor heading
Windows NT design	o The domain model to use o Deployment of domain controllers o Deployment of other applications on NT servers where Exchange will be installed
Network infrastructure	o Existing network traffic patterns and available bandwidth o Impact of Exchange-related network load o Impact of other applications that may be introduced along with Exchange o Current implementation of the TCP/IP infrastructure, including DNS, DHCP, and WINS o Predicted growth rate in network traffic over the next three years
Exchange organization	o Location of sites o Number of servers within sites o Workload allocated to servers o Allocation of users to servers
Hardware for servers	o Hardware platform for Exchange servers (Intel or RISC) o Impact of other applications such as SMS, SQL Server, or file and print services o Configuration details including RAID and UPS
Client desktop environment	o Operating system o Other applications that will be run with Exchange o Choice of client software to connect to Exchange o Hardware platform, including any requirement to introduce new PCs or upgrade existing PCs
Connectivity	o Connections to other messaging systems, including the determination of the exact degree of interoperability (simple text or compound messages) o Directory synchronization with other messaging systems o Connections to other information sources such as NNTP, FAX, voice mail, or pagers
Extensions	o Third party add-ons o Electronic forms o Client extensions developed with MAPI
Operational procedures	o Backup and Restore procedures o Disaster recovery plan o Allocation of privileges and permissions o Document retention policy, including the policy for the creation and maintenance of public folders o Plan for distribution of software upgrades (new versions and service packs) to clients and servers o Operation of Advanced Security, if desired o Virus checking for Exchange

Table 1.2   *Elements of an Exchange implementation plan (continued)*

Major heading	Minor heading
Training	o System administrators o System designers o Help Desk and support staff o Programmers o Users
Pilot systems to verify all aspects of the previous plans	o More than 3 servers, using the same hardware platform as will be used in production o Connected in more than one site o Using network infrastructure o Featuring range of client platforms o Including more than 50 users o Including all third party products and client extensions

1.4   Getting Exchange up and running

What sort of a computer will you need to run Microsoft Exchange? The answer is, of course, that it all depends on the type of user community you tend to support. If you just want to run Exchange for a small pilot for up to 20 or 30 users you shouldn't need anything more than a reasonably well-equipped desktop system, preferably one equipped with a fast (100MHz or above) Pentium-class processor and at least 64MB of memory. It must be emphasized, however, that this is very much a basic configuration that has absolutely no room to grow.

The stakes get a little higher once you start to look at a system intended for production use. First you'll need a high-specification system running Windows NT V3.51 or V4.0 to run Exchange V4.0 or V5.0. Note that it is probable that you'll need to run Windows NT V4.0 (or later) to run versions of Exchange after V5.0. The operating system clearly forms a critical part of the overall system equation and it is reasonable to expect that future versions of Exchange will leverage off new features in Windows NT. However, it takes time to plan and implement operating system upgrades across a large number of systems, so this is yet another factor to incorporate into any deployment plan.

I wouldn't bother with a system equipped with an Intel 80486-based CPU unless you really only want to connect a couple of clients for testing purposes. Go for a high-end Pentium Pro or Alpha-based system and make sure you have plenty of memory. Disk space, although getting cheaper all the time, is still a factor to consider and you'll need 250MB to get the software up and running. The space used afterwards will depend on the number of messages handled by the system and the type of messages and attachments generated by your user community. Clearly a system dealing with users specializing in large Word for Windows or PowerPoint attachments will consume disk space quickly. Microsoft recommends that you consider a striped disk set for better performance, but you shouldn't have to go this far to be able to run a pilot. In all cases it's best to have the Exchange software installed on a different drive to Windows NT. More details about hardware configurations and performance can be found in Chapter 4.

In general, Exchange server software is not supported on the workstation edition of Windows NT. The Exchange administration program (ADMIN.EXE) can be run on a NT workstation (but not on a Windows 95 client). In this situation the administration program communicates with server processes running on a remote server via RPCs. None of the server processes such as the MTA or System Attendant can function or are supported on a Windows NT workstation. Windows NT server differs from the workstation edition in a number of aspects, including support for features that enable higher resilience, for instance, disk striping. But the level of difference is hardly enough to impose any technical limitation so perhaps some hard-coded restrictions have been inserted. In view of the onerous task involved in supporting, testing, and qualifying software across the wide variety of platforms supported by Windows NT a restriction like this would be very understandable.

Apart from Exchange you may have to install other software components on your Windows NT server before everything hangs together. For example, you require TCP/IP for Windows NT if you want to use TCP/IP as the protocol to tie servers and gateways together. Microsoft Mail sites will need to install the Mail Connector, and anyone dealing with Macintosh clients will need Windows NT Services for Macintosh.

The architecture laid out for Exchange server and clients is reasonably modular. Well-defined components work together to achieve tasks such as the dispatch of messages or directory look-ups, and because all the components are based on a single architecture (MAPI) there is no restriction on the source of the various components. Essentially, each of the components provides a service to users, so the common term used for Exchange components is "service provider."

Hundreds of independent software vendors and other third parties are working to integrate their own products with Exchange. The nicest integration is to be able to present new functionality, such as voice mail, to Exchange as if it is a standard part of Exchange. In short, to create a new service provider.

Apart from adding new functionality to Exchange it is also possible to build a client-centric service provider which enables standard Exchange clients to connect to other mail servers. The usual implementation is to install software (some DLLs) on the client to intercept MAPI calls made by clients and redirect them to a different server, translating the functions en route into the server's own API if the server doesn't support MAPI. This is the approach taken by third parties that wish to allow clients such as the Windows 95 Universal Inbox to connect to their own servers.

From a user perspective it's all a matter of describing the different service providers you want to use in the form of a profile. A profile typically details the type of message transport in use, the directory that can be used to locate addresses in, and the type of message store that's available. A profile might specify that Exchange server is used for message transport, the Exchange global address book is used for directory, and the Exchange information store is used as the message store. A profile can also detail multiple transports. For example, it is possible to configure an Exchange client to be able to send messages via Exchange, FAX, and CompuServe mail.

You can have multiple profiles to deal with the different circumstances you process mail in. A PC used by multiple users will have a different profile for each person, if only to specify that a connection should be made to a different mailbox and/or server for each user.

Communication between clients and servers is carried out by RPCs (Remote Procedure Calls) using named pipes, NetBIOS, or Windows Sockets over a range of network protocols including IPX/SPX, NetBEUI, and TCP/IP (but only TCP/IP implementations that support Windows Sockets). The Exchange designers selected RPC as the mechanism for client/server communication precisely because it supports so many different underlying network protocols. RPC connections between clients and servers enable a high degree of service robustness. You can stop and restart Exchange services on a server, or even the server itself, and clients will not receive any error messages unless they attempt to communicate with the server. When the server reappears or the services are restarted clients reconnect seamlessly, giving the impression to users that a single continuous link has been maintained.

In the 1996–98 period, as Exchange servers replace Microsoft Mail Post Offices, the NetBIOS/NetBEUI combination is likely to be the most common network base for Exchange. However, in most corporate situations I've seen over the past few years there has been a steady march towards the combination of Windows Sockets and TCP/IP. I see no reason why this trend shouldn't continue as Exchange is accepted in corporate installations, especially in light of the fact that people are so excited about Intranet applications that depend on TCP/IP.

1.5   One-stop system management

Market analysts have rightly criticized PC LAN-based e-mail systems over the years for the high cost per seat associated with these systems. Once a decision is reached to move towards a client/server model there's not much that can be done about the cost of the PC hardware and software, including network cards and other items required to link a user into the corporate network. All of these costs are based on items that have largely moved into the commodity category and similar expense is incurred no matter which vendor's e-mail system is used.

While hardware and software costs have descended in real terms people costs have risen. Due to the number of parts contributing to the whole system and the complexities involved in connecting all the parts together PC LAN-based e-mail systems require more hands-on maintenance time per user than older mainframe or mini-based systems. A lot of time is spent in fire fighting mode getting users' mail through rather than proactive preventative maintenance. Where two or three full-time people might administer a large centralized system serving a thousand users it is common to find the same number taking care of a hundred users. Even worse, valuable user time is absorbed doing work that they are not trained for, such as PC software installation or printer maintenance. Overall, it is the human factor that has contributed more than any other to the overall high cost per seat in the PC environment.

Exchange is designed to permit a single point of contact for system administrators for all components that might require management intervention through the Exchange administration program. All of the servers in a site can be managed from a single workstation, and each individual server can cope with far more users than a single older-style post office. Using a highly graphical, point-and-click interface for system administration is most appropriate when not too many items need to be displayed or manipulated. The Exchange administration program is wonderful for low-end or medium-sized systems, but information can be slow to find and then displayed in situations where there are, for example, thousands of mailbox entries in a single recipient's container.

In much the same way, occasionally the graphical design limits the information about an item that can be viewed. For instance, when tracking a message it would be nice to be able to view more information about a selected message, but because the graphical interface is designed to show a particular set of data you can't. These comments are mild criticisms of the administration program, which is, in general, a very commendable step forward in messaging administration.

Some of the safeguards built into the graphical interface of the Exchange administration program can be circumvented by running the program in "raw mode." Raw mode is invoked by specifying the /R switch when ADMIN.EXE is started. Using raw mode is like playing around with explosives. If you know what you're doing and you take care there's a fair chance that you won't do any damage. On the other hand, you've got to remember that raw mode gives you direct control over the directory structures normally safeguarded by the graphical interface, and that if your finger slips when typing a command (or when responding to a prompt) it's entirely possible to wreak havoc. In this context havoc means causing enough internal damage to necessitate a complete restore of the Exchange directory store. Deleting a container or other important structure in the directory is a pretty good example of what I mean. Raw mode certainly isn't intended for day-to-day use. Because its use carries such a high potential for accidents it cannot be recommended unless you proceed with great care.

1.5.1   Managing connections to other systems

The majority of corporate messaging systems are heterogeneous in nature. In other words, you don't have a single mail system deployed throughout the different departments, groups, and work teams that collectively form the enterprise. A lot of the reasons for this situation are historical. Different people installed different systems at different times, and the systems have become embedded into the body of the enterprise. Connecting all of the different systems is skilled work, and it's usually something that takes a reasonably high percentage of the available system administration effort.

Generally speaking, because a wide range of well-integrated off-the-shelf connectors is available for Exchange, it is relatively easy to link Exchange into corporate messaging environments. If you're upgrading from a DOS-based post office you'll find that the combination of Windows NT, Exchange, and the Exchange connectors deliver a far more stable, robust and powerful base for the messaging system than you had before. The net result is that less connectivity problems are encountered on a day to day basis, reducing the overall workload for the people who have to manage the e-mail system and releasing skilled people for more useful activities. Because the connections are up and running all the time, users also benefit through the much more predictable and reliable nature of the service.

On the other side of the coin, those upgrading from mini- or mainframe e-mail systems will experience the same type of reliability in multi-system connectivity they probably enjoy today. In these cases the added value delivered by Exchange is ease of setup and maintenance. I have never experienced connectors that are quite so easy to install and configure as those that are integrated into Exchange or the optional connectors available as add-ons afterwards. Again, the net effect is to ease the load on system administrators. The data to back up these assertions of ease of use and maintenance is described in Chapter 7.

1.5.2   Software upgrades, patches, and service packs

Any step that contributes to high system availability and a consistent level of service is good. The advances in one-stop system management delivered in Exchange server will be welcomed by system administrators. But the nature of software technology and the demands of both users and the market mean that new hardware and software appear on a very regular basis. A system will therefore never be fixed in time and plans must be made to evolve the system in a planned manner in order that advantage can be taken of the advances and new technology. You can be sure that faster and more capable hardware will be available; new versions of Exchange server and clients will ship; and the desktop applications such as word processors and spreadsheets will evolve. Over a three-year period you can expect to see at least two new releases of Windows NT, Exchange server and clients, and the desktop applications. Will this new software feature in your plans? How will the new software be made available to users without undue disruption and while maintaining the advances in system reliability achieved through the deployment of Windows NT and Exchange server?

Microsoft's System Management Server (SMS) technology can provide an answer to the problem of managing PC desktops. SMS is to desktop application management and distribution what Exchange server is to PC e-mail systems: a radical step forward in the right direction. SMS allows system administrators to distribute and manage application software across networked PCs. It's easy to plan for an update of Exchange server software, even if a number of servers have to be updated at the same time within a site. Normally there is a ratio of hundreds of clients per server so the work necessary to update all the clients to the required software revision level is quite a different matter. SMS helps to solve the problem, allowing all the Exchange clients to be updated in a controlled manner precisely when the new software is required. A full description of SMS and its capabilities lies outside the boundaries of this book. Hopefully you'll consider the common and very real problem of software distribution posed here and look at the answers available to you. Windows NT, Exchange, and SMS combine well together and enable true one-stop system management and for that reason you should take a serious look at SMS.

Table 1.3   *Exchange software version numbers*

Exchange Build Number	Meaning
837	Exchange V4.0 RTM ("Release to Manufacturing")
838	Exchange V4.0 Service Pack 1, May 1996 (SP1)
993	Exchange V4.0 Service Pack 2, August 1996 (SP2)
994.64	Exchange V4.0 Service Pack 3, November 1996 (SP3)
995.54	Exchange V4.0 Service Pack 4, April 1997 (SP4)
1389.7	Exchange V5.0 Release Candidate 1[1], December 1996
1457.11[2]	Exchange V5.0 RTM, February 1997

(1)   You shouldn't run Release Candidate software in production after the release to manufacturing variant is available. Apart from anything else, you'll get very little sympathy from Microsoft support should anything go wrong.

(2)   The original released build was 1457.10. This build was released to customers (via the Web) as a 120-day promotional offer, but only for a couple of days in March 1997. 1457.11 is the official and supported build for Exchange V5.0.

Handling server upgrades is a problem that is easier in one respect (because there are less servers than client systems to be updated), but harder in another (because the effect of a bad upgrade is felt by multiple clients). The Microsoft Exchange developers appear resolute in their determination to make software updates quickly available to customers. As shown in Table 1.3, three service packs[4] were issued fairly rapidly after Exchange V4.0 was released in 1996. The indications delivered at the 1996 Exchange Deployment Conference were that people should expect to see service packs being issued at roughly 90-day intervals. The delay in issuing service pack 4 for Exchange V4.0 can easily be explained. The engineering group was, after all, fully occupied getting Exchange V5.0 out the door.

Not all of the service packs have to be installed, but some do. For example, Service Pack 2 (sometimes referred to as Exchange V4.0a) must be installed on a server within a site before Service Pack 3 or Exchange V5.0 can be installed. Service Pack 2 for Exchange V4.0 is huge (30MB) and contains lots of new functionality, including support for

[4]   A service pack is a collection of bug fixes, sometimes referred to in Microsoft-speak as the latest mature build of a product. Service packs are usually cumulative, but this is not always the case. In other words, if you install Service Pack 3 you are in fact installing all the fixes included in Service Packs 1 and 2. Look at the properties of a server to discover the build number and service pack level installed on that server. The operation must be repeated for each server within a site, and each site within an organization.

Far East languages and the Macintosh client. All ExchangeV4.0 kits manufactured beginning in July 1996 included Service Pack 2, so you may have installed it without even realizing that this was the case.

In general, service packs for Exchange are cumulative. In other words, you can install the latest service pack without having to install any of the previous service packs. Service Pack 3 is an exception to the rule and is referred to as a "delta release" because Service Pack 2 must be installed beforehand. The sheer size of Service Pack 2 and the number of changes contained in it, including an upgrade to the directory store, are the reasons for making Service Pack 3 a delta release. Microsoft product management is pretty frank in admitting that too much was bundled into Service Pack 2. The future intention is to comply with the goal of issuing cumulative service packs, and this is what we should see for Exchange V5.0.

In some senses, Service Pack 4 is cumulative. Even so, it still requires Service Pack 2 to be present before it can be installed. Service packs contain both server and client code, but there are different requirements to install the client upgrades. Experience with all of the various service packs and versions released to date shows that there appears to be no problems running "old" versions of clients against upgraded servers. Exchange V4.0 clients are able to run quite happily against V4.0a servers, or even V5.0 servers. While it is good to apply client level patches it's not always practical to do so, especially for hundreds or thousands of PCs (if the client software is installed on PC local hard disks). Most installations avoid installing client patches unless they are experiencing a bug that's fixed by a service pack.

Normally there's no great harm in installing a service pack quickly. After all, they contain fixes to problems that the Exchange developers have tracked down and rectified. Microsoft PSS representatives generally urge customers to apply any available service packs as the first step when a problem is detected. However, service packs do not get the benefit of the extensive external beta test program that most Microsoft products are subjected to, and bugs can lurk beneath the surface, ready to explode at the most inconvenient times. Two such situations have already occurred with the service packs issued for Exchange Server V4.0. Service Pack 2 included many important or even essential fixes for the MTA, but it introduced a problem with the Internet Mail Service. Service Pack 3 addressed many of the reported issues with the Internet Mail Service, but it introduced a bug that stopped some third party products working, such as Cheyenne's ArcServe backup utility. The problems in the service packs were addressed through quick fixes issued from Microsoft and made available through their FTP site[5], but the sheer fact that these bugs arrived through service packs made many system administrators uneasy.

The situation is compounded by the close inter-relationship between Exchange and Windows NT. Service packs are also issued for Windows NT, so what's the correct and safest combination of Windows NT, Exchange, and the various service packs? At the beginning we all knew that the answer was Windows NT V3.51 SP4 and Exchange V4.0, but as software evolves, bugs are found and fixed, and service packs appear, the waters get murkier and murkier.

Table 1.4   *Valid combinations of Windows NT and Exchange Server*

	Exchange V4.0	Exchange V4.0 SP1	Exchange V4.0 SP2	Exchange V4.0 SP3	Exchange V4.0 SP4	Exchange V5.0
Windows NT V3.51 SP4	Base Platform	OK	OK	OK	OK	OK
Windows NT V3.51 SP5	OK	OK	OK	OK	OK	OK
Windows NT V4.0	Not supported	Not supported	OK	OK	OK	Not supported
Windows NT V4.0 SP1	Not supported	Not supported	OK	OK	OK	Not supported
Windows NT V4.0 SP2	Not supported	Not supported	OK	OK	OK	OK
Windows NT V4.0 SP3	Not supported	Not supported	OK	OK	OK	Base Platform

The release of Exchange V5.0 somewhat addresses the situation because a definitive version of Exchange is delivered and a firm statement can be made as to what revision levels for Windows NT should be used. We can all start off again from a base of Windows NT V3.51 SP5 or Windows NT V4.0 SP3, but the merry-go-round recommences with the appearance of the first service pack afterwards for either Exchange or Windows NT. Life was certainly never meant to be easy, at least not for system administrators. Table 1.4 is my attempt to list the valid or recommended combinations of Windows NT and Exchange.

Will the situation improve in the future? Some trends are emerging that will affect the attitude we take towards service packs. First, Microsoft is now beta testing service packs instead of rushing to issue

---

[5]   Ftp://ftp.microsoft.com/bussys/exchange/exchange-public/fixes is a good starting point for Exchange bug fixes released by Microsoft.

code to anyone who cares to request it. This step has been forced on Microsoft by the debacle of Windows NT Service Pack 2, a collection of bug fixes that introduced some nice new bugs of its own. We should therefore expect that any future service pack has at least been through some degree of extensive testing in the field, albeit not to the same extent as with a full software release.

The second trend is more interesting. Issuing a new software release costs a lot of money (sources inside Microsoft put the cost around the $1 million mark). There is a constant pressure to keep software competitive by including new features, yet there is matching pressure not to force the pace of software development because some customers can't keep up. From an Exchange perspective its development group relies on Windows NT, yet exerts no real pressure on the Windows NT development group. Exchange is just another product for Windows NT, one that has to join the push forward to new releases like Windows NT V5.0. There is, however, a commitment for Exchange to support new releases of Windows NT very soon after those releases are provided to customers. If this wasn't done then Exchange would potentially be in the ludicrous position where it couldn't support a new release of Windows NT, but competing products could.

Handling new versions of Windows NT (and any other dependencies) is a tricky task. Neither the engineering group nor customers want a proliferation of different versions of Exchange. We already have enough complications today. Service packs offer the engineering group a potential way out. Instead of incurring all the cost of building a complete new product release, new functionality is slipped into a service pack. Customers who don't need the new functionality don't have to install the service pack, and the apparent pace of change (measured by new product releases) is kept under control.

Microsoft has already used service packs to introduce new functionality—Exchange V4.0 Service Pack 2 fixed problems, but it also added support for Far Eastern languages. According to Microsoft sources, during the 1997–98 period we can expect service packs to add support for 16TB information stores, Wolfpack clustering APIs, and potentially even Windows NT V5.0. Again, if you don't need the service pack you don't need to install it, and if Microsoft gets their cumulative service pack strategy right you should be able to elect for selective upgrades, installing software at your pace rather than the vendor's.

1.5.3   Deploying new software

Many large companies that I work with have rules that prohibit the introduction of new software versions until they have been tested for between 60 to 90 days. Testing means that the software is installed on servers that are closely monitored. Ideally the test servers replicate the production environment; they have any third party product (like a backup product) installed, all the different connectors are used, and the spectrum of clients operated by users are connected to the server. I recommend that the test environment be established as a site within the production Exchange environment, so that the test servers can fully participate with all the other (non-upgraded) servers.

It may seem dangerous to introduce a test site into the production environment, but this is the only real way to isolate and identify any potential interoperability problems that might otherwise show up when the first few live servers are upgraded. Keeping the test servers in a separate site isolates them and allows easy disconnection, if required, from the rest of the organization. A certain degree of control has to be exerted. For example, new connectors that will take over routing of messages for the rest of the organization to destinations like the Internet should not be installed on test servers; thousands of test entries should not be imported into the directory (and thereafter replicated around the organization), and so on. It is relatively easy to create a set of guidelines where the differing needs of the operations and planning staffs are met. Remember that any reasonably sized organization (more than 10 servers) will have to engage in rolling upgrades when the time comes to install new versions of Exchange or Windows NT. During the upgrade period a mixture of "old" and "new" servers will be in production. Creating and operating a test site within the production organization only brings the inevitable forward.

Usually it's only large companies that can afford the relative luxury of operating such a comprehensive test. But then again, it's a lot more serious to introduce a new bug via updated software to multiple, often geographically dispersed servers, a scenario that is more relevant to large companies than their smaller counterparts.

Seeking to minimize the disruption of service levels delivered to users is definitely a good tactic for everyone to adopt. This means that you shouldn't try and upgrade at every opportunity. Instead, try and group upgrades together so that you don't have to intervene with the servers too often. Twice a year is more than enough. Remember, each time someone has to perform a software installation it will cost money. People won't be able to use the systems so they'll be less productive, each server has to be manually upgraded, and the servers must be closely monitored immediately after the upgrade to make sure that everything works right. All of this activity can cost thousands of dollars, so it's wise to try and balance the need to be up to date with software revisions with the demands of the business to provide a cost-effective service.

The best advice I can give is:

- Keep in touch with the current software revision levels for Windows NT, Exchange, and any other product you use. The Microsoft Web site (www.microsoft.com/exchange) is updated with details of new service packs as soon as the packs are released.

- Review the contents of the service packs and make a decision whether you need to install the update. The README.TXT file normally lists the bugs that have been fixed and references an article in the Microsoft Knowledge Base for each bug. You can review the articles to discover more details about the bug fixes, if desired. It is difficult to realize the value of the patches from a quick browse through README.TXT, so be warned that it can take a considerable effort to research each Knowledge Base article and compare its contents against your experience of your own operating environment. This is work that should be done while the service pack is tested.

- Always test service packs before deploying them into production. Some people like to let others take any heat generated by bugs in service packs by waiting at least a month before upgrading anything. During this period monitor sources like the Internet mailing list for Exchange to see if anyone else has hit a problem.

- Upgrade all servers as quickly as possible after the decision is made to proceed. There's no point in having some servers running a different software version. All it does is make support more difficult.

- Take backups (of both Exchange and Windows NT) both before *and after* the upgrade is performed. The reason for taking a backup before any software upgrade is obvious; the reason for taking it afterwards is because it is entirely possible that the internal structures (or schemas) of the directory and information stores may have been changed when the service pack was applied. Any attempt to restore a store using a backup taken before the upgrade may not succeed! There is no need to backup Windows NT after the software upgrade, unless you feel paranoid (or more secure if it's taken).

- Plan the upgrade. Make sure that users are aware that the systems may be unavailable for stated periods and that the help desk and other system administrators understand why the upgrade is being performed.

Remember that installing a new server is only the start of a journey. Along the way you'll spend a lot of time and money keeping the server running. Your goal should be to expend minimum effort for maximum return.

1.5.4   Upgrading to Exchange V5.0

Upgrading a computer from Exchange V4.0 to V5.0 is a relatively painless process. Like everything else to do with Windows NT and Exchange, proper planning is an absolute prerequisite. Coming into work and suddenly deciding "it's a great day to upgrade a server" is not the right thing to do. New software must be tested to validate that it will work properly in your production environment in association with any specialized or third party software you operate.

Most system administrators have their own recipe for software upgrades. It's good to have a basic checklist to follow, so here's mine:

1. The initial step is to select the first server within a site to upgrade. Because the directory is altered during the upgrade process you must perform the upgrade on the bridgehead server within the site first. The concept of bridgehead servers is explained on page 409.

2. Make sure that the computer is at the correct revision level of Windows NT by installing any service packs that are required (for example, Service Pack 3 for Windows NT V4.0). If upgrading from Windows NT V3.51 to V4.0 make sure that this is done first, and give the system at least a couple of days (weeks is preferable) to stabilize before proceeding with the Exchange upgrade. Upgrade the Internet Information Server to the required revision level (V3.0 or above) if you're interested in supporting Web client access.

3. Take a full backup of the Exchange directory and information stores. Shut down the Exchange services afterwards and then take a file-level backup of the Windows NT and Exchange directory structures. Windows NT is backed up to make sure that you can roll back to a set of system files and registry in the state before the upgrade occurred. The Exchange directory structure is copied for the same reason. Remember that Exchange files can be spread across a number of disks, so make sure that all relevant disks are copied to tape.

4. Stop all applications and other services to ensure that the installation procedure can upgrade any files it needs to. Many applica-

tions now use MAPI in one way or another, and if they are active they will lock a file and prevent the upgrade proceeing. MAPI32.DLL is a good example of a file that is often locked by an active application.

5. Running the EDBUTIL utility to make sure that your information stores are as compact as possible before commencing the upgrade is a strictly optional step. The installation process for Exchange V5.0 performs an in-line modification of the stores, a process that can take quite a long time on slow servers or when large stores have to be processed. Compacting stores makes them smaller and speeds the upgrade process. Compaction takes longer than the actual store upgrade, so any real timesavings will accrue afterwards when backup times are reduced.

6. Install Exchange V5.0 using the normal setup program. To avoid contention with files moved onto the system during the installation, make sure that all mail-enabled programs and services (anything that might possibly use MAPI) are stopped before beginning the upgrade. Everything happens quite quickly—a Pentium 166 MHz system with a 1GB-information store is usually upgraded in under an hour. The larger the information stores the slower the upgrade will be. As noted above, the database schema used by the information store is changed in V5.0, so the internal structures must be manipulated to reflect the new schema. Updating the stores is often the longest part of the upgrade procedure, and the time required depends on the speed of the CPU and disk I/O subsystem on any particular computer. Large servers that support stores greater than a few megabytes may take a couple of hours to get through the store upgrade phase.

7. If the system runs the Exchange Key Management Server component it must be upgraded using its separate installation program.

8. Test the server by connecting a client to it and verifying that everything works. An Exchange V4.0 or Outlook client is quite happy to connect to an Exchange V5.0 server. Conversely, an Exchange V5.0 client is able to connect to an Exchange V4.0 server.

9. Notify users that the server is back on the air and available for use. Ideally the users should receive some information about the server's new capabilities if they are interested in items such as newsfeeds, Web access, or POP3 clients.

10. Upgrade any client install share points with Exchange V5.0 client installation kits. Notify the personnel assigned to perform client upgrades that the install points are available.

After an Exchange V5.0 server is introduced into a site, either as a new server or as the result of an upgrade, special procedures (provided as part of the Exchange V5.0 kit) must be followed if a decision is made to create a new server running Exchange V4.0. I must say that I cannot see the point of installing Exchange V4.0 software on a new server in a site where an Exchange V5.0 server is already active. It seems better to me to use the new version of Exchange everywhere once you've begun using it. Once an Exchange V5.0 server is operational within a site let it settle in and allow the new directory schema to replicate to the other servers before you upgrade the next server in the site. There is no good reason to rush to upgrade servers one after the other unless you want to set a new speed record for upgrades.

Servers upgraded to V5.0 correspond quite happily with their V4.0 counterparts. Because all communications between servers in a site are accomplished through RPCs it is valid to upgrade only one server to V5.0 and keep all other at V4.0. For example, you might decide to upgrade the server that supports the X.400 and Internet connectors in a site, but leave the servers that just provide messaging (private folders). Another valid reason is a wish to introduce the new cc:Mail connector into a new server within a site. Finally, sites distributed across large geographic areas inevitably need time to arrange the basic logistics of an upgrade and it would be impossible not to envisage a situation where you'd want to perform a rolling upgrade. In a similar vein, because communications between sites can be made by RPCs or SMTP or X.400 messages there is no requirement (apart from Microsoft's desire to have everyone run the very latest software) to uplift all servers to V5.0 in the shortest possible time.

1.5.5   Do clients need to be updated too?

Planning to upgrade a set of servers, even when there are 50 or more to do and they're spread across a large number of different countries, is a project that shouldn't cause too many problems. It's a totally different manner to plan the upgrade of several thousand clients, especially when the upgrade issue wasn't considered too carefully when the clients were first deployed.

If client software is accessed from a shared file service then the upgrade is straightforward. The file service is upgraded and everyone proceeds to work, perhaps not even noticing the tasteful new splash screen displayed when the Exchange V5.0 client starts up. On the other hand, if temptation has won out and client software is cheerfully spread across the hard disks of hundreds or thousands of individual PCs, the upgrade challenge takes on a new dimension. Just how will you arrange to visit all the PCs? How long will it take to upgrade each client? Does anything else have to be upgraded at the same time? Are all the PCs physically available? Who takes care of notebook PCs—their owners or the PC support team? How will the new client software be distributed to everyone who needs it?

Given the challenge, and the cost involved in rolling out new client software to lots of PCs, the question "do the clients really have to be upgraded to use the new version of Exchange?" must be asked. The first thing to understand is that aside from the POP3 and Web clients, Exchange clients communicate with the server using RPCs. The RPC mechanism between clients and servers has not been changed, so it is totally feasible to connect an Exchange V4.0 client to an Exchange V5.0 server, or an Exchange V5.0 client to an Exchange V4.0 server. Basic messaging functionality will work, but (very logically) any new feature supported by the Exchange V5.0 server cannot be used by Exchange V4.0 clients. This fact is brutally obvious, and is included here for the sake of completeness.

In practice, running a slightly outdated client isn't very harmful and I think that it's perfectly acceptable to consider running with a mixture of Exchange V4.0 clients and V5.0 server for a couple of months after the Exchange V5.0 server is installed. Microsoft, of course, would prefer you to upgrade because it's easier for them to support the latest version of any software. If you experience problems with clients and contact Microsoft support you'll probably be told that you must upgrade before they can help you, so at this stage you can proceed to upgrade any client affected by the problem (bug) that you've found. Operating a production environment composed of a mismatch of client/server versions isn't a recommended strategy. It is far better to bite the bullet and take whatever steps are necessary to ensure that you can deploy new client software easily and quickly. As we've seen with the server, new versions and service packs appear all the time, so it is a wise investment to install the infrastructure, such as SMS, to support automated client upgrades.

1.5.6   International versions

Although this book is written in English it is an undeniable fact that Exchange is popular throughout the world. Following the success of the international versions of Windows 95 and Windows NT, Exchange Server and its clients are available in a number of different languages. You can connect a client running in any language to a server running in another language. A client community can operate software in multiple languages and connect to a server running in another language. The sole issue is whether or not clients can read the content of messages created in different languages.

Table 1.5   *International server and client versions for Exchange*

	Exchange Server V5.0	Exchange V5.0 client	Outlook client
English[1]	▣	▣	▣
French	▣	▣	▣
German	▣	▣	▣
Japanese	▣	▣	▣
Spanish		▣	▣
Swedish		▣	▣
Italian		▣	▣
Dutch		▣	▣
Portuguese		▣	▣
Brazilian		▣	▣
Korean		▣	▣
Traditional Chinese		▣	▣
Simplified Chinese		▣	▣
Norwegian		▣	*(2)
Danish		▣	*
Finnish		▣	*
Czech		▣	*
Hungarian		▣	*
Polish		▣	*
Russian		▣	*
Greek		▣	*
Turkish		▣	*
Hebrew		▣	*
Arabic		▣	*

(1)   English language versions are available in "International" and "US & Canada" editions. The difference is the type of encryption technology bundled with the server. The "US & Canada" edition offers 64-bit encryption while the international edition uses 40-bit.

(2)   The client is not available in this language. The English language variant is substituted in the box containing Exchange server software.

For example, if you create a message using the Greek client, can it be read with the German client, or the Japanese client, or even the Russan client? The issue is not specific to Exchange. Instead, it is all to do with the code pages installed on client computers. People running computers in Greece use a different code page to represent and display the Greek character set to that used for the Russian character set. If you receive a message that has been composed in Greek and attempt to read it without loading the Greek character set you probably won't make very much sense of what you see. The rule is, if you expect to read messages composed in a particular character set, make sure that the relevant code page is installed on your PC.

The English-language server CD includes software for many different language clients, while the French, German, and Japanese servers offer a more restricted choice. The range of client languages outlined in Table 1.5 is not definitive. It merely represents the situation as at the date that Exchange V5.0 became available. In Chapter 2 we'll discuss how client software will evolve over the next few years, and a by-product of that evolution will be the gradual insertion of Outlook as the standard client for all languages.

1.6   Is Exchange a mail system or groupware?

"Groupware" is a strange term, which means very different things to different people, but it's basically all about helping groups of people to work together in more intelligent ways. In terms of application software groupware is very different to electronic mail because the focus tends to be more on widening information sharing rather than the often purely singular interchange involved in the sending and receipt of an electronic mail message.

Software vendors vary in their definitions of just what groupware is exactly. Much depends on the aspect of groupware that their products excel in. Microsoft's edge in messaging leads to an assertion that electronic mail is the most important groupware application, with electronic forms and good interpersonal scheduling close afterwards. Lotus, on the other hand, considers information sharing and bespoke application development to be at least as important as electronic mail. Both can be right, because each customer situation poses different requirements. I think groupware can be broken down into a number of discrete areas of functionality or user requirements as described in Table 1.6 below. For each area I've indicated my view on whether Exchange provides a solution to the requirement.

Remember that the assessments offered in Table 1.6 are mine, and you will probably have different views on the subject. From the table you can see that Exchange offers a great deal of potential in most areas of groupware. The weakest area for Exchange is unquestionably workflow processing, and this is where competing products will no doubt stress their own capabilities. In rebuttal there are many third party software developers who are able to provide more sophisticated work-flow solutions that can be integrated into Exchange.

Table 1.6   *Exchange groupware capabilities*

Groupware applications		Exchange capabilities
Interpersonal messaging	Used by almost everyone in an organization. Can be thought of as one to one communications.	Strong, the basic function of an Exchange server.
Structured document repository (file cabinet)	Location available to applications to store objects. Usually accessible from multiple client applications and often network-enabled, allowing access to documents from points distributed across a WAN.	Medium, based on mixture of public and private folders.
Bulletin boards	Used to make relatively static information from central sources that are available to users on a read-only basis. Can be thought of as one to many communications.	Strong, using read-only public folders.
Workflow/electronic forms	Structured form of messaging where "intelligent" items are routed from user to user, following rules that determine the processing steps taken at each stage.	Weak. Electronic forms do not provide the type of comprehensive workflow functionality available in workflow-specific applications. See note on Exchange and workflow.
Interactive conferencing	Many to many communication where users have the ability to post their ideas in electronic forums.	Strong, using writeable public folders.
Time management/ scheduling	Applications that allow users to schedule meetings and appointments with each other. Often includes requests to schedule fixed items such as conference rooms, projectors, or white boards. Electronic mail is commonly used to transport meeting requests between users or across a network.	Strong (Schedule+)

1.6.1   Exchange electronic forms

If Exchange is primarily a mail server, albeit one that includes notable attributes like an X.400-compliant MTA, would there be any reasons to consider Exchange to be an advance on the previous Microsoft messaging system? Of course, the answer is yes, mostly because Exchange is far more reliable and scaleable than any Microsoft Mail post office, but perhaps a more compelling reason is rooted in its groupware capabilities. Exchange V5.0 scales new heights through its support of a wide array of new clients and protocols, moving even further away from the "just a mail server" label.

In any demonstration of Exchange you're bound to run into electronic forms somewhere along the line. Electronic forms are positioned as the way to accomplish groupware applications, capable of meeting many different needs. Groupware applications fall into many categories. Some groupware applications use intelligent document routing functionality enabled by a messaging infrastructure to move business documents around an organization. Exchange certainly has the messaging infrastructure and can move documents around, but its workflow capabilities are limited in comparison to specialized workflow products (see page 36). Other groupware applications focus on collaborative working, functionality enabling people to share information in a more developed and intuitive manner than they can through the simple exchange of mail messages. Lotus Notes has built a huge market around replicated document-oriented databases that allow easy sharing, and its market share has established Lotus Notes as the de facto groupware standard in many people's eyes.

Exchange approaches groupware from a messaging perspective rather than building applications around document databases. Public folders provide the foundation for Exchange's groupware functionality. These are repositories whose contents can be automatically replicated to "replicas" located on other Exchange sites. Exchange servers sharing a common location (a site in Exchange terminology, with the caveat that a site can expand over a wide geographical area as long as the requisite network bandwidth is available) share public folders. A user connecting to any server within a site can look at the same set of public folders, access controls permitting, of course.

Public folders can store any type of object. Electronic forms are an intelligent form of object, which contain code that can be executed when users access the forms. A set of sample forms applications is provided with the Exchange server to form a toolkit that can be drawn upon by programmers to develop site-specific applications. The toolkit contains commonly required applications such as electronic conferences, bulletin boards, and a range of intelligent forms like travel requests. The electronic forms designer component can be used to design forms from scratch, and programmers are able to take the code automatically generated by the forms designer and enhance it with Visual Basic to complete the necessary functionality for production-quality applications.

Visual Basic is both the major strength and weakness of Exchange electronic forms today. Strength is delivered by the ease of development delivered through the Exchange Electronic Forms Designer (EFD) utility, capable of generating basic electronic forms applications, and the use of Visual Basic to write additional code to extend the application if required. Anyone who has worked with Visual Basic will be able to use the EFD as its interface is very similar in layout and use to the Visual Basic development environment.

Visual Basic delivers a lot of power and goodness to Exchange, but because Visual Basic is limited to Windows platforms the electronic forms it creates cannot be used on anything but a Windows PC. Apple Macintoshes and UNIX workstations cannot use electronic forms, nor indeed can people who are still using video terminals or DOS PCs. For this reason it is unlikely that there will be very widespread deployment of electronic forms applications in production environments. In short, today's electronic forms are fine to demonstrate what might be possible, but they cannot be used unless everyone is connected to an Exchange server.

The future is different. Microsoft recognizes the weakness of Visual Basic. Sources indicate that future electronic forms will be built with HTML and ActiveX components, much like the Web client is today. The attractiveness of HTML forms is obvious—they are platform independent and so can be used everywhere, even if people contributing to the flow of business documents don't use Exchange. Control over routing can be exercised by a combination of Exchange and the Internet Information Server, with form-specific code coded up with ActiveX controls and held in Active pages associated with the form. The Web client is an obvious signpost to the future, so don't be surprised if and when Exchange moves its focus for e-forms to HTML-based forms soon. This feeling was confirmed for me by the announcement (March 11, 1997) from Jetform Corporation, a Canadian company, of its support of the Exchange V5.0 Active Messaging component in its Jetform Workflow engine. Active Messaging (see Chapter 2) allows Web browsers to contribute to and participate in workflow processes in a platform-independent manner, and is a real signpost to the future.

With such a fundamental change in sight, the wisdom of devoting any serious development time to building electronic forms with the EFD and Visual Basic must be questioned. Microsoft has indicated that any form built today with EFD can be migrated to whatever standard is adopted in the future, but there's a question mark over forms that are extended with bespoke Visual Basic code. My advice is to leave electronic forms alone for the moment until the future is clarified. There's enough work to be done to get Windows NT, the network, and a basic Exchange infrastructure deployed and stabilized before spending much time on forms development.

1.6.2   Client and server extensions

The EFD is able to initiate complex applications, and programmers can complete the application with Visual Basic but this combination does not always deliver a complete application development environment. Exchange addresses this requirement through the MAPI interface which can be used with Visual C++ to build client or server extensions for Exchange.

Client extensions add menu options or command buttons to the interface, and provide the code behind the interface. Third party products, like Fulcrum Find!, a text search and retrieval package, usually have to build client extensions to integrate their code with Exchange clients. Server extensions perform background processing, for example, to gather statistics or perform maintenance operations on mailboxes. The Exchange Resource Kit includes examples of both client and server extensions, albeit without the actual source code. You'll have to buy a book such as "Inside MAPI[6]" for detailed explanations of how to approach MAPI development and see some solid examples of source code that can be loaded directly into Visual C++.

Microsoft is busy seeking opportunities to add value to Exchange and create the utmost degree of synergy by weaving Exchange into the fabric of as many applications as possible. One obvious example is to mail-enable the Microsoft desktop "Office" applications like Word for Windows and Excel. Another is the integration between the Microsoft Internet Explorer (Microsoft's version of a World Wide Web browser) and Exchange. The setup wizard for the Internet Explorer is able to install "Internet Mail" as a valid Exchange service provider.

Outside Microsoft a wide range of Independent Software Vendors (ISVs) are engaged in the task of writing extensions for Exchange. Quite logically, most extensions focus on the concept of the Universal Inbox, extending its capabilities to accommodate technologies other than electronic mail. The integration of Delrina's WinFax Pro product to add sophisticated FAX support for the inbox, or the incorporation of voice mail capabilities are good examples of typical third party extensions to the Universal Inbox.

1.6.3   Exchange and workflow

It's possible to implement simple workflow with electronic forms, but not to accomplish the more complex and complicated routing steps that are usually associated with workflow applications. These routing

---

[6]   Authored by De Cruz/Thayer. Published by Microsoft Press (1996).

steps include parallel and serial routing, joins and splits, quorum voting, intelligent decision points and branching, and other features.

Microsoft announced a plan to add workflow capabilities to Exchange in April 1996 with the unveiling of MAPI-Workflow Framework (MAPI-WF), engineered in conjunction with Wang Computers. Documentation and sample code appeared during 1996 but MAPI-WF has still not yet been included in shipping releases of Exchange at the time of writing. The Internet has a lot to do with the reason why MAPI-WF has not been included in Exchange V5.0. The Internet Engineering Task Force is working on extensions to the MIME standard to allow workflow and other data to be carried around in MIME-encoded documents. There's a lot of value in this approach because MIME is a standard that isn't owned by any one company. Thus, there is every chance that many different companies will support the MIME workflow extensions in their mail servers, allowing workflow applications to flow between different mail servers.

Paper business documents have never been really threatened by electronic versions. Up to this point in time there has never been a generally agreed upon standard for workflow or the intelligent exchange of application data, so if you wanted to create workflow applications within an enterprise everyone who participated in workflow cycles had to use the same mail server. The closest to standard so far is EDI, but it favors highly structured documents such as purchase orders and isn't really appropriate to build rather less structured documents like vacation requests. In a heterogeneous messaging environment where departments quite often selected and deployed their own choice of mail server it is still impossible to implement workflow applications and their popularity decreased after the initial flush of enthusiasm. The only people who have really succeeded with workflow were those who succeeded in creating largely homogeneous environments, with just one mail server deployed everywhere. Not many large companies are in this category.

Microsoft sources say that they are keeping a close eye on the workflow and other extensions now being discussed for MIME. Workflow is not the only area affected by this work—it's likely that the Secure/MIME (SMIME) standard will be built into a future version of Exchange to replace or supplement the current implementation of message encryption. Until the MIME extensions are ready and agreed upon, people who need workflow solutions must consider third party products like KeyFile, JetForm, Reach, Filenet, Ultimus, Wang, ViewStar, and StaffWare. All of these products are integrated (albeit to varying degrees) with Exchange, so it is totally possible to consider creating workflow applications for Exchange today. Most of the third party workflow products support other mail systems so it is even feasible to meet the challenge of heterogeneous messaging environments.

1.7   Integration with other Microsoft products

There are several different office product suites available for Windows. If you select Exchange as the basis for your messaging system does it matter if you choose a word processing, spreadsheet, or presentation graphics application, or an integrated suite from another vendor?

All the current releases of desktop applications from the major vendors such as Lotus and Corel/WordPerfect support the major aspects of Windows integration such as OLE. On the conceptual level there should be no difficulties attaching files generated by common Windows applications such as Lotus 1-2-3 or WordPerfect to messages created by an Exchange client, or storing similar files in public folders for replication throughout an Exchange network.

However, while things may work on a purely practical level it's safe to assume that Microsoft desktop applications will enable a more complete degree of integration. For instance, look at ability to use Word for Windows as the message creation editor for the Windows 95 Exchange client. You'll need Word for Windows V7 (from Office 95[7]) before "WordMail" is possible, but it's a nice example of how you can take a standard word processing editor and utilize it for as many tasks as possible, including message composition. The integration isn't perfect at this stage—the ability to insert the text from other messages or add digital signatures to messages is removed once Word-Mail is used—but I'm sure these small points will be ironed out over time. In a purely practical sense it's more important to consider whether your PC is capable of invoking Word for Windows every time you want to create a new message. Word, after all, is quite a heavy-duty application.

Sites that don't use Office 95 or Office 97 (both of which require a 32-bit platform—either Windows 95 or Windows NT) must be content with the standard message creation editor, perfectly capable in its own way but lacking the extended range of features available to a full-function word processor like Word.

Note that no matter whether Word for Windows or the normal rich text editor is used to create message text the content is always

---

[7]   You need a patch for Office 95 to upgrade it to Office 95a before some of the advanced features such as "Post to Exchange folder" from Word or Excel work properly.

stored and sent in Microsoft Rich Text Format (RTF). This ensures that all clients are able to read messages when they arrive, even if Word for Windows isn't installed. In the future the native storage format will evolve to HTML, but this shouldn't be an issue from a client perspective, as the server will continue to ensure that content is always provided to clients in a format they can handle. Microsoft has already begun the process of moving towards HTML through the Office 97 application suite and I expect that all Microsoft applications will support HTML natively by the end of 1998.

Other features that can be gained from a purely Microsoft desktop environment include the ability to use the Exchange or Schedule+ address book as the source for mail merge operations carried out by Word for Windows. The Outlook contacts folder can also be used. Applications can use MAPI functions to post documents or worksheets directly into a public or private folder. It's difficult to see other applications creating an integration with Exchange that goes to the length of accommodating address books for mail merges, but it should be possible to build code to bridge the gap between an application and Exchange folders. MAPI is, after all, a publicly documented interface.

Exchange extracts and displays OLE properties from objects created by OLE-compliant applications when those objects are imported into Exchange. For instance, the author, title, and summary information for an Excel worksheet are stored as OLE properties, so if a worksheet is dragged from the DOS file system and dropped into an Exchange folder, the user is not prompted for a title as it's extracted automatically. Of course, this magic is only viable if users care to fill in the information held as OLE properties. The feature is not restricted to Microsoft applications either, as any application is able to support OLE if they desire. However, it's fair to say that the most complete implementation of OLE across a complete suite of applications is found in the Microsoft Office suite.

If you are going to switch to a purely Microsoft desktop environment it may be best to do so in conjunction with a change to the desktop operating system as this will concentrate all the changes in a single operation. Switching to the latest version of Windows and the Microsoft Office suite at the same time is something that many corporate installations are considering today, but remember that such a changeover may have other impacts like hardware upgrades.

At the end of the day the decision about which desktop applications are going to be used depends on many factors, including some historical aspects and how the people who actually use the applications feel about things. An attempt to change someone's word processor or spreadsheet can be taken as a personal insult, especially if people have accumulated personal libraries of useful macros or other shortcuts. The retraining requirement plus the cost of switching applications, no matter how tempting the trade-in offers seem, are other points to bear in mind.

1.8   Exchange and the Internet

The Internet has been around for years, but over the past few years there has been an explosive growth in interest from both the computing and non-computing communities in the potential possible from a global information highway. The establishment of the World Wide Web (WWW) and easy availability of WWW browsers such as Netscape, Mosaic, and Microsoft's Internet Explorer has brought the power of distributed computing home to many people. The ease by which anyone with an Internet presence can make information available to others by establishing a WWW site is stunning when considered against the problems that the same exercise would have met a few short years ago. Look at the number of newspaper and magazine advertisements published today that include URLs[8] for Web sites. If you pick up a magazine from 1995 or before you'd perhaps find one or two examples. Now URLs are everywhere, despite their technical and non-user friendly nature.

Another interesting aspect to consider is the influence that Internet-evolved standards are having within corporate computing networks. Once the focus was on using functionality like the World Wide Web or TCP/IP as a basis for presenting a corporate external face to the world, but now there's more and more use of technology from the Internet within internal networks to form the Intranets[9]. Developments such as secure tunneling (the ability to make a direct connection from the Internet through a firewall to an internal network via an encrypted communication channel) meld the Internet with Intranets to present what's apparently a single seamless network to users. Indeed, the real growth over the next few years is likely not to be in the Internet itself, but rather in the development and deployment of Internet-originated technologies within corporations as people move towards a more distributed way of working.

---

[8]   URL = Universal Resource Locator, a network pointer to a page on a Web site. Enterprises commonly publish the URL for their "home page," the entry point to their Web site. For example, http://www.digital.com is the URL pointing to the home page for Digital Equipment Corporation.

[9]   An Intranet is a network built from Internet-type components (World Wide Web, TCP/IP networks, etc.) but which operates purely within the boundaries of a single company or enterprise.

In terms of electronic mail it's a sobering thought that the numbers of people equipped with Internet mail accounts may already have passed or will soon pass the number of mail accounts operating in corporate systems[10]. The Internet has truly delivered e-mail to the masses. Metcalfe's Law, part of the lore of the computer industry and named after Bob Metcalfe, the inventor of the Ethernet networking protocol and founder of 3Com Corporation, states that the power of a network increases with the square of the nodes installed in the network. In other words, as PCs are added to a network people have more and more opportunity to share information using those PCs via e-mail, the Web, traditional file and print services, and other mechanisms. All of this means that the available network bandwidth had better increase in line with the extra nodes, or else the performance delivered to users will steadily degrade over time. This fact is as true for private networks as it is for the Internet.

Some observers of computing trends have pointed to the evolution of WWW browsers to include e-mail functionality and asked whether a compelling case exists for enterprises to consider jettisoning their messaging and information distribution infrastructures in favor of a move to an Internet-based solution. Cost is a major reason for such a move even being considered. Comparing the cost of Internet connections together with WWW software versus the costs of installing and operating networks, servers, and clients internally appears to make a great case for a move to do business on the Internet because, generally speaking, everything can be done much more cheaply. Today the degree of functionality available in Internet-centric e-mail systems is lower than a fully-fledged system such as Exchange. These systems will never be as functional as long as they are based on protocols such as POP3, where clients pull messages down from the server for local processing. These systems work, but only as long as you are content to use the same PC all the time and never want to move from PC to PC within an organization. IMAP4, a more developed version of an Internet client/server messaging protocol, delivers more functionality than POP3, but still not as much as a system based on proprietary standards, like Exchange or Lotus Notes.

The promise of low-cost connectivity seems compelling but while the costs involved in connecting a single individual to the Internet are cheap, the costs of achieving consistent, secure, and reliable messaging across the Internet for hundreds or thousands of people aren't necessarily so low. The costs of scaling a system up for thousands of users in-

[10] "Electronic Mail and Message Systems" (April 29, 1996) reports 47,260,000 LAN-based mailboxes and 30,810 host-based mailboxes installed as of March 31, 1996.

crease dramatically if a high value is placed on system availability, data security, and 100% guaranteed message delivery. Internet messaging tools exist, but other applications like scheduling, workflow, and collaborative authoring don't. The Internet already creaks and groans (in an electronic sense) during heavy processing periods, chiefly when the working hours for people on the east and west coasts of the United States overlap. Perhaps moving to a structure that's already having problems handling the load isn't such a wise move for a corporation?

Even if a general move isn't going to be made to use the Internet as a corporate infrastructure the desire still exists within corporations to achieve whatever leverage is possible from the resources available within the Internet. Seeking to create close links between the information held in internal systems and the information available externally (subject always to the installation of a good firewall to prevent unauthorized access) is a good strategy to take.

1.8.1   How Exchange supports the Internet

Exchange is a good Internet citizen. By this I mean that Exchange V5.0 supports all of the most common Internet protocols for messaging, directory, and data access. Look at the list of the ways Exchange can interact with the Internet:

- POP3 mail clients are able to connect to an Exchange server and use Exchange to send and receive messages. The same functionality will be extended to IMAP4 clients in a future version of Exchange.

- Any Web browser that supports frames and JavaScript can connect to Exchange and use even more of the server's functionality. Where POP3 clients are interested in a very simple exchange of messages, Web clients can send and receive mail, browse any folder in a mailbox, access public folders, and look peoples' names up in the Exchange directory. Anonymous access to public folders is also supported, so Exchange can act as a repository for documents published to external people. These features are enabled through the support of the HTML and HTTP protocols, JavaScript, and Microsoft's own ActiveX technology. LDAP is supported for directory access.

- The SSL (Secure Sockets Layer) protocol is supported to allow Web clients to log-on to Exchange in an encrypted manner.

- The NNTP (Network News Transport Protocol) protocol is used to allow Exchange users to read the content of Internet newsgroups through public folders. Automatic feeds come in from NNTP to public folders, relieving the necessity for multiple people within a company to subscribe to and track news-groups, thus making better use of valuable network connections.

All of the features described above are new for Exchange V5.0, so this release can be described as the "Internet release." Details of how the various protocols are implemented in Exchange V5.0 are distributed throughout this book, with Chapter 2 containing most information. Exchange V4.0 wasn't too bad in terms of Internet support either. The Internet Mail Service (connector) is a highly capable SMTP mail server that supports all the important protocols required to send messages to Internet recipients—SMTP, MIME, UUENCODE, and BINHEX. Exchange V5.0 builds on these capabilities and adds new features, described in Chapter 7.

All of this goes to prove that you should have no doubt in the capabilities of Exchange to play a full role within a company Intranet or the general Internet. The server is certainly as capable as anything else that's available today, and it scores highly on usability to create a combination that is a compelling solution for many people. Of course, Exchange will never be regarded as a "true" Internet server because it runs on Windows NT and not UNIX (a totally facetious view is that a server must be able to awk, grep, and ls with the best to score 100% as an Internet citizen). From a practical and pragmatic view Exchange delivers everything most people want in an Internet mail and information server.

Introducing so many new protocols in a single release is certainly accompanied by a degree of risk. The engineering team must now focus effort across multiple protocols and sources of data, many of which they have no control over. Dealing with independently defined (open) protocols is both a joy and hardship for companies like Microsoft, and I expect that some of the new Internet components in Exchange will need time to become as robust as other parts of the server. If we look at other core components like the MTA, the store, and the Internet Mail Service, experience with Exchange V4.0 shows that problems were detected as soon as people put Exchange into real-life production environments. This is inevitable for any product that is used on a global basis in thousands of different companies, and Microsoft moved quickly to fix the problems, albeit with multiple service packs. Nevertheless the fact remains that the problems were addressed and the core components are now very solid. The same profile can be expected for the new Internet components.

Above all, the comprehensive support of Internet protocols within Exchange is a great pointer to the future. MAPI will continue to be the essential foundation for Exchange, at least for the foreseeable future, but Internet protocols are now a pervasive part of the server and possibly the most important piece of the client jigsaw. Internet protocols will prosper inside Exchange and anyone interested in this product needs to become fully conversant with HTTP, HTML, POP3, IMAP4, NNTP, SMTP, MIME, and so on.

1.9   Challenges for Microsoft Exchange

Every new software product that arrives on the technology scene faces challenges that must be overcome before the software is deemed to be successful. Some of the challenges are inherited from the environment the software is deployed into; others arise from people who work with the software or in the links to other products established by APIs or network connections. Exchange is not built with magic, nor can the server perform tricks. Along with its own set of challenges, the eventual success of Exchange is influenced by many of the same challenges that face other messaging products. This section outlines, in fairly broad strokes, the most important challenges. Details of how you might face those challenges and how to be successful in your implementation follows in later chapters.

1.9.1   The Microsoft legacy

When Exchange V4.0 first shipped, the immediately obvious obstacle in the way of success for the product was the fact that Microsoft had no history in the design and implementation of enterprise-level messaging systems. In fact, Exchange can be described as the first family of e-mail products that Microsoft has engineered from scratch. The previous generation of e-mail clients, post offices, and connectors was largely bought in from an external company in the form of a product called "Network Courier," and then released as Microsoft Mail. The fundamental principles of LAN-based e-mail systems established in products like Network Courier and Lotus cc:Mail are preserved to this day in Microsoft Mail, and I think it's fair to say that the evolution of Microsoft Mail since its purchase has been in a series of small steps rather than a total redesign.

It's important to realize that the Microsoft Mail clients and its Post Office (server) are far removed from the Exchange program and, apart from the fact that Microsoft Mail clients can be incorporated in an Exchange environment via the Microsoft Mail connector, there is no direct link between the two. It would therefore be unfair to draw any conclusion about Exchange from past experience with Microsoft Mail.

Moving on from a basic e-mail client, Exchange is intended to be much more than a "mail user agent"[11]. Bundled into Exchange is a messaging server, a messaging backbone, a directory service, and the connections that enable the "universal inbox." Implementations from other vendors have not attempted to build all this functionality into a single product, preferring instead to spread it across several products that can, if required, be interconnected to form a logical MTA. The fact that Microsoft has little or no background in this type of messaging technology allows a fresh and brand new look at MTA designs, and maybe it's the right way to go! Certainly the level of integration established across the different components of Exchange has set a new standard for the electronic mail industry.

1.9.2   Competing in the corporate messaging market

One fundamental truth of client-server computing is that older methods of piloting system implementations are obsolete and invariably produce inaccurate results. When I started working with mainframe computer systems we used to pilot new software by running test suites against a limited set of users, carefully recording results as we went. Those results were then used as the basis to determine the likely sizing for full-scale implementations of whatever system we had in mind. In simple terms, if the pilot was run for 20 terminals (users) then roughly 5 times the resources were required to support 100 users, and so on.

The "test then multiply" methodology survived the mainframe era. Suitably modified, I have seen it used to size PC LANs. For example, how much disk to attach to a server, and so on. The same methodology just does not work in client-server implementations because it is so hard to accurately predict what will happen when the system goes live.

In working with e-mail systems over the last fifteen years or so I have found that users learn more about the system every day they're connected. People keep on trying to do new things and learn through a process of trial and experiment. Where users might start by sending two messages a day, soon they're up to ten, and then on to twenty. Where once someone would limit themselves to a few brief lines in an electronic memo, tomorrow they write their life story. Where two or three addresses are the norm on messages, numbers grow to a stage where large (200+) distribution lists become the norm. Where users would never consider rich text attachments, they progress to attach anything and everything that can exist on their hard drive, including

---

[11] A very basic definition of a mail user agent is a program that allows users to compose, read, and send messages. Many additional options can be built on top of this basic set of functionality.

multi-megabyte files. Overall, the average size of messages is going up and up and some large organizations have experienced a ten-fold increase in average message size (from approximately 4K to 40K) in the period 1991–95. This trend can be expected to increase and the average message size may well reach 100K in some networks by the year 2000, or even sooner if the artistic side of users finds fulfillment in the increasingly graphic capabilities of today's desktop applications. Some software vendors are trying to help the situation by building compression capabilities into their products. Microsoft Office 97, for example, is able to create much smaller files in comparison to its predecessors, especially if graphics are incorporated into documents. This book was a 22MB document in Word 95, but decreased to 5MB when I upgraded to Office 97. The same effect is seen for PowerPoint presentations, which often contain graphics. The efforts of the software vendors are laudible, but I fear it's a race against the desire of users to create even more richly graphical documents. The day of the plain typewritten document is long gone.

What affect will it have on your e-mail system if someone attaches a 20MB video or multimedia presentation to a message and sends it to all their friends throughout the network? You may think that a fifteen or twenty megabyte file is never going to be circulated via e-mail within your organization, but I have seen larger files than this sent out across a number of customer networks many times already. Large PowerPoint presentations originating from marketing departments are particular culprits. Most mail servers receiving such large messages don't perform quickly or smoothly, and some collapse under the load.

The increasing volume and size of messages mean that messaging systems are becoming more and more loaded as time goes on. If systems are not monitored and tuned on a continual basis the old adage that all performance always degrades over time (the best performance you ever see is immediately after a new system is switched on for the first time) comes into play and service levels for users degrade.

Running an Exchange server is not the same as running a Post Office on a LAN. There is more to think about, Windows NT is a more complex operating system than DOS, Windows, or Novell NetWare (or Intranetware), and connectivity with other messaging environments is more of an issue than ever before. Exchange servers will support larger user communities than any LAN-based Post Office, so more users are affected at one time if anything goes wrong with the server. There's a whole new skill set to learn too, littered with masses of new acronyms calculated to wear out valuable system management brain cells. Hopefully the remainder of this book provides some illumination to guide the way.

1.9.3   Achieving stability

I am often asked, "when will Exchange be stable?" The flood of service packs and new versions issued by Microsoft is one very good reason why the question is asked. Microsoft is selling Exchange to the corporate sector, a place where people fondly remember the stability of mainframe and mini-computer messaging systems (one software release a year, no massive changes, and so on). Those days are gone now.

Stability is an interesting question, because it's not just Exchange that has to be taken into the equation. A messaging environment is constructed from the underlying operating system, the mail server, and its clients. There is no doubt that the combination of Windows NT, Exchange, and the ever-increasing family of clients that can be connected to Exchange are collectively in a state of flux today. The bad news is that the period of flux will continue for at least two years; the good news is that if proper planning is done it should be possible to minimize the impact of change and maximize the leverage that can be achieved from the new developments.

Among the major changes that will occur in the next two years are:

- Windows NT V5.0; in particular, the advent of the Active Directory.
- Windows NT clustering (the "Wolfpack" API, otherwise known as Microsoft Cluster Manager), and the ability for Exchange servers to be combined into closely connected clusters. The initial release of Wolfpack will provide loose clustering, basically server failover, but close coupling can be expected as the Wolfpack API matures.
- Support for 16TB information stores, with all the associated knock-on effects on the file system and backup products.
- 64-bit Windows NT.
- Rationalization of client options.

The impact of all of these developments is discussed throughout this book. I don't pretend to have the answers. At this stage all I can do is describe what I think is going to happen and why I think it's important. After that it's up to you to get the planning right, and make sure that your company is prepared for change.

1.9.4   Planning leads to success

Judged on the number of companies considering its deployment and the number of clients that have been installed, Exchange is already a successful product. In September 1996 IDC estimated that 750,000

Exchange clients were already operational, six months after the product first shipped, the fastest ramp-up achieved by any new messaging product. When Exchange V5.0 shipped on March 11, 1997, Microsoft announced that 2 million client licenses had been sold, so the pick-up in sales continues to rise. IDC, and other consulting companies, have predicted that Exchange and Lotus Notes will both have over 18 million users by the end of 1998.

Statistics tell the story you want. Getting 750,000, 2 million or whatever number of clients into production is certainly an impressive achievement, but maybe the impact of the number is lessened when you consider the huge size of the Microsoft Mail installed base, allied to the long waiting period for Exchange V4.0 to be shipped. I prefer to say that only 2 million clients were installed because major corporate customers had fully realized the amount of careful and detailed planning required before large-scale global deployments could be successful. Everyone should learn from this caution. To be successful we need to do an amount of planning proportional to the size of your company. That's what the remainder of this book is all about—planning for success with Microsoft Exchange Server.

2

Exchange Clients

2.1   Introduction

Building a robust and reliable server infrastructure is only one part of the messaging story. Clients are equally important. The good news is that Exchange is able to support more and more clients as time goes by. The bad news is that there's possibly too much choice today. It's great for users to be able to pick and choose between lots of different clients so that literally everyone has a different client program on their desktop. In this scenario the server is the point of unification for all the different clients, making sure that everyone can communicate together. Unfortunately, diversity of clients is often a support nightmare, so some intelligent decisions need to be made up front to select the clients for deployment.

MAPI, or Messaging Application Programming Interface, is used by Microsoft to build high-end clients such as Outlook or the 32- and 16-bit versions of the Exchange client. MAPI was the only interface available to clients to communicate with Exchange Server V4.0, but the range of available interfaces expanded to accommodate some non-proprietary standards in Exchange Server V5.0 through the support of protocols such as POP3, HTTP, HTML, and LDAP[1].

The seamless introduction of these protocols is a tribute to the internal architecture of Exchange, built from the start to support multiple protocols and present them as external interfaces for other programs. It's also a fair indication of a trend that is likely to continue in the future when Exchange may expand its range of protocols to incor-

---

[1]   POP3 is the third version of the Post Office Protocol, commonly used to connect Internet mail clients to mail servers. It is a basic interface in that it does not support the range of features commonly offered by high-end interfaces like MAPI. HTTP, the Hypertext Transfer Protocol, and HTML, the Hypertext Mark Up Language, are the interfaces used by Web browsers and servers to communicate together. LDAP, the Lightweight Directory Access Protocol, is used by mail clients to access X.500-like or compliant electronic directory services.

porate new standards as they become established in the electronic mail market.IMAP, the Internet Mail Access Protocol, is a good example of a potential candidate for future support. In 1996 IMAP lags behind POP3 as the protocol of choice for the majority of Internet mail servers, but this situation will reverse itself as new and upgraded versions of mail servers appear that include IMAP support. When IMAP becomes the de facto standard for mail clients to access mail servers in the Internet world, the internal architecture of Exchange will enable the engineers to support IMAP as quickly as they wish to do so.

With the arrival of Exchange V5.0 a number of questions present themselves. These questions need to be assessed carefully within the context of an implementation and deployment plan:

- What client platform should be used? The choice here ranges from DOS through Windows V3, Windows 95, Windows NT, and Apple Macintoshes.

- What client interface is used? Perhaps MAPI to gain full access to all of the features of Exchange, or maybe POP3 because there's an installed base of Internet mail clients already in place?

- How will traveling or roving users be supported? Maybe using the normal client that people use when they're in the office, or maybe something like a Web browser when they're on the road and a low-capacity network connection is all that's available.

- What hardware will clients use? Maybe the client hardware in place can't support the demands that will be made by certain client types, limiting options to something like a Web browser. How will UNIX workstations and 80386-class Intel systems be incorporated into the environment?

- Perhaps some exciting new technology like Citrix's WinFrame (www.citrix.com) can be used to meet certain client demands?

In this chapter I look at these and other questions in an attempt to understand what's really important and help you make intelligent decisions. One thing's for sure: the area of client technology is rapidly evolving and will change between the time this text is committed to a page and the time you read it. Always check to see what's currently available before making your mind up.

2.2   MAPI: The rock Exchange is built on

Over the last few years great attention has been paid by the computer industry to application programming interfaces, mostly because programming to a set of well-documented and understood functions which are supported by multiple products is very much easier than having to create different interfaces for each product.

MAPI is part of a general set of APIs called WOSA, or Windows Open Systems Architecture. Each API within WOSA addresses a specific need. MAPI takes care of messaging, TAPI (the T stands for Telephony) caters for telephone-based applications, and so on. None of these APIs are formally sponsored or coordinated by an industry standards body. It is the sheer market force generated by Microsoft that has moved the WOSA APIs into the lead position for PC development. Other competing interfaces in the messaging area, such as VIM (Vendor Independent Messaging), an interface chiefly espoused by Lotus Development and implemented in their Lotus cc:Mail product, have long been bypassed by MAPI, which is now the de facto interface used by PC applications when they want to integrate support for external messaging products.

While it seems that MAPI is yet another example of where Microsoft has imposed a standard on the computer industry in this case there are many benefits in having a single pre-eminent standard for desktop messaging. The most obvious benefit is reduced cost, achievable because software developers now only have to code to a single standard rather than supporting many. Paradoxically, the single standard could also lead to increased choice for system implementers and users because more products may decide to make themselves "mail-enabled" through MAPI, figuring that if everyone is including support for messaging functions in their product they should too.

2.2.1   The different faces of MAPI

The first implementations of MAPI were seen in versions of Microsoft Mail released in 1993. These implementations were not complete in that the full power and scope of the interface had not been built. In fact, just enough functions were available to build a basic messaging system such as Microsoft Mail, leading to the implementation being referred to as "Simple MAPI," "sMAPI," or "MAPI-0." Simple MAPI is composed of a total of twelve functions including those necessary to log onto a server and then to create, address, send, and read messages. Even the biggest Microsoft fan cannot claim that Microsoft Mail is anything but a simple e-mail client, and indeed this is a strong selling point for the product as users don't tend to need very much training before they become productive. However, it is also a weakness because a lot of functionality available in competing products from other vendors (for example Lotus cc:Mail or DIGITAL TeamLinks) is not supported by the Simple MAPI interface.

Simple MAPI can be viewed as a first step towards the full MAPI interface. Extended MAPI, or MAPI V1.0 is far more comprehensive and capable of accommodating the needs of many different messaging systems.

MAPI can be described as a multi-layered architecture. From top to bottom the different layers are:

1. Client applications. For example, the Exchange client, Outlook, Schedule+.

2. Client Interface, or the mechanism by which client applications make calls to the MAPI subsystem. Four MAPI interfaces are offered to allow client programs to connect:

   ○ The original Simple MAPI interface.
   ○ CMC, or Common Mail Calls.
   ○ OLE Messaging.
   ○ Extended MAPI.

   Only the last of these interfaces can be regarded as an implementation of the full range of MAPI functionality as envisaged by its designers, and this is the interface used by the Microsoft Exchange Server and clients. OLE messaging follows the general trend of Microsoft application programming interfaces towards well-defined object-oriented interfaces. Exchange server and clients use extended MAPI, which is the most flexible and powerful interface.

3. The MAPI run time system and the message spooler.

4. The Service Provider Interface.

5. The individual Service Providers. The Service Provider Interface and the three major service providers are discussed in detail on the next page.

The run time component and the message spooler form the layer between MAPI client interfaces and service providers. The run time component is a DLL that contains a set of base objects and the APIs used by other components. The API contains all the functions necessary to establish a client session with MAPI, to initialize everything correctly, to read profiles to determine what services a user normally connects to, and how to retrieve information such as folders, messages, and other items from a MAPI service provider. The message spooler is an independent process that manages the flow of messages in and out of the system. On Windows 95 and Windows NT systems you'll see a process called MAPISP32 running when the message spooler is active. Not all MAPI service providers use the message spooler, but it is certainly used by Exchange.

As MAPI is an open interface or at least one that's published into the public domain, doesn't this mean that anyone can write a client and connect it to an Exchange server? The answer is that it all depends on what you want to do. The interface between Exchange clients and Exchange server is built on OLE messaging, the most complex and functional interface. The Exchange server also makes use of a number of MAPI extensions to build functionality like public folders. So where it's true that building a client using MAPI will allow a connection to be made, the degree of integration afterwards depends on much of the MAPI interface and any particular extensions are supported by a specific implementation. Certainly there shouldn't be much difficulty in sending and reading messages, but dealing with public folders or electronic forms requires a lot more work on the client side.

2.2.2 MAPI service providers and clients

Applications have very different messaging needs. Most popular desktop applications only want to be able to send copies of documents they produce as attachments to messages created and dispatched without requiring users to leave the application. This is the approach taken by products such as Word, Excel, and PowerPoint. It's a highly functional approach because it lets users get on with their jobs without having to start up a separate mail application.

Figure 2.1 *MAPI Services and service providers*

Each service is physically represented by one or more DLLs

Full-blown e-mail applications such as the Exchange client typically deliver a lot more functionality. They can read, forward, and reply to messages as well as being able to simply generate and send messages. MAPI provides the messaging subsystem for Windows PCs, and facilitates the requirements of desktop and mail applications through the set of interfaces we've just discussed. The different interfaces—Simple MAPI, CMC, OLE Messaging, and Extended MAPI—are all layered on top of MAPI itself. In effect MAPI is the collection point for all messaging commands issued by applications on a Windows PC.

A set of Service Providers, or SPIs, is arrayed beneath the MAPI layer. Service Providers are the implementations of driver programs which action the commands issued by clients through the MAPI layer. You can think of Service Providers as the glue connecting MAPI clients to services that are, in turn, physically represented by software running on a server computer somewhere in the network. Microsoft and other software vendors may provide a single service, or collect together a number of different services that can be provided to clients by a mail server. Exchange delivers all of the services necessary for a high-end messaging system. The most important services are:

- *Message Store:* how messages are organized and accessed in a structured repository. For example, the set of folders in an Exchange mailbox. Message stores are defined as a well-organized hierarchy of folders and messages, where folders are objects that can contain other folders as well as messages. Message store providers also handle the creation and submission of messages.

- *Message Transport:* how messages are physically dispatched to their eventual destination.

- *Address Books:* sources of addressing information that can be made available to end users. Exchange provides an on-line address book (the directory store) and off-line address book (the OAB and PAB).

MAPI takes the responsibility of deciding whether its own subsystem is able to handle a client request, or which service provider should take on the task. Table 2.1 outlines how MAPI and the different Exchange service providers might interact during a simple client session.

On Windows PCs MAPI service providers are built in the form of one or more Dynamic Link Libraries. This implementation allows the code for each service provider to be loaded as required by clients.

Table 2.1   *Interaction between service providers*

Client action	Responsible components
Start up an Exchange client and connect to an Exchange server	MAPI
Display the list of folders in the server mailbox	Message store provider
Create a new message	Message store provider
Respond to CTRL/K keystroke to validate some addresses added to message header	Address book provider
Send the message	Message store provider, then message spooler, then transport provider
Delete the message from the outbox folder	Message store provider
Exit from Exchange and Log Off	Message store provider, then MAPI

When an Exchange client is invoked it consults its "profile" to discover what set of services it is configured for. Profiles are named lists of message services and configuration data that are created and managed by users. Users may have multiple profiles configured on a single PC. For example, you might configure a profile for use in the office when a wide range of messaging servers are available, and another for use when you're traveling, when the only server that can be connected to is Exchange (via a RAS dial-up connection).

The installation procedure for service providers writes details about the capabilities that can be offered to clients into the system registry. Clients are then able to browse through the set of available services when they configure a profile. Figure 2.1 illustrates the set of MAPI services typically configured for an Exchange client. Details of the Dynamic Link Libraries can be gained by viewing a service provider's properties.

The standard Windows 95 kit contains MAPI service providers for Microsoft Mail, FAX, and the Microsoft Network. You can also add an Internet (POP3) provider from the Windows 95 Plus! kit. When you configure an Exchange client in this environment you are able to select one or all of these service providers to use. And when Exchange Server is available you can install the Exchange service provider and use it to connect to the Server. Third parties provide MAPI service providers to allow clients to connect to their servers and if these are available you can configure a client for them as well. The resulting profile might well contain entries for four or more providers, all of which will be connected to when the client starts up.

Figure 2.2
*The Windows
messaging
subsystem*

Figure 2.2 illustrates how all of the components in the Windows messaging subsystem work together. At the top clients use calls to messaging functions to create and send messages. The functions are processed by MAPI. Responsibility for processing the messages is handed over by MAPI to the service providers configured in the user's profile, and eventually the messages arrive at a server computer that takes care of delivery. Extended functions such as the address book, Schedule+ meeting requests, or e-forms are handled in the same way, the difference being that the service providers (and the server) must be able to process these type of messages.

2.3   A wide range of Exchange clients

A wide range of client platforms is available for Exchange. Clients[2] shipping with the Exchange Server include Windows for Work-Groups, Windows 95, Windows NT, and good old DOS. The DOS cli-

---

[2]   Microsoft also refers to the Exchange client as a "viewer." This may be in line with the concept of "Information Exchange" where the server becomes a common receptacle for information arriving from many different sources—interpersonal e-mail, faxes, voice mail, and so on. In this scheme the client can be considered a universal information viewer because it contains all the functionality and features necessary to deal with all the data that arrives at the server.

ent is a short-term tactical solution to cater for organizations that have considerable populations of low-end PCs still in place, and is limited by the basic functionality available to DOS. Don't expect to be able to handle embedded OLE objects, for instance. Of course, a purely cynical view of the situation is that providing someone with the DOS client is possibly one good way of convincing them that life could be a lot richer and that they should really start using a more modern platform!

Notable for its absence in the client line-up is support for a native UNIX solution, chiefly to address the UNIX workstation market. Primarily due to their understandable focus on Windows, Microsoft has never provided a solution for UNIX workstations. UNIX is a popular and powerful platform for mail servers used by many millions of people, but UNIX workstations, although popular with their users, is a very minor player in terms of the total potential market for client licenses when compared to Windows in all its shapes and forms.

With these points in mind the lack of a native UNIX client from Microsoft is not at all surprising. However, corporate messaging environments demand accommodation for all the different platforms typically found on user desktops, including UNIX workstations. Two solutions are available to fill the gap.

First, you can consider emulation software that allows Windows programs to be run on UNIX systems. Emulation software works by basically trapping calls made to Windows API functions and translating the calls into UNIX code. Good emulation software will allow applications like the Windows 95 Exchange client to run on a range of UNIX systems, including Sun Solaris. Performance isn't too bad either, especially if the workstation has a fast processor (as most of the latest generation has) and there's plenty of memory available. At the end of the day code that runs natively is a better solution than emulation, leading on to the solution currently espoused by Microsoft.

The second option for UNIX users is to consider accessing an Exchange server via an application that can run as a native-mode UNIX program. In this scenario the UNIX program communicates using a protocol understood by both the program and Exchange. Using a Web browser to talk to Exchange via the Web connector is one way; using a UNIX mail client and the POP3 protocol to connect to Exchange is another. Looking at things from the reverse angle, the POP3 service provider for the Exchange client allows the client to connect to a POP3 mail server (such as Netscape's mail server or DIGITAL's AltaVista mail server).

In both cases you may be limited by the fact that neither interface (Web browser or UNIX mail client) is designed with the express intention of leveraging the capabilities of Exchange Server, so many of the server features may be unavailable. However, you should be able to read information and create and send messages, which is all that many people are really interested in. The situation certainly isn't as good as would pertain if a true native UNIX client were available, but at least you are able to connect UNIX users in.

While it's undeniable that Windows has grabbed the lion's share of the desktop market there are considerable and often influential groups of Apple Macintosh users in most major corporations. In comparison to their undoubted success with Microsoft Mail for Windows, Microsoft hasn't had a good record in the Macintosh messaging space over the years. In late 1995 Microsoft transferred Microsoft Mail for Macintosh (and some 750,000 clients) to StarNine Technologies, who were promptly taken over by Quarterdeck (the company made famous by its QEMM memory management product). Quarterdeck Mail for Macintosh shipped in 1996 and has reasonable interoperability between it, Microsoft Mail for the PC, and Exchange.

Microsoft's own Exchange client for the Macintosh was not released with Exchange V4.0, eventually arriving some four months afterwards with Service Pack 2 (August 1996). The Macintosh client is limited in some respects. For example, it can't process electronic forms designed with Visual Basic, but it does deliver the basic e-mail features people need to be able to access and work with messages. Schedule+ support for the Exchange client for Macintosh is provided as part of the Exchange V5.0 release.

An important improvement from previous LAN-based mail systems is the provision of out-of-the-box remote (modem-enabled) access. In the previous Microsoft Mail product users had to purchase a separate add-on module to upgrade their client for remote access. The most common way to establish remote connections is via RAS dial-up connections to Exchange server, a good example of how Exchange has leveraged off a standard component of the Windows NT operating system.

To complete the line-up, OS/2 Warp clients, the great unwashed of the Windows community (in Microsoft's eyes), are able to run the Exchange 16-bit client under the OS/2 Windows subsystem. Communication with the server is accomplished via TCP/IP. I have never attempted to set up and operate such a configuration so I am unable to add any other value other than noting that such a combination exists. The question of whether an OS/2 client will ever work happily in an Exchange environment is left for experimentation on the part of those of you who have an OS/2 installed base to support. Given that many

POP3 and Web browsers are available for OS/2 I think I would look in those directions for a solution rather than trying to convince OS/2 to run a Windows client.

2.3.1   The facts about the Universal Inbox

While I'm discussing clients, let me take the opportunity to pour a judicious amount of cold water on one of the biggest fables around Exchange—the "free" Exchange client that first appeared in Windows 95 and then in Windows NT V4.0. Building on the precedent established by the provision of the Microsoft Mail client in Windows for WorkGroups and Windows NT V3.*, basic messaging functionality is provided in all Windows 95 and Windows NT systems. In both systems the foundation for electronic mail is referred to as the Universal Inbox. Some fog and confusion is introduced into the picture when the Universal Inbox boldly labels itself "Microsoft Exchange" when the program starts up, so a quick review of the actual facts of the matter is probably necessary at this point.

Figure 2.3
*Components of
the Windows 95
Universal Inbox*

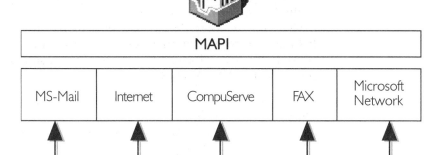

The concept behind the Universal Inbox—to provide a single consistent location for all electronic communications to arrive into—is a compelling vision, and Microsoft has done a good job in defining the structure for the single location, especially in Windows 95. As well as acting as a single location for incoming communications (see Figure 2.3) the client is able to act as a fully-fledged message user agent, creating and sending messages via a variety of systems, each of which is defined as a messaging service provider. However, the standard Universal Inbox isn't as comprehensive a mail client as the full-blown

Exchange client as it provides only the same degree of send/receive/ process messaging capabilities as the older Microsoft Mail clients. The Universal Inbox isn't the same as Microsoft Mail and it would be incorrect to represent it as such, if only because the underlying internal structure follows the same architecture as the full Exchange client.

Now that you're suitably confused between the Universal Inbox and the "full" Exchange client let me reassure you that you're not very different in this respect to many other people. To help address the issue Microsoft renamed the Universal Inbox and began to refer to it as "Windows Messaging" from June 1996 on (the client included with Windows NT V4.0 announces itself as Windows Messaging). Now there is a clear differentiation between messaging as incorporated into the desktop operating systems and the fully-fledged Exchange client. To back the point Microsoft released an updated version of Windows Messaging at the same time. This client incorporates fixes made during Exchange development and can be downloaded from the Microsoft Web site. However, it will take a while before Windows Messaging becomes the commonly used term so I'll continue to refer to the Universal Inbox for the rest of this book.

So what can you do with the Windows 95 or Windows NT Universal Inbox? First, you can use it as a direct replacement for current Microsoft Mail clients by configuring the Universal Inbox to connect to a Microsoft Mail Post Office. Then you can expand your horizons by enabling additional messaging service providers. For example, Windows 95 includes the components needed to connect your universal inbox to a FAX service, CompuServe[3], and the Microsoft Network. An additional service provider for Internet mail is available in the Microsoft Plus pack for Windows 95. The Internet service provider is interesting because it allows the Windows 95 client to connect to a large number of UNIX-based mail systems, downloading messages via the POP3 protocol and then acts as an SMTP client when sending messages. Other Internet service providers are available from Netscape and as part of the Microsoft Internet Explorer.

Service providers enabled by installing additional software onto a PC bring plug-and-play to the world of messaging. The concept is an important part of the way that the Universal Inbox has been built to bring many different forms of electronic communications together in a single consistent place. It's an exciting concept because it means that

---

[3]   The CompuServe service provider is not installed automatically. A service provider for CompuServe is packaged in the Windows 95 kit and can be found in DRIVERS\OTHER\EXCHANGE\COMPSRV. Use the SETUP.EXE in the directory to install the new provider. An updated service provider which addresses some bugs in the original is also available from CompuServe (see the WINCON forum).

people can configure their mailbox the way they want to, as long as a service provider exists to connect them to whatever information sources they need.

Figure 2.4 *How the Exchange server service provider fits into the Universal Inbox*

The free service providers will meet the needs of many people, but a separate license must be purchased and the Exchange client components upgraded before the Universal Inbox can connect to Exchange, as shown in Figure 2.4. Encountering a requirement to upgrade client software is hardly surprising because Windows 95 shipped some seven months before Exchange. Most of Windows 95 was finalized in the early summer of 1995, and many of the important internal client-centric features in Exchange changed considerably between the release of Windows 95 through the final builds before eventual product ship in March 1996. Apart from updating the service provider for the Universal Inbox, the upgrade is necessary to expose server-centric features such as the rules engine and to enable server-based time management via Schedule+. If you're running an earlier version of Schedule+, such as the version provided with Office 95, this software can be updated at the same time. The upgrade is quick and simple, and carried out by connecting to a share-point on a Windows NT server where the installation kit for the client software is located.

In summary, while it's an attractive notion to have a free mail client on all desktops, there's no such thing as a free lunch and the financial analysis for a general move to an Exchange infrastructure must factor in the costs of client licenses.

2.3.2   No luck for older terminals

"Green screen e-mail" is the term used by a certain Microsoft sales representative of my acquaintance to describe host-based messaging systems. The term accurately describes the green (or other color) glow of the 24 × 80 screen used to log onto mainframe or mini-based computers to access older messaging systems.

Exchange offers no method for connecting unintelligent clients like IBM 3270s or the other classic Video Terminals (VTs). If you want to run Exchange you have to face the fact that PC clients are the only way forward. Most installations have gone a long way to sorting out their desktop infrastructure over the past few years and there has been a steady decline in the number of VTs in use. However, I know of quite a few sites where VTs are still counted in hundreds, mostly because they are cheap to install and support and many users only require simple text-based messaging. If you have a substantial VT population you'll either have to remove Exchange from your list of potential messaging solutions or pay the ante and replace VTs with PCs, with all the attendant costs involved.

2.3.3   Basic Exchange client functionality

How many features of your word processor or spreadsheet do you actually use? How many have you mastered to a degree where you can use the feature without reaching for a manual or conducting a frantic search through the application's help file? If you're anything like me you'll only ever use about 20% of an application's features, unless it's something that you use every day. Electronic mail is an application accessed by most users every day, so the range of features offered by the application is important and it's more likely than even esoteric features will be discovered and used by quite a few people.

The Exchange clients are highly functional. There are probably more options available on menus, especially if the long versions of the menus are turned on, than most people will ever care about. All of the options are presented in an attractive user interface that is utterly consistent with the rest of the Microsoft office applications. If you're accustomed to using Word, Excel, PowerPoint, and Access you'll be totally at home with an Exchange client, such as the Windows 95 client pictured in Figure 2.5. Even the more esoteric options hidden away on the farther reaches of Tools.Options, such as the feature which allows messages to be sent after a certain delay, show evidence of careful research into the finer points of graphical user interfaces.

Figure 2.5 *The Exchange client for Windows 95*

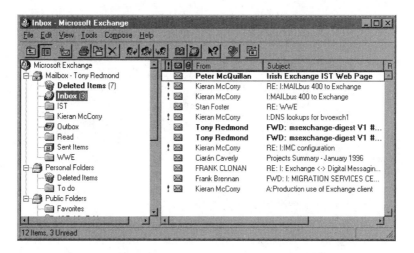

Let me give an example to illustrate what I mean. An option to submit a message to a server for delivery later on is common to quite a number of messaging systems, where the feature is sometimes referred to as "deferred mail." Most other implementations ask the user to specify a time and date to send the message. There's little wrong in this approach, but the Exchange developers have taken a slightly different view that may make the option more approachable to some users. In Exchange you can ask for a message to be sent after a range of different delays, for instance 1 to 999 minutes, or after 3 days, or 4 weeks, and so on. Instead of requesting an absolutely accurate date and time, which is the correct technical or engineering solution, the emphasis is placed on accommodating humans and the fuzzy logic that humans tend to use. "When do I want this message to go?"; "In about two days' time...." You may or may not like the implementation, but it's good to see people trying to do things slightly differently than it's been done before.

While I like the overall functionality delivered in the Exchange client, all is not sweetness and light. The ability for a user to autoforward or redirect messages from a client option is a startling gap, mostly because this is a feature that's commonly found on other high-end messaging clients. Autoforward usually means that the server automatically forwards messages on to a different address after they are delivered in a mailbox, normally leaving a copy of the forwarded message in the mailbox. Redirection occurs on the server, with messages being intercepted and never reaching the original recipient's mailbox, so no trace of the redirected messages will be found. The system administrator can redirect messages on behalf of a user by setting the redirect property on a mailbox. I think that most people who have ever used an autoforward feature would agree that it would be much better to be able to do this without boring system administrators.

Table 2.2 breaks down the most important features of the standard Exchange clients (16-bit or 32-bit) into four categories. Note that the Microsoft Outlook client adds a whole range of new options, all of which operate quite happily with an Exchange server. A curious omission from Outlook is the ability for users to set their passwords on the server. Exchange clients allow passwords to be changed through the "Exchange Server" properties accessed through the Tools.Options menu choice.

Table 2.2   *Exchange client features*

Mailbox Maintenance	
Open	Open a set of folders
Move	Move an item from one folder to another
Copy	Copy an item from one folder to another
Delete	Move an item to the "Deleted Items" folder
Rename	Change the display name for an item
Find	Search a store according to a set of criteria supplied by the user
Find Public Folders	Search the public information store (5.0)
Properties	Display the properties of an item
New folder	Create a new folder in a selected store
Add to favorites	Mark a folder as one that you refer to frequently
Import	Import messages stored in a mailbox
Send on behalf	Give permission to another user to send messages on your behalf
User Interface	
View...	Turn off/on viewing of folders, toolbar, and the status bar
Sort	Define different sort orders for folder contents
Filters	Apply a filter to folder contents so that only items which pass the filter are displayed
Personal views	Design your own view of a store
Cover memo creation	
Create	Create a new memo
Send	Send a memo

Table 2.2 *Exchange client features (continued)*

Reply	Reply to a memo you've received. Options are reply to sender or reply to everyone who received the note
Forward	Forward the memo to another user
Post Note	Post a note to a folder
Post Form	Post an electronic form to a folder
Editor	Rich text format (RTF) or Word for Windows (V7.0a onwards)
Spell Check	Spell check the contents of a memo, including automatic check before dispatching a memo to the server
Tools	
Synchronize	Synchronize local folders with the server
Remote mail	Access mail over a telephone connection
Inbox Assistant	Define rules for execution when messages arrive on the server. For example, delete any message with "For your information" in the title
Out of Office Assistant	Create informative messages to be sent to correspondents when you aren't able to respond to your messages
AutoSignature	Apply supplied text to messages before they are sent
Address Book	Personal repository for e-mail addresses
Application Design	Design a public folder
Schedule+	Time management and PIM (Personal Information Manager)
Customize Toolbar	Customize the client toolbar
Services	Configure the services you wish to use. For example, Exchange Server, Personal Folders, Personal Address Book, Microsoft FAX, and so on
Security	Message encryption and digital signatures

Mailbox maintenance is the feature which enables a user to manage his or her own working environment and organize the information they receive and work with. A user interface is common to all graphical products, but Exchange clients offer a few unique features in their implementation. Cover memo creation is the set of features used for the core activity, creating and sending messages. The features in the Tools category mark the real difference between Exchange and the majority of PC-based electronic messaging clients that have appeared before. While many of the features in all categories have appeared before in other products, the real difference is the breadth and depth of the features as a collective whole.

A viewer for different file formats is a feature currently missing from Exchange clients. Viewers typically allow files generated in different formats to be displayed in a Read Message window, avoiding the need to start up a separate application to view file contents. Viewers are more important in a heterogeneous messaging environment where different word processors, spreadsheets, and graphic packages tend to be used across the total user population, leading to inevitable difficulties when one user generates a document in a certain format and sends it to others who haven't got the application installed on their PC. A number of third parties are working to address this need. Two of the best are OutSide In and Quick View Plus, both of which are capable of dealing with all the common PC file formats and quite a few of the more esoteric formats that float around a network.

2.3.4   Exchange clients from non-Microsoft sources

We've already discussed how the user configurations for the Windows messaging subsystem are defined in terms of a profile. A profile describes the services the user wishes to access and the MAPI providers that enable such access. A graphic illustrating typical components configured within a MAPI profile is shown in Figure 2.6.

Figure 2.6 MAPI
Clients and
Providers

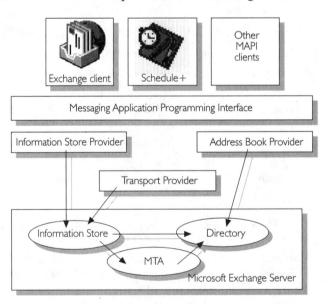

If multiple users share a PC a separate profile is quite probably defined for each. It is quite possible for a user to maintain several profiles, each of which describes a totally different environment. For example, one profile might detail a connection to Exchange Server for use when transporting new messages while another specifies that a Microsoft Mail Post Office is to be used instead. Each of the different providers might be capable of making different features available to clients, so these differences can be configured as part of the profile too.

The attractive notion of having a single universal client as the access point to many different messaging services has encouraged many vendors to consider building the necessary software components to link Microsoft Exchange clients (both the full Exchange client and the Universal Inbox) to their own mail servers via MAPI. DIGITAL has built two separate products (called Digital Drivers for MAPI[4]) to connect Exchange clients to DIGITAL MailWorks for UNIX or ALL-IN-1 (OpenVMS) servers, allowing enterprises to deploy UNIX-based or OpenVMS-based messaging servers while continuing to use the well-integrated desktop functionality available in the Windows 95 clients.

The DIGITAL drivers are good examples of full MAPI service providers. The MAPI Service Providers enable DIGITAL mail servers to be defined to MAPI clients in terms they understand. As a message store (in DIGITAL messaging terms a store is referred to as a file cabinet), the transport by which messages pass between the client and server, and a directory of mail subscribers to replace or supplement the Exchange Global Address List. Apart from incorporating a huge new range of potential clients, building a MAPI service provider conveys a number of advantages to vendors. For example, changes normally don't have to be made on the server as all the work to translate MAPI functions to server-specific calls can be encapsulated in the service provider DLL that's installed on each client. This fact alone means that existing servers can continue to operate, in effect gracefully evolving to support new client connections without realizing the fact. While the server side is insulated from change, using MAPI means that a whole client user interface is picked up free of charge, giving the vendor the option of concentrating solely on the server if that makes commercial sense.

Figure 2.7 shows the Exchange client for Windows 95 connected to a DIGITAL ALL-IN-1 server running on an OpenVMS system. As far as the user is concerned all they see is the Exchange user interface. The only hint that it might not be an Exchange server humming in the

---

[4]   The first version of the Digital MAPI driver (for MailWorks for UNIX) shipped in November 1995. The ALL-IN-1 driver shipped in summer 1996.

background is a few discrete mentions of ALL-IN-1 when mailbox contents are listed or when users configure the services they wish to connect to. Even Lotus Notes, the major competitor for Exchange in the battle to win the hearts and minds of people for selection for corporate groupware and messaging deployments, provides a MAPI service provider for Exchange. The Lotus Notes service provider allows an Exchange client to connect to a mailbox on a Lotus Notes server (Release 4.0 or later). Once connected you're able to drag and drop from one server to the other, preserving the data as well as most of the attributes of messages and other items.

Figure 2.7
*Digital's
ALL-IN-1 server
accessed by the
Exchange client
for Windows 95*

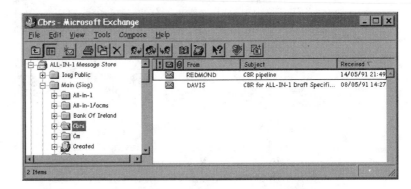

Another good example of how MAPI can be used to build extensions for the Exchange client environment is the provision of an additional directory service that can be shared between Exchange and other clients. See the discussion and screen shot beginning on page 501.

While a general movement towards a common client for all sorts of electronic communications makes sense in many aspects, especially when client software is bundled with the desktop operating system, there will be situations when the Exchange client doesn't fully exploit the capabilities that a third party server can offer. Perhaps the MAPI specification doesn't completely accommodate features of other servers and no amount of magic programming can make the client work with the server. Or maybe the server offers more in terms of features such as workflow or document management. In these cases vendors, such as DIGITAL, will continue to supply their own client software.

Utilizing MAPI to permit enterprises to select clients from one source and servers from another, while all the time presenting users with a seamless service, is a compelling example of the power of the MAPI concept.

In general I think it's fair to say that mixing different MAPI clients with different MAPI servers is great as long as you're interested in purely messaging functionality. In other words, all you want to do is create, send, and read messages. However, if a particular client or server offers specific functionality you may not be able to access it with all possible combinations. Some testing may be required to establish exactly what's possible with what combination in your particular environment. For example, will public folders be accessible from non-Microsoft clients that connect to an Exchange server? Will Exchange clients be able to utilize the mail delegation functionality as implemented in another vendor's MAPI-enabled server?

Another issue to consider is that third party service providers need to keep up to date with developments in the Exchange program. The advent of the Outlook client required software vendors to issue new versions of their service providers. In 1997 DIGITAL updated their code to add new functionality in OpenVMS mail servers as well as to support Outlook, while Lotus has also upgraded code to allow Exchange and Outlook clients access to Lotus Notes (Domino) servers.

A purely cynical view of the situation, which is perhaps accurate in many respects, is that open systems work best as long as you buy all the open components from a single vendor. Along this line it may well be inevitable that MAPI components originating from Microsoft will always offer the highest degree of integration and interoperability with the Exchange server. This is somewhat inevitable where client and server components are built by a single vendor. The Microsoft clients will also look and feel exactly like other Microsoft applications, again hardly surprising because all the desktop applications make use of common programming libraries. Vendors selling alternate clients for connection to Exchange servers or servers for Exchange clients have to make a compelling case and provide significant added value before a real case can be made for those alternate solutions to be considered. Better integration with other messaging systems installed within an organization, an integrated set of converters and viewers, or better customization capabilities are all good arguments to go towards another client, especially if you want to establish a situation where a common client (one that's capable of connecting to all servers) is used throughout your organization.

I do not recommend that you consider using client-level software such as service providers as the primary tools for migration from other mail systems to Exchange. It is attractive to imagine that you might be able to ask users to shoulder the burden for the migration of data to Exchange. However, the sheer amount of work and number of repetitions required to drag and drop messages from the old system to Exchange is too onerous in most cases. Remember that you're asking people to review all the messages in the old system, decide whether they want to take them to Exchange, and then perform the physical action of dragging and dropping. Users also have to create a new folder structure in Exchange to receive the messages they wish to move. It may take a user an hour or two (probably more) to review and process an old mailbox, but a very large number of hours is required if you scale the number of hours up across the entire user population. You won't be popular when you explain to upper management that several thousand people hours are going to be lost (in terms of other productivity).

In essence, MAPI service providers are coexistence tools, not for migration. Use the service providers to introduce Exchange to client desktops. Service providers span the gap between the introduction of Exchange within your messaging systems and whenever the Exchange client/server combination becomes the primary user environment. Other migration tools do a better, cleaner job of bulk movement of user files to Exchange.

2.4   Exchange and Outlook

With such an array of available clients how can you make a choice as to which one (or ones) to deploy? Before making any decisions, let's take a quick look into the past and try and figure out what the lessons learned there tell us for the future, especially when put into context with the developments in train within Microsoft and the industry in general.

Figure 2.8 *The Outlook client*

When Exchange shipped first the only clients that were available came from Microsoft. These clients can be described as heavy-duty e-mail clients because they are designed for a specific purpose. The Exchange clients deliver a lot of functionality, but even with the integration of e-form applications and extensions like Schedule+ they are relatively single-minded.

The next generation of Exchange clients came in the form of Outlook (Figure 2.8), initially introduced as part of the Office 97 application suite. Outlook takes a different view of the world. Instead of focusing primarily on e-mail, Outlook attempts to apply the same basic user interface to a whole range of information sources to form a desktop information manager, something that people can use to access and manage all of the different data sources they need to work with. Overall, Outlook is a much more comprehensive client than the standard Exchange client, but it is only available for 32-bit Windows desktops. Exchange still figures very much as the preferred mail server behind the scenes, but again, Exchange is only one of the information sources for Outlook, albeit the most important one.

Lots of people will buy Office 97 and won't necessarily have Exchange at their disposal. They can still use Outlook as their mail client by connecting it to another mail server, such as an Internet messaging system via a POP3 interface (referred to as the Outlook Internet E-Mail Driver). Expect to see Microsoft put considerable effort into Outlook add-ons and enhancements to make the client work as smoothly as possible with Internet mail systems. Just like Exchange wants to become the server of choice for as many different types of mail clients as possible, the Outlook client wants to be the client of choice for as many different mail servers as possible. Delivering the widest range of functionality is the best way to ensure user loyalty, although the tactic of providing a free mail client along with every Office 97 kit will also be a great help in achieving the "client for the masses" goal.

There still is a large population of Microsoft Mail clients in use today. It is probable that Microsoft Mail Post Offices will serve a growing population of Outlook clients until these installations can migrate to Exchange. There is a reasonable case to advise people using the Microsoft Mail client today to migrate to Outlook immediately to use it along with the rest of Office 97. The clients can then switch their messaging focus to Exchange when the necessary infrastructure (network, Windows NT, and so on) has been put in place. This approach delivers more functionality to users quickly, relieving pressure on the implementation team and hopefully leading to more satisfied users.

A new version of calendaring software is included in Outlook, one that focuses on server-based folders rather than the mixture of server and local resources that powered Schedule+. Microsoft plans to ship a module to allow Schedule+ users to read Outlook calendars by the middle of 1997, so it should be available by the time you read this book. A batch-mode utility to migrate large numbers of Schedule+ calendars to Outlook should also be available then. Both of these programs are required to help corporate users migrate to Outlook.

Figure 2.9
Recalling a message with Outlook

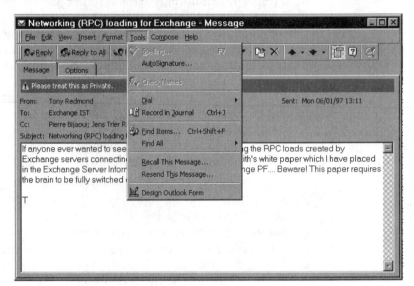

Remember that Outlook can be bought separately from the rest of the Office 97 applications, so there's no reason to wait until you're ready to upgrade from earlier versions of Word, Excel, and so on. Outlook works quite happily with Office 95 applications, or even earlier versions like Word for Windows V6.0.

2.4.1   Outlook and Exchange

Curiously there are two slightly different versions of Outlook. The first was delivered with Office 97; the second is included with Exchange V5.0[5]. Why might this be so? In many respects, Microsoft is a company whose software is driven by marketing pressures. Outlook is an essential part of Office 97 so it had to be ready to ship at the appointed date. But Outlook also had to work well with Exchange V5.0 and three full months elapsed between the ship dates for Office 97 and Exchange V5.0. That time was used to fix some bugs and improve product quality, meaning that if you plan to deploy Outlook you should use the software distributed with Exchange and not Office 97.

---

[5]   The version numbers for the two versions are 8.0 (Office 97) and 8.01 (Exchange V5.0).

Among the changes made in the Outlook client shipped with Exchange V5.0 are:

- Updated MAPI modules and service provider DLLs to connect to Exchange Server.

- The AutoUpdate feature, which is able to sense whether a newer version of the Outlook client is available on a network share. If this is the case a prompt offers the user the option to update their client software.

- Better handling of MAPI tables allows performance improvements when the client needs to collapse or expand folder lists.

- The sort method for the "By Conversion Topic" view is changed to sort (more logically) by the most recently received message rather than alphabetically.

- The OUTLOOK.PRF (Outlook preferences) file which is used to configure a default profile for a new user now includes Exchange in the list of service providers, and configures the profile to direct new mail to be delivered to a server mailbox rather than a PST file.

- Support of the new features in Exchange V5.0 such as per-recipient send options, address book views, NNTP publishing user interface, and sub-folder favorites.

As outlined at the end of this chapter, it is likely that Outlook will remain the focus for Microsoft client development for Windows platforms. Today's Exchange client is not likely to receive much additional development over the next few years because splitting scarce development resources across two competing clients is hardly a good idea. Microsoft's past history gives no indication that they'll be happy to continue building multiple clients so some rationalization is inevitable.

2.4.2   Outlook forms

Exchange clients have always offered e-form capabilities. As reviewed in Chapter 1, there are some deficiencies with the current implementation that prevent e-forms being generally adopted outside a pure Exchange environment. Outlook has forms of its own, and these are different to the forms created with the standard Exchange Forms Designer.

The major differences between Outlook and Exchange e-forms are:

- Outlook forms are fully 32-bit. Exchange forms are 16-bit.

- Outlook forms are much smaller than Exchange forms, mostly because they don't contain any interpreted code. Everything in an Outlook form is compiled, so they perform faster too.

- Outlook forms support advanced security features (digital signatures and encryption).

- Outlook forms can contain template documents for Office 97 applications. For example, the sample Expense Claim form (see the Microsoft Web site) contains an Excel template that can be used to enter expense data. Exchange forms are limited to documents rather than templates.

- Outlook forms support a wider range of field types than Exchange including formula fields, combination fields, and fields with preset validation criteria. Outlook forms also support ActiveX controls, including Internet controls, so a far closer integration with Web resources can be built.

- Outlook forms can be programmed with VBscript, the common "macro" programming language for Office 97 applications.

- The Outlook forms designer is a much-enhanced version of its Exchange counterpart. For example, it includes an AutoLayout feature that automatically positions controls on a form. Features like this make it much easier (and quicker) to develop forms, in turn making it more likely that people will devote effort to building forms.

With such an impressive list of features it is easy to assume that Outlook forms can provide a solution for everyone. However, while Outlook forms are much more functional than those built with the Exchange EFD, they are still limited to Windows desktops. As long as you only ever need to deal with Windows, Outlook forms will do a great job, and allow you to exploit the "one application for everything" concept that Outlook brings to the desktop. In the future, when forms applications move away from proprietary standards towards a platform independent form, probably HTML, forms like those generated by Outlook will be much more interesting for the people who aren't connected to an Exchange server.

2.5   Lightweight clients

The Exchange or Outlook clients provide a very high level of functionality, but they are not suitable for everyone. As we've just discussed, these full-function clients require a fairly modern and well-specified hardware platform before they can be used, and there are no Exchange clients available for some operating systems, such as any variant of UNIX.

Many corporate environments have hundreds or even thousands of low-powered PCs still in use. It is common to find 80386- and early 80486-class systems that have been happily running DOS, Windows V3, old versions of Windows applications that don't take up quite as much system resources as today's editions, and maybe even terminal emulators to access mainframe or mini-computer e-mail systems. On such PCs it is difficult to achieve an acceptable degree of performance with the Exchange clients. The DOS Exchange client is a notable exception, but I cannot think of a single corporate project I have worked with that has regarded the DOS client as anything other than an interesting side street, certainly not something suitable for deployment on user desktops. Old Apple Macintoshes (basically anything that's not powered by the PowerPC CPU) are often in the same situation, especially if they don't have a lot of memory or local hard disk.

Without unlimited finance, no one can propose a complete replacement of these systems, yet a solution must be found as otherwise a block is placed on Exchange implementation projects. Without client desktops capable of connecting to the server there's no point in installing the server. Without client desktops to use there's no point in replacing the current e-mail system. The desire to implement Exchange, or any high-end messaging system that uses a graphical user environment, founders on the rock of a low hardware base.

Another common situation is to find that plans exist for a complete overhaul of user hardware, normally as part of an effort to move desktops from Windows V3 to Windows 95 or Windows NT. Both Windows 95 and Windows NT require a great deal more hardware than Windows V3, so the need to invest in some new hardware is a well-recognized part of the upgrade effort. Application upgrades are usually factored into the deployment of a new version of Windows, and the Exchange client or Outlook can be included in this set of tasks. The Exchange implementation project is contingent on new hardware being deployed as part of the general desktop upgrade. It is an advantage that the upgrade will eventually occur, but the implementation of Exchange can be slowed if the general upgrade does not progress quickly.

Lack of support for a certain operating system, limited finance, and dependency on other projects are therefore three significant challenges for implementation project managers to overcome. Microsoft's answer is to allow "lightweight clients" to access and use the resources of an Exchange server, and so act as an alternative to the Exchange or Outlook clients. Microsoft is not generally associated with the engineering or provision of lightweight clients. The exception that proves the rule is Microsoft Internet Explorer, which can connect to Exchange using either the POP3 protocol or via the Web access service. However, in general, lightweight clients might be defined as software built to use Internet protocols that have now been enabled for Exchange through server support of those Internet protocols. Today, these protocols include:

- Post Office Protocol (POP3)
- Hypertext Mark Up Language (HMTL)
- Hypertext Transmission Protocol (HTTP)
- Lightweight Directory Access Protocol (LDAP)
- Secure Sockets Layer (SSL)

Anyone can write software that uses one or more of these protocols to access the messaging and other capabilities of an Exchange server. The lightweight clients are broken down into two major families:

1. Messaging-only clients, those that use the POP3 protocol to access an Exchange server. In the future the IMAP4 protocol will be supported, expanding the variety of clients in this category.

2. Web browsers that use the combination of the Web Active Server (on a Windows NT server) and the normal HTTP/HTML Web protocols to access messaging, public folder, and scheduling functionality from an Exchange server.

Both families of lightweight clients can use LDAP to access the Exchange directory, providing the individual implementation of the client software supports the LDAP protocol.

There are a wide variety of e-mail clients that use POP3 to connect to a mail server. Some of the POP3 clients are of a much higher quality than others, but the sheer number of available clients is testimony to the popularity of the protocol. Apart from the major players (Microsoft and Netscape) in the Web browser market, there are other browsers available that can connect to Exchange. Some Web browsers are POP3-capable, so can access Exchange using POP3 or Web protocols. The latter is usually the better option, if only for the fact that much more functionality is available.

A large proportion of Web browsers and POP3 e-mail clients are given away free or provided on a shareware basis so they are undeniably cheap to deploy. Best of all, versions are available that will run quite happily on low-end Apple Macintoshes, any variant of a UNIX workstation, as well as the most basic Windows-capable PC. All lightweight clients interoperate happily with full-function Exchange clients, so deployments of Exchange can therefore proceed released from dependencies imposed by software unavailability, low hardware base or lack of finance. From a marketing perspective the ability to connect POP3 and Web clients into Exchange expands the potential client market quite dramatically. How many Web browsers are in use today? No one knows—the only sure thing is that the number is already measured in the tens of millions and increasing all the time. Apart from the pure marketing element there's also a great deal of strategy being played out as Exchange expands the set of clients that are able to access and use its services. In competitive situations, where Exchange is head to head with other products, comparisons between the different products under review are made across a wide variety of points. If Exchange tops the list of servers in terms of the breadth and variety of clients it supports, then the server is shown up in a very good light. Also, the initial implementation of the server may be very much easier if supported clients are already being used on peoples' desktops.

Free or shareware software is one thing, but there's no such thing as a free lunch and client connectivity is no different. According to Microsoft software licensing policy, all clients, Exchange or lightweight, require a Client Access License (CAL). By selecting POP3 or Web clients you can certainly avoid paying for Exchange client software, but licenses must be registered on the server.

We'll discuss the good and bad points of the specific lightweight clients over the next few pages. Before moving to specific details it's worth noting that all the lightweight clients share a common attribute, that of maintaining a passive rather than active connection to the server. Exchange and Outlook clients connect to servers via RPCs so communication is two-way. Active clients are able to accept and react to the instructions sent out by the server. For example, a dialog should be displayed because it is the result of a rule being executed or the contents of a folder updated because a message has just been deleted. The simplest example is the broadcast announcing that a new message has arrived. All of this work is done through RPCs. Passive clients merely make demands of a server and do not react to server attempts to have intelligent conversations. Thus, whereas a Web browser is capable of displaying the contents of the Inbox, it is unable to maintain an active count of new messages. If users wish to discover how many new messages are in the Inbox they must make an explicit "refresh new mail count" request to the server.

2.6   POP3 clients

POP3 clients are the simplest (or even lightest) clients capable of connecting to an Exchange server. A wide range of POP3 client software is available on the market. Some of this software is free, yours for the expense of a download from a Web site somewhere. Other clients are available as commercial products, and clearly the degree of sophistication and functionality that's available from any client depends on the amount of work that's been put into it. The commercial products, like Eudora Pro, Pegasus, or DIGITAL TeamLinks, are complete in terms of functionality, and usually offer more features than those just devoted to message retrieval and sending. But if all you want is a simple mail program that can handle messages in a basic manner then one of the free (or shareware) programs will probably do the job.

The messaging functionality that can be built for any POP3 client is constrained by the limitations of the POP3 protocol, defined, like SMTP, by the Internet Engineering Task Force (IETF). The protocol concentrates on simple messaging and ignores high-end features like public folders or scheduling. Simplicity has its benefits too. Generally speaking, POP3 clients impose the lightest load on the server of any client. The model used involves off-line work to process messages followed by quick connections to the server to send any messages waiting and fetch any messages that have arrived since the last connection. The process of downloading messages from the server inbox to the client is rather charmingly referred to as "scraping." Table 2.3 lists points of client functionality and indicates whether these are available to POP3 clients.

Table 2.3   *Functionality available to POP3 clients*

Feature	Available to POP3 client
Access to any messages and attachments delivered into a user mailbox	Yes
Can read Rich Text Format content in messages	Yes (contents are MIME-encoded)
Access and browse Exchange directory	Yes – via LDAP
Create new folders or otherwise manipulate folder hierarchy	No – POP3 only supports a simple inbox
Browse private folders on server	No – POP3 has no concept of private folders
Browse public folders on server	No – POP3 has no concept of shared or public folders
Use Exchange or Outlook electronic forms	No – POP3 has no concept of anything but a simple message
Set Out of Office Assistant	No client option available to set conditions Out of Office Assistant

Table 2.3   *Functionality available to POP3 clients (continued)*

Feature	Available to POP3 client
Set AutoSignature text	No client options available to define text for addition to end of messages
Use Schedule+ functionality, view calendar, accept, view or create meetings	No – POP3 has no concept of scheduling
Use Exchange rules	No – POP3 has no concept of rule processing

As POP3 is a protocol in the public domain there are many different visions of what a client interface should look like. The protocol makes no demands on software designers; it merely states how a client can connect to a server and retrieve messages from it. The design of the user interface is left completely in the hands of software engineers, who are only limited by their own ingenuity and the constraints applied by the simplicity of the protocol. POP3 clients therefore vary greatly in terms of style, content, and quality. There are acknowledged market leaders who count their users in millions, such as Eudora or Pegasus, but there are other products too that are deserving of consideration. The Exchange client is a fine POP3 client—a POP3 service provider has been available since V4.0, so it is entirely a legal combination to connect an Exchange client to an Exchange server using POP3. An exercise perhaps in technical exactitude, but not the most effective way to use this particular combination.

Figure 2.10
The Eudora Lite client after downloading some messages from Exchange

Figure 2.10 shows the shareware version of Eudora [6] after a number of messages have been downloaded from an Exchange V5.0 server.

---

[6]   The shareware version is called Eudora Lite. It can be downloaded from http://www.eudora.com

During a download messages may be removed from the server inbox, so if you use an Exchange client to connect to the same mailbox immediately after a POP3 download there might be no trace of any of the messages that the POP3 client now has control over. In addition, all formatting and rendering information in the messages is removed, leaving simple text content. Attachments are preserved and can be accessed. Most POP3 clients move attachments into a download directory where the attachments can be dealt with in the same manner as DOS files. Format tagging and file names might be lost, depending on how the client deals with attachments and whether they can process long (32-bit) file names.

In terms of simple messaging POP3 clients work well with Exchange. Difficulties arise when you look at any extended functionality. Table 2.3 lists some of the extended messaging features that you'll miss by using a POP3 client rather than the Outlook or Exchange clients, but there are other things too to consider. For example, there is no option in a POP3 client to set a new password for a user account in a Windows NT domain. What happens when an account password expires? The technology answer is simple—there's a passwords applet available in the control panel of Windows 32-bit clients, but it's an extra step that users have to take. Training needs to be altered to reflect this fact, and the help desk prepared to take calls from users who have just discovered that they can't access their mailbox because their account password is expired.

In theory (only because we don't yet have real-world experience of connecting hundreds of POP3 clients to a server), Exchange can support more POP3 than MAPI clients. Certainly, the test results achieved by Microsoft in their test laboratories indicate that very large POP3 user communities (numbered in the thousands) can be supported by a medium-range Exchange server. Microsoft has compared the number of POP3 clients supported by Exchange with the results of other POP3 servers, and Exchange looks pretty good. As always, the results achieved in a software laboratory must be taken with a large pinch of salt. Even so, because of the intermittant nature of the pull and push mechanism used to retrieve and send messages, it is reasonable to expect that POP3 clients will place less demand on the server. The number of inbound connections to the Internet Mail Service is the notable exception. Each POP3 client connects to the Internet Mail Service to send messages, so a server dealing with a population of POP3 clients needs to be configured to handle the increased number of connections. The default value (set through the Advanced tab of the Connections properties for the service) was 20 in V4.0. The value remains the same after an upgrade, so if you want to support a lot of simultaneous POP3 client connections you should increase the value.

2.6.1 Microsoft Outlook Express

The Internet Mail and News client, part of the Internet Explorer, is Microsoft's own POP3 client. The client is renamed as "Outlook Express" since the release of Internet Explorer V4.0 (1997), reflecting Microsoft's desire to create a common identity for all its clients (Outlook, Outlook WebView, and now Outlook Express).

Microsoft claims that Outlook Express offers the most features of any freeware client. The list of supported protocols is certainly impressive, incorporating POP3, SMTP, NNTP, HTML, IMAP4, and LDAP. Together with the straightforward and attractive user interface, the rich protocol list prompts people to ask why they shouldn't just use this client instead of Outlook. Consider this list of reasons to use Outlook Express rather than the MAPI-based Exchange or Outlook clients:

- The same development group that works on the MAPI version of the Outlook client engineers Outlook Express.

- It can be expected that Microsoft will keep Outlook Express competitive with similar clients from Netscape and other vendors.

- A server can support more POP3 clients than MAPI clients.

- Because there are fewer features to cover, it is easier to train people to use Outlook Express.

- Outlook Express is integrated with web browsing capabilities, so we have two important application areas integrated into one program.

- Best of all, Outlook Express is (currently) free. However, remember that you still need an Exchange CAL to connect any client to an Exchange server.

Quite a compelling case can be argued for Outlook Express! But before we all rush to return unused copies of Exchange or Outlook clients to Microsoft, let's reflect on some of the functionality that you'd be giving up.

- Richer feature set for messaging functionality (recall message, deferred mail, inbox assistant, etc.)

- Public folders

- Server and local stores, including local slave copies of server-based private and public folders

- Scheduling (Schedule+ or Outlook calendar)

- Contact management/PIM functionality

- Client extendibility (MAPI or electronic forms)
- Advanced security

The major advantage of Outlook Express is the fact that Microsoft is engineering the product, making Outlook Express the preferred POP3 client for Exchange. Outlook Express should remain very competitive, largely because Microsoft needs it to be so to maintain pressure on Netscape. It's undeniable that Outlook Express will always be handicapped by the constraints of the POP3 and IMAP4 protocols and so lag behind the full Outlook client in terms of functionality. However, even with these limitations, it should always be a more than adequate client for people who are just starting with e-mail, or those who really don't require the features of a high-end client. Also, if you need a solution that works on low-end hardware that might struggle with the demands of Outlook and the rest of the Office 97 suite, Outlook Express is an excellent way to help to introduce Exchange.

2.6.2   Internet Mail Access Protocol (IMAP4)

While POP3 is a messaging protocol supported by many mail servers and clients it is relatively simple and not really suitable to meet the needs of a sophisticated messaging community. The deficiencies in POP3 were recognized long ago and efforts have been ongoing to replace it with IMAP4, the Internet Mail Access Protocol. In comparison to POP3 few mail servers and clients support IMAP4, but this situation is expected to change very quickly in the 1997–99 period.

Exchange V5.0 does not support IMAP4, but the work to do so is ongoing. If it weren't done Microsoft would run the risk of losing support for the next generation of Internet mail clients. Prototype implementations showing special versions of Exchange supporting IMAP4 clients have already been demonstrated at industry events in the United States (April 1997). The final implementation of IMAP4 support is likely to be very similar to that of POP3. There will be some obvious differences because the protocols are so very different, but this won't be obvious to the user.

Like POP3 the user interface of IMAP4 clients is left totally to the software designer. The protocol states what it is able to do, and after that it's up to the software designers to construct a user interface around the features available to them. Unlike POP3, the IMAP4 protocol allows for server-based folders other than the inbox, and accommodates the concept of shared folders. It will therefore be possible for IMAP4 clients to access public folders on an Exchange server, much like the Web and NNTP interfaces can today.

2.6.3 Secure connections?

The POP3 and IMAP4 protocols do not specify that any particular means of enforcing secure communications between server and client should be incorporated into client software, allowing great flexibility for designers to incorporate common security mechanisms such as Kerberos. Including a mechanism like Kerberos is not automatic and the majority of POP3 or IMAP4 clients don't support anything except basic clear text authentication as defined in RFC 1225.

Clear text authentication isn't very secure. All the information necessary to establish a connection to the server is dispatched in clear, 7-bit ASCII text, available to anyone who cares to monitor the network using a tool such as the SMS Network Monitor. As an example of what I mean, let's look at how a client notifies a POP3 server that it would like to connect to a mailbox.

First, the client sends a signal to the server over a TCP/IP link to port number 110. The server responds to indicate that it is able to accept client connections, and the client sends the name of the mailbox it wishes to connect to.

```
User <username> <CR> <LF>
```

The server responds with either +OK or –ERR to indicate that the mailbox name is known. The client then proceeds to send the password associated with the mailbox. Again, this data is sent in clear text.

```
Pass <password> <CR> <LF>
```

If the password is correct the server locks the mailbox for exclusive access and the client can proceed to issue the necessary commands to retrieve and send mail. In an Exchange context account names and passwords are exchanged under the control of the Windows NT authentication service, but the fact remains that the protocol determines that everything is dispatched from the client to the server in clear text. For comparison's sake, the Exchange and Outlook clients use the standard Windows NT encrypted RPC-driven challenge/response mechanism. Because the POP3 and IMAP4 protocols allow great latitude in this area, it would be possible for a third party client to support the Windows NT challenge/response mechanism but no such client is yet available. Perhaps the Microsoft Internet Mail client will do so in the future.

2.6.4   Who are you getting mail from?

As we've discussed, the POP3 and IMAP4 protocols accommodate different security implementations, but they do not mandate that any security arrangements should be in place before a client connects to a server. Connecting the clients to Exchange means that some security is in place, albeit with clear text transmissions. However, there is another challenge for security-minded system administrators.

From time immortal, an SMTP client has been able to give itself any identity it wishes. In this instance, identity is the SMTP address displayed to people who receive messages from the client. Thus, I am able to connect to Netscape mail and announce myself as

```
bgates@microsoft.com
```

and merrily generate messages as such. You can't do this from all clients, but the vast majority of POP3 clients certainly permit it, including Netscape, Eudora, and even the Microsoft Internet Mail client. Clients that generate SMTP messages through a connector or gateway, as in the case of the Exchange or Outlook clients, are not given the opportunity to misrepresent themselves because the server stamps all outgoing messages with the sender's true identity.

Of course, sophisticated recipients who understand messaging generally mistrust messages that come in from people they don't know, and are likely to examine the information in the message header. The routing a message has taken within the network is clearly obvious from its header, so the true identity of a sender can be revealed. Look at the example in Figure 2.11. Is the message really from Bill Gates? Of course it isn't. The message was generated by customizing the personal preferences for Netscape Communicator (V4.0) to insert Bill Gates as the sender for all messages. Unwary recipients would only detect the problem if they browsed through the message header to find out exactly where the message came from. You'd expect a true message from Bill Gates to come through a server somewhere in the Microsoft domain, but that isn't the case here. Instead, the message was sent from a PC called VORLON somewhere in the local domain. Clearly a case of someone having fun at my expense!

Normal human beings don't tend to look too closely at message headers. In fact, they never do. The mail server therefore takes an almost moral responsibility to protect people against SMTP crooks. Exchange can't force good behavior on client software that it doesn't control, so any protection must come at the point where SMTP messages enter the Exchange environment—the Internet Mail Server.

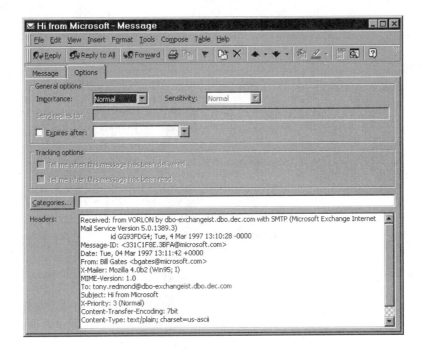

Figure 2.11 *A message from Bill Gates? Not likely!*

The default behavior in Exchange V4.0 is to match addresses in any incoming message against the directory. This is an attempt to create a user-friendly feature, because the unfriendly SMTP addresses are resolved into more readable display addresses fetched from the directory. Users can work with resolved addresses in the same way as they can with any other directory entry. For example, you can right-click on an address to see its properties, and if the address has been resolved in the directory, you'll be able to view other directory information (like manager, telephone number, e-mail addresses, and so on).

Let's assume that a message apparently comes in from

```
Peter.McQuillan@xyz.com
```

and that there's a matching entry (custom recipient or mailbox) in the directory. In this case, if directory resolution is enabled, the server changes the display address to Peter McQuillan, or whatever the display name was in the directory. Matching is, of course, performed against the list of mail addresses that can be maintained for each directory entry.

Friendliness is fine when everyone plays by the rules. But we have to defend against the antics of people who might use the weak points of SMTP to insert rogue messages. Exchange V5.0 makes a major change to help solve the problem. The default behavior of the Internet Mail Server in V5.0 is to no longer attempt to resolve incoming SMTP addresses against the directory. Instead, addresses are left as they come in, unless you explicitly instruct the server to perform resolution. Given the world we live in this is probably the best way for the Internet Mail Server to behave. Microsoft also intended to add a feature where a security flag was placed on all messages arriving in from the Internet. This feature didn't appear in the late betas (but was described in the documentation) and was removed from the shipping product. It may well appear in the future.

All servers installed with Exchange V5.0 from scratch do not perform name resolution. Servers upgraded from V4.0 maintain their previous behavior. If you want to change the server to be in line with latest practice you'll need to amend the system registry by changing the following key:

```
HKEY_LOCAL_MACHINE\System\CurrentControlSet\Services\MSExchangeIMC\Parameters\ResolveP2
```

Set the value to 0 to stop the Internet Mail Service performing name resolution. The registry value needs to be added if it is not already present.

2.6.5   Testing connections

Configuring and testing new types of clients always presents a challenge to system administrators. The POP3 connection is easy to test using a TELNET connection to port 110. The connection essentially mimics the interaction between a client and the server. Instead of client software driving the connection by issuing a series of commands to connect, authenticate, and retrieve messages, the POP3 commands are issued manually. You can monitor the response to the commands and determine whether the link is operating as expected.

In the example, we'll assume that the server name (DBO-EXCHANGEIST) is known to the local DNS. We'll connect to my own mailbox. First, use TELNET to connect to port 110 on the server. Make sure that local echo is turned on for the TELNET session, as otherwise you won't see characters you type echoed back to the screen.

After a successful connection is made the Exchange Server then announces its presence, together with the build number. Now enter the user name. Because Exchange uses Windows NT and there is a potential difference between the Windows NT account name and the Exchange mailbox name you may have to pass a fully specified name. That is, pass the Windows NT domain name, the Windows NT account name, and the alias for the Exchange mailbox.

```
+OK Microsoft Exchange POP3 Server 5.0.1389.6 ready
User OFFICESI\T_Redmond\TonyR
+OK
pass abc1238658
+OK User successfully logged on
```

In this set of commands we have connected to port 110 on server DBO-EXCHANGEIST in the OFFICESI Windows NT domain, and issued a request to connect to my mailbox. Note the use of the alias for my mailbox (TonyR). The characters in the password are echoed to the screen, which isn't great if someone is looking over your shoulder. A short pause may be experienced after the password is provided. This is accounted for by the need for the POP3 server to authenticate the credentials with a domain controller. Standard·Windows NT security is not bypassed by POP3 clients.

Once a connection is made we can issue other commands to manipulate the contents of the mailbox. Remember that the POP3 server only deals in terms of an inbox folder, so that's exactly what you'll be working with. For example, to list the contents of the inbox (not a good idea with a big inbox), type:

```
List
```

Each message is listed sequentially together with an id number. No other attributes (title, author, etc.) are listed. Messages have to be retrieved from the server before a client is able to discover attributes. To retrieve a message, type the RETR command and the number of the message. For example:

```
RETR 1
```

Retrieves the first message in the inbox. This is not the latest message. Rather, it is more likely to be the oldest message in the inbox. The connection has been adequately tested so we can close it off with a QUIT command.

Testing the POP3 connection in this way is quick and direct. Any potential client-specific configuration issues are eliminated and if successful, you've proved that Exchange is configured correctly and able to serve clients.

2.7   Browsing the Web with Exchange

We all know the impact of the Web. Acknowledging that impact and accommodating the huge spread of browsers as clients for Exchange is clearly a strategic step for Microsoft to take. It's also one of the most interesting aspects of Exchange V5.0, if only because of the way that the technology now being put in place may point the way to future desktops.

2.7.1   Active technology

Web pages started life as passive entities. You clicked on a page, followed hyperlinks around the Web, but basically everything was quite static. The CGI (Common Gateway Interface) marked the next steps along the Web evolutionary path, allowing people to build scripts and link commands into pages so that some real processing could be performed when requested by users. However, the interaction between CGI scripts and users is asynchronous and still relatively passive. The advent of Java changed the way developers looked at Web pages because now there was a way to build code (or intelligence) into pages. Suddenly a rush began to understand where the limits for Java-enabled pages lay, what applications could be built, and how the ever-growing Web could be harnessed for commercial advantage.

Sun Microsystems were the originators of Java and have been the chief proponents of a general move to Web-enabled applications, facilitated by new network-capable devices engineered by Sun and other vendors. After a slow start Microsoft began to catch up with the quantum leap in Web technology and has now formulated a strategy known as the Active Platform. Exchange is an important part of the Active Platform because it delivers messaging functionality that's immediately useful to many people. Solving a Microsoft problem with non-Windows clients is a side effect of enabling Exchange for Web access, albeit one that will help Exchange gain acceptance in some companies that couldn't previously deploy it.

As with all new technologies the Active Platform promises something to everyone. Developers get an easy-to-use platform to build new Web applications. Users get a "seamless browsing experience, regardless of the operating system being used" (a phrase taken from a Microsoft market bulletin, and one that I don't really understand!). Anyway, three core parts form the Active Platform:

- **Active Desktop:** Technology that will be built in at the operating system level (in other words, initially incorporated into Windows 95 and Windows NT) to leverage the capabilities of other Active Platform components.

- **Active Server:** Built into all versions of the Internet Information Server from V3.0, this is the server component of Active Platform, responsible for handling client requests generated by applications such as the Web client for Exchange. The software application that uses the Active Server to access Exchange is known as Active Messaging.

- **ActiveX:** A set of reusable development components including controls, documents, scripts, and a Java Virtual Machine (a software-based machine to run Java code). ActiveX controls are possibly the most famous component, mostly because of the wide exposure of the Windows development community to Visual Basic VBX and OCX controls. Two immediate advantages are gained from this background. First, ActiveX can be regarded as mature technology with a lot of developers who know the broad concepts. Second, there are a lot of controls that started life as VBX or OCX files that have now been converted to ActiveX controls. ActiveX documents, or the capability to view non-HTML documents like Word or Excel files via a Web browser, are an important component in an Exchange environment where these types of files are often attached to messages or placed into a public folder.

The value of controls that can be dropped into a project and immediately add functionality is obvious to anyone who has ever programmed with Visual Basic, and the same approach is being taken with ActiveX. The difference is, of course, in this case the target environment is composed of Web pages that include ActiveX controls (active pages), with each control taking responsibility for a particular task. Today, ActiveX controls can only be used by Windows 95 and Windows NT desktops. This is a challenge for Exchange, because it wants to be the server of choice for the widest possible client population, so special processing is built into Active Messaging to emulate the processing normally done by the control when non-Windows clients are connected. Microsoft has documented ActiveX for The Open Group, an industry body that encourages cross-platform technologies. However, it is not yet clear exactly which software developers (apart from Microsoft) will support ActiveX in the future. There's certainly a fair amount of discussion in the Web world about the impact of ActiveX. The anti-ActiveX people believe it's the leading edge of a Microsoft plan to make the Internet as Windows-centric as most desktops are today. The jury is out on this opinion, and we'll just have to wait and see how things develop.

As mentioned above, Active Messaging takes care of the interaction between Exchange and the Internet Information Server. Let's see how this is done.

2.7.2   How Web clients connect to Exchange

Figure 2.12 illustrates how Exchange supports Web clients. The server-side application is called Active Messaging or the Exchange Active Server. Active Messaging provides the interface between the Internet Information Server and Exchange and is implemented as two dynamic link libraries. The functions contained in these libraries allow client requests to be interpreted and dispatched to Exchange for execution. In a similar manner the results of these requests are returned to Active Messaging and transformed into HTML instructions that can be displayed by a browser. Note the emphasis on processing performed by servers. Today's Web client is very passive and merely serves as a display device for the Active Messaging application. Future developments such as Dynamic HTML, which allow web browsers to cache and manipulate data that originated from a server, may split processing between clients and servers a little more evenly, but not today.

When a browser is used as a client to an Exchange server it is called Outlook WebView, a term that delivers a marketing benefit of associating Web clients with the altogether more comprehensive functionality delivered by the "real" Outlook client (which, of course, uses MAPI). I don't like long names that don't really mean anything, so I'll continue to refer to a browser connected to Exchange as a Web client.

Figure 2.12
*Components
of the Web
connection*

The Web client is, in fact, a working application assembled with Active Messaging components. Let's have a look at what those components are:

- Any standard Web browser can be used, as long as it supports JavaScript and frames. Netscape Navigator V3.0 or later, or Microsoft Internet Explorer V3.02 (with the appropriate patches) or later are good choices. Frames are used extensively to divide the browser screen into a user interface which somewhat approximates to the interface you'd see if you used an Exchange client. JavaScript, or more correctly, VBscript is used in association with Active Pages (pages that have embedded ActiveX controls) to accomplish complex processing, such as executing a lookup against the directory or creating a new message.

- The Web client connects to Exchange over the HTTP protocol by reference to a standard URL. The URL points to an active page (ASP file) on a Windows NT server running the Internet Information Server. The Internet Information Server can run on a Windows NT V3.51 system, but this configuration cannot support the active pages required by the Web client. If you want to support Web clients you need Internet Information Server V3.0 or later running on Windows NT V4.0 (SP2 or later). Apart from anything else, a higher degree of security is possible with Windows NT V4.0 because it supports the SSL for network authentication.

- The initial page for Exchange offers users an option to either connect to their own mailboxes or connect anonymously. All of the processing on this page is performed by an ActiveX control and ActiveX scripts communicating with an ISAPI application (the Active Server) running on a Windows NT server. The Internet Information Server converts ActiveX scripts to byte code on an as-needed basis. An anonymous connection is restricted to viewing a nominated set of public folders that an administrator has decided should be available to users who have not or cannot be authenticated. Mailbox access is only available after a dialog is conducted to establish which mailbox to connect to and the user has provided the Windows NT account and password for that mailbox. Using SSL the password information can be sent encrypted to the server, otherwise it's dispatched in clear text (OK in a pilot or restricted trial, unacceptable in a production environment).

- Dialog between the Active Server and Exchange is conducted using MAPI. The Active Server accepts HTML format requests from the browsers and translates them into the equivalent MAPI function calls. The Exchange server sees the requests coming from the Active Server as if they were MAPI function calls generated by an Exchange or Outlook client. When the Exchange server responds, the MAPI responses and any RTF-format message content is automatically translated by the Active

Server into HTML before it passes to the Web browser, and the Active Server also takes care of dispatching any relevant applets.

Active pages are basically the same as normal HTML pages. The big difference is the fact that they contain embedded code written in a language that will be very familiar to any Visual Basic programmer. For example, the code necessary to display the current time in an active page is:

```
<HTML>
Hello World! The current time is <%= time() %>
</HTML>
```

Combined into a text file with an .ASP extension this code is enough to make a browser proclaim:

```
Hello World! The current time is 6:13 PM
```

Not awe-inspiring, but enough to illustrate the point.

The source code for Active Messaging is split across a set of HTML pages, GIF graphics, and active pages. The code is organized into a set of directories, one for each language (USA, Germany, Japan) supported by the server. Each language root directory has a set of sub-directories, and you'll find the actual source code here. For example, the \anon directory contains all the code used to connect anonymous clients to Exchange whereas the \inbox directory has the code to display the contents of an inbox folder.

Active Server applications are not compiled. Instead, .ASP pages hold interpreted scripts that are processed by the server when requested by a client. Interpreted scripts are easier to change than compiled code, even if they are slower. The speed issue is largely addressed by the fact that scripts are executed on the server, masking any great difference from a client perspective. Interpreted code also allows the same application to run across multiple client platforms. The same script runs on the server no matter how many client platforms are used. It is the responsibility of the clients (browsers) to display the data returned by the server. In the case of an active server application, clients receive HTML formatting instructions that result from scripts being run on the server.

Some magic is required to make active server applications work. When a server receives an HTTP request to open an active page it scans the page to locate any script commands. In the normal course of events when dealing with simple, static pages that only contain HTML instructions a Web server retrieves the data and passes it untouched to a client browser. The activation of an active page causes the server to pause, to interpet the script commands and then execute them, and only then will data be sent to the client. In the case of Exchange the script commands in the active pages interact with the Active Messaging component to log-on to a server, fetch inbox contents, and other details like the count of new messages. The HTML Rendering Object Engine (see next page) helps to create a good looking client interface, even given the obvious limitation of browser technology today. The resulting pages are always dynamically generated and reflect the current state of the data held on the Exchange server. As noted earlier, the relationship between a browser and an Exchange server is passive, and updates must be explicitly requested before a browser can display them.

Some questions have been asked whether the use of active pages represents a potential security hole. Could hackers break into Exchange and access unauthorized data because they can "see" the script code that drives the active pages? The answer is "no." The script code is public, and merely contains the instructions necessary to control the connection to Exchange. Data is provided by the server according to the same permissions and rules that any other client is governed by. All of the data passing between a Web browser and Exchange is invisible to the active page and cannot therefore be intercepted or otherwise affected by the act of a hacker.

Figure 2.13
Using Internet Explorer to access an Exchange mailbox

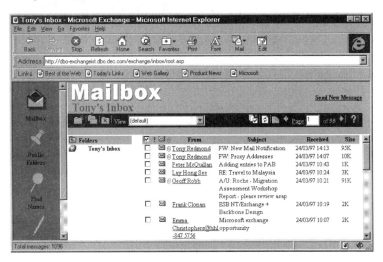

From the perspective of software engineering, such an implementation is not new. Lotus has accomplished much the same feat in their Domino project, and DIGITAL created similar features in the ALL-IN-

1 Web Gateway in 1995. However, Microsoft has brought the concept to a new degree of integration and has created a remarkably usable and visually attractive Web client. Figure 2.13 shows the contents of my inbox folder being listed. The layout and appearance of the Web client looks remarkably similar to the Outlook client, and as noted earlier, now that Microsoft has concentrated client development into a single development group, the clients should grow closer over time.

In addition, the components used to build the Web client can be used to create other Web-centric applications and it will be interesting to see how application developers respond to the challenge of levering the Active Server in the next few years. Jetform Workflow is the first example. As mentioned in Chapter 1, Jetform Workflow (V2.0) allows Web browsers to participate in workflow processes built around Exchange. Jetform provides its own ActiveX control, which is responsible for generating workflow commands and data and sending it via Active Messaging to the next person in the workflow cycle. That person might use a Web browser, but on the other hand, they might also use a different client, one that also supports Jetform. The combination of Active Messaging and Jetform Workflow makes it entirely feasible to build a totally platform-independent workflow process, something that has been very difficult if not impossible in the past.

Active Messaging allows read-only access to mailboxes on an Exchange V4.0 server. This is not a supported configuration and if you're interested in supporting Web access to mailboxes the server should be upgraded to Exchange V5.0.

It's worth noting that the Active Server and the Exchange server it corresponds with do not have to reside on the same physical computer. The network load is reduced if the two servers co-reside, but it is quite possible to distribute processing across multiple computers. After all, the calls made by other clients come into Exchange across the network, so there's no reason why the Web client should be any different.

2.7.3   Subsets of Active Messaging

There are two major subsystems within Active Messaging:

1. The Messaging Object Library
2. The HTML Rendering Object Library

The messaging object library looks after client requests to connect to Exchange (log-in and authentication) and navigation within folders, both public and private. All of the functions necessary for messaging operations (send, read, delete, attach or detach documents, look up an address in the directory).

The HTML rendering object library provides a set of functions to render outputs from Exchange into the HTML and JavaScript suitable for processing by Web clients. The rendering library is used to build the user interface for the Exchange Web client, but its functions could obviously be used for other applications. The library includes functions to create columns, groups, sorting, filtering, and conversation threads.

Perhaps the most important service delivered by the rendering library is to enable support of browsers that aren't engineered by Microsoft. If the target browser doesn't support a Microsoft-driven technology like ActiveX or VBscript, the rendering library is able to output the (lowest common denominator) combination of HTML and Java commands to build and populate the user interface.

2.7.4 Web client functionality

There's much that can be done with the Web client, but there are some things that can't. Table 2.4 lists the reduced or missing functionality that's available from the Web client.

Table 2.4 *Unavailable or reduced functionality in Web clients*

Issue	Comment
Full access to all folders in user mailboxes	Yes, although if a fast network is not available access slows down as the number of folders in a mailbox increases.
Full access to all public folders (in line with access control lists)	Yes, although the same comment applies as for folders. If many messages and items are stored in a folder it can take some time to transmit details down to the Web client.
Processing attachments	The client can read attachments but can't currently upload attachments to messages that it creates.
No message encryption or decryption	The Web client cannot access the X.509 certificates necessary to encrypt or decrypt messages.
No off-line folders (OST)	Web clients have no concept of off-line folders and synchronization.
No personal stores (PST)	Web clients only deal with server-based resources.
New mail count not dynamic	Server cannot update client with information about new messages.

Table 2.4   *Unavailable or reduced functionality in Web clients (continued)*

Issue	Comment
Limited views	The format and content of views are hard-coded into the Web client and cannot be customized by users.
Rules cannot be set, but profile-independent rules are executed.	Inbox Assistant is not available.
Extended client options: AutoSignature; Out of Office Assistant	Only the Out of Office Assistant is supported
Schedule+ interface not complete	Not currently available, should be provided soon.

There isn't too much missing, and it's certainly possible that future iterations of the Active Server components will add missing features or address some of the reduced functionality. Scheduling and the ability to upload attachments to messages are obvious examples of mainstream functionality that should be available in mid 1997. Updated modules will probably be provided as part of a service pack or as optional downloads from the Microsoft Web site.

2.7.5   Reasons for the Web client

Why has Microsoft developed and delivered a Web client? Here are a number of potential reasons to consider:

- First, the Web client delivers a solution for UNIX workstations. UNIX workstations are nowhere near as numerous as Windows PCs, but their users are usually a pretty vocal bunch. Microsoft doesn't have a good record in integrating the UNIX community into their software applications, but the need is greater than ever before now as Microsoft seeks to deliver truly enterprise solutions.

- Second, the Web client allows quicker deployment. It can take a long time to roll out large numbers of Windows 95 or Windows NT clients in a company, especially if the whole user desktop is being redesigned. Almost everyone has access to a Web browser, so they can now be given an Exchange mailbox and start working with the server. Later on, when planning is complete and the new desktops are ready, a more full-feature client (Exchange or Outlook) can be provided. At this stage users can continue working with all the messages and public folders they had used with the Web client.

- Third, the Web client delivers a solution for low-end Apple Macintosh and Windows (or even DOS) clients. Not everyone has a Pentium PC or PowerPC Macintosh, yet they may be required to use Exchange because everyone else is going to use Exchange. The department or cost center may not be able to pay for new hardware immediately, so the Web client allows people to continue using older hardware until the necessary budget is available. The same point can be made in favor of POP3 clients, especially Outlook Express.

- Fourth, it's difficult to get the infrastructure necessary to transparently support roving users in place if you don't lay the foundations from the start. If the organization is in a situation where people have Windows or Windows NT installed on the hard disk of their PC the PC is very "personal." It is difficult for people arriving at a remote office to use a PC without having to create a new profile. Not everyone is happy to create a new profile or mess with other PC settings, so the Web client allows quick and easy access to mailboxes without any great effort.

- Finally, it is conceivable that some people will want to pop into their local cybercafe to quickly read their e-mail back home. Web terminals are appearing in the most unlikely places—airports, shopping malls, maybe even drive-in restaurants soon. Should we all expect to be able to get back to a server to check our mail? Maybe, maybe not. The technology is certainly available to make this happen, but Exchange is only one piece in the jigsaw. Security across the Internet is a more fundamental challenge, and any Web connection from a public place must be controlled and secure. The advent of technologies such as PPTP (Point to Point Tunneling Protocol, available with Windows NT V4.0 Server) and encrypted tunnels through firewalls (like DIGITAL's Alta Vista Tunnel) make such connections more feasible. Once we have a secure connection to the home server the sole issue to solve is network capacity. There is no magic in the Active Server to relieve Internet bottlenecks and deliver great response to a waiting Web client, and while the Internet remains a touch clogged this issue will always be there.

I doubted the ability of any Web browser to allow people to process mail across an Internet connection until Microsoft proved me wrong by setting up a "test-drive" site that anyone could connect to. I was able to log-in to a test account there, browse through an inbox, and create and send messages nearly as easily as I can within my own company's network (Figure 2.14). Given a fast server (Microsoft used an Alpha computer), and good access to the Internet (and suitable firewalls in place) it is entirely conceivable that people could access their mail using Web clients anywhere in the world.

Figure 2.14
Accessing a mailbox with a Web client across the Internet

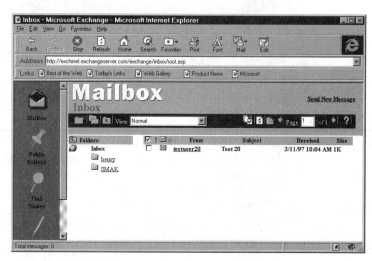

Searching for an altogether more cynical reason, one can't help looking at the Web client as a preemptive strike against Netscape. Why bother with a Netscape mail server when you can use the very best of Netscape client technology in conjunction with Exchange? Just point a Netscape browser at the URL for Exchange and connect!

2.7.6   Network Computers

Everyone is aware of the debate around the role of the Network Computer (NC) versus the PC. Microsoft is definitely on the side of the PC and proposes to continue to evolve the PC to make it easier to use and maintain. The NC, supported by companies like Oracle, Sun, and Netscape, has little or no local disk storage and downloads all the application software it requires from large servers situated around the network. Despite Microsoft's antipathy towards the NC, Outlook Web View is a great NC application, better (because it's here now) than some of the other applications the proponents of the NC constantly refer to.

The NC could take the place of a lot of unintelligent video terminals in use today. It could also replace a large number of PCs, especially those used by people who never really exploit the power of the PC but remain connected to the LAN all day long. In these cases Outlook Web View is the right client option for deployment.

2.7.7   Anonymous access

Putting items into public folders allows Exchange users to share the information, but access is restricted to the Exchange community. You must own a mailbox and possess a set of Windows NT security credentials before the server is happy to allow you to view the contents of public folders. Restrictions like this aren't at all important if you operate in an Exchange-pure environment, but they can be very frustrating during migrations, when people haven't fully moved across to Exchange, or if a set of cross-platform clients are operated. Imagine the frustration for a user who receives a message saying that a presentation can be found in a certain public folder, or learns that some valuable marketing data has been posted in a spreadsheet in another folder?

Anonymous access means that a client is able to connect to Exchange without providing a set of security credentials. Today anonymous access is limited to Web clients, but as the IMAP4 protocol allows for public folder-like structures it is entirely conceivable that the same mechanism could be used for these clients in the future.

Access must be limited because the client making the connection has no identity and cannot possess the normal rights and privileges attributed to mailboxes. Normally, the right to access a folder is controlled by an access control list composed of mailbox names (or more precisely, the X.500-like directory name for the mailbox). Exchange permits anonymous access by creating a pseudo-name called "Anonymous" which allows administrators to nominate which folders they'd like unidentified clients to be able to view. Anonymous access is not granted by default. You must select each folder that you want to allow access to and modify its access control list to allow anonymous clients into the world of public folders. Reviewing and modifying the access control list for a large hierarchy of public folders is quite a task, but it's better to do this rather than granting anonymous access by default.

Restricting access to a nominated set of folders is one step, but it needs to be supplemented through special arrangements for Web clients. Exchange and Outlook clients see the full public folder hierarchy when they access public folders. This is possible because the full hierarchy is replicated to all servers in an organization. However, you definitely don't want to allow anonymous clients to browse the complete public folder hierarchy because:

1. The names of some public folders may contain hints to the contents, and those contents may be commercially sensitive.

2. Publicly-available folders are most likely going to be used as repositories for documents and other information you'd like people outside (or inside) the company to access. You don't want

people to be distracted when they access public folders, a possibility that certainly exists if they could browse through the complete hierarchy. Focusing on a selected set of folders serves as signpost to the information you want to disseminate.

3. Web browsers would have to download all of the hierarchy before it could be displayed. Clients accessing organizations with large public folder hierarchies might encounter performance problems.

Exchange provides a simple solution to the issue by allowing system administrators to build a set of shortcuts to the public folders they'd like to make available to anonymous clients.

As shown in Figure 2.15, the shortcuts are configured as properties of the HTTP protocol object within a site. Shortcuts are specific to a site, so clients that connect to one site will not necessarily see the shortcuts to folders on another site unless the local system administrator has created a shortcut to a local replica. An alternative is to provide a URL to redirect queries to other servers who also host sets of shortcuts.

Figure 2.15
*Configuring
Public Folders
for anonymous
access*

Web clients access public folders in exactly the same way as they access mailboxes, as you can see from Figure 2.16 (see page 101).

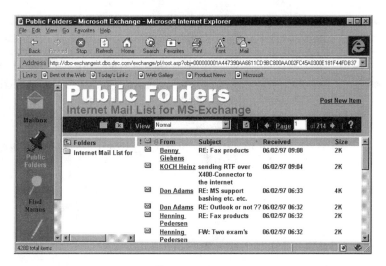

Figure 2.16 *Web Client accessing Public Folders*

2.8   IMAIL: The protocol engine

All Exchange clients, including the lightweight variety, connect to the Information Store service. Up to V5.0 the only supported protocol was MAPI, with clients sending requests for information via RPCs. Exchange V5.0 introduces IMAIL, a new software layer within the information store, together with the POP3 protocol stub that's necessary to allow POP3 clients to connect in. Web clients still connect via MAPI, but only indirectly, as the MAPI calls generated by Web clients are created and dispatched on their behalf by the Active Server.

We now have two ways into the information store: POP3 and MAPI. A third method will be implemented shortly to support IMAP4. MAPI is tied more closely than the other two methods because it can talk directly to the store and supports the RTF format used to store content within the information store. Exchange is expanding the number of protocols supported by the server all the time. The application world is moving quickly towards HTML (or a more developed version of HTML) as the de facto standard for platform-independent content storage. These two influences mean that changes must be made to allow support for new protocols to be incorporated seamlessly, and to support the introduction of HTML as the native content format used by Exchange. IMAIL, the protocol engine, is a hidden jewel introduced into the Exchange V5.0 information store to provide the foundation for the future.

As illustrated in Figure 2.17, the task of the IMAIL software layer is relatively simple. It sits between the information store, where messages, attachments, header information, and other items of data are stored, and the different protocol stubs supported by Exchange. As data is moved between the store and the different protocols the IMAIL engine is able to convert the data from the format used by the store to the format most acceptable to the calling protocol. Thus, when a POP3 client retrieves messages from the store, the IMAIL engine takes care of extracting the RTF message content and packaging it up into whatever the requesting client can accept. The information in message headers is likewise extracted from the information store and sent down to the client. When IMAP4 is supported IMAIL will take care of its needs as well.

Figure 2.17 *The role of the IMAIL protocol engine*

IMAIL is already used to perform RTF to HTML content conversion for the Web client. RTF will remain a valid native content for the information store, but the announced direction for Exchange is to move towards a situation where HTML becomes the preferred native format. This move shouldn't be surprising because we are already seeing evidence of the same switch in other Microsoft products (the Office 97 application suite is an obvious example), and it will happen gradually, as the opportunity and need arises. The next major version of Exchange is likely to be the time when HTML supplants RTF as the server's native format, unless other development priorities rule this step out. In any case, when the time comes the IMAIL protocol engine will be there and ready to handle the RTF to HTML and HTML to RTF format conversions that will be required.

2.9   Schedule+

Apart from its comprehensive electronic mail functionality, Exchange comes complete with a good time management and personal organizer application called Schedule+ (see Figure 2.18). There are a few different versions of Schedule+, the most notable being:

- The Exchange version of Schedule+ operates in a client/server mode which facilitates group scheduling across a distributed network whereas the Office 95 version is primarily designed for standalone operation.

- The Exchange version of Schedule+ stores scheduling information in special folders managed as part of the Information Store.

- The Exchange version of Schedule+ is managed as an integral part of Exchange. This means that you don't have to make any special provision for managing the scheduling information as it's all taken care of for you by normal system management procedures like backup.

In summary, Schedule+ is a fine personal calendaring system. Meetings can be set up between different users, and a certain amount of resource scheduling (for example, booking a conference room) can be achieved. The version of Schedule+ integrated with the Exchange clients includes many items found in low-end project management, personal information systems, and contact managers (all terms I sometimes feel have been generated and then used to help sell software packages). Outlook takes everything further and delivers more features and functionality.

Figure 2.18
Schedule+

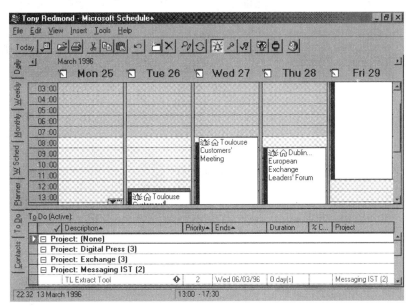

2.9.1   Dealing with the past and the future

Schedule+ has, of course, been available for a long time. V1.0 was integrated with Microsoft Mail. The close integration of messaging and scheduling was a major selling point and contribution to the success of Microsoft Mail. It is not surprising to learn that Schedule+ V1.0 used the same file-sharing architecture as Microsoft Mail. Substantial changes were therefore required to upgrade Schedule+ and fit it into the client-server architecture of Exchange. As we've discussed, Schedule+ V7.0 first appeared as an application within the Office 95 suite, and the Exchange-compliant version of Schedule+ evolved from this release.

The net effect of the changeover from file sharing to client-server was a howl of anguish from users. People accustomed to opening other users' calendars (with permission) to scan for an appropriate time to set up a meeting suddenly found that they were restrained to a simple indication of whether people were free or busy at a particular time. Information about free and busy time slots is maintained in a hidden folder on the Exchange server, and it's possible to share free and busy data with Microsoft Mail users through the MS-Mail connector. Users are able to schedule events with other people, no matter whether they use V1.0 or V7.0, via the connection between Exchange and Microsoft Mail.

Scheduling is one thing. Knowing what effect the new schedule has on people is another. It's not possible for a Schedule+ V1.0 user to open a Schedule+ V7.0 calendar, so work habits are disrupted as users upgrade from V1.0 to V7.0. Seeing that someone is busy is one thing, but it's far less information than users were accustomed to. Being able to open someone else's calendar enabled people to establish where the calendar's owner was at any point in time, who they were meeting, and whether they'd be able to physically attend an event. There's no point in scheduling a meeting for 3 p.m. in New York when one of the important attendees is in Dallas until 1:30 p.m. The calendar indicates a free slot at 3 p.m., but it's impractical.

The classic answer to the problem of incompatible software versions is to move users to the new release of Schedule+ as quickly as possible. This is easy to do in a small installation, more difficult in a large site, and normally only possible over an extended period in large, distributed enterprises.

Microsoft Mail users were the only people affected by the changeover. People who started with Exchange, or migrated from another messaging system, never realized that a problem even existed, but the new scheduling software included with Outlook affects everyone who uses Exchange and Schedule+. The prospect of having some people using Microsoft Mail and Schedule+ V1.0, some with Exchange and Schedule+ V7.0, and others using Outlook's calendaring is too awful to contemplate, even with the availability of an Outlook driver for Schedule+ (32-bit only). So a decision has to be made to avoid the upgrade to Outlook and sacrifice the additional features it offers (albeit only for 32-bit platforms), or to move over to Outlook as quickly as possible, possibly as part of the upgrade to Exchange server V5.0.

As a user I find little to complain about in Schedule+. Perhaps it would be nice to be able to view an overview of the calendars for a group of different users, subject to permissions, but this is a small point. As a system planner attempting to deal with a mixed bunch of Microsoft Mail, Exchange, and Outlook clients complete with their differing implementations of scheduling, I might have a different view. There's no doubt that pain is being felt en route to what will hopefully be a more integrated, cross-platform calendaring and scheduling application with technical implementation surviving more than a single version. The calendaring in Outlook is the closest we have to a totally integrated scheduling system at the moment. When everyone gets to Outlook, or Microsoft delivers software that can coexist with previous versions without losing functionality, we'll get to where we want to be.

2.10   Selecting the desktop environment

Windows NT is the only operating system option for an Exchange server, but as we've just reviewed, there is a reasonably wide choice of DOS or Windows-based clients. Given that all of the Windows-based Exchange clients offer roughly comparable functionality, which desktop operating system offers the best option for large-scale deployment of Exchange clients?

Most large customers I have worked with in the last year or so have reduced the choice for client desktop operating system to two: Windows NT workstation or Windows 95. DOS is seen as a solution only for the rapidly reducing population of 80386-powered PCs (in corporate computing environments), while Windows V3.1 and Windows for WorkGroups are crippled by the flaws in the old Windows architecture that are so readily exposed if a user attempts to run more than two large applications together at the same time. Moving to Windows NT or Windows 95 on the desktop will cost money for application upgrades and extra hardware, but the costs are somewhat offset by reduced help desk calls generated by frustrated users complaining of depleted system resources.

Windows 95 arrived in a blaze of publicity in August 1995, easily winning the all-time award for hyped-up software. Despite all the talk about the evolution to 32-bit desktop computing, Windows 95 hasn't quite achieved the full status of a 32-bit operating system because its kernel remains a hybrid mixture of 16- and 32-bit code. Microsoft probably would have liked to have more 32-bit code in Windows 95 but time and the need for backwards compatibility for applications dictated that some 16-bit code survived. The resulting mix works well, most of the time. Windows 95 is far more reliable than Windows V3.*x*, and users can plan for a complete day's work without factoring in the need to reboot to recover leaked system resources. While more memory is needed, far more applications can be run together and Windows 95 will cope with the load. Using Windows 95 as my day-to-day workhorse platform I typically run Word, PowerPoint, Excel, and multiple mail clients together at the same time without problems.

Windows NT had a slow start but has greatly improved since its early days. The workstation edition of Windows NT V4.0, suitably equipped with the Windows 95 user interface shell, is the top of the range user desktop environment available today. While Windows 95 increased reliability and robustness over the previous version by a user-perceived factor of 10 or more (based on my own personal experience), Windows NT is even more reliable, secure, and network-aware. In addition, Windows NT is hardware-independent and not tied to the Intel *x*86 architecture, allowing screamingly fast desktop systems to be built around high-end RISC CPUs such as the DIGITAL Alpha chip.

Interestingly, although Windows NT sales are higher than ever before and continue to set new records each reporting period, Windows NT workstation still can't compete with Windows 95. According to International Data Corporation, approximately 2.2 million copies of Windows NT workstation were shipped in 1996, against 60 million copies of Windows 95 (shipped since its release in August 1995). This data backs up my own experience that the majority of major corporate enterprises have standardized on Windows 95 on the desktop. The main reasons being because Windows 95 requires less hardware resources, offers better support for plug and play, and under the terms of many support contracts, doesn't carry an upgrade fee to move from Windows V3. Windows NT, on the other hand, has better security and is more robust, but it carries an upgrade fee (the standard price is $95). When all the costs are put together Windows 95 looks much more attractive.

Which desktop operating system should you use? Certainly I would not recommend Windows V3.*x*. Apart from the restrictions imposed by Windows in its 16-bit implementation, Microsoft is not developing Windows V3.*x* any further. The old saying that "when the horse is dead, it's time to get off" comes to mind here. Windows 95 or

Windows NT represents the best option for the future, but both require a considerable investment to install across all desktops in any medium to large enterprise. Because it is priced for the home/small office market Windows 95 is the cheaper of the two options. As noted above, Windows 95 still scores over NT in terms of Plug and Play and power management, meaning that if you're interested in using notebook computers Windows 95 is the best choice.

In desktop environments Windows NT is a little more expensive, but it is built on a firm 32-bit code base and is a more robust and secure operating system. Microsoft's direction towards a Windows NT desktop environment is also pretty clear, so if you can afford the extra cost then Windows NT workstation is the option I would go for. You are paying more now, but it's probably a better long-term bet for the future.

Selecting the desktop operating system is only the start. Apart from a potential requirement to upgrade hardware with additional memory and faster CPUs, if you install a new desktop it's likely that you'll also want to review the application software in use too. Migrating everyone from Microsoft Office V4 to Office 95 or Office 97 costs money, and then all the terminal emulators, databases, programming languages, and other applications might require new versions too if real advantage is to be taken of your new 32-bit desktop. Putting all the costs together that might be incurred in evolving towards a 32-bit desktop it's easy to see how a $60 product[8] could become a major push factor behind a decision to invest between $500 and $2,000 per desktop.

One way to keep costs down is to adopt a "one-upgrade" approach. In other words, when you change the messaging system to Exchange you do so as part of an ordered, coordinated upgrade for the entire desktop environment. The move may involve the following operations:

- Hardware upgrade or replacement for existing PCs. Adding new memory to accommodate the demands of Windows 95 or Windows NT, or just switching out old PCs for new.

- Installation of the new desktop operating system.

- Configuration of network protocols. For example, you may wish to switch over to TCP/IP as a universal network protocol. If so, the PCs need to be configured correctly in terms of an IP

---

[8]   Exchange clients are priced differently depending on the number of clients purchased and the country they are purchased in. I've taken $60 as an average price for the purpose of illustration only. Contact your local Microsoft office to get current price information about Exchange servers and clients.

address, connection to WINS, DNS and DHCP servers, and so on. You may need to configure the PCs to run multiple network stacks—TCP/IP for client to server connectivity and Novell IPX for file and print services are a pretty common combination.

■ Installation of desktop applications. Configuring client software for Exchange is obvious, but you'll probably need to upgrade the office application suite, terminal emulators, and so on. After everything is upgraded the applications may need to be configured to connect to the right printers, etc.

■ Training of users to deal with the new environment.

People generally find it easier to move in one operation rather than to be constantly bothered by a series of upgrades spread over an extended period. Change disrupts users, but the cumulative disruption caused by a series of upgrades is generally more than experienced in a single upgrade operation that deals with everything at one time. Apart from the effect on users, it is also cheaper to concentrate the efforts of technical and support staff on a set of "one-time" upgrades. Every time a technical person touches a desktop to upgrade an application or the hardware it costs money. Minimizing these interventions will save money in the long run.

Selecting the right platform to deploy Exchange clients is an important part of your overall computing infrastructure for the next few years. But Exchange clients are only a small, low-cost part of the overall equation. The question therefore needs to be asked whether a $60 client can drive the whole desktop in terms of its evolution and technical environment. Only you can answer that question.

2.10.1   Hardware resources for clients

The rich functionality contained in the Exchange clients is implemented in millions of lines of complex code. Large programs that offer extensive functionality fight a constant battle between the constant demands from users for increased functionality and the need to up the minimum hardware threshold. Complex code, no matter how optimized, has to be loaded into memory sometime, the modules, executables and other data files representing the program must be stored, and all the machine instructions generated by the code will be executed on processors. If there isn't enough memory, disk space, or processing power available to handle the demand generated by the program it will either not be able to execute or will run slowly. Everyone wants programs to run fast, but users, no matter how hard they lobbied for the new features, frown on any slow-down produced through the introduction of new functionality. This is the conundrum for all engineering groups.

The minimum specified hardware base for Exchange clients is different from the minimum practical base. The difference is, of course, in that Microsoft certifies that Exchange clients will run with a certain hardware configuration, but they don't specify the level of performance, perceived or otherwise, a user will experience with the configuration. This tactic isn't unique to Microsoft as all software vendors seek to qualify products against low hardware configurations in order to increase the total potential user base for their product. While the Exchange client for Windows V3.x will run on an 80386-powered PC with 8 megabytes of memory the performance will be slow and unacceptable.

If you're coming from a Microsoft Mail background expect to have to take a long hard look at current hardware resources on user desktops before migrating to Exchange. Microsoft Mail is a much simpler product in terms of architecture and implementation and is therefore able to comfortably perform on a PC with a far lower specification. Expect to have to add extra memory to the majority of your PCs and eliminate any low-end PCs that are in use. Don't expect to be able to use 80386-powered systems for anything else but DOS systems.

The situation can be further complicated in terms of overall client hardware configurations if you want to upgrade applications and desktop operating system at the same time, for example to move to a Windows 95/Office 97/Exchange desktop environment. It seems that every desktop application is gently expanding in size and complexity as features are added in each new release, and each addition has to be paid for somewhere. Consider the complex interconnections underpinning a message composed by a user with the Exchange client for Windows 95 using Word for Windows as the cover note editor. Now drag an Excel worksheet from the Windows Explorer and drop it into the memo. Then double-click on the newly embedded icon to start Excel so that the figures in the worksheet can be verified before being sent. Three highly functional applications working smoothly together in a relatively seamless manner under Windows 95. Is it any wonder that PCs need to have faster CPUs today than the largest mini-computers had at the start of the 1990s?

Table 2.5 suggests some sample configurations for desktop computing environments that must support Exchange client as well as a mix of commonly used personal productivity applications (Word, Excel, and so on). These configurations are not the minimum specified by Microsoft for any of the operating systems. Instead, they are the minimum configurations I recommend to people who come to me for advice.

Table 2.5   *Sample configurations for desktop clients*

Desktop Operating System	CPU	Memory	Basic Hard Disk requirements
DOS (V5 or above)	Intel 80386 upwards	8MB upwards	200MB upwards
Microsoft Windows V3.1 or Windows for WorkGroups	Intel 80486 25MHz upwards	12MB upwards	300MB upwards
Microsoft Windows 95	Intel 80486 33 MHz upwards	16MB upwards	400MB upwards
Microsoft Windows NT 4.0 workstation V3.51 or V4.0	Intel 80486 50 MHz upwards; any DIGITAL Alpha CPU	20MB (Intel); 32MB (Alpha)	512MB upwards
Apple Macintosh System 7.5	PowerPC	8MB	200MB upwards

The central ideas driving the recommendations are to create a system that works well (all the time) and has scope to grow and accommodate increased demands generated by users, or new versions of operating systems or applications. The recent history of computing tells us that any system that appears to be slightly over-configured today will be the smallest usable system in the very near future, and that future comes closer every day.

2.11   Windows CE

Windows CE (previously codenamed "Pegasus"), a cut-down version of Windows for Hand-Held PCs (or H/PC) was first released in November 1996. Windows CE is based on a stripped down sub-set of the Win32 APIs. Some reports place the amount at roughly 30% of the code base in Windows 95, but this shouldn't be taken to imply that Windows CE is based on Windows 95. In fact, Windows CE is more like Windows NT in many respects. For example, all characters used in Windows CE are 16-bit UNICODE, totally unlike the mix of 8- and 16-bit characters used by Windows 95. Out of the box, Windows CE includes a number of applications, including Pocket Word, Pocket Excel, and a messaging client. Some of the more advanced features of the full-sized applications, such as grammar checking, are removed to reduce the demand on system resources.

Despite its cut-down nature, Windows CE is an elegant 32-bit pre-emptive multitasking operating system with a built in database. Interestingly, like Windows NT, Windows CE is designed to be cross-platform and is currently able to run on Hitachi SH3, NEC, and MIPS processors. Plans are in place to support processors from ARM, Motorola PowerPC and any x86 CPU. Much of the code is execute-in-place, meaning that it can run directly from ROM and doesn't need to occupy valuable RAM. Everything has to fit into 2MB of memory, the minimum configuration for an H/PC. The more up-market versions come with a whopping 4MB! Anyone who is really interested in using these devices for more than a few casual notes should invest the extra money to equip their H/PC with at least 4MB. Computers at the upper end of the H/PC spectrum can accommodate up to 32MB.

The functionality of all the pocket applications is minimal when compared to their grown-up equivalents. Such a comparison misses the point—who really cares that Pocket Word isn't able to exert the same page formatting control as Word for Windows, or that Pocket Excel doesn't have all the modeling functions built into the regular version? I don't think I shall ever be tempted to do any heavy-duty writing on an H/PC if only because their small keyboards represent a large challenge to my uncoordinated fingers! Peering at a (small and dim) monochrome 480 × 240 LCD dot panel, even with the ever-improving clarity that LCD panels achieve, is also not something that I'd care to do for an extended period. It's hard enough to deal with the screens on notebook PCs. Second generation H/PCs will provide larger and clearer screens, and HP has already shipped systems equipped with 640 × 480 backlit screens. Even such relative luxury is still possibly not enough to consider writing for more than a page or two.

H/PCs are intended to compete with pocket organizers, the classic example being the Psion range of hand-held computers. The applications included in H/PCs must be able to pass information to and from PCs and allow their users to work on a document, spreadsheet, or other item away from the office. Based on the success of other hand-held computers, H/PCs are likely to be attractive to people who spend a lot of time shuttling between meetings and other appointments. These folks want to jot down a few ideas as they occur, or to use these tiny computers for a form of "emergency e-mail." You won't do very much more than make a few notes, as the tiny keyboard is not conducive to any major writing endeavor. However, it's certainly more than possible to write up meetings and other events with the intention of polishing up the text with a desktop PC later on.

Attempting to craft something like a book on a H/PC misses the point of the device however. The major advantage of combining Windows CE with a H/PC is its compatibility with common desktop applications, plus the excellent synchronization features that allow users to upload and download files from PCs. Similar in concept to the Windows 95 briefcase, you can easily set up an H/PC to synchronize its contents with a desktop PC. Microsoft provides an H/PC Explorer application (for Windows NT and Windows 95) to allow you to browse thorough the H/PC's contents when it is connected to a desktop system.

A POP3 messaging client is bundled with Windows CE, so it can connect straight into an Exchange server. Windows CE also supports PPP networking, which provides the foundation for its communication with desktop PCs. A more feature-rich Exchange client is also available, and an Outlook client will appear sometime in 1997.

H/PC messaging clients connect to servers using dial-up connections. Windows CE supports many standard PCMCIA modem cards, so dial-up is as easy as in Windows 95. However, standard AA batteries power H/PCs, and these are rapidly exhausted once modem activity starts—understandable because PCMCIA cards are designed for the power supplies in "real" notebook PCs. An AC adapter is an essential tool for anyone who wants to use one of these devices on the road. Some H/PCs, such as the Philips "Velo" incorporate a built-in modem, but you'll still need a good power supply when you connect to the network. Multitasking is another way to drain power. Switching between Pocket Word, Pocket Excel, and the mail client is possible, but the computer has to manage all the context switches and does so in memory, creating a drain on the battery.

Palmtop PCs, similar to the H/PC concept, have incorporated editions of electronic mail clients before, so this isn't a new concept. Hewlett-Packard palmtops, for instance, are provided with a cut-down version of Lotus cc:Mail. You can't compare the functionality to that of the Exchange client for Windows 95 or Windows NT, but it does a reasonable job of reading messages, and creating and sending mail. Those who are really serious e-mail users will probably not be satisfied by a Windows CE PC, and opt instead to use a high-spec notebook.

2.12   Using the crystal ball

Lots of people like making predictions, and some make predictions about subjects they know little or nothing about. Trying hard to avoid that trap, let's look into the crystal ball to see how client technology might evolve in the next few years. My own view is that:

- In the 1996–98 period (at least) Exchange clients will continue to be available for people who want to use high-end e-mail clients. During that period it's likely that these clients will deliver the highest level of pure e-mail functionality, including e-forms. Exchange clients are also the only solution for 16-bit (Windows V3.*x*) and DOS clients, if these platforms remain important to you.

- The direction taken by Outlook is an important point to the future in that it delivers a single point of desktop data access and management. Over time rationalization will occur and a single client will emerge. Given the enormous effort to incorporate Outlook in the Office 97 project it is almost 100% certain that Outlook is the focus for all future client development within Microsoft. Outlook will therefore become the de facto Exchange client for all 32-bit platforms. The Exchange client will remain for 16-bit platforms but will not receive any future development, except perhaps for a few bug fixes. The same logic applies to Schedule+, which has now been surpassed by Outlook scheduling and will receive no future development effort.

- New versions of Outlook shipped in 1997–98 will move to incorporate even more support for Internet standards. Expect HTML to become the default content format in addition to support for protocols such as LDAP, IMAP4, POP3, and SMTP that will allow Outlook to be a highly functional client for other servers. It's interesting to speculate on what the combination of an Outlook client and a Netscape mail server might accomplish!

- Microsoft has another client—the Internet Mail and News client—shipped as part of Internet Explorer. This client will be able to use Exchange via its POP3 (now) and IMAP4 (later) interfaces, but will never approach the degree of integration and functionality that the Outlook client will enjoy when connected to an Exchange server. Microsoft renamed the Internet Mail client to Outlook Express for Internet Explorer V4.0 release, reflecting the desire to create a family of client products that share a range of common services. Expect all clients shipped by Microsoft (Outlook, Internet Mail/Outlook Express, Web browsers/Outlook WebView) to eventually share the same user interface so that training costs can be reduced and users are more easily able to move between clients. The common user interface will be very close to the Outlook interface we see today.

- The incorporation of Web browsers into the range of possible Exchange clients expands the potential audience for Exchange considerably, but should you use a browser and drop specialized e-mail clients? Remember that Exchange is Microsoft's mail server for the Internet, and that Microsoft, as a company, is very heavily focused on the Internet. Web access and browsing will appear as a basic part of Windows clients over the next year or so, and if this is accepted, we can then project the evolution of Outlook to incorporate some degree of Web capabilities. However, the Web client will remain as the platform-independent option and will never have the same array of features that can be built into a "full" Outlook client.

- Windows CE and H/PCs are interesting devices, but only for a small section of the user community. But keep an eye on this stuff—you never know what might happen!

Some of this stuff is happening already. The important thing is to keep your eyes open and realize what's going on, then interpret the data as it arises and decide whether it is important for you. There's certainly no reason not to continue to deploy the standard Exchange clients today rather than stopping an implementation project to wait until your company is ready to install Office 97 and Outlook on user desktops. If you haven't started to roll out Exchange clients you're probably better deploying Outlook rather than the standard client because Outlook delivers more functionality, some of which, like the integrated contact manager, will be welcomed by users and other aspects, like archiving, will be a boon to system administrators. Outlook also offers some neat messaging features that are not supported by the standard Exchange clients. For example, you can use Outlook to recall a message from recipients who have not yet read it, a useful thing to do after sending a message that's maybe a little too hot and heavy (like telling your bosses exactly how they should be doing their job). Regretfully, Murphy's Law says that messages you'd like to recall are read quickly by recipients before you get a chance to issue the recall command.

The same argument holds with respect to Web browsers. Yes, you could decide to concentrate primarily on Web browsers today and start using Netscape Navigator or Internet Explorer to work with Exchange e-mail, public folders, and scheduling functionality as well as continuing "normal" access to Web resources. But perhaps the degree of functionality available to Web browsers is a touch immature in comparison to its dedicated Exchange or Outlook client counterparts. Given today's technology and the degree of development reached by the Web/Exchange components, in most cases the most pragmatic and functional approach is to use an Exchange or Outlook client to process e-mail, schedule meetings, or work with public folders, no matter how much the Web paradigm appeals. The day when the Web browser is as functional in all respects to purpose-designed programs may come, but it's just not here yet. The development environment for Web tools has to become far richer before it is able to deliver code that matches today's Visual C++ programs. I have no doubt that Microsoft is working hard to bring Web development tools up to speed (the appearance of tools like Visual Java is evidence of this), and in the next two years I expect Outlook Web View to grow more and more in terms of features.

Every additional client variant deployed increases the pressure on support resources. Every additional client makes it harder to plan software upgrades to ensure that people are using relatively up to date software. Every additional client requires extra training, and perhaps a new set of training or support material, if your company produces these items. In short, each new client means extra cost, even if the client software is free. For these reasons it is unwise to get too carried away with all the different clients. Select one, focus on it, and deploy it successfully. Then see if you really need another client and have the resources necessary to deploy, support, and maintain the new client in production. It's nice to have freedom of choice, but maybe it's even nicer to have a supportable client environment.

It's always good to attempt to remain pragmatic and focused when technology is changing so rapidly. It's bad to fall too deeply in love with the latest and greatest technology. Select what seems right for you today and deploy a client environment with a plan to keep it stabilized for the next two years. At the end of that period the fog will have cleared and you'll be in a good position to go through a similar exercise to plan for the following two years. One thing's for sure: expect change in the client area. We will be using different client technology in the future; the only question is when that future will arrive.

3

Establishing the Infrastructure for Exchange Server

3.1   Introduction

Every computer system or application is built on a set of basic concepts that must be mastered before an implementation can be considered. This chapter is my attempt to explain what I believe are the most important concepts relating to an implementation of Microsoft Exchange Server. We'll look at Windows NT, the basic organization of the Exchange messaging infrastructure, how to connect servers together, and the impact of Exchange on a network.

More detailed discussions about some of the points raised in this chapter, such as how to select and deploy the different connectors to link sites and other messaging systems together, are described in detail in Chapter 7.

Figure 3.1
*Organization,
sites, and servers*

Exchange and its clients are packaged and sold as shrink-wrapped software that you can purchase at many retail computer outlets. Unwrapping the packaging and taking out the CDs is done in a blink of an eye, but it's unwise to continue to rush forward and run the SETUP utility to install the new server. Successful Exchange implementations require a lot of detailed up-front planning and system preparation, especially if you plan to operate a multi-server, multi-site, distributed organization. The process of planning begins by understanding how an Exchange Server environment is developed on top of Windows NT.

3.2   Organizations, sites, and servers

Anyone considering the implementation of a messaging infrastructure built around Exchange needs to understand what the terms "organizations," "sites," and "servers" mean within the context of the overall system.

The organization you create to implement Exchange represents the total messaging enterprise and is layered on top of the Windows NT security model. The organization can be described as the full messaging infrastructure, and is composed of one or more Exchange sites.

A server is a computer running the Windows NT Server operating system, with Exchange server software installed on top of the Windows NT operating system. Note that there is a differentiation between Windows NT Server and Windows NT workstation, the two variants of the operating system. A computer running Windows NT workstation can be an Exchange client, but is not able to act as an Exchange server.

A site is often a single physical or geographical location where one or more Exchange servers are situated. Communications between the different Exchange servers forming a site are carried out with synchronous RPCs so the network links between the servers must be capable of supporting the load generated by client-generated calls in a very responsive manner. It is also important that the network connections within a site are reliable and predictable, and not prone to failure, as this will affect the replication of data between the different servers in the site.

Knowing how users communicate with each other is good information to have when planning where to locate servers or how they might be formed into sites. Keeping messages on a single server provides the fastest possible delivery service for users, so it's a good idea to locate users who need to communicate on a frequent basis on the same server. Building a site from a collection of user groups who pass information between the groups is a logical progression of the same idea. Clearly it's easiest to build up message patterns when you already operate a mail system, but even if you don't have an existing system to monitor it pays to spend some time on the subject to try and develop some educated guesses. Any data based on reality will result in a much better initial implementation of Exchange server than would otherwise occur if users are allocated to servers in an unstructured manner.

If you do have an existing system look for opportunities to improve the current message flow. It's a sad fact of life that many systems have evolved through passive management and there is no guarantee that users are allocated in an optimum fashion today. Don't be afraid to move users from server to server (within a site) after the implementation begins, if that seems to make sense.

Network connections are an important influence on the decision whether a location will be a discrete site or join other servers in (usually) close physical proximity to form a site. An office serving many people might, for instance, be deemed to be a site in its own right because its network connections to the rest of the organization cannot sustain the predicted traffic generated by the flow of messages in and out of the server. Unlike other messaging systems, Exchange server uses a type of specially encoded message to replicate data, so items like directory updates must be taken into account when predicting network traffic. It is also a reasonable argument for a single server to become a site because of the number of supported users. However, in situations where many users are to be supported multiple servers will always provide better system availability, as you'll eliminate a potential single point of failure.

Once a site is established all of the Exchange servers that collectively form the site share a single collection of data relating to connections (to external systems), and recipients and other directory information. All of the servers in a site can be administered from a single central location. General wisdom is that it's better to limit the total number of sites within an organization if at all possible because this makes everything easier to manage. While there are no real limits to the total number of servers that can form a site, you should restrain yourself to no more than 50 servers in a site. The logic behind this recommendation is simply based on the fact that it's easier to manage fewer servers than more.

3.2.1 Network connections between Exchange system components

Perhaps it makes things easier to associate the network links that tie things together with the terms that have just been introduced. A range of different types of links is normally used to create the network infrastructure that ties an organization together. Consider a multi-national enterprise with offices in Europe, Asia, and the United States. Three separate geographical areas are involved in this scenario, and each is likely to have different characteristics in terms of the connections that are available. Within the United States it is generally easier and cheaper to establish high-speed, high-bandwidth connections between locations than in Europe or Asia. Within the organization therefore you

might find satellite inter-continental links, 64 Kbps land-line links between offices in an individual country, and fiber-optic FDDI extended
LANs connecting locations in a single metropolitan area.

Within a site the range of network links is much simpler. Exchange
servers in a site share a common repository of information, but this is
impossible unless the connections between the servers are fast enough
to accommodate the data that passes around. Consider directory replication. In a site, directories are replicated automatically in the form of
messages generated, sent, and processed as background operations. An
automatically updated directory ensures that messages are not addressed incorrectly and permits users to send messages to new recipients as soon as they are added to the system. Substantial networks are
required to carry all the information between servers, so much so that
you'd be forgiven in thinking that network vendors sponsor Microsoft!

Exchange clients are normally connected to their servers via a LAN
so the connection is fast and only limited to the speed of the LAN, for
example, 10Mbit/second for Ethernet. You shouldn't ever encounter
problems transferring data between servers and clients unless message
contents are huge or the LAN itself is saturated. Abnormal conditions
will sometimes occur to interfere with the perceived transfer speed
(for users), such as when many users at one time access very large messages, but in general LAN throughput shouldn't be an issue.

3.2.2   Two or more organizations

As we've seen, the model used by Exchange attempts to encapsulate a
complete enterprise in terms of a single self-contained unit called an
organization, breaking the enterprise down into sites and eventually
servers. The model works well for smaller enterprises where cooperation is easier to achieve but poses some challenges for larger corporations. If the corporate operating model stresses decentralization with
each department taking charge of its own computing destiny, then
multiple Exchange organizations can easily evolve, perhaps one for
each country or one for each operating unit. What can be said about
these situations?

Apart from its messaging connectors Exchange is equipped with no
mechanisms to facilitate the transfer of information from one organization to another. According to the rules no form of public folder sharing is possible, encryption will be stripped from messages as they leave
one organization for another, and directory entries cannot be replicated automatically. Workarounds must be found to transfer information, either via the messaging service or with some homegrown manual
processes.

A little lateral thinking reveals that a certain level of inter-organization data exchange can be accomplished as follows:

- Messaging between the two organizations shouldn't be a problem. If both organizations use TCP/IP networks and can connect to the Internet the easiest way to establish a messaging connection is via the Internet Mail Service. Using TCP/IP as the base protocol for an X.400 connector is also more than feasible.

- It is possible to create rules for public folders so that when new information is posted it is automatically sent to a recipient, which could be a public folder in the other organization. Deletions cannot be handled by rules, so manual notifications of deletions are necessary if the different sets of public folders are not to become very much out of step with each other. Also, conflicts that occur when multiple users change public folder contents at the same time cannot be detected, as would be the case within a single organization.

- Directory information can be exported from each participating organization and imported into whatever other organization is interested in it. Directory exports are in the form of CSV (Comma Separated Value) files that can be mailed to an appropriate recipient. The contents of the export file need to be edited before they are imported as the mailbox recipients from the exporting organization are custom recipients for the importing organization. Editing can be done with a variety of tools, including a spreadsheet, but as it's a repetitive operation following well-defined rules it's best to write a program to do the job.

As Exchange grows in popularity I'm pretty sure that either ISVs will create a toolkit to make inter-organization transfers easier or Microsoft will upgrade Exchange to allow super-organizations to be created from a group of subsidiaries. After all, not every enterprise has the luxury of being so well coordinated to fit into a single self-contained unit.

3.3   Windows NT, domains, and security

Apart from mail encryption and digital signatures, Exchange provides no special security features of its own. Instead, Exchange relies on all of the security facilities built into the Windows NT operating system. For instance, users must be able to authenticate their identity to Windows NT before they can ever connect a client to an Exchange server. Providing a valid account name and password during the initial log-on from a client to a Windows NT server authenticates a user. The Windows NT NetLogon service validates the account name and password against the Security Account Manager (SAM) database, and if the authentication check is successful a user process is created on the client. After it is created the process is granted the set of rights allocated to the user account in the form of a security access token. The access token contains information about the user and can be used to check whether a user is entitled to access a file or other object, for instance, a Microsoft Exchange mailbox.

Because Exchange is so tightly integrated with Windows NT you must take account of the Windows NT domain and trust models that are already in place, or design a model that will accommodate the needs of the messaging system. No implementation of Exchange will succeed if the underlying Windows NT structure is unstable. It is important to note at this point that restructuring a domain is not a matter of setting a few switches or parameters followed by a reboot of all the systems in the domain. In most cases, changing anything fundamental in the domain structure requires a complete re-installation of Windows NT on each system in the domain. Given the potential workload generated by reinstallations as well as the impact on users and an organization, this is clearly not something that any reasonable system administrator wants to even consider.

Just to get a formal definition in place, a Windows NT domain is a logical set of workstations and servers that are managed as a single unit. The domain shares a common security policy and user account database, as encapsulated in the SAM. The SAM is stored as part of the Windows NT registry and contains information about global and user accounts, including the user name, password, groups which the account is a member of, any restrictions that might be in place, and the account's SID (Security Identifier). All of this data is doubly encrypted.

The minimum requirement for a domain is one system running Windows NT server software, which acts as the Primary Domain Controller (PDC) and holds the copy of the domain's SAM. A domain can also contain many other servers and workstations distributed across a wide area. Because all servers in a domain share a common SAM it is only necessary to create a user account once for each domain. Once equipped with a valid account name and password a user is able to connect to resources by logging on to any of the server computers within the domain. A domain can contain one or more Windows NT servers and manage a wide array of clients including Windows NT workstations, Windows for WorkGroups, and DOS.

3.3.1   Domain controllers

Within each domain at least one server will be allocated the task of authenticating all the log-on requests from clients. This server stores and maintains the security database for the domain and implements all the changes made by applications throughout the domain. For example, if a user is granted the necessary access rights to be able to manage some-one else's mailbox, the fact that the access rights have been granted will be registered in the security database. A small domain will have one server, referred to as the Primary Domain Controller, and there can be only one PDC per domain. However, large domains typically implement one or more backup domain controllers to enable opera-tions to continue should anything happen to the PDC. These servers are called Backup Domain Controllers (BDCs) and they hold copies of the security database. Changes to the security database are automati-cally replicated between the PDC and the BDCs, normally every five minutes. The copies of the security database therefore should never be more than 5 minutes out of date, although it is possible for some small inconsistencies to arise if replication has not been completed.

PDCs are computers and all computers, no matter how reliable the operating system and reliable the environment, are prone to operating problems. If the PDC experiences a problem such as a system crash or becomes unavailable due to a network outage, one of the BDCs can be promoted to become the PDC on a temporary basis until normal ser-vice is resumed. This switchover arrangement allows the domain to continue to operate while the original PDC is off-line. When the origi-nal PDC is available again any changes the backup controller has made to the security database are automatically replicated back and synchro-nized.

Apart from the possibility of taking over from the PDC in case of failure, BDCs can also be used to balance the load generated by user authentication requests and so provide a degree of fault tolerance in this respect. When this happens the authentication requests are chan-neled to the BDC for verification in a totally transparent manner. Us-ers are certainly not aware which server is responsible for handling their log-on. In large installations it's wise to avoid PDC saturation at peak times such as the start of the business day by sharing the authenti-cation load across BDCs. The general recommendation is to have a BDC for each physical LAN or site running Exchange. Up to 2,000 us-ers can be serviced by a BDC.

In any relatively medium to large Windows NT installation the PDC will have to satisfy a reasonable workload of authentication re-quests and updates to the security database. Whatever the speed in which updates are applied to the security database, it is critical that au-thentication requests are serviced quickly and users can complete the log-on process quickly. For this reason it is unwise to install Exchange on the same Windows NT computer that acts as the PDC. A more practical consideration is the fact that if Exchange is running on the same computer as the PDC it is difficult to restore the Exchange information and directory stores from backups to an operational state should a problem occur. We'll discuss this particular issue in Chapter 5 (see page 284).

3.3.2   Types of servers

The retail versions of Windows NT are broken down into server and workstation software. We've now seen that Windows NT supports different kinds of security workload for a server. This leads to a point where we recognize that there are systems running Windows NT server, which never participate in security processing (as a PDC or BDC). These servers are dedicated application servers, or sometimes called non-domain servers.

Application servers off-load security processing to a PDC or BDC, allowing all the resources of the server to be dedicated to a specific application or set of applications. Because of the potentially heavy demands made by a messaging system, it is a good tactic to plan to install and operate Microsoft Exchange Server on systems acting as application servers.

In a small domain it is possible to have a server that acts as the PDC, provides file and print services to a set of users, and runs Microsoft Exchange server. However, there is a limit to the number of users that can be supported in this case, depending on the hardware configuration that's installed. When the time comes for expansion the natural option is to install a dedicated application server into the domain and move the majority of Microsoft Exchange processing over to the new server, perhaps leaving workload like directory synchronization with external sources or a specific connector on the original system.

3.3.3   Trust relationships

Windows NT uses trust relationships to link domains in terms of the actions a user can take. If domain A trusts domain B it means that a user from domain B will be able to log onto a server in domain A, and then access resources controlled by domain A. Access is permitted because the trust relationship between the domains attributes rights and permissions for objects controlled by domain A to any registered user from domain B. Of course, there are some limitations to what a user from a trusted domain is allowed to do or the data they can access, but this simplified explanation will serve for now.

Shared mailboxes provide a good example of the domain trust mechanism in action. Shared mailboxes can serve as common repositories for messages sent to organizational units. For example, inquiries about new products could be sent to a mailbox controlled by the marketing department, and any user who has permission to access the mailbox can process the messages arriving there. If all the accounts that need to process messages in the mailbox connect to the same server or site then the question of trusted access does not arise. However, if you wanted to allow a remote user to access the mailbox, that user must belong to a trusted domain as Windows NT will not allow a non-trusted domain to even see the mailbox.

3.3.4 Windows NT domain models

Understanding an existing Windows NT domain and security model or designing an appropriate domain model (if you are starting to use Windows NT) are important pieces of an Exchange implementation plan. In fact, getting the domain model right or understanding how best to leverage off an existing domain model is probably the single most critical item on the path to a successful implementation.

There are four distinct Windows NT domain models that can be implemented within an organization. These are:

- Single domain model
- Single master domain model
- Multiple master domain model
- Complete trust domain model

Obviously if you don't have a Windows NT infrastructure already in place you have total freedom over the type of domain model you select. Lots of enterprises have experimented with Windows NT since it was first released in 1993 but may not be using Windows NT for anything other than a desktop operating system or to provide shared file and print services to other Windows clients.

Windows NT is probably the finest desktop operating system available today and it certainly does an excellent job of providing shared file and print services. But many implementations to provide file and print sharing tend to be carried out in a local or departmental manner and do not pay special heed to the needs of the organization as a whole. In other words, you can very quickly install Windows NT servers and connect clients in to form your own domain, but if everyone does this for their own department the resulting Windows NT infrastructure is fragmented. It's also highly likely that no comprehensive set of trust relationships exist. We'll return to the question of what tactic to take in this instance, but first let's review the options open for domain models.

3.3.5   Single domain model

The single domain model (see Figure 3.2) is by far the simplest domain model that can be implemented for Windows NT. It is also the most common model selected for departmental-style implementations, especially where Windows NT has replaced another network operating system such as Novell NetWare as the base for shared file and print services.

Figure 3.2
*Windows NT
single domain
model*

Within the single domain model all users are registered in a single security database, but there are practical and technical points that need to be borne in mind. Windows NT V3.5 increased the upper limit for the number of user accounts that can be registered in a domain from 10,000 to a theoretical limit of 40,000. However, the logistics involved in managing such a large number of user accounts almost always means that another model is considered well before the "old" limit of 10,000 is attained, unless there are lots of system administrators waiting around for work to do.

The technical limitation of 40,000 is not actually a simple matter of Windows NT reaching a magic number and then refusing to register any more users. Instead, the upper limit is determined by the size of the SAM database file in conjunction with the amount of physical memory available on the PDC. Microsoft recommends that the size of the SAM is kept below 40MB. Databases larger than 40MB have been tested in software laboratories and work, but it's wise to pay attention to the firm recommendations from Microsoft. A quick calculation of 40MB for 40,000 users appears to indicate that the details of each user account occupies 1K in the database and indeed it is possible to create a situation like this, as long as no global groups or machine accounts[1] are created.

Within any large user population the normal situation is to operate with a selection of global groups, if only to reduce the level of system administration overhead required to control access to shared resources, so it's highly unlikely that no groups will be active. Group details occupy varying amounts of space, depending on the number of members within the group. Microsoft suggests using 4K as an average for each group, driving down the space available within the SAM for individual user accounts and decreasing the theoretical maximum from 40,000.

Within a single domain model no trust relationships are required because no other domains are known. If you are a small, single-site enterprise with a small number of users (well below 10,000) then the single domain model is a natural choice. This model allows fairly simple and straightforward centralized management of all user accounts and global resources, including those used by Exchange.

The major drawback is that the PDC can become overloaded and slow down other computers if it is not capable of handling the authentication demand created by the user community. Each authentication request or log-on is processed by the PDC, so it must be able to process those requests at peak time. Clearly slow network links to servers and clients located in different parts of the domain can contribute to the problem. The authentication workload can be somewhat off-loaded to BDCs, but the PDC still has a lot of work to do in circulating security information updates to its backup controllers. Concentrating the security workload in a single PDC is the major reason why the single domain model is not recommended for large numbers of users or an enterprise that is distributed across many sites.

A lot of goodness can be gained by simplifying the domain structure to create a seamless environment for everyone to work in. We've just discussed some technical limitations that might get in your way and force the deployment of multiple domains, but there are some practical issues too. The management tools in NT are primarily designed for small to medium domains and have some problems dealing with very large domains. For example, User Manager for Domains caches SAM data before displaying it to system administrators. If you attempt to change details of a user account in a large domain, like the password, it can take a long time before the data is displayed and

---

[1]   Machine accounts are automatically created by Windows NT to allow workstations or servers to participate in the security model

you're able to work with it. The problem is exacerbated if slow network links are used. One of the domains in DIGITAL has a SAM that's 24MB large today (28,000 user accounts), and it can take over half an hour for User Manager for Domains to display on a server in a location with slow links. Third party management tools are available for Windows NT, but it can be quite expensive to deploy these in large companies as they are typically priced on a per seat basis.

The Active Directory in Windows NT V5.0 promises to address many of the issues discussed here and allow domains to scale much higher than is possible today, but the deployment of Windows NT V5.0 remains at least two years away for most large corporate customers. Based on early information, it seems pretty clear that many of the tools that work on the Active Directory will be built using Web components, accessing information via active pages and the Internet Information Server. Look at what can be done today in the Web client. It's totally feasible that the same degree of functionality could be implemented for system administration tools.

3.3.6   Single master domain model

Once a number of different sites are present within an organization you might start to consider expanding away from the single domain model. The natural evolutionary step is the single master domain model, named because a single central domain is established as a point of unification for subsidiary Windows NT servers. User accounts and global groups are registered in the central domain but local resources can be managed from the subsidiary servers. Because of the reliance on the central domain it's essential that systems to act as BDCs are maintained.

Figure 3.3
*Single master
domain model*

Figure 3.3 illustrates a single master domain created for a company called World-Wide Systems Incorporated. It is possible to create a model where authentication is carried out in one place for log-ons and other security requests originating in Asia, the U.S., Europe, and Aus-

tralia, but this would only be practical if extremely fast and dedicated network links are available all the time. Possibly a better and more realistic example would be a single master domain established to serve all users within a large metropolitan area like London or New York, with the individual subsidiary servers distributed to different locations within the area.

3.3.7   Complete trust domain model

Once an organization grows past approximately 10,000 user accounts a single domain often becomes unwieldy. Two options exist, one usually regarded as fairly difficult to set up and administer while the other is fairly simple, albeit less structured. The simple option is the complete trust domain model, a way of distributing the management of all resources to different domains located throughout an enterprise. Each domain creates and manages its own user accounts and groups, for instance. No attempt is made to unify the domains together, but each domain trusts the others so resources such as Exchange public folders can be shared. The model is very flexible because new domains can join at any time, but it can also be somewhat chaotic because no strong central coordination is achieved.

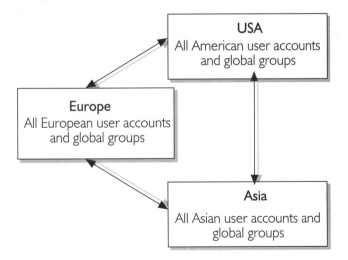

Figure 3.4
*Complete trust
domain model*

The complete trust domain model (Figure 3.4) removes the upper limit of 10,000 users and can therefore be considered to be scaleable. Connecting two or three domains together in this manner to allow people to share information certainly does the job. If you are not worried about having a complete trust relationship with the other domains the simplicity of the model has much to recommend it, especially if Exchange is the major Windows NT. However, if you require better coordination, centralized management, or the ability to partition your Windows NT infrastructure in a more controlled manner the complete trust domain model may not be appropriate.

3.3.8   Multiple master domain model

The two-tier domain model (Figure 3.5) is the most scaleable model. The first tier contains a set of master domains that maintain two-way trust relationships between each other. User accounts are registered in one or other of the master domains. The trust relationships between the domains mean that all user accounts are known throughout the enterprise.

Figure 3.5
Multiple master domain model

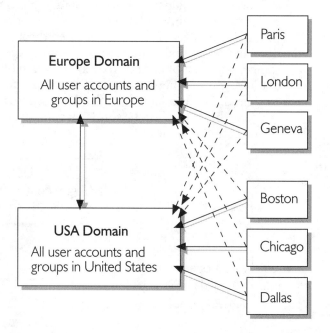

The second tier is composed of domains serving discrete sections of the overall organization. These sections might be created along departmental, organizational, or, as shown in the figure, geographical divisions. The responsibility for managing resources resides at the second tier. Note that the second-tier domains all maintain one-way trust relationships with the first-tier domains. This means that the second-tier domains trust any information provided by the first-tier whereas the opposite is not true.

Each new domain added at either tier increases the number of trust relationships that must be managed so it's wise not to become too enthusiastic when creating first-tier domains. Try and establish a fairly high-level picture of the overall enterprise at the first-tier, using convenient divisions such as the continental sections as illustrated. Enterprises broken down into operational divisions such as Manufacturing, Sales, Marketing, and so on can consider using these divisions but geographical lines are probably more practical because network links are normally organized like this, with very fast connections within a physical location and slower connections maintained between countries. Once again it's important to have BDCs deployed within each second-tier domain, just in case.

Because of its relative ease of management that scales well over thousands of user accounts, most large distributed enterprises, including the internal networks operating by Microsoft and DIGITAL, use either the master domain model or multiple master domain model. DIGITAL, for example, has three master domains called DIGITAL1, DIGITAL2, and DIGITAL3, respectively serving North America, Europe, and the Asia/Pacific regions.

The examples of the master domain model presented here are based on a geographic separation of resources. Even if you're not very widely distributed in a geographical sense there is still a case for adopting the master domain model. In this instance you'd create a resource domain for Exchange (and perhaps other applications). The Exchange resource domain will have no user accounts—they'll all be in the master domain, so the only accounts that operate within the domain will be the service accounts required for Exchange administration and inter-service communications. Placing all the Exchange servers into their own discrete resource domain is a great way of cutting down the administrative workload by creating an integrated Windows NT environment that can be managed totally separately from other applications and user accounts.

In summary, if you are considering a large-scale implementation of Windows NT (initially) leading to a deployment of Exchange, the master domain model and the multiple master variants are both leading contenders.

3.3.9   Making a decision about the domain model

The domain option selected by any other company is not necessarily a recommendation that a particular domain model is best for your situation. However, my experience of working with many large companies to create a suitable Windows NT infrastructure for the implementation of Exchange has been that almost all of these companies have selected a variant of the master domain model. In some cases this decision has required those companies to discard their existing Windows NT implementation, mostly because it was either fragmented or deployed without any regard to the requirements of an application like Exchange which is so tightly integrated with Windows NT. We'll discuss the topic of working with existing Windows NT domains in more detail in just a few pages.

Making the decision about the Windows NT domain model to use is possibly the most critical of all the decisions you'll have to make as you approach an Exchange deployment. It's certainly the first decision to make, and the one that influences many of the other deployment options down the line. I have one major recommendation to make at this point in time. Make sure that the people who are making the decisions have enough knowledge about Windows NT and Exchange before the decisions are made. This means that whoever's involved in the decision should get some training (attending a one-day overview seminar or a similar event is not enough—go and get some proper training) so that they fully understand the implications of selecting one domain model over another. Making decisions based on what someone thinks they know rarely, if ever, leads to success.

3.3.10   Don't forget WINS and the rest of the Windows NT infrastructure

The decision about the domain model is important but it's not the only item on the Windows NT agenda. The point has already been made that Exchange is inextricably linked with Windows NT and depends on that infrastructure. Bitter experience over a large number of deployments reveals that the most common problems are not due to Exchange but rather flaws in the Windows NT infrastructure.

WINS (Windows Internet Naming Service) is an important part of the Windows NT infrastructure for any distributed organization. WINS tracks the association between TCP/IP addresses and computer names, and in a distributed environment it's likely that there will be several WINS servers to manage the set of TCP/IP addresses and computer names used by a company. The history of WINS implementations has not been smooth. Originally, general wisdom held that WINS servers should be distributed around a network to keep them close to concentrations of computers, but this opinion has moderated through experience so that implementers typically have smaller numbers of WINS servers than before. The WINS software suffered from some bugs too, most if not all of which have now been addressed. Certainly, Windows NT V4.0 does a much better job of managing the WINS database than NT V3.51.

Exchange servers should all have fixed TCP/IP addresses. There is nothing dynamic about a server computer! Once an entry is made into WINS for an Exchange server that's the address it should use all the time. If this is the case, does a dependency exist between WINS and

Exchange? The answer is that it all depends on your network and how the WINS servers are distributed.

For example, there have been instances where public folders were re-homed onto a server because the original home server couldn't be found due to a WINS problem. In one case a whole collection of public folders were re-homed to a server in Australia because the original owning server (in the United States) couldn't be contacted for a few days by the Australian server. It seems that Exchange assumed that the home server had been removed from the network and decided to adjust the public folder hierarchy to take account of the new situation! When the WINS problem was fixed and the original home server could be contacted by the Australian server, all of the folders were removed, an unfortunate side effect of public folder backfill. For this reason many experienced system managers keep entries for all Exchange server in each server's LMHOSTS file. Hopefully the future unification of Exchange and Windows NT directories will go a long way to eliminate problems like this.

WINS is important, but so is DHCP (for client address allocation), SMS (for software updates and client inventories), and file and print sharing. The impact and deployment of other BackOffice applications like the Internet Web Server also need to be considered. Everything needs to be brought together into a comprehensive and sensible plan for Windows NT. Third party products also need to be factored into the plan, especially if they are used to help manage the Windows NT environment. Unfortunately people implement on a fractured, uncoordinated manner and fall into the black holes that lurk in bad deployments. The blame is then often attributed to Exchange because it's the most obvious application in the hands of users.

3.3.11   The Exchange Service Account

A privileged Windows NT account is required for the installation and operation of Exchange. The standard Windows NT Administrator account can be used for this purpose, but it's a good idea to create a special account in each domain to use for all aspects of Exchange administration, including installations. Apart from anything else, using a different account creates a clear separation between Windows NT and Exchange administration. Often the same people will take care of everything, but in large installations it is quite common to have different teams looking after general system administration and messaging. In these situations it's best to allocate each team their own working environment so that they don't interfere with each other.

Use an account name such as EX-ADMIN or EXCHADMIN, but make sure that the same name is used on all servers where Exchange is installed. Some people, especially those who wish to run the most secure environment possible, don't like using names that convey any idea of the purpose that an account is used for. In these situations the usual approach is to use an account name like ZZYYYXX, the logic being that no hacker is going to guess that such an account is privileged. The same logic dictates that the normal Windows NT administrator account should be disabled and another account created for administrative purposes.

Using the same service account is mandatory within a site, and it makes everything easier to administer if the same account is used throughout an organization. This is another good reason to put all the Exchange servers in an organization into an Exchange-specific resource domain. The service account should have the same privileges as the standard Windows NT Administrator account. You may need to include the service account into any administration groups that are used to manage Windows NT.

The Exchange installation procedure grants special rights and permissions over Exchange objects to the account used to perform the installation (usually the service account). If you want to use other accounts to manage Exchange servers afterwards you'll have to grant those accounts the necessary permissions to deal with whatever objects they are interested in. Tracking down all the places where permissions have been granted is a little tricky, so it's best to leave the original account used for installation alone if at all possible.

3.3.12   Getting help—automated tools

The Microsoft TechNet CD-ROM (May 1996 edition onwards) contains two software tools that help to collect information about essential characteristics of the Windows NT and Exchange organizational structures that are best for your enterprise. These tools are:

1. The Windows NT Domain Planner

2. The Exchange Server Modeling Tool

Both tools are also included in the Exchange V5.0 Resource Kit. The basis of the tools is simple. A question and answer session is conducted using "wizard" technology. In the case of the Domain Planner you answer questions such as the total number of users, whether you want to administer all servers centrally, and so on. After all questions are answered you can generate a report containing the recommendations arrived at by the wizard. If you don't like the recommendations you can go back and modify earlier answers (see Figure 3.6) and see if the recommendations change.

Everything you enter into the domain planner is captured into a configuration file. In turn, the domain information held in the configuration can be fed into the Exchange modeling tool. This reflects the close and intimate relationship between a solid implementation of a Windows NT domain structure and eventual success with Exchange being deployed on top of that structure.

The Exchange modeling tool offers similar opportunity to input details about the type of Exchange organization you want to build. The questions cover points such as the different network connections available to link sites, which sites will host public folders, whether messages can flow constantly or if they'll follow a schedule, and so on. The design is arrived at through a process of constant refinement, and the graphical nature of the tool allows you to quickly see the current situation at any time. Figure 3.7 shows how site details are input. As you can see, it's possible to experiment with different scenarios to analyze how a change will affect the overall situation. At the end of the exercise the modeling tool creates an organizational diagram (Figure 3.8). Note the representation of the different external connectors (X.400 and SMTP in this case).

Figure 3.8 *An organizational diagram built by the Exchange modeling tool*

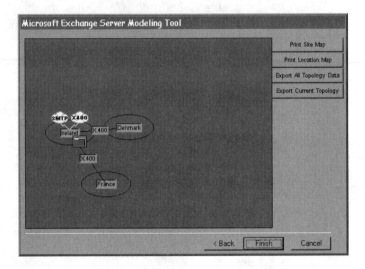

Both tools store the data they record and analyze in Microsoft Access databases. It's possible to open either EXSERVER.MDB (for Exchange) or OLPGDATA.MDB (for the NT domain tool) and have a look at the data. If you can figure out all the relationships you'd even be able to create your own extensions. Most people, I imagine, will be quite happy to leave the data to the tools.

I've used quite a number of automated system design tools in my time. Those available for Windows NT and Exchange provide an excellent starting point for the design exercise. Apart from anything else, using tools like this forces you to collect information together in a logical fashion, something that's extremely valuable in itself. If you feel that you lack knowledge or experience with Windows NT or Exchange you can engage in the data collection exercise yourself and then bring the data along for analysis and review by an expert.

Treat the recommendations issued by the tools as an input to the design process, not the final and absolute decision. Automated tools are all very well, but human knowledge and experience often produce insights that have critical influence on the shape of the best possible design.

3.3.13   Installing Exchange on top of an existing Windows NT infrastructure

As discussed previously there are going to be a large number of situations where Windows NT domains are already operational within enterprises. The question now arises of how to incorporate or leverage an existing infrastructure for use with Exchange.

If the enterprise is small and a single domain is in use then introducing Exchange is a straightforward process, providing the network in place is able to handle the volume of additional traffic introduced through Exchange messaging and replication activities.

Planning is more complicated where several different domains are already in use. Lots of companies start using Windows NT as a replacement for shared file and print services that had previously run in a Windows for WorkGroups or Novell NetWare environment. It's easy to fall into the trap of implementing Windows NT in line with a workgroup rather than a corporate model. In other words, the server is installed to fulfill a specific purpose, to provide file and print services to a small client workgroup. Each workgroup is a separate domain. No real attempt is made to consider inter-working with other domains outside the immediate physical location, so the servers in London don't know about the servers in Paris, or New York, or anywhere else. Why should they, if all that's being provided is local file and print services?

Figure 3.9
Browsing a very large Windows network

Look at the set of Windows NT domains illustrated in Figure 3.9, the result of browsing the internal DIGITAL network. Having 939 domains visible to the network (and there are probably a lot more lurking under the surface) is a classic example of domains gone wild, almost to a point where it is impossible to know what each domain has been set up to do. Networking is taken for granted within DIGITAL. DIGITAL operates the largest commercial network in the world. At one time there were over 40,000 computers attached to the internal network, so it's not altogether surprising or frightening to discover so many Windows NT domains in use. DIGITAL has used Windows NT since the operating system became first available as a beta test. There are many technical people inside DIGITAL, and many of those who are quite capable and happy to set up and maintain a new domain. These two influences, along with no centralized control being exercised on domain creation, lead to hundreds of domains. Is it a problem? Probably not, as long as the people who created the domains in the first place remain happy to manage them, and there are no fights about domain names. Is it desirable? Absolutely not—flexibility is important, but anarchy is unwanted.

It is worth noting this point that the project teams who implemented Windows NT and Exchange as corporate services within DIGITAL ignored what had gone before and did not attempt to use any existing domains. This was a very wise decision because it removed any of the convoluted interconnections, like trust relationships, that would otherwise have been required.

Enterprises distributed across large distances where LAN connections are not possible can use the complete trust domain model to unify domains that are already operational, as long as there aren't too many domains. The complete trust model requires trust relationships to be set up between all the different domains. The bulk of the work to establish the trusts is a one-time operation. Maintaining the trust relationships isn't too difficult if new domains are not added. Bringing new domains into a set of trusted domains requires a new and separate relationship to be created between the new domain and each one of the existing domains. This can rapidly get nasty because the number of trust relationships expands to a point where there are just too many to easily manage. For example, in a situation where 20 domains are involved in a complete trust relationship, a total of 380 (19×20) trusts must be set up between the different domains. Creating 380 trusts is one thing; managing 380 trusts over an extended period of time is quite another.

Trust relationships (Figure 3.10) come into play if sites are to span domain boundaries. When a new server is installed the installation program requests details of an existing server in the site and then attempts to retrieve information about the site from that server. A Windows NT trust relationship is enough to allow the two domains to see each other, and this permits the installation program to make the request to the remote server for site information. However, if the account being used to perform the installation does not possess permissions to administer the organization, site, and configuration objects on the target server it won't be able to update the remote server's configuration. Failures to possess the necessary permissions will cause the RPC queries to be rejected by the target server and the installation procedure will not be able to proceed.

Figure 3.10
Trust relationships

It's altogether too easy to forget to set up a trust relationship, in turn leading to problems with Exchange features such as public folder affinity, single seat administration, and message tracking. Administrators sometimes make mistakes and remove trusts, leading to similar problems for Exchange. Worse again, if a site connector is in use to connect sites across two domains the removal of the trust relationship will instantly stop messages flowing between the sites. For all these reasons it is best to avoid trust relationships if at all possible, lending weight to the argument that a complete Windows NT redesign should be undertaken before any Exchange deployment begins.

In situations where you're faced with a large number of independent domains steps should be taken to rationalize the situation and form a more unified Windows NT infrastructure before any deployment of Exchange is begun. Normally this means that you have to design and implement a new Windows NT infrastructure from scratch. If the existing domains have only been used to provide shared file and print services it shouldn't be too hard to connect the desired services to the new domain and then move or even recreate user accounts. Some user accounts may need to be renamed if the same account name has been used in multiple domains.

Clearly creating a new Windows NT infrastructure is not a task to be undertaken lightly. It is an exercise that won't be cheap in terms of time and effort, and few people will understand why anyone would want to redesign an infrastructure that's successfully providing users with good service today. Of course, these people (some of whom are likely to occupy senior roles within your company) are looking at the situation at a pretty superficial level and don't understand the issues involved. Good communication of all the reasons why it's important to have a solid, integrated, and scaleable Windows NT infrastructure as a base for Exchange will therefore be important.

Remember that Exchange sites can map domain models in different ways. Sketching out the basic shape of the Exchange organization to illustrate where sites and servers will be located and the names each site and server will have is a very fundamental and important step in the planning of any Exchange implementation. A site can map a domain on a one-to-one basis and this is the most probable implementation where domains and sites are created to serve different geographical locations (London, Paris, Geneva, and so on). And as we've seen, sites can also be built from servers spanning different Windows NT domains as long as the necessary trust relationships exist.

3.3.14   Pirate Exchange organizations

Computer professionals love new technology (a complete generalization I know, but useful for the purpose of illustration). As such, they like to deploy new applications. Sometimes the desire to deploy new applications, like Exchange, conflicts with the need to plan the implementation to the necessary level of detail that's required by corporate deployments of Windows NT and Exchange. I've been in a number of projects where some departments in a company are started to operate Exchange servers that have been installed with little or no coordination with other departments. There might be one Exchange organization in production, but then again, there might be several different Exchange organizations up and running. The latter scenario is very difficult to manage because each additional organization will eventually need to be integrated into a whole.

Suddenly being given the job to create a unified messaging environment from an already-installed loose collection of Exchange organizations, sites, or individual servers is a variant of the problem created by an existing Windows NT infrastructure. One of the joys of Exchange is the ease with which the server software is installed. Forty minutes or so after the shrink-wrap is removed the server can be up and running with clients happily sending messages to each other. Once you have a Windows NT server you can install Exchange and unfortunately sometimes people get carried away and Exchange servers can proliferate within an organization, perhaps as a result of different organizational units carrying out their own pilot deployments. I refer to unauthorized or uncoordinated Exchange implementations as "pirates." People running Exchange like this may think they're delivering a valuable service to their users, but the long-term implications of early and unplanned deployment carries a heavy price to pay. I see four major issues with pirate deployments:

1. Pilot implementations should be treated as early deployments of the corporate model. If they are not they're not very valuable (what do they prove?) and will have to be redone. We'll return to this topic later in Chapter 9.

2. If early implementations are not in line with the Windows NT domain model and the Exchange organizational model that are eventually used for the corporate deployment, there is a very high percentage chance that the software (NT, Exchange, or both) will have to be re-installed. Adjusting domains, site names, or server names after a server goes into production is difficult, if not impossible.

3. No utilities exist today to incorporate an external Exchange server into an organization. You cannot merge Exchange organizations together. In passing I'll note that no utilities exist to split out an Exchange server from a site either. However, the manual tasks to perform such a split are fairly straightforward.

4. Pirate implementations may not comply with other standards under consideration for the corporate deployment. For example, items like public folder creation and permissions, document retention policies, operational policies such as backup software and hardware, server platforms, and so on. It's certainly easier to bring these inconsistencies back in line with corporate requirements than it is to fix problems with Windows NT or the Exchange organization, but why should you have to do the work?

Pilot implementations need to be planned. There is no point in going through all the effort and incurring all the expense involved in a pilot if the work must eventually be discarded. Yet pilot implementations will have to be discarded, software re-installed and re-configured, and users may loose data if every system administration does their own thing, creates their own NT domain structure or defines their own Exchange organization model. The need imposed by the Exchange directory to define naming conventions for the organization, sites, servers, and mailboxes means that it is very difficult to take a server that's being operated by one department or another and incorporate the server into a corporate Exchange organization. As noted above, no tools or utilities exist today to merge Exchange organizations, or import a complete organization into another. If a "pirate" server does not match the organizational model created for the corporate implementation then Exchange will have to be re-installed on that server.

The close relationship between Windows NT, Exchange, and the individual servers that collectively form a corporate-wide implementation makes re-installation inevitable. The question therefore needs to be asked of anyone who considers deploying Exchange early, before everything is planned and ready to go: "Are you ready to accept that the work you're doing will be discarded once the corporate deployment starts?" In most cases, the enthusiasm of the potential pirates is tempered with the realization that their work will have to be redone.

So what can you do to integrate standalone systems into an Exchange infrastructure which spans the enterprise? There are two basic approaches.

1. Leave the existing servers in place and integrate everyone with a unified messaging backbone to connect all the different servers together. In this scenario each location that operates an Exchange server retains its existing user accounts, server names, and other attributes and is treated as a separate and distinct Exchange organization (rather than site).

2. Start over by designing the Exchange infrastructure from the base up so that all the servers are connected together into sites within a logical Exchange organization. In this scenario all the existing servers will eventually be assimilated into the new infrastructure. Because of the dependence on Windows NT domains, security, and networking this process will inevitably be more painful for some user communities than others.

Clearly the first approach is faster and easier to implement. It devolves the responsibility for operation away from a central coordinating body to the system managers in individual locations, and this may make the approach attractive to managers of central MIS groups who struggle with shrinking budgets. All that the central group has to provide is the messaging backbone and this can be based on SMTP or X.400. A centrally coordinated corporate directory is an optional extra.

Requiring servers which are already up and running to basically stop operations and change to come into line with standards determined for a corporate Exchange infrastructure will clearly impact system managers and users alike. Software will probably need to be re-installed to change organization, site, or server names, meaning that users will have to save the contents of their mailboxes to personal stores (PST files), or discard whatever they had stored in their mailboxes and start over again. Servers may have to join different Windows NT domains to allow public folder affinity. Connectors may have to be re-installed and communications re-established with other messaging systems. User accounts may need to be renamed to come into line with whatever corporate standard is felt best. If you've just been running pilot systems the best idea may well be to stop and start from scratch again, but clearly this approach is more difficult for all concerned if the system has been operational for any length of time. This is another good reason to pay attention to the overall design for Windows NT and Exchange before attempting a corporate implementation.

3.3.15   Franchised sites

Pirate organizations operate totally independently of a centrally managed deployment. Sometimes you want to be able to allow people to deploy Exchange on their own, taking responsibility for delivering service to a particular user community while remaining a full participant in a company's deployment. These deployments are franchised sites.

The main characteristics of franchised sites include:

- The site serves a distinct user community. It may be a physical location such as the London site. On the other hand, it may be an organizational entity, such as the Human Resources department.

- The site takes full responsibility for the deployment of whatever servers they wish within the site. Hardware configurations and designs remain totally under the control of the people managing the site, although they may well take advice from a central group.

- The site connects into the central core organization via an agreed type of site connector. Typically the X.400 connector is used because it allows the greatest degree of control over network traffic. The connection is made to a nominated server within the core organization.

- The site does not install other connectors unless on an agreed basis. No one wants sites to introduce connectors without consultation as an unplanned growth in the number of connectors merely complicates the organizational routing table for everyone.

- The site shares a common address space with the rest of the organization, including other franchised sites. Because of this the site must agree to follow naming conventions, especially for user display names.

- The site establishes a directory replication connector to the core organization and participates in the organization GAL.

Franchised sites allow distributed management. Many corporations have distributed administration already and are interested in the concept. If you've been running a local Microsoft Mail or cc:Mail Post Office you're already well aware of local administration!

Franchising has many advantages. However, it can't work without a strong core implementation in place to link all the franchised sites together. It also can't work if everyone does not have the discipline to comply with the practices that allow everyone to work together. Finally, local administration cannot be done if local administrators are not trained to the same level of professionalism and knowledge as the people who plan, design, and carry out the central deployment. The last point is possibly the most important.

3.3.16   The consequences of not getting Windows NT 100% right

Exchange is a messaging system so it's not altogether 100% correct to say that its servers must share the same Windows NT security context before successful operation is possible. Putting all the Exchange servers in a separate resource domain or establishing a reliable set of trust relationships between a set of domains will make things easier to set up and manage. Connections between servers and sites, for example, flow much more easily if their underlying connections are underpinned by a well-planned, solid Windows NT design. But if you're in a position where it's impossible to bring all the servers together into a single domain or trust relationships prove unreliable for one reason or another it is still possible to create a messaging infrastructure, albeit at the expense of lesser functionality.

The most important point to recognize is that all communications between Exchange servers, including replication, can be accomplished through the interchange of messages. As long as a network capable of supporting the TCP/IP protocol is in place and the servers can "see" each other across the network, messages can be exchanged and data replicated. So what functionality does not work? Here are the most important issues:

- Public folder affinity is not possible.
- Single seat administration cannot be performed.
- Message tracking doesn't work.
- Server monitors don't work.

Public folder affinity (see discussion beginning on page 236) will not work unless a client is able to authenticate itself to the server controlling the public folder. If I have a client connected to a server located in Domain A, and the public folder is stored on a server located in Domain B, then the client must be able to authenticate itself in Domain A and B before the servers will allow affinity to proceed and the client to access the contents of the public folder. If all the servers are located in the same domain or appropriate trust relationships are defined between the different domains then authentication is achieved during the initial client log-on.

Most companies like the idea of being able to manage a complete network of Exchange servers from a central server (or workstation). But again, the administration program must be able to authenticate itself to a server before the server is happy to accept administrative instructions. If the administration program is used to browse an Exchange organization and then selects a computer in another domain, an attempt is made to log-on to that computer, which is of course impossible if the appropriate rights are unavailable.

Message tracking (see discussion in Chapter 11) is based on the availability of message tracking logs, held in a network share called "tracking.log" on each Exchange server. Message tracking can only follow the path of a message from one computer to another as long as the trail can be established through examination of the message tracking logs, so the network share on each server in the path must be available to make full tracking feasible[2]. If the servers reside in different domains and trust relationships are not in place the network shares cannot be accessed and tracking halts at the stage when the message exited the domain.

Server monitors (also discussed in Chapter 11) can be used to establish whether important Exchange services, such as the Store, System Attendant, or MTA are up and running on one or more target servers. RPCs are sent to the target servers to glean information about the services the monitor is interested in, but the RPCs will not be responded to if they come from an un-authenticated source.

Over time it may be the case that other functionality is unavailable when a unified security context cannot be established across all Exchange servers in an organization. We simply don't know the minds of the Exchange engineers on this topic. As such, I believe the best thing to do is to attempt to create the most solid Windows NT infrastructure that's possible, and then execute the Exchange implementation on top of that solid foundation.

---

[2]   Tracking must also be turned on for the different components (connectors and the MTA) that handle messages if tracking logs are to be filled with valuable information.

3.4   Layering the site design on top of the network

When designing the Exchange organization for your implementation will you:

- Create a small number of large sites?
- Create a large number of small sites?
- Create a mixture of large and small sites?

The automated tools mentioned earlier in this chapter (see page 134) can help to clarify the best solution to your requirements. Sometimes the decision will be made for you. If you don't have fast network links between servers that are capable of handling the RPC load generated to synchronize site-wide shared data structures such as the directory then you won't be able to combine the servers together into a site. Anything less than a dedicated high-quality 64 Kbps link (the recommendation generally given by Microsoft) provides too little bandwidth for site connectors to operate in a satisfactory manner. It's often difficult for enterprises, especially outside the United States, to justify the operation of such high-speed links just to connect some mail servers together. In these situations careful attention must be paid to the location of servers and how servers are combined together into sites. Everything is layered directly on the network and if the network can't carry the load the Exchange organization cannot function.

Be wary of assuming that just because a network connection is there its total available bandwidth is available for use by Exchange. In most instances other applications will want their own slice of the bandwidth, leaving Exchange with whatever is left over. Another issue to consider is that a line rated at a certain speed may not deliver the maximum bandwidth all the time, perhaps because of some low-quality links that occur at places along the line. Indeed, in many cases there is a significant difference between a line's maximum theoretical bandwidth and its committed information rate (CIR).

The CIR is a much more reliable indication of how much information a line can transmit because it represents the information transfer rate which the network (or network provider) is committed to transfer under normal conditions. The CIR is always averaged over a period of time before it is determined, and this takes account of any retransmissions required because of low line quality. RPCs in particular are sensitive to low line quality, so a line that apparently provides 64 Kbps bandwidth might only achieve an information transfer rate of 32 Kbps or less due to RPC time outs and other errors. Aside from a line's CIR, bandwidth tends to be absorbed in many different ways. For these reasons it's wise to begin planning on the basis that 128 Kbps links are used for RPC-based site connectors with 256 Kbps links deployed to connect servers together within a site. You can tune the bandwidth back if you like, but always with detailed knowledge of exactly what's passing across the network.

Now that I've stated a rule let's acknowledge that exceptions will always be found. Large network pipes are best for Exchange, but reliable data transmission depends on the capacity and quality of the network link. There are instances where people have experienced difficulties transmitting RPCs between sites over 128 Kbps links, and other examples where the RPCs were happy to travel over a 9.6 Kbps link. Line quality dictates whether data flows easily, so the 128 Kbps link was obviously very low quality while the 9.6 Kbps link was high quality. The short-term solution to the problem experienced across the 128 Kbps link might be to increase capacity to 256 Kbps or greater, on the basis that increasing the size of the pipe will let more data through. The solution will probably work, but it doesn't address the underlying problem that provoked the issue in the first place.

When you look at any anecdotal evidence of an Exchange implementation and examine the network connections in use, consider how much data flows between sites, and between servers within sites. The amount of data to be carried is an important influence on the network that we need, but it's often an issue overlooked during the planning phase. Take the example quoted as using 9.6 Kbps links. If only a small number of messages were sent between users in the different sites, and there wasn't a lot of public folder replication, and not many changes were ever made in the directory, then it's entirely possible that the small pipe is more than able to handle the load. However, if people make energetic use of e-mail, use e-forms, replicate public folders that contain large Word documents, PowerPoint presentations, and other files, and regular directory synchronizations are performed with directory data taken from other messaging systems, then the network load between the sites is going to be much heavier. Attempting to link heavily trafficked sites together across 9.6 Kbps connections may work, but only at the expense of slow message delivery and potential message queues building up in the MTAs on all sites. In addition, the resilience of the network will be quite low, and if network outages occur, it will take a considerable amount of time before message backlogs can be cleared. Large network links really come into their own when it's time to clear a lot of work.

No example is enough evidence for anyone to make a firm recommendation that you should have 9.6, 56, 64, 128, or 256Kbps links installed in your company. The starting point is to base the core site design on the way data flows through the transmission network. Then use local experience of network conditions, measurements of data transmission rates, errors, and evidence of any time-outs known to occur to help decide how much bandwidth you need, but above all concentrate on achieving line quality as without quality the RPCs will find it difficult to get through.

3.4.1   The mistake of depending on the examples of other companies

Many companies start planning on the basis that there should be as few sites as possible in the organization, and concentrate on building very large sites even over widely distributed geographic areas. The experiences of the Exchange implementations in Microsoft and DIGITAL are often quoted as examples of how to build and operate very large sites. Microsoft's North America site, for instance, has over 160 servers in it. DIGITAL also has a very large site spanning North America, the difference between the two implementations largely being the size of the servers. Microsoft deploys relatively small servers, so there are a lot of them. DIGITAL prefers large servers (a graphic illustration of the power of Alpha technology), so there are much fewer—less than 20 in all of North America with the largest server supporting over 2,700 mailboxes.

Simple figures conceal a lot of details about both implementations. Microsoft has a lot of servers concentrated in a small area (the campus at Redmond, Washington). DIGITAL also has a large number of users concentrated in a small part of America, in this case in the New England area. Both implementations depend on high-quality, high-bandwidth networks (including satellite links) because both companies have invested heavily in an extremely capable network for internal communications over the years. Both companies also depend on electronic mail and other forms of communications, like internal Web or electronic forums, to share information.

Not all companies have the luxury of such extensive and capable networks, at least not on the scale deployed within Microsoft or DIGITAL. So is it reasonable to select the same implementation model if the underlying foundation is radically different? The answer, of course, is "No." A little additional probing past the headline points of both implementations reveals that:

- Microsoft has a number of small sites in South America. Those sites are not connected by permanent high-speed links, so RAS dial-up connectors are used to link servers in the sites into the rest of Microsoft. The network connection is limited to the 28.8 bps modem speed.

- DIGITAL has more users located in Europe and the Asia-Pacific regions than Microsoft. In many instances the network link back to a hub site is 64 Kbps, but that link is not solely available for Exchange and must carry traffic from many other sources. Because Europe is spread across multiple international boundaries and many telecommunications providers it is both harder and more expensive to put high-speed network links in place. Thus, DIGITAL has found that it is impossible to run a single site across Europe. The current European implementation has two sites concentrated around network hubs. More sites will probably be developed as the deployment spreads into countries where networks are less developed, such as Eastern Europe. The sites are linked together with X.400 connectors because they are more reliable and robust across low-speed links than site connectors.

- Communications in Asia-Pacific are also expensive and the people are widely dispersed. Creating a single site is impossible when there are several thousand people to serve. DIGITAL therefore operates three sites in the region, and connects everyone up with X.400 connectors.

With these points in mind I think it reasonable to look at the Microsoft and DIGITAL implementations in order to learn, but not to assume that just because these companies have deployed Exchange in large sites within America that this is the only and best way to proceed. There is no reason why any company's culture and implementation should directly influence your implementation, unless you want this to happen and understand the consequences. The network places the most immediate and important constraint on the way Exchange sites are built and linked together, and this point must always be paramount in the minds of those who architect an Exchange solution.

3.4.2   Learning never stops

All products go through different stages in their lifecycle. Exchange is still in the early stages of its lifecycle and it follows that many people are still learning a lot about effective ways of deploying Exchange, and the trade-offs and decisions that must be taken as an implementation plan or design is arrived at. A lot of the experience we have today comes from early adopters (the companies who were brave enough to agree to put Exchange into production very early on—their nickname is the "Bravehearts"); Microsoft's own implementation of Exchange; and books, conference papers, and other consulting studies. Much of this information is valuable and should be carefully considered when building new organizations, but to date it has necessarily been created from a reasonably narrow base and can't be considered as the absolutely best way to do everything.

Judging by experience of the lifecycle of other messaging products, the really ingenious and clever deployment techniques only come about after some years, really after people have had time to see the product in action and think through how they could improve matters. Unless you pay attention to all available sources of information and ideas some of the new techniques will pass you by and you'll never be able to take the kernel of the new learning and apply your local knowledge to put the techniques into practice for your company.

3.4.3   Inter-site communications

Every server in a site communicates with its peers on a regular and unregulated manner. In other words, you can't prevent a server talking to its peers *when it wants to* rather than when you'd prefer it to. Servers exchange details about configuration changes, they update each other with directory information, and messages are routed between servers without regard to the network or any schedule. Sometimes, when I try and illustrate this point in seminars, I compare Exchange servers in a site as insecure human beings with a constant requirement to reassure each other that everything's OK. At the end of the day all you can say is that each server will connect to its peers on a regular basis to establish a full-mesh network. Nothing can be said about the amount of data that will travel across the links, because that amount is highly dependent on the way Exchange is used within a company. Another interesting point is raised by the RPC mechanism used by servers to communicate together. RPCs are sensitive to network quality, and if that is not high enough RPCs will time out or otherwise fail to get through, leading to a large number of retransmissions.

Firm and quantitative data can only be gathered as a result of a data collection exercise, watching the data flow between servers and measuring how much is sent out and received. The bottom line here is that you shouldn't introduce servers into a site unless permanent, robust, and highly capable network links exist between the server and every other server already in the site. In short, you need a high-speed, high-capacity network. If the network links between servers are incapable of offering a solid, reliable, and generous supply of bandwidth to satisfy the sometimes seemingly insatiable demands of the servers, then you are better off to create separate sites and connect them together with site or X.400 connectors.

In general the recommendation is to limit the number of sites within an organization. While moving objects within a site is easy, moving users and servers between sites is a difficult, manual process. Putting effort into the organization/site design is important. Ask yourself questions like "How can we expand without breaking the organization if a large number of new users needs to be added?" or "What happens if our company sells a building, de-centralizes, or otherwise physically changes the shape of the company?" A design should be flexible and able to expand (or contract) as business requirements dictate.

An organization with more than fifty sites is going to be moderately difficult to manage. A site with more than twenty servers in it will also be difficult to manage. Try to restrict the number of points of management, at least at the beginning. It is very easy to add a site or server to your Exchange organization afterwards, if required, but organizations that start off sprawled and scattered don't tend to regain any coherent shape without great effort on the part of system administrators.

3.4.4   Locations with small number of users

Sometimes you won't want to put a server into a location. Perhaps the network doesn't extend there or maybe there aren't enough people to justify the expense and effort required to bring an additional system into production. Local sales offices that host two or three people are a common example of such a location. What can you do to connect these people in with the rest of the organization? Two choices exist:

1.   Run an extended WAN connection to the location

2.   Use telephone connections

The number of clients that can be connected over a WAN link depends on the bandwidth delivered (the more bandwidth, the more clients) plus the type of work that the clients do. A 64Kbps link will support many users (up to 20 or so) if they are just going to read and send a few messages on a sporadic basis. On the other hand, the same link will be hard pressed by a relatively small number of users who insist on working with large documents that are stored in public folders. Sending large attachments (greater than a few hundred kilobytes) across an extended WAN link will degrade performance for everyone else, and there's always the temptation to use the bandwidth for other activities, such as surfing the web, terminal connections to mainframe or mini-computers, and so on.

Educated use of network resources increases the number of users that any link is able to support. For example, if users are coached to make connections to the server every couple of hours or so, synchronize their folders, and then work off-line until the next connection time, most of their work will be done off-line and the network will only have to handle bursts of activity. It's not easy to convince people to be so disciplined. Most individuals will fall into the habit of assuming that the network link is available all the time for their exclusive benefit and proceed to work on that basis.

Telephone connections are best used when the number of users in a location is very small, possibly between 1 and 5. In this instance users must be disciplined because each connection is going to be charged for, and the longer people spend on line the higher the charges. I have known of cases where a senior manager became distracted when working over a telephone link, and left the PC connected to the line overnight. That connection was from a hotel, and the call had been placed to a server in another country. The end result was a bill well into the thousands of dollars, an extreme example perhaps, but a useful war story to tell to users when you're trying to encourage good habits.

Telephone connections require a RAS infrastructure to be in place too. You'll also need the fastest possible modems at both ends of the connection.

People often rule out telephone connections as an option if the remote locations are in another country. The thought of international phone call charges mounting up on a regular basis is enough to push network planners to try and secure dedicated network connections to foreign offices. The logic here is that it's better to pay network charges up front and deal with a known figure that can be factored into a budget rather than live with the unpredictable nature of telephone bills. I can't fault the logic, but sometimes a little lateral thinking can result in another solution for international calls.

The Internet is everywhere and it's easy to make cheap, even free telephone calls to local "points of presence" serviced by an Internet Service Provider (ISP). If this is the case, then why not use the Internet to channel network traffic from remote clients back to an Exchange server? The normal answer is "security." No one wants their mail to be read by hackers who might intercept messages as they move across the Internet. But technology exists today to allow encrypted tunnels to be built between clients and servers across the Internet, and so transfer messages and other data in a very safe and reliable manner. One such technology is DIGITAL's AltaVista Tunnel.

AltaVista Tunnel encrypts IP packets as they leave clients, and decrypts the packets as they arrive into a private network. The result is a Virtual Private Network (VPN) built between the client and the private network. The tunnel is built through PC client software, which is responsible for initiating and managing the tunnel across the Internet, and an AltaVista Tunnel Server, which is located inside the firewall that guards a company network. The AltaVista Tunnel Server decrypts the data sent across the VPN, and routes it to the end destination, in our case, an Exchange server. No change has to be made by the local ISP, who remains blissfully unaware that their services are being used to build a VPN. If the ISP were to monitor the transmissions between an AltaVista Tunnel client and the Internet, all they'd see is perfectly normal IP packets.

You may think that using an encrypted tunnel across the Internet still represents a risk, probably because you need more information than can be presented here to help you become more comfortable with the concept and technologies used to implement the tunnel. Encrypted tunneling does work, and has been used in a number of projects to facilitate people in remote locations or users who move from place to place and need to connect in when a RAS environment isn't available. Perhaps the biggest benefit is the way that costs are reduced by eliminating expensive international telephone calls in favor of cheap local calls to an ISP. The downside is speed. Although more than acceptable for most of the time, the Internet is congested, and there's no doubt that messages sometimes take longer to transmit and receive than would be the case if you had made a dial-up RAS connection. However, given the cost benefits, tunneling is still an interesting option for anyone who needs to connect small offices cheaply.

3.5   Connecting up an Exchange organization

Once you have an Exchange server up and running and some clients happily connected and sending mail to each other the next natural step is to consider how you can connect your server to others. Connecting a new server into an existing site isn't an issue because connectivity is largely transparent and is automatically accomplished when the new server joins the site.

The major options for connecting Exchange sites together are:

- Direct RPC connections between Exchange sites (aka Site Connectors)
- Using the Internet Mail Service to connect Exchange sites together
- Using the X.400 connector to link Exchange sites together
- Using an SMTP-based backbone
- Using an existing X.400 backbone (in other words, a non-Exchange MTA)

These methods are listed in order of convenience. In other words, making a direct connection between two Exchange sites over an RPC-based connector is a quick and easy way to get things going. It is also the lowest cost option and probably the way that most people will use when they start to connect sites together. However, it is an Exchange-specific solution and only suitable where a low to medium volume of messages need to be transported within the boundaries of a single physical LAN or WAN. The basic and most fundamental thing to understand here is that if the network cannot support and reliably deliver the RPCs between servers in the different sites you shouldn't even begin to think about using site connectors. The X.400 or SMTP connectors are able to function over lower-quality and less capable networks, and are the pragmatic choice when the network is not able to deliver permanent, high-speed, robust connections.

3.5.1   Selecting a corporate messaging backbone

Once the requirement arises to connect to other messaging systems, inside or outside your organization, another approach must be taken. At this stage a fundamental decision about the corporate messaging structure may have to be made. Are you going to use SMTP or X.400 as the basic messaging backbone? This decision is one of the most important that messaging system implementers must make.

X.400 is an internationally agreed upon standard designed to enable interoperability between different messaging systems. The standard describes the structure and format of messages, and how they can be exchanged between different systems. It is issued in the form of a set of recommendations that can be used by vendors when they build messaging systems. Microsoft Exchange Server complies with the set of recommendations issued in 1988 and is able to connect to systems that support either the 1984 or 1988 recommendations.

SMTP is the messaging protocol generally used to send messages throughout the Internet and is designed to operate over TCP/IP networks. Initially drafted in 1982, SMTP is an old protocol now, even older than the first set of X.400 recommendations. Originally designed to facilitate the transmission of simple text messages between systems, SMTP has evolved (not always gracefully) through the add-on of different extensions to the protocol. The extensions have allowed SMTP to compete on an almost equal basis with the underlying richness promised by the more comprehensive nature of the X.400 recommendations. Continual evolution through add-ons rather than a complete redesign of a protocol is not always the best way to bring a protocol forward. Some industry observers have asked whether it's not time to carry out a full review of SMTP so that it can survive and prosper past the year 2000. An exercise like the effort carried out for the TCP/IP protocol which resulted in TCP/IP V6.0 would be good for

SMTP at this point in its lifecycle, but no such project is in view at present.

Exchange uses the Internet Mail Service to allow connections to SMTP-based mail systems. You can use the Internet Mail Service to send messages to other messaging systems, as long as you can connect to the other system via TCP/IP and it is able to accept SMTP-type messages either directly or via an SMTP gateway. Alternatively, you can use the Internet Mail Service to tie Exchange sites together over a TCP/IP network.

Debates about the best messaging backbone have raged over the years. Over the last decade X.400 has traditionally proved to be more popular in Europe than in the U.S., possibly because of the high level of support the majority, if not all, of the public telecommunications carriers in Europe have given to establishing X.400-based messaging services. Indeed, in the United States, there is at times almost visceral antipathy towards X.400 and any messaging system associated with the set of standards. Even the mention that an X.400 connector might be used to connect some Exchange sites together is enough to provoke a strong reaction, with people rushing to deploy site or SMTP connectors instead, just in case they might be infected with the X.400 "disease." This is a silly reaction. Just because a particular technology is built on a set of standards that you mightn't particularly appreciate is no reason to ignore X.400 connectors. The current implementation of Exchange is, after all, largely modeled on the broad outlines of the X.400 and X.500 recommendations, yet it is totally possible to deploy Exchange without realizing that X.400 is playing a part. In the same way, it is possible for X.400 connectors to be deployed without anyone outside the administration community knowing about it.

Table 3.1   *Comparing X.400 and SMTP*

	X.400	SMTP
Security	✓	
Reliability	✓	
Target population		✓
Cost		✓
Technical complexity	Difficult	Easy
Ease of interoperability		✓
Ease of operation/administration	Difficult	Easy
Ease of use (addressing)		✓

The Internet was slower to spread in Europe and the number of Internet connection points and choice of public providers is still far lower in Europe (the number grows all the time). A purely cynical view of the X.400/SMTP debate is that X.400 was designed by a committee so it's bound to be overly complex and bureaucratic whereas SMTP has evolved through practical implementation so it's more down-to-earth. The truth lies somewhere in between.

Table 3.1 looks at X.400 and SMTP backbones from a number of perspectives important to system administrators. These are personal opinions and you're quite welcome to agree or disagree. X.400 offers more inherent security features than standard SMTP, but these are largely offset by Exchange server's ability to encrypt and apply digital signatures to messages before they are transmitted over either backbone (within a single Exchange organization). In some respects an X.400 backbone tends to be more reliable than an SMTP equivalent, if only because of the superior notification options supported by X.400, including non-repudiation of messages. It should be noted that a draft specification intended to allow SMTP to support delivery and read notifications is currently under active consideration, and this may well erode the current advantage held by X.400. At the end of the day SMTP scores heavily in terms of its target population (the number of people reachable through SMTP), the cost of deployment, and the ease of use when it comes to addressing.

Using the Exchange directory to mask the complexities of addresses necessary to reach remote correspondents makes the point about addressing somewhat academic. However, if an SMTP type address is exposed to a user it's obvious that:

```
Tony.Redmond@dbo.mts.dec.com
```

is a little friendlier and more understandable than:

```
/C=IE/A=EIRMAIL400/P=DIGITAL/O=DIGITAL/OU=DBO/G=TONY/S=REDMOND
```

Addresses can change as they move from network to network so an address that starts off being stated in a fairly simple form (as shown above) can become very cluttered and hard to decipher, even for people who are very au fait with messaging standards.

Possibly the most important difference from a user perspective is the way that an SMTP backbone enables easy interoperability for compound messages. These are messages composed of both cover memos and attachments or embedded objects. SMTP backbones use the MIME protocol to encode compound messages, and almost every messaging system available today is able to understand and interpret MIME. The SMTP and MIME combination makes it very much easier for people to send each other messages containing Word documents or Excel spreadsheets than through the sometimes extreme contortions necessary with X.400. The pragmatic approach of user-driven standards as seen in the Internet beats the conformance-driven approach of X.400. Making things easier for users has a bonus for system administrators too because less time has to be spent setting up the connections between servers and the backbone, tuning parameters to enable complex messages to travel from one system to another, and responding to user queries when problems arise.

Ease of use and administration also makes SMTP a more attractive option from the point of cost. Time is money, so the less time spent setting up and managing the backbone the better for all concerned. Compare the time taken to configure the Internet Mail Service and the X.400 Connector to see how much more configuration effort X.400 requires. The extra effort also requires more knowledge of X.400 and OSI that implies training and experience on the part of the system administrator, or an additional cost to buy in expertise from external consultants.

Lest it be assumed that I overly favor SMTP over X.400 let me review some of the arguments often used in rebuttal by the proponents of the X.400 recommendations.

The establishment of the X.400 recommendations has enabled bridges to be built between vastly different messaging systems. The recommendations are well understood and supported by many public electronic mail carriers and PTTs (public telephone authorities) throughout the world. Because X.400 is supported by so many organizations it's easy to make connections between different companies. Finally, the construct of X.400 messages follows an agreed scheme that preserves content as messages move from one system to another. All are valid assertions, but the value of the arguments is being eroded all the time by the sheer weight of the SMTP/MIME combination driven forward by the Internet juggernaut.

3.5.2   Factors governing the choice

Both X.400 and SMTP allow you to build and maintain connections between Exchange sites. The decision as to which to use depends on a number of factors including whether an X.400 or SMTP infrastructure is already in place and type of connections you want to make with other people outside your company.

For example, if you are migrating from a situation where a well-established X.400 backbone is in place to link different messaging systems together and to provide connections to external companies, then it might well be best to leave the existing backbone alone and concentrate on integrating Exchange in with the other messaging systems using the X.400 connector. Remember that Exchange isn't limited to just one X.400 connector (within an organization) and two or more might be used; some to connect Exchange sites together and another to link Exchange to the corporate backbone.

If your organization only uses X.400 for external connections or another OSI application, such as Electronic Data Interchange (EDI) transactions with trading partners, the best idea is probably to leave the X.400 backbone in place for its present purposes and establish a single X.400 connector between a designated Exchange server and the backbone. In circumstances where sites are upgrading from Microsoft Mail or Lotus cc:Mail to Exchange and no messaging backbone exists the easiest option is to go with SMTP, but only because there are fewer steps to take to connect sites together with the Internet Mail Service than there are using X.400 connectors.

My personal preference is to use X.400 connectors to link sites whenever available network bandwidth will not support the deployment of the RPC-based site connector. The preference is driven by a simple fact—the X.400 connector is the only one that supports scheduled connections, enabling a far greater degree of control to be exerted on data transmitted across the network. This simple fact is enough to always recommend X.400 over Internet Mail connectors in large corporate messaging environments. SMTP messaging systems do not incorporate the concept of scheduled connections, although there is nothing to stop the Internet Mail Service including such functionality in the future.

Despite a preference to use X.400 connectors, my prediction is that 75–80% of all Exchange implementations that need a messaging backbone will use SMTP, and the rest will use X.400. Some people will select SMTP because it's simpler; others because they regard X.400 as being some sort of European standard that's being foisted on the rest of the world; and a few more because Internet protocols in general, including SMTP, is where all the action appears to be at present. In most large networks some sort of gateway will connect the two backbones, mostly because the messaging world is still so diverse. At this point it's important to emphasize that the selection of SMTP as a corporate messaging backbone does not rule out the selective deployment of X.400 technologies within Exchange. In fact, because the original design of Exchange was closely aligned to the X.400 recommendations in many places you don't get much choice in the matter and will end up using X.400 even if you don't really want to.

Some system administrators propose to use SMTP to connect Exchange servers together using the Internet as the glue in between. Again, I think this is a reasonable plan to get systems connected quickly, but some of the attributes of the Internet, such as its openness and availability to all, are not conducive to the creation of a reliable, dependable, and secure messaging system. For example, do you know what route messages will travel along as they proceed through the Internet? Can you be certain that other people aren't going to be able to intercept your messages and gain access to commercially sensitive information which could potentially damage your company? Also, what guarantee have you that messages will move across the Internet in any guaranteed time, and will the operations of your company be compromised if the message flow is interrupted by network problems within the Internet? A lot of the same issues arise within internal networks, but at least the network is under your control and can be managed as such. The advent of technologies like PPTP (Point to Point Tunnel Protocol), included in Windows NT V4.0 onwards, certainly delivers an answer to the problem of data protection as it passes across the Internet, but the other points still need to be considered as there's no easy answer immediately obvious today.

Knowledge of your existing messaging environment, the systems involved, how they are connected, the external connections in place or required and how you want the overall messaging environment to evolve are important inputs to the SMTP/X.400 backbone decision. Because this decision is so critical and its effects pervade all parts of the messaging infrastructure it's critical that the decision is right, so if you don't have the right level of knowledge and experience it's a good idea to seek help. The details of how to go about connecting into SMTP and X.400 backbones are covered in a later chapter. You may want to read these sections before considering your options.

3.5.3   Using Exchange connectors or X.400 backbones to connect sites

It is possible to create an organization of Exchange sites, each of which uses an X.400 connector to link to a corporate X.400 backbone. In this scenario messages are routed out of Exchange via the X.400 connector to the backbone, over the backbone and then delivered to the X.400 connector of the recipient's site. Sometimes this is the only option to take because a direct connection cannot be made between the Exchange sites, but if a direct connection is possible the question must be asked as to why the backbone is involved at all? Wouldn't it be simpler to keep all the messages within the Exchange organization and only involve the backbone if a message were being sent to a non-Exchange recipient?

The answer is that the backbone does introduce another step, one that is strictly speaking, unnecessary. There can be good reasons for routing messages across the backbone. Many X.400 backbones allow messages to be logged and tracked, enabling messaging administrators to verify the well-being of the overall messaging environment by checking that the flow of messages is never halted. The logging data can also be used for charging purposes, or to analyze the performance of the backbone, identify bottlenecks, and plan for growth.

The benefits of routing across a backbone have a downside too. Some administrators do not understand that Exchange uses messages for everything—replication of data for the directory, public folder hierarchy, and public folder content; configuration data; and then the normal interpersonal messages that are expected. Transmitting all of the data sent between Exchange sites across a backbone may introduce new strain on the backbone, possibly one that the backbone is not configured to support. Extra network resources will be consumed to send messages to and from the backbone. Finally, routing messages across the backbone will probably be slower than over a direct site to site connection, so the quality of the messaging service is not as good as it could be. The quality represented by consistently fast message delivery is subjective. If users are migrating from a LAN-based system like Microsoft Mail where message delivery times across an extended network are usually slower than mainframe or mini-computer based systems then routing across a backbone is not a problem.

Keeping messages inside an Exchange organization as far as possible reduces network demand, speeds message delivery, and is easier to set up and administer. Therefore, the rule of thumb when planning systems is to use native Exchange connectors whenever possible, and only use a backbone to connect Exchange to other messaging systems. Note that this rule holds for connections to Microsoft Mail and Lotus cc:Mail systems because native Exchange connectors are available. The old adage is that exceptions prove the rule, but if you make an exception be sure that you understand the consequences of the decision in terms of the issues discussed above.

3.6   Naming systems

The name given to a Windows NT system is not only the name that the computer is known as within your network, it's also the name that Exchange will use when the software is installed. With this fact in mind it is clearly important to define a well-structured and easily understood naming convention for Windows NT systems intended to run Exchange.

A good naming convention allows system administrators to gain an immediate snapshot of a computer's role in the overall scheme with a quick look. This requirement immediately rules out any name that might be defined as "cute." For example, it's a bad idea to name all computers after cartoon characters because there's a reasonably small pool of names to choose from. There's no indication of what a computer might do or where it might be located if it is given a name like "Goofy," "Happy," "Sneezy" and so on.

Exchange is designed to be an organization-wide system so the naming convention must reflect this aim. Any organization is likely to include a number of geographical sites, and each site may have one or more computers that act as mail servers. This three-tier structure can be expressed in the naming convention. For example, let's assume that the XYZ Corporation is located in three sites in Asia, Europe, and the United States. The initial servers in the three sites might be named as follows:

```
XYZASIA001
XYZEUROPE001
XYZUSA001
```

As servers are added in the three sites it's easy to see that the numeric value at the end of the name is incremented by one to create a name for the new computer that's unique and conveys some idea of the overall organizational structure.

You can take this idea further and incorporate as many different levels as you like. Larger organizations that operate many Windows NT domains might like to include the domain name as the second element in server names. As an example, if the XYZ Corporation operated with manufacturing and sales divisions, each of which was represented by a different Windows NT domain, the names for the computers might look like this:

```
XYZMANASIA1
XYZSALESASIA1
```

Note that this scheme implies that the divisions operate different Exchange sites in addition to the two Windows NT domains. You also have to make sure that the server names don't exceed the 15-character limit imposed by Windows NT. Just to complicate matters, some versions of SMS (V1.0 through V1.2) cannot perform remote control of systems with 15-character NetBIOS (computer) names.

There may be situations, especially with smaller offices, where multiple organizational units are represented in the same place, perhaps a location that has a slow network link back to the rest of the organization. Clearly it would be silly in this situation for the users from each unit to have different Exchange servers, so the server naming scheme might need to have some flexibility built in to allow for such circumstances.

Creating an arbitrary naming convention is an activity that system managers may enjoy, but users sometimes find confusing. Sometimes the need for a structured naming convention is obvious, but in situations where sites span single geographical locations such as Dublin, London, and Paris, the naming scheme for Windows NT domains and Exchange sites could be based on city names or other geographical terms. A naming scheme based on Australian cities is used for illustration purposes in many places in the Exchange administration documentation.

Geographically based schemes provide the immediate and obvious advantage of creating a very familiar naming convention that is totally obvious to all. Given that sites are named on a geographical location, for example "Dublin," the servers within a site might be named DUBLIN001, DUBLIN002, or DUBLINSALES, DUBLINORDERS, and so on. If you plan to connect to other X.400 messaging systems it is not recommended to use the underscore character in any name associated with Exchange (server, site, or organization). Exchange passes information about itself to the receiving X.400 systems and some can't handle underscores in system names, leading to undeliverable messages. To avoid problems in the future use hyphens instead of underscores to separate parts of server and site names as shown above[3].

3.6.1   Naming the organization and sites

We've just discussed the somewhat esoteric topic of how to name Windows NT servers. Applying a well-designed naming convention to Windows NT servers makes it easier for system administrators to instantly recognize a server's location and purpose, but it's only going to be possible if you're able to install and commission the servers from scratch. Any installation that's been operating Windows NT for some time won't have this luxury and will have to do with the server names that are in place. In the case of the installation illustrated in Figure

---

[3]   The advice on using hyphens as separators holds as long as other products don't have problems with server names that include hyphens. For example, SQL Server (for all versions up to and including V6.5) cannot perform replication if system names include hyphens! The lesson here is to check all angles before settling on a naming scheme.

3.11 where existing servers called DBO-EXCHANGEIST, DPSW08, OFFICENT1, and OFFICENT2 form the "Dublin" Exchange site. This is a practical real-life example of where Exchange has been installed on four existing Windows NT servers that have been combined to form a site. It would be wonderful if you always had the chance to create and implement a logical naming scheme throughout an organization, but this won't always be possible.

Figure 3.11
Different servers in site "Dublin"

You may not be able to do anything about the names given to Windows NT servers, but you do need to plan out names for the Exchange organization and the sites that will comprise it. These are important decisions that shouldn't be made on the spur of the moment because these names are used as the basis of the unique entries created for objects held within the directory as well as messaging addresses. Directory information is propagated to many places within the Exchange environment so it's impossible to change the name of the organization or a site in a single place. If you need to change the name of the organization you need to re-install Exchange on every server within the organization while a change to the site name implies a re-installation for every server in the site. In effect, you will be rebuilding the organization or site from scratch.

Cryptic, heavily coded, or artificially short names are not necessary for site names. All system administration is carried out through the rich graphical interface provided by the Exchange administration program. Use fully spelled out names that make sense and look good. In general it is best to avoid commas and hyphens in organizational and site names if at all possible. While there is not a general prohibition on these characters, past experience with many different applications demonstrates that curious problems often arise when they are used. For example, the Key Management Server component wouldn't work in Exchange V4.0 if the organization or site name contained a comma. The problem is fixed in Exchange V5.0.

3.7   Installing a new Exchange server

The process of installing a new Exchange server is straightforward. Two basic scenarios can occur:

1. Installation of a server for a brand new site, including the first site in a new organization

2. Installation of a new server within an existing site

In all cases you should know:

- The name of the site you are creating or wish to join.

- The name of the organization (if not already selected).

As normal with Windows applications, installations are performed by running SETUP.EXE. You'll be asked to provide the organizational details noted above, and if you want to join an existing site (and organization) you'll be asked for the name of an active server in that site. The installation process must be able to access the Exchange configuration data for the site before the new server can be introduced.

Sites joined across Windows NT domain boundaries must have a trust relationship between the two domains before the installation is performed. Without a trust relationship in place the installation procedure will not be able to make the necessary contacts between servers in the different domains.

3.7.1   Removing a system from a site

Removing a system from a site is accomplished by selecting the server from the administration program and then selecting the delete option (or press the delete key). The administration program must be run on another computer holding administration permission for the target server as a server isn't allowed to initiate the process of deleting itself.

Exchange will check that it is safe to proceed (the server is not currently active) and advise on the consequences of the action. For example, mailboxes or connectors will be lost if not moved; public folders may be discarded completely or their replicas re-homed onto other servers, and so on. If the server is the only one in a site the result is to remove the site from the Exchange organization. Neither step should be taken without carefully planning the removal. After all, you have planned the construction of the organization in terms of the deployment of sites and servers, why not pay the same attention if you have to adjust the plan by removing something?

Before proceeding to delete a server make sure to:

- Move all user mailboxes to another system in the same site, or to a system in another site. These steps are accomplished using the procedures described on page 215.

- All public folders hosted by the server have been relocated to another server. In other words, make sure that at least one other replica of each public folder exists elsewhere.

- Check all connectors hosted by the server. Sometimes it won't matter if you remove a server that hosts a redundant or excess connector, but it's a pity not to ask a simple question and end up deleting the sole Internet Mail Service used by everyone in the organization!

After all user mailboxes, public folders, and connectors have been relocated to other servers it's a good idea to wait a couple of hours to allow the details of the changes you've made to replicate around the rest of the organization. In large distributed organizations it is probably safer to wait at least a day or so to ensure that all replication activity is complete. You never quite know where messages might be queued and delayed due to a temporary network outage.

Check that everything is working normally after the changes have been replicated. If public folders have been moved to other servers, check that the folder replicas are on the right servers. Then shut down the server to see if that affects anything. If this test proves negative you can proceed to reboot the server. After the reboot, proceed to delete the server. After the server has been removed you can run the setup utility to remove all the installed components.

3.8   Permissions

We've just discussed the requirement for trust relationships to exist between two domains that wish to join sites. Trust relationships are only part of the picture as there are two different types of permissions involved in Exchange. Trust relationships correspond to Windows NT permissions, required to access Windows NT itself and then assume the privileges to perform administrative functions. After access is gained to Windows NT there are a number of separate Exchange permissions used to manage and control access to Exchange resources. Exchange permissions are totally different and separate to Windows NT permissions. This fact often causes confusion when people can't understand why they aren't able to "make" Exchange do something despite having all known Windows NT permissions granted to their account.

3.8.1 Naming contexts

Exchange stores configuration data within containers arranged in a hierarchical structure. Four naming contexts are established within the container hierarchy. Windows NT accounts can be allocated permissions within each of these naming contexts. Once a Windows NT account has been granted a set of permissions for a particular naming context within the hierarchy it also automatically inherits the same permissions down through objects arranged beneath the naming context.

The four naming contexts are:

Enterprise container (1)
➡

                Site container (2)
                ➡

                                Configuration
                                container (3) ➡
                                Recipients
                                container ➡

                                                  Schema
                                                  container (4)

Thus if a Windows NT account is granted a set of permissions over the site container it also inherits the same permissions over the configuration and schema containers. The recipients container is an exception. Permissions for this container are inherited from the site container, but not from the enterprise (organization) container. Permissions are modified or granted by double clicking on an object and then selecting the permissions property page. It can take several seconds for Exchange to display the permissions property page within large organizations that span several domains. This is because contact must be made with all the different service accounts in the different domains before their details are listed amongst the properties. Many of the problems seen in replicating directory or other information between sites lie in the fact that the Exchange site service accounts do not possess the necessary permissions for containers in remote sites. In summary, to avoid replication difficulties, the site service accounts should be granted the Exchange Admin role (or a role with equal or greater rights) on both the configuration and site containers in both sites.

3.8.2 Defining permissions for Exchange

Windows NT accounts assume permissions for Exchange through a collection of rights and privileges collectively referred to as a "role." A role defines the exact type of access a user has to objects held within a container. A set of default roles is provided with Exchange. These are:

- Admin
- Permissions Admin
- Service Account Admin
- View Only Admin
- User
- Send As

The account used to install Exchange is allocated the Permissions Admin role. The site service account is granted the Service Account Admin role. The difference between these roles is that the Service Account Admin role holds all available rights whereas the Permissions Admin role lacks the replication, mailbox owner, and send as rights (see Table 3.2).

Table 3.2 *Rights used to define roles*

Right	Meaning
Add Child	Gives the account the ability to create a new object underneath this object. For example, to add a new custom recipient to the recipients container.
Modify User Attributes	Modify the user attributes associated with an object.
Modify Admin Attributes	Modify the administrative attributes associated with an object.
Delete	Delete an object.
Send As	Send messages from a mailbox. This permission allows a user to send messages from a mailbox as if the owner of the mailbox had connected to it. It is different to the "Send on Behalf" option because the messages appear to have come from the mailbox's owner and are not marked as having been sent by another user on behalf of the mailbox's owner.
Mailbox Owner	Able to log on to a mailbox and use it to send and receive messages.
Logon Rights	Log on to any server within a site using ADMIN.EXE (the administrator program).
Replication	Replicate directory information with other servers.
Modify permissions	Modify permission for the object.

The site service account is also granted the Windows NT Logon as a Service and Restore Files and Directories permissions for the local computer. These permissions allow the site service account to start the various Exchange services and to perform essential system backup and restore operations.

If you don't like these roles or believe you need additional roles you can proceed to define a new role by deciding which rights or permissions should be incorporated into the role. An Exchange right defines a specific action that a Windows NT account can perform within an Exchange context. The available rights are listed in Table 3.2.

Bringing everything together, the different Exchange permissions allocated to the set of pre-defined roles are listed in the table below.

Table 3.3 *Roles and permissions*

Roles ➡ Permissions ⬇	Admin	Permissions Admin	Service Account Admin	View Only Admin	User	Send As
Add Child	✓	✓	✓			
Modify User Attributes	✓	✓	✓		✓	
Modify Admin Attributes	✓	✓	✓			
Delete	✓	✓	✓			
Logon	✓	✓	✓	✓		
Modify Permissions		✓	✓			
Replication			✓			
Mailbox Owner			✓		✓	
Send As			✓		✓	✓

The question of exactly who should be allocated permissions for Exchange objects should be addressed in all implementation plans. Send As permission is especially interesting because it allows someone to send a message which appears as if it's been sent from someone else. There is absolutely no indication to show that someone who has no connection to the apparent sender originated the message. Most senior managers or auditors find this a slightly difficult concept to appreciate.

People who have been granted the Permissions Admin permission are able to grant themselves the Send As permission, so the general advice is to restrict Permissions Admin as far as possible. There is no reason for first-level administrators to have Permissions Admin. All the permissions necessary to manage mailboxes or perform day to day maintenance on an Exchange server are encapsulated in the Admin permission, so that's what an administrator should normally be allocated. Only the very highest level support personnel, those who already occupy positions of trust within an organization, should have Permissions Admin, and it's probable that only two or three people in a small organization, or one or two people in each location in a large organization, will need Permissions Admin. Regular audits should be conducted to assess who possesses different levels of permissions and make adjustments as required.

You should also ask yourself whether all Windows NT administrators should also hold administrative permissions for Exchange. My view is that there is no logic to dictate that every Windows NT administrator should be an Exchange administrator. Should someone who deals with file and print services be able to manage Exchange, possibly messing around with settings on an X.400 or directory replication connector? Of course this shouldn't be the default case, and the ability to manage Exchange should only be given to people who really need it. Again, make a list of the Exchange administrators and don't distribute the right too widely as otherwise it will be impossible to keep track of who's making changes to system configurations.

3.9 Third party products

Microsoft is a very aggressive software company and its products never stay still for very long. The list of features in Microsoft products grows at a rate that its competitors find difficult to keep up with. With such activity, is there any role for third party products to play in an Exchange deployment? The answer is "Yes," and largely so because Microsoft concentrates on building the base messaging functionality and providing a framework that third party developers can leverage off.

Microsoft Mail had a large and committed community of third party developers that busily produced all manners of extensions that could be added to a Microsoft Mail system. These developers are slowly but surely moving their products across to pursue new revenue streams with Exchange, and the number of third party products grows all the time. The more success Exchange enjoys, it is inevitable the more add-on products will be available. The trick then is to identify which areas of functionality are likely to be most useful, and then focus on buying products in those areas that are well integrated with Exchange and exhibit a high level of quality.

Experience gained over 15 years of corporate messaging projects indicates that the major areas of interest for third party products are likely to be:

- Backup software (see page 295)
- Virus checkers (see page 272)
- Full text retrieval packages
- FAX connectors
- Connectors and gateways for external messaging systems like PROFS, SNADS, Lotus Notes, or public X.400 services
- Directory synchronization tools to help build, populate, and maintain a corporate directory
- Extensions to the Universal Mailbox concept. For example, products that integrate paging and voice mail technologies with Exchange.

Some of these areas are not going to be useful to everyone. Small installations will probably be happy to use the standard backup software provided with Windows NT. Installations dedicated to messaging are unlikely to be too interested in full text retrieval systems, and those who don't have to communicate with legacy mail systems won't need connectors for those systems.

FAX connectors are a special case. Unlike the majority of the areas listed above, the selection of FAX connectors is heavily influenced by the availability of local expertise and support in addition to approval from the local telecommunications authority or PTT. Many countries insist that FAX connection software is certified before it can be used, largely to prevent the introduction of automated systems that might introduce an uncontrolled stream of faxes into the public network. There are many, many FAX connectors available for Exchange and a healthy discussion about FAX connectors takes place in the Internet mailing list dedicated to Exchange. After you've researched who the local suppliers are, what level of expertise they possess, and what software is available, it is a good idea to review the comments about the different connectors in the mailing list. At least you'll get relatively unbiased opinions there, unlike the propaganda issued by the more disreputable software vendors.

Paging and voice mail technology integrated with Exchange is available today. Like FAX connectors these technologies can require local regulatory authorization, so they are not yet available everywhere. The basic idea is simple. Software and hardware extensions are created to direct paging and voice mail messages from sources like a

PABX to user mailboxes. Outgoing messages to pagers are also supported. The technology works, but the resulting messages (for voice mail) are relatively large and great user discipline is required if the information store is not going to be filled with voice mail.

Integrated full text retrieval systems like Fulcrum Find! or Verity's Search 97 help with any medium to large public folder deployment. Public folders have a habit of growing to a stage where it becomes difficult for users to navigate within the hierarchy. If navigation is difficult, finding the right information becomes impossible and people stop using public folders. You might even find that people revert to using NT file shares instead! Indexing won't solve the problem of a badly designed public folder hierarchy, but it does help people to find information fast. I don't suggest that you index all folders (unless you really want to), but certainly select the folders you think will be most popular and index those.

Whatever third party products you are interested in, it is essential that they are incorporated into a pilot or other pre-production environment to ensure that the components really work. The products need to be tested against different combinations of Windows NT, Exchange, and their service packs so that you know which combination works and which will not. You need to know how quickly the products will support a new version of Exchange (client and server extensions may be involved), as well as any dependency a product may have with another software or hardware component. The help desk needs to know the support chain for the product, who to call, how issues can be escalated if required, and what degree of local expertise is available. Finally, licensing needs to be negotiated. It's easy to fix a price for a single server or group of users, but what happens when the use of a product expands within a company? Do you want to negotiate a price based on the initial user group or one that allows for easy and cost-effective expansion should the product be successful?

The complexity of integrating all the different pieces into an overall implementation rises as the number of components increase. Make sure that you make the right choice, have a clear view of the value added by the products you introduce, and know how the products will evolve in step with Windows NT and Exchange over the next few years. With these precautions in place you shouldn't have too many problems with third party products.

4

Selecting Hardware for Exchange Server

4.1   Introduction

Hardware resources are an emotive topic. Software engineers want their software to work well and not encounter difficulties imposed by what they see as insufficient system configurations. System administrators want to run with correct configurations too, but are often restricted by operational or financial constraints.

In general, Microsoft Exchange Server requires more hardware resources than the computers used for LAN Post Offices. This reflects the demands of the Windows NT operating system as well as the expensive functionality available within the server, especially in the system management subsystem. Installations upgrading from Microsoft Mail need to reconsider the system configurations they use today to see whether the computers can be used with Exchange Server. Anyone else beginning to use Exchange needs to go through the same process of analysis and determination of the right configuration for their needs.

It's foolish to begin any project with "just enough resources." Always plan to be successful and expect growth to happen. Electronic mail systems are characterized by rapid growth in user interaction with the system. As people become more familiar with electronic mail they'll send and receive an increasing volume of messages and provoke more demand on the system, and if the system can't handle the demand users will perceive a reduced level of service.

The important elements of any Windows NT computer configured to run Exchange are:

- The power of the CPU
- The amount of memory (RAM)
- The number and capacity of the hard disks
- The speed and capability of the connection to the network

These elements need to be combined together in proportion to each other to form an effective recipe for good performance. Too much of a resource can be as bad as too little. A little extra memory may, for example, help to compensate for a lack of sheer CPU processing power, but it can also disguise the underlying problem. In this case you might overcompensate totally and throw lots of memory where the real problem is the slow CPU. In general it's fairly safe to say that systems configured to run Exchange need to have a fast CPU, lots of memory, a fast network connection, and lots of disk space. In terms of disk space remember that it's the number of spindles (physical devices) rather than the sheer amount of storage space that's important.

I am always a little suspicious of vendor-provided system sizing tables. Vendors, through no fault of their own, are forced to measure system performance and throughout in artificial circumstances. No one can predict how your local user community will interact with the computer on a daily basis, so the workload used in system tests is created to represent the work that "average" users produce. Now show me an average user!

Sizing data and recommendations derived from that data will inevitably improve in accuracy as Microsoft Exchange Server is implemented in different situations. The reasons for this statement are simple:

- Customers will provide realistic data taken from real-life situations back to Microsoft, and this data will be reflected in the testing scenarios used to produce sizing tables.

- Consultants, Microsoft, and customers will all gain experience from operating Exchange and will be better able to size systems based on that experience. The way people use the system and the load produced by users are especially important factors in this experience.

- New versions of Exchange will become available, and the performance characteristics of the new releases should reflect the experience gained from real-life operation.

Nevertheless, if you want to get a server up and running today what can you do to adjust vendor-provided sizing information?

4.2   Sizing an operational system

A good first step is to gather information from your current system, if you have one. Clearly an operational electronic mail system can provide a wealth of valuable and up-to-date data about user workload, and this will enable you to create a set of parameters to measure against the vendor tables. For example, you should know how many registered users are allowed to use the system, and also how many of those registered users actually connect at any one time. Some installations have a high ratio of registered to active users, sometimes as high as 10:1. However, in my experience the most common ratio is around 2:1. In other words, if there are 100 registered users, 50 are connected at any one time.

After you know how many users you have to cater for you can proceed to estimate the demand created by that population. Electronic mail is not like transaction processing. The same volume of work is not seen during the entire day. Most installations I have worked with over the years experience a number of "hot points" during the day when the demand for system resources is at its highest. Typical hot points include just after the start of the working day, usually around 9 a.m. each morning, around lunchtime, and again towards the end of day. At these times users want to send or receive mail, perhaps to complete tasks to meet deadlines. Heavy message traffic has the potential to cause bottlenecks as the system struggles to process message queues, so clearly it's important to size the system so that it can cope with the maximum predicted traffic plus a comfortable margin for error.

Tracking the flow of messages in and out of an existing messaging system and understanding where those messages originate from and go to is invaluable data when sizing a new system. If some sort of message log is available, you should be able to determine figures for:

- The total number of messages processed each day. It is useful to determine the average number of messages processed each day over a reasonable period of time, for instance a month. Try to analyze the highs and lows in the traffic pattern so that you can see the peak demand.

- The number of messages sent each day by users in your organization. Users can be categorized in terms of the message traffic they produce, and it is helpful if you know how many of your users fall into each category. I use categories like "Light," "Medium," and "Heavy." We'll discuss various numbers that could be used to categorize users later on in this chapter.

Again, expect demand to grow over time. Users will generate more messages as their experience grows. You might not like some of the messages that are generated, especially those that don't have a direct connection to any particular item of business, but I think it's a sign of success when users become so accustomed to electronic mail that they use mail for just about everything!

4.2.1   Knowing what the system will do

Electronic mail is only one potential source of load for a computer system. All the other applications that will run on the system generate load and remove resources from the pool available to Exchange. Thus, to create an accurate prediction of the resources required to provide good service quality to users, you must be aware of the load likely to be produced by other applications and Windows NT system services.

All computers that run Microsoft Exchange Server software within a site offer the same set of core functions to users. These functions are:

- The Information Store
- The Directory Store
- Mail Transfer to other servers.

The other Exchange components that can be distributed across different servers within a site are:

- Connectors to other electronic mail systems
- Public folders
- Exchange administration
- Site to site connections.

All of the other components are optional and can be distributed across different Exchange servers within a site. For example, in a small site (up to perhaps 100 users) it makes sense to have a single client installation point. If you already have a server acting as a shared application area, perhaps for the other Microsoft Office applications, it would be logical to make that server the place where clients access the Exchange installation kit. Depending on the speed and saturation of the network a larger site might determine two or more client installation points. After the initial burst of installations an installation point does not normally generate a great deal of day-to-day network traffic, so its overall impact on the network and host computer will probably not be heavy. However, this is not a reason to place an installation point on a server that is already stressed.

A "standard" Exchange server with one performance profile can quickly change. Consider the new possibilities presented by Exchange V5.0 with Web and POP3 clients joining in. The system performance profile changes as the Internet Information Server is activated to accommodate Web clients, although this might be compensated for as the Web and POP3 clients generally make less demand on the system than Exchange or Outlook clients. The performance profile might also be altered through the addition of new applications such as a FAX connector or full-text retrieval package.

Administration is the only constant across all Exchange sites. The load generated by all the other optional components is highly site-dependent. Sites migrating from another mail system are likely to generate a high volume of message traffic through a gateway to the original mail system until all users are migrated over to Exchange. If you don't use public folders at all, or only use them to distribute small files then the replication load is not going to be heavy. But if electronic forms are used or large documents are stored in public folders, or there is a high and consistent level of remote access to the public folders then a substantial load can be generated for the server.

When facing the first implementation of Exchange within an organization it is difficult to predict what load will be generated by any of the Exchange services. This fact isn't at all surprising because the same is probably true of any moderately complex application. A great deal of intelligent guesswork is needed to come up with a configuration that will last in terms of adequate performance for more than a few months.

Figure 4.1
*Different
applications
distributed
across servers in
a Windows NT
domain*

To complicate the entire sizing equation, the Windows NT systems you might want to use for Exchange server may already be providing other applications to users. One of the attractive points about Windows NT is its ability to construct a logical domain composed of many different server computers all connected by network links. Building a complete Windows NT environment to create the foundation for Exchange will inevitably use more applications than just messaging. People considering Exchange who focus in on Exchange and ignore the needs and requirements of all the other applications often miss this fact of computing life. Of course, vendors add fuel to the fire of confusion by publishing benchmark results for a particular application, and then detailing the exact hardware specifications of the systems under test. These results are accurate, but often must be adjusted to factor in the demands of more normal application mixes, as well as the load placed by network communications.

4.2.2 Putting everything on a single server

You can opt to try and put all your applications on one server. This is an acceptable course of action as long as you:

- Don't have many users to service
- Don't have a requirement for a resilient system
- Don't mind going through severe pain and heartache if the system ever develops software or hardware problems
- Don't have any budget limitations so you can buy the largest and fastest Windows NT system on the market.

As these circumstances don't arise very often the more common course of events is to distribute applications across servers. This approach allows system administrators to match available hardware configurations to application demands, so you end up with a situation where hardware is optimally used rather than perhaps being discarded as being of little use. For instance, a computer can be allocated the task of acting as the Primary Domain Controller and nothing else. A low-end 80486-class system could easily act as the Primary Domain Controller for a domain supporting a relatively small user community. The same system might also be used for shared file and print services. Making use of older systems in this way allows newer hardware to be reserved for new applications, like Exchange.

Some of the common options for distributing application load across individual servers within a domain are illustrated in Figure 4.1. The need to distribute an application differs from organization to organization and depends on the way that the application is used, if at all. For instance, if you run an Exchange-pure messaging system then there is no need for SMTP or X.400 connectors to other messaging backbones, so apart from the network connection overhead you remove the need to translate messages from internal Exchange format to the formats supported by the backbones in question. Because of all the different factors in the equation it is difficult for anyone to give hard guidelines for system sizing and load distribution without a detailed examination of current configurations in conjunction with some fairly accurate estimates of future demand.

The worst situation to be in is where Exchange and another application constantly contend for system resources. It is easy to see where some areas of contention might arise. A system acting as a Primary Domain Controller, or even as a Backup Domain Controller, for a large domain needs to provide fast responses back to authentication requests generated across the domain, so operating an X.400 connector to a heavily traveled public X.400 service on the same system is not wise. In the same way, a system acting as an SQL database server is hardly likely to be a good Exchange host.

In these situations it is usually wise to leave the existing system alone and install a new computer for Exchange. This stops any prospect of application contention and creates a degree of resilience because applications are better distributed. You'll also be able to configure one or more systems especially for Exchange and won't have to compromise because of existing hardware. The configuration you install is also more likely to last longer, require less administration, and provide better service to users. Overall, initially it's a more expensive approach but better over the long term.

4.2.3   Where system load comes from

So far we have discussed the load created by Exchange services and some additional Windows NT applications. However, the system load generated by Exchange and Windows NT represents only two parts of the overall equation as so far we haven't discussed the load imposed by user activities, such as reading and sending messages. Even supposedly skilled and experienced people can generate user load unwittingly. For example, people connected to a server I manage complained bitterly about its performance, yet everything worked smoothly whenever I looked at the system performance monitor, or was working with the system itself. The answer lay in an OpenGL screen saver that I had turned on for the server in a fit of security consciousness. The screen saver worked, but whenever it was active it generated a huge load on the server (taking up to 100% of the CPU) to create all the pretty and intricate graphic images displayed on screen. This was a small, but telling point!

Table 4.1 attempts to summarize the different loads that might be placed on a server. All potential loads are not listed here and the load will differ from environment to environment. Use the table to create an idea of the work you expect your servers to handle.

The total load imposed by user activity tends to increase proportionally as the user population grows. However, unlike other elements in the load that maintain a consistent and constant demand on system resources, the user load arrives in peaks and furrows and is not distributed evenly over time. The classic view of messaging systems is that three peaks occur during a working day—first thing in the morning as users arrive and want to read mail; at mid-day as users send a couple of messages before lunch; and at the end of the day when users strive to clear their desks.

Table 4.1   *Different loads placed on a server*

Users	Exchange Services	Windows NT Applications
Reading messages	MTA activity	Primary or Backup domain controller
Creating and sending messages	Connectors	DNS/WINS/DHCP
Searching folders	Replication	Web server
Updating the contents of public folders	Executing rules	SQL Server
	Monitoring links and servers	System Management Server
	Key Management Server	SNA Server

At first glance, Exchange is hardly likely to be different to other messaging systems in this respect. People will still want to read and send mail throughout the day and hot spots will occur. As long as real human beings create the workload the same type of demand is created. However, Exchange facilitates off-line working and servers that support large populations of mobile users often experience radically different peak loads than those supporting office-based workers. Consider the load generated by five hundred users who come into an office, connect their notebook computers to the LAN, start Exchange, and synchronize folders. All of a sudden, the server is swamped with requests to send messages or download copies of items into off-line folders. At this time the information store becomes extremely busy as it attempts to satisfy client demands, and the LAN also experiences a heavier-than-normal load. The demand is artificial because it is driven by client computers talking to the server at a speed that's comfortable to computers, but would never be generated by humans. After all the synchronization operations finish the load on the server declines to a more acceptable state.

Given that peaks will occur it is wise to configure systems that can accommodate peak demands without too much stress. Any system that runs at 90% load (for memory, disk, or CPU) is unlikely to be able to deal with sudden increases in demands. In reflecting on this point it should be understood that the additional demand will not come from Exchange or Windows NT services. Rather, users will generate it, and users will experience bad service times from the system if it cannot react or respond to the demand as quickly as it should. Systems also tend to degrade in performance over time, reflecting the eternal struggle between fragmenting disks, user demands, and system tuning and maintenance activities and the efforts of the system administrator to keep things running. With all these factors in mind it is clear that an attempt to operate an under-configured system close to the edge of its performance envelope generates a high potential for horrible performance.

4.2.4   Categorizing users

Should you attempt to categorize users? In other words, should you attempt to analyze the demands made on Exchange by the different people who use the system?

I think it's always good to know what's happening on the servers you're responsible for. Each user is different, but it is possible to place users in a number of broad categories, and then use that information to predict the likely demand those users will place on system and application resources. Going through this exercise before system implementation is good, but repeating the exercise on a regular basis is even better as the information gained will allow you to more accurately predict the time when additional system resources need to be introduced. Proactive system management is harder than reactive system management, but it provides a much higher degree of service to users because system performance and response will be more predictable and less prone to sudden interruptions.

Table 4.2 suggests one set of categories that could be used to analyze users. The decision process used to determine the boundaries for each category wasn't very scientific, but the categories serve as a starting point for the discussion. For instance, if you follow the categories precisely no user who sends messages would ever be responsible for managing a public folder. This isn't likely to happen in reality, so you should try and adjust the criteria laid down for each category to match your own view of the situation. User communities vary greatly, and it is a mistake to look at a simple number and base every decision on that. Look at the type of people you want to serve (traveling, office-bound, other), the type of work that they do, and the applications they want to run to adjust the gross picture to a more refined value.

Table 4.2   *Categorizing user types*

	Type of user					
	Very heavy messaging	Heavy messaging	Public folder maintainer	Medium messaging	Light messaging	Intermittent access
Number of items in private folders	2,500 to 5,000+	1,000 to 2,500	circa 100	500–1,500	200–750	Under 100
Number of private folders	50 to 300+	50–200	10	40–100	20–50	5–10
Total size of data held in the private information store	50–300MB	30–60MB	1–5MB	20–40MB	10–25MB	1–5MB
Number of outbound messages generated daily	50–100	35–75	1–5	10–40	3–10	1–2
Number of inbound messages received daily	75–200	25–50	1–10	15–40	5–20	2–5
Number of public folders owned/ maintained	0	0	5–10	0	0	0
Load factor	10	6	4	3	2	1

The table assumes that all clients use Exchange or Outlook clients. Lightweight clients exhibit different characteristics, normally making lesser demands on a server. For example, POP3 clients make intermittent connections to the server to upload and download messages. The concept of browsing through stores, defining rules, or many other advanced features are simply not implemented. Thus, given any server configuration, many more lightweight clients can be supported by a server. Because everything depends on user work habits it's impossible to quantify the difference except in gross terms, but it should be possible to support at least twice as many lightweight clients on a server than Exchange or Outlook clients.

In the model described in Table 4.2, a user in a category is defined as capable of placing a certain load on a server. This is expressed as a multiple of the load generated by a user who makes intermittent access, or someone who reads a couple of new messages every day. Thus, a user in the very heavy messaging category generates roughly ten times as much load as an intermittent user. Think of a user in the heavy messaging category as someone that is logged on all day long and seems, at times, to do little else but create, send, and read messages.

Clearly a system supporting users in the first two categories will exhibit significantly different characteristics than a system in the last two categories. One obvious difference is the amount of disk space that will be required to support the volume of message traffic generated by the users, and in turn probably lead to further requirements to optimize disk performance through RAID-5 arrays or disk mirroring.

The next chapter contains a discussion on how users occupy space with messages in the Exchange information store. For now, let's consider a simple example of how the different types of users impact the information store. As illustrated by the categories described above, users generate different loads and traffic patterns, resulting in varying demands on the information store.

Today the Exchange architecture imposes a sixteen-gigabyte limit for the private information store where user messages are held. This creates an absolute upper boundary for the size of the user community that can be supported on a single server. Some quick calculation reveals that you can allocate 32MB each to 500 users, seemingly a nice comfortable amount to work in, but only enough for users placed in the "medium" category described in Table 4.2.

When calculating the number of users that can be supported by any one system it's unwise to allocate up to the limit. Users of messaging systems tend to fill any space they're allowed and leave you with nothing for maneuvering. Try allocating 20–25MB to each user as a start, but remember that a theoretical allocation is useless unless there's physical disk space available to meet user demand. If every user is going to occupy 60MB within the private information store you'll end up with a theoretical maximum user population of approximately 266. At the other end of the scale if users are allocated only 5MB each the potential user population soars to 3,200, a very considerable difference. The load generated by users can therefore limit the potential user population per server, and it is definite that you'll need more servers around if your users tend to fall into the heavy use categories.

Keep the view you've formed about your own user community in mind when the information store is discussed in order to arrive at a conclusion about the size of store (and hence disk space on the server) you'll need to operate. Note that determining limits in this way is artificial. Other factors, such as data migrated from legacy systems, the use of personal information stores, and the effects of commonality across the store influence the amount of space available to users. The answers determined at this stage are just for the purposes of initial sizing, and will need to be adjusted further once you understand if and how data is going to be migrated to Exchange, and how users are to be allocated across servers. The subject of commonality is discussed in the next chapter.

4.2.5   Selecting the right hardware platform

Unlike its lower-end desktop cousins, Windows NT is designed to be hardware independent. The Hardware Abstraction Layer (HAL) masks the complexities of different computer hardware architectures (the original set of architectures was Intel, Alpha, RISC and Power-PC[1]) from Windows NT system software and the applications built on top of Windows NT, including Microsoft Exchange Server.

Simply put, the function of HAL is to intercept instructions issued by applications or the operating system and translate them into the hardware-dependent code required by whatever specific processor type is in use at the time. HAL supplies the magic that allows Windows NT to work across different platforms, but its existence does not assure availability of any particular application. Just because an application is available for the Intel platform does not imply that the application can run on the PowerPC. An application must be compiled for each target platform to create a suitable binary executable, and this is the reason why the Exchange CD-ROM includes separate installation kits for each of the supported platforms—at the time of writing computers built around the Intel $x86$ and Alpha architectures.

With so much freedom of choice in mind the important thing is not to become focused on one particular platform unless absolutely necessary, perhaps because a strategic buying decision has been made to go with one platform or another. Use the flexibility of the Windows NT HAL implementation to select the right computer for the task in hand.

---

[1]   The power of HAL has certainly been illustrated by the implementations of the operating system across the different platforms. However, NEC, the major manufacturer of MIPS processors discontinued sales of MIPS-powered NT servers and workstations in late 1996. Microsoft and NEC committed to continue support for customers who operate MIPS systems, and Windows NT V4.0 is available for MIPS. The bad news was followed by the news that IBM and Motorola had discontinued support for Windows NT on the PowerPC platform, considerably weakening the HAL story. However, future versions of Windows NT and its applications will only be available for Intel and Alpha processors. 64-bit Windows NT will be supported on the Alpha platform (first) and then the new generation of Intel processors.

4.2.6   Typical hardware configurations

The content of any publication ages over time. Whether or not the value of the content decreases with age is another matter, but one thing's for sure—the pace of hardware development makes it impossible to offer guidelines for configuring systems that last for any length of time.

CPU speeds increase all the time. The speed of the latest processors is a little awesome for those of us with fond (or less fond) memories of early mainframes. Alpha processors have moved from 150MHz to 500MHz in the 1993–96 timeframe, with future processors predicted to go near the 1,000MHz level well before the end of the century. The first Alpha Windows NT system (the AXP150) is now rated well down the power scale. The same is true of Intel-powered systems where the Pentium chip has been cranked up to 200MHz, and has now been supplemented (or even supplanted) by the Pentium Pro, the first Intel processor that's optimized for a pure 32-bit environment. The race to develop faster and faster CPUs goes on, and I know that the speeds quoted here will look slow in just a few years.

While processors get faster memory gets cheaper, at least in relative terms, and disk storage has reached the stage where the MB/$1 plateau has been achieved in many world markets. The combination of increasing processor power, affordable memory, and cheap large disks means that even very large and powerful Windows NT systems are well within the reach of restrained budgets. If falling prices help free money from your budget and a little extra to spend it's probably best to put it into peripherals that make systems easier to manage such as uninterruptible power supplies (UPS), automated tape loaders, and RAID-5 disk arrays.

Vendors commonly publish suggested configurations for systems to support specified workloads. For example, you'll need a Pentium-powered system equipped with 64MB of memory and at least 8GB of disk to support a 200-strong Exchange user community. This is a very basic configuration, one that will have to be upgraded as users become more proficient with the system and demand more of it. Guidelines like these are a useful starting point, but they should not be treated as the sum of all knowledge. The problem is that each operating environment is different, so the results obtained in your installation will be different to those seen by Microsoft when they measure the performance and throughput of Exchange. Users behave differently and some will do very strange things that are never factored into simulated system workloads. Network overhead is also different across installations, and of course, system performance tends to degrade over time due to factors such as disk fragmentation. All of these things contribute to differences between performance results achieved in software laboratory conditions and those seen in real life.

Table 4.3 summarizes the hardware situation at the time of writing. As I've said above, the situation is likely to change over time.

Table 4.3　*Comparing processors for exchange*

Hardware family	Pros	Cons	Suitable for
Intel 80486	Cheap!	Old	Dedicated servers such as Primary Domain Controllers, File and Print servers, or small Exchange servers
Intel Pentium	Performance at lowest cost	Obsoleted by the Pentium Pro	Smaller servers
Intel Pentium Pro	Optimized for 32-bit Windows NT and applications	Relatively expensive	Most production-class Exchange servers
Alpha systems	Sheer power	Requires more memory than Intel-based systems	High-end servers and messaging connectors

To try and put a more practical slant on the matter let's take each of the categories outlined in Table 4.3 and build a system configuration to meet a set of requirements. With the high pace of change in CPU performance a chart like this is only able to offer some generic recommendations, so no attempt has been made to list all possible combinations. Base hardware configurations will change over time as particular chips come down in price or new processors are introduced. Take these suggestions as a base point to start from and adjust for the latest developments on the market.

Note the configuration for the system dedicated to the Internet Mail Service, an example of how to deploy an Exchange server that does nothing else except concentrate on a single task. The growing volume of corporate connections to the Internet and the amount of messages flowing through those links means that many organizations need to consider a scenario that includes a system dedicated to the Internet Mail Service. Depending on traffic patterns you may need one system dedicated to outgoing messages and another dedicated to incoming.

The ideal situation is to build dedicated servers. Budget constraints may limit your capability in this area, but if you are given the budget try and split the different type of work across separate physical systems. In order of desirability try to:

- Keep connectors separate from systems serving user mailboxes.
- Keep directory replication connectors and servers used for directory synchronization with other e-mail systems away from connectors.
- Keep public folder servers away from user mailboxes, especially if heavy use is made of public folders and contents are frequently replicated.

Table 4.4   *Sample server configurations*

Requirement	CPU	Memory	Disk	Extras
Primary Domain Controller or File and Print server	Intel Pentium 100MHz or above	32MB	2GB	
Exchange messaging server for testing or to serve small (10–100) user communities	Intel Pentium 166MHz	64MB	8–12 GB	RAID-5
Exchange messaging/public folders server for a small user community	Intel Pentium 166MHz	64MB	8–12 GB	RAID-5
Exchange messaging/public folders server for a medium (100–400) user community	Dual Intel Pentium 200MHz or medium Alpha	128MB/ 256MB (Alpha)	16–20 GB	RAID-5 array, UPS
Exchange messaging/public folders server for a large (400–800) user community	Dual Intel Pentium Pro or high-end Alpha	256MB	24–32 GB	RAID-5 array, UPS
Computer dedicated to the Internet Mail Service	Dual Intel Pentium Pro 200MHz or mid-range Alpha	128MB	4GB	UPS

Performance tests carried out by Microsoft reveal that Exchange is sensitive to disk throughput at the high end of the performance spectrum. This means that if you want to build large servers you must be prepared to add lots of disk capacity. Large disks provide lots of capacity, but having multiple spindles available to spread the load and support disk striping is better still. If in doubt, use the Performance Optimizer utility (see Chapter 11) to check your current configuration and make suggestions to possibly improve the distribution of files across the available spindles. Experiences with very large systems running inside DIGITAL suggest that no more than six physical drives should be combined together into a single logical drive. You can add more, but no real improvement will be seen. Look to replace drives with larger capacity drives to add capacity instead. For example, replacing 6× 4GB drives with 9GB drives adds an extra 32GB (on a gross level) to a logical drive.

During the discussion on the information store (from page 238 onwards) a suggestion is offered to use a FAT-formatted drive for Exchange transaction logs rather than an NTFS-formatted drive. There is a significant penalty to pay in terms of wasted space allocated to small files in FAT-formatted drives once they go beyond 512MB in size. However, the transaction logs are created as large (5MB) files so this issue doesn't arise.

Remember that the Performance Optimizer cannot distinguish the difference between partitioned drives created on a single physical disk. Each drive on a system is measured in exactly the same way, so the suggestions made to redistribute files across partitioned drives may not be optimum and require reassessment once the Performance Optimizer offers its suggestions. As referred to above, more physical disk spindles are generally better from a performance perspective than a single large disk. In other words, given the choice of a single 4GB disk or 4×1GB disks you'll get better performance from the latter option. The way the Performance Optimizer analyzes disks proves that you should never place too much trust in automated utilities. They're a great starting point and a guide towards better performance, but they are not infallible.

Servers powered by Pentium processors are likely to be the general workhorse systems chosen for Exchange deployment in 1996–97. New processors tend to fall in price after they have been available for a while and competitors have started to appear, so the Pentium Pro will start out as a more expensive option which should become the baseline system for Exchange from 1997 onwards. If the pace of development seen over the last three years is maintained the Alpha processor will maintain its lead in terms of sheer speed. Unlike its competitors Alpha is a 64-bit processor and the net effect of this is an increase in the amount of memory required on Alpha-powered systems in comparison to others.

A heavily loaded Exchange server demands a lot of a CPU. The sheer speed of the Alpha processor makes it an excellent choice for systems supporting large user populations or those that handle a high message interchange workload. Systems that act as X.400 or Internet connectors must translate messages from internal Exchange format to the formats used within X.400 or SMTP backbones, and this work can generate a lot of processing especially with large messages or those addressed to big distribution lists. Similar workloads are generated by incoming messages arriving from the X.400 or SMTP worlds.

If you're unsure about the potential of any particular configuration to support Exchange, perhaps that of a system which you have on hand ready to go, you can run the Exchange Load Simulator (LoadSim). The load simulator program creates a workload for the system and measures how it responds. A full description of the program can be found in Chapter 11.

4.2.7   Preparing for success

My personal approach is to over-configure a system rather than attempt to get it just right. In other words, to expect the system to be successful and grow over time. The "just right" state lasts about one week after a system goes into operation and after that it's a constant battle between system administrators (who want to preserve as many resources as possible) and users (who have quite the opposite viewpoint). Apart from the general contest between users and administrators a number of other factors may have an impact on system performance after they go into production. Common factors include:

- New applications are added. For example, a web-based application using the capabilities of the Microsoft Internet Information Server to is put into production. Some of these applications may have the capability to be "mail-enabled" through MAPI, and if enabled will use Exchange to create and send messages.

- The characteristics of user workloads change, as people become more familiar with the system. Instead of small, simple messages large, complex, multi-attachment messages are generated and sent. Heavier use is made of Schedule+. Electronic form applications are created and put into use. Users begin to move away from using messages to share information to the more powerful, but also more demanding, paradigm enabled by public folders.

- Heavier use is made of Internet or X.400 connectors. For instance, because the Internet Mail Service provides very easy access to Internet messaging resources, users start subscribing to news groups and other mailing lists, resulting in a new source of external messages arriving into the system.

- New features are incorporated into the overall messaging service. For example, Electronic Data Interchange (EDI) communications with trading partners, voice mail, a FAX gateway or a paging service is added, and so on.

For these reasons it's better to fight the battle to get the necessary budget to build a really well configured system from the start. Apart from anything else, deploying a high-end system will enable you to use the same system for a number of years from the point of initial deployment, avoiding the need to interfere with hardware configurations. Altering hardware configurations means taking a system off-line and interrupting service to users. Change brings its own benefits in that you can upgrade hardware, but it also delivers a potential for something going wrong during the upgrade and extending the time when the system is unavailable. Building redundancy and growth into systems from the start avoids the situation of having to continually patch in new hardware or other resources and play catch-up with user demands. Having additional memory, disk space, and CPU power from day one gives an element of assurance that the system will last a reasonable amount of time before it begins to creak at the edges.

4.2.8   Large versus small servers

As far as I am aware no prize has yet been made available for building the largest Exchange server in the world. DIGITAL certainly holds this particular blue ribbon, with over 2,700 mailboxes on a server (the server is dedicated to messaging, no connectors or other activity takes place on the system). Most of the other large servers that I know of in production today are in the 1,000–1,200 user range.

In general, at this point in time, it is unwise to put too many users on a single server. The situation will certainly change as additional features such as system clustering are added to the product. Until this happens my recommendation is to try to balance your user community across the set of available servers, keeping no more than 500 or so on any individual server. More than 500 users on a single server makes administration unwieldy and extends the time necessary to perform regular housekeeping or maintenance operations. For example, finding the necessary disk space to run EDBUTIL to reorganize the information store gets more and more difficult the larger the files become.

LoadSim allows you to conduct automated tests on selected hardware configurations. Microsoft and hardware vendors use LoadSim to determine how many users can be supported on different CPUs. The results of these tests indicate that many computers (albeit sometimes equipped with multiple CPUs) are capable of supporting over 1,000 users. The upper limit (as tested) is set by 8-CPU Alpha systems tested at up to 20,000 users. Treat such figures cautiously. They are fine in theory but not in practice, not least because the 16GB limit for a server's information store places a practical limit on the number of users that can be comfortably supported on a server. There's no point in configuring a system to support 2,000 users if they aren't able to create and send messages because there's no disk space available.

Although Exchange is clearly capable of supporting many more users on an individual server, the Microsoft group responsible for coordinating the internal implementation of Exchange determined that there should be no more than 315 user mailboxes on an Exchange server. This reflects a pragmatic solution to the need of e-mail users within Microsoft where they are allowed 50MB of disk space each in the information store. Sizing systems for user communities of similar size allows consideration of a wide range of hardware configurations. You can configure for the bare minimum, allow room for growth, or expect success and over-configure initially in order to deal with an expected growth for computer resources as users become more familiar with the system or as new facilities are introduced.

Many experienced administrators of high-end messaging systems advocate mixing different types of users on each server so as to spread the workload generated by user activities evenly across all servers in a site. Spreading users across a set of smaller servers avoids a single point of failure and increases the amount of space within the private information store that you can allocate to each user. Smaller systems are cheaper to buy and you have a wider range of hardware to choose from. You may even be able to use existing hardware after applying disk and memory upgrades rather than buying expensive new high-end computers. However, there are disadvantages. Lots of different servers in a site increase the overall complexity of the installation and drive up the time required to accomplish day-to-day housekeeping tasks, such as backups. You may have to spend time moving user mailboxes from server to server in an attempt to balance the load, and the range of hardware installed within a site may make maintenance harder, especially for older hardware.

For instance, there is no point in grouping all the really heavy messaging users together on a single server unless you want to equip that server with the resources needed to handle their demands. Another tactic worth bearing in mind is to try and have as high a degree of message locality on each server. In other words, try and allocate users who need to send messages to each other on the same server so that the processing by Exchange's various connectors is reduced to a minimum. The same tactic can be taken with public folders, placing them close to the users who need to access the data held in the folders most often.

4.2.9   Two small servers is not equal to one large server

If one server can support 250 users will two servers similarly configured support 500 users? The answer is "No." Once multiple systems are connected together, within a site or between sites, the processing required to synchronize the systems together absorbs a certain amount of performance. In addition, the benefit of the single message storage model is eliminated, as messages must now be transported between users on the different servers.

How much system performance is absorbed by the connectivity overhead? There's no good or clear answer to that question because it all depends on the number of servers within a site and what type of work users do. Each server within a site periodically updates the other servers, forming a full-mesh network. The servers pass directory updates and other data to each other, similar to the way that all domain controllers communicate together within a Windows NT domain. Because each Exchange server talks to all the other servers it follows that the addition of a new server into a site exponentially increases the number of RPC connections made between servers and the amount of data transmitted on the network. After the requirement to keep servers synchronized is met the systems are then able to deal with interpersonal messages sent between users.

If messages can be kept on the same server they are processed in the same way as on standalone systems. The usual rule of thumb applied when estimating the percentage of messages that will be sent off the system is 80/20. In other words, 80% of all messages will be delivered to a local recipient, but 20% will have to be processed by a connector. There is a difference in the way connectors process messages that must be taken into account too. If the message is destined to go to another server at the site it can be sent directly. The same is true of messages that pass over a site connector, but any message that travels across an X.400 or Internet connector must first be translated into the connector's native format. Servers that act as bridgeheads for connectors or directory replication will also have more work to do, and this will affect performance further.

Clearly not all systems will obey the 80/20 rule. It is important to try and keep people who communicate together on the same server and this is the reason why workgroups or departments are usually allocated to the same server. If this isn't possible and a department ends up being split across multiple servers it is inevitable that a higher percentage of messages will end up traveling off-system.

For planning purposes it is better to over-estimate the reduction of users. Based on experience gained over a number of projects, my view is that the user population supported by any server should be reduced by 30% once systems are connected. Therefore, if benchmark testing reveals that a certain system configuration is capable of supporting 1,000 users, then two systems connected together will only support $(1,000 \times 2) \times 0.7$, or 1,400 users. It is unfortunate that hardware vendors only publish figures for the number of Exchange users supported on a single server. Conducting benchmarks for a distributed network is much more difficult because all networks are different, so it's always going to be up to the people with most knowledge of the network to determine the overhead and how this impacts the number of users that can be supported.

It is very much easier to configure systems if they are dedicated to a single purpose, so this advice only holds for Exchange servers that are pure messaging servers. Adding any connector, other application, or other workload will affect the number of users a server can adequately support, perhaps to a surprising degree. Your mileage will vary, a good reason to run your own set of load simulation tests.

4.2.10 Resilience through clustering

In simplistic terms clustering is the ability for a group of computers to transparently share common information while allowing computers to join or leave the group without interfering with the service provided to users. People who use a clustered computer system see a single identity for the cluster and are not normally aware of the complex interaction that takes place behind the scenes to make all the component systems work together.

Clustering is important for messaging systems because it allows you to build highly available resilient systems. Messaging, for many enterprises, rapidly becomes a mission-critical application, and whenever a problem occurs to interrupt the messaging service, howls of pain can be heard throughout the organization. For example, it's easy to see why a marketing department would be annoyed if the server hosting the public folder where all the latest pricing information is located goes down. Or how people who communicate with external organizations might have their plans interfered with if the server where the X.400 or SMTP connector is located goes off the air. A personal observation of mine is that there is less tolerance for interruptions the higher up users are within an organizational structure, leading to situations where it is imperative that the messaging system is available for as close to 100% as possible.

The first production-quality clustered systems were delivered in the middle 1980s when Digital Equipment Corporation developed VAXclusters. VAXclusters originally required a very tight hardware-based connection between the individual systems within the cluster, but were evolved to allow looser coupling over network-based connections. A later development expanded clustering to accommodate different computer families and allowed the 32-bit VAX family of systems to be clustered with 64-bit Alpha systems, all using the single OpenVMS operating system.

Microsoft is currently working on its own implementation of clustering for Windows NT systems, and is expected to ship the "Wolfpack" technology during 1997. At that stage a modification will be made to Exchange to support clustering, probably in the form of a service pack. Initially, only two Exchange servers can be connected in a cluster, but this limitation should be lifted to make it possible to connect more servers together as the Wolfpack APIs, Exchange, and Windows NT evolve.

You'll therefore have to install upgrades for Windows NT and Exchange to be able to use clustering. It is also possible that system hardware configurations will need to be altered as not all disks and controllers may be suitable for clustering. With clustering on the horizon it clearly makes sense to buy modern disks and controllers with new systems or system upgrades as these are most likely to be able to support clustered systems after the software is available.

The Microsoft implementation isn't the first, as products are already available from DIGITAL (mid 1996) and AT&T[2], and Compaq. Other clustering vendors may have come to market in the time between the date of publication and when you read this book, so it's worth searching the Web to see what the latest situation is. As part of the technology exchange within the DIGITAL-Microsoft Alliance for Enterprise Computing, DIGITAL has provided details of its Open-VMS and Windows NT clustering technology to Microsoft. Microsoft has developed its own clustering, but it's fair to say that the information from DIGITAL has had an influence on Wolfpack. DIGITAL has also committed that its implementation of clustering will upgrade to Wolfpack as soon as Microsoft releases its software.

The features of the DIGITAL clustering solution include:

- Works across Intel and Alpha processors, and supports the shrink-wrapped version of Windows NT

- Requires no hot (or cold) standby system, so you don't need to keep a system hanging around doing nothing until a problem occurs

- Is not a port of clustering technology from another platform (such as OpenVMS or UNIX), and is optimized for Windows NT

- Requires no special hardware or interconnection devices.

The DIGITAL cluster software connects systems together with SCSI adapters on a shared SCSI bus, allowing systems to share disk devices (standalone or RAID arrays). Fail-over capability is included, so

[2]   AT&T's clustering product is called LifeKeeper for Windows NT.

that if a problem happens the clustered services (such as the Exchange information store) or a shared resource (like the install point for Exchange client software) are maintained. From a client perspective, an alias is given to the cluster as a whole to use when addressing cluster resources, so users don't have to know how many systems actually form the cluster and what their individual server names are.

One way of looking at clustering is to draw an analogy between it and the way Exchange allows a site to seamlessly expand itself across a number of individual servers, all of which share common data structures. When you want to add users from a new department all you need to do is to install a new Exchange server and have it join the existing site. Once data has been replicated the new server is up and running as a full and participating member of the site. A clustered system works at a lower level, but also allows you to expand the overall power and resources available to users by allowing you to introduce new hardware when required without affecting the hardware that's already installed.

Do you need to cluster the systems you use for Exchange? Clustering helps high-end Windows NT servers to attain a higher degree of overall system availability, but the current implementation of Windows NT clustering is based on NT file sharing and doesn't accommodate the type of database application that Exchange basically is. More resilience is therefore gained through a RAID-5 array (discussed further on in this chapter) than through clustering.

The decision as to deploy clustering or not depends on the role Windows NT servers play within your organization. In circumstances where a lot of small sites supporting single servers are in use there probably isn't much call for clustering. The exception to this rule is for sensitive servers or those that require the highest possible degree of resilience. On the other hand, if you have a number of large servers, each of which supports several hundred users you'd be wise to consider some sort of clustering to drive down the probability that an unforeseen problem will deprive users of the services (that can take advantage of clustering) for any length of time.

The combination of 64-bit Windows NT, clustering, and 16TB information stores offer the potential of building very large Exchange servers. However, this combination is unlikely to be well tested and validated for production use until mid to late 1998. Earlier deployments will happen, but anyone rushing to use this technology will be at the leading and bleeding edge. In the interim a better approach is to use the other technologies we already understand to achieve high levels of server resilience.

4.2.11 Protection through fault tolerance

Most high-end Windows NT servers have multiple disk drives and applications are carefully distributed across all available drives in order to maximize the disk I/O capability of the system as well as minimize the effect of a failure. I believe that the majority of systems used to run Exchange in a production mode will automatically have configurations that mark them as high-end systems. In circumstances where reasonable hardware configurations are available keeping everything on a single drive is similar to keeping all your eggs in one basket: tidy, but prone to leave an awful mess should anything go wrong.

RAID, or Redundant Array of Inexpensive Disks, is a method of combining several inexpensive disks into what appears to be a single large physical device, largely replacing older methods implemented mainly for mini- or mainframe computers. The fault tolerant features enabled by RAID technology make it an item to consider when configuring medium to large systems for use by Exchange server.

It is possible to implement RAID in hardware or software, and indeed Windows NT facilitates both approaches. Hardware implementations are normally preferred, largely because the hardware can be optimized to provide a much higher level of overall disk performance than is possible with a software implementation. RAID comes in different levels, from 0 to 5, and each level offers an increased degree of fault tolerance at higher expense. Windows NT servers support RAID levels 0, 1, and 5 in software, but all six levels can be supported by hardware implementations. Apart from fault tolerance RAID can also achieve higher disk throughput through disk striping, a technique that creates a logical disk from a set of physical disks.

Disk striping increases performance by spreading I/O reads and writes across the physical disks in the set. In the case of an Exchange server that has large public and private information stores concurrently accessed by many clients, far better performance will be seen if the stores are placed on a striped disk rather than large physical devices. A simple step towards better performance is to place the public and private information stores on separate physical disks.

Any server deemed to be critical, such as those supplying messaging services to large user communities, should be equipped with some degree of fault-tolerance for disks that store essential information. The choice for Windows NT servers are mirrored disks, duplexed disks, or stripe sets with parity. When a disk is mirrored it means that a perfect duplicate copy of the contents of a disk partition is kept on a second partition, so that when a write operation is made to the primary partition the same data is written to the mirrored partition at the same time.

Disk mirroring provides the same level of fault tolerance as RAID-1. It provides a reasonable degree of protection against faults as long as errors are confined to a single partition and do not afflict the physical disk where the partitions are located or the disk controller that the disk is attached to.

Disk duplexing expands the concept of disk mirroring by removing the mirrored partition to a second disk controller. The technique used to assure data protection is similar to mirroring. Extra protection and resilience is afforded by spreading the two write operations across two separate disk controllers. A further advantage is achieved because the I/O load generated by the write operations is split, so there is less danger that an individual drive will become saturated by the I/O operations generated by applications or even Windows NT itself. Windows NT always attempts to read from the drive that it regards as the fastest path to the required data, so a slight potential increase in read access to data can also be considered an advantage gained by splitting activity across two controllers.

Striped disks with parity checking are the basis for RAID-5 fault tolerance. In a RAID-5 array the equivalent of one disk is dedicated to the storage of backup information, but the actual backup data is spread across the entire array[3]. RAID-5 permits multiple read and write operations to proceed simultaneously.

If RAID is operational and a drive fails the array should continue to operate. In these situations the array will mark the failed drive as bad (the correct term is orphaned drive) and continue to use the good drives that remain. However, at this point in time fault tolerance disappears and the bad drive must be replaced as soon as possible.

In a RAID-1 (disk mirroring) environment it is normally sufficient to replace the faulty disk with a new one and then take steps to break up the mirror set and then introduce the new volume to the set. All of this is done with the Windows NT Disk Administrator utility, and when the new volume has been successfully added Windows NT will copy the data from the other volume in the set. After the copy is completed and both drives mirror each other fault tolerance is resumed.

Roughly the same concept applies with striped arrays, the difference being that a new physical disk is added to the set. At this stage the backup data from the rest of the array is restored to the new drive and the full array becomes active again.

---

[3]   Striped disks with parity demands a minimum of three disks in the array.

Hardware implementations of RAID use "hot-swapping" when drives become faulty. This means that as soon as a fault is detected in a disk it can be removed from the array and substituted with a new disk while the system is active. DIGITAL StorageWorks controllers take this a little further by allowing a hot spare, or a disk that remains inactive until a problem occurs at which time the controller automatically switches the faulty disk out of the array and brings in the hot spare.

Fault-tolerant disk technology evolves all the time and you should pay attention to new developments as they arise. The detail provided here is hopefully enough to inform you about some of the options available to help create a high-availability Windows NT system and form a solid base for Exchange. A messaging system that continually breaks down is good to no one and it's normally very visible within an organization. For that reason alone (job preservation for system managers), make sure that all important systems in your installation are satisfactorily protected against disk faults.

4.2.12   The importance of the I/O subsystem

Why pay so much attention to the I/O subsystem? The reason is simple. On low-end systems you don't have to worry so much about the speed at which disks transfer information. There won't be too many users to stress the system and an investment in extra memory will probably pay a higher dividend than installing a high-speed disk controller. Also, with only a few users to support you probably don't want to spend a lot of money to protect the disks because the extra hardware drives up the overall cost per seat. Good backup practices (and good luck) will protect the system against accidents.

On high-end systems the situation is different. These systems may support hundreds or thousands of users and are well configured in terms of CPU (or multiple CPUs) and memory. All the work done by the users generates a great deal of I/O and a bottleneck is immediately created if the I/O subsystem cannot handle the load. In addition to the work generated by users the operating system must run faster to manage all the different processes and threads, resulting in an increased demand for system paging and even more pressure on the I/O subsystem. Thus, if attention is not paid to the I/O subsystem the bottleneck becomes more and more evident. The system is unlikely to exhaust CPU or memory resources because everything must wait for the disks to catch up.

As noted earlier, the largest server in production worldwide (at the time of writing) operated by DIGITAL is an Alpha supporting over 2,700 mailboxes. During the day the CPU is seldom very taxed, operating at between 40% to 60% load. However, this is only possible because the I/O subsystem has been configured with a high-end RAID-5 controller and the fastest possible disks. Such an example is not unusual and is true for Pentium or Pentium Pro systems as well as Alphas. It's also true for other operating systems such as OpenVMS and UNIX. The lesson is if you don't treat high-end systems as a whole and ignore parts of the configuration the best possible performance will never be achieved.

4.2.13 Designing a luxury hardware configuration for Exchange

Given that the system configurations discussed so far are pretty basic and that I have expressed a view that you should build well-equipped servers from the start, what type of configurations should be considered if budget is not a limiting factor? Here are some suggestions for you to consider.

CPU

Get the fastest possible CPU you can get your hands on—you'll use it! Consider multiple CPUs, but don't go overboard. Two CPUs is good, and Exchange will be able to use them, but tests have shown that the current versions of Exchange don't make as good use of multiple CPUs (past two) as other applications, such as SQL/Server. A dual-CPU Pentium Pro system is a good choice, as is a dual-CPU Alpha processor.

Pentium Pro systems come with built-in secondary (L2) cache memory, so I don't need to worry too much about this aspect of system sizing if I select a Pentium Pro as the system processor. However, if offered the chance to use a (cheaper) high-end Pentium CPU, make sure that it is equipped with as much L2 cache as you can afford. Upping the L2 cache reduces bus contention and normally delivers more beneficial effect on system performance than a simple CPU upgrade, which may not be altogether effective if other system components, like the motherboard, are unable to fully handle the speed of the upgraded CPU.

Disk

Apart from Windows NT (the executables) and other applications, we have three main sources of I/O on an Exchange system, each of which needs to be isolated from the others. The three sources of I/O are the information store, transaction logs, and MTA work directory. Systems experiencing heavy traffic through the Internet Mail Service should also look at a separate disk for the IMS work directory (\IMCDATA). Isolation across separate physical disk devices delivers the highest possible performance while also allowing us to build a high degree of resilience to software or hardware failure.

The I/O generated by the MTA work directory and transaction logs is very different to that produced by the information store. In addition, the degree of resilience required by the information store is much higher than the other two. A RAID-5 array should always protect the information store (and directory store) on any Exchange server used in production environments, and our luxury configuration is no different. Make sure that the array contains some hot spare disks, ready to be inserted into the array if a problem occurs. Hot spares ensure that the array can be kept operational all the time, even if a disk fails.

To get the optimum balance between protection and performance the system should be equipped with a hardware-based RAID-5 controller with a bus adapter. Hardware-based RAID systems are always faster and more flexible than software-based equivalents. For example, if a disk fails in a hardware-based array, you can plug in a "hot spare" and proceed. The array will take care of any required adjustments automatically. Software-controlled arrays, on the other hand, need to be reconfigured before new drives can be added. RAID0+1 (striping and mirroring) will deliver better performance at the cost of reduced protection. If you need sheer performance and believe that you'll want to dynamically increase the amount of disk space available for information stores, then RAID0+1 (with mirroring performed at the host, and striping at the controller) may provide a better choice. The difference here is that RAID-5 expansion requires you to reconfigure the array and then restore the databases from a backup, not a task that you'll want to take on very often.

If money is no object then you can consider using a combination of striping with parity (RAID-5) and mirroring (RAID-0). This is a RAID-6 (sometimes called RAID-10) solution, commonly implemented in server configurations designed to support many hundreds of users for intensive applications. RAID-6 delivers great robustness and reliability at the expense of additional cost for all the extra disks required to mirror the RAID-5 striped set. RAID-6 also delivers the best possible performance from any disk configuration, although a lot of the performance is very possibly due to the hardware controller.

You can get RAID controllers that are integrated in the system backplane, but these controllers are slower than those that are separate from the backplane. You'll appreciate the extra speed if things go wrong, a disk fails, and the array needs to synchronize itself. Read-ahead caching on the controller should be disabled because it slows down I/O performance for databases like the information store. Because of the way that Exchange writes details of database transactions to a log Microsoft recommends that the write cache is disabled on SCSI controllers. With a write through flag Windows NT might signal that a write operation is complete before the actual write is made to the transaction log. If a system crash happens before data is written to disk, it may lead to a situation where the transaction log contains potentially corrupt data. Always use a battery backup to protect the array.

Don't focus on just the physical space available on a disk when considering the question of equipping the system with drives. Systems can avoid I/O bottlenecks (indicated by large I/O queues that are present on a constant basis) by increasing the number of physical disks rather than focusing on very large disks. For example, a RAID-5 volume of $10 \times 2GB$ disks is faster than a volume composed of $5 \times 4GB$.

Data written to transaction logs is always written to the end of file. Optimum performance is gained by placing the transaction logs on their own separate disk. Head movement is restricted to slight movement to add transactions to the end of file or when new logs are created. Our luxury system has a separate 2GB disk for transaction logs. Apart from speed we gain another advantage in that it is highly unlikely that the system will ever stop because there is no available space to create a new transaction log! Strictly speaking the transaction logs don't need a whole pile of resilience because the information store is well protected by the RAID-5 array, but as we're building a luxury system we should add a level of protection by building a small stripe set to hold the logs. Alternatively, the transaction logs can be protected by mirroring, or, if you're really into protection, by being copied across the network to another system at a regular interval. Copying transaction logs may seem a touch excessive, but it might be very valuable if a catastrophic situation occurs and the server is physically destroyed. The combination of transaction logs and a full backup of the information and directory stores is enough to recover an Exchange server.

The amount of I/O generated by the MTA depends greatly on the type of work done by the Exchange server. Systems that are dedicated messaging or public folder servers (or both) probably won't need a separate disk for the MTA work directory. Any system that acts as the focal point for a lot of other systems (bridgehead server, or server in a site that connects together lots of other sites) may experience a lot of messages passing through the MTA. In these situations it is advantageous to place the MTA work directory on its own separate disk. Select the fastest possible disk for this task, because you want to switch the messages through the MTA as quickly as they'll go. No great degree of mirroring or other protection is required.

Memory

Our luxury system should have lots of memory, but only up to 256MB or so. There is some anecdotal evidence that Exchange V4.0 doesn't make much use of additional memory past 256MB, although some personal observations appear to indicate that the server will use extra memory if it is provided. However, 256MB is quite enough to handle the needs of more than 1,000 users, so don't throw away good money by over-equipping on this point. Do pay attention to the system page files, and attempt to reduce system paging as much as possible by deploying a number of page files across the different disks on the system. Do not put a page file on the dedicated disk allocated to transaction logs.

Tape Drive

A system is only as good as its weakest point. There is plenty of resilience built in for the disks, but that's no reason to avoid taking backups on a regular basis. Buy the fastest tape drive you can so that you can take a full backup of the information store and directory, if possible, every night. Remember that today's Exchange databases can be up to 16GB each in size, but tomorrow's can grow to 16TB. When dealing with this type of files any increase in backup speed is very useful. Digital Linear Technology (DLT) tape drives is the fastest available today, so they should be your starting point. Drives that compress data as it is streamed out to tape are preferable.

Don't forget to back up all the other information on the system, like Windows NT and application executables and the system registry, at regular intervals too. Full backups of the Exchange databases will make it much easier to get a system back on line and working should a problem ever occur that necessitates a restore. Combine the fast tape drive with backup software that can take advantage of the drive's speed. Windows NT backup is OK, but it's slow, so spend some time looking for a good third party backup utility.

UPS

All production Exchange servers need to be reviewed to decide whether or not a UPS is required. In many parts of the world, where electricity supplies are known to fluctuate, the decision is easy, and a UPS is added to system configurations without a moment's thought. In other places, where a reliable electricity supply is assured the decision is less clear. Accidents happen, even in the most reliable of circumstances, so adding a UPS to our luxury configuration is not a hard decision. Look for a device that has a long battery life as this will enable a system to continue working during all but the most severe power outages.

Futures

Given the ever-changing world of computers it is impossible to say what new features will be added over the years. CD-ROMs were new a few years ago, now an 8× CD-ROM is normal. It's important to continually review developments in both the hardware and software markets so that you're able to take advantage of new technology when it becomes available. Clustering is of particular interest to those who want to build very large Exchange servers, and it's likely that this technology will make demands on both the software and hardware environments. Our luxury system is designed to be a high-end system, so it should be configured to accommodate new technologies like clustering when they become available.

In general all parts of the configuration should be bought with an eye on robustness, performance, and expandability. Components (including disks, controllers, and power supplies) that are hot swappable are especially valuable. CPU boards that can be upgraded with new CPUs or by installing additional CPUs provide a useful mid-life kicker to systems. Wolfpack clustering will be available for Windows NT servers before the end of 1997 so any high-end systems should be built with this feature in mind. For instance, will the disk and SCSI controllers be able to support clustering? It's hard to be exact at this point in time, but a reasonable guideline is given by the requirements of current clustering solutions such as DIGITAL clusters for Windows NT.

Finally, our system should be equipped with the capability for remote management and monitoring. If something goes wrong, like a controller or disk error, we want to know about the problem as soon as possible. The system should be capable of sending messages to an engineer when problems occur so that any downtime is minimized.

4.3   A growing strain on existing network resources?

Does your LAN and WAN operate in a satisfactory manner today? Of course you'll say "yes" and why wouldn't you? But the facts are that many LANs are tied together with so much string and good wishes and just about manage to limp along on a wing and a prayer. If you're in this type of situation then you need to consider whether you can even attempt to implement Exchange in such a flimsy network environment.

Even if your network is in good shape Exchange is going to impose some extra demands. If you replace several LAN Post Offices with one or more Exchange servers you may find that people will start to use the system more because message delivery is more reliable. They'll also like the additional functionality that Exchange provides. Clearly with such a range of network capabilities it is important to plan how information is exchanged between the different systems.

All Exchange servers should be equipped with the best and most capable network adapter you can afford. Don't try and limp by with an old or low-throughput adapter because its flaws will be revealed once the pressure goes on. Given that client-server systems place a huge emphasis on network stability and throughput it's important that you provide a solid base for your clients to connect to servers and for the servers to service the clients. Servers designed to support large numbers of clients should be equipped with multiple LAN adapters and caching controllers on disks to ensure that network and disk I/O demands generated by clients can be met. Equipping the servers with fast CPUs, fast disks, and lots of memory will be wasted investments if the server can't pump data down to clients as quickly as it would like to because of an old or underpowered network adapter.

4.3.1   Sources of network demand

What are the potential sources of additional network demand? First, there is a general increase in the average message size being seen within messaging networks. In the old text-based environments an average one-page message, complete with all its header information and whatever other data was necessary to transmit the message from originator to recipient could comfortably fit into the 4K–6K range. The advent of rich text messages complete with all the huge attachments regularly generated by the current suites of desktop office products has driven the average message size up dramatically. As we've already discussed in Chapter 1, some installations report an average message size of 40K, some see higher, and all expect the average message size to grow. The features and functionality of desktop applications encourage users to incorporate highly graphical items in their documents, and all the glitz must be paid for in size.

Users gain in confidence all the time. Electronic mail was once an application to be approached with care, but not any more. The electronic age makes e-mail just another way to communicate and users create more and more messages all the time. Added to the increased comfort zone there are more ways to create messages through mail-enabled applications. Almost every application today can add a "Send Message" option to its menus. External message feeds from other organizations and the Internet drive up the number of messages within the system. If just a few users subscribe to some Internet news groups you can expect to see many hundreds of messages coming in from that source on a daily basis.

You can help users to work with Exchange in an intelligent manner and restrict their use of system resources. Most of this is done through good habits instilled into individuals through training (a good reason not to skimp on user training during any implementation). An example of a good habit is using public folders to share documents rather than mailing large documents around to multiple recipients during a review cycle. Training allows you to divert people away from using neat client features that, although attractive, impose a real strain on the network.

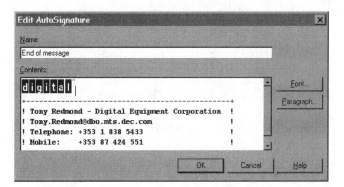

Figure 4.2 A really bad user habit – inserting a logo into auto signature

Including a bitmap image of the corporate logo in an Auto-Signature is a good example of how a feature can be misused, the reason being that several kilobytes of bitmap data will be appended to every outgoing message. Figure 4.2 illustrates how easy it is to include a logo into the auto-signature feature. In this case the overhead is relatively low at 2K per message, but only because the bitmap was available in 16-color format. It is entirely possible for users to insert a complicated graphic that's only available in 256 colors! As long as you can use the standard Windows cut and paste facility to move a graphic around it can be slotted neatly into an Exchange auto signature. And of course, users aren't necessarily going to insert the corporate logo. All manner of smiling faces, cute cats, or other icons can be pasted into an auto-signature. Those interested in discovering where the contents of their auto-signatures are held should look for a file called AUTOTEXT.SIG in your Windows directory. The file's stored in Rich Text Format and can be edited with NotePad or WordPad (if you want to see the native RTF formatting commands), or Word for Windows to see the auto-signature in all its glory.

You can also help to enforce good user habits by placing restrictions on some of the available gateways or connectors. Not allowing users to send messages larger than 1MB seems like an intelligent step in the right direction. If a user has a good business need to transmit a message larger than this they should really find out if there's a better (faster or more functional) method to accomplish the same task before possibly clogging up a vital e-mail link. Directives (or "Tips on how to use the system better") can easily be brought to users' attention by distributing easy-to-reference hint sheets.

The enhanced functionality available in Exchange and its clients imposes some additional demands of its own. It's great to be able to distribute public folders throughout the organization, but there's an overhead incurred by the messages sent to get data from one place to another. The automatically synchronized Exchange directory is great, but again more messages are generated and exchanged between systems to keep the directory synchronized. And if you turn on advanced security there'll be authentication requests generated too.

Finally, just to make the situation even more complicated network planners must take account of the impact of the World Wide Web, whether it's used in an Intranet or out on the Internet. Users love being able to browse remote locations to discover new information and that information is generally presented in a very graphical and attractive manner. But again, the network must be able to handle the load generated by shipping all the data from one place to another. System administrators and network planners in quite a few corporations that I work with are now discovering that Web traffic is taking more and more network capacity. I think this trend will continue over the next few years, and the net effect will be a continuing and growing demand for more and more network bandwidth.

These are just some of the potential sources for growth in network demand. Implementing a new messaging system often focuses minds on the infrastructure required by the new system, so this is a good time to perform a health check on the underlying network and take steps to ensure it is able to cope. Without a good network you have little chance of a good implementation of Exchange Server.

4.4   Tuning Windows NT for Exchange

Exchange is an application that runs on the Windows NT operating system. This simple statement implies that Windows NT must be kept in good health if Exchange can ever deliver any reasonable quality of service. New hardware can be installed to address performance degradation but if the system isn't properly tuned then the degradation will inevitably return. Few can afford to get into the very expensive cycle of constant hardware upgrades. It's much cheaper to install a reasonable configuration from the start and then make sure that the system is tuned on a consistent basis.

Normal tuning rules apply. If the system is paging heavily you either need to add more memory, increase the page file size, introduce additional page files on lightly loaded disks, or redistribute the file I/O generated by applications across all available disks. If one disk is a bottleneck it may be possible to redistribute applications to other disks, and so on. Just because a server is running Exchange there is no reason to approach it in any manner other than normal.

There are a few minor points relating to Windows NT that should be born in mind for Exchange servers. These are addressed by instructing the system to behave in a manner most appropriate to the service-oriented workload generated by Exchange. Use the control panel to make the changes.

- The system applet is used to tell Windows NT how to divide its attention between background (services) and foreground (interactive) demands. A typical Exchange server runs a lot of services so you should elect to give background applications more of a boost than foreground. Running an interactive application will be a little slower, but messages will be processed faster.

- The network applet is used to tell Windows NT how to deal with the network. The setting we're interested in here is "Maximize Throughput for Network Applications" (Figure 4.3), in effect saying that the system should devote more of its time to handling the demands of applications that generate network requests, like the RPCs used to communicate with other servers in a site.

- The system applet can also be used to resize the system page file. An Exchange server tends to use a large amount of virtual memory, so the system page file needs to be large enough to handle the demand without resorting to an excessive amount of paging. The workload generated by the system will determine the correct size for the file, but it's difficult to know what this will be until the system goes into production. In the meantime a good rule of thumb is to set the page file size to be the amount of physical memory plus 125MB. Thus, a system with 96MB physical memory should start with a page file of 96 + 125 = 221MB. Paging should be carefully monitored after the system goes into production and adjustments made if necessary afterwards.

Figure 4.4
Setting Windows NT network properties

Figure 4.4 shows Windows NT system properties being set. I took this screen capture from my notebook PC, which is configured to run Windows NT and Exchange. The notebook boasts a high specification (150MHz Pentium and 56MB memory) but its primary use is as a notebook computer, not a server. The settings made reflect its use and shouldn't be taken as a guide for a production computer.

5

Managing Exchange Servers

5.1   Introduction

Exchange won't manage itself. Time, commitment, and energy are all required to keep an Exchange server operational. Much of the internal workings of Exchange servers remain hidden from the eye, and at times it is downright difficult to know exactly what a server is doing, let alone influence the server to do what you'd like it to do. Messages pass between servers without let or hindrance, network bandwidth is absorbed without permission, replication takes place in the background, and disk space is silently filled up. The GUI administration interface hides all of this in a mass of property pages, drop-down lists, and check boxes. The administration program is nice to look at, but sometimes it would be nicer to have some more information coming out of the server. System usage statistics and reports is generally a weak area for Exchange.

When things go well Exchange is a joy to administer, but when things start to go wrong and the system falls down around your ears you'll need to have some idea about how Exchange works from a management perspective. Good system management practices for Windows NT and Exchange reduce the chances that something will go wrong as well as helping people get out of trouble when problems appear.

This chapter reviews some of the day to day issues that system administrators have to deal with, and discusses how the issues might be approached. There is never only one good way to deal with a problem, so be prepared to look at the solutions outlined here and then make your own mind up as to how you'll do things.

5.2   Exchange services

Exchange is not engineered as a single monolithic process. It is broken down into a number of separate processes, each of which runs as a

Windows NT service. The collective group of these services make up the application we call an Exchange server. The table below lists the most important of these services together with the name of the executable that you'll see in the list of active processes. All the executables are stored in the \EXCHSRVR\BIN directory.

Table 5.1 *Major Exchange services*

Name of service	Executable
System Attendant	MAD.EXE
Directory	DSAMAIN.EXE
Information Store	STORE.EXE
Message Transfer Agent	EMSMTA.EXE
Internet Mail Service	MSEXCIMC.EXE
Internet News Service	EXCHINS.EXE
Directory Synchronizer (MS-Mail)	DXA.EXE
Key Management Service	KMSERVER.EXE

The Services applet of the Windows NT control panel controls how services are run. Figure 5.1 lists the services running on a computer, and shows that a number of Exchange services are active. Note the startup state for each service.

Figure 5.1
Exchange services

All of the Exchange services are "automatic," meaning that they will be started up without manual intervention each time the computer is booted. This is the preferred state, as anything else will force the system administrator to select each service and start it up after a system reboot. Not only is this boring work, but it's impossible to be there each time a computer is restarted.

Figure 5.2
Changing the
startup state

Selecting the service and then clicking on the startup button can change the startup type for a service. Apart from the startup type, the dialog (Figure 5.2) reveals the account name used to run the service. When the service starts up Windows NT uses the account name and password information furnished here to conduct a log-on and establish security credentials. If the password information is incorrect credentials will not be issued and the service will fail to start. The account name used is the Exchange service account (see page 133). Exchange is slightly special in this respect because password information is held in two places: in the SAM (accessed and managed via the control applet) and in the Exchange directory, where the password information is held as a property of the site.

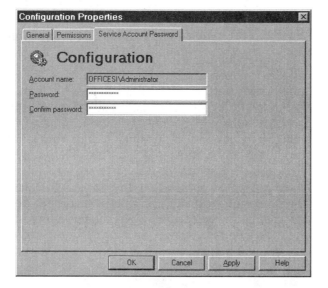

Figure 5.3
Changing the
service account
password

When an Exchange service is started a check is performed to make sure that the password provided matches the password held in the directory, and if they don't match the service will terminate abruptly on the basis that a potential security breech has occurred. Never use the Windows NT User Manager for Domains utility to change the password for the Exchange service account. Always set the password for the Exchange service account by amending the properties of the site object, as shown in Figure 5.3.

5.2.1   Shutting things down

Exchange does a lot of work in the background. Part of the reason for this is the attitude taken to user-initiated work, which Exchange always gives priority to over system work. For example, if a user request to send a message is detected, Exchange will stop what it's doing to accept the message. Working like this means that users get best response from the server, but it does mean that even where there doesn't seem to be too much obvious activity, the server is probably busily dealing with work like flushing transactions out of memory and committing them to the database.

Shutting down a busy Windows NT server can take a few minutes from the time you instruct the server to begin the shutdown process to the time when the server has finally ceased operation. Shutting down a busy Exchange server takes even longer. There are a number of background processes that must be halted, and before those services can be stopped they may have operations to complete or data to save. Connectors finish dealing with new messages, the information store must commit any outstanding transactions to its databases, the message queue must be flushed, and so on. All of this activity means that a busy server can, in some conditions, take between ten to twenty minutes to shut down.

There is, of course, the temptation to lose control and hit the "power-off" button. After all, Exchange has a great transactional database that is able to automatically roll-forward any outstanding transactions when the information store service starts up. It is correct that Exchange will take care of any outstanding transactions that had not been committed to the database when the system starts up. That's what the checkpoint file is for (discussed later in this chapter). However, the brutal power-off approach to life brings other dangers—like a corruption of the MTA queues. If Exchange is shut down abnormally then checks must be performed when the server is restarted. Some minutes might be gained by powering a computer down quickly, but all those minutes will be paid for when the server restarts because a number of internal checks must be performed to ensure that everything is OK. Checking the MTA queue files on a large server can take quite a time!

Apart from the amount of work to do to close all the services down properly, it seems that the amount of inter-process chat that goes on during the close down procedure contributes to the overall slowness. Many experienced system administrators recommend that you manually terminate the Exchange System Attendant[1] process before commencing a general system shutdown. There's no obvious logic to this assertion, but closing down the System Attendant forces all other Exchange services to shut down gracefully, one after the other. It is perhaps the graceful and coordinated way that the Exchange services shut down before a general shut down commences that contributes most to faster elapsed times. The only reason I can come up with is that Windows NT can give the Exchange services the chance to close themselves down efficiently without any contention with other applications and services. As always, your mileage may vary, but it's something to try if you get frustrated with long system close down times.

5.2.2   What do I connect to?

Exchange is a messaging system built in the client/server paradigm. This mouthful, so beloved of the marketing fraternity and the computing purists, means in reality that we have clients making network connections to server computers in order to use the services offered by the servers. But in an Exchange context, where are those connections made to?

All connections between Exchange clients and servers are made via RPCs. The connection is made between the client application (for example, EXCHNG32.EXE or OUTLOOK.EXE) to the information store service (STORE.EXE). Each connection results in one or more threads being created within the information store service process. The store allows access to user mailboxes, public folders, and directory information. Clients that don't specifically use messaging, like Schedule+, also make connections to the information store because they need to access data held in special folders, such as the free and busy information about user schedules, which is stored in a hidden public folder.

Exchange uses Windows NT for security purposes. Each connection must be authenticated, or possess security credentials trusted by the domain where the Exchange server is located. The default mecha-

---

[1]   From the purely trivial perspective, I can't help wondering why the System Attendant executable was given the name "MAD.EXE". Is this service the mad dog of the Exchange world?

nism is to use network credentials that are already established, those created as a result of a client logging on to a domain. If those credentials are not available, or the Exchange server is located in a different domain to the one that the client logged onto, a log-on dialog will be presented to allow the user to enter the account name and password. This information is then used to create security credentials (if valid) and allow the client to connect to the server.

Passwords entered into log-on dialogs are never sent to the server, as this would create a potential danger that password information might be intercepted and decrypted en route. The Exchange server and the client both share a common secret—each knows the password, so the password can be used as the basis for a challenge/response sequence that establishes whether the client is authorized to use the account that they have nominated. The server encrypts a random string with the account's password and sends it down to the client. The client is now challenged to decrypt the string and return it (the response) to the server. If the string can be decrypted successfully the server accepts that the client really must be who they say they are, and will issue the necessary credentials. This is a simplified version of the steps in the challenge/response sequence, enough to establish that a client must either possess credentials or be able to establish bona fides by responding correctly to server demands.

5.2.3   Using alternative credentials

We've seen that the default mechanism for client connections is to use existing security credentials gained by logging on to a domain. Normally this is exactly the right thing to do. It is very convenient to use existing credentials because it avoids the necessity for users to enter password information a number of times. However, there are times when you'll want to override the default credentials and force a challenge/response dialog to appear. For example:

- You're logged into one domain and want to use an Exchange server in another domain.
- You're logged into a domain and want to use an Exchange server in the same domain, but access a mailbox that's associated with a account that you are not already logged into.

In these instances you can instruct Exchange to override its normal mechanism and always prompt for security credentials. Use the client Tools.Services option to view the information services you connect to, as illustrated in Figure 5.4. Select "Microsoft Exchange Server," and access its properties. Click on the "Advanced" tag. The "Use network security during log-on" check box controls whether Exchange uses existing credentials (checked, the default) or not (clear the check box). The setting becomes active after you exit and log-on again.

Figure 5.4
Advanced properties

5.3   Transferring users

It's hard to achieve perfection when the time comes to allocate users to servers, unless of course you only have a single server to work with. In any large system the time will come when you have to redistribute user accounts across servers, to balance the user-generated messaging load on each server or perhaps to keep users who communicate together on the same server in order to reduce off-server message traffic.

Figure 5.5
Moving a user's mailbox

Moving a user's mailbox from one server to another within a site is child's play. Select the "Move mailbox" option from the Tools menu in the Administration program (Figure 5.5), select the user to move and the server they are to be moved to, and leave Exchange to do the work. The contents of the user mailbox are moved by sending messages from the source server to the target, emulating what would happen if someone forwarded each message in a mailbox to a mailbox at a new address. Because everything is done through the messaging service one or more transaction logs will probably be created during the move, depending on the size of the mailbox being moved. It is usual that the physical space occupied by a mailbox is increased after a move, largely because all the messages in the mailbox are not shared when they arrive on the target server.

Because Exchange servers in the same site share the same directory and configuration information and are normally connected by high-speed links it's feasible to allow the software to take total control of:

- Locking the user's mailbox so that no new messages are delivered while the move is in progress. Messages are queued and delivered to the relocated mailbox once the move is complete.

- Moving all the folders and messages from the private information store on one server to the private information store on another.

- Updating the directory to indicate that the user's mailbox is now hosted on a new server. Apart from ensuring correct delivery from external sources this step ensures that other servers within the same site copy new messages to the correct private information store.

The process of moving all the information in a user's mailbox may take time to complete, especially if the user has managed to build up a large mailbox or the servers involved are busy. It's best to perform all moves during off-peak server times and after the user has been "encouraged" to delete any unwanted messages from his or her mailbox. If the user won't cooperate with the request to clean the mailbox out, you may have to convince them by threatening to use the "Clean Mailbox" option (see discussion starting on page 262). Because of the obvious potential difficulties that might occur it makes sense not to attempt to move a mailbox when the user is logged in. This is yet another good reason to move mailboxes when everyone's gone home and the systems are quiet.

Moving someone from one site to another or from one organization to another is not so straightforward. No options exist to do the job for you, so it's pretty much a manual task that requires coordination between the system administrators for the source and target systems. Indeed, the relative complexity of the steps required in moving a user from one site to another has been enough to convince some very large enterprises to combine several physical locations into one very large site. The logic behind such a step, which on the face seems pretty surprising, is that if you've got very high speed private networks already in place you might as well go ahead and build a big logical site from the distributed physical locations. For example, one large company has built a site from five locations within the United Kingdom. With the site in place the administration workload is simplified and reduced, but I believe it is too early today to determine whether easier system administration can be justified by throwing expensive network links at the problem. Given that Exchange servers are pretty "chatty" within a site and network bandwidth is in constant demand by any and all applications it's possible that all the extra bandwidth might be taken up without any great benefit being accrued. Another factor is that Exchange system administration should mature to accommodate trans-site operations. In the meantime, the people who made these courageous design decisions will see whether or not their logic is flawed. You might like to ask the same questions when considering the design for your Exchange organization. But unless you expect to have to administer a highly mobile workforce I wouldn't generally recommend such a radical solution.

Moving back to the subject at hand, the basic steps to move a user from one site to another are:

1. Have the system administrator on the target site create a new mailbox for the user. After this is done, hide the user's original mailbox from the global address list using the "Hide from Address Book" option when editing mailbox details. This prevents two mailboxes for the one user appearing in the global address list. You should also modify any distribution lists that the user's old mailbox featured in by changing each list to include the new mailbox.

2. Set a redirect address for the old mailbox on the source server to transfer all newly arriving messages to the new mailbox on the target system. All new messages arriving on the old server should now be forwarded to the new mailbox.

3. To speed up the transfer process ask the user to delete all unwanted messages held on the server or do the job for them with the "Clean Mailbox" option.

4. Create an auto-reply message stating that the user has moved to a new server. This step is optional and is really only important if the user is physically transferring location and won't be able to answer messages for a few days.

5. Move the contents of the user's server-based mailbox to a personal information store (.PST file). This is a manual process that requires the user (or the administrator) to log on and move the messages with drag and drop operations.

6. For any reasonably sized mailbox the PST file will be quite large. You will need to make arrangements to transfer the PST file to the target system, possibly through a simple FTP copy.

7. Disable the Windows NT account for the user on the source server to prevent them logging on once the transfer process is complete.

8. On the host system the user can import their messages from the PST file into their new mailbox. Or, better still, they can use the PST file as an archive for messages processed before their move.

9. After you are happy that the new mailbox is operational you can delete the old mailbox, erase the directory entry, and generally clean up any trace of the user on the source system. This will also remove the redirect address and the auto-reply message, if set.

These steps take no account of items like distribution lists where the old mailbox is included. Distribution list memberships must be updated manually. If you're using advanced security no special steps have to be taken for intra-site transfers. However, moving users with secure messages from one site to another requires care if they are to be able to access their messages afterwards.

The Exchange V5.0 Resource Kit includes a tool to automate the movement of users across sites. If this tool proves effective in practice then it will mark a major step forward. However, I have not yet had a chance to use the tool to transfer a user with a very large mailbox, or to attempt a transfer across a low-bandwidth network connection. The tool must be able to cater for these situations if it is to be of benefit to all corporate customers.

5.4   Replication

Most system administrators who work with messaging systems are familiar with the concept of individual interpersonal messages arriving at and being dispatched from the system. This is the basic currency of any messaging system and there is nothing particularly new in the way that Exchange deals with interpersonal messages. Replication, on the other hand, is a somewhat more uncommon technique when applied to messaging systems. The major proponent of replication to this point in time has been Lotus Notes, where replication is used as the basic method to distribute information to servers throughout a network.

Replication means that data is copied from an originating computer to other computers according to some predefined rules. In an Exchange environment replication occurs in two main areas:

1. Directory entries are replicated to servers that share a common directory. Entries are made, amended or deleted by the server responsible for user accounts or other entries held in the directory. Once the entry is made the "owning" server communicates with the other servers in the network to update them with the new information. Replication is performed with a special type of encoded messages, and it can take anything from five minutes to several hours before the process of replicating an update to all servers in an Exchange network is accomplished. Latency in data updates is an inherent fact of life when replication is concerned. The speed at which replication takes place depends on how many servers are in the network, the connections between those computers, and the other traffic that flows between the servers. Directory entries do not impose a great strain on the network because the size of the messages containing replication data is quite small.

2. Objects placed in public folders can be replicated to copies of the folders held on other Exchange servers so that users connecting to those servers can access the information held in the folders as quickly as possible. Like directory entries public folders are associated with an originating server, the location where objects contained in the folder are managed. When a decision is made to share the contents of a public folder with another Exchange server, a replica of the public folder is created on the "foreign" server. Thereafter, whenever a change is made to the original public folder the amendments will be automatically replicated to the replica folders on all the servers that maintain an interest in the folder. Replication is performed by a background process and does not happen immediately.

Updates can also be applied to objects via replica folders. In this case the changed data is replicated back to the original source folder and the update applied there. However, the distributed nature of Exchange which underpins the ability for updates to be applied in this manner opens up the question of what happens when updates arrive concurrently for the same object from two different replicas. We'll discuss what actually happens when multiple users make changes to a replicated document later on in this chapter.

Directory entries are all pretty similar in size, so the traffic pattern and network load generated by directory replication is predictable and should not change dramatically over time. Occasionally there may be major changes in the directory, for example, when a large group of people using a new server joins the network, but in most organizations the volume of directory changes is low, ranging from 1% to 5% of the user population per week. Replication of public folders and directory entries is only possible when servers are connected together; thus, each system participating in replication must be licensed to run one of the available connectors.

5.4.1   Public folder replicas and affinities

Generally speaking there are two ways to distribute information in a networked environment. One method is to place multiple copies of the information at different points throughout the network, basically in an effort to keep information close to users in terms of the network resources required to gain access to information. The second approach is to establish a single point of reference to hold the definitive copy of the information, perhaps supplementing the definitive copy with a number of distributed read-only copies. Exchange supports both models. Support for multiple distributed copies of information is gained through public folder replicas. Support for a single definitive point of contact is achieved through public folder affinity. In essence, public folder affinities allow local pointers to be maintained to remote folders held elsewhere on the network.

Figure 5.6
Replication and affinity. The two methods of distributing information in public folders

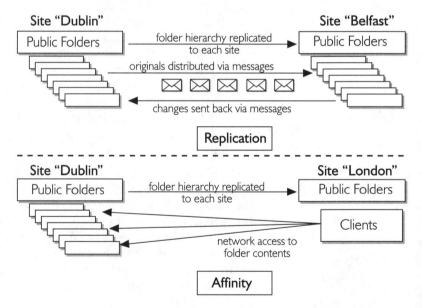

Servers exchanging mail messages with each other accomplish public folder replication. The messages, of course, contain the data being replicated. You can limit the size of the messages used during replication operations to prevent the replication of very large objects interfering with the smooth operation of the MTA. Getting interpersonal messages through quickly is much more important than delaying system-generated background messages a little.

Figure 5.7
*Defining
affinity values
for a site*

Affinity is not automatic. It must be configured as a property of each site so that servers know what other sites are available to handle user requests to access information contained in public folders where replicas are unavailable in their "home" site. Affinity is defined by allocating costs to other sites (see Figure 5.7). The lower the cost (the range is from 1 to 100) the more a site is favored by clients seeking information. Clearly, the site with the lowest cost is always going to be accessed first.

The argument for folder replicas, or multiple synchronized copies of folders established at different locations distributed around a network is based on three points.

- Synchronized copies of public folders distribute the processing load generated by user access to folder contents. This improves response time for users because they will generally be accessing content from a location close to them rather than from some remote network location.

- Synchronized copies of public folders established at strategic locations within a network can dramatically reduce the amount of long-distance or wide area network traffic generated by users attempting to access folder contents.

- Synchronized copies of folders maintained on multiple servers mean that users will always be able to have access to the information, often mission-critical, held in replicated public folders. If one server becomes inoperative users are automatically and transparently switched to another location holding a synchronized copy to access information.

Users are completely unaware that public folder replication occurs because Exchange hides everything from them. As far as users are concerned they are able to see a public folder and access its content, and they don't really care that substantial programming and network magic has been performed to enable them to view a document, form, or other object with such ease. Because users retrieve information directly from a copy held on their own server, access to information is as fast as it can possibly be. With such strong arguments for replication why would anyone choose to incur the potentially long delays in accessing a single definitive copy of information held on a remote server?

Replication is, by far, the mechanism that receives most attention in documentation and marketing material. Some of the reason for its high profile can be assigned to competitive pressure, but perhaps replication is viewed as a more high-tech option.

All the Exchange servers in a site automatically share the same directory and set of public folders. Thus, no replication is performed to update the servers within a site. Replication is only necessary when you want to share information between Exchange servers in multiple sites. Even then you can force another site to connect to remote public folders through "affinity," a facility managed by the system administrator on the sites that wish to connect to public folders stored on other sites. Affinity is only possible when the two sites share a high-speed connection capable of handling the traffic generated by users accessing the contents of the folders.

The concept of public folder affinity (see the bottom part of Figure 5.6) establishes a mechanism where a single copy of a public folder is maintained in a set network location. The content of the folder is accessed there from all points of the network. Public folder affinity offers a number of potential advantages over replication that are attractive in concept:

- No network overhead is incurred to replicate new objects and changes to different sites throughout the organization
- No latency is experienced between the time when changes are made and the same data is available to everyone throughout the network
- There is no need for conflict handling, and finally, information is not duplicated in different locations.

Affinity can only work if a network connection can be made to the server that hosts the public folder. Two different requirements must be fulfilled if the affinity approach is to succeed. Clearly a network path must be available on a consistent basis. There is no point in deciding to use affinity if your network is unreliable. Users will just be unhappy because they won't be able to get to information when they want to. Secondly, users must be authenticated or possess the necessary security credentials to access the information on the server that it's stored on. Sometimes the security credentials gained through a user's original network log-on will be sufficient, but only if the Exchange servers are all in the same Windows NT domain or are able to mutually authenticate each other's users through a set of trust relationships. If you're unable to assure organization-wide authentication then affinity is not the best choice and you'd be better off to use replication as the mechanism for public folder content distribution.

In all instances, whether public folders are distributed via replication or accessed via affinity, Exchange always sends a copy of the public folder hierarchy from each site to all the other sites in the organization. This is a logical step to take otherwise the system administrators in remote sites wouldn't know about the existence of any of the interesting folders they might otherwise connect to. There is no requirement to replicate any or all folders to all sites. System administrators have a great deal of control over folder replication and are able to select particular folders to be replicated to their servers from any other server in the organization (see Figure 5.8).

Figure 5.8
Selecting Public Folders for replication

All of these points are valid and should be considered before taking the replication option. In the example illustrated in the bottom part of Figure 5.6, whenever a user in the London site wishes to access an object stored in a public folder serviced by a system in the Dublin site, Exchange makes a transparent network connection between the two sites to retrieve the object's content. When an item is fetched, a copy of its content is moved into the Windows temporary directory and is operated upon there.

The case for affinity is harder to argue in terms of user convenience. However, because a single copy of information exists within a network it can be regarded as definitive. This can't be said of a replicated folder because the possibility always exists that a change to the content has been made somewhere in the network and hasn't yet arrived on the local server. Lots of organizations will be attracted by the concept of a single definitive source of information, especially when that information is critical corporate information, but you have to make a decision whether your network is able to facilitate fast (or at least acceptable) access times to the information. If there are many slow links in the network replication is possibly a better solution.

5.4.2   The replication of public folder content and hierarchy

Replication of public folders occurs in two distinct steps—hierarchy and content.

As mentioned in the last section, the public folder hierarchy is automatically replicated between all servers within an organization. This means that every server knows about all the public folders that are available on any other server within the organization. It also means that every user is able to see a full list of public folders when they click to expand the public folder portion of the overall folder hierarchy. A user's next step may be to double-click on a folder to access its content. If a local replica is unavailable or affinity has not been put in place to allow network access to the content an error message is displayed.

You can't do anything about public folder hierarchy replication. It just happens automatically, so the challenges are really what tactics to take to control content replication and how to avoid users becoming frustrated when they cannot access content. As I've already mentioned, keeping all your Exchange servers in a single, unified Windows NT environment is the best way to facilitate affinity, but if you can't use affinity then arrangements must be put in place to implement a replication strategy.

Public folder content can be replicated according to models commonly referred to as the "push" or "pull." In the "push" model the ad-

ministrator of the system hosting a public folder decides on which other servers a new replica of the folder should be created. The system
administrator of any server that already holds a replica can push out
new replicas of folders to other servers. This is done by expanding the
set of public folders (at the top of the organization configuration
shown in the left hand pane of the administration program), selecting
the desired folder, selecting its properties, and then nominating the
new target server in various sites to send the new replicas off to. For
example, in Figure 5.9, the system administrator of the server called
RUCKS [2] has just chosen the DBO-EXCHANGEIST server in the
Dublin site and instructed Exchange to replica the contents of the folder "RUCKS Test Folder" to DBO-EXCHANGEIST. It's as simple as
select and click, and contents can be replicated around the world without too much effort on the part of an administrator. All the work is
done later on by the messaging system, which must transport possibly
many megabytes of data across the network to create the new replica.

Figure 5.9
Pushing a new
replica to a
remote server

The system administrator on any target server is not aware of this
action. Any administrator can decide to push a replica towards another
server, and because replication is performed using the messaging system, as long as there's a valid messaging path between the servers the

---

[2] RUCKS is a word with special meaning to rugby fans where it refers to a particular game situation. I've had a
server called RUCKS in my personal network for many years!

content will be sent off to its new home. The only indications that a new replica has been established are an increase in the count of replicas and a growth in the disk space occupied by the public information store on the target server. Most administrators will not be even aware that a new replica has arrived!

Whereas the "push" model is controlled from a server that already hosts a replica (remember that all replicas are treated as equivalent masters), servers that don't already have a copy use the "pull" model. In this case the system administrator of the server that wants to create a new replica browses through the public folder hierarchy until the desired folder is located. At this stage we can select the folder and click the "add" button, as shown in Figure 5.9. As soon as the change is applied Exchange will proceed to request the host public information store to begin transmitting the folder contents to the requesting server. Content is always transmitted in a series of messages, so it may take some time before the local replica is available for user access. Again, the owner of the original public folder has no idea that a new replica has been created.

Does it matter whether you pull or push? Of course it doesn't, as long as you want to create the new replica, and understand the consequences of your action. In most cases the consequences are no more than an increase in the volume of messages generated within the system. The more replicas, the more messages are required to ship data around for all changes—additions, deletions, and amendments. If the public folder hierarchy is allowed to grow without restraint a danger is created that the sheer number of folders within the hierarchy cloaks valuable data. In the same way, if multiple replicas are created without restraint, a danger exists that valuable network bandwidth is absorbed by unnecessary messages being transmitted between Exchange servers.

It's interesting to reflect on the philosophy inherent in a system that allows uncontrolled distribution of replicas to occur. There is no way that a system administrator can prevent an administrator of another system deciding that a folder created on their system should be pushed over the network, or indeed to create a local replica and pull content from your system. The reverse is true too. There is no method to prevent a remote system administrator rejecting an attempt to create a replica on their server. The replica may arrive, but as soon as its presence is noticed the local administrator can remove it, sending the folder back to where it came from.

When replicas are created the folder access control list (ACL) may prevent people seeing the actual content when it arrives. But because the public folder hierarchy is automatically replicated everywhere and the facilities exist for replicas to be created outside some type of central control, a danger clearly exists that unwanted replicas might be created.

Implementation plans should address this issue by stating clear guidelines for the creation of replicas. In other words, who can create replicas and the conditions replicas should be created under. Regular checks should also be performed to see how many replicas exist for each folder (available as a property of the public information store—see Figure 5.10), especially those that might contain sensitive information, and where those replicas reside. Finally, statistics should be kept to track the growth of the number of public folders and what use is actually being made of their contents. It is also useful to know who is creating the public folders and have a procedure to allow people to inherit control of folders when the original owners move on to other responsibilities.

5.4.3   How replication occurs

Replication between servers is controlled by the Public Folder Replication Agent (PFRA), part of the public information store. The PFRA takes care of monitoring changes made to public folders, but only for folders where replicas exist. The list of servers that hold replicas, or instances, of the folder is maintained as a property of the folder. After changes are made the PFRA takes care of dispatching details of the changes to all of the other servers that hold replicas. Updated content, commands to delete items, and details of new items posted into a folder are sent through a special form of messages sent by the public information store on one server to the public information store on another. The messages contain the content in MDBEF format and hold a unique change number. The change number identifies the order in which a change should be applied to a public folder.

In addition to the relatively simple task of sending updates to other public information stores, the PFRA maintains historical information about the state of each message in each replicated folder. Every update generated for a replicated folder is allocated a change number, composed of a unique server identifier and a store counter. The change number is therefore unique to a server. Conceptually, a simplified representation of a change number might look like this:

```
DBO-EXCHANGEIST\PUBIS\0174345
```

The change number shows that this is change number 174,345 generated by the public information store on the DBO-EXCHANGEIST server. Of course, real change numbers are created in an encoded fashion that makes sense to computers, not humans, so this example is purely to illustrate the point. The PFRA maintains a list of all predecessor change numbers for a store, meaning that the agent is able to recognize the most recent or current message.

The simplest replication task involves new items. When a new item is added to a public folder the PFRA creates a new change order and sends it along with the content of the new item to all of the other servers that hold instances of the folder. The receiving stores insert the content into their copy of the folder. Deletions are similar operations, except that content is not sent. In this case the message to the servers holding instances instructs them that the item should be removed from their replica.

If permissions allow, all servers are entitled to modify items. Modifications are always applied to local instances, so the local PFRA takes responsibility for informing the other servers that a change has occurred. When a modification message arrives to a public information store it replaces the original content, but only if the modification is more current than the existing message. The store uses the change number on the message and the predecessor change list to determine whether the message should be applied. If the store discovers that it has content that is more up to date than the content in the replication message it realizes that a potential conflict exists, and a conflict resolution process begins. That process is more fully explored on page 279.

5.4.4 Backfilling public folders

Backfilling describes the process by which a server updates an instance of a public folder when information is lost due to system outages. Backfilling also occurs when a new instance of a folder is created.

System outages include hardware crashes, which may lead to the public information store being restored on a server. A restored store is out of date and lacks the content replicated since the backup was taken. When a server is restarted after the restore, replication messages will begin to arrive again. At this stage the public information store will look at the change numbers on the incoming replication messages and update its predecessor change list. Gaps will exist in the predecessor change list, forcing the store to look to fill the gaps, or backfill.

The server begins the process by generating a backfill entry, literally a placeholder inserted into the store to indicate that some data is missing. It then proceeds to dispatch requests for assistance to two other servers (chosen at random), that also hold replicas of the folders that are missing information. The request specifies the missing content and requests the receiving server to generate a message containing the content and send it back to the public information store. Eventually the other servers will respond and messages with the missing content will arrive. At this point the backfill entries can be replaced with real content and the predecessor change list updated.

5.4.5 Public folder ownership and access control lists

All public folders have nominated owners. Or rather, all public folders should have at least one nominated owner. Owners are user mailboxes that have complete control over a public folder, typically used to manage the access control list for the folder (defining, in turn, the people who can access the folder and the degree of control they exercise over the folder's contents).

Sometimes folders lose owners. This isn't carelessness on the part of the folder, or a bug. It's just a by-product of normal system maintenance. The access control list for a folder is composed of distinguished directory names that must point to a valid entry in the directory. If a user mailbox is removed from the directory, the entry in the folder's access control list that pointed to the mailbox is null and void and is therefore removed. We end up with a folder that has no owner. This isn't a disaster. You can use the administration program to manipulate the properties of a public folder, including client access and permissions. So all you need to do to amend folder ownership is to select the folder and then add one or more mailboxes from the GAL to the access control list, marking them as "owners."

Because access control lists are composed of directory entries it therefore follows that any type of valid directory entry can be inserted into the ACL. Individual mailbox entries are the obvious default option for ACLs, but custom recipient entries don't make much sense because you must be able to use Exchange before access can be gained to public folders. Distribution lists, on the other hand, are very useful because they reduce the amount of system administration overhead required to maintain ACLs. Figure 5.11 shows a typical ACL being manipulated. Two mailboxes have been nominated as the owners of the folder while a distribution list (Ireland SI Management) is used to establish a more general level of access. No access is permitted by default, or to anonymous (Web) users.

Figure 5.11
*Client
permissions
for a public
folder*

Using distribution lists to control access to folders creates a situation where a single entity, or group of entities (lists), are managed in place of a lot of individual mailbox entries. As mailboxes are added to or removed from the distribution list users gain or lose access to public folders, all done through simple maintenance of a distribution list. Remember too that system administrators don't have to maintain distribution lists as this task can be allocated to users.

Each folder maintains its own ACL. When a new sub-folder is created it inherits the ACL of its parent. However, in Exchange V4.0 when a change is made to a parent folder it is not automatically reflected in any sub-folders, so any change such as a new user being granted permission to access the parent folder needs to be made to any sub-folder as well.

A welcome change is made in Exchange V5.0 where additional properties are made available to control how changes are propagated to sub-folders. Figure 5.12 demonstrates the degree of control available during the propagation process. The most used of these properties is likely to be client permissions, but it's good to see that other major properties such as replica age limits have not been overlooked in the implementation.

Figure 5.12
Propagating properties to sub-folders

Deleting a directory replication connector can have the unfortunate side effect of affecting folder ownership. When a directory replication connector is deleted all the directory entries associated with the connector are removed from the directory store. An immediate disconnect can therefore arise between folder ACLs and the directory. If a substitute directory replication connector is established and the remote site has not changed the format of its directory entries (for example, by changing its site name), then no damage should arise. However, if the format of the directory entries has changed then they will no longer match the folder ACL and users will no longer be able to access folder contents.

Exchange (from V4.0 SP3 on) flags a warning about running the DS/IS consistency adjuster after a directory replication connector is removed. The actual warning is shown in Figure 5.13.

Figure 5.13 *The
solemn warning
about the
consequences of
running the DS/
IS consistency
checker*

The DS/IS consistency adjuster is available through the advanced properties of a server, and is used to verify that every object in the store has a matching entry in the directory. Obviously, after a directory replication connector has been removed and all its associated entries eliminated from the directory a large number of inconsistencies probably exist. If the DS/IS consistency adjuster is invoked at this stage the following will occur:

- The permissions on public folders will contain only mailboxes from one site or the other (depending on whichever site modified the permissions last)

- The home server of public folders from the site that has been disconnected will be reset to a site they were not created in; therefore administration of these public folders can be done only in the other site. The algorithm driving how public folders are re-homed is not totally clear to me, but Exchange certainly appears to have a preference to re-home to the server where the last known change (to the folder) was made.

Essentially, if the DS/IS consistency checker is run immediately after a connector is removed a real mess can occur. One company that experienced the effects of an unwanted consistency check referred to the re-homing of public folders as a "complete meltdown of the public folder hierarchy," after being forced to spend hours of administration effort resolving the conflicts and moving public folders back to their proper home server. Re-homing folders may require many megabytes of data to be replicated around the organization to get the proper replicas in place before the adjustments can be made. After experiencing the effects of bad DS/IS practice myself I can testify to the way that it can spoil your whole day.

5.4.6 Fixing orphan public folders

If you unwittingly run the DS/IS consistency adjuster and find that some folder re-homing has occurred, you will have a number of orphaned public folders to deal with. An orphaned public folder is one with no owner and is the direct result of the consistency adjuster being unable to resolve any entry in the folder's ACL against the directory. Thus, the ACL is empty, or possibly contains just the default "anonymous" access (which should be at the level of "none") introduced in Exchange V5.0.

Orphaned folders originate somewhere. As we've discussed, orphans are normally created when a site connector is removed. If the disconnected site is ever to rejoin the organization you can leave the orphan folders alone. You'll still have to adjust their ownership when the site rejoins, but you should not rush to do anything else because any action you take against an orphaned folder will be replicated to other copies once connections are available again.

However, if the original site is never going to rejoin the organization the orphans represent some debris that must be cleaned up in the public folder hierarchy. Failure to reset ownership and delete the folders will leave errornous entries in the hierarchy that only results in confusion for users. For example, if users attempt to access an orphan folder they'll be told:

```
The folder could not be opened. The contents of this public
folder are currently unavailable. Either the Exchange server
computer servicing this public folder is down or the public
folder has not been replicated to this site.
```

Attempts to access the properties of orphan folders from the administration program also fail. The message in this case also complains that replication is not complete. These errors occur because the attempts to access the content of the orphan folder result in zero data. Alternatively, from a client perspective, the access attempt is rejected because the user has been denied access. In either case the solution is the same. You must add an instance of the orphaned folders to the local public information store, then reset permissions so that a local user takes ownership (normally the administrator), and then delete the orphans. Cleaning up a set of orphaned folders is easier in Exchange V5.0 because permissions can now be propagated down through subfolders of a parent folder, but the work still needs to be done and will occupy valuable system administration time.

The bottom line is that the DS/IS consistency adjuster should only be run if a site is being permanently removed from an organization.

Properly run, the adjuster creates any necessary directory objects for all folders in the public folder hierarchy, maintaining permissions for the users (within the remaining sites) on the folders.

5.4.7   Network traffic generated by public folder replication

Objects stored in public folders are highly unpredictable in terms of size and content and no assessment can be given as to the traffic and network load generated by the replication of a public folder until its content and usage pattern are analyzed within a specific production environment. Instead, some broad guidelines can be given and taken into account when designating the owning server for public folders. For example:

- Public folders used as document repositories may not have many updates, but the size of the objects held in the repository can span an enormous range. PowerPoint presentations equipped with highly graphic pictures, OLE-enabled worksheets and documents, and perhaps even a set of speaker notes can quickly occupy 10 megabytes. Word for Windows files, such as those used to hold the content for this book, are normally smaller, unless screen captures and other bitmap images are featured. Excel worksheets tend to be smaller again but swiftly grow when some graphs are included. Remember too that the basic unit of replication is the item or document, and not a page, section, or field where a change was made. For these reasons it's a good idea to make smaller subsets of objects available whenever possible. Store chapters of a document rather than putting everything into a single file.

- Replicating a large object can saturate a network link for several minutes and hold up more urgent message traffic. With this in mind I think that it's important not to make too many changes to documents if you want to use a public folder as a point for revision control.

- Public folders used as points for interactive information dissemination, such as electronic conferences or bulletin boards have a higher volume of changes made to folder contents but the data involved in the changes is typically smaller. Public folders that use electronic forms produce similar network loads.

- Exchange treats all replicas equally (see discussion later on in this chapter). Thus, no difference is perceived (by the Exchange replication technology) between a replica created on a server running on a low-end 80486 CPU connected by a 56 Kbps circuit and another running on a high-end server equipped with 4

Alpha CPUs that's on an ATM circuit. Look at the network link to a server before deciding to place a replica there.

- Rules defining when replication occurs can be defined for each server. If the information contained in a public folder is not especially time critical, you can place the folder on a server which only performs replication outside normal business hours. Of course, business hours are different throughout the world because of work conventions and time zones, so don't assume that replicating large documents at 6 p.m. each evening will not interfere with other, more important network traffic.

The status of the replication activity on a server can be viewed in a number of different ways. A quick way to check that everything's in order is to look at the replication status via the properties of the Public Information Store (Figure 5.14). As you can see, each folder is listed with its current synchronization status. Another easy way to check is to look at the MTA queues. If there are large numbers of messages generated from the Public Information Store queued for transfer to the bridgehead server[3] in any other site there may be a problem with the connector to that site. Using a continually active server or link monitor (see Chapter 11) to check the connections to the bridgehead server in each site is a good proactive way to avoid unpleasant surprises.

Figure 5.14
Displaying the replication status

---

[3]   See the discussion on bridgehead servers in Chapter 7.

5.4.8   Replication philosophy

The design philosophy behind public folders means that everyone's view of a public folder is the same no matter where the folder is physically located. No one instance of a public folder is the master copy. All instances of a public folder enjoy the same standing within the organization. Users are automatically directed to the replica with the lowest connection cost. Even within a site it can make sense to distribute replicas of heavily used folders to each server so that user requests don't have to travel off the local server.

Locating data close to users is the major advantage delivered by a system of distributed, replicated public folders. However, there are some disadvantages. For example, it is possible to put a copy of a public folder on a laptop's hard disk for use in off-line mode. Changes in folder contents are replicated down to the copy on the PC when it is connected to the network using the normal folder synchronization process. Exchange's logical behavior in treating every copy of a folder in exactly the same peer-to-peer manner can lead to an interesting side-effect if the laptop's owner deletes objects from the folder, thinking of course that the copy of the folder on their PC is totally under their control. Eventually the deletions made in a copy of a public folder are enforced in every location where the folder has been replicated to, potentially becoming a rather unpleasant surprise for the other readers of the folder. The lesson here is to be careful in allocating delete permission to public folders. Unless people really need to have delete permission they shouldn't receive it, following the old system administration principle that sometimes users need to be protected from themselves.

The way you must approach balancing public folders across servers is another interesting side effect of how public folders have been implemented. It's common to find that public folders begin life on one server just because the folder's owner happens to have his or her mailbox on that server. An assessment of whether that server is the most appropriate location for the folder is not performed, so you can end up with an array of popular, high-traffic folders on a server that's already struggling to keep up with the demands of normal messaging or other applications.

To move a public folder from a server you must first create a new folder replica on the target server and then wait until the contents of the folder are replicated to the target server. Replication may take some time to complete, especially over slow links or when the folder contains many megabytes of information. Once replication is complete you can remove the original public folder by removing it from local

Public Information Store. Use the "Instances" property page for the Public Information Store to remove a public folder from a store. You will not be able to remove a folder in this manner if only one instance of the folder is available. Use an appropriately permissioned client to delete a single instance of a public folder.

After an instance is marked for removal Exchange will delete the contents of the folder from the information store and direct any future client connect requests for the folder to whatever replica is currently available at the lowest (network) cost.

5.4.9 Hiding public folders

The public folder hierarchy is replicated automatically from site to site within an organization. This is a nice feature if you want to publish the names of your site's public folders to everyone else, but sometimes it's nice to be a little more private.

Let's assume that you want to set up a public folder for use by a restricted group of users. You can, of course, protect the folder's contents through suitable permissions, but let's assume that you don't even want people to see the folder's name within the folder hierarchy. In short, you want to create a hidden public folder.

Hidden public folders cannot be created in the top level of the folder hierarchy. There is no mechanism to indicate that a top-level folder should be hidden. But sub-folders can be hidden and protected as follows:

- Create a top-level folder and give it a suitable name. For example, "Executive Information."
- Set the default permission on the new folder to "None."
- Create a sub-folder under "Executive Information." For example, "Secret Information."
- Set permissions on the "Secret Information" sub-folder to allow the users you want to have access to its content. If you are granting access to more than a couple of users you may want to create a distribution list and grant permissions to it. Users in the distribution list will then inherit the access permissions for the folder.

Users without the necessary permissions will be able to see the top-level folder, but any attempt to open the folder will display nothing. Only users with permissions will be able to see the sub-folders and other objects placed into the "Executive Information" folder.

5.5   Maintaining Exchange Information Stores

In Exchange V4.0 and V5.0 the maximum size of an information store or database is 16GB, possibly a limit that seemed to be well in advance of anything that people would need to use when it was first set. As we've seen, the ever-expanding size of messages and attachments has driven the requirement to support larger stores much faster than people might have expected. A server in DIGITAL reached a 15.5GB private information store in early 1997, after roughly 6 months of production activity. Spirited use of the EDBUTIL utility to compact the store and judicious transfer of user mailboxes to other servers managed to keep the server from hitting the magic 16GB limit, but there's no doubt that production servers will hit the ceiling soon. Just like the original 640KB memory limit in DOS, the limit is architectural and will be lifted in future versions of Exchange to allow servers to manage stores up to 16TB. Based on past experience of massive e-mail systems capable of supporting up to 10,000 users, I don't think that Microsoft will need to move past a 16TB limit in a hurry.

By default, each server has two stores—the private and public information stores, so a single Exchange server can manage a maximum of 32GB of data. There can be many servers within a single Exchange site. The number of servers operated within any individual site therefore dictates the maximum available storage for a site. Users store messages in the private information store of their host server. You can balance disk space usage across the servers in a site by moving user mailboxes from server to server. As this can be a tiresome activity that must be accomplished when people are not using their mailboxes it pays to carefully plan the allocation of users across available servers.

A computer running Exchange does not necessarily require the presence of both public and private information stores. It is possible to configure a server to be "messaging-only" in which case only a private information store is operated. The converse case is to have a server dedicated to public folder access only, in which case no user mailboxes are allocated to the server. Smaller sites are not likely to operate dedicated servers, but in larger sites a good case can be made to exploit Exchange's flexibility in this manner by deploying servers configured for particular tasks. For example, one large server with a fast CPU and large disk arrays might manage all the public folders for the site, leaving general messaging activity to a set of smaller servers.

When you create a site it is important to consider whether all servers will host both types of store or if different servers will take on different tasks. The "General" property page for the Private Information Store (see Figure 5.15) is used to define the server location for the associated Public Information Store. When a user creates a new public folder it is normally created on the same server that hosts the user's mailbox, but if the location of the Public Information Store is redefined the new folder is created on the other server.

Figure 5.15
General properties of the Private Information Store

Exchange V4.0 allows servers to be operated without private information stores. This policy is prohibited in V5.0 because the mechanism for inter-site directory replication has been changed. The private information store is now used to hold the messages generated for directory replication, so it is no longer possible to delete the private information store from a server.

5.5.1   The type of database used by Exchange

Relational database technology forms the heart of Exchange. The data contained in user mailboxes, public folders, and the Exchange directory are held in three databases called PRIV.EDB, PUB.EDB, and DIR.EDB; the stores that contain all the important information used by an Exchange server. Understanding the technology and knowing how to keep these databases healthy is clearly important if you want to avoid problems with Exchange.

Exchange uses a variant of Microsoft's "Jet" [4] database technology called "Jet Blue," an object store which is roughly similar to a tradi-

---

[4]   JET stands for "Joint Engine Technology," an internal Microsoft database project.

tional relational database. A lot of myths and rumors have built up around the database used by Exchange. One popular story alleges that Exchange uses SQL Server for all database access, while another says that Exchange uses the same database engine as the popular desktop Access product, probably because Access is also based on Jet database technology (but not the same development as Exchange). As mentioned above, there are some similarities to a relational database such as those implemented in SQL Server and Access, but the two implementations are very different beasts. Both SQL Server and Access deal in rows, tables, and joins like other database applications while Exchange is very much focused on the definition of a MAPI message store.

Based on "Jet Blue," the Exchange developers have designed the information store to be optimized for the type of activity produced by users creating and sending messages, or the traffic generated by directory and public folder replication. Remember that a large number of messages are generated, sent, and deleted to carry out behind the scenes database synchronization. Public folder replication, system attendant updates for configurations, and directory updates are all examples of messages that go through the database without too much notice being taken (unless things go wrong). When added to interpersonal messages the traffic generated by background messages was enough to require the Exchange architects to pay special attention to database efficiency in terms of message throughput, leading in turn to the decision reached to use Jet Blue.

Apart from its high-volume message processing capacity the chosen database confers other advantages. In addition to having a smaller "footprint" (amount of memory that the code occupies) than an SQL-based equivalent, the Jet technology allows for a number of unique features such as record level locking and "on the fly" indexing. "On the fly" indexing means that Exchange automatically indexes the values contained in object properties as objects are added to the database. Good indexes are a critical factor in allowing users to execute very fast searches despite specifying complex criteria. For instance, looking through a large information store for all instances of documents authored by "Tony Redmond" which mention "Exchange server" in the title would take a long time unless the author and title attributes (or rather, MAPI properties) are indexed in some way.

The closest thing a MAPI message store has to the concept of a join across tables is a "multi-valued property." If a document stored in a public folder has multiple authors (properties) there is no need to create separate tables for document and author and join them just to see who the different authors are. This is another example of a major difference between Exchange and other Microsoft database implementations.

Even if Exchange does not use a relational database, that's no good reason not to learn from the lessons learned from many years of relational database use in high-availability production environments. The best example of this in practice is the transaction rollback and roll-forward capabilities built into the Exchange information store, plus the elimination of the requirement to halt the server to perform backup operations. Using the correct tools (those that know about the capabilities of the information store) backups can be taken while users are accessing the information store, a characteristic of high-end transaction systems.

Over the long term the plan of record for Exchange is to move from its own database to Microsoft's strategic object store, or OFS. Microsoft people are careful to emphasize that the transition to OFS will follow a conservative approach and should be seamless to end users and administrators alike.

5.5.2   Major characteristics of the Exchange database model

Exchange is designed to meet the ACID (Atomicity, Consistency, Isolation, and Durability) test for database transaction integrity. Exchange uses transaction logs to achieve atomicity. In other words, if a system interruption occurs the information store will attempt to apply any outstanding transactions when the information store service is restarted. Outstanding transactions are those that are held in logs but have not been committed to the database. Incomplete transactions, which may be found at the end of a log, are ignored. They are normally the result of transactions that are in progress when the system outage occurred.

The process of transaction log checking and committal occurs automatically every time the Exchange databases are started, and because all transactions are applied to the database in a controlled manner a great degree of consistency is achieved. The multi-threaded nature of the Exchange information store service allows database operations to proceed as if each transaction was the only one currently active. Although many different user-initiated operations may be proceeding simultaneously, each is isolated and dealt with on an individual basis. Finally, the separation of transactions into logs and database, and the ability to conduct automatic transaction recoveries after system outages gives Exchange a high degree of durability.

Moving away from the requirements of the ACID test, let's focus on some of the major characteristics of the Exchange databases. These are:

- Single-instance storage
- Atomic transaction model
- High throughput
- Designed for on-line 7 × 24 × 365 operation

5.5.3   The single message storage model

Unlike PC LAN-based electronic mail systems, which typically create copies of messages for each recipient, Exchange uses a shared message model. In other words, a single copy of a message is stored on a server and all of the users who have access to the message hold a database pointer to the single copy within their folders. The shared message model is well tried and tested and has been in use with other messaging systems, such as DIGITAL's ALL-IN-1 server, since the early 1980s. There are a number of obvious advantages in a shared message model. For instance:

- Disk activity is reduced because the system doesn't have to create, delete, and otherwise manage multiple physical copies of messages. This is especially important when message content is large and the average size of messages is increasing. Think of the disk activity required to create 100 copies of a 100K message. Now scale it up for 250 copies of a message (perhaps one circulated to everyone in a site) that has a very large attachment.
- Disk space required for message data is much reduced because no redundant copies are created.
- Because of the two previous points the shared message model is the most scaleable type of electronic file cabinet or message container.

Apart from making effective use of storage, the single instance model also effectively increases the maximum size of the information store from its 16GB physical limit upwards towards a higher logical plateau. Charging the size of a message (and its attachments) against the quota of each recipient does this. If a 10K message is sent to three recipients, then 10K is physically taken up in the store but 30K is logically occupied (10K for each recipient). Depending on how many users share messages and how long users retain those messages (in a single instance model the number of sharers is inevitably reduced over time), the "commonality" factor allows the logical limit of the store to expand many times. In production use you'll probably see commonality factors between 2 and 3, meaning that the 16GB store can, to users, store up to 50GB of messages. In production use you will probably never approach these limits because:

1. Most servers don't have 16GB of available disk space to allocate to information stores

2. Warnings should start to sound if you see the database growing to approach its physical limit. At this time you need to start thinking of other plans—either cleaning up user mailboxes to remove debris from the store, or installing a new server into the site and moving some mailboxes across to it.

While it is very scaleable and uses least disk space, a shared message model imposes some additional load on the mechanism used to register messages. The database used in the Exchange server information store is responsible for tracking user access to messages through pointers, and must make sure that "hanging" pointers, or pointers belonging to messages no longer wanted by any user on the system, are removed. The actual message contents are removed from the system once all the relevant users have deleted their pointers, in effect reducing the count of interested parties to zero. The database must also track the movement of messages from location to location within the overall filing system, and all this must be done quickly and without being obvious to users. Note that the single message model only extends to the confines of a single server and does not span a site. A message sent to several users in the same site will be delivered to the private information store on each server connected to by the recipients of the message. It is therefore possible to have several copies of a message within a single site, albeit only on the servers whose users have an interest in the message.

The space occupied by user mailboxes within the private information store can be viewed by selecting the Private Information Store properties for a server and then the "Mailbox Resources" page (see Figure 5.22). Mailboxes can be restricted by individual quota (set as a property of a mailbox) or general quotas applied to all mailboxes (set through the General properties of the Private Information Store). Limits can be set for Exchange to issue warning messages and then to prevent users from creating and sending new items.

5.5.4   Atomic transactions

The atomic transaction model used by Exchange means that any messaging operation (add, change, delete) is composed of a set of clearly defined steps which collectively form a transaction. Exchange will never commit a transaction to the database unless all steps have been followed, meaning that theoretically it is impossible to write invalid information, for example a corrupt message structure, into the database. All transactions are actually written twice; first into a transaction log, and then into the database. The write-ahead logging scheme is a common implementation in high-end database systems (for example, SQL Server or Oracle) and helps Exchange achieve its goal of high transactional throughput. The Exchange database is capable of handling a very heavy transaction load and is not going to be the limiting factor in scaling systems. Other items such as the physical size of the store or the lack of clustering are more likely to throttle back the number of users you'll connect to a server.

Table 5.2   *Major tables in the Exchange information store*

Table	Use
Message	The RTF text for each message plus some other information is stored in a row.
Attachments	Each attachment to any message is stored in a row in this table.
Message/Folder	Each folder has a separate table created to hold header information for all the items stored in the folder.

Exchange is designed for 7 x 24-hour use, 365 days a year. There is no requirement to stop the server to perform maintenance. The database is defragmented on-line and backups can proceed with users connected and working with the server. Much of Exchange's capability in this area come from the transaction model that's used, as we'll see below.

Before plunging into the details of the transaction model we need to understand the basic structures within the Exchange information stores. Relational databases are organized into tables. Exchange is no different; its database is also organized into a set of tables, the major ones of which are detailed in. There are other tables in the information store, but these are the ones that are most interesting.

5.5.5   Exploring the information store

User mailboxes are built up in folders, and folders can be nested. All folders are referenced as rows in a single Folders table in the database. The data held for a folder is pretty simple—a unique identification number, the name of the folder, the name of its owner, a count of the number of messages stored in the folder and another count to indicate how many are unread, and the number of the folder's parent, if it is nested within another folder. When Exchange builds the folder hierarchy for a user mailbox it first finds all the folders owned by that user and then sorts the folders into parent/child order before presenting the hierarchy to the user.

Every folder can be sorted differently, so a separate table is built for each folder. The rows in this table contain header information for the messages in the folder—items like the author, subject, date received, message size, and (very important) a unique number to help retrieve the message content from the database. Maintaining a separate table for each folder allows Exchange to very quickly retrieve and display the contents of a folder, no matter how many items are contained in the folder and whatever sort order is chosen by the user. Compare the speed in which Exchange can open and display details of messages in a folder that holds a few hundred messages with other mail systems; now click on a field to sort it and Exchange immediately responds. This just wouldn't be possible if separate message tables weren't maintained.

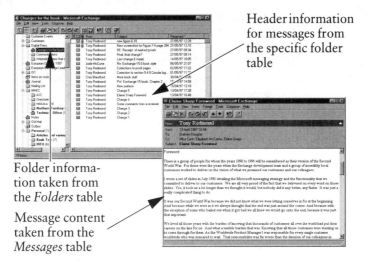

Figure 5.16
How users access information store database tables

Header information for messages from the specific folder table

Folder information taken from the *Folders* table

Message content taken from the *Messages* table

Folder tables don't hold the actual content for items. All content is stored in two tables, one for messages and one for attachments. The link between message tables and content is made by unique identification numbers. When a user double-clicks on a message to read it Exchange examines the id number in the message folder table and uses it to retrieve the content from the messages table, and perhaps attachments if any are present. The message table is where the reference count is kept. This is the field that's reduced as users delete messages from their mailboxes. Once the reference count reaches zero the row holding the message is removed from the message table, freeing the space used for message content within the store. Unfortunately, as we'll see later on, while the logical store within the database is freed up, the database never shrinks in size if the EDBUTIL utility is not used to rebuild the database.

Figure 5.16 illustrates how users look on Exchange and where the data they view originates. In this case we're viewing some folders in the private information store. The folders listed in the left-hand pane come from the single large Folders table. Information about the items contained in the currently selected folder is displayed in the right-hand pane. This is header data that is fetched from the table that's set up and maintained for each individual folder. When a user double-clicks on an item to read it, Exchange launches a read message form and combines header information (which is already available) with content retrieved from the Messages table.

5.5.6   Exchange databases

The two most important data structures requiring regular and consistent backups are the Information Store and the Directory Store. The Information Store, containing public and private folders and other system-wide objects, is split between two separate database files called PRIV.EDB and PUB.EDB whose default location is the \MDBDATA directory. The Directory Store, holding information about recipients, other servers, and connectors, is held in the DIR.EDB file located in the \DSADATA directory.

Table 5.3   *Exchange databases*

Database/file	Purpose	Default location
PRIV.EDB	Private Information Store. Location for all private folders.	\EXCHSRVR\MDBDATA
PUB.EDB	Public Information Store. Location for all public folders.	\EXCHSRVR\MDBDATA
DIR.EDB	Directory Store	\EXCHSRVR\DSADATA
EDB.LOG	Current log file for Information Store transactions	\EXCHSRVR\MDBDATA
EDBn.LOG	Backup transaction log file	\EXCHSRVR\MDBDATA
EDB.CHK	Database checkpoint file	\EXCHSRVR\MDBDATA
RES1.LOG	Reservation log file used to hold transactions if disk space is exhausted	\EXCHSRVR\MDBDATA
RES2.LOG	Reservation log file used to hold transactions if disk space is exhausted	\EXCHSRVR\MDBDATA

Table 5.3 summarizes the major databases and associated files used by Exchange Server's Information and Directory Stores.

While the \MDBDATA directory is the default location for the information stores there is no requirement for you to keep the stores together in the one directory. Keeping everything together is neat and tidy but it concentrates disk activity to a single place, a situation that will eventually lead to the disk being swamped with I/O requests generated by database activity. If you want to optimize disk performance it's best to keep the two stores apart on separate drives, and also to move the log files (more on log files shortly) to another drive.

Figure 5.17
*Amending
database paths*

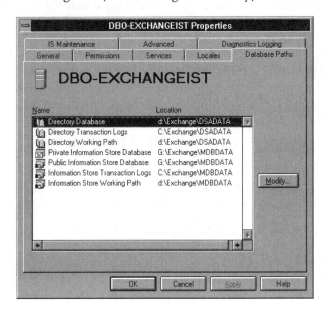

On all but the smallest or disk-starved servers the Performance Optimizer will recommend that the various files used by the Information Stores and Directory are spread across all available disks. It is logical to spread the I/O load generated by any application across all available disk spindles, and the approach taken by the Performance Optimizer is in line with well-established system management practices. Keeping everything on one or two disks will deliver satisfactory performance for small user populations, but performance will steadily degenerate as the number of users grows or the demands created by the users increase. You can amend the location of any of the files through the "Database Paths" property page (see Figure 5.17). Note that Exchange does not support the placing of its database files on a networked drive. All databases must be stored on local disks.

5.5.7   Interaction between transaction log files and the information store

Exchange uses a set of log and other files to ensure that the information stores are kept up to date. Each transaction (a new message, for example) directed to an information store is recorded into a transaction log file called EDB.LOG as well as an area in memory. This avoids the need to constantly write information directly into the information store databases, generating large amounts of I/O for the system to process. Updates are deferred, gathered together into efficient "chunks," and then committed from memory to the information store when time and system demand allows.

When a user sends a message a transaction is begun. For example, to write a new message into the store we have to:

- Begin the transaction
- Insert the message content into the Messages table
- Insert any attachments into the Attachments table
- Insert the header information into the Inbox folder table for each recipient
- Update the Folders table to increment the number of messages and unread count for the Inbox folder for each recipient
- End the transaction
- Commit the transaction to the database

When complete the transaction is written into a queue in memory and also into the current transaction log (EDB.LOG).

Figure 5.18
Transactions
for the
information
stores

Because transactions are written to a log file and then into the information store it follows that the database can never be considered to be totally up to date until the transactions in the log file are taken into consideration. If no users are using the system for more than five minutes it is fairly safe to assume that all the transactions in memory will have been written into the database. You can "force" transactions to be written in two ways. First, by using a backup utility to create a backup of the Exchange databases. We'll discuss this operation in more detail later on. The second way is to close down Exchange's information

store service. In both cases it's important to check the system event log
to ensure that no error messages have been recorded to indicate problems occurred when the database was updated.

Because transactions are preserved log files, a physical record of
the processing that has been performed for the database is always
available. The transaction log files can be used in the event of a problem with the information store when transactions can be rolled back
from the logs into a recovered copy of the information store to bring it
up to date. For this reason it is dangerous to delete transaction logs
without first knowing that their contents will no longer be required.

EDB.LOG is the name of the "active" log file. In other words,
EDB.LOG is the file that details of new message transactions are written into. A new log file is created after approximately 5 megabytes of
transactions (message operations) have been recorded. When the current transaction log is filled up EDB.LOG is renamed and a new version of EDB.LOG created. On a very busy server lots of transactions
flow through the log files and it's not uncommon to see very many separate files created over the working day. You can force log file creation
by importing large amounts of data into the information store, notably
when the migration wizard is running.

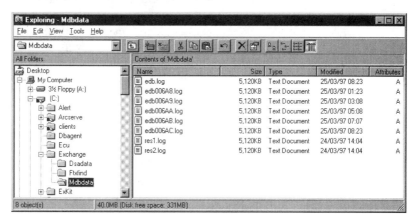

Figure 5.19
*Files in the
\MDBDATA
directory*

Each log file is allocated 5MB when it is created. This step ensures
that all transactions can be written without running the risk of suddenly exhausting disk space. If File Manager reports that a transaction log
is anything other than 5MB (5,242,880 bytes) it is likely that the log is
corrupt. In this case you should check the event log for errors, stop Exchange, take a backup, and then restart Exchange services. All the log
files should have been erased and the database brought fully up to date.
Check too that the disk where the log files are stored hasn't encountered any hardware problems.

Log files are numbered sequentially using a file-naming scheme of EDBxxxxx.LOG, where xxxxx is a hexadecimal number from 0 to f). After a few days of moderate messaging activity you end up with EDB00001.LOG, EDB00002.LOG, and so on (see Figure 5.19). Depending on the number of messages generated on your system and the frequency that backups are taken it's common to find that the \MDB-DATA directory stores ten or more log files.

Systems that engage in heavy replication activity turn over transaction log files quickly. Replication (see page 218) occurs when servers update each other about the contents of public folders or directory information. Servers can be very "chatty" if allowed to do so. For example, servers will send each other frequent snapshots of the public folder hierarchy, just to make sure that everyone knows where all the different public folders are located. The snapshot information is circulated in the form of messages, and these must be logged in exactly the same manner as interpersonal mail. Systems handling large numbers of directory changes, either in the startup period when many additions are being made, or if they act as the point for directory information dissemination to other servers also generate lots of work for transaction logs. You can cut down on the number of messages being produced by replication activities by scheduling replication to occur at particular times of the day rather than whenever Exchange feels the need. Scheduling in this manner also reduces traffic through whatever connectors you use to link sites together, thus preventing any potential delays for interpersonal mail that might otherwise creep in.

The \MDBDATA directory is the default location for both the transaction logs and the information store. It's more efficient to move the transaction logs away onto a separate physical disk so that the disk I/O activity generated by message traffic is divided across multiple spindles. From a performance perspective some anecdotal evidence exists that transaction logs should be placed on a FAT-formatted drive. The assertion normally being that:

1. Fewer overheads are incurred by the system when writing files to FAT drives than NTFS.

2. Transactions are written in a sequential manner to the end of the logs. Thus, no sophisticated indexing or file structure management is required.

Your mileage may vary! In all cases, FAT or NTFS, make sure that the disk where the transaction logs are created has plenty of disk space. The very best thing is to allocate transaction logs to their own disk as it is very embarrassing for a system administrator if the information store suddenly shuts down because no more space exists to create a new log.

The EDB.CHK file acts as a database checkpoint. Its function is to track the transaction log files and make sure that they are synchronized with the databases. When the Exchange database engine starts up it checks EDB.CHK to determine the current status of the database and takes whatever action is required to enable the database to commence operations in a stable state. At this stage any transactions in the log file that have not been recorded are applied. If you are ever unfortunate enough to suffer a major corruption of the database you may be able to get up and running fast by restoring a recent backup and starting the server. If possible, all of the transactions that occurred since the backup was taken will be applied and the database restored to full working order. Of course, this type of restoration depends on good quality backups being taken at regular intervals.

When backups are taken the transaction log files are automatically purged by the backup utility. The process of purging basically zeroizes EDB.LOG, to ready the log to accept new transactions. All other log files (EDB00001.LOG and so on) are deleted and the disk space returned to the system. Cleaning up log files in this manner is logical because the database has been written to backup media in a consistent state with all outstanding transactions applied before the backup is allowed to begin, so there is no longer any need for the log files to be retained. As the log files can take up quite a bit of disk space the automatic deletion is welcome, but if you want to be cautious you can always back the log files up before commencing the database backup.

Two special log files, called RES1.LOG and RES2.LOG (the reservation logs) are used by the system to ensure that there's enough disk space available for Exchange to complete operations in a controlled manner should the computer run out of disk space. In other words, if disk space is exhausted, Exchange can use the space allocated to RES1.LOG and RES2.LOG to complete whatever it needs to do before halting.

In any case where Exchange discovers that there isn't enough space available on a disk to create a new transaction log, an error condition is generated which causes the information store to shut down, hopefully in a graceful manner. When a shutdown occurs it is possible that transactions are waiting in memory to be written to a transaction log and of course this isn't possible because there's no disk space. The current log files are also full, which is the reason why the error condition has occurred in the first place. Exchange resolves the immediate problem, what to do with the in-memory transactions, by writing them first to RES1.LOG and then, if necessary, to continue writing on into RES2.LOG. It's not altogether clear to me what happens if there is more than 10MB of transactions waiting in memory, but it's perhaps fair to assume that such a volume and quantity of transaction data would never be held in memory. After all transactions are flushed into the reservation logs Exchange will shut down.

5.5.8   Source of transactions

Interpersonal messages are the most obvious source of transactions, but in an Exchange environment many other types of messages are generated on a daily basis. Remember that public folder and directory information is replicated over the mail system, and these messages contribute to the overall message volume experienced by a system. If you look at the various sources that typically generate messages you'll find:

- Interpersonal messages
- Directory replication
- Public folder hierarchy replication
- Public folder contents replication
- System attendant messages
- The migration wizard
- The Move Mailbox option

It's a good idea to throttle back the replication schedule for public folders and the directory to wider intervals than the defaults (every 15 minutes) just to reduce the message load on a system. Extending replication intervals also relieves some of the demand for disk space for transaction logs (unless you use circular logging) and helps to prevent any embarrassing episodes such as the Exchange services being shut down prematurely because there's no more disk space available to create any more transaction logs.

5.5.9   Circular logging

Circular logging is the default transaction logging behaviour implemented when Exchange is installed. Circular logging is a scheme where transaction logs are "re-used" after the transactions that they contain have been committed into the database.

Circular logging is supported for both the directory and information store (the same setting applies to both the private and public information stores). Exchange is instructed to use or ignore circular logging through the advanced property page for a server (Figure 5.20). The affected services (directory and information store) need to be stopped and restarted before a new setting becomes active.

Figure 5.20
*Enabling
circular logging*

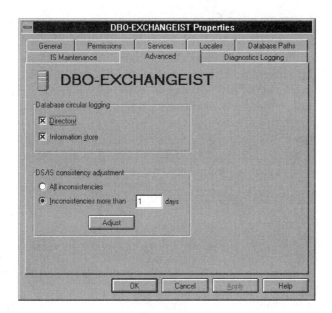

Systems running circular logging normally use between one to four transaction logs, but under times of heavy messaging activity it is possible to see a few more logs created. If you experience this situation, for example during a period when you use the migration wizard to import lots of user data onto a server, be assured that the logging scheme will return to its normal situation the next time the Exchange services are started (normally following a system reboot).

Using circular logging means that Exchange is less likely to run out of disk space, but you will lose the capability to replay transactions from a log should it be necessary to recover a database after a hard disk crash. All you can do is restore the last available backup tape and go forward from that point.

The logic behind making circular logging the default is simple. A lot of Exchange servers will be low-end systems designed to support small populations, and there may not be a skilled system administrator around to look after disk space. Getting rid of administrative tasks in this environment makes a lot of sense, but if you expect to run a high-end server that supports a couple of hundred users it's madness to consider using circular logging.

If you implement circular logging it's important to note that incremental and differential backups of the Exchange databases are not possible. When circular logging is enabled full backups must always be taken. Because circular logging negates the additional protection afforded through the logging mechanism you may want to take file-level backups of the Exchange databases as well as online backups. File-level backups are only possible when all the Exchange services are halted.

The information store is designed for use in a situation where regular and frequent backups are taken. Good system management practices dictate that any system supporting important data should be backed up, and in view of these points it is hard to make a case to use circular logging instead of the system of creating and erasing multiple log files. After all, provided you take backups you shouldn't run into situations where the disk space occupied by the transaction log files is excessive and causes problems for the system.

5.5.10   Checkpoint files

During normal operation transactions in the in-memory queue are written into the private or public information store when the system is a little quieter and messaging activity is not so intense. The database checkpoint file (EDB.CHK) keeps track of the buffers that have been written out of memory and into the database, so Exchange knows at any time what transactions remain in the logs and are waiting to be written into the database.

As mentioned earlier, you can "force" Exchange to flush transactions out of memory and write them to the database by stopping the Exchange information store service. This happens when a system is shut down gracefully. If a system is forced to stop abruptly, for example when a power outage occurs, it is more than likely that some transactions will not have been written into the database. However, the transactions will be in a transaction log and can be replayed when the information store service is restarted after the system is powered up again.

During a recovery operation, the data in the checkpoint file determines which transactions are replayed, basically by comparing a time-stamp in the checkpoint file against the transactions in the log files. If the transactions in the logs are newer than the time-stamp in the checkpoint file they will be replayed and written into the information store. Note that replayed transactions don't just include new messages and attachments; they can also include deletions and updates. If many transactions remain to be replayed when a system powers up then the information store update can take a few minutes to complete.

Whereas it is convenient to have EDB.CHK available before beginning a recovery operation it is not a prerequisite. If Exchange finds that the checkpoint file is not available it will read the transaction logs to determine the point at which transactions had been committed to the database.

5.5.11 Soft and hard database recoveries

Replaying transactions after a power outage or similar failure is referred to as a "soft recovery." The database is available and just needs to be updated from the transaction logs. The checkpoint file is consulted when the information store service is started and any outstanding transactions are written into the database. Soft recoveries are pretty automatic and sometimes you won't even be aware that a recovery has occurred. A "hard recovery" is different. This scenario occurs when a hard disk failure or other hardware fault has corrupted a database and you have to retrieve an old copy of the database from a backup tape. You have, of course, taken backups, and even more to the point you've tested the backups and know that you can retrieve the data from the tape!

When dealing with hard recovery situations you'll have to restore all the last full backup of the database that you have available plus all the transaction logs that have been created since. When the information store service starts up it will recognize that the database is out of date and proceed to replay transactions from the logs. Because hard recoveries rely on the availability of log files it is obvious that if the log files are on the same drive as the database you run the risk that corruption will affect both database and log files and so make any recovery exercise impossible. This is a pretty fundamental reason for you to separate the database and transaction logs on any Exchange server intended for production work. Indeed, most large production systems place transaction logs on their own separate disk.

The use of a relational database and the way folders, messages, headers, and attachments are stored within the database makes backup and restore operations a very interesting exercise, even if you never considered the way that transactions are stored in memory, log files, and the database. As I'm sure you are aware, it is not currently possible to restore a single mailbox or document from a backup tape, and when you consider what would be required to retrieve all of the logical components that make up a physical mailbox (just think about how many tape scans would be needed), you'll appreciate the type of processing that a "bricked" restore involves. It is little wonder that this functionality is unavailable today.

5.5.12 Transactions for the Public Information Store

Transactions applied to PUB.EDB, the database used by the public information store, are also written into log files. However, there is a slight difference in behavior in the way that the database expands in size as new objects are added to the store. If you watch PRIV.EDB for a while, even on a fairly heavily used system, it won't expand very often. But if you watch PUB.EDB as new items are added to public folders you'll see that the file appears to grow dynamically. The difference in behavior is logical because the additions, deletions, and modifications of objects held in the public information store occur at a very much lower rate of activity than the often-frenetic throughput of messages arriving and departing the private information store. Applying updates to PRIV.EDB in bulk from memory is a more efficient way of writing information while preserving a high level of performance.

Both the private and public information store databases can be compacted with the EDBUTIL utility to reduce their size by optimizing internal structures and eliminating redundant data. Details on ED-BUTIL are presented later on in this chapter.

5.5.13   Exhausting available disk space

As a general rule for all messaging servers you can never have too much disk space, just in case. I have seen instances where the Information Store exhausts the space available on a disk. In most cases the problem occurred on systems that had been on the threshold of available disk space for some time, meaning that it was always a struggle to find available disk space for any application let alone one that has to manage shared files on behalf of many users. Failure to pay attention to system administration compounds this particular problem as all systems tend to accumulate files over time, albeit perhaps files that should be automatically cleaned up by the application that produced them. The reality of mail systems is that the amount of disk space used for messages can quickly mount up, so it's important that all system configurations are sized with a reasonable degree of seemingly excess disk space to allow for unplanned growth

The most common cause for space exhaustion is where one or more users create large messages with many attachments. When the message is sent its content is moved from the client to the server and Exchange attempts to add it to the Information Store. If space is unavailable or becomes exhausted at this point the Information Store will not be able to extend itself to store the new message. This causes the Information Store to automatically shut itself down, as manual intervention is required from the system administrator. A warning message will be sent to the Windows NT system log (see Figure 5.21) and can be viewed through the system event viewer. Users will immediately know that a problem exists because clients will be unable to log-on to the server, in essence because the server will not be able to send details of the folders in the user's mailbox to the client due to the unavailability of the Information Store service.

Figure 5.21
*Windows NT
Event Viewer
showing that
we've run out
of disk space*

Possible solutions to the problem are:

- Increasing the available space on the disk where the Information Store is located by deleting unwanted or unnecessary files.

- Moving the Information Store to another disk. Files belonging to Exchange server or other applications might also be moved at the same time.

- Replacing the original disk with a larger disk. You'll need to restore a full backup of the original disk to the new disk before operations can begin again.

- Using circular logging for the Information and Directory stores. This is not recommended on any production-level server.

In most instances the first solution is both the most immediate and pragmatic, although I would take immediate steps to consider the other two solutions over the long term. If the disk where the Information Store is located runs out of space on one occasion it is likely to do so again in the future.

The Information Store isn't the only service that will shut down gracefully in the event that a lack of disk space is detected. The Exchange MTA will stop working if it detects that there is less than 10MB available on the disk where its working directory (\MTADATA) is located. The MTA working directory is prone to accumulate many small (and some not so small) files on systems that are under heavy load, and it may take the MTA a lot of time to clear those files. The performance characteristics of Exchange give most weight to user response. In other words, any request for service from a user will be attended to first before Exchange will proceed to process any outstanding background work.

Large MTA queues are often observed on heavily loaded systems, and those queues translate into files in the \MTADATA directory. The solution to the problem is simple—clear out some files on the same disk as the \MTADATA directory and restart the MTA service. Do not delete files in the \MTADATA directory without knowing what you are doing as this will inevitably result in a loss of messages.

5.5.14   Limiting user disk space

You can limit the amount of space a user can occupy within a store, and if you have the opportunity to set limits and so encourage good habits within users by forcing respect for disk space from the start, you should seize your chance quickly. Users who are allowed free range will run rampant and occupy as much space as they can, a good proportion of which is unlikely to store messages and other data of great strategic importance.

Figure 5.22
Viewing space
used in the
Private
Information
Store

Limits (defined in kilobytes) are set on an individual user mailbox (see Figure 5.23) or on the private information store as a whole, in which case the same limits are set for all user mailboxes. As illustrated in Figure 5.23, two different limits can be specified. The limit set by checking the first box determines the point at which a user will start to receive warning messages generated by the system attendant.

Figure 5.23
*Limiting space
for a user
mailbox*

The second check box determines the point at which users won't be allowed to send any more messages. If "Never" is checked for the information store limits, users or particular users will be allowed to continue occupying space until the disk fills up and reaches its physical storage limit or (more unlikely) the information store reaches its 16GB design limit. Users who have exceeded their quota will not be able to create new messages, but they'll still be able to receive messages that arrive for them. It is therefore possible for a user to grow the space they occupy within the private information store after restrictions have been placed on them.

Interestingly, if users exceed their quota in the private information store Exchange will also stop them putting anything into a public folder. No doubt this restriction is in place to stop "smart" users getting around quotas by moving messages and other objects out of their private space into the public area. The only way a user can resolve the problem of an exceeded quota is to delete messages (and make sure that the Deleted Items folder is emptied) until they go under their quota or to have the system administrator give them a temporary increase in quota. Temporary increases in user quotas usually become permanent unless the system administrator is vigilant!

While encouraging you to impose limitations on the space within the database allocated to individual users, make sure that reasonable amounts are allocated. There is nothing so boring or time-consuming for a system administrator as having to answer a continuous stream of requests for increases in allocations. Apart from taking up time to respond to each request, the requirement to ask for more space just to send a few more messages (for this is what it will appear in the mind of users) will cause irritation and reduce overall satisfaction levels with the system.

A proactive approach to system management dictates that every step should be taken to ensure that unpleasant surprises don't occur. Running out of disk space counts as one of the surprises no system manager wants to have, so you should perform manual or automated checks each morning to ensure that:

- The disk(s) where the information stores are located have sufficient free disk space. Start to get worried when less than 150MB is available on a system serving less than 100 users, or 300MB on a system serving more than 100 users. Systems serving very heavy mail users may want to increase the warning threshold for free disk space. Remember that a single large message can chew up several megabytes very easily.

- Backups have been taken and the log files for the information store (for example, EDB00001.LOG, EDB00002.LOG, and so on) have been deleted.

- No user has exceeded their disk space allocation. If someone has they may be unaware of the fact, so take steps to contact them and then help the user free up some space.

Every night the Exchange System Attendant checks for people who have exceeded disk quota. If someone is discovered to be approaching their quota a message is sent to the offending user to indicate that they may not be able to send any more messages. You can instruct the System Attendant to perform checks and send warning messages many times each day, if you think this is necessary. Once the System Attendant determines that someone has actually exceeded their quota a stop is placed on any further send operations. Users will be able to create new messages, and save them to their local disk, but they won't be able to send them until they free some of their allocated quota within the information store.

5.5.15   Freeing up some space

There is no automatic way for a system administrator to free space by deleting obsolete messages from the public or private information store. Space is returned to the information store when messages are deleted. However, as we'll discuss later on, the space is returned to the database and not to the Windows NT file system. Recovering file space from the database requires additional steps, discussed on page 305.

Figure 5.24
*Message from
the System
Attendant to
tell a user their
disk space is
exhausted*

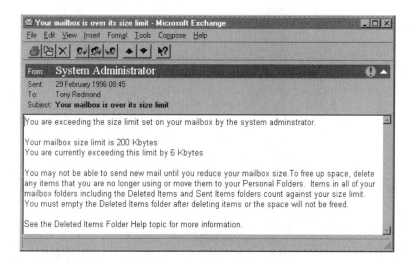

Deletion is a two-stage process as the messages are first moved into the "Deleted Items" folder, and then only permanently removed from the store when the contents of this folder are purged. Users can set their working conditions from Exchange clients to purge the contents of the "Deleted Items" folder automatically when they exit. This is one of the choices available from the dialog displayed from the Options entry on the Tools menu. Purging the "Deleted Items" folder is not default behavior for the client, so users must change the setting manually. As pointed out before, setting default values for options like this is a very good reason to use the Exchange Setup Editor utility before client installations start.

It's somewhat surprising to find that there are no system housekeeping facilities to produce reports of the number of messages each user has in their mailbox and the amount of space these messages occupy. This is a pity, because reports of space utilization taken on a regular basis (for example, every month) provide invaluable data for use when planning the growth of a messaging system. You can, of course, use the Exchange Administration utility to view the contents of the private information store, and note the data presented there (Figure 5.22). But it would be nice to be able to export this information in the form of a spreadsheet or other formatted data, as this would make the data much easier to work with. The STORSTAT utility from the Exchange Resource Kit (see Chapter 11) provides another option to analyze the contents of a user's mailbox.

Figure 5.25 *The*
Clean Mailbox
option

Reports on various aspects of Exchange can be obtained if you buy third party add-on products. The best reporting utility for Exchange I have seen to date is Crystal Reports for Exchange[5]. A copy of Crystal Reports for Exchange is included in the Exchange Resource Kit.

Unlike the public information store where administrators can set expiry limits on folders, messages held in the private information store never expire (they remain in the mailbox as long as the user wishes to keep them there). Administrators can intervene and clean up a user's mailbox without their permission by using the "Clean Mailbox" option on the Tools menu (see Figure 5.25), but the sudden disappearance of a whole pile of messages from their mailbox is not likely to make a user very happy. It's probably better to reserve the clean mailbox option for the most intransigent users and restrain yourself to warnings for the others, unless of course you follow the "I know best" school of thought for system administration. It's not immediately obvious from the user interface or documentation, but you can select multiple mailboxes for the "Clean Mailbox" option to process with the CTRL/Click and SHIFT/Click key combinations to either select a range of mailboxes or a set of individually chosen mailboxes.

Along the same line as the point already made regarding the generation of statistics about the information store, it would be nice if Mi-

---

[5]   The version of Crystal Reports shipped in the Exchange V4.0 Resource Kit only works for Intel systems. If you're running another type of server you'll have to copy the source files (message tracking logs and so on) to an Intel server before running Crystal Reports to extract statistics. This isn't a difficult task, just mildly frustrating. The version of Crystal Reports in the Exchange V5.0 Resource Kit supports Intel and Alpha.

crosoft could provide a fully supported and integrated system house-keeping procedure to clean up user mailboxes on a regular basis. For example, a useful procedure would remove all messages over 30 days old from specified folders such as "Sent Items" as well as deleting the messages waiting to be removed from the "Deleted Items" folder. A mailbox cleanup agent is part of the Exchange Resource Kit (see the section in Chapter 11), and this add-on provides the missing functionality, albeit at an added cost.

If limits are not in place and mailboxes are left to take care of themselves it is quite a normal state of affairs to find that the private information store grows gradually over time as messages accumulate. When people hit storage limits they are forced to exercise a form of triage over the contents of their mailboxes, deciding what should be kept and what can go. Once they've cleaned up their mailboxes users can proceed to create and send some more messages.

5.5.16   The space used to store messages

How much space within the information store is required for each message? The answer depends on the size of the cover note, the number of message attributes (addressees and so on), and the attachments. I conducted some very unscientific experiments with a selection of sample messages to see what type of storage requirement was reported for each message type. The results of my experiments are shown in Table 5.4. Be aware that your mileage will vary depending on the types of sample messages you create and the size of attachments you include with messages, but the basic results should be pretty well the same.

Table 5.4   *Storage requirements for different types of messages*

Message type and contents	Size of message reported by client
Simple text message containing 65 words sent to 1 mailbox	610 bytes
Simple text message with 1 page cover note sent to 8 mailboxes	3K
Compound message sent to 5 mailboxes with 1 page cover note, 79KB Word attachment, and 18KB Excel attachment	100K
Compound message sent to 10 mailboxes composed of 5 page cover note and 1.004MB PowerPoint attachment	1,104K

Aside from the actual content of messages, the overall size is greatly affected by the number of people messages are addressed to. Inside DIGITAL it is common to receive messages (some generated automatically) dispatched to hundreds of people. These messages are usually 50K or greater in size, and it's disappointing to open such a message to find that the actual content is no more than a couple of lines of text.

The shared message model used by Exchange means that all mailboxes on a server share a common copy of a message and its contents. The mailbox resources data reported by Exchange only indicate how much space within the information store is occupied by messages that individual users have a pointer to within their mailbox. This is quite a different figure to the amount of space within the information store that the messages for an individual user solely occupy. In other words, if a user sends a 1MB message to 10 other users, the next time you look at mailbox resources you will see that all of the users associated with the message, including the originator, have had an apparent increase of 1MB in the resources they occupy within the store. This isn't actually the case as just a single 1MB chunk is used to store the message. The commonality within the store achieved by sharing the single 1MB message with 10 other users just contributes to a form of optical illusion.

Any individual user will have a mixture of these message types within their mailbox, and it's probable that the average user will have more small messages than large. If you assume that the space reported by the Exchange client provides the more accurate of the two sets of figures, we can use them to create a rough forecast of the space likely to be occupied by any particular type of user. For example, let's take a user with the mixed set of messages as shown in Table 5.5.

Table 5.5   *A mixed message set*

Number and type of message	Average size	Total space required
300 simple messages	600 bytes	180K
100 multi-addressee 1 page messages	3K	300K
75 compound messages	100K	7,500K
25 large messages	1000K	25,000K

In this instance the total requirement is calculated as 34,980K or almost 35 megabytes. This figure contains a considerable safety margin as a good proportion of the messages are likely to be shared with other users on the same server, unless the predominant communications pattern is off-server to other sites or messaging systems. Even the simplest messages described in our model (those sent to a single addressee) start off by being shared, so the 35 megabytes of apparent storage might well be less than 20 or 25 in reality. This figure is in line with other shared-model messaging systems that support PC clients where reasonable planning rates for "average" users dictate 20–30MB for personal messages. People who send lots of mail, of course, are quite another matter and I have known some capable of easily occupying entire disks (over an extended period of one or two years) with the volume of messages they generate.

5.5.17   Commonality and the maximum size of the information store

Commonality, or the degree of sharing for messages within the shared database, is another factor to take into consideration when looking at disk space usage patterns. The level of commonality in shared message systems decreases as messages age. In other words, if a message starts out being shared by ten users over time some of those users will delete their pointer to the message, eventually reaching a point where a single user "owns" the space occupied by the message. On large systems (more than a couple of hundred users) the degree of commonality is higher than on smaller systems because there are more people to share information, leading to a reduced chance that a message needs to be sent off the server to reach its final destination. For this reason it's wise to encourage users to gain the good habit of automatically filing or deleting messages as they are read and not letting messages pile up aimlessly in a cluttered mess.

The current maximum 16GB space available in the private information store is enough to allocate 50 megabytes to over 300 users, a figure higher than the average user population for all but the very largest Exchange servers. The 16GB physical limit for an information store is very much a theoretical limit because the apparent or logical total size of messages held in the store is increased by the commonality imposed by the single message model. As explained earlier, if ten users access a single 100K message the store logically allocates and shares a megabyte between the users. The physical increase in the store is just 100K, give or take the additional bytes used to store message attributes. Thus, on a system with a high degree of message commonality the information store can apparently hold more than you might think.

The maximum size for an information store restrains the number of clients that can be supported by an individual server in a very practical sense. Administrators have to decide whether they want to support hundreds of clients with small space allocations, or provide a larger allocation to a smaller number of clients. The very practical nature of this trade-off makes some of the claims for massive numbers of supported clients for specific server configurations only valuable in a theoretical sense. There's no point in being able to connect 600–800 clients to a high-end server if they're only allowed to store 50 messages each, unless of course this is precisely the type of system you really want to operate! Personal Folders, as we'll discuss in just a little while, can be used as a workaround to the 16GB limitation, but the real long-term answer will come when Exchange is able to handle information stores much larger than those available today.

Another way of looking at the number of clients that can be supported by a system is to consider the assertion that the majority of computers running Windows NT today have far less than 16GB of disk storage in total, let alone 16GB to give over to the Information Store. If this is true, and I have seen no evidence to the contrary, then available hardware resources will be the first limit to overcome. Another factor that must be considered is that after a server has been in use for some time a set of power users might each occupy a gigabyte or more of disk space, considerably limiting the user population that can be supported by that server. There's a common answer to all these issues: install another server in the Exchange site and transfer some of the users to the new server.

It's been interesting to see just how quickly people can fill a store and approach the limit. Servers that support communities migrating from other mail systems are more affected than those used by people who start from scratch. The reason for this is simple. When you migrate data (old messages) it is loaded and stored in user mailboxes in the private information store. Afterwards the migrated data is like a stone around the neck of the store. It seldom reduces in size quickly (how many users do you know to clean out old messages on a regular basis?) and reduces the space available for new messages, forcing the store towards the 16GB limit much faster than if the store held no migrated data. Compacting the store with the EDBUTIL utility (see the discussion from page 305 onwards) makes little difference because the old information is so static, so all the system administrator can do is look at a store racing towards the limit. The largest servers in operation already have stores in the 10–14GB range, so someday soon the race to the finishing post will stop.

No one quite knows what will happen when an information store reaches 16GB. Based on knowledge of how things happen when disk space is exhausted on the drive holding the store or transaction logs, it is safe to assume that the information store service will attempt to conduct an orderly shutdown. Users will be logged off as the store winds down. Transactions in memory that have not been committed to the store will be written into transaction logs and stay there until the store can be restarted. The store will have to be shrunk before the service can restart, so the immediate course of action is to run EDBUTIL. Before this can happen you have to find enough disk space to create the temporary database created during the compaction process. Finding a spare 16GB is not always easy!

As soon as EDBUTIL is finished a smaller store should be available. At this stage the information store service can be restarted and all the outstanding transactions will be committed. Users can access their mailboxes, but before this happens you should transfer a number of users (a hundred or so for a start) to another server in the site to reduce the chances that the store will hit the limit again in the near future. If possible, transfer the mailboxes to a brand new server, otherwise select the server in the site with the largest amount of free space to grow into.

Microsoft has publicly committed that the maximum size will be increased up to a limit of 16TB in a version of Exchange after V5.0. 16TB is a size that will offer enough space for even the most voracious of user communities. The sheer amount of disk space that a 16TB store makes possible—remember that the same limit will apply to the private, public, and directory stores—will present some new challenges for system administrators. You'll be able to allocate hundreds of megabytes to each of hundreds or thousands of users, but how will their backup devices and media be able to cope with such large stores? What form of disk farms will have to be put together to support such a monstrous store? Because it will only be the very largest servers that will want to use such large stores, resilience and robustness will be absolute pre-requisites, so the basic disk space will need to be supplemented by RAID arrays. The issues pile up the more I think about the challenge of managing 16TB files. Thankfully that's another day's work!

5.6   Managing the Public Information Store

Users who have been granted permission to create, write to, or edit information held in public folders control the contents of the Public Information Store, the repository for all public folders on a server. The public information store shares the same 16GB physical limit per server as the private information store, but again this is more than enough space for all but the most demanding or retentive installation. Indeed, a server's available disk space is likely to be exhausted before you ever approach the theoretical limit for the store.

Public folders are always created in the public information store on the home server of the user's mailbox who creates the new folder.

5.6.1   Issues to consider in planning public folders

Among the issues to consider when planning the implementation of the Public Information Store you should:

- Pay attention to the information that's being placed into public folders. Public folders should not be used as a dumping ground for all and sundry.

- Restrict the permission to create top level folders in the public folder hierarchy to a limited group of users. It's a recipe for confused storage if everyone is allowed to create folders at the top of the hierarchy. Top level folders represent the entry point to the public folder hierarchy so it's essential that a well-designed structure be instituted at this point. Users who have the permission to create top level folders are able to allocate permissions on the folders they create. In this respect, users with permissions to create top level folders can be regarded as guardians or administrators of the Public Information Store.

- Ensure that data is removed from public folders as soon as it is no longer valuable. You can arrange for data in public folders to expire after a set period, and this is a convenient feature where data held in certain folders has a regular and predictable life. However, it would be difficult to impose expiration times on public folders used by people as a point of reference. For instance, it is inappropriate to store documents describing a company's personnel policies and procedures in a public folder with a 60-day expiry. It is very appropriate to set a 60-day expiration limit on a public folder that stores bulletins relating to training courses or other events with a readily determinable life-span.

If you have lots of information that must be made available in public folders you might consider:

- Establishing a server to use as host for a set of "archive" public folders. Data can be transferred from the "live" set of folders to the archive server after a set period, for instance, every month, perhaps using some automated rules. The traffic to a set of archive public folders should be lighter than its live counterpart so you can factor this into network traffic planning.

- Splitting public folders over a set of servers rather than one specific server. Remember to ensure that everyone who needs access to the public folders has good network links. If you are moving public folders from one server to another you should also make sure that any affinities are transferred as well.

5.6.2   Public folder favorites

From a user perspective having hundreds, perhaps thousands, of public folders to choose from represents a rich vein of knowledge whose contents may hold the answers to many questions. But so much data is hard to track and it's easy to miss important items that are added to a public folder used for particular purposes, such as a folder used for project reports or new sales opportunities. As systems age the public folder hierarchy tends to become less structured and organized unless great attention is paid to the elimination of folders no longer required and careful control maintained on the creation of new folders for possibly unneeded purposes. Duplication and wholesale proliferation of folders always happens if control is not applied, leading to a situation where public folder anarchy exists and information becomes impossible to find. The fact that the public folder hierarchy is automatically replicated to all servers within an organization means that control must only lapse on one server before unwanted folders are created and shown to users. It's hard to stop the system administrator of any individual server losing control, but the designers of Exchange have helped to get around the potential information overload by establishing the concept of "Favorite" public folders.

Each user maintains a unique list of favorite public folders. A public folder is included in a user's list by marking it with the client's "File.Add to Favorites" option. When a public folder is marked in this way Exchange knows that it must monitor the contents of the public folder for any new items that are added. New items are indicated by the maintenance of a folder unread count displayed in the same way as the presence of new messages are indicated for the Inbox folder (see Figure 5.26) A quick visual scan of the Favorites section shows any folder where something new is stored.

Figure 5.26
Public folder favorites

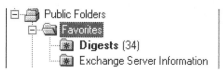

Public folder favorites is a very useful concept. The more folders are added, the more valuable the concept becomes, so users should be encouraged to use favorites to organize their own hierarchy of selected folders from the time they begin using Exchange.

5.6.3   Setting time expiration limits

Public folders experience different usage characteristics to private folders. Consider the following points:

- Folders are often created for a specific purpose and receive considerable activity for a period of time. For example, a folder might be created to hold documents relating to a particular project. While the project is active the folder is in daily use, but once the project finishes a danger exists that the folder loses relevance but remains in situ, clogging the store up with unwanted material.

- Larger items tend to be stored in public folders. Messages flow in and out of private folders, and messages are usually quite small in comparison to the documents and other items placed in public folders. Thus, a small number of items can occupy a considerable amount of space within the store.

- Public folders may be maintained by a number of different people. Not all of the maintainers will be efficient when it comes to controlling the content of "their" folders. Some folders will be dynamic and only contain up-to-date information. Others will be stagnant and hold data that was valuable some time ago but is totally unnecessary today.

Figure 5.27 Age limits imposed on specific public folders

Apart from a steadily growing demand for disk space, the larger the public information store, the slower maintenance operations like backups will be. You should therefore consider whether age limits should be placed on any or every public folder. Age limits dictate how long material will be retained in a public folder. Once an item exceeds the age limit the system attendant process automatically removes it, normally once a day.

By default there is no age limit applied for public folders. You can specify an age limit that applies to all folders created in a public information store or set specific age limits on certain folders. For example, if you have a public folder used to distribute training announcements it's probable that you won't want to keep announcements that are more than sixty days old. Age limits can also be set on replicas of foreign public folders maintained in a store. The precedence rule is as follows:

1. If set, the limit on a folder is complied with.

2. If a general age limit is set for all public folders in a public information store it is applied to remaining folders.

3. If no limits are in place within a public information store but an age limit applies for all replicas of a public folder, that limit will be applied, but only for the folder in question.

Setting a general age limit for new public folders is a good idea. Try 90 or 120 days as a starting point. If no one complains then this limit can remain as a default value. It will take some time before the default limit can take effect so in the interim you can analyze the public folders that are actually in use to try and determine what content is actually stored and how long it needs to be kept. The next stage is then to decide whether specific age limits need to be set on certain folders. Before you set any limits you should consult with the folder's owner as they may understand the effect of the limit on the folder's contents better than you.

5.6.4 Displaying the space allocated to public folders

A quick glance at the \MDBDATA directory reveals the physical size of the Public Information Store, but knowing what's actually occupying the space is more important. It's a good idea therefore to browse through the display generated by the Public Folder Resources property page (Figure 5.28) to see just where all the space is being used.

If you've set time expiration limits on some or all public folders the resources used will change all the time. The folders you need to pay attention to are those that consistently increase in terms of number of items and the space occupied. You should try to determine why the folder keeps on growing and see whether you can restrict the growth in any way. Sometimes the answer is simple. For example, the folder is used as a repository for documentation belonging to an ongoing project. You'd expect that this folder would grow as the project progresses and then can be cleaned out after the project finishes. Folders assigned to hold information about products can be expected to occupy a lot of space (graphics occupy much more space than plain text), but perhaps only hold a relatively few items.

Figure 5.28
*Displaying
resources used
by public folders*

It is good system management practice to know what's going on in a server. Reviewing the number of items in public folders and the space they occupy gives you essential system management data and helps you tune your system more effectively. Once you know more about the contents of public folders than indicated by just the raw size of the information store you can make decisions at the folder level. For instance, public folders experiencing lots of activity should be located on servers capable of handling the traffic whereas folders storing very large items should be allocated to servers with lots of free disk space.

5.6.5   Virus checking

Any Exchange message can include an embedded object. Embedded executables are an obvious source of potential contamination from viruses, whether included in messages received from outside the organization or those perhaps unwittingly passed on by people working inside. Most users are now aware of the problems posed by executable-based viruses and system administrators have taken steps to address the problem. For example, some sites disable floppy drives while most have implemented some sort of automatic virus checking for system memory and .EXE and .DLL files whenever PCs are booted.

The first document-transmitted virus appeared in the Word for Windows "Prank" macro in 1995. Recognizable by the presence of the "Payload" macro, the virus worked by inserting itself into NOR-MAL.DOT, the default Word for Windows document template. The virus is activated and infects a PC whenever a document containing its macros is opened. The virus is irritating but harmless, and easy to clean up. All it ever did was display a dialog box, but so much more damage could have been wreaked if the virus's author had included some more malevolent instructions. Word for Windows' macro language, Word-Basic, is capable of including calls to Windows API functions and file operations which can, in turn, inflict grave damage on user files. For instance, it's easy to write a macro that will automatically delete all sorts of important system files whenever the macro is invoked.

Many Windows products have their own macro language, and the majority of these languages are already pretty capable of making the same type of damaging system calls. Exactly the same effect as the "Prank" macro could be created with an Excel macro written in Visual Basic for Applications, or in a WordPerfect for Windows macro. Macro languages are being improved all the time. They're also being made easier, so vicious macros can be written without too much programming expertise. These developments make system administrators nervous because users don't seem to exercise the same level of care and attention when they deal with documents or spreadsheets. The lack of care when opening documents is perhaps natural because so many documents flow around a messaging system, but it means that viruses created as document macros spread rapidly once they've been introduced into an installation. As such document viruses are a major challenge for messaging system administrators, especially so in the case of systems like Exchange which place a high degree of importance in information sharing through distributed document repositories such as public folders.

What can you do to defeat the best efforts of document virus creators? There are three basic approaches:

1. **PC-centric.** Most of the commercial virus checking packages now available have been updated to include checks for known document viruses. In general, checking is performed whenever a document is opened. This approach is effective providing the virus checker is installed and used on every PC. It's essential that the virus checker is kept up to date to ensure that new viruses can be detected soon after they are generally encountered, and arrangements must be made to distribute new releases of the virus checker to all PCs, including notebooks. Traditional PC-based virus checkers focus on DOS files, so they're not much good in catching infected files stored in a PST, OST, or Exchange mailbox, although the virus checkers will be able to deal with infected files if a scan is made before files are imported into an Exchange container. The best option is to select a virus checker that is able to

deal with Exchange data structures as well as traditional DOS devices and file shares. One such example is Thunderbyte for Exchange[6].

2. **Server-centric.** Some virus checkers can be run on a server to scan all the documents held in a file system or electronic file cabinet. In the case of Exchange you need a virus checker that understands the internals of the public and private information stores, as otherwise it won't be able to check documents stored therein. Checking documents held in user directories is fine, but the real danger exists from documents that are stored and distributed via the messaging system. The first commercial server-based virus checker to support Exchange (Cheyenne Anti-Virus Agent for Microsoft Exchange Server[7]) appeared in October 1996. The Anti-Virus Agent works with Cheyenne's InocuLAN 4 for Windows NT to detect and cure viruses in documents attached to Exchange messages. The Agent is implemented as a Windows NT service and works in real-time to detect and cure infected files attached to messages as they enter an Exchange server (from all sources). ScanMail for Microsoft Exchange is another interesting product (from Trend Micro Inc[8].) which takes much the same approach to solving the problem by scanning for viruses as they arrive on an Exchange server.

3. **Firewall-centric.** This approach uses a virus checker to check the contents of SMTP messages as they arrive into a messaging environment. MIMESweeper from Integralis[9] is a good example of the type. While it's true that the majority of viruses will arise from external sources, especially the Internet, only scanning SMTP messages will ignore messages arriving from other sources. For example, messages delivered from other X.400 MTAs, or even messages generated by internal Exchange users who have (unwittingly) attached a document containing a virus.

Using a combination of the approaches described above provides a more resilient solution. The combination of server- and firewall- based checking is a good team, and should catch the vast majority of any viruses that come into view. There's lots of activity in this area and I expect other products to appear. Before making any choice you should take the time to search the Web to see if you can find better options to pursue. One mistake with a virus can be very expensive. Disinfecting a

[6]   See http://www.thunderbyte.com
[7]   See http://www.cheyenne.com
[8]   See http://www.antivirus.com
[9]   See http://www.integralis.com

system, especially a large networked system, will take a lot of time and effort and it's probable that the system will be unavailable to users while the viruses are being eliminated. Be proactive and ensure that your system is protected!

5.6.6   Access rights for public folders

Roles, a collection of permissions defining the actions a user may perform on a folder and its contents, are used to control personal access to a public folder. Apart from "Owner," the role automatically given to the user who actually creates a new public folder, the default role is called "Author." A user holding the "Author" role is allowed to place new items in the public folder and edit items that they have put into the folder. Exchange comes with a number of predefined roles to enable you to get up and running with minimum effort and not worry about having to sit down and define roles and what each role can and cannot do. The default roles are shown in Table 5.6.

Table 5.6   *Default Roles for Public Folders*

Role Name	Allocated to	Rights
Owner	User who creates a public folder	All, including control over permissions allocated to other users
Author	Default role allocated to other users	Add new items to the folder and edit items they have provided
Publishing Author	People who will provide information to the folder and use the folder as a work area	Able to process own work and create sub-folders
Editor	User who will work on information posted into the folder by others	Edit, read, and delete all information
Non-editing Editor	User who will review work posted into the folder by others	Read and delete all contributions
Publishing Editor	Second highest level (after user) of control over the folder	Edit, read, and delete all contributions Able to create sub-folders
Reviewer	People who you want to read but not interact with folder contents	Read only access
Contributor	People who you want to provide content to folders and forget about it afterwards. On the surface, a rather strange role.	Write only access

If you don't like the rights defined in the default roles you can create your own.

Figure 5.29
*Setting
permissions
on a folder*

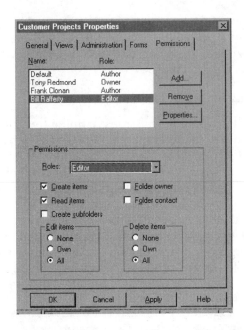

Roles are changed or allocated to users by selecting a public folder and viewing its properties. The Permissions tab allows you to add to or remove users from the list of people who have rights over the folder (see Figure 5.29). Roles can be allocated to individual mailboxes or distribution lists. Using a distribution list is a convenient way of allocating the same role to a large group of people in a single operation. It's important to understand that roles allocated to individuals supersede roles gained through membership in a distribution list. The same dialog allows you to define a new role, should the need exist.

Owners of public folders assume certain responsibilities. Apart from being able to control the access and permissions other users enjoy on a public folder, owners are the only people who are entitled to create rules via the Folder Assistant. Just like the Inbox Assistant, the Folder Assistant is a rules-based agent that monitors objects placed in folders. If the objects meet the criteria stated in a rule the Folder Assistant will swing into action and execute whatever action is required. For instance, a public folder is created to accept a feed from an Internet Newsgroup. A rule might be created to monitor new objects as they arrive and reject anything that does not originate from the Newsgroup.

Remember our discussion about moving users from one server to another within a site? When users are moved all their private folders held within the Private Information Store are automatically moved from the source to the target server. However, any public folders that were created by the users before they are moved are retained on the original server. Any new public folders created after the move is complete will be created on the new server, but if a sub-folder is created for one of the public folders on the original server, it too will be stored on that server. This is quite logical when you think about it, but some people expect that all public folders will be transferred along with a user's private folders.

5.6.7   Using public folders to reduce messaging activity

People will always have the temptation to circulate large files by attaching them to messages. Good examples of what I mean are documents under review by a committee, when a document might go through several review cycles before eventually being approved. Attaching the file to a message is quick and easy and makes sure that everyone the sender wants to see the particular file receives a copy. Whether or not the recipient ever looks at their copy is quite another matter.

While undeniably easy to use, sending large files as attachments does not make the most effective use of the functionality available to users. It is much more efficient and reduces the chance of redundant information being stored in many places throughout the network to place a copy of whatever file needs to be circulated in a public folder. A short message can then be sent to act as a reminder to the circulation list that the file awaits their attention.

Public folders are an obvious source of shared information, but they're not the only one. If your Windows NT environment is designed in such a way as to allow general access to files no matter where they are located within the network you can even include a shortcut to a file, or even a program or installation kit within a message. And of course, Exchange supports embedded URLs to allow speedy access to specific Web pages.

After receiving messages containing pointers to public folders, shortcuts, or Web pages people can then go and retrieve the information as they wish. In the case of public folders, if the folder allows write access they can even make their contributions by directly annotating the document in place so that everyone can see the comments as they are made. Beware of clashes occurring if two or more users attempt to update the document in the shared folder at the same time.

Using a public folder to replace large attachments won't always be possible, and it requires people to make decisions about the method to be used to distribute information to others. Users coming from other mail systems where public folders or similar mechanisms weren't available may not take kindly to the idea at all. But even if you can convince some groups within the user community to pay attention to the way they distribute and share information it will be a contribution towards increased system effectiveness. Users learn from each other (perhaps by a process of osmosis), and if one group sees that there's a better way to do something the new method will spread, slowly at first, but soon to become common practice.

5.6.8   Using public folders for collaborative authoring

Public folders make it easy to distribute any type of information among Exchange servers. Collaborative authoring, the collective creation of objects, chiefly documents, depends on easy access to the item being created by all contributing authors. Systems designed to facilitate and control the steps involved in the collaborative authoring process are sold under the label "Document Management Systems." Can Exchange fill this role?

The answer is a qualified "yes." Exchange certainly scores highly on its abilities to

- Organize information in a structured manner within the public folder hierarchy

- Control access to information held in public folders through permissions, and to allow different people to fulfill different roles during the creation and editing of documents

- Distribute initial documents and changes applied thereafter to interested parties in a seamless manner through folder replication.

Problems lie in the way Exchange allows multiple users with write or edit permission to concurrently change documents stored in public folders. The underlying reason why the problem exists is that Exchange has not implemented any system of document check-in or check-out. In other words, a user cannot reserve a document for exclusive write access while they make changes to the content, and then automatically release or cancel their reservation once the edit is complete. Consider the following scenario:

1. User1 selects a document in a public folder and begins an edit session.

2. User2, logged into the same server, selects the same document and also starts an edit session.

3. User1 completes the changes they wish to make and exits the editor. Exchange saves the changes back into the public folder.

4. User2 completes their changes and exits the editor. Exchange flags that the document was changed since User2 began working with it and so cannot be changed again (see Figure 5.30). User2's changes are then discarded and cannot be applied to the item. The work is not actually removed from the system as User2 can save the item as a file and then import it back into the public folder. However, this is a two stage manual process.

Figure 5.30
Error saving a document

Clearly no user will be happy with such a situation. Three separate problems have been encountered. First, no warning was given to User2 that User1 was already working on the same document. Second, no indication is ever given as to which user actually has a document open or was responsible for making the last changes applied to the document. The original author's name is always shown and manipulating the document's properties cannot change it.

Given that these problems exist is there any way that they can be avoided to enable Exchange to be used as a collaborative document authoring system? The answer again is a qualified "yes," but achieving a satisfactory status requires users to be disciplined about how changes are applied to documents in public folders because a manual system for change control needs to be established and implemented. Two methods come to mind:

1. All changes to documents are made after a copy is made through a drag and drop operation to a DOS directory. Changed documents are inserted as new objects when they are ready. The advantages of this method are that the last author name can be seen and that changes are never discarded.

2. All changes to documents are made after they are moved to a special "Work" sub-folder. The same properties will be retained for documents, but it's immediately obvious that someone is working on a document if it is in the "Work" folder.

Given a little thought, many variations on these themes can be constructed. As no document change history is made available by Exchange you might like to consider creating a note in each folder that could be updated by users as they make changes.

5.6.9   Conflicts arising from distributed updates

All manners of conflicts can potentially arise when multiple users scattered around a network attempt to change a document. The only real way to avoid conflicts is to lock documents against changes by not allowing anyone except a specified group of users to have permission to edit objects held in a public folder. Others can read and comment, but nothing can be changed. This enforces a simple rule that the author (or their nominees) is the only person permitted to make changes to a document. In this scenario people who want to suggest changes have to mail them back to the author who then takes charge of assessing the proposed change and eventually integrating it into the document. This is a reasonable way of working in many cases, but not always.

Exchange recognizes that instances will occur when multiple concurrent changes are made to objects distributed across multiple instances of folders. As we've seen, a mechanism is in place to intercept changes made to objects held in public folders before changes are finally applied.

Let's go through a fairly common scenario. Two users located in two different sites begin an edit on a document stored in a public folder. It doesn't matter which user starts first, just that both are engaged in edits at the same time. When both are finished they exit from the editor, and all appears to be successful as the edited object is applied to the local copy of the public folder. Thus, if each user were to immediately start another edit they'd see the changes they made last time around. Problems only appear once the replication engine has had time to kick into gear and communicate with the home server for the folder.

Changes to objects stored in public folders are posted back to the home server according to the replication schedule for the folder. In most instances replication occurs every fifteen minutes, although the actual elapsed time before the effect of replication is seen can be longer than this if the home server is unavailable for some reason or a long message queue needs to be serviced before the replication message is processed.

As soon as the home folder server detects that multiple changes have been made it begins a consultation process with the contributing authors to attempt to resolve the conflict. In effect the computer is throwing up its hands at the illogical behavior of humans and sending the problem back to the humans to have them sort it out. Computers, of course, are extremely logical and would never be guilty of attempting to make multiple concurrent updates to a single object. At least, not to something like a Word for Windows document which was never designed to support multiple concurrent updates!

Figure 5.31
*Message
notifying that a
conflict exists*

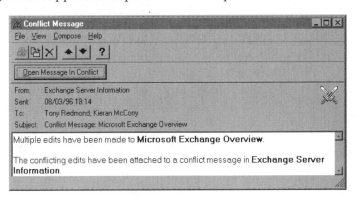

Special messages are generated and dispatched to all of the users who have attempted to make a change to the object, plus anyone who is registered as having "Owner" permission on the folder. Figure 5.31 illustrates an example message sent to two users (Tony Redmond and Kieran McCorry) who attempted to make a change to a document called "Microsoft Exchange Overview" in the "Exchange Server Information" folder. The crossed-swords icon is used to provide a visual indicator for conflict messages when viewed in the Inbox folder.

Figure 5.32
*Instructions
given to resolve
a conflict*

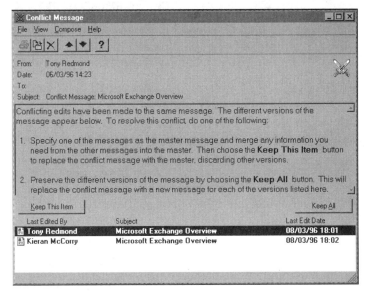

When a user receives a conflict message the natural reaction is to go to the relevant public folder and see what's happened. If the user double-clicks on the object in conflict Exchange displays a dialog giving details of the conflicting changes and offering the user a choice of what to do next (Figure 5.32).

The options are:

- *Keep this item*. This means that the user has selected one of the changed objects that have provoked the conflict and now wishes to treat this object as the definitive version. All other changes are discarded. The authors who contributed the other versions should be contacted and their changes, if available, merged manually into the new definitive version.

- *Keep all items*. This is the more author-friendly version. It means that all of the versions offered for consideration are kept, each as a separate object stored in the public folder. Later on, if desired, the separate items can be reviewed and their content drawn together into a single version.

If you allow distributed users to contribute to documents in a replicated environment you must set ground rules to cater for instances when conflicts occur, or better still, establish a method for working which avoids conflicts. Computers can resolve problems that are stated in a logical sense, but they have no chance in the resolution of different thoughts and ideas arriving in from multiple users.

5.6.10   Using Exchange as a document management system

Given the issues around conflicts and the problems associated with multiple concurrent edits can Exchange be used as a document management system? The characteristics of a document management system include:

- A structured document repository
- Access controls to define who can do what with the objects stored in the repository
- Object check-in and check-out facilities
- Object audit trails
- A flexible high-speed search engine capable of scanning large quantities of information to identify objects meeting user-specified criteria.

Exchange exhibits the first two characteristics in a very positive manner. The last three points are not currently met by the standard Exchange software, although a combination of third party offerings may be enough to establish the basis for a document management system.

As we've discussed, an object check-in and check-out facility can be emulated through permissions and user discipline. It's harder to implement audit controls, something to track who did what to a document, for what reason, and when. You could implement a log in each folder and require users to complete it, but this depends on users complying with the request.

What is sure is that Exchange public folders can act as a more than adequate replacement for the shared directories on file servers that are used by many companies as document repositories. Ever since the first NetWare file servers arrived on the market people have used file services to allow users to share documents together. It's not just NetWare now. Companies use Windows NT, DIGITAL PATHWORKS, and other products too. All these systems allow people to share information, but they are more restrictive than public folders.

High-end document management or text retrieval features can be incorporated into Exchange through third party products such as Fulcrum Find!, KeyFile, PC DOCS, or Verity's Search97 product[10]. In terms of text retrieval the usual approach is not to ever search through the physical contents of public folders. Instead, background processes periodically scan public folders and construct an index that can then be searched against. Much greater flexibility and power is gained when searching, but at a cost of an additional load on the server (to build the indexes and run the search engine). There is also a danger that a relevant object might not be located because it has not been indexed since it was added to the public information store.

5.7   System Backups

A very wise person once said that an important difference between electronic mail and word processing applications was that when a word processor stopped working its effect was normally confined to a single user and perhaps a small quantity of documents, but when an electronic mail system collapses everyone is affected and normally it's the people at the top who notice fastest (and complain quickest).

Electronic mail systems depend on many different hardware and software components to keep everything going. If any element fails to operate in the required manner data corruption can occur. If the hardware suffers a catastrophic failure, or the site where the computers are located is afflicted by some disaster, you'll need to know the steps nec-

[10] Check the latest third party product list as new products are added all the time.

essary to get your users back on-line as quickly as possible. In all these instances system backups are a prerequisite.

Backups, in their purest sense, are snapshots of a system's state at a certain point in time. All of the data available to the system should exist in the backup and should be restorable to exactly the same state if required. Backups can be written out to many different forms of magnetic or other media, although the most common type is some form of high-density magnetic tape.

The standard backup utility (NTBACKUP.EXE) provided with Windows NT V3.51 is not suitable for taking backups of an Exchange server due to the nature of the complex connections between the information stores and the transaction logs (see the discussion starting on page 239). When Exchange is installed the standard Windows NT backup utility is replaced with an enhanced version. The enhancements made to NTBACKUP.EXE are:

- Support for the transactional nature of the Exchange information and directory stores. In particular, the capacity to deal with the fact that the contents of the stores are represented by database files, transaction logs, and transactions that might still be queued in memory.

- Ability to perform on-line backups. In other words, to copy the information and directory stores to tape without having to shut down Exchange services. Users continue to work during backups.

- Extension of the NTBACKUP.EXE user interface to allow system administrators to select which sites and servers they wish to backup or restore.

Figure 5.33
Selecting a server from an organization before backing it up

Figure 5.33 shows an Exchange organization displayed in the Backup utility's window. The system administrator can select the server or servers they wish to backup, and whether or not the directory or information store, or both, should be processed. The concept of single seat administration means that it is possible to conduct all backups and restore operations from a single server. However, the practical network limitations encountered when shipping many gigabytes of information over the network to a single server during backup operations means that you'll probably want to run backup from a server in each site, or even on each server.

Don't make the mistake of introducing a third party extension to your system that conflicts with the requirements of Exchange. And don't fall into the trap of retro-fitting older software, such as a Windows NT service pack (patch kit), which might over-write the change to enable the Windows NT Backup utility to support on-line backups of the Exchange information and directory stores.

5.7.1   Creating a backup strategy

Although Exchange does an excellent and almost automatic job of keeping its databases in shape, contributing to a high system availability level for users, hardware failures can and will occur. And when it's your turn to experience a hardware failure on the server you'll be glad that backups exist.

System failures come in three broad categories.

- Disk failure.

- Other non-critical system component failure. For example, the monitor for the server develops a fault.

- Critical system component failure. For example, the motherboard or other associated component experiences a fault that cannot be quickly rectified.

Any failure situation requires some fast but calm thinking in order to make the correct decisions to get everything up on-line again. If the system cannot be brought back up, can you substitute another similar system and restore application data? If it's a particular system component, can it be replaced or can the system configuration be altered to work around the problem? Having backups around won't replace making the right decision, but they're a great safety net.

The MTBF (Mean Time Between Failure) rate for hard disks is improving all the time. This doesn't mean that you will never experience a hard disk failure, but it does mean that you are less likely to have one over any particular period of time. A high MTBF is no guarantee that the disk won't fail tomorrow, so the challenge for system administrators is to have a plan to handle the problem when it arises.

Without RAID-compliant disks, if something does go wrong with a disk you'll have to stop operations and fix the problem or swap in a new drive. Once the hardware problem is fixed you'll have to restore the data, and of course this simple statement assumes that you have copies of all the application files that were stored on the faulty drive, and possess the capability to move the data onto the new drive. Backups come into their own here!

Having the capability to take on-line backups is one thing. Making the backups is quite another and there is a temptation to leave backups to the side and concentrate on more interesting work. This is a short-term and dangerous attitude. Nightly backups of the information and directory stores taken in tandem with full weekly backups of the server taken as a whole (in other words, including Windows NT, all the other applications, as well as the Exchange server files) must be taken if any guarantee as to the integrity of the messaging system is to be given to users.

Figure 5.34 *A successful backup*

The database-centric nature of Exchange poses a particular challenge for restore operations. There is no getting away from the fact that if a restore is necessary it's going to take much longer than you may realize. The length of time required to backup and restore databases from a production Exchange server may come as a surprise to some. It's easy to forget just how long it takes to move data to backup media. The private and public information stores both have the capacity to expand quickly, so your backup times will grow in proportion. After a server has been in production for a number of months you might find that it's time to consider looking for faster or higher capacity media to help reduce backup times. Remember too that it's not just

Exchange data that must be backed up. Windows NT, user files, and other application data all contribute to the amount of data and length of backup operations.

It is also important that the correct levels of service packs are applied to Windows NT and Exchange before commencing any restore operation. The database structure has changed a number of times as Exchange evolved from V4.0 through service packs to Exchange V5.0, and you cannot restore a database from a backup taken with a higher software revision level. In other words, don't expect to be able to restore a backup taken with Exchange V4.0 SP3 to a server running Exchange V4.0 SP2. This rule does not hold true for all combinations of service packs and versions, but there's enough truth in it to make a strong recommendation that backups should be restored to servers running identical software versions.

All of the factors discussed here must be accounted for in the operational procedures you employ at your installation. Consider this question: how long will it take to restore one gigabyte of data from your backup media using the backup software you employ? Now, how long will it take to restore three gigabytes, or maybe ten gigabytes, or how about a full-blown sixteen-gigabyte private information store? And what about the public information store? And the directory store? And all the other applications you may want to run?

In most circumstances, even when suitable hardware is waiting to be hot-swapped into your production environment the answer is counted in hours. Even when the restore is complete you may have other work to do before Exchange is available for use again. For instance, messages and other items waiting in the transaction logs may have to be written into the private and public information stores. Exchange does this automatically, but applying masses of transactions at one time delays the startup operation. Users will be yelling at you to get the system back on-line as quickly as possible, so it's going to be a time when stress levels are rising, which just adds to the piquant nature of the task.

I'm not trying to scare you about restores. Instead, I'm trying to point out an essential fact of system management life. You must be prepared and able to conduct a well-planned restore of essential data in order to be successful. No one wants to explain to a CIO why the messaging system was unavailable for one or two days while staff fumbled their way through a restore. We'll discuss restores a little more later on in this chapter, but remember to secure your job continuation program by being prepared ahead of time.

Knowing how to properly use and safeguard backup media is an important part of a backup strategy. Think of the following questions: After the backups are performed how will the media be moved to a secure location? Is the secure location somewhere local or remote? When will the tapes or other media be used for backup purposes again? How can the backups be recovered quickly if needed?

5.7.2 Taking backups

The simplest way to perform a backup is to double-click on the NT-BACKUP icon and start things off, as illustrated in Figure 5.35. Easy as this is to do it's often inconvenient to take backups interactively. Backups should be taken on a regular basis and you're not always going to be around to start things off.

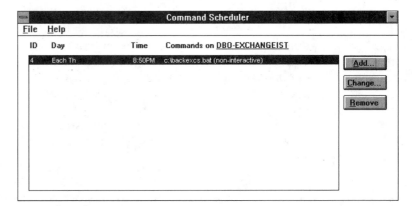

Figure 5.35
Scheduling a daily backup with the WINAT utility

WINAT.EXE (see Figure 5.35) is one of the utilities available on the Windows NT Resource Kit. WINAT provides a GUI for the standard Windows NT AT.EXE (command line scheduler) utility and allows you to schedule tasks for execution in the background without human intervention. WINAT is similar to many other third party scheduling programs that are available. These programs often have extended feature sets that ease the scheduling process, but WINAT provides enough functionality to get the job done in many cases. However, as we'll see later on, third party backup utilities come with significantly better scheduling capabilities that become very important for corporate installations.

WINAT schedules batch files (.BAT files) to execute at specified times. Before you can use WINAT you'll need to write a simple batch file and create the commands to tell NTBACKUP.EXE what components should be backed up. You can take both on-line and off-line backups. On-line backups are those taken with all Exchange services active. Off-line backups are taken after all Exchange services have been stopped. Exchange has been designed to fully support on-line backups, so there's no reason why you shouldn't plan to take on-line backups all the time. Off-line backups permit system registry data relating to the Exchange configuration to be included in the backup. As such, an off-line backup is a more accurate and complete picture of an Exchange server, albeit one taken at the expense of stopping all services beforehand.

The complete set of parameters for NTBACKUP is described in Chapter 15 of the Exchange Administrator's Guide. A two-line batch file to take a backup of the information and directory stores on the DBO-EXCHANGEIST server is shown below:

```
NTBACKUP backup DS \\DBO-EXCHANGEIST IS \\DBO-EXCHANGEIST /v /d "On-line backup of
DBO-EXCHANGEIST" /t normal /l
Exit
```

Coding up the commands to stop and start Exchange services before and after an off-line backup is easy. You need to include a NET STOP command for each Exchange service before NTBACKUP is invoked, and a matching NET START command for each service afterwards. For example:

```
REM Stop the Internet Mail Service
NET STOP MsExchangeIMC
REM Stop the Information Store
NET STOP MsExchangeIS
NTBACKUP backup C:\ D:\ E:\ /v/d "Off-line backup for DBO-EXCHANGEIST" /b
REM Start things up again
NET START MsExchangeIS
```

As you can see, there are differences in the NTBACKUP commands used for on-line and off-line backups. On-line backups specify whether the information or directory store, or both, should be backed up whereas off-line backups ignore the stores and concentrate on backing up the files contained on specified disks (C:, D:, and E: in the example shown above).

5.7.3 How on-line backups process Exchange databases

The Jet database engine used by Exchange allows on-line backup with users connected and actively using the information and directory stores. It follows that transactions can take place during the backup process, for example when users create and send messages. During on-line backup processes a number of special-purpose files known as patch files are used by Exchange to track these transactions.

A separate patch file can be created for each store. The files are called:

- PRIV.PAT—Private Information Store Patch File
- PUB.PAT—Public Information Store Patch File
- DIR.PAT—Directory Store Patch File

The process of backing up an Exchange database follows these steps:

1. A patch file is created for the database. For example, PUB.PAT.
2. The current transaction log is disabled and prevented from accepting new transactions (this only happens with the private and public information stores).
3. The database and log files are written to the backup media. During this time any transactions written from memory are directed to the patch file.
4. The block on the current transaction log is removed to allow it to accept transactions from memory again.
5. The contents of the patch file are written to the current transaction log.
6. The patch file is written to the backup save set.
7. The patch file is deleted.
8. The next database to be backed up is selected.
9. After all databases have been backed up all the transaction logs containing data now fully written and checkpointed in the database are deleted.

Patch files are created in the \MDBDATA directory. You will only be able to see them during a backup process.

5.7.4   Restoring an Exchange server

Having backup tapes taken on a regular basis and then carefully stored away is clearly a great step towards assuring data security, but having the ability to restore data from the backup tapes is an equally important part of the overall equation.

Some sort of hardware failure is the most common reason why a restore is required. It's also possible for the information or directory stores to be corrupted in some manner, perhaps as a side effect of an intermittent hardware fault. In this case, the utilities ISINTEG (see page 301) or EDBUTIL (see page 305) may be able to rectify the problem and allow normal processing to continue. If not, a restore is required. In all cases where database corruption has occurred it's a good idea to have the hardware checked out to eliminate it as a potential underlying cause. There is no point in restoring a backup onto a server where a problem lurks deep in the hardware.

Let's assume that a hardware failure has happened. You can't use the server where the failure occurred. What steps need to be taken to get a substitute server up and running? Here's an outline checklist:

1. Create a new server with a hardware configuration as close as possible to the original computer. This includes disks, tape drive, memory, and any special devices.

2. Make sure that the correct version of Windows NT (complete with any required service packs) is installed.

3. Connect the new server into the domain structure. The substitute system should have the same name as the failed system. The substitute should assume the same role in the domain structure. In other words, if the failed system was a Backup Domain Controller (BDC) the substitute should become a BDC. If it was a simple server with no role in user authentication that's fine too. The most complex situation is where the failed system was the PDC (see next page).

4. Install Exchange Server on the substitute. Use the same site and organization name as the failed system. Use the same Exchange service account. If joining an existing site use SETUP /R to install Exchange. The /R switch tells Exchange that configuration information for the newly installed server should not be replicated to the rest of the organization.

5. You should also install the Exchange client software so that you can test the effectiveness of the restore once it's completed.

6. Run NTBACKUP.EXE and restore the directory and information stores from the backup.

7. If the restore was performed from an off-line backup, run ISINTEG -PATCH to update the GUIDs (Globally Unique Identifiers) in the information store. ISINTEG does not have to be run if the restore is performed from a backup taken when Exchange was on-line.

8. Use the Exchange client to check accounts and make sure that messages can be sent and read. Use the administration program to check that the correct correlation exists between Exchange mailboxes and Windows NT accounts.

9. Make sure that all connectors are operating properly. Check directory replication connections if the system being restored should act as a directory replication bridgehead for the site.

10. If you can only restore the information store and are unable to restore the directory, use the Directory Consistency checker to scan the information store and create a new directory object to match each information store object

11. Run the Exchange Performance Optimizer utility (see Chapter 11) to optimize the Exchange configuration.

A strong recommendation has already been made not to run Exchange on the same Windows NT computer that acts as the Primary Domain Controller, or PDC (see page 122). The link between the Windows NT security database (SAM) and how authentication for access to directory objects is performed is the major reason behind the recommendation. When you only have one server to do everything it's impossible to avoid having Exchange and the PDC on the same system, but in all cases where multiple servers are in use you should definitely separate the two.

If you rebuild a system that acts as a PDC a new SAM is created. When the time comes to restore the Exchange directory any attempt to authenticate against the new SAM will fail, the net effect being that no Exchange service will be able to start and you won't even be able to log onto the Administration program. The information store can be restored and you can use a brand new directory to create mailboxes to access data in the store, but it's obvious that a lot of work is needed to recreate mailboxes and other directory information, and then propagate it to the rest of the organization. Apart from anything else there's lots of potential for error and confusion.

On the other hand, if the system being restored is a BDC, a copy SAM will be retrieved from the PDC when the system is rebuilt. Note that you'll need to use the Windows NT Server Manager to demote the system from BDC status and then promote it again after Windows NT has been reinstalled on the computer. This step is necessary to ensure that the SAM data is copied correctly from the PDC to the new BDC.

The simplest case to handle is where the Exchange server being rebuilt takes no part in user authentication. In these cases it is sufficient to rebuild Windows NT and Exchange on the server as outlined above. User authentication will be accomplished by reference to the PDC and/ or BDC in the domain that the server joins during the rebuilding process.

5.7.5   Processing single mailboxes

One specific item of functionality not provided by the standard Windows NT Backup utility is the ability to save or restore a single mailbox. The standard Backup utility operates on the information or directory stores as whole entities, so if you want to restore a single user's mailbox (sometimes referred to as a "brick" or "bricked" restore) you have to restore the entire information store.

Restoring a user's mailbox is a task that system administrators probably won't welcome with open arms. Experience with other messaging systems indicates that over the course of a server's productive life there is more than a 50% chance that you'll encounter a situation where a user mailbox is deleted in error, or a user deletes some important files in error and only realizes their mistake some time later. Given the human capacity to err the latter situation is more likely to arise. It's difficult to restore the complete information store onto a production server. You could do this, but only through a set of complicated steps involving:

1. Shut down the production server.
2. Take a backup of the information store.
3. Restore the backup of the information store that contains the mailbox you wish to restore or otherwise recover.
4. Start up the Exchange information store, but don't allow users to log on and make sure that no external connectors are active.
5. Log onto the mailbox and move all the messages you wish to recover from the mailbox to a personal information store (PST file). You can drag and drop individual messages or select all the messages in the mailbox and copy them in one operation to the PST.
6. Shut down Exchange.
7. Restore the backup taken in step 2.
8. Restart Exchange and allow users to resume work. Make sure all connectors and directory replicators are restarted successfully.
9. Provide the user with the PST and instruct them how to access the recovered messages from the PST.

Executing this complicated set of actions will take at least four hours on any reasonably sized server. Shutting down a production system for four hours and depriving users of their e-mail is not a recipe for generating popularity, so another tactic needs to be considered.

The obvious solution is to restore the information store onto another Windows NT computer and use that as the basis to retrieve the necessary messages. To do this you'll need:

- A Windows NT server with the same version of Windows NT and Exchange installed as on the production server. We'll call this system the "recovery host."

- A tape drive on the recovery host capable of reading the backups created on the production server.

- Exchange (on the recovery host) must be configured with the same organization and site name as the production server where the backup originates. If the organization and site name do not match you won't be able to restore the backup taken from the production server.

Equipped with a suitable recovery host you can proceed to restore the backup tape, log into the user's mailbox, and extract the necessary messages to a PST. The pressure to do all of this is much less than when you've had to take a production server off-line, so you can take your time and make sure that everything's done correctly.

Lacking the capability to restore a single mailbox from a backup is an obvious flaw in the current Windows NT backup utility. It remains to be seen whether the flaw will be addressed in a future release of Windows NT or Exchange, but until that time this feature is high on the list of desirable items to look for if you consider buying a different backup utility from a third party.

5.7.6   Restoring single documents

Users delete documents and messages that they really want to keep all the time. It's easy to hit the delete key when an important message is highlighted, sending the message off to the Deleted Items folder. If you realize the error in time the message can be retrieved from Deleted Items, but it's a different matter if the user logs off from Exchange and the Deleted Items folder is emptied. Unlike other messaging systems the messages managed by the Exchange information store never exist as individual files. Messages, documents, and other objects added to the information store reside in the database as binary objects, or BLOBS in database terminology. In other words, within the database messages are stored as collections of binary information which make little sense to anything else except the information store. As we've seen there are many advantages to this scheme, but there's a dark side too.

Documents or messages deleted in error can only be recovered by restoring a user's entire mailbox. The restore is only going to be possible if the document or message existed in the mailbox at the time when the backup was taken. Nothing can be done to recover the missing item if it was created and deleted since the last backup.

5.7.7 Restoring the contents of public folders

Accidents can happen to user mailboxes, and users are more than capable of deleting objects from their mailboxes in error, and much the same type of accidents can happen to the contents of public folders. What can be done to recover an important document that's been deleted from a public folder? The first thing to do is to check whether a copy of the document exists in a replica folder elsewhere in the organization. Changes, including deletions, have to be replicated before they are effective throughout an organization. It is therefore possible to go to a public folder replica on another server and recover a copy of the desired document before the deletion command is replicated. However, it must be acknowledged that such a recovery depends on realizing that the document shouldn't have been deleted as soon as the action is performed, quick access to a remote server hosting a replica (directly via the network or perhaps through a phone call to the local system administrator), and a large slice of luck.

If your luck runs out and you don't manage to get to a replica in time there is no alternative but to refer back to a backup. Much the same problems exist for the restore. You don't want to stop the production server to recover the document if at all possible, so using a separate recovery host is the best approach. After the document is recovered to a PST you can move the document from the PST back into the public folder.

5.7.8 Third party backup utilities

NTBACKUP is all very well, but as we've seen it's a pretty basic backup engine. The job gets done, and the Exchange databases will be written safely to tape (or another backup medium), but the interface and features available in NTBACKUP leave a lot to be desired, especially when you're dealing with high-end servers. The same situation existed for Windows NT before Exchange came along, and for that reason there are many highly functional and feature-rich third party backup utilities available for Windows NT today. Most of these products have created add-on modules or new version releases to support Exchange, so NTBACKUP is not the only option. Table 5.7 lists some of the major third party backup products that support Exchange. Use the Web address to get information about the latest product features to help decide which is best for you.

Table 5.7   *Third party backup utilities*

Company	Product	Web address
Cheyenne Software (a division of Computer Associates)	ArcServe	`http://www.cheyenne.com`
Seagate Corporation	Backup Exec	`http://www.seagate.com`
Barratt Edwards International Corporation	Ultrabac	`http://www.ultrabac.com`

It's always difficult to justify the additional expense of buying a package to replace a standard utility, especially when there is a standard utility that appears to do the job in an adequate manner and there's a need to install the new software on many different servers. Backups are a system manager's parachute and if they don't work when they are needed then anyone involved may soon be looking for a new job, so it is reasonable to regard backup software as a very important part of the management armory.

A specialized package often provides very useful features that are missing in the standard utility. In practice there are three major enhancements that a third party backup utility might provide over the standard NTBACKUP program:

1. Scheduling

2. Speed

3. Control

We've already reviewed how the AT and WINAT utilities can be used in association with NTBACKUP to schedule backups (see section 5.7.2 beginning on page 288). However, the scheduling capabilities that are possible with this combination are rudimentary, to say the least. Third party backup utilities usually include a complete scheduling engine that allows any type of backup to be processed at whatever interval (daily, weekly, or monthly) that's desired. In addition, these scheduling engines tend to be very much easier to use, and make it possible to select different parts of Exchange for backup at different times. It is also possible to include important files and even the system registry when backing up a server.

Exchange permits on-line backups to be taken. In other words, there is no requirement to stop the different services (information store, directory, system attendant, and so on) while the backup is proceeding. It might therefore appear that speed is of little concern. After all, you can start a backup off each morning and have it running alongside users as the day proceeds. This is true, but it's only a partial picture. Backups can proceed on-line, but restores can only be done with a "silent" server. If backup software processes data quickly it's normal that restores are quick too, and this fact is very interesting when the files being restored might be several gigabytes in size. Up to the version of NTBACKUP shipped with ExchangeV5.0, all of the third party backup software tested (in a very unscientific manner) on my own server was significantly faster than NTBACKUP. A very quick test on a reasonably lightly loaded server (no more than 10 users logged on during the backup period) revealed the following:

- Size of information stores   623MB
- System   100MHz Pentium/
                                             96MB memory
- Tape drive (model)   HP 35480A
- Tape   4mm DAT
- Time taken with NTBACKUP
  (Exchange V4.0 SP3)   57 minutes
- Time taken with NTBACKUP
  (Exchange V5.0)   24 minutes
                                             (best time)
- Time taken with Cheyenne ArcServe   32 minutes

With very large information stores clearly on the horizon Microsoft knew that NTBACKUP was too slow. The changes made in Exchange V5.0 (increasing the tape block size for DLT drives and speeding the rate data is written to tapes) helped performance. Sources inside Microsoft engineering indicate that they are still constrained by the tape drive speeds, but they continue to work to improve matters.

In practice I found that achieving faster backups with the new version of NTBACKUP appears to be highly dependent on the workload on the server when the backup operation is active. Systems under load write data to the backup tape much more slowly than systems that are lightly loaded. In a few months' use of the enhanced NTBACKUP utility the backup times were quite erratic, ranging from 24 minutes to nearly an hour for roughly the same quantity of data. As an example of what I mean, the backup status illustrated in Figure 5.34 shows that approximately 706MB of data (740,217,480 bytes) was written to tape in just over 1 hour and 9 minutes. The screen capture was taken from the same system used for the test described above, although in this instance the system was heavily loaded as the backup was running.

No doubt the other backup software developers will view this result with both interest and some degree of trepidation, and will work to recapture their speed advantage. The commercial backup packages seem to be less affected by system workload, possibly because they usually employ more sophisticated techniques to control the streaming of data out to tape. Even if the new version of NTBACKUP is faster, remember that speed is only one of the issues to consider and some of the other points, like scheduling and control, may be more important in the long run.

Because of the unscientific nature of the test these results do not serve as an endorsement for any particular software. Your mileage will vary, depending on your own system configuration and the circumstances under which the backup is taken, so you should make your own tests before making any decision. Don't forget that there are other important aspects that can affect backup times. Using DLT tape drives instead of 4mm DAT drives will improve backup times dramatically because DLT drives are able to stream data out to the tape much faster. For example, that 15.5GB private information store inside DIGITAL I referred to earlier is backed up using the standard NTBACKUP utility (Exchange V4.0) in approximately 3½ hours on a DLT tape.

Increased speed and reduced backup times make it more feasible to take full backups every day rather than a more normal cycle of full backups every week with incremental backups taken on the days in between. The advantage gained here will only accrue if you have to restore the server. You'll be very happy to find that it's much easier and faster to restore from a single full backup than to go through the hoops and loops of restoring from the last full backup followed by all the incremental backups since. With large servers that have stores greater than 10GB (in total) the backup times may be a touch too long to take full backups every day, but with smaller servers it's certainly a tactic you should consider.

The final advantage that can be gained from third party utilities is control. NTBACKUP is quite content to overwrite the same tape with a new backup every day if the tape is left in the tape drive, as some people have discovered to their loss. Commands such as "eject tape after backup is complete" prevent accidents happening and contribute to data security. This type of problem is unlikely to occur in data centers where skilled operations staff work, but it's entirely possible in places where people only know how to insert tapes into drives. Effective tape handling is critically important for installations dealing with large stores that span more than one tape. You don't want to get into a situation where a backup never actually completes because someone forgot to take out the first tape and insert a new tape at the appropriate time.

A number of the third party backup utilities also allow you to backup the system registry, disks, and the Exchange databases in a single operation, much easier than having to make (and restore) three separate backup tapes.

·In the future, both NTBACKUP and third party utilities should be able to address a major bugbear of Exchange—the ability to restore a single user mailbox from a backup rather than being required to restore the entire private information store. This facility was promised by many software vendors around the time that Exchange V4.0 first shipped, but rapid decommitments arrived when the difficulty of reassembling a mailbox (or extract a single message or other item) from a backup was realized. Work is ongoing to provide the underpinnings to allow mailboxes to be assembled from a backup more easily, but no software has appeared to date. Apart from the sheer convenience of being able to process just one user's messages, the time taken to complete the operation is a lot less than if you have to process everyone's messages.

If you decide to use different backup software than NTBACKUP, make sure that the same software is used everywhere. Don't allow yourself to get into the situation where some sites (or even worse, some servers within a site) use different backup software or different backup devices. With backups it pays dividends to keep things simple and that means creating the same backup environment everywhere— the same software, tapes, and drives. Due to the different ways that software can stream data out to tapes, it is highly unlikely that one backup software package will be able to read a tape created by another. Once you allow diversity the potential is created that a backup tape, for one reason or another, cannot be restored onto a system. And Murphy's Law dictates that this situation will occur just after a server hosting 500 users has crashed and cannot be got back on-line.

It's important to understand that while third party backup software can provide some valuable advantages, it's another piece to be fitted into the system configuration matrix. New releases of the backup software must be qualified against existing versions of Exchange, and then against new versions of Exchange. The backup software should also be checked against service packs of both Exchange and Windows NT. The Exchange development team cannot check their product against every third party extensions, so it's entirely possible that the installation of a service pack will introduce a problem that only comes to light when a backup operation is attempted[11]. Or, even worse, dur-

---

[11] While it may seem inconceivable that an Exchange service pack will cause problems for backup software it did happen with Exchange V4.0 SP3. A minor bug in the service pack prevented products like ArcServe connecting to the information store, so backups could not be taken. The problem was quickly fixed and an updated module posted on the Microsoft Web site, but the fact that the situation happened is a cautionary tale for all of us.

ing a restore. The complex interaction between Exchange, Windows NT, and any third party product adds weight to the argument that all combinations of software products (including patches) should be well tested before being introduced to production servers.

5.7.9   Key Management backups

If you are operating the Key Management Server you should arrange for the security information to be backed up on a daily basis. This information is stored in the SECURITY\MGRENT directory on the central Key Management Server system. Losing security data through hardware failure without having a backup available can have catastrophic implications. All of the users who have been enabled for advanced security will not be able to encrypt messages because their security credentials will have disappeared. Even worse, they won't be able to decrypt messages they received previously.

5.8   Information Store maintenance

Exchange performs maintenance operations against the information store in two distinct manners:

1. On-line maintenance performed as the server is operating

2. Off-line maintenance procedures activated when something goes wrong.

5.8.1   On-line maintenance

Like most databases, the internal structures within the information store become less efficient over time. Data is not stored in an effective manner and becomes fragmented throughout the database. Taking Exchange off-line to compact the databases stops people using the server, so an on-line maintenance facility is included to keep things in order and defragment or re-order data within the private and public information stores.

On-line maintenance is scheduled by first selecting a server and then the "IS Maintenance" property page. The schedule, if active, is then displayed and can be changed if desired (see Figure 5.36). On-line maintenance is also possible for the directory, in which case it's controlled by setting the "Garbage collection interval" on the general property page of the DS Site Configuration object.

The effect of on-line maintenance is slight on most servers. Unless you are running close to the limits of your hardware's capabilities users shouldn't notice a significant degradation of server responsiveness as the information store is verified and any internal inconsistencies corrected. You can avoid any potential conflicts between the demands of users and the system maintenance processes by scheduling the maintenance to occur when a reduced number of users are active. As you can see from the maintenance times set in Figure 5.36, I like maintenance to occur when everyone is safely tucked up in bed or otherwise engaged in activities that don't require electronic mail.

Figure 5.36
Schedule for on-line Information Store maintenance

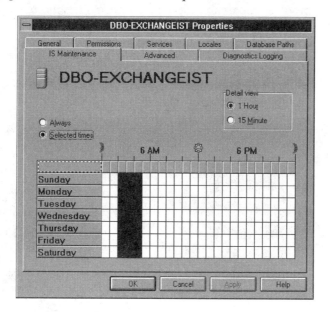

5.9   Off-line maintenance

Two off-line maintenance utilities for the information store are provided with Microsoft Exchange Server. These are:

- ISINTEG: Information Store Integrity Checker
- EDBUTIL: Exchange database utility

Both ISINTEG and EDBUTIL can be found in the EXCHANGE\BIN directory. Both are command line utilities run in a DOS (command) box, with an extremely minimal interface. The Exchange information store service (and any associated services such as the Internet Mail service) must be stopped before the utilities are run. Further details of how to use the utilities can be found in Chapter 17 of the *Exchange Administrator's Guide*.

5.9.1   ISINTEG—The integrity checker

ISINTEG is designed to find and remove errors from public and private information stores. The utility is able to run in two modes; test and patch. In test mode a scan is performed against an information store to determine whether any errors exist. Potential errors include incorrect reference counts for an object, table errors, or the discovery of objects that are not referenced anywhere within the store. Optionally, errors found in test mode can be fixed by ISINTEG as they are discovered. All errors are reported to a log file. ISINTEG is used in patch mode to repair an information store if it will not start up after being restored, for example, after a disk failure. Patch mode rectifies any inconsistencies that exist in an information store to ensure that data is not overwritten and that all data within the store is available to users.

Figure 5.37
ISINTEG
options

The most common reason why ISINTEG might be required occurs when the backup used to restore an information store was originally performed by a backup utility that doesn't support the on-line nature of the Exchange information store. In these instances ISINTEG runs in patch mode, using a command line like:

```
C:\EXCHSRVR\BIN\ISINTEG -PATCH
```

All databases have some form of index used to catalog information. Exchange uses indexes built from 64-bit hex strings that are referred to as Globally Unique Identifiers, or GUIDs, which partially depend on the date and time when the identifier is created. Each store (directory or information) has some base GUIDs that are created when the store is first established, and all of the objects created in the store from that time are allocated a GUID derived from the a base GUID. If a database is restored you are basically rolling back time, so you affect the date and time portion of the algorithm that creates new identifiers. Therefore, the potential now exists that the store might create a GUID that over-writes an identifier that's already allocated to another object within the store, with all the resulting confusion that would ensue. Af-

ter an off-line backup is used to restore a database ISINTEG can validate the base GUID and update the store so that all new GUIDs are created correctly.

Restores performed from on-line backups do not require the store
to be patched separately afterwards, mostly because the base GUIDs
are checked and adjusted during the restore process. This is a good reason to always use the Windows NT Backup utility or a third party replacement utility that supports on-line backups of Exchange.

By default, ISINTEG produces a log file detailing what it has done.
If you look at the bottom of the ISINTEG command line options illustrated in Figure 5.37, you can see that a large number of switches for
various tests are available. A full run of ISINTEG performs all the tests,
each of which validates a different part of the database. The log file
should be checked afterwards so that you know exactly what's gone
on. The default file names are ISINTEG.PRI for a run against the private information store, or ISINTEG.PUB for the public information
store. I immediately rename these files to ISINTEG_PUB.TXT and
ISINTEG_PRI.TXT to allow me use a text editor to view their contents.
It's a pity that the Exchange engineers created yet another file type for
what is purely a simple text file.

Edited highlights of an ISINTEG log file from a run against a private
information store are shown in Figure 5.38 below.

```
Microsoft Exchange Information Store Integrity Checker v4.993.3
Copyright (c) 1986-1996 Microsoft Corp.    All rights reserved.

Started:    11/06/96 13:30:23

Store path: g:\Exchange\MDBDATA\PRIV.EDB
Store size: 147333120 bytes
Output log: isinteg.pri
Check mode: check and fix

Starting test 1 of 24, 'Categorization Tables'
Finished Categorization Tables. Time: 0h:0m:0s
Starting test 22 of 24, 'reference count verification'
Fix: Message[0001-0000001EBABD].RefCt: Deleted message table row
Fix: Attachment[0001-0000001EBABA].RefCt: Bad count - prop(1)<>calc(0) .. Fixed
Fix: Attachment[0001-0000001EBABC].RefCt: Bad count - prop(1)<>calc(0) .. Fixed
Finished reference count verification. Time: 0h:0m:17s, number of fixes = 3
Starting test 24 of 24, 'Row Count'
Warning: table DeliveredTo row count: Calc(1) <> Prop(0)
Warning: table Folders row count: Calc(600) <> Prop(0)
Warning: table Mailbox row count: Calc(28) <> Prop(0)
Warning: table ACLList row count: Calc(10) <> Prop(0)
```

```
Warning: table PerUserRead row count: Calc(505) <> Prop(0)
Warning: table ReplidMap row count: Calc(38) <> Prop(0)
Warning: table NamedProps row count: Calc(360) <> Prop(0)
Warning: table DeletedAttachments row count: Calc(2) <> Prop(0)
Fix: The performance monitor counters are set to the correct values
Finished Row Count. Time: 0h:0m:0s, number of warnings = 8, number of fixes = 1


. . . . . SUMMARY . . . . .
Total number of tests : 24
Total number of warnings : 8
Total number of errors : 1
Total number of fixes : 4
Total time : 0h:4m:5s
```

Figure 5.38
Extract from
ISINTEG

Two of the tests performed by ISINTEG encountered errors. Test 22 validates that reference counts for messages and attachments are correct. If the reference count is too low it is increased, avoiding the potential of the item being removed prematurely, and if the reference count is too high it is decreased so that it will be deleted at the right time. The final test[12] validates the count of rows in each of the tables in the database and makes changes as required.

Should you run ISINTEG to check the contents of the information store on a regular basis? The answer is that it all depends. If you're a cautious person (or paranoid, depending on your point of view) and really want to know that the store is functioning at 100% then you can take the time to run ISINTEG at regular intervals. It doesn't take very long to run ISINTEG to validate the structures in the store and fix any problems that it comes across. The time taken to run ISINTEG depends on the size of the store, the speed of the CPU, and the speed of the I/O subsystem, but it is certainly much faster than EDBUTIL. The command line to validate and fix the private information store is:

```
C:\EXCHSRVR\BIN\ISINTEG -PRI -FIX
```

And for the public information store:

```
C:\EXCHSRVR\BIN\ISINTEG -PUB -FIX
```

Including the –VERBOSE switch in the command line forces ISINTEG to output details of everything it does, perhaps far more information than you care to view.

---

[12] The number of tests performed by ISINTEG has varied from version to version. As you can see from the sample output, Exchange V4.0 performed 24 tests. Exchange V5.0 performs 19 tests for public information stores and 21 for private information stores. The different number of tests reflects some consolidation and optimization work that has been built into the ISINTEG utility.

Running ISINTEG in fix mode can reveal problems that you never even contemplated. Judging by my experience, systems that have run beta test releases of Exchange, where errors are expected to arise, may have large numbers of inconsistencies (incorrect counts in tables, etc.) in the store, so it is a good idea to run ISINTEG after you upgrade to the commercially released version. Apart from these instances there is really no great need to run ISINTEG unless you want to know what's happening or begin to experience database errors that cannot be explained by events you know about (like a problem with a disk).

In all instances, if you use ISINTEG to fix or patch a store, make sure that you take a backup afterwards.

5.9.2   EDBUTIL—the compactor of Exchange databases

While ISINTEG could be described as operating on the content of an information store, EDBUTIL operates at a higher level, concentrating on the internal database structures that underpin an information or directory store. EDBUTIL is able to physically compact a store, rearranging database contents into an optimal manner, and returning unused space to the disk system.

The private information store experiences lots of message activity. New messages arrive, are read, and then hopefully deleted or filed away. All this activity results in separate database transactions, potentially leading to a database that becomes fragmented very quickly. The exact time when an unacceptable level of fragmentation occurs depends on how many people use the system and how many messages they send and receive. The private store will continue to grow even on servers where new messages are delivered to user PSTs. The reason is simple—messages have to transfer through the store en route to a PST, something that may not happen immediately unless clients are connected to Exchange. After messages are transferred to the PSTs they are deleted from the store, but the space the messages occupied during their stay in the store may not be recovered until the store is compacted.

As a matter of practice I run EDBUTIL every few months on my group's production server to defragment the private information store and return some valuable disk space to the file system.

Table 5.8 lists some representative results from EDBUTIL runs against the different stores on a small Exchange server (Pentium 100). The stores had not been compressed for two months before EDBUTIL was run. Recovering 300MB from the public information store may seem surprising, but the server in question hosted a number of public folders fed from Internet mailing lists. In addition, a number of public folders were used for working documents that were added and deleted to the folders as projects progressed. Public stores hosting folders that are largely static will not see the same type of reduction. The bottom line from the results shown is that 37 minutes' work returned 423MB to the file system, a more than worthwhile investment in terms of time.

Table 5.8 *EDBUTIL results with different stores*

Store	Size before EDBUTIL	Size after EDBUTIL	Elapsed time for EDBUTIL run
Public Information Store	774MB	472MB	24 minutes
Private Information Store	340MB	220MB	14 minutes
Directory Store	7.5MB	6.5MB	42 seconds

Logically, the larger the server the more disk space will be recovered. Apart from improving internal efficiency (because the database pages are arranged in the most efficient manner), backup and restore operations will be quicker and perhaps the most interesting reason why you want to defragment information stores on a regular basis.

Figure 5.39
EDBUTIL in action

Another good example of when EDBUTIL might be used is after a large number of mailboxes have been moved from one server to another within a site. The space originally occupied by the moved mailboxes can be recovered by running EDBUTIL to compact the private information store. In general, it's fair to assume that all systems will be taken off-line, even in the most demanding production environment. Software upgrades and patches have to be applied, and hardware maintenance performed. These interruptions in normal service provide opportunities to run EDBUTIL and recover some disk space.

The time taken by EDBUTIL depends on the speed of the CPU—fast Alpha servers can process databases at the rate of 3–4GB/hour, while small Pentiums should certainly be able to process data at 1GB/hour. Figure 5.39 shows the display at the end of an EDBUTIL run. Note the primitive progress bar, which, although basic, does a reasonable job of telling you how far EDBUTIL has gone with the database. If the system is quiet EDBUTIL will process data faster than if other work is proceeding at the same time. The length of time taken to rebuild a database is one very good reason not to run EDBUTIL during normal working hours.

After time, disk space is the second requirement imposed by ED-BUTIL. You'll need a lot of temporary disk space (at least twice the size of the database being compacted) during the compaction because the database is rebuilt by reading data a page at a time, checking the page, and then writing it into a temporary database called TEMPD-FRG.EDB. When all the pages in the database have been read and no errors were detected the old database is deleted and TEMPDFRG.EDB is renamed in its place. You can instruct EDBUTIL to keep the old database if you'd prefer. Rebuilding a database page by page is a reasonable approach to take, but it can be difficult to find enough disk space to hold the temporary database, especially when the database grows past 4GB or so. By default, TEMPDFRG.EDB is created in the same directory as the store being processed, but the /P switch allows you to select another file name or directory. It's not always easy to find enough space on the same drive! Note that you cannot use a network drive as a location for the temporary database. Exchange doesn't support network drives as valid locations for stores. The temporary file is renamed to become the "real" database after compaction is complete, so if a network drive was permitted as a valid location for TEMPD-FRG.EDB you might conceivably end up in a situation where a newly compacted database was in an illegal location.

Always take a full backup after compacting a database. The internal structure is changed because the pages are rearranged in order, so it is not possible to roll forward any transactions in transaction logs held in backup sets. Thus, it is not possible to fully recover the database from backups taken prior to the compaction should a problem occur.

Unfortunately there is no mechanism to scan a database to discover how much "white space" (space that will be recovered when the database is compacted) is within a database at any time. The constant movement of messages in and out of the store creates little spaces in the database, and the on-line defragmentation performed nightly merely rearranges space in the database to pack information in more tightly. The end result of defragmentation is an area of unused space at the end of the database. Exchange will use this space to store new messages, but space will never be returned to the file system until EDBUTIL is run. It would be nice to be able to make a quick check, preferably with the database on-line, to discover how efficient the internal structures are and how much disk space would be recovered if EDBUTIL was run. Perhaps these features will appear in a future version.

After compacting and database repair the last use of EDBUTIL is to upgrade a database's internal structures or provide information about those structures. This option is only ever taken upon advice from Microsoft. Why might this happen? Who knows—the internal structures in the store have changed as Exchange has evolved. Such changes are expected when a product is being developed, but internal changes were also made during the upgrade from V4.0 to V5.0. The need to conduct separate upgrades for a store outside the boundaries of a product version change can be envisaged, but it shouldn't happen often. The only reason I can think of is where a problem in the store requires a special software patch, normally provided by Microsoft product support. Before or after the patch is applied one or more of the stores might need to be updated.

5.9.3 Life on the dark side—Repairs performed by EDBUTIL

Compacting a database is a pretty simple affair. Read a page from the source database and write it out to the target, continuing until all of the input pages have been read. No attempt is made to determine whether the input pages contain valid data and can be used after they are written into the compacted database.

EDBUTIL offers a repair mode that is able to validate the database pages as they are processed. However, this isn't a mode you want to find yourself using if at all possible. Typically repair mode is only ever used if a problem is detected in the database, possibly during system start-up when the information store service refuses to start and reports one or more errors to the system event log. Errors occur when the store can't read the database and are pointers to a sick file that must be repaired.

Before rushing into repair mode let's consider what happens when EDBUTIL operates in repair mode. Each page is validated after it is read from the source database. Validation means that a checksum is calculated and compared against the checksum stored for each page. If the checksum matches, the page passes and is written into the output database. If the checksum doesn't match, the page is discarded and EDBUTIL proceeds to the next page.

Discarding pages results in data loss. Quite what data is lost depends on whatever is stored in the page. Pages can store many different types of information relating to the various tables held in the database. Consider the following scenarios:

- Pages containing data for the folders table results in the loss of potentially many different folders.

- Pages containing data for the messages table results in the loss of content for a number of messages.

- Pages containing data for a folder table results in the loss of header information for messages in specific folders.

The most catastrophic loss is the first. If folder information disappears then all the content and attachments held in those folders are no longer accessible.

With potential losses like this it follows that EDBUTIL's repair mode is very much a last resort. It is much preferable to restore the database from the most recent full backup plus all the intervening transaction logs, and then let Exchange perform a soft recovery (roll-back of all outstanding transactions) when the information store service is restarted. Of course, reverting to a recent backup is only possible if good backup disciplines have been followed and the backup sets are available.

In summary, the message about EDBUTIL is simple. EDBUTIL is a valuable utility for system administrators because it's the only way to recover disk space from a store. It is recommended that EDBUTIL is used on a reasonably regular basis to compact stores, especially the private information store. However, avoid using its repair mode unless absolute necessary—backups are important!

5.9.4 Limiting user log-ons to the information store

After performing off-line maintenance operations it is likely that you'll want to check the server out before allowing users to log-on. This poses a small problem for Exchange, because its normal behavior is to start its services and begin to immediately accept client connections to the information store. A block must be inserted if you want to prevent total access or (more likely) restrict access to a nominated set of individuals.

Microsoft Knowledge Base article Q146764 describes a registry setting that can be used to control user log-ons, and so create the type of block we need. It's a hidden feature of Exchange. The basic idea is to provide Exchange with a list of distinguished names of mailboxes (users) that it will allow clients to access via the information store. A client that presents a distinguished name that isn't on the list will be refused access. Thus:

```
/o=Digital Equipment Corporation/ou=Dublin/cn=recipients/cn=TonyR
/o=Digital Equipment Corporation/ou=Dublin/cn=recipients/cn=BillR
```

Means that only the users with these distinguished names are allowed log-on to the information store. How can you find out the right format and content to pass for distinguished names? Select a mailbox and examine its raw properties, something that requires you to run the Exchange administration utility in raw mode. See Chapter 8 for more details on distinguished names and raw mode administration.

The magic registry key is:

```
HKEY_LOCAL_MACHINE\SYSTEM\CurrentControlSet\Services\MSExchangeIS\Logon Only As
```

You shouldn't find this value in the registry on any active server. If it's there, someone has attempted to insert a roadblock and, for one reason or another, has left the value around. The idea is to provide Exchange with a set of distinguished names (each on a separate line) of mailboxes that are allowed to gain access. If the registry parameter is left blank it means that all users should be prevented from gaining access!

The correct way to use this feature is as follows:

1. Stop the Information Service.

2. Take a copy of the system registry.

3. Run REGEDT32.EXE, the registry editor.

4. Add the new value to the registry, typing the value as described above and illustrated in Figure 5.40. The parameter data type is REG_MULTI_SZ (multiple string values).

5. The registry editor displays a data box to collect information for the new value. Type the distinguished names of the mailboxes you will allow access to. Put each mailbox on a separate line.

6. After all names are added, click on OK.

7. Exit REGEDT32.EXE.

8. Restart the Information Store service.

9. Test that the specified mailboxes are able to access the store, and that those that aren't on the list cannot. Mailboxes not on the list should be told that the set of server folders couldn't be opened.

Figure 5.40 *A hidden feature! How to allow just your friends to log on*

After you are finished working with the server and are ready to allow general access, use the registry editor to delete the key. Do not forget this step as leaving undocumented and unsupported registry settings floating around is not good system management practice.

5.10 Keeping messages secret

No one likes to think that their messages might be read either en route to a recipient or by someone other than the recipient after messages have reached their final destination. Exchange encrypts all messages by default to ensure that message contents are secure as they are transferred between servers and clients. Users aren't aware of this encryption and no client or server options are available to disable it.

Optional functionality is available to allow you to encrypt and decrypt messages and their attachments as they pass from sender to recipient. Messages can also have electronic signatures applied to them to prove that a specific individual generated the content. User-driven encryption is not something that you introduce into your messaging environment on a whim as it requires some detailed up-front planning and introduces at least some, and potentially substantial, additional work for system administrators. Such a sweeping statement is true even of a messaging system that has worked hard to integrate encryption as seamlessly as possible, which is the case in Exchange where encryption/decryption and electronic signatures are collectively referred to as "Advanced Security."

The Advanced Security features of Exchange are available to anyone who buys either the Exchange Server Enterprise Edition or who adds the Exchange Connector to an Exchange Server Standard Edition. Advanced Security is controlled by a component called the Key

Management Server (KMS). Exchange client software performs encryption and decryption. Nothing is done on the server. In passing, it's worth noting that the DOS client does not support Advanced Security.

Recent examples of legal discovery actions throughout the world have awakened people to the danger of putting something in an e-mail message that they wouldn't like someone else to see in the future. It's difficult to explain to a lawyer that a remark about a competitor's product, or even someone else in your company, wasn't more than a throwaway thought on your part. Once committed to e-mail that thought becomes a fact that might be presented in court one day. In the United States, where the majority of discovery actions have occurred to date, the situation is complicated by a concept known as "negligent waiver of privilege," meaning that an insecure message sent between two people in the same company can constitute a waiver of the lawyer/client privilege. In this context, insecure means that the message is not encrypted and could be read by someone else, such as a system administrator.

Consider a situation where two managers are discussing the termination of an employee and one is unwise enough to send an e-mail saying "I never really liked him/her from the start." What would a trial lawyer do with such a statement in front of an employment tribunal? The moral of the story is clear. Encryption of business-sensitive messages provides added protection against potential legal difficulties in the future, at least in the United States. The question therefore is whether the advanced security features of Exchange have the correct balance of usability and features to protect your enterprise. I believe the features are certainly there; to a large degree the question of usability (and therefore compliance) depends on how advanced security is implemented.

5.10.1   Different types of encryption

Exchange Server uses the RSA security system and supports both the DES and CAST encryption algorithms. RSA is a public-key encryption system that can be used for both encryption and certification and is probably the most widely used public-key encryption system in use today. RSA was originally developed in 1977 by Ron Rivest, Adi Shamir, and Leonard Adleman at the Massachusetts Institute of Technology. The initials of the authors' surnames make up RSA.

DES (Data Encryption Standard) is a complicated algorithm for the encryption of data designed by the U.S. National Bureau of Standards. The intention behind DES was to create an algorithm that is extremely difficult to break, certainly well beyond the capabilities of anyone equipped with copious time and anything else than a supercomputer or a networked array of workstations. Even with such powerful hardware resources the 56-bit key used by DES[13] to create a binary encryption key with 72 quadrillion possible combinations is enough to make any attempt to break the code a relatively fruitless activity.

CAST is a proprietary encryption method developed by Northern Telecom (who sold a license for their "Entrust" technology to Microsoft for inclusion into Exchange). CAST was originally developed as a more flexible encryption scheme than DES, mostly because it allows for a variable input key of between 40 and 128 bits.

The exact nature of the algorithm used by your particular server depends whether you are in the United States or not. The 56-bit (DES) or 64-bit (CAST-64) encryption algorithms are treated by the United States government as militarily-sensitive items and are therefore only provided with Exchange servers shipped in the United States and Canada. Other countries are restricted to the lowest available form of the CAST algorithm based on a 40-bit key. The real difference between the U.S. and anywhere else is therefore the size of the input key used for encryption (64-bit or 56-bit versus 40-bit). It's obvious that the size of the input key determines the amount of computing effort required to break an encryption code, so the encryption used in the United States and Canada is much more secure than elsewhere.

In a practical sense the presence of different encryption algorithms in use within a single Exchange organization doesn't affect matters in the least because non-U.S. servers are able to decrypt messages originating from the U.S., and vice versa. The difference lies in how messages are encrypted in the first place rather in how they are eventually decrypted.

For comparison's sake it's interesting to note that Lotus Notes Release 4 also uses 64-bit keys in its international versions[14]. However, the last 24 bits of each key are registered in escrow with the U.S. government, reducing the amount of key-cracking to 40 bits. Of course, giving the U.S. government a head start when the time comes to crack a key is done just in case someone wants to officially read your mail at some point in the future.

Governments generally like to know what people are up to, and steps are often taken to put obstacles in place to stop people protecting their privacy. The U.S. government, for example, was really upset

---

[13] The specification for DES is contained in the Federal Information Processing Standard Publication 46 of January 15, 1977.

[14] Page 738, "Using Lotus Notes 4," Que Books 1996.

when Phil Zimmerman, the author of the PGP (Pretty Good Privacy) encryption algorithm, placed his code into the public domain through the Internet. Following much the same line, the French government do not permit the import of any encryption software into France[15], so any Microsoft Exchange server used in France cannot include the encryption functionality. Even if a server located in France cannot generate encrypted messages people using the server will still be able to read encrypted messages originating from elsewhere. Microsoft cannot be criticized for shipping different encryption technology to different countries. As a U.S. company, Microsoft is limited by law to the software they can provide, and the implementation in Exchange is similar in many respects to the approach taken by other products, most notably the Lotus Notes server which supports a mixture of United States and "international" keys to encrypt messages.

I'm not sure that it really makes a lot of difference to the average user whether their messages are encrypted with 40, 56, or 64 bits. Huge amounts of computing horsepower are necessary to decrypt even a single message encrypted with a 40-bit key. The resources required are sizable enough to prevent anyone but national security agencies and other government bodies from even attempting to browse or intercept the volume of messages generated on an average server. And anyway, the content of the majority of messages is hardly earth-shattering and is of little commercial or other importance. If you're really interested in probing the outer edges of message encryption perhaps you should investigate messaging systems that support the U.S. Defense Messaging System (DMS) standard. A variant of Exchange Server V5.0 that supports DMS is now available.

The security component of Exchange dictates which algorithm is used when a message is encrypted. Thus, if a message is addressed to someone outside your organization (a custom recipient, in other words) Exchange will not allow encryption to occur and messages will be sent in clear text. This approach is reasonable as it's clearly folly to send an encrypted message out across an SMTP or X.400 link to a recipient who potentially uses another mail system that knows little or nothing about Exchange-style encryption. Intelligence is also applied when encrypting messages circulating within an organization. If a recipient is connected to a server located outside the United States or Canada a 40-bit key and algorithm is used automatically.

With Exchange V4.0 advanced security was only possible within the confines of a single Exchange organization. The reason for this

[15]   The prohibition against encryption software is described in Decree 92-1358, dated December 1992.

limitation was simple: there was no defined mechanism for organizations to share or synchronize directory information together, so the data used in the encryption/decryption process could not be exchanged between organizations. In Exchange V5.0 the situation is a little different. There still is no way for organizations to send each other their security data on an organizational level, but it is now possible for individual users to set up security arrangements between themselves and other people who may use a different Exchange organization. Figure 5.41 shows how someone (in this case, myself) can create a special type of message to send to another user. The special message contains the sender's public keys. When the message is received the public key information can be extracted and inserted into the recipient's PAB, much the same way as key information is held in the Off-Line Address Book (more on this later on in this section). As you can see, the message can contain other information too, allowing a complete PAB entry to be created.

Figure 5.41
Sending security keys with Exchange V5.0

Welcome as this development is, the ability for users to exchange key information between each other is a short-term solution to the problem. It does nothing, for instance, to address the cases when a user changes their public key, or when keys are revoked or reissued. It is far more desirable to have the ability for Exchange organizations to be able to automatically share directory information between each other on a scheduled basis. That functionality is not yet with us, but it should be in the future.

5.10.2 Basic points about encryption

Before plunging into the inner details of how advanced security works we need to create a broad sketch of the security implementation. The basic points regarding message encryption, or message sealing, as implemented in Microsoft Exchange Server are as follows:

- Encryption is accomplished through a mixture of public and private keys allocated and controlled by a single nominated Exchange server within your organization. This server runs an optional component known as the Key Management Server. It is obvious that this computer must be located in a secure environment as if it is physically accessible or becomes unavailable the entire encryption scheme is compromised. Because of its need to be as secure as possible the files for the Key Management Server must be located on a disk using the Windows NT NTFS file system. The server must be capable of providing as high a degree of available service (ideally 24×365) as a hardware configuration can make possible.

- 512-bit RSA public/private key pairs are used to verify a sender's authenticity. The RSA MD5 message digest algorithm is used for calculating the unique hash used to check message integrity. These techniques are similar to those employed by other encryption products available today. Microsoft didn't build this technology from scratch. It is licensed from Northern Telecom, who sells the base encryption functionality as "Entrust™ Security Technology."

- Each user who will encrypt messages must be individually identified to the server to allow a temporary token to be generated. The temporary token is then used to allocate public and private keys for an individual.

- Messages are encrypted with a one-time "bulk" encryption key generated by the server. After the message is encrypted the bulk key is in turn encrypted using the public key for each recipient. Thus, if a message is addressed to ten different users, the bulk key for the message is encrypted ten times using ten different public keys. When an encrypted message is received it is decrypted by fetching the bulk key using a recipient's private key, and then the retrieved bulk key is used in turn to decrypt the content of the message.

Clients (Exchange or Outlook) perform all encryption. No encryption is done on the Exchange Server, which merely serves to transmit the encrypted message from one user to another, and to act as a store for the X.509 certificates. Because client software is used to encrypt messages it follows that it is eminently possible to export the technology on a laptop PC, or even import it into a country, no matter what the wishes of the respective governments are. Some countries, including the United States, require their citizens to keep records of the occasions when they export (albeit unknowingly) the encryption software along with the rest of the client, and these records can be demanded for inspection by government officials. This requirement may change over time, but it's an interesting indication of the attitude that governments have to encryption technology when it's incorporated into (almost) consumer products.

5.10.3   Keys and Certificates

The concept of keys is clearly very important when attempting to understand how advanced security works. Signing and sealing of messages is controlled by a scheme of private and public keys in line with the ITU X.509 set of recommendations for authentication information. Each mailbox enabled for advanced security receives a key pair composed of a public and private key. Public keys are provided as fixed-length strings that are published and made known to any process that needs to encrypt information destined for that user. Two public keys are used, one to encrypt messages before they are sent, and one to read electronic signatures on received messages.

Private keys are also stored as fixed length strings. However, their values are kept private to the user and never revealed. The private keys are stored in an encrypted file (with an extension of .EPF) stored on the user's computer. As in the case of public keys, two separate private keys are used within the Exchange security scheme. One for message decryption and one to apply electronic signatures. Table 5.9 summarizes the key types and when they are used.

Like passwords, it's easy for human beings to forget their private keys. With Exchange advanced security losing a key isn't a total disaster so there's no need for users to write their keys down on a piece of paper that can be kept in a convenient location. If users forget their private key the key server can allocate a new key.

Key pairs are managed by Exchange through X.509-compliant special security certificates created and managed by the Key Management Server. When fulfilling the role of certificate manager the Key Management Server is known as the Certification Authority or "CA" because it is responsible for creating and maintaining the security key pairs and special certificates.

Table 5.9 *Private and Public Key usage*

	Encryption/Decryption	Electronic Signatures
Sending messages	Public key used to encrypt message contents	Private signing key used to apply signature
Reading messages	Private key used to decrypt message contents	Public signing key used to interpret applied signature

Certificates are an authentication mechanism used by many security schemes. In Exchange certificates are used to transport users' public keys throughout the organization so that they are available to any process which needs them. They are replicated via the Directory Service and contain:

- A unique serial number for each certificate which the Key Management Server generates.

- The encrypted password of the Certification Authority. This is sometimes known as the CA signature.

- The directory name of the Certification Authority. This allows clients to send messages back to the Certification Authority via the mail system.

- The directory name for the user who holds the certificate.

- The user's public keys for either signing or message encryption.

- The expiry date of the certificate, if set by the Certification Authority.

Two certificates are issued to each user who is enabled for advanced security. One certificate holds the public signing key, the other the public encryption key. A copy of the CA's own certificate is also distributed to each user. This certificate is stored in the user's .EPF file along with the user's personal certificates.

A wax blob impressed with the seal of office of a mayor or other public official and affixed to a formal document is a reasonable analogy for a special certificate, which fulfills the same role in attesting that the item it is associated with has been authorized by a specific individual (or public body).

5.10.4   Electronic signatures

Much of our discussion so far has been focused on message encryption. Exchange also allows messages to be "signed" by users to enable non-repudiation and message integrity. These features utilize additional keys, known as signing keys, which are quite separate from those used to encrypt and decrypt message content.

Non-repudiation means that a message can be associated with a specific individual who cannot deny that they sent a message (because it has been electronically signed by them). Of course, just like passwords, non-repudiation only works if individuals do not reveal their signing keys to others. It is also very unwise to keep copies of signing keys taped to the bottom of a keyboard.

Message integrity can be assured by creating a "hash" value, an algorithmically derived value calculated by passing the contents of a message through a complex set of computations. The end result of taking such an electronically mixed snapshot of a message's contents is a unique numeric value, the hash value. Before sending the message the hash value is encrypted with the sender's private signing key. When the message is received its contents can be verified by creating another hash of the contents using the same algorithm and comparing it against the original hash which is fetched from the message using the originator's public signing key. Any difference in the two hashed values indicates that the message has been changed since the originator signed it.

5.10.5   Installing advanced security

The installation of the Key Management Server is easy and accomplished by running the SETUP.EXE in the \EXCHKM directory from the Exchange Server CD. After the installation is complete the Key Management service starts up and functions in the same manner as any of the other Exchange services, such as the System Attendant.

The installation of the Key Management Server involves the creation of two passwords, both used to decrypt, or unlock, the "lockbox" which protects the Master Encryption Key for the Key Management Server. The master encryption key protects all keys held within the security database.

The first password is written to a file called KMSPWD.INI on a floppy diskette that you'll be asked to provide during the installation. If you want to you can avoid writing the information to the floppy, but this decision can lead to future inconvenience because the password will then have to be manually input each time the Key Management Server is started. If the floppy disk containing the password is not available whenever the Key Management Server is started you'll be asked to insert it, and failing this, the server will not start up because the master encryption key cannot be accessed. Remember, without access to the master encryption key the server cannot even begin to process security requests, so make sure that the floppy containing the master encryption password is always available. Don't leave the floppy in the computer's floppy drive because the computer will attempt to use its contents to boot an operating system the next time it is restarted, and Windows NT doesn't boot too well from a key management server floppy disk! Floppy disks are very prone to error, especially when they are used over a long period of time. It's therefore a good idea to copy the diskette containing the password and store the copy in a safe place.

The second password is created for use by the system administrators every time they attempt to carry out any management operation that involves the Key Management Server. For example, if you select a recipient and attempt to enable them for advanced security you'll be asked to enter the password. As it can get quite tiresome to continually be prompted for a password Exchange allows you to decide whether the password should be "remembered" for up to five minutes at a time. This allows you to get on with the task at hand such as enabling a whole group of users for advanced security.

A default value for the security administrator password is provided (the password, strangely enough, is set to "password") and you should change it as soon as possible after the installation is complete. Remember to share the password with anyone who will participate in any security management operations. At first glance it may seem that the management of the Key Management Server involves lots of passwords being demanded; it's logical when you think of the attitude that should really be adopted when you approach the implementation of a secure messaging system. Either you want to have a secure system or you don't. There really isn't a half-way point in this respect.

As noted previously, a single central Key Management Server is allocated the role of creating and managing all security keys allocated to users within an Exchange organization. In all advanced security implementations the central Key Management Server is installed first. You can switch and change the Key Management Server across different systems, but only within the same site. This process is accomplished by simply copying the security database, security DLL, and service to the target server. If you make a mistake and want to move the Key Management Server to a system in another site you'll have to withdraw all the existing keys and issue new ones, adding up to a lot of work that's easily avoided by making the right decision in the first place.

The effect of the initial Key Management Server installation is to create the "CA" object in Exchange Server's configuration container. Once created, details of the CA object are replicated to all the other servers in the organization in the same manner as other configuration data. Using the CA object as a marker prevents another server becoming the central Key Management Server for an organization, but only after replication has occurred. It is technically possible that two administrators install the Key Management Server component in different sites at the same time, something that will result in chaos after replication occurs and two certification authorities vie for primacy. Advanced security needs to be planned, not just dropped into an organization on an ad-hoc basis.

Figure 5.42
Stages in implementing advanced security for a user

Although the central Key Management Server is the sole definitive source of security keys within an organization, the Key Management Server software should be installed on a server in each site. These installations can be thought of as secondary Key Management Servers. They don't allocate or control security keys, but allow local recipients to be enabled for advanced security by routing any security-related messages back to the primary Key Management Server for action.

All security-related operations such as credential generation and verification are channeled back to the central system where the central Key Management Server is running, so clearly it's important to carefully select the right server to take on this role. The central Key Management Server should be located on a system that has good network links and is able to undertake the load generated by security processes. In small organizations it's not normally a problem to determine which server should be nominated to act as the host for the central Key Management Server, but larger organizations need to look at how advanced security is going to be used in the organization before making the choice.

Once the decision is made to implement advanced security and a suitable server nominated you should take steps to ensure some level of physical security for the server. This implies that the server should not be easily accessible to users and that as few people as possible should be able to log-on to the system in a privileged mode.

5.10.6 Enabling advanced security

Before anyone can use the advanced security features of Exchange the system administrator must authorize or enable the user for these features. This process can be performed individually, or for a whole group of users at one time. Authorization can only be accomplished after the Key Management Server component is installed and running.

Table 5.10 *Security components*

Location	Component	Use	Filename
Client	Security DLL	Contains code to sign/verify or encrypt and decrypt messages.	ETEXCH.DLL (16 bit) ETEXCH32.DLL (32 bit)
Server	System Attendant	Interacts with clients when advanced security is enabled. The System Attendant works with the Security DLL to store and manage key pairs as required by the system.	
	Key Management Server	Allows the System Administrator to use the Security property page to enable advanced security for users.	SECADMIN.DLL
	Key Management service	Accepts and actions requests from the Administrator program and the functions contained in the Key Management Security DLL.	
	Key Management database	A collection of files managed by the Key Management service. These files contain security information about clients.	\SECURITY\MGRENT directory
	Security DLL	Functions to enable the server to respond to security requests generated by clients.	SECKM.DLL

Before examining the details of the steps taken to enable a user for advanced security, it's important to know how all the different security components fit together. Security components are divided between Exchange clients and the Key Management Server and are shown in Table 5.10.

Once everything is installed you can begin to enable individuals or groups of users. As illustrated by Figure 5.42, enabling a user is a 4 stage process.

1. Temporary security credentials are requested for the user.

2. The credentials are provided to the user.

3. The credentials are used to enable advanced security from a client.

4. The security server recognizes that the credentials have been properly used by a client and allows the user to begin using advanced security.

Figure 5.43
Temporary
security
credentials

With the exception of mass generation of temporary security credentials using the SIMPORT.EXE program, the same process is repeated when users are enabled en masse. Let's look at each stage in a little more detail.

Temporary credentials (sometimes called a token) are generated by selecting the security property page for a recipient from the administrator program and clicking on the "Enable Advanced Security" button. The Key Management Server then proceeds to create temporary security credentials for the user and displays them to the system administrator, who should note the credentials down exactly as they are displayed. The credentials can be thought of as a password for the user to identify themselves to the security server during the later phases of enabling. At the same time the public and private encryption keys are generated and stored in the security database on the server.

After the temporary credentials have been noted the system administrator must pass them to the relevant user. This should be done in a reasonably secure manner, preferably not by writing the password down on a slip of paper or yelling it across a crowded room. In small sites it's probably best for the administrator to visit the users and coach them through the remainder of the process. This isn't practical for large installations where the issuing of keys and their provision to users might fully occupy a system administrator for quite some time. Assuming that it takes an average of fifteen minutes to create the temporary credentials, note them down, visit the user, and enable security from the user's client, only four users can be processed in an hour, or 32 in an eight hour day. Chasing users to enable security isn't a good use of a system administrator's time, so in this situation it is best for the administrator to concentrate on the task of generating the temporary credentials and noting them down before passing the credentials to one or more others, possibly users who have been nominated to help with this task, who will then visit users to pass on the credentials and help complete the whole process as quickly as possible.

Figure 5.44
Enabling
security

Administrators in remote sites must make arrangements for credentials to be first generated and then passed over by an administrator in the site where the central Key Management Server is running. Credentials can then be passed out locally, again in as secure a manner as possible. After receiving their temporary credentials each user then enables advanced security from a client by selecting the "Security" property page from the Tools.Options menu option (Figure 5.44). The user must now type in the temporary security credential and provide a password of their own (which must be at least six characters long). This step generates the public and private key pair to be used for electronic signatures.

As mentioned earlier, the special security certificates generated for the user and the copy of the CA's own special certificate is written into a file with an .EPF[16] extension. This file is normally stored in the Windows directory, for example: C:\WIN95\TONYREDM.EPF. The

---

[16] EPF = Encrypted Password File.

security file is encrypted using a CAST-64 algorithm to prevent unauthorized access. The security file must be available before encrypted messages can be read or sent. Local availability of the .EPF file has implications for users who roam from workstation to workstation to read their mail. It is possible to copy the .EPF file to a floppy and point the client to the floppy when it attempts any security operations, and this is possibly the best way for roaming users to cope. Indeed, keeping the .EPF file on a floppy disk guarantees maximum security at the expense of relying on relatively fragile media. If people opt to use floppy disks to hold EPF files make sure they know that they need to have a copy available just in case problems occur.

After the user enables security from a client an encrypted message is automatically generated and sent back to the Key Management Server to indicate that the user has provided credentials and a satisfactory password and wishes to begin using advanced security. This message contains the public signing key, which is in turn stored by the Key Management Server.

The Key Management Server checks the credentials and, if they are satisfactory, generates a message back to the user to inform them that they can now begin to use advanced security. The user receives the message from the "Security Authority," the name that the Key Management Server represents itself by to users. This message includes some hidden data containing the encryption key pair that was earlier generated by the Key Management Server as well as the pair of X.509 certificates to use later on for signing and encrypting messages. A copy of the CA's X.509 certificate is also enclosed. Before the message can be read the user must provide the password they originally specified when they received the original enabling message. This step ensures that the same user is involved at all stages of the enabling procedure. If the password matches, the encryption key pair is written into the .EPF file and once it is present the user can begin to encrypt and sign messages.

By default security certificates are valid for one year from the date of issue. As a user approaches the end of a certificate's validity the Key Management Server sends them a message to request whether the certificate should be updated for another year. This process continues from year to year unless the security administrator issues a certificate that is valid for a specific period.

Security keys can be recovered anytime after they have been issued. This would be in cases where a user loses (or forgets) their password or corrupts the security file on the PC. Another reason is because the user suspects, for one reason or another, that their password is compromised, possibly because they shared it with someone else on a temporary basis. Along the same theme, the administrator can revoke security keys if any reason arises to believe that a user should not be able to use the features of advanced security. Revocation works by the server writing the number of a user's certificate into a revocation list maintained in the directory. Once a certificate has been added to the list no other user can encrypt a message for that user.

5.10.7   Using advanced security

After a user is enabled for advanced security they can proceed to encrypt messages and attachments and apply digital signatures. Users can select to encrypt or sign every message by default, or elect to encrypt or sign a specific message. Encryption isn't much good if no one else is able to decrypt the message, so Exchange checks any message before attempting to encrypt it to determine whether the recipients will be able to decrypt the message. This process occurs just before the message is sent. If Exchange believes that even one recipient on a message will not be able to decrypt the message it will stop sending the message and notify the user, as shown in Figure 5.45. Digital signatures can be applied to messages sent to users who have not been enabled for advanced security.

Figure 5.45
Non-secure
recipients

Because recipients are checked to ensure that they have been enabled for advanced security and will be able to decrypt messages you cannot encrypt messages when working off-line unless a copy of the Off-line Address Book (or OAB—described in Chapter 8) has been downloaded. Amongst the information about users extracted from the directory, the OAB contains copies of X.509 certificates, so public keys are available for encryption purposes. However, if the OAB has never been downloaded or is out of date then the keys will be unavailable, a record may not exist for a user that has been added to the directory since the OAB was last downloaded, or some of the public keys may be obsolete. For this reason, people who travel and need to generate encrypted messages on the road should always download an up-to-date copy of the OAB before they leave the office.

Common reasons why Exchange will determine a user cannot receive encrypted messages include:

- They have not been enabled for advanced security

■ The message must pass through a gateway before it can be delivered to the recipient. In general any attempt to get encrypted information through a gateway fails. As discussed earlier, Exchange V5.0 and Outlook clients are able to send special messages containing public keys to users in other Exchange organizations that may be connected via X.400 or SMTP backbones. In these cases, when both parties at either side of the backbone possess the necessary key information to allow encryption/decryption to proceed, encrypted messages can pass through connectors. However, encrypted messages can never be sent to non-Exchange recipients such as an IBM PROFS or Lotus Notes user.

Figure 5.46
Icons for signed and encrypted messages

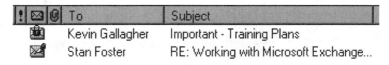

Encrypted messages or those bearing digital signatures are indicated by using a different icon when messages are shown in a folder. The lock icon indicates that a message is encrypted, while the pen icon means that it has been digitally signed (Figure 5.46).

5.10.8   Location of security objects

We've been through a lot of fairly complicated and interlinked structures which work together to allow someone to encrypt or sign messages. Table 5.11 describes the location of each security object after advanced security has been enabled for a user. As you can see, there are four main locations.

Table 5.11 *Location of security objects*

	X.509 certificate	Key Management Security database	User's personal EPF file	Exchange Directory Store
User's directory name (mail address)	▭			
Signing certificate			▭	
Encryption certificate			▭	▭
Private encryption key		▭	▭	
Private signing key			▭	

Table 5.11 *Location of security objects (continued)*

Public encryption key	✉			
Public signing key	✉	✉		
Certificate expiration date	✉			
Unique certificate number	✉			
CA signature	✉			
CA directory name (mail address)	✉			

5.10.9 Making a decision about advanced security

Advanced security is one of those features that seem awfully attractive on the surface, so why won't it be immediately implemented in all organizations that operate Exchange? Table 5.12 lists some of the advantages and disadvantages of advanced security.

System administration workload is the biggest issue influencing the decision whether to implement advanced security. Small organizations or those able to dedicate a person to fill the role of security administrator won't experience too many problems handling the work, but the same cannot be said for larger sites or organizations.

Before making a decision consider:

- Who is going to act as the security administrator?
- Who is going to be the back-up to the security administrator to handle their work when they are on vacation or sick?
- What is the maximum number of users in the organization that are going to be security enabled?
- Where are these users located? How and when are they going to be enabled for advanced security? How are the initial credentials going to be provided to users, especially users remote from the security administrator?
- How will roaming users access their .EPF files as they move from workstation to workstation?
- What server is best to act as the Key Management Server? Does it have an appropriate hardware configuration to handle the expected load? Is it capable of providing a highly available service to users?

- How physically secure is the chosen Key Management Server? Where is it located and who has access to it?

- When will the security data used by Key Management Server be backed up? Is this operation included in regular system maintenance activities?

Do not attempt to enable advanced security unless you are happy with the answers to these questions. Cleaning up a bad security implementation and starting over again will require a lot of work and cooperation from users, especially when new credentials have to be issued or a new, different Key Management Server installed. In the latter case users won't be able to read any messages encrypted with credentials issued by the original Key Management Server, proving the point that it's very important to get your security implementation right first time.

Table 5.12 *Advantages and disadvantages of advanced security*

Advantages	Disadvantages
Users can apply digital signatures to messages so that the messages cannot be repudiated.	A lot of work is imposed on system administrators to generate, distribute, and manage security credentials.
Users can encrypt messages before they are sent, and decrypt messages received from other users.	Encrypted messages can only be sent to other recipients who are "security enabled."
Encrypted messages can only be accessed when a user's personal security password is provided, even if another user's mailbox is accessed by a privileged user.	The .EPF file must be physically available before messages can be decrypted.

If you decide that you can't implement advanced security it is still possible to protect sensitive information. For example, it is possible to use application-specific password protection for documents and spreadsheets. Users can set their own passwords to protect items stored in their private folders and shared passwords can be determined and used by groups who want an extra layer of protection for confidential information in public folders. I know of quite a number of installations that have opted to protect information in this manner. It's certainly not an infallible scheme, but it is simple to operate and is enough to stop casual unauthorized browsing through data.

Managing Exchange Users

6.1   Recipients, mailboxes, and people

Users are the most important part of any system, and perhaps especially so in the case of systems that automate common office tasks and enable better human interaction. Without users there's simply no point to an electronic messaging server. In this chapter we'll look at the challenges involved in day to day operation of an Exchange server, covering topics like setting up and managing the user community, distribution lists and so on.

Figure 6.1
Contents of a recipients container from a small Exchange server

Anyone who has ever faced the task of managing a mail server knows that people have to be registered before they can use the system. Exchange server is no different in this respect. Users have to be registered and allocated space to hold their messages, but Exchange is a little different because a wide range of valid mail destinations, including people, are registered together in a single directory. Some or all of the recipient types are supported by other servers, but possibly not in as complete a fashion as Exchange. Valid recipient types are:

- **Mailboxes.** This is the most common type of recipient. Everyone who wants to use Exchange to send and receive interpersonal messages must be able to access a mailbox. Several users can share a mailbox, and it is possible for someone to delegate access to their mailbox to other users (see section on mailbox surrogacy later on in this chapter).

- **Distribution lists.** A distribution list is a collection of recipients of any valid types. When messages are sent to distribution lists copies are dispatched to every recipient that appears in the list.

- **Custom recipient.** Someone who uses any other messaging system. For example, an Internet user who receives mail via SMTP, or someone who receives messages sent via an X.400 link between Exchange and another X.400-compliant messaging system such as AT&T Mail.

- **Public folders.** A folder is a sub-section of the information store, used to arrange information in a logical order. Unlike folders in the personal message store, information placed in public folders becomes available to anyone who has access to the folder.

By default, details of user mailboxes and distribution lists are stored in the Recipients container in the Exchange directory (see Figure 6.1). Two interesting aspects of mailbox entries in the Exchange directory are:

- You don't have to reveal all mailboxes by adding them to the Global Address List. The "Hide from Address Book" checkbox on a mailbox's Advanced property page controls whether a mailbox is included in the Global Address List. Senior management or other individuals occupying sensitive posts are often excluded from directory listings, the e-mail equivalent of an unlisted telephone number.

- The Directory Restrictions property page controls the addresses a mailbox can send messages to as well as the people the mailbox will accept messages from. You can use these properties to restrict users to a subset of total possible recipients, or to stop messages arriving into a mailbox from people you'd rather not receive mail from. Contract workers who join an organization for a short time and need e-mail connectivity are candidates for restricted send options. Senior management might also like to be protected from a flood of messages, so they are candidates for restricted delivery options. Controlling a large exclusion list for send or delivery restrictions can be quite time-consuming, but you can cut down on the work by using distribution lists instead of specifying individual mailboxes, as shown in Figure 6.2.

Figure 6.2 *Using a distribution list for delivery restrictions*

6.1.1 Breaking up the directory

Multiple containers can be defined to hold recipients, allowing you to break up large user communities into more manageable chunks. Apart from anything else, dividing recipients up into different containers makes it easier for users to select from a set of particular addresses when they add recipients to mail messages.

Figure 6.3 *Selecting a custom recipient from a special container*

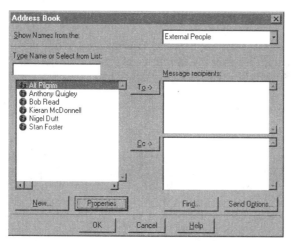

Figure 6.3 shows addresses for a new message being selected from a special container called "External People." This container holds all the custom recipients defined system-wide. It's easier for someone to look through a small container holding all the addresses of a specific type, in this case, everyone external to the company, than it is to wade through a potentially very large global address list. It is also very much faster to conduct a search for a specific name in a smaller segment of the overall directory than to scan through the complete global address list.

Public folders are fairly special entities. As such they deserve a separate discussion removed from the topic of how to set up and name the accounts used by people to access Exchange.

6.1.2   Distribution lists

Exchange can currently store a maximum of 5,000 objects in a distribution list. Note the word "objects." An object can be an Exchange mailbox or a custom recipient, but it can also be another distribution list, leading to a situation where distribution lists can contain nested distribution lists, greatly expanding the total possible user population that can be addressed through a single list. However, while it's nice to know that it's technically possible to create a mega-distribution list to address thousands of users at a single keystroke, once a list contains more than 100 users or so perhaps public folders offer a much better way of distributing information to wide interest groups.

Because Exchange treats them like any other recipient, distribution lists are useful when setting permissions on folders, much along the same lines as delivery restrictions. When permission is given to a distribution list all members of the list inherit the permission. The advantage lies in the fact that it's very much easier to grant permission to a single entity, the list, than it is to manage separate permissions for each individual on the list. And better still, when people join a distribution list they'll inherit permissions granted to the list, and when they are removed from the list the permissions are revoked.

6.2   Managing user mailboxes

We've already discussed the topic of well-designed server names. If you've been running an electronic mail system, including PC LAN-based systems, you're also aware that each user must be uniquely identified to allow proper control of access to the system and also, possibly more important from the user perspective, to make sure that messages are delivered correctly. To accomplish this each person wishing to use the Exchange messaging system is allocated a unique identifier, otherwise known as an account or user name.

Successful operation of Exchange requires management of user accounts and mailbox names. Plunging forward to create accounts and mailboxes without considering the long term ramifications of what you're doing may work for a 20-user operation. But you're bound to run into problems when the system expands and has to accommodate more accounts or mailboxes, so it pays to consider your options before starting.

All messaging systems impose their own requirements in terms of the number of characters that can be used in an account name, and which characters may legally appear in the name. Some installations have well-defined guidelines as to how account names are made up, although some of these ideas are a little obscure. For example, if your organization allocates numbers to staff members it may seem sensible to use the same staff numbers as the basis for allocating e-mail account names. In reality however such a scheme falls down badly as the resulting addressing scheme is very unuser-friendly. I hold badge number 150847 in DIGITAL's personnel system, but I'd hate to be thought of as a mere number, or to have other people forced to address messages to me as 150847. National social security numbers are unique and are sometimes proposed as the basis for an even more unuser-friendly account naming convention. Thankfully it's illegal to use social security numbers in this way in many countries. But, strange as it may seem, there are organizations who think it's a good idea to use cryptic, esoteric naming schemes.

The most sensible principles to remember when considering what type of account naming scheme is appropriate for your organization are:

- *Logical.* Users shouldn't have to go through mental contortions to remember the account name for the people they want to send mail to.

- *Friendly.* Some logical schemes are well, too logical. Look for a compromise between logic and user-friendliness.

- *Straightforward.* Avoid complexity at all costs.

Surnames are often considered to be the first and most obvious basis for planning a naming scheme, and it's often possible to use surnames in small e-mail systems. However, the statistical fact is that the more users a system supports the more chance there'll be that common surnames exist. In a small system supporting 50 users you might only have one "SMITH" (or the equivalent most common name in a country or language), but I'll guarantee that in a system supporting more than a hundred or so users there'll be more than one surname clash to contend with.

6.2.1   Accessing your mailbox

Everyone who wishes to use Microsoft Exchange server to send and receive messages must have access to a Windows NT account. Normally, a Windows NT account is associated with a single Exchange mailbox, although a privileged account is able to use its elevated permissions to access a mailbox apparently reserved for another account. You could, for instance, log into the computer's privileged Administrator account, run the Exchange client program, and define a profile to connect to a mailbox allocated to another account. This is quite legal and understandable, if not altogether desirable from a user perspective. All that's happening is that standard permissions are being used to over-ride the protections on a mailbox. Being able to log-in to a user's account in this way is a useful feature for an administrator, but it can be disconcerting for users to discover that their mailbox can be accessed in this manner, especially as no permanent trace or audit record is left that a mailbox has been accessed from a different account[1].

Exchange is little different from many other messaging systems that permit privileged administrators to "take over" user mailboxes for debugging or maintenance purposes. System administrators (and sometimes operators) basically have access to any data held on a computer unless special steps are taken to restrict their access to specific information. This fact is something to think about when appointing people to fill positions with access to such a range of sensitive information. The advanced security features of Exchange (discussed later on in this chapter) help by preventing unauthorized access to encrypted messages. Even if someone else is privileged enough on the Windows NT level to be able to access your mailbox they shouldn't be able to read encrypted messages unless you hand over your security password.

The implications of privileged user access to electronic mail should be factored into your security policy and the consequences of unautho-

[1]   The log-ons property page for the Private Information Store lists the mailboxes which access the Private Information Store together with the Windows NT account last used to access each mailbox. This information provides the only obvious sign of instances where a privileged account was used to access a user mailbox. However, the information is transient and is over-written each time a mailbox is logged on to. It is possible to log the use of privileges to access user mailboxes by turning diagnostic logging on for the log-on category for the MSExchangeIS Private service through the Diagnostics Logging property page for a selected server. When log-on diagnostics are enabled privileged access to user mailboxes is recorded in the Windows NT event log. You can see these events by viewing the log (look for events 1011, 1016, or 1009).

rized access to messages clearly spelled out. A wide variety of views are present in the computer industry on the nature of information held in electronic messages. I believe the majority of companies treat the contents of electronic messages as private to the sender and recipients and take steps to ensure that no unauthorized access is tolerated. However, the increased incidence of "discovery" actions taken by lawyers in attempts to uncover potentially damaging revelations about incidents or business dealings is causing companies to review the data contained in electronic mail systems with an aim of protecting themselves if the time comes to defend such an action.

How would you deal with a request to search your system to identify and recover all messages relating to a specific topic? Would it make things harder if the request focused in on a particular range of dates? I've been involved in a couple of discovery cases where lawyers requested copies of all messages sent by a particular group of users over the period of a month two years back from the time of asking. Fulfilling such a request is an expensive and time-consuming exercise. Exchange does not offer any text search and retrieval functionality capable of meeting such a request, so the only option in this case is to check the mailbox of each user on the list to see what it contained during the particular period. In fact, the standard find option provided in the Exchange clients (see Figure 6.4) is only capable of searching the cover memo text of messages and won't, for instance, search through a Word document or a PowerPoint presentation.

Figure 6.4
Searching for a
message

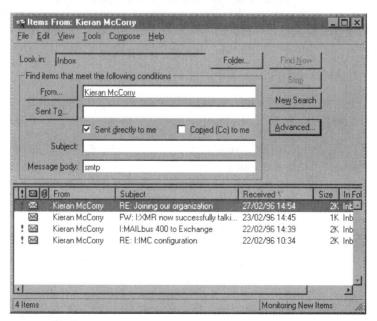

Note that the "search subfolders" option is disabled automatically whenever a search involves folders that may span multiple servers. While it is reasonable to expect a search to be able to conduct a fast scan through all the folders in a specific folder tree when the folders are stored locally, it's quite another matter to attempt to do the same thing when the folders may be scattered throughout the network. Executing live, distributed queries would take a long time to complete. It's a problem that database vendors have been looking at for quite a time, but so far no good answers have arrived.

In a discovery situation before any check can be made the system must be restored back to the exact state it was at the time in question. This point raises the question of just how long you need to keep system backups around in today's legally-charged atmosphere. Is two years enough? Probably not. If you take full system backups at regular intervals you should plan to keep the backup tapes around for at least five years, just in case.

6.2.2   Mailboxes and Windows NT accounts

Mailboxes can be created when new Windows NT user accounts are set up or by using the Exchange Administrator program to create a new mailbox for an existing Windows NT account. In most situations there will be a one-to-one mapping between users and mailboxes, but it is also possible for several users to have access to a shared mailbox, such as in the case where a group of users need to monitor messages arriving at a mailbox set up as a generic recipient. For example, a mailbox created to receive requests to register for training events, or a mailbox that people can send messages to report problems to the help desk.

Windows NT account names tend to be rather terse and pretty un-user-friendly, and are limited to 20 characters. For example, my account names on the two servers I connect to regularly are T_REDMOND and TONYR. Exchange treats everything associated with the server as an object in one form or another, and the Windows NT account name is an attribute of a user object, albeit one that's pretty important. However, you're not limited to account names as Exchange also allows for a more complete name as another user attribute, so I can be referred to as "Tony Redmond." A complete user name is sometimes referred to by users as a "pretty name," probably because it's nicer to look at on-screen or in printed format than the shorter computer account names. While it's by no means essential to have two names for an account, from the human interface point of view it's also possibly true that people feel better addressing messages to "Tony Redmond" than "TONYR."

Using surnames as the basis for Windows NT account names meets the criteria of being logical, friendly, and straightforward. So it makes sense to persist and try and use a variation of pure surnames as the basis for a naming scheme. How about adding an initial to the surname so that I, for instance, become "TREDMOND." This is more unique but incurs the disadvantage of throwing all our account names out of synchronization, mostly because it's easier and more logical to view a user directory when it is ordered in the same way as the telephone directory —in surname order.

It's therefore better to use initials as a suffix rather than a prefix, giving us "REDMONDT." Now all the names are sorted according to the same order you'd expect, making it easier for users to follow. If Tony Redmond and Tom Redmond are on the same system we can add another initial to create a difference. For example, "REDMOND-TY" and "REDMONDTO."

Some installations separate the surname from the initials with a character such as "," (comma), or "." (period). Underscores ("_") should be avoided in electronic mail addresses because some mail systems are unable to deal with addresses that contain underscores. My preference is to use a period as a separator, but only because this has been successfully used within DIGITAL for many years and has therefore withstood the test of time.

Thus, the preferred Windows NT account name is a choice between "REDMOND.T" or "REDMOND.TONY". Remember that 20-character restriction. It may limit your options in situations where you have to cater for very long names, so be prepared to be flexible.

6.2.3   Exchange user names

After you've successfully managed to log onto your Windows NT system you can proceed to connect to Exchange Server. Mailboxes have a number of user name attributes that link Windows NT accounts with the correct Exchange mailboxes. These are:

■ **Display Name.** The name that appears in the Administrator window (and used to select mailboxes when their details are changed or otherwise worked with by an administrator). This name can be up to 256 characters long, so even the longest name in the universe should fit. The display name is sometimes referred to as the "pretty name" because it is seen when addressing messages, as part of a distribution list, or in the header information when a message is viewed or printed. Because the information from Global Address List cannot be customized when recipient information is viewed by users large organizations often include some additional data in recipients' display names to allow users to distinguish between common names. For example:

```
John Smith (Sales)
John Smith (Training)
```

If department names aren't enough consider using locations or other hints. For example:

```
John Smith (Sales - London)
John Smith (Training - Geneva)
```

The display name is also shown when the contents of a recipients container is viewed using the administration program.

- **Alias Name.** An alias can be up to 64 characters and is used to associate other mail addresses with an Exchange mailbox. As such, the mailbox alias must be unique on a server. Exchange will stop you if you attempt to allocate an existing alias to a mailbox. Apart from its use within the directory the alias is used as the "account name" portion of an SMTP address. Many experienced system administrators like to set the Exchange mailbox alias to be the same as the Windows NT account name.

- **First Name, Initials, and Last Name.** These are all optional naming attributes that can be up to 32, 2, and 64 characters long respectively. While you don't have to enter this information it is useful to do so, especially in an X.400 environment where these attributes form part of fully qualified X.400 originator/recipient addresses.

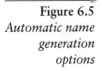

Figure 6.5
Automatic name
generation
options

The auto-name generation feature of Exchange, as shown in Figure 6.5, is able to generate a display and alias name for a new recipient when you enter details of the first name, initials, and last name. If you don't like the names generated by Exchange feel free to override the defaults and create your own versions. For example, you might decide to generate aliases based on the new recipient's surname and the first letter from their first name. To do this, select the Options menu from the Administration utility, select the "Custom" radio button for Alias name generation, and type %Last%1First into the provided field. If you change the scheme used for automatic name generation midway through adding mailboxes or custom recipients some newly generated aliases may clash with entries already in the directory when you attempt to add them. Fixing this problem is easy—all you need to do is create a custom alias for the affected recipient or mailbox.

When addressing messages Exchange clients allow you to enter the full display name, a mailbox's alias, or a user's surname in the TO:, CC:, or BCC: controls. Names are always checked before messages are sent from the client to the server. Names that are successfully validated against the global address list (server or off-line) or the personal address book are underlined in the control to show that Exchange has recognized the address and knows how to route the message to it. Names that are not underlined have not been validated but Exchange will validate the names when the message is sent and before it is actually passed on to the MTA for onward dispatch. If a name cannot be found in the global address list by reference to the full display name, a mailbox alias, or a surname, Exchange signals this to the client and refuses to accept the message. At this stage the user must "fix" the address, possibly by perusing the global address list to select the address they actually want, before resubmitting the message to the server.

6.2.4 The value of mailbox naming conventions

If the value of a discussion about mailbox naming conventions appears small to you I think you're probably running a small organization, one with less than 1,000 mailboxes. The challenges involved in managing and dealing with multi-thousand mailbox deployments escalate after the first thousand, and past this point it is essential to pay close attention to details. Consider two questions:

1. How long will it take to display a GAL containing five, ten, or twenty thousand when a user attempts to browse through the GAL before addressing a message?

2. What's the most logical way to organize a large GAL? How will users expect to have the information presented to them? In sur-

name order (like most telephone directories) or in first name order (the default used by Exchange)?

Figure 6.6
GAL display
orders

Jane Doe	Archer, Julian
John Jones	Doe, Jane
John L. Robb	Jones, John
John Rogers	Robb, John L.
John Smith	Rogers, John
Julia Sommerville	Smith, John
Julian Archer	Sommerville, Julia

You can't do much about the time necessary to browse a large GAL. Indeed, the problem of a large GAL is much less severe for MAPI clients (like Outlook) than for Web and POP3 clients that use LDAP to access the directory. The sole problem is time. How long will people wait for the client to retrieve and then display information from the directory? With MAPI clients the delay is measured in seconds, but LDAP clients can take much longer than this.

Given that browsing a large GAL can take some time it clearly pays to use an efficient approach to browsing, and that's where a good mailbox naming convention is valuable. If mailbox display names are generated using the standard First Name Last Name syntax the GAL is displayed sorted by first name. But people have largely accumulated the habit of consulting directories sorted by surname, so it is more effective to use the same sort order in the GAL? Compare the two orders illustrated in Figure 6.6. Which seems more logical to you?

6.2.5 Maintaining mailbox details

Exchange allows system administrators to enter lots of information about user mailboxes, possibly more details than you would ever want to know about users, including who their manager is and who their direct reports are (if they have any).

One possible flaw in the implementation is the fact that only system administrators, or rather people who hold the privilege to run the Exchange administration program, are able to amend user mailbox details. The logic behind this stance is easy to understand. User mailbox details are used as the basis of the directory and are replicated to other sites within the organization. It is therefore important to have a certain level of quality control and consistency imposed on the information entered into the directory.

To achieve quality in the directory users are not able to change even the most non-sensitive fields, such as their telephone numbers. Everything has to be done by system administrators, and I can foresee many help desk requests from users to change small details about the information that's been entered into the directory.

Other implementations of corporate messaging systems allow users to update their own details in the directory, so is this a competitive disadvantage for Exchange? Not really, those same implementations have discovered to their pain that user-initiated directory updates produce a lot of potentially unnecessary network traffic to propagate user-initiated changes throughout the organization. Restricting users from endless fiddling with their own details stops this traffic and helps to maintain the quality of directory information. A lot depends on corporate culture and previous expectations. If people expect to be able to amend personal information, likle telephone numbers and office details, only to find they can't with Exchange then you can expect a certain level of grievance. In these situations it's best to address the grievance head-on by explaining to users the reasons why they can't update the directory. But be prepared to seek another solution in the event of major push-back, possibly by writing a client extension that permits a certain degree of access to the directory. This topic is discussed more in Chapter 8.

6.2.6   Mailbox surrogacy

Mail surrogacy or delegation is where users are authorized to take control of other users' mailboxes for specific purposes.

Figure 6.7
*Delegating
access to a
mailbox*

The classical example of this functionality in action is where a secretary or administrative assistant controls a senior manager's mailbox. Even today, a minority of very senior executives actually process their own electronic mail and some are still at the stage where they demand that their messages are printed each day for their perusal. They then mark the printed copies of the messages with their comments or replies and leave the marked-up messages with their secretary who takes care of generating an appropriate response.

In the early days of electronic mail systems tended to be unsophisticated when compared to the systems in use today. Delegation was accomplished in an easy to work but totally insecure manner when users would give their system password to whoever was going to process messages on their behalf. System administrators hated this method because it totally compromised system security, but users find it easy to understand, especially when passwords were handed over on scraps of paper that could be conveniently posted on their pinboard or securely stored in their desk drawer!

Figure 6.8 *Mail delegation from the client*

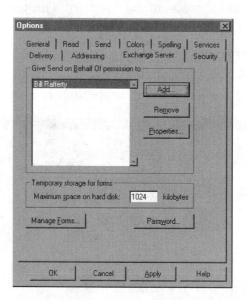

As electronic mail systems evolved attention was paid to eliminating the security hole caused by such a general interchange of passwords. Facilities to allow other users to connect to all or specific parts of mailboxes began to appear in the early 1990s, but even so many users persist in their old habits and continue to exchange passwords today. Exchange takes a comprehensive approach to the problem by:

- Not restricting users to only allowing one other account to access their mailbox. Any number of users can be granted the permission to send on behalf of a particular mailbox.

- Allowing system administrators to control the permission centrally by using the Administration utility (see Figure 6.7) to edit details of user mailboxes while also permitting users to issue their own permission using the client Tools.Options menu choice (Figure 6.8).

A newly delegated mailbox does not automatically appear after permission has been granted. Users must reconfigure their profiles to access additional mailboxes and then reconnect to the server after permission is received. Exchange does not break any new ground in mail delegation. However, it does build on the lessons learned in other messaging systems and has made the whole process a little easier.

6.3   Client installations and settings

The Windows registry holds MAPI user profiles on all 32-bit platforms. A MAPI user profile consists of information about a user's working environment including the mailbox and server they connect to as well as the services they have configured. The normal set of services include Microsoft Exchange Server and the Personal Address Book, and traveling users will probably configure Personal Folders as well. Optional services such as Microsoft Mail or Internet Mail can be configured as required, and all the details written into the registry.

Figure 6.9
Exchange profile settings held in the Windows 95 system registry

Figure 6.9 shows the Windows registry editor, REGEDIT.EXE, being used to view details of a user's profile on a Windows 95 client. The registry key in this case is:

```
HKEY_CURRENT_USER\Software\Microsoft\Windows Messaging Subsystem\Profiles
```

The system registry is also used to store user-specific settings for Exchange on Windows NT. On a Windows V3.* the settings are held in a standard application initialization file in the Windows directory. For example:

```
C:\WINDOWS\EXCHANGE.INI
```

Application initialization files group settings into a series of sections, each of which holds values applicable to a specific part of the application. An initialization file can be edited with any ASCII editor, such as the Windows Notepad editor, but care should be taken when editing as it's all too easy to slip and make an inadvertent change that doesn't quite have the intended effect. Always make a copy of an initialization file before making changes. Just to be complete let me note that the settings for DOS clients are stored in a file called EX-CHANGE.PRO.

6.3.1   Setting default client options

From a support perspective it's a lot easier if everyone uses the same client options. By defining a default set of client options you also have an opportunity to enforce good housekeeping habits, such as erasing the contents of the Deleted Items folder when a client logs off[2]. This simple option prevents large amounts of unwanted objects accumulating, probably unnoticed, in the Deleted Items folder and frees up space in the private Information Store. Many users are reluctant to change settings at all on the basis that if the client works it's a bad idea to attempt to fix or make things better by changing options. In view of this, establishing a good default set of options is something that should be considered early on in a deployment. After all, it's much easier to have the system make a change when a client is installed than it is to travel around and visit multiple PCs afterwards.

Exchange provides a Setup Editor (also known as the STF editor) to enable administrators to change options for kits installed in a shared installation point. A shared installation point is a location on a server where clients can connect to when they wish to install software. Installation points can be created automatically when you install the Exchange client software on a Windows NT server. A separate installation point is created for each client platform.

---

[2]   Always emptying the contents of the Deleted Items folder when exiting is good housekeeping but it has a potential side-effect too. See the discussion on restoring deleted documents starting on page 294.

Use the following steps to alter user settings with the Setup Editor.

1. Review the options available to each client you support (DOS, Windows NT, Windows 95, Windows V3.1) and decide which default settings you would like to change. The best way to conduct a review is to actually use a client for a period of time.

2. Start the Setup Editor from the Microsoft Exchange Administrator program group.

3. Select the installation point for the client you wish to change.

4. Make the changes as shown in Figure 6.10.

5. Close the Setup Editor.

Changes made with the Setup Editor are written into the EXCH-NG.STF files in the selected installation point.

Figure 6.10
Exchange Setup Editor

All clients installed after you make changes with the Setup Editor will pick up the new default values. Note that you can revert to the default set of options shipped with Exchange by clicking the "Default" button on the Setup Editor form. Clients that were installed before you make the changes will not be affected.

6.3.2   The question of network protocols

Establishing good communications between clients and servers is a fundamental part of a successful deployment of a client/server messaging system. In the case of Exchange, clients communicate with the server using remote procedure calls (RPCs), which are able to use a range of network protocols. Each protocol is attempted in the order stated in the protocol binding order, a setting specific to each PC. If a network infrastructure is in place and working then clients should be able to fit in and connect to the server without any difficulty. Problems occur when parts of the network infrastructure are unreliable or the PC attempts to connect using a protocol that isn't supported within the network.

It's common to hear Windows 95 users complaining that the Exchange client takes many minutes to start up. Lots of people have written entries on this topic to the Internet mailing list for Exchange, and they can't understand how their PC is so slow when a co-worker is able to start up and get working within a few seconds. The answer lies in the bowels of Windows 95 networking and afflicts this client in particular.

Table 6.1 lists the protocols that can be used by a Windows 95 Exchange client to connect to a server. The protocols are listed in the default order that the installation procedure writes them into the system registry. This is important, because if your site doesn't support a protocol or wants to use a particular protocol you have to adjust the contents of the registry to force Exchange to do the right thing. Time-outs occur when the client attempts to make a connection to the server using an unsupported protocol, or when an attempt is made to resolve the server name via a mechanism (like DNS) that isn't totally reliable. Network time-outs are the reason why some users can't start up Exchange quickly and others can. Those who start up quickly use PCs where the network protocol binding order is stated in an optimum manner, while those who start slowly are attempting to connect over many and varied protocols that just can't be used for one reason or another. It's really that simple.

Table 6.1   *Network protocols for Windows 95 clients*

Protocol as set in registry	Meaning
NCALRPC	Local RPC calls (client and server on the same system).
NCACN_IP_TCP	TCP/IP transmitted over Windows Sockets. The server is located using DNS, a local hosts files, or a raw IP address. NETBIOS is not used.
NCACN_SPX	Novell SPX using the NetWare Bindery to locate the server. NETBIOS is not used.
NCACN_SP	Named pipes. The server is located using a NETBIOS computer name, WINS, or LMHOSTS.
NETBIOS	The default NETBIOS protocol.
NCACN_VNS_SPP	Banyan Vines.

Of course, if you can't connect at all then there is a fundamental network problem that has to be resolved. Something like making sure that TCP/IP is correctly configured on the PC with a valid IP address allocated, and so on. No manner of adjustments made to the network protocol binding order in the registry can compensate for issues such as a badly defined or missing IP address.

As already noted, the problem of badly stated protocol binding orders is specific to Windows 95 clients. The protocol binding order can be changed by editing the appropriate value in the system registry, as shown in Figure 6.11. The setting is specific to Exchange, so the registry key is under the Exchange root within the registry. You can help solve the problem by making sure that the correct binding order is used on each PC. The easiest way to make sure that the correct binding order is used on all PCs is to alter the setting with the Setup Editor.

Figure 6.11
Modifying the Windows 95 network protocol binding order

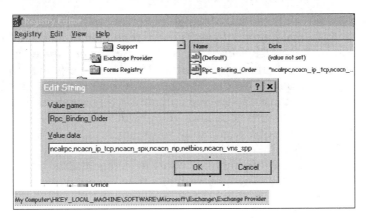

For example, in a Novell NetWare environment you should move NCACN_SPX to the top of the protocol binding order, whereas if you want to use TCP/IP it's clear that NCACN_IP_TCP should be at the top of the list. You can remove protocols that are never used. Also, in TCP/IP environments make sure that DNS is operational and can be accessed by each client.

6.3.3 "Hot" PCs and roaming users

A hot PC is one that isn't always used by the same person. It might be a PC used in a multi-user shift environment, or just one that's available for visitors to use when they arrive at an office.

User mailboxes, public folders, and directory information are all maintained in separate databases on an Exchange server, so users can connect to the information held in these containers from all PCs.

There are some files and other information that can cause concern to those who move around. These include:

- MAPI user profiles
- Personal Information Stores
- Off-line folders
- Advanced Security Encrypted Password Files
- Personal Address Book (PAB)
- Autosignature file
- Profile Information

Most of these sources of data are discussed in separate sections in this or other chapters. For the moment we'll concentrate on their involvement in the act of roaming from PC to PC.

Personal Information Stores can be located on any disk. In the normal course of events users create personal stores on local hard drives, although I know of some cases where stores have been successfully used on floppy diskettes. If a store is held on a floppy it's easy to move from PC to PC, but there are some disadvantages, including the high potential for media corruption (in comparison to hard drives) and the relative lack of space. Floppy diskettes are really only suitable for moving stores containing simple messages, not large amounts of complex documents. In most cases it's more realistic and useable to place personal information stores in personal directories on a networked file server. The only problem then occurs when people want to work in a location where they can't access the file server

Off-line folders are snapshots of server-based folders that allow users to work with the folder contents when they are disconnected from the server. People who move from PC to PC and are able to connect to their server won't need off-line folders. Problems only occur when server connections aren't possible and off-line folder files aren't available. Exchange requires users to make an initial connection to the server before they can use off-line folder files, probably to ensure that the folder hierarchy is correctly synchronized between the server and client. This means that you can't just take an off-line folder file from one PC and move it to another and expect it to work. First you'll have to create a profile (or update an existing profile) and indicate that off-line working is required, and then make a connection. Catch-22 if the network's unavailable!

Encrypted password files are only necessary when advanced security is enabled. Someone who wishes to encrypt or decrypt messages, or apply digital signatures to messages must be able to access their password file. It's easy to move the password file from PC to PC, but it's embarrassing and frustrating to find yourself in a remote location after forgetting to copy your password file before you left home base.

The PAB is typically stored in a location such as \EXCHANGE \MAILBOX.PAB. Losing access to your PAB becomes a minor annoyance if you wish to use another PC, especially if the PAB contains the addresses for many external correspondents who don't have an Exchange mailbox. The "Briefcase" feature of Windows 95 can be used to move a PAB from one PC to another (along with many other files), and then synchronize any changes that may have occurred when you return to the original PC. However, using the briefcase in this manner requires a discipline that lots of people just don't have so some frustration is likely. It's also important that you don't overwrite a PAB belonging to someone else when you move your PAB onto a PC, so it's good to recommend to users that they give a more appropriate name to their PAB, such as REDMOND.PAB.

It would be nice if PAB data could be stored in a folder in the private information store rather than a DOS file. Using an OST, the PAB could still be made available for off-line working. Unfortunately this is not the case and we are left to deal with the issue of PAB mobility. The Outlook client stores "Contacts" information in a folder in the store, so hopefully this is a pointer for the future. It's not quite a final solution because the Contacts folder is only able to hold information about individual people, including their e-mail addresses whereas the PAB is also able to store personal distribution lists. In the meantime the best idea is to place the PAB on a network drive and direct the client to go there. A client locks the PAB when it is in use so you'll need to educate users to always log out when they leave a PC. Otherwise you'll end up in the situation where someone moves to a new PC, attempts to log on, and can't connect to his or her PAB.

Figure 6.12
Extract from
AUTO-
TEXT.SIG
(autosignature
file)

```
\rtf1\ansi\ansicpg1252\deff0\deftab720{\fonttbl{\f0\fswiss MS
Sans Serif;}{\f1\froman\fcharset2 Symbol;}{\f2\fswiss\fprq2 Taho-
ma;}{\f3\fswiss\fprq2 Arial;}}
{\colortbl\red0\green0\blue0;\red0\green0\blue255;}
\deflang6153\pard\plain\f0\fs17\i Tony Redmond, Technical
Director, Mail and Messaging Practice (Northern Europe)
\par Digital Equipment Corporation
\par
\par \plain\f0\fs17
\par \pard\plain\f2\fs17\i \plain\lang2057\f3\fs20\cf1\ul
mailto:Tony.Redmond@dbo-exchangeist.dbo.dec.com\plain\f0\fs17
\par }
```

Autosignature information is kept in a file called AUTOTEXT.SIG. Unhappily the file is stored in the Windows default directory, so it poses a particular challenge for users who move between computers. The file contains the RTF source code for one or more sections of text. The normal situation is for the file to contain just one section, the default signature applied to new messages when they are sent. Optionally, the signature file can be appended to replies and forwarded messages. For example, an extract of the RTF code in my signature file is shown in Figure 6.12.

Sending a couple of messages without your normal signature isn't a great disaster. Most people will accept this as a side effect of moving away from their normal PC. The challenge is greater for users who roam as a matter of practice. You'll have to arrange for their signature file to be stored somewhere on a server and retrieved and copied to the Windows directory whenever the user logs on to a PC. A separate procedure is required to remove the signature file (and possibly replace it with the file that was present before the user logged on) upon log-off. The Outlook client uses a different version of the autosignature file. Make sure that you know which client you're dealing with.

MAPI profiles contain details of user working environments. On a shared PC it's quite possible to find many different profiles set up, one for each person who's passed by and used the PC. When you move to a PC you've never used before you'll need to either create a new profile or change an existing one to reflect items like:

- The name of the server you want to connect to
- The name of your mailbox
- The network protocol binding order
- Whether you want to work with off-line folders
- The name of your PAB

Manually configuring a new MAPI profile or changing an existing profile to suit your tastes are not tasks that every user will enjoy. The steps necessary to move a complete working environment from one PC to another are reasonably complex and full of potential error, but it's important to say that roaming users who use shared PCs normally only want to access a basic messaging service. They want to quickly use a PC to see whether any important messages have arrived, or have the chance to send a few messages of their own. Given that this is the case system administrators can accommodate the requirement of roaming users by ensuring that it's possible to connect PCs to all the servers in an organization. Users who require more advanced facilities, such as security or access to a personal information store, can be coached or instructed how to make their own arrangements, or you can go the whole way and use the Exchange profile generator to automatically create profiles for roving users.

6.3.4   The profile generator

The profile generator is a program called PROFGEN.EXE, an unsupported utility provided via TechNet or available from the Microsoft Web site. It works in conjunction with NEWPROF.EXE, the program that users see when they manually create a new MAPI profile. Together the two programs work to automatically generate a profile for a user when they first log-on to a client computer. PROFGEN can be used with Windows V3, Windows 95, and Windows NT clients, although Windows 95 and Windows NT clients are easiest to set up.

To achieve full roving capability, users should store PST and PAB files on personal network shares. The network shares should use a consistent drive letter for all users. Many sites use H: (for home drive). In addition, user profiles need to be configured so that they follow the user from PC to PC. Windows NT and Windows 95 have slightly different mechanisms to achieve the "follow me to the next PC" effect, but the basic idea is the same. Once the user authenticates himself or herself within a domain their registry settings can be downloaded from the domain controller to the PC. MAPI profile details are among the data that can be downloaded. Full details of PROFGEN can be found in the BackOffice Resource Kit, but there are a few important points that should be made here. You should also read the Knowledge Base article Q148595 for details of roving Windows profiles.

Figure 6.13
Extract from
DEFAULT.PRF

```
[Service List]
Service3=Personal Address Book
Service4=Personal Folders
[Service3]
PathToPersonalAddressBook=H:\EXCHANGE\MAILBOX.PAB
ViewOrder=1
[Service4]
PathToPersonalFolders=H:\EXCHANGE\PERSONAL.PST
```

The Exchange setup editor should be used to create a new default client preferences file (DEFAULT.PRF) so that the pointers to PAB and PST files are directed to the user's home drive. The client preferences file is in simple text format and can be edited with Notepad or a similar editor afterwards. The setup editor won't make the changes to point user files to a networked drive, so after all the other default settings are made, exit the setup editor and open the preferences file with Notepad. Make changes similar to those shown in the extract in Figure 6.13.

Once a properly configured preferences file is available you can add a line in users' Windows NT log-in scripts to call PROFGEN. The idea is simple. If a MAPI profile for the user already exists on the PC then exit, otherwise call PROFGEN to generate a new profile based on the information held in DEFAULT.PRF. You'll know if this step works because the file is renamed to DEFAULT.PR~ afterwards. PROFGEN is called like this:

```
\\servername\share name\PROFGEN C:\EXCHANGE\NEWPROF -p H:\EXCHANGE\DEFAULT.PRF
```

PROFGEN starts up and calls NEWPROF to generate the new profile, instructing it to use the preferences file pointed to with the –p switch. If you like, the –1 (create log file) and –s (use the GUI interface from NEWPROF) switches can also be specified. It's a good idea to create a log file the first time out!

Clearly none of this can work unless you configure the server and client environments to support home directories and log-in scripts. By default this isn't done, so it needs to be incorporated into the Windows NT deployment and implementation plan.

6.4   Remote mail

Roaming users want to be able to get to their mail anytime, anyplace, anywhere. There are two basic approaches that can be taken to retrieve messages from an Exchange server when you're working off-site. These are:

1. Use the Remote Mail facility (see the Tools menu on the client). This option is only available if you connect in off-line mode.

2. Make a dial-up connection to the server computer and work on-line as if you were connected via the office LAN.

Each approach comes with its own set of advantages and disadvantages. You'll probably want to experiment with both to see which approach is best in your own environment.

6.4.1   Using the Exchange Remote Mail facility

The basic idea behind the Remote Mail facility is to make a quick telephone connection to the server, send any messages that are queued and waiting to go, and grab details of messages that are waiting in your inbox. The connection can then be broken, leaving you to browse through header information for the messages in the inbox. You can mark which messages you'd like to retrieve, leave the others alone, or even decide that you want to delete some without reading. Another dial-up connection is then made to grab the full content of the marked messages. This type of interaction is pretty typical of the way you'd want to do things when you're concentrating on just processing new mail or want to keep phone bills to an absolute minimum. One major disadvantage about the remote mail facility is that you can't work with folders other than the inbox (and the outbox folder indirectly when sending messages).

Some method of communicating between your PC and the server must be established before you can use remote mail. The easiest way I know is the combination of the dial-up networking feature in Windows 95 and Windows NT RAS. Dial-up networking is one of the reasons why Windows 95 is so good to use on notebook PCs. Windows NT V4.0 workstation edition is also OK in this respect, but for now I think Windows 95 remains the easier option for notebook users who represent the bulk of the people interested in remote mail. You are not compelled to use Windows 95 and dial-up networking if you don't want to. The sole criterion is the ability to make a reliable connection between the PC (client) and the server computer. Likewise, while RAS is very convenient because it's a standard part of Windows NT, you can use one of the other approved network modem managers you want on the server, such as Shiva LanRover.

Figure 6.14
*Configuring
a dial-up
connection*

Dial-up networking allows you to configure all the details of how a network link is established to a server computer over a telephone link. As you can see from Figure 6.14, all of the important information such as telephone number to dial, the modem type to use, and the server capabilities are easily accessible. Advanced options, for instance the ability to use a text box to input commands directly to the modem (sometimes useful when dealing with strange and wonderful telephone systems occasionally encountered around the world) are also available.

After testing to ensure that your dial-up connection actually works and contact can be made with the server, you can proceed to use remote mail. The properties option ties things together by allowing you to associate the dial-up networking connection you want to use with the remote mail option. Dial-up networking is located on one tab of the property page. The other tab, holding the options that affect how the interaction between the client and server are conducted during the telephone connection, is a little more interesting (Figure 6.15).

Figure 6.15
*Properties of
the Remote
Mail connection*

For example, you can set a filter on the items that the remote connection will process. I use a filter specifying that I'm only interested in messages of 20K or less, to ensure that I am not bothered by very large messages. More importantly this filter stops me attempting to download messages with large attachments over a slow or expensive connection. Large documents, presentations or other file attachments can always wait until I get back into the office and connect to the LAN.

Remote mail properties also allow you to set up a schedule for connections. If you're on the road and want to make a connection each night to pick up and send messages you're probably not going to be too interested in a scheduled connection. Instead, the connection will be made when you're good and ready, perhaps when you're relaxed and ready to face whatever's in the mail after a good dinner. Scheduled connections are of most use to people who are located in offices that don't have permanent links back to the server. In most cases these are locations that don't have enough users to justify the expense of installing and operating a permanent network connection, so people have to dial-in and collect their mail at regular intervals if they're to stay in touch. Scheduled connections enable messages to be sent and fetched automatically, according to the schedule that's created. You might, for example, decide to connect four times a day, or every hour, or maybe only at 5 o'clock every evening. Scheduled connections are one major advantage of the remote mail facility.

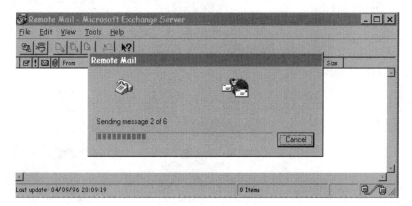

Figure 6.16
Sending messages via the Remote Mail facility

Once all the properties are set a telephone connection can be made. Once the connection is made user credentials are examined (domain, account name, and password) and, if OK, you'll be logged on to the domain. At this stage a link exists between the server and client. Remote mail always checks first to see whether any new messages are waiting to be sent. Exchange is quite happy for you to work in off-line mode.

Any messages you create and send when working off-line are held in a special folder (you can rename the folder if you like—I call mine "Items en Route") that is checked whenever a connection is made to the server. Any messages waiting in the "en route" folder are immediately dispatched by being transmitted from the client to the Exchange MTA for onward delivery (Figure 6.16).

After any waiting messages have been sent remote mail turns to retrieve header information for messages in the inbox that meet the criteria stated in the filter. Headers provide a snapshot of the messages waiting in the inbox, including details of the originators, date and time sent, subject, and size. The size is important because it determines the time it will take to download the complete message, if that's what you decide to do later on. Exchange predicts the time required to download a message by comparing the speed achieved with the modem connection against the size of the message. Anyone who has ever downloaded a file from an on-line service like CompuServe, America On-Line, or a Web site knows that predicting download times is, at best, an inexact science because there's nothing to prevent a connection degrading or something like a server hiccup interrupting data transfer. However, it's useful to have an idea as to how long it is likely for an operation to take and the remote mail facility does a fair job in this respect.

Figure 6.17
*Browsing
through details
of messages in
the Inbox*

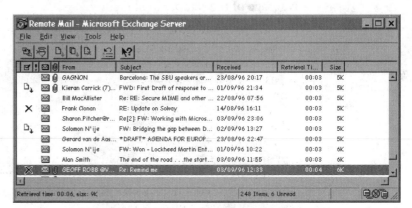

If no filter is specified header information is retrieved for all messages. When available, the header information is presented in the remote mail window, allowing you to browse through and mark the messages you're interested in. In Figure 6.17 you can see that several messages have been marked. Different icons indicate the action that will be taken for each message. The first message is marked to be downloaded, the second to be deleted, and so on. Two separate download actions are available. You can opt to download messages from the inbox on the server and leave copies of the messages on the server, or chose to download messages and delete them from the server. Leaving messages on the server is a good idea if you're not the only person to access a mailbox, but otherwise I recommend cleaning up after a download by deleting the messages from the server. Remember, you can always use the synchronize option later on to make sure that the server inbox matches the content of the off-line inbox. As a matter of practice, I usually synchronize all folders before I go away on a road trip and after I return to the office. This ensures that I have up-to-date material at my fingertips wherever I am.

Retrieving the actual content of messages is done by making another telephone connection and instructing Exchange to pick up the messages you've marked. At the cost of a little extra time on-line you can do everything over a single connection. That is, make the connection, send any waiting messages, download headers, browse and mark, and then retrieve the messages you've marked. Telling remote mail not to disconnect the link after headers are retrieved allows everything to be done while maintaining a single connection. Once the headers are available you can make a quick review, select the ones you want, and proceed to download. The telephone link can be broken at any time with the disconnect menu option or command button.

There's a reasonable amount of functionality in the remote mail facility. It's certainly superior (and faster) to the equivalent functionality offered by other PC mail clients such as Microsoft Mail. Indeed, users extensively criticized the remote mail capabilities of Microsoft Mail in the past because of its relative unreliability and slow throughput, so anyone upgrading from Microsoft Mail to Exchange will notice an immediate and significant improvement. However, I've got to say that working in such a disconnected manner is not my favored approach. Seeking to minimize costs through bursts of communication between client and server seems to be the best method for people working with slow modems, unreliable telephone lines and low-spec computers. Given the speed of today's modems and a desire to use telephone connections to access more than just e-mail, the fact that you can only work with Exchange and a restricted set of folders is the final nail in this feature's coffin. At least, it is from my point of view!

Some evidence exists that the Outlook client transmits more data to an Exchange server than is the case with an Exchange client. For this reason Outlook is slightly more inefficient than the Exchange client in a remote-working environment. Over time, I expect that Outlook will be optimized and this differentiation will disappear.

6.4.2   Working remotely

Fortunately there is an alternative way to work remotely. As we've seen, Exchange is quite happy for a client to talk to a server across a wide range of network protocols. Point to point protocol (PPP) is a variant of the TCP/IP protocol specially developed to efficiently handle remote connections over a telephone line. Once again, the combination of Windows 95 dial-up networking and Windows NT RAS scores heavily in the ease-of-use stakes.

My preferred approach is to establish a PPP connection to my server and connect the client across that link. The following advantages are accrued:

- As soon as the connection is made, the client performs automatic synchronization of folders whose contents have been changed since the last on-line connection. Messages created and sent are dispatched to their final destination. Other actions such as deletions or modification of objects in folders are also synchronized with folders on the server. Automatic synchronization is a real boon to people who have to work remotely on a regular basis.

- All folders are available in both the private and public information stores. I can therefore refile messages from the inbox into other, more appropriate folders, as they are read.

- E-form applications are available and can be used.

- New message notification works. Not a big advantage, I know, but it is sometimes very useful to know that a new message has arrived, especially if you're in the midst of a series of messages flying between a group of people.

- All Inbox Assistant rules work.

- The same network link can be used for other applications. For example, I use the same PPP connection to browse the Web at the same time it's being used to connect me to Exchange. Basically you can work as if you were in the office, albeit at a reduced pace.

Working across a PPP link is my preferred way of connecting when I'm on the road, but it may not be the most cost-effective. Once connected there is always a tendency to stay connected for just a little too long. However, the higher communication bills are being offset somewhat by the use of faster modems and I believe that the extra flexibility and power delivered by this way of remote working makes me more productive.

It's worth noting that the way Exchange clients talk to the server contributes to a great deal of robustness for dial-up communications. Clients do not have a continuous connection with the server. Instead, they communicate via RPCs on an as-needed basis. In other words, if a client wants some information it asks the server and then receives whatever the server cares to provide. Otherwise the chatty discourse that other clients and servers engage in is not present. The advantage here is that the telephone connection can be dropped (hopefully you'll notice) and re-established without forcing you to stop working, apart of course from the necessity to use whatever software you have to reconnect. In certain parts of the world it's quite common for lines to disconnect at frequent intervals, and if you were forced to restart sessions all the time the opportunity to process e-mail would rapidly lose its charm.

Data sent between the client and server is compressed to minimize the amount of connect time. You can see this for yourself by monitoring the number of bytes sent by a modem when sending messages, or moving a document into a public folder. My own observations lead me to believe that a compression ratio of approximately 2:1 is achieved, although this clearly varies with the type of information being sent.

The human tendency to stay connected too long can be moderated by disciplined habits. One habit I try to adopt is to make a connection (which immediately sends any messages that I had previously created and sent), immediately synchronize my inbox folder, and then disconnect. The effect is to populate the inbox folder in my off-line store with an exact replica of anything that's on the server, reducing the length of the telephone connection and thus the cost (very important when you look at the outlandish surcharges applied to telephone calls by many hotels). I can then begin to work off-line and process these messages, generating whatever responses I wish.

Two problems with working on-line trip me up from time to time. First, downloading a full inbox (more than 100 messages) can take a long time, especially if you don't first carefully review the messages to ensure that none contains a large attachment. Second, once disconnected and working off-line you won't be able to refile messages and stay organized. There are partial solutions to these problems. In the first case, it's important to make a quick browse through the inbox and refile any messages with large attachments into another folder (I use one called "To Do"). You can refile messages into other folders, but only if you've marked them to be available when working on-line and off-line. Once this is done you can cheerfully refile to your heart's content, but you must remember to synchronize all the folders once you get back into the office as otherwise all your refiling will be for nothing.

6.4.3 The Inbox Assistant and dial-up connections

Unfortunately there's a small side effect of the way the Inbox Assistant works that can slow down working on a dial-up connection. The majority of the rules handled by the Inbox Assistant can be processed when a client is not connected to the server. This is different to the rules services implemented by other e-mail clients, which require a server connection before any rules are processed. A rule requiring messages to be moved to a folder that's not in your mailbox is a notable exception. People commonly use rules like this to move incoming messages from specific individuals to different folders (some of which may be public or others in a personal information store), but these rules are only processed when a server connection is made.

If, like me, you subscribe to a number of Internet mailing lists that generate a fair amount of message traffic daily you can arrive at a situation where you log on, find that the Inbox is cluttered up with messages from all the different mailing lists, and then find that the Inbox Assistant busily goes to work to move messages out of the Inbox to their predetermined locations. The only problem is that while the Inbox Assistant is busy a great deal of traffic is generated on the asynchronous telephone link and you won't be able to do much work while all this is going on. Even with a 28.8 modem processing 50 or so messages can take a few moments, so prepare by having a good cup of coffee at hand. I'm pretty sure Microsoft will do something about this in the future but for now the way the Inbox Assistant processes "move to other folder" requests leaves a little to be desired.

6.5   How rules work

For the most part, the Exchange clients are pretty straightforward. Messaging functions work like you'd expect them to, but rules seem to cause people a lot of problems. At least, that's been my experience over a number of deployment projects.

There are a number of reasons why people possibly can't use the Inbox Assistant and its rules as effectively as they might. First, user training tends to skip over rules, tending instead to concentrate on basic functionality such as how to send and receive mail. Second, as we've just discussed, some rules only work when clients are connected to the server. Third, there's no really good explanation of rules and how they work in any documentation.

Figure 6.18
Defining a rule
for the Inbox
Assistant

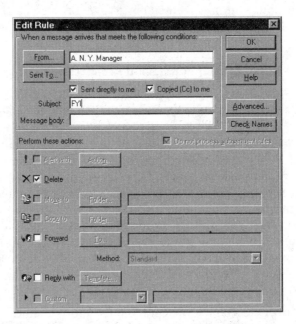

I can sympathize with the difficulties that people have applying rules to electronic mail. In 1988 I contributed to a project to implement rules processing for one of DIGITAL's electronic mail systems. That effort eventually resulted in a patent being granted, but no one could ever get to grip with the rules. They were difficult to explain in concept, and hard to put into practice. Microsoft has solved some of the problems by making the Inbox Assistant very approachable, but it's still not simple. Setting up a new rule, for example, is very straightforward and to a large degree can be accomplished in a couple of point and click operations (Figure 6.18).

So how do rules work with Exchange? In a sense, rules can be divided into those that can operate on a folder under all circumstances and those that are "profile-dependent." In other words, rules that can only be executed if a client is connected to server through a specific profile that's associated with the rule.

Rules are composed of a set of actions, properties defining the criteria that must be met for the rule to be triggered, and some other assorted properties, chiefly flags, but also a sequence number that determines the order in which rules are assessed. Rules are stored in a table in the folder they are associated with. The Inbox Assistant only works on the Inbox folder, so all rules used by the Inbox Assistant are held in a table in the Inbox folder. Rules can be set for other folders, but only by the owner of the folder. The table used to hold rules is invisible, and can never be seen by a client.

When a new message is delivered to a folder (private or public), the rules table is opened by the server. Each rule is then evaluated according to the sequence number property. When a rule is evaluated its stated criteria are checked against the properties of the newly-delivered message. If the evaluation determines that the criteria are met, the actions associated with the rule are applied. For example, a message containing "FYI" (For Your Information) in the title might be automatically moved into the Deleted Items folder!

Some actions cannot always be applied. For example, if the action states that a copy of the message should be moved to a PST the action cannot be performed if a client is not connected to the server. The same is true of movement to public folders. In this instance the public folder may be available on the same server that the rule is being applied to, but access to the folder may require authentication in the form of a log-on to a Windows NT account. These rules can be regarded as being profile-specific. Exchange notes rules that are profile-specific by examining the actions associated with a rule when each rule is created. If the server determines that an action cannot be performed a special stamp is placed on the rule to indicate that it requires client intervention. The stamp also indicates the user profile that created the rule.

Actions that a server cannot perform are stored away until a suitable client connection is next available. The actions are stored in items called Deferred Action Messages (DAM) in a special hidden folder called the Deferred Action Folder (DAF). DAMs contain any data required to fulfill the rule that could not be executed by the server and also a reference to the message that triggered the decision to create the DAM. Each time a client connects to the server it interrogates the DAF to discover whether there are any DAMs available for it to process. Each DAM is examined to see whether its properties match the current profile. If a match is made, the action is then performed.

All this sounds quite complicated, but it's pretty simple once you understand how rules are resolved by the server and how the rules are linked to user profiles. Unfortunately explaining this type of implementation to users often isn't easy!

One final point to consider about rules. There is a 32K "packed data" limit for the rules created for any folder. The maximum number of rules fitted into the 32K depends on the size of the rules defined and the amount of data required for a rule. For example, a rule to move messages into a folder, for a single recipient, takes about 660 bytes. Hence there is no defined limit for the maximum number of rules that can be assigned to a folder. On average it is between 40 and 50 rules per folder. The following error will be displayed when the number of rules exhaust the 32K memory limit:

```
Changes to the rule could not be saved. There is not enough
memory or the rules are too complex. Try deleting some rules.
```

6.6   Using personal stores

Exchange is built around the information store as the repository for messages and other items created by users. The information store has many notable attributes—high performance, single message instance storage model, availability from any client, and so on. However, the information store also suffers from a number of drawbacks. Personal information stores can be used to offset some of the disadvantages, while off-line stores supplement the usefulness of server-based storage.

6.6.1   Making effective use of personal information stores

Personal information stores are files that reside on users' local drives, either those on a PC or space allocated to users on a network device. You can even create a personal information store on a floppy disk, a feature that allows stores and their contents to be quickly transferred from one PC to another. Personal information stores are commonly referred to as PST files and are used to hold personal folders, a term that differentiates the content from that held in private or public folders, both of which are server-based. Messages are stored in two formats within a PST—RTF and ASCII, because it is conceivable that some clients will be unable to read RTF-style messages.

Figure 6.19
Entering a PST password

PSTs can be encrypted and compressed to enhance security and minimize disk space storage, and if a password is set on a PST users must provide it before a client will open the PST. The encryption depends on a user-supplied password, but there is no mechanism to recover data from an encrypted PST if a user forgets their password. Not even Microsoft can "break" into an encrypted PST. Unfortunately this fact is not normally realized until after the first incident of a user forgetting their password for a PST that contains some very important documents.

Figure 6.20
Configuring mail delivery to a PST

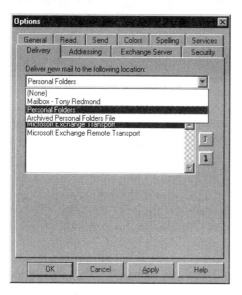

PST files allow users to create and manage their own private document archives. As we've seen it's obvious that any server is going to have some storage limitations in terms of either the total available physical disk space installed on drives connected to the server or the space allocated to individual users within the private information store. It's easy to run out of space, especially if you're in the habit of creating or circulating messages with large document or worksheet attachments. In these situations space can be freed within the private information store by moving files to a PST. Moving messages into PST files effectively "unshares" the message in private information store insofar as a separate copy of a message is created and moved to the PST.

Encouraging users to work with personal folders is fine as long as individuals use the same PC all the time. But if people move from one PC to another they'll leave information behind them. In these situations it's best to concentrate on server-based storage (which can be accessed from any PC) and leave personal folders to those who can use the same PC all the time. One way to accommodate roaming users (those who move from PC to PC) is to place their PSTs in their directory on a networked file server. If you do this remember to tell users to always fully log-out from each PC they use, otherwise they won't be able to connect to their PST when they move to another PC.

If the same person uses the same PC all the time then personal folders can provide an additional advantage in that Exchange can be instructed to deliver messages to an inbox in a PST. Mail delivery to a PST is configured using the Delivery tab of the client Tools.Options menu option (see Figure 6.20). Don't rush to divert messages from the server to the PST because there are a few points that need to be considered before making what is, to some extent, a pretty radical change in a basic function of the messaging system.

When messages are delivered to a PST they are held on the server until a user connects and then the messages are transferred down to an Inbox folder in the PST. If you decide to redirect mail the Exchange client automatically transfers all messages currently stored in the Inbox folder down to the PST, and then deletes them from the server.

Delivering mail to a PST is commonly used by installations wishing to build Exchange servers that support many hundreds or thousands of users. If server-based mailboxes are used the space available to each user is constrained by the 16GB limit on the private information store (in Exchange V4.0 and V5.0), but if PSTs are used then the storage on the server is largely transient because messages are only held there until the PST is available. Users can therefore be allocated relatively small quotas within the store (10MB or less), allowing many more users to be supported on a single server.

Diverting message delivery from the private information store to a PST eliminates the effect of the shared message model, removing a major benefit normally enjoyed by Exchange. Quite obviously, a message delivered to a PST cannot be shared. The storage model therefore moves from being database-centric to something similar to that used by Microsoft Mail (where messages are stored in MMF files). All of the disadvantages in the Microsoft Mail model, including the storage of multiple redundant copies of messages are inherited to achieve an advantage that doesn't really seem to be worth the price.

Another important factor to consider is that using a PST for mail delivery means that only users with physical access to the PST will ever be able to read messages sent to the mailbox's owner, eliminating the potential problem of unauthorized but privileged users reading other people's mail. Adopting this solution is a double-edged sword and a price is paid for privacy. In some cases, especially if a company believes that mail messages are of short-term use, responsibility for backing up and securing the messages in the PST passes from the system administrator to the user once messages are redirected into a PST. In most other cases where the PSTs used for mail delivery are held on networked file services, the responsibility for backing up the PSTs remains with the system administrators. Backing up individual PSTs is easier than backing up a very large information store, chiefly because there is a wider range of backup software available that is capable of processing individual files (the PSTs). Restoring an individual file from a backup tape is much easier than restoring a user mailbox from a backup of an information store, and this fact alone makes the use of PSTs an interesting item for consideration until the time comes that Exchange supports "bricked" restores.

While on this point it's interesting to note that Exchange clients automatically disconnect from a PST after 30 minutes of inactivity, allowing system administrators to plan to take file-level backups of PSTs stored on shared file services even if users insist on leaving their PCs logged on (hopefully protected by a password-enabled screen saver). The next time a client operation commences that uses an item in the PST Exchange will automatically re-establish the connection.

Many installations try and encourage users to view the private information store on the server as a repository for working documents, or those that must be available no matter which PC is used to connect to the server. In this model users are supposed to move files to a PST once the files are no longer current or perhaps become less important. The model assumes a fair amount of discipline on the part of users, something that's not always easy to find, and also devolves responsibility for data security to users once files have been moved away from a server-based store. One of the undoubted advantages of server-based storage is the assurance that someone else will take care of backing up all your important data. People aren't so good when the time comes to create backups or copies of local data on a PC.

Exchange does not limit users to a single PST. It is entirely possible to configure multiple PSTs for use, perhaps having one file on a networked file service and another on the local DOS device, with maybe a third on a floppy disk. Putting a PST on a floppy disk may seem strange, but it's certainly a valid method to transfer files from one PC to another, or one user to another. Each PST is individually configured into a profile. By default, the display name of each PST is "Personal Folders," so things can get slightly confusing if you don't change the name afterwards to reflect the use that the PST will be put to. For example, "Network Personal Folders," "Archived Folders," "Mail Folders," and so on. The display name of a PST is easily changed by selecting the PST from the client and then bringing up its properties, as shown in Figure 6.21.

Figure 6.21
*Changing the
display name of
a PST*

It would be useful if the actual location (file name) of the PST was available through its properties, even in read-only mode, but if you want to find out where a PST is physically located this must be done through the client Tools.Services menu option (Figure 6.22). No aspect of Personal Folders can be configured or otherwise controlled by system administrators through the administration program. Remember—these are personal folders.

Table 6.2   *Pros and cons of using Personal Stores to supplement server storage*

Pros	Cons
A PST can be stored on any available device, including floppy disks.	A PST can't be shared between users. For example, you can't use a PST to share documents between a manager and a secretary. Users who leave a PC logged on can inadvertently block their own access to a PST if they move to another PC.
PSTs can be used to transfer files between users, including users in different Exchange organizations.	A PST can be encrypted to protect its content against other users, but if the password is lost there is no way to recover it.
A PST can expand to any size up to a theoretical 2GB limit, subject to available disk space. The largest PST in use is at least 400MB (there is a limit of 16,000 items in a single folder). Thus, users can be allocated more space in the information store, getting around the 16GB limit.	Delivering mail to a PST removes the benefit of single instance storage. Also, the space required to store a message is doubled because they are held in RTF and ASCII.
PSTs can be backed up with any file-level backup utility.	If people use PSTs they must make sure that the files are actually backed up. There is an increased chance of message corruption because there is no rollback/transaction log mechanism available for PSTs.
PSTs are easier to restore than the Exchange information store.	Deferred mail messages won't be sent unless the client is actually connected to the server.
The Auto-Archive feature in the Outlook client uses PSTs to store archived items.	Inbox Assistant rules won't be processed unless the client is connected to the server.
PSTs provide an easy way for Microsoft Mail users to move to Exchange because they can convert MMF files to PSTs.	There is a decreased ability for system administrators to monitor disk usage because messages and other items can be stored on the server and scattered across user PSTs.
	Extra network traffic is generated to move information to and from PSTs. Messages for delivery to a PST are held on the server until a client connects, and if a lot of mail is waiting the initial connect can take quite a long time.
	PSTs are not available to Web clients.
	The administration program "Move Mailbox" option does not move items stored in PSTs. These must be manually moved.
	PSTs may not be available to roving users. For example, people who want to work with the same data at home and in the office.

Users moving to Exchange from Microsoft Mail will find personal information stores a very natural extension of the mode of working they had become accustomed to. In a Microsoft Mail environment it is normal to pull messages from a post office server down to a mailbox file held on the PC. In an Exchange environment the situation is somewhat reversed, as the normal way of working is to leave messages on the server rather than moving them to the PC. Users can move messages down to a PST if they wish, albeit through a drag and drop operation rather than having the mail system do it automatically. Installations moving from Microsoft Mail should carefully consider whether they want to migrate the many megabytes of user messages into the private, server-based, information store. In my opinion it is best to leave messages where they are—on the PC by converting the Microsoft Mail format mailbox to a personal information store. Apart from reducing the demand for server resources, this approach means that users can be migrated to Exchange much more quickly than otherwise possible.

Figure 6.22
*Personal
Folders
properties*

Training sessions clearly offer an opportunity to encourage good work habits such as the effective use of PSTs. Hint or cheat sheets can also be used to get your point across and so relieve some pressure on server-based resources. As with most features there are pros and cons that need to be understood before you can make the most effective use of them. Table 6.2 (page 369) summarizes the most important issues to understand about PSTs. Make sure you understand the impact of these issues before you rush into using PSTs.

6.6.2   Off-line slave replicas (OSTs)

Off-line folders are replicas of server-based folders, stored in special files with .OST extensions. An off-line folder file is created automatically when you configure a user profile and indicate that you want to be able to work in off-line mode. Thereafter the off-line folders are made available when you elect to work in off-line mode rather than connecting to a server. Examining the advanced properties of the Microsoft Exchange Server service reveals the file name of the OST.

Exchange and Outlook clients can use off-line folders to store and access information without being connected to the server. In one way the concept behind off-line folders can be thought of as snapshots of server-based folders (the folders held in OSTs are, in fact, true slave replicas of server-based folders). In another they can be thought of as a more intelligent version of personal folders, but only because facilities are provided to automatically synchronize an OST with the contents of server-based folders.

Aside from synchronization, the most fundamental difference between an OST and a PST is that an OST is tied to a specific MAPI profile. If you don't log in and authenticate using the profile originally used to create the OST then the client will refuse to open the OST. This is because the profile stores an encrypted "cookie" created from the mailbox's unique ID. The mailbox unique ID can only be accessed when connected to the server, so it follows that an initial connection must be made to create the cookie and store it into the MAPI profile. Every time you attempt to work in off-line mode afterwards the profile is read to determine whether the cookie exists. If the profile is unavailable the OST will refuse to load, issuing a warning that you must connect to the server (to recreate the cookie) before you can use the off-line folders. Not using the right profile is the most common reason for not being able to access an OST. Deleting and recreating the server mailbox is a more radical version of basically the same reason. In this instance the next time you connect to the server the master ID for the server mailbox will not match the data held in the profile and the OST will refuse to load.

Because OSTs contains slave replicas of server-based folders they can be used to recover information from accidentally deleted mailboxes. Let's assume that a mailbox is removed by a system administrator, only for the administrator to then discover that the mailbox should have been retained. All the database rows and tables relating to messages in the mailbox are discarded by the information store immediately a mailbox is deleted, so there is no way to recover the mailbox on the server except by restoring a full backup of the store. If an OST is available, you can start the client and opt to work in off-line mode. All of the deleted messages are available in the OST and can be moved out of the OST to a PST. Once the movement is complete you can log out of the client, delete the OST file, and reconnect to the server. The old OST is invalid because the mailbox ID is changed when the mailbox is deleted and recreated so there's no point in attempting to use it. Anyway, the messages we're interested in are safely held in the PST and once we're connected back to the server the messages can be dragged from the folders in the PST to folders on the server. Following that, synchronizing with the newly populated server folders can rebuild a new OST.

Any profile can be used to open a PST because these files are profile-independent. If PSTs were not profile-independent they couldn't be used to transfer user files from one site to another, or from one user to another, or even (conceivably) for archiving. Table 6.3 contains a more exhaustive list of the basic differences between OSTs and PSTs.

Table 6.3   *Differences between PSTs and OSTs*

	Personal Information Store (PST)	**Off-Line Store (OST)**
Valid locations	Any DOS device.	Any DOS device.
Storage type	Permanent, persistent storage in its own right.	Transient storage that's inextricably linked to the contents of the master (server) folders.
Can be opened by	Any Exchange or Outlook client, using any MAPI user profile.	Any client, but only using the same MAPI profile that originally created the OST.
Synchronization	None—all movement between the PST and other stores is user-initiated and performed manually.	Automatic for server-based personal folders upon each connection to the server. Specific synchronization must be requested for replicas of public folders, or of any personal folder when connected to the server.
Encryption options	Optional encryption with a separate password (individually defined for each PST).	By default, OSTs are automatically encrypted. No password used (because of OST association with server mailbox).
Managed through	By configuring a Personal Folders information service (Tools.Service).	Off-line Folder File Settings tab from Advanced properties for Exchange Server information service (Tools.Services).
Multiple PST/ OST possible	Yes.	No.

An .OST file can be created anywhere, including network drives, but the usual location is somewhere like C:\WIN95\REDMOND.OST. I don't like storing anything in the Windows directory, so recommend that you create a separate directory to hold user-specific information. All my Exchange files (OST, PST, and PAB) are held in a directory called C:\REDMOND\EXCHANGE\, a name that instantly indicates that the files belong to me and are associated with the Exchange application. Placing an off-line folder on a network drive may seem pointless, but it does mean that off-line folders will be available if you log in and wish to work in off-line mode from different PCs.

The set of special mail folders—Inbox, OutBox, Sent Items, and Deleted Items are automatically added to off-line folders if off-line folder use has been configured in the user profile. These folders allow you to process messages while disconnected from the server. For example, you can create and send messages to anyone you want. In this case Exchange holds the messages in the OutBox folder and automatically sends them the next time you connect to the server. Sending messages in this way is done by synchronizing the contents of the OutBox off-line folder with the OutBox folder on the server.

Figure 6.23
Off-line folders

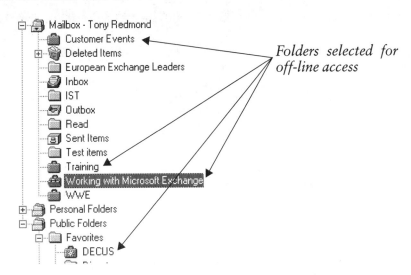

All of your personal server-based folders allow you to set properties to determine whether the folder is available off-line. Replicas of public folders can also be made available off-line, but only if you first add them to your set of favorites (see the discussion later on in this chapter). Use the synchronization page in a folder's properties to mark a folder for off-line access. Once a folder's properties have been set to enable its use off-line the fact is indicated by marking it with a briefcase rather than the normal folder icon (see Figure 6.23). This is in line with the briefcase paradigm established in Windows 95 to enable users to synchronize files between two PCs.

The contents of folders marked for off-line access can be synchronized with the server using the client Tools.Synchronize option. You can elect to synchronize a single selected folder or all folders at one time. Of course, only the special mail folders plus any other folder marked for off-line access is synchronized when the "all folders" option is selected. Unless you really must have everything available to you when you work off-line it's a good idea to restrict the number of marked folders plus the number of items stored in these folders. Even when synchronizing a single folder the whole process can take several minutes to complete if there are several hundred messages to deal with. Inbox and Sent Items folders tend to accumulate messages so give these folders a good clean out every so often to save yourself some time.

Figure 6.24
Off-line folder
synchronization
log

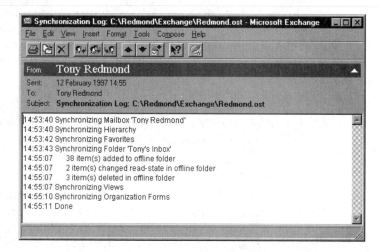

Automatic synchronization of the OutBox folder is performed when a client connects to a server to make sure that any message generated by the user when working in off-line mode is sent to its final destination. If changes have been made to any other folder when working off-line, including replicas of public folders, those changes (additions, updates, and deletions) will also be synchronized back to the server-based folders. After all synchronization operations you can see exactly what happened during the synchronization process by viewing a log that ends up in the Deleted Items folder. As you can see from the sample log illustrated in Figure 6.24, the synchronization process updates new and deleted folders in the folder hierarchy as well as the actual folder contents.

Accidents happen, and it is possible that an OST file becomes unavailable for one reason or another, the most common being that a PC's hard disk experiences a failure and no backup exists. Unlike a PST, it is easy to recreate the OST, albeit with some minor problems. After the disk is restored or replaced, remove any trace of the OST if necessary, then use the Tools.Services client option to access the properties of the Exchange Server service. The Advanced tab allows you to define the name of a new OST. Enter the name for the new OST and click on OK. Exchange checks whether the file exists, and when the OST cannot be found, offers to create a new file. Accept the offer. Log-off and log-on again, and the OST is now available. However, recreating the OST removes the folder properties controlling whether a folder is available on-line only or both on-line and off-line for all folders except the special folders (Inbox, Deleted Items, and so on). Before synchronizing the other folders, including public folder favorites, you must mark each folder you want to use in off-line mode.

Apart from their obvious use in processing messages off-line folders are very useful for anyone who travels. You might, for instance, want to make a copy of all documents relating to a particular project before going on a trip. During the trip changes might be made to some or all of the documents, and when you get back to base you can synchronize the changes back with the data held in the server-based folder. Conflicts can occur when synchronization is attempted. If this happens you'll have to resolve the conflicts manually as there are no intelligent agents available to help out.

6.6.3 Archiving

Users, despite the suspicions of some system administrators, are only human. As such they will accumulate mail messages and other items in their mailboxes in the same way as they collect anything else. Some people will be very neat and tidy, maintaining an efficient and effective folder structure. Others will let chaos exist with messages piling up in folders that were created for a purpose long forgotten. Most users exist between the two extremes. They do their best to keep their mailboxes reasonably clean, eliminating dead wood from time to time, but generally there's a lot of excess information kept hanging around, occupying valuable space in an information store on the server.

Archiving is an attempt to provide some automatic assistance to users. In the context of a messaging system, archiving means that messages that meet certain conditions are moved from the "live" store to a "passive" store. In Exchange the live store is a user's mailbox in the private information store while the passive store is a PST file, where the conditions for archiving are age-based. In other words, move messages once they exceed a certain age—28 days, 15 weeks, or maybe 6 months. The net effect of moving messages from the live to passive store is to reduce the amount of information held on the server, although the actual physical size of the private information store will not be reduced unless the store is compacted with the EDBUTIL program (see page 305). Reducing the space occupied in server-based stores is good from a system administrator's point of view. More space is created for new items, optimal use is made of disks, and backup times are reduced.

In Exchange, archiving is client-driven and the server plays no great role, apart from actioning client requests during the archival process. Not all clients include archiving functionality. To date, only the Outlook client is equipped with options to archive items automatically, or to archive items on an explicit basis according to criteria defined by the user.

Figure 6.25
*Archiving items
from a selected
folder*

A client can archive messages in two ways. First, the Outlook client has an "Archive" option on the File menu, producing the dialog shown in Figure 6.25. The default option presented by the dialog is to create an explicit instruction from the user to the client to review the contents of selected folders (and sub-folders) and archive any items contained within that are older than a specified date. Alternatively (by clicking the first radio button in the dialog), a scan can be performed against all folders that have an auto-archive property set, and all items that meet the criteria stated in the property will be processed. For instance, if the "News" and "Views" folders both have an auto-archive property of "archive after 3 months," then the scan will examine these folders to locate any message older than 3 months, and will then move any such messages to the passive store (the PST). PSTs can, of course, be located on any DOS device—even a floppy disk. Placing PSTs used for archiving in user directories on networked file services is probably the best approach because these directories are more easily backed up to tape than local hard disks. Both the Exchange and Outlook clients support the concurrent use of multiple PSTs, so it's possible to have a

PST for the purpose of archiving on a network file service and another PST to use for personal documents on a local hard disk.

Figure 6.26
*General
auto-archive
options*

The second archiving method is called "auto-archiving," a two-step process. Before any automatic archiving can be performed the parameters for archival must be set by defining the auto-archive property for the mailbox. This is done via the auto-archive property page accessed from the Tools.Options menu choice.

6.6.4 SCANPST—First aid for PSTs and OSTs

There are plenty of utilities available to maintain the contents of the server-based stores. There's also a need to ensure that the DOS-based stores are adequately protected against inconsistencies that can arise through normal operation. Over a period of time it can be expected that not every RPC sent between the client and server or vice versa will complete; that network interruptions will occur; there may be errors reading or writing data to the hard disk; and PCs might be powered off abruptly while a PST or OST is open by an Exchange or Outlook client. The files themselves might continue to work in an apparently normal manner, but sooner or later a problem will come to light.

With an OST you can opt to create the file from scratch, as described earlier. The sole drawback to this arrangement is the length of time taken to synchronize the contents of all the server folders down to the OST. Problems in a PST take on a different dimension because the folders in a PST are not replicas of anything else; they are the sole containers for the data they hold. A tool that is able to "fix" a PST to get around the problem is therefore a pretty important weapon in an implementation team's armory. That tool is SCANPST.EXE, and it is found in the same directory as the Exchange client software.

SCANPST can only be run if it can gain exclusive access to the PST or OST you want it to process. After the target file is opened a series of 8 tests is performed to establish whether any inconsistencies exist in the internal structure of the file and the links between folders and items stored within. If any inconsistencies are detected you'll be given the opportunity to repair the file, or, in the case of a successful run the program reports the number of items processed and will go no further (Figure 6.27). There is no need to run SCANPST unless a problem is encountered. There's no harm in running the program either, and it does provide a certain peace of mind for the more paranoid of the Exchange community.

Figure 6.27
Successful
SCANPST run

7

Connecting Exchange

7.1   **Exchange connectors**

A messaging system that's only able to communicate internally or with other systems of the same kind isn't much use in today's heterogeneous world. This chapter reviews the methods an Exchange server can use to connect to other electronic messaging systems.

Connectors are the components that provide links between the Exchange MTA and other messaging systems, normally over an intermediate network connection. Two types of connectors exist—site connectors and external connectors. Remember that the basic Exchange server package only includes the site and Microsoft Mail connectors and you need to either purchase the Enterprise edition of Exchange or individual copies of the Internet or X.400 as required by your installation.

As the name implies, site connectors are used to send messages between one Exchange site and another within a single organization. In fact, four different connectors can be used to link sites together:

- Direct site connector
- X.400 connector
- Internet Mail Service (previously called the Internet Mail Connector in Exchange V4.0, and often shortened to the IMC or IMS)
- Dynamic Remote Access Server (RAS) connector

Direct site connectors operate through Remote Procedure Calls (RPCs) between the connected servers. This is the preferred connection in a LAN environment or when a permanent high-speed connection exists between two sites. The dynamic connector depends on Windows NT Remote Access Server and it is used when a dial-up connection is made between two sites to send mail to each other. The connection between small branch offices where a single server is located for a small group of users and a larger central department is a good example of the type of situation where a RAS connector might be used. Naturally you'll need to ensure that RAS is configured on the servers involved in the transactions, and provide telephone lines and modems to make the physical connections.

In addition to standard asynchronous connections made over the telephone RAS can also be used over X.25 links. X.25 is a little more complex because you have to install an X.25 card and software in the computers that will talk together. Currently the only X.25 card and software supported by Windows NT are provided by Eicon Technologies. Eicon have one- and four-port X.25 cards available. These cards work with version 3 (release 2 or 3) of the Eicon X.25 software. A Microsoft speaker at the 1996 Exchange Deployment Conference announced that plans were in place to upgrade the current X.25 interface to incorporate the Windows Sockets protocol. When this happens it's more than likely that many other vendors will produce X.25 cards and software for Windows NT, giving much more choice than available today.

Apart from the options available to connect sites together, Exchange servers are able to send messages to each other over X.400 and SMTP connectors, even when the systems are in the same Exchange organization. Conceptually the primary function for X.400 and SMTP connectors can be viewed as to exchange messages with non-Exchange mail systems. In reality these connectors are going to get far more use in linking Exchange servers together. They are also a useful fall-back option for situations where it may be more convenient to piggy-back onto an existing corporate messaging infrastructure than to establish one especially for Exchange. For example, if an SMTP messaging backbone is already operational and used to tie together all the different systems used within an enterprise, the best course of action might be to use the Internet Mail Service to send messages across the SMTP backbone instead of site connectors.

Reaching outside the organization, the major external connectors provided with the enterprise edition of Exchange Server are:

- Microsoft Mail
- X.400
- Internet (SMTP)
- Lotus cc:Mail (available from Exchange V5.0)

The Microsoft Mail connector facilitates backwards connectivity with the messaging system that's replaced by Exchange. This is important not only because the installed base of Microsoft Mail systems are a rich vein of opportunity for the initial deployments of Exchange, but also because the migration period from one messaging system to another often covers quite a long time, especially in larger organizations. The Microsoft Mail connector also allows installations to continue using MS-Mail gateways to other mail systems that they may have previously installed.

This connector is very important to Microsoft because it answers an immediate problem for the many thousands of Microsoft Mail installations—"how can I connect to Exchange." The answer is, of course, "Easily—through the Microsoft Mail connector." Thus, this connector is an intensely strategic weapon in the battle to get installations migrated to Exchange. There are other routes—you could certainly use either X.400 or SMTP to link Exchange to Microsoft Mail, but it just wouldn't be as straightforward, seamless, or easy, all arguments that carry enormous weight with system administrators.

We've already discussed how the X.400 and SMTP connectors can be used to connect sites in an Exchange organization together. Now we see them in a different light, facing externally rather than the purely internal view taken so far. The X.400 and SMTP connectors are very important to the overall success of the Exchange program, but in a different way to the Microsoft Mail connector. Unlike Microsoft Mail, whose development was totally under the control of Microsoft, X.400 and SMTP, offer the promise of openness in the electronic messaging world, and most international or large-scale organizations will use one or the other, or even both methods to tie different organizational units or sites together. Without easy and out-of-the-box connectivity to X.400 and SMTP, Exchange would face a much harder struggle for general acceptance in corporate environments. Equipped with the ability to connect over both X.400 and SMTP, Exchange is in a much stronger position, if only because of the fact that many other messaging systems require you to purchase additional components or gateways before they can connect in a similar manner.

While SMTP and X.400 now represent the generally accepted methods for widespread electronic mail, this hasn't always been the case. Corporations have been deploying electronic mail since the start of the 1980s, and there's an often-bewildering array of systems in operation today. Whereas many of the older systems might be tagged with the "legacy" label and they might be scheduled for replacement by a newer system like Exchange, in the long term a connectivity need still exists. A set of add-on connectors is therefore available and must be purchased and installed separately.

The Lotus cc:Mail connector appears with Exchange V5.0. This connector is a strategic weapon in the war of hearts and minds waged between Microsoft and Lotus. The aim is simple. If Lotus cc:Mail users find it easier to move to Exchange than Lotus Notes (the preferred option for IBM/Lotus) then that's what they'll do. Easier means easy to connect, more functionality, and ease of migration. The latter point is addressed by the cc:Mail migration tools provided with Exchange, and now the cc:Mail connector comes along to bridge the remaining gaps.

The Lotus cc:Mail connector works in roughly the same way as the Microsoft Mail connector. In other words, the connection to Exchange seems to be just another cc:Mail post office within the cc:Mail network. So far so good, but this isn't the real value to cc:Mail users. That value is delivered by the ability of Exchange to act as an SMTP or X.400 server for cc:Mail users. Remember that messages introduced into an Exchange organization by any connector can be routed by Exchange to any other connector, so messages sent by cc:Mail users can be routed by Exchange out to Internet (via the Internet Mail Service) or X.400 addressees (via the X.400 connector), or indeed to FAX, PROFS, or any other messaging service connected to Exchange. This functionality is certainly something that could be delivered by connecting cc:Mail to a Lotus Notes environment, but it's harder to configure and certainly doesn't work automatically, without a great deal of configuration. To me, this is the biggest win for cc:Mail users and it will be interesting to see if they agree, and a lot of cc:Mail installations migrate to Exchange. Microsoft certainly hopes so.

7.1.1 Optional connectors

The Exchange MTA is responsible for delivering all messages sent to recipients who do not reside on the originating server. This task includes communication with other Exchange servers over all types of site connectors, X.400 MTAs, and gateways to other messaging systems. As illustrated in Figure 7.1, the MTA does an excellent job as a single point of contact or message switch for messages arriving into the server from many different sources. The clearly defined nature of the connection engine allows third parties to build new connectors and the introduce them to the MTA in a very clean manner. Once installed a connector takes care of accepting messages from a particular source before providing them to the MTA for eventual delivery to user mailboxes. The process of acceptance may involve format translation before messages can be given to the MTA. For example, the Internet Mail Service converts newly arrived messages from SMTP/MIME format to the internal format used by Exchange. In much the same way outgoing messages may also require conversion by a connector before they are handed over to an external messaging system.

The list of optional add-on connectors is expanding all the time. Check with your local Microsoft office or Microsoft Solution Provider for the current list. At the time of writing the set includes connectors for:

- AT&T Mail

- IBM SNADS (System Network Architecture Distribution System)

- IBM PROFS and OfficeVision/400

- Verimation MEMO

- MCI Mail

- MHS (Message Handling System)

- FAX

Some of the connectors are very specific both in terms of geographic relevance and mail systems that are supported. AT&T Mail and MCI Mail are, for instance, not generally available or used outside the United States, so European and Asian sites probably won't be interested in them.

Figure 7.1 *The Exchange MTA acting as a message switch or connection engine*

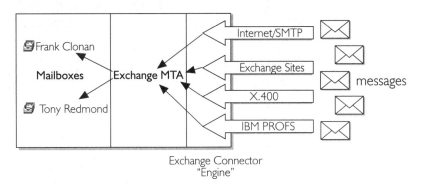

All of these connectors are built by third parties and often there's a reasonable choice between different offerings. For example, if you want to connect IBM PROFS to Exchange you can chose between the Attachmate Extra connector or an equivalent LinkAge connector. There's a bewildering array of connectors available for FAX, tribute to the wide and deep development community that had previously developed FAX gateways for Microsoft Mail. All of these folks seem to have turned around and upgraded their software to work with Exchange, so there's an extremely wide choice, far too many to mention any here.

Some connectors are designed to help in the transition from certain messaging systems to Exchange. The connectors for IBM PROFS, OfficeVision, and SNADS are good examples of this type. PROFS and

SNADS were both popular mainframe-based electronic mail systems that were deployed in many "true blue" sites in the 1980s, but their popularity waned as minicomputer and then PC LAN-based mail systems took over as mainframe computers were downsized.

PROFS is often used as a sort of lowest common denominator for connecting different mail systems together. For example, you can connect Lotus Notes mail into a Soft*Switch gateway and connect via the gateway to other systems. In this example the Lotus Notes messages, and the users who generate the messages, appear to be PROFS messages and users. PROFS and SNADS are no longer sold or supported by IBM so corporations using these systems need to consider their migration path. Microsoft would very much like that migration path to lead to Exchange, whereas I suspect IBM might prefer to move people to OfficeVision (based on AS/400 computers rather than mainframes) or even Lotus Notes. The availability of connectors for PROFS and SNADS "helps" people to consider Exchange as a more than viable migration option.

MHS-type electronic mail systems represent the other end of the spectrum to the large corporation PROFS deployments. MHS is quite a simple system which is based on file sharing, much like Microsoft Mail. As such it suffers from the same type of architectural and scaleability weaknesses that afflict Microsoft Mail and is therefore a prime candidate to evolve towards Exchange. Again there's an element of competition here and I assume that Microsoft has quite deliberately chosen to make the MHS connector available to place pressure on users of Novell NetWare systems, the major proponent of MHS mail. Apart from the argument about what electronic mail system to use, there's an underlying battle between Windows NT and Novell NetWare, a battle that Windows NT appears to be slowly winning in the marketplace. The logic of "if you're going to move to a better mail system, why not upgrade your shared file and print services as well?" plays to the strengths of the Exchange/Windows NT combination very well.

As mentioned above, there are many FAX connectors available, but alas, not for its telematics counterpart, telex. It's undeniable that FAX has largely taken over from telex in most situations, but telex is still important in certain circumstances. Directives to airlines to carry out preventative aircraft maintenance operations are usually, if not always, sent by telex because of its unique status as a document accepted in legal disputes.

7.1.2   Connector licensing

From a management perspective it's important to realize that you don't need to install and configure connectors on every server or even within every site. As long as the connector is configured properly and appears in the address space the MTA will be able to route messages to the connector. For example, if you have ten Exchange servers in three sites and you want to send messages via X.400 and SMTP you could install the following:

■ One server to handle all external messages. This server is configured with the Internet Mail Service and X.400 connector.

■ Three servers configured with site connectors. These servers act as the bridgehead servers for the three sites within the organization and are responsible for passing messages between the different sites. We'll discuss what "bridgehead" means in a little while.

■ Six servers which act as pure messaging or public folder servers.

In this instance all messages for X.400 and SMTP recipients are routed to the server where these connectors are configured and operational. No other servers are able to directly send messages to X.400 or SMTP recipients, but all servers are aware that the X.400 connector and Internet Mail Service are available and able to route messages via these connectors. Because Microsoft licenses connectors on a per server basis it therefore follows that all 10 servers must be licensed to use the connectors installed within the organization. You could create a mix and match license patchwork from 10 licenses for Exchange along with 10 licenses for each connector. But it's easier and more convenient (and possibly cheaper, depending on the prices pertaining in your country) to purchase 10 copies of the Exchange Enterprise Edition because it contains everything you need.

7.2   Maintaining the Message Transfer Agent and connectors

Internally, the Exchange MTA is a true implementation of the X.400 messaging model. In other words, all of the recommendations described in the X.400 standards issued by the ITU in 1988 are complied with. The MTA processes data internally according to the X.400 model, and X.400-type messages are sent across the network when the MTA on one server communicates with the MTA on other Exchange servers, be they within the same site or the bridgehead server in another site connected via a site, X.400, or a dynamic RAS connector. The last point is not often understood, but it's very important. While the Windows NT RPC mechanism is used to transport messages across the network used to link a site or dynamic RAS connector, X.400 P1/P2 format messages pass "on the wire." Exchange may well use its own data format to transport content (MDBEF), but the fact remains that the messages being sent are built according to the X.400 recommendations. And of course, messages sent across X.400 connectors naturally comply with the recommendations. It is only in the case of other connectors, such as the Internet, MS-Mail, or cc:Mail, that data conversion must occur and messages are transformed into the format demanded by the foreign connector.

X.400 messages are divided into envelopes (P1) and content (P2 or P22). Another interesting point is that the MTA usually only ever works on the P1 part of messages. The actual content is never touched unless the MTA is forced to open the message to effect data conversion, and that's only ever when the message is going to be transported across a foreign connector. Think about sending a message to a distribution list. When you read a copy of the message you see the name of the distribution list in the message header. No matter how many people the distribution list is eventually expanded to when the message is delivered you'll never see the names of the members of the list displayed in the header. This is because clients display the P2 part, or content, whereas the MTA has performed distribution list expansion when it processed the P1 part of the message.

7.2.1   The work done by the MTA

We've mentioned in passing some of the work done by the MTA. A more complete list includes:

- Message routing and flow. The most basic and important task of the MTA is to route messages according to the addresses placed in the envelopes. Remember that Exchange messages come from other sources than users, so the MTA takes care that messages are directed to the public information store, other MTAs, the directory service, and so on. Messages sent to local recipients are directed to the private information store. The MTA includes retry logic to make sure that messages are directed along different paths to their eventual destination if the premier or preferred path becomes blocked. The MTA also takes care of the creation and dispatch of non-delivery and delivery notifications.

- Distribution list expansion. Note that it is possible to expand distribution lists on the server that originates the message or on the server that hosts the distribution list. In the latter case messages must be routed via the home server before the list can be expanded. Distribution list expansion is expensive in terms of

CPU. Each object in the list must be examined separately, and each object could, in turn, require expansion. However, if the directory is replicated everywhere (which it should be) then it's probably best to perform distribution list expansion on each server and not route messages back to home servers.

- Loop detection. Obviously distribution lists can be nested inside other distribution lists. Unless loop detection code is implemented it would be possible to have distribution list "Team A" called by distribution list "Team B," and have the "Team B" list nested inside "Team A." Loop detection prevents the thread that expands the list getting very confused and makes sure that people on the list only receive one copy of the message.

- Message fan-out. A message might be sent to 100 recipients, but only 3 connectors might serve those recipients. The MTA applies intelligence to determine how many copies of the message have to be sent to the different connectors or other MTAs in order to effect the most efficient delivery.

- Format content conversion. Clearly the different connectors require different formats of messages routed their way. Some of this conversion occurs within the connector. For example, the Internet connector converts messages to SMTP/MIME format. The MTA must take care of any format conversion required before messages are dispatched. A good example of this is where a connection is made to a 1984-compliant X.400 MTA. In this case message content must be downgraded from the 1988/1992-type formats used by Exchange to the much simpler 1984-type formats used by the foreign MTA. Conversion between different character sets used by X.400 MTAs such as IA5 and ISO-Latin-1 is also performed by the MTA. The set of template files (.TPL) in the MTA work directory (\EXCH-SRVR\MTADATA) defines how the MTA deals with other X.400 systems. The template files include the ASN.1 rules for conversion between format types. Having template files allows encoding problems to be fixed through simple edits of one or more files and prevents the need for the MTA code itself to be recompiled or otherwise rebuilt.

While the Exchange MTA and its associated connectors are usually very reliable and self-maintaining it is necessary to keep a watchful eye to make sure that messages are flowing at a regular and predictable rate. Before looking for signs that everything's all right we have to know what to look for and what we might see.

7.2.2   **Monitoring MTA queues**

The easiest way to check message flow through the MTA is to select the queues property page for the Message Transfer Agent and then view the list of queues and the number of messages in each queue as shown in Figure 7.2.

Figure 7.2
Viewing MTA
queues

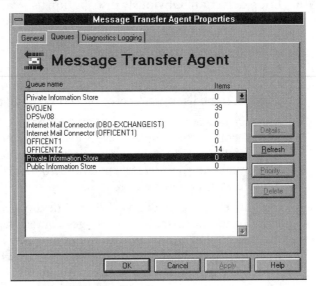

Your own knowledge of a connector and its normal traffic pattern will tell you whether an abnormal number of messages are in the queue. Clearly the best case is to have zero or very few messages in each queue because this indicates that no delay is being experienced in transmission. If you see that a number of messages have built up for a connector consider whether any unusual activity has recently taken place on your server which might have generated a large number of messages. For example, these activities can generate many messages for a connector:

- Moving public folders from one server to another.

- Adding or amending a large amount of information stored in public folders.

- Modifying the contents of the directory by adding, changing, or deleting recipients.

- Importing or synchronizing directory entries from another messaging system.

■   Unblocking a connection to another messaging system, which results in a large number of messages being delivered to a bridgehead server.

Taking the screen shot shown in Figure 7.2 as an example we can see that 39 messages are queued for BVOJEN and 14 for OFFICENT2. Both of these are servers, one located in a remote site (BVOJEN), the other server in the local site (OFFICENT2). You should know what's happening with all local servers so it's the first and easiest problem to investigate. In this case the answer was easy—the server was off-line for hardware maintenance, but there can be more problematic situations to resolve such as a server failing due to hardware or power problems. Monitoring queues helps to identify these situations by forcing system administrators to ask questions as to why queues should be building up for a local server.

The BVOJEN situation is a little harder to resolve because the server is remote. First we must know the type of connector used to link our site with BVOJEN. Knowledge of the Exchange environment (sites and servers) should provide the answer. In this case BVOJEN acts as the bridgehead server for the Belfast site and it is connected with a site connector.

Figure 7.3
Viewing the queue contents for a site connector

The next step is to determine whether the server is operational and whether the necessary Exchange services are running. Link and server monitors (see Chapter 11) help by revealing whether a network connection can be made to a server (link monitor) as well as the Exchange and other Windows NT services that are currently running (server monitor). If you haven't already created and implemented some monitors you should do so now and review the results as soon as they are obtained. Assuming that the server in question is running and the MTA is active on the server you should then review the contents of the queue to see if you can determine why so many messages are there.

Figure 7.3 shows the messages at the beginning of the BVOJEN queue. The contents are ordered in message priority (High/Medium/Low) sequence. Interpersonal messages are scattered among the messages generated by background system activities. You'll find messages from the Directory Service, the Public Information Store, and the System Attendant, reflecting the messages sent to replicate information between servers. The order of messages in the queue shown in Figure 7.3 looks a little strange at first glance. Why, for instance, is there a message generated by the Directory Service at 18:50 on April 1 (right at the bottom of the list) when messages generated by the same service throughout April 2 are at the top? The reason is simple: messages move up and down within the queue as attempts are made to send them. As problems have clearly occurred sending messages to the BVOJEN server over a period of days the messages from different days have become intermingled. You can manually intervene if you like by giving messages different priorities, but in most cases it is easier to let the Exchange MTA deal with the messages in the order they are presented.

I prefer to give interpersonal messages most importance, so the first step I take when dealing with a blocked queue is to immediately increase the priority of all interpersonal messages to "High." This action forces interpersonal messages to the top of the queue and makes sure that they will be sent first when the block is released. The logic behind this attitude is simple. Users complain when they receive non-delivery notifications, but the system components are much more patient and are content to wait for their messages to get through eventually.

The internal ordering of the queues also appears to give large messages a slightly higher priority than small messages. Once I've bumped all the interpersonal messages to the top of the queue I then like to move the small messages forward, the only reason being to clear the queue faster (at least on the surface). If the queue doesn't start to go down after all of this it's time to stop and restart the MTA on the target server, or perhaps restart the MTA on your server if lots of different queues are backing up. Restarting an MTA forces an internal reset and may clear out a problem that you can't see through the GUI.

In this instance the problem wasn't connected to Exchange Server at all. The network link between the two sites had become saturated because some large software kits were being copied from one computer to another. This goes to prove that all potential reasons must be considered when problem solving.

7.2.3   The MTA sliding window

A "sliding window" protocol is used by the MTA to transfer messages to other MTAs or gateways. This means that the MTA sends a certain amount of data, waits for an acknowledgment that the data has been received correctly, and then proceeds to send more data, continuing the process until the whole message is transferred. For comparison, many other messaging systems attempt to send complete messages as single entities, an approach that delivers satisfactory results with small to medium messages. Problems can occur when larger messages are sent, especially with network links that aren't very reliable. Given that the average message size continues to grow due to the influence of large and complex attachments, the sliding window protocol is a reasonable solution for a messaging system that is designed to cope easily with large messages.

System administrators can influence the sliding window by setting a number of properties for the Site MTA (using the Advanced page). The important properties are:

- Checkpoint size—the amount of message data to send before the MTA inserts a checkpoint. The default is 30K.

- Recovery time-out—the amount of time after an error occurs before the MTA will wait for a reconnection. If the connection cannot be reestablished the message fails and is returned to the queue. The default is 60 seconds.

- Window size—the number of checkpoints that can remain unacknowledged before the MTA will suspend data transfer. The default is 5.

In most instances the default values are appropriate and should only be changed if you suspect that the MTA is unable to process messages in a satisfactory manner. For example, if you suspect that the network is experiencing some problems that are causing messages to fail (evidence of this would be provided by a queue building up for a connector that doesn't normally have a queue of more than a few messages), then you might reduce the window size from 5 to 2 in order to force the MTA to send less data before an acknowledgment is received. Reducing the checkpoint size from 30K to 10K is another step that could be taken in a situation where network problems are being experienced.

7.2.4   MTA data files and the MTA work directory

If you browse through the MTA work directory you'll come across some data files named DB000001.DAT, DB000002.DAT, and so on. These files are used by the MTA for items such as message queues, internal indexes used by the MTA, and temporary storage of mail messages en route through the MTA. Collectively they are referred to as the MTA database.

Of course, the MTA database isn't a database in the same sense as the JET databases used for the information store. But there's a very good reason to elect to use the NT file system to build a file-driven data store, which is in fact what we have here. Consider the work that the MTA is expected to do. There's no real sense of data retention because the MTA should be accepting messages and redirecting them to their proper direction all the time. The only reasons why files should remain around for any real length of time are because:

- The system is under heavy load and messages can't be processed by the MTA as quickly as they arrive. In this case files will build up in the MTA work directory, but they should be deleted fairly quickly as soon as the system load reduces and the MTA is able to get access to CPU and memory.

- There's a network or other problem (perhaps a connector is stopped or has terminated abnormally), causing messages to accumulate in the MTA work directory. In this case the solution is simple: get the network connection back in operation or investigate why a particular connector stopped and return it to normal operation.

The installation process creates an initial set of 35 data files which are required to initiate MTA processing. As processing proceeds the set of files changes with the demand placed on the MTA. The number of files is influenced by the number of messages in the queues or other work in progress, but on fast systems where there are no problems sending messages through any of the attached connectors you shouldn't ever see more than 250 files or so in the directory. However, this figure depends on the size and workload of a system. If you run the Performance Monitor and tune the system to handle a large user community, say 600 users, then the MTA will increase the number of files that it uses in an attempt to handle the predicated load generated by such a user community.

When messages arrive into the MTA they are written to disk. Messages are also written into a cache in memory (one of the reasons why EMSMTA.EXE appears sometimes to occupy more memory than you think it might). Processing data held in memory is always faster, so the MTA attempts to do as much as possible with the messages stored there. The MTA is multi-threaded, so multiple operations can be concurrently executed against single message objects. For example, a message sent to a large distribution list might be sent by one thread to an MTA on another server in the same site, to the Internet connector for transmission to an SMTP addressee, and to an MS-Mail connector to be sent to an MS-Mail addressee. A scheme of message roll-in and roll-out of the cache is implemented to accommodate heavy processing times when there mightn't be enough memory available to handle the number of messages arriving to the MTA.

Two registry entries control the number of files that the MTA uses for transient message storage in its work directory and to state a threshold value for the maximum size for a transient file. The two entries we're interested are can be found in the

```
Hkey_Local_Machine\System\Services\MSExchangeMTA\Parameters
```

section of the registry and are:

- DB File Handles, determining the number of the file handles kept and using for caching.
- DB File Size Delete Threshold, defining the maximum size of a file to be kept. Any file exceeding the threshold is automatically deleted after it is finished with.

Even with the fastest and most efficient file system it would not be good for performance to have file creation and deletion going on all the time. On heavily loaded systems it is quite possible to fully occupy the disk I/O subsystem with the demands of file creation and deletion if a new file is created for each new message. The MTA therefore maintains a set of files that it attempts to reuse. A separate handle (literally an I/O channel) is kept for each file by the MTA, allowing it to flush the content of a file after a message has been dispatched and reuse the on-disk storage to capture the content of a newly arrived message. Thus the overhead of file creation and deletion is kept to a minimum. It is entirely possible that users will send ridiculously large messages over time. Messages containing video clips are a particular favorite of mine, and such messages occupy many kilobytes or even megabytes of storage. The threshold parameter controls whether the MTA retains large files within its set. For example, let's assume that the threshold is set to 300KB. If a new 400KB message comes in the MTA will create a new file to hold its content. Once the message has successfully passed through the MTA it will immediately delete the file and not seek to retain the file to be reused.

7.2.5 When problems occur in the MTA work directory

Note the caveat in the last section—"where there are no problems ... through any of the attached connectors." Once problems occur files start to accumulate in the \MTADATA directory, and you can get an unpleasant surprise at the rate that these files build up. For example, if a connection between one site and another is inoperative for a few days several thousand messages are queued by the MTA. A simple test I performed involved disconnecting a server from the network over a three-day period. The server was connected to the Exchange organization via a site connector to another site that served as a hub to five other sites, a factor that contributed to an increase in the messaging load. During the disconnected period over 3,500 messages built up in the MTA queue for the unavailable server, and when that server was reconnected to the network it took nearly two hours for the queue to be cleared. In this instance the two servers were connected over a LAN, so network bandwidth was not an issue and the messages cleared from the queue pretty rapidly. In another scenario, where the bandwidth between the two sites is not so copious, the queue will be reduced much more slowly.

Figure 7.4 *A large MTA queue*

The problem of large MTA queues is not unique or confined to site, X.400, or Internet connectors. Exactly the same situation can arise if a server is disconnected from its partner servers within a site. If servers remain unavailable for any length of time a queue of messages will build within the MTA. The queue will only be cleared when the missing server is restored to action and restarts the Exchange MTA service. In fact, because you have no control whatsoever over the messaging activities that take place between servers in a site the number of messages in the queue builds up very rapidly. On the other hand, because intra-site connections are normally LAN-based, the queue will be quickly reduced once all the servers are available again.

Apart from the obvious system workload that arose once the servers were able to resume normal operation across the site connector, another potential performance issue came into play because the 3,500 messages were also stored as .DAT files in the \MTADATA directory. Most systems are able to manage several thousand files in a directory, but significant strain is placed on system resources if more than 20,000 files are allowed to accumulate. If you doubt what I say test the theory by allowing some thousands of files to build up in a directory and then attempt to list the files with the Windows NT Explorer (or even just a simple DOS DIR command in a DOS command window). The system will take a little time to satisfy your request, so keeping the number of files in the \MTADATA directory down to a reasonable level is important in terms of system performance.

Putting the \MTADATA directory on its own physical disk is a good way to assure that the system will deliver optimal performance. You'll be assuring that the system has the fastest possible access to the work files required by the MTA. But even if you can afford the luxury of a separate \MTADATA disk, you should still pay close attention to MTA queues and never let them mount up to a situation where more than a few hundred messages are waiting to go across a connector. Placing the \MTADATA directory on a separate disk helps to avoid another potential problem by reducing the likelihood that the MTA will be forced to stop because it is unable to create new .DAT files in its work directory. During normal operation, with messages flowing freely, disk space exhaustion should not occur. As we've seen, messages and queues are represented by many individual files ranging in size from 8K right up to the size of the largest individual message. If message queues start building, disk space will be consumed, eventually leading to exhaustion if action is not taken to start messages flowing again. The MTA will shut itself down if it detects that less than 10MB of disk space is available on the drive hosting its work directory.

It is a fact of system management life that servers will become unavailable during day to day operation. Wise system planners never base system designs on an assumption that computers and network connections will operate on a basis of 100% availability. Power outages or planned building, computer, or network maintenance can all affect availability. If interruptions in service are not catered for you can end up with a situation where servers take many hours or even days to deal with the work load that has accumulated when normal communications were unavailable.

We've already discussed how a simple site connector can build up a queue of over three thousand messages during a network outage. Hub sites, those that act as a central network point of contact for other sites, are especially sensitive to network problems. Consider a situation where a site acts as a hub for a number of the other sites. If network connections are lost to one or more of the "spoke" sites, the MTA queues in the hub site will start to grow. Messages arriving in from sites that are still connected must be held until they can be sent. The longer the network connections are unavailable, the bigger the queues will grow. In one case in my experience a hub site had a network problem for four days. At the end of that period there were queues of over four thousand messages for the three spoke sites the hub could not communicate with. Clearing the backlog took almost two days, and the system that acted as the central hub did not provide good performance to its own users while it cleared the backlog. The lesson from this is clear: if you operate hub sites, make sure that there are at least two servers in the hub site, and spread the connections to other sites across all available servers. This won't stop network problems arising, but at least it will divide the queues across a number of servers and help to get everything back working sooner once the network problem has been resolved.

Where can so many thousand queued messages come from? If you view the contents of any MTA queue you'll see that messages come from the system attendant, the public information store, the directory, and interpersonal messages generated by users. The vast bulk of the messages are normally system-generated, that is, those generated to keep systems up to date with each other's configurations or to replicate data for the directory or public information store. The number of background messages generated by servers can be restrained by amending replication schedules for public folder replicas and directory connectors. If network bandwidth is an issue or no assurance exists that connections will be available on a regular and predictable basis close attention should be paid to the schedules set for these items. Why, for instance, do you need to replicate directory information every 15 minutes when perhaps 1-hour or even 2-hour intervals will suffice?

You might use some or all of the suggestions given below to avoid problems occurring with large MTA queues:

- Check MTA queues on a regular basis (at least twice a day) to ensure that no queue is building up for an unknown reason. If a large queue is present try and determine why the queue has accumulated and take action to rectify the situation.

- Consider the effect that system outages have on message queues and try to avoid breaking the connections between Exchange servers if at all possible. Review your Exchange organization to try and work out how various network failures might affect message flow between the different sites. Don't power down systems within a site unnecessarily as this will provoke large queues too.

- Put the MTA work directory (\MTADATA) on a disk that isn't heavily used (not the same disk as the database transaction logs). Check that space is available to create work files on the disk, especially at times when message queues begin to build up. The MTADATA directory can be moved away from its default location (the same disk as the Exchange executables) to a more suitable location with the Performance Optimizer (see Chapter 11).

- Throttle back the schedules for directory and public folder replication so that an unnecessarily high volume of messages isn't generated between servers.

- Spread the connector load across several systems in a site so that, if a network problem occurs, the queues accumulate on several servers and so can be processed more quickly once the problem is resolved.

The MTA creates additional data files for messages and queues as required. Because the files are all used for internal processing no one can be sure as to the exact contents or use of any particular data file. It is therefore very unwise to take the chance of deleting any of the data files. You might be deleting a message, or a connector queue, or something else needed by the MTA. In much the same way as the information store transaction logs, leave these files alone and let Exchange take care of them.

7.2.6   Expanding distribution lists

Before we get to the details of how a message is routed by the MTA to its ultimate destination it's important to understand that the MTA must first expand the contents of any distribution lists in the message recipients. An Exchange distribution list may not be a simple object. It can contain addresses for mailboxes, custom recipients, public folders, and other distribution lists. The process of expansion must be performed recursively until all lists, including those nested within any original distribution lists, are conclusively resolved.

Distribution lists are not resolved when a client sends a message to the MTA. At this stage the message is passed, without interference, from the client to the private information store. Distribution lists are always expanded by the MTA after the message has been delivered by the private information store. The rule therefore is if a message contains a distribution list it is always sent to the MTA for resolution, even if the distribution list only contains local mailboxes. For this reason the MTA service must always be active, even on servers that aren't connected to anything else.

7.2.7   Message routing algorithm

The following algorithm is used by the MTA to decide how a message can be delivered to an external recipient.

- According to the contents of the GWART, what connectors are available? Which of the active connectors on this system can handle the message?

- The retry count should not have been exceeded for any connector being considered. A check is performed to ensure that the maximum number of retries for a message has not been exceeded. This ensures that a message is returned with an "undeliverable" status to a user within a reasonable time after sending. Note that retry counts cannot be specified for site connectors, so it's possible for messages to stay in a site connector queue being retried constantly until they expire after a few days, at which time they'll be returned to the originator as undeliverable.

- Scan for active connectors. Which of the connectors that are able to process the message are active on the system right now? Dynamic RAS or X.400 connectors often operate only at specific times during the day. If two routes are available and only one is active (albeit even apparently at a higher cost), then it's logical to dispatch messages via the active route. The valid states for connectors are listed in Table 7.1.

- Lowest retry count. Which of the active connectors have the lowest retry count? In other words, which connector is most likely to be able to dispatch the message first time around? The initial check was to ensure that the message retry count had not reached its maximum value; this check is to determine which connector has been attempted the least number of times.

- Not currently trying. A check is performed to ensure that an active connector isn't currently processing the message.

- Lowest cost. Given all else, if two or more connectors are available, which connector can transmit the message at lowest cost? We'll discuss how costs are allocated to connectors later on in this chapter.

- Local over remote. If a local connector is available to handle the message, send it locally rather than attempting to use a remote connector.

Table 7.1 *Connector states*

Connector Status	Meaning
Active now	The connector is currently active and is available to process messages. Active connectors are always selected first by the MTA. Standard site connectors, the Internet Mail Service, and the Microsoft Mail Connector do not have activation schedules. Thus, they are always "Active Now."
Will become active in the future	The connector is scheduled to become available sometime in the future. If several connectors are suitable and in this state the MTA selects the one scheduled to become active first.
Never	The connector is unable to make connections at present. This state might arise when a connector is temporarily disabled.
Remote initiated	The connector cannot be started locally. Instead, its use is always initiated by a remote MTA.

Hopefully a suitable connector is determined at the conclusion of these steps and the message can be sent on its way. It may well be that several connectors present themselves as willing and able to dispatch the message, and if so, the MTA attempts to balance the connection load by making a random selection from the set of suitable connectors.

After all that, if a message is returned immediately or very soon after it is sent it's a good indication that the message is either badly addressed or the address space for the target connector is badly defined. The MTA always tries to reroute a message immediately if it encounters a failure on its first attempt. If the message cannot be rerouted it will remain in the MTA queue for the relevant connector and have its retry count incremented by one. The properties of the Site MTA object define the default retry interval (normally 600 seconds—10 minutes), and the maximum number of retries. These properties are known as the "Open Interval" and "Max Open Retries" respectively.

If the message exceeds the maximum number of retries it will be returned to its originator wrapped in a non-delivery notification. The user can then, if they wish, click on the "Send Again" command button to see whether the message can get through. It may well be, for instance, that a connector who depends on a specific network link is unavailable because of hardware or other problems. In this case lots of non-delivery notifications can be generated, causing considerable frustration to users and lots of calls for the help desk. The sole silver lining in this particular cloud is that the useful "Send Again" command button on the non-delivery notification gives users a chance to send the message again with little difficulty.

7.2.8   What gets sent, where, and how?

When Exchange sees that a message has been sent to external recipients it passes the message to the MTA to begin a process called message routing, or the determination of how that message is going to be delivered to its recipients. Message routing requires the MTA to check what connectors are capable of getting the message to a recipient as well as at what cost, no matter how many connectors the message must pass through en route to its final destination(s). The calculation of cost is based on figures entered by system administrators when connectors are added to an Exchange server. The final calculation is a cumulative figure composed of the cost required to navigate from connector to connector on different Exchange servers. The simplest cost to determine is, of course, when a direct connection is made from one site to another.

Connectors are configured using the Exchange Administration program. The two most important items specified when a connector is configured are:

■ Address Space: literally, the types of mail addresses that can be handled by the connector. Directory replication ensures that all servers within an organization know about all the connectors installed on other servers. Thus, the MTA is able to consider all connectors for potential message dispatch. The process of reviewing all possible connectors for message delivery is known as selection.

■ Connected Sites: the list of sites to which mail can be sent through the connector.

After a connector is configured the remote routing table for the server is rebuilt in order to make the new connector active. In effect this includes the new connector in the site address space so that the connector can be assessed and possibly used whenever the MTA reviews the addresses on an outgoing or incoming message. An address for the new connector is also added to each user record in the directory so that messages arriving via the connector can be delivered correctly. For example, the SMTP type address is used to indicate user addresses that the Internet Mail Service should handle. The administrator can define the set of sites serviced by the connector when the connector is configured.

The information relating to connectors is stored in the configuration container and is replicated by the directory service to adjacent sites. The system attendant and MTA work together to create a routing table known as the Gateway Address Routing Table (GWART) to use when routing messages. Servers maintain their own GWART. You can think of the GWART as a set of address information relating to all possible routes that can be used to deliver messages.

The GWART is stored in the directory and can be viewed through the Routing property page of the Site Addressing object (see Figure 7.5). The routing table is also available as a simple text file in the \EX-CHSRVR\MTADATA directory. Two copies are kept:

- GWART0.MTA—the current routing table
- GWART1.MTA—the routing table prior to the last change

Figure 7.5 *Site Address Space*

These text files are created each time a change is made to the routing table. You can force Exchange to recreate the routing table by pressing the "Recalculate Routing" command button (Figure 7.5); otherwise the routing table is rebuilt automatically at scheduled times.

Connectors are installed on specific servers, but every server in a site needs to know how to route messages as a whole, rather than an individual case. Normally one server in each site takes care of the task of rebuilding the routing table. In large sites supporting multiple connectors a rebuild can be a fairly intensive exercise, certainly not one to allocate to a server supporting many hundreds of users, or one that's scheduled to occur at 9 a.m., just as all the users log-on and begin reading their mail. Rebuilding the routing table involves a scan through the address spaces from each server within the site and the connectors installed on all servers. The resulting routing table is then distributed throughout the site via the directory, the same mechanism used to update other sites within the organization. Depending on how directory entries are replicated throughout your organization it may take some time before all servers are made aware that a new connector has been added or a change (such as an update for the routing cost of a connector) been made.

As you can see from the Site Addressing properties illustrated in Figure 7.5, the routing table contains a subset of complete addresses. In other words, the table contains only the necessary elements to identify the route that a message should take. The table is divided into three major types of addresses:

1. **Type "EX"**: These entries refer to native format Exchange addresses (distinguished names) and relate to site connectors. The illustration shows a single "EX" entry corresponding to a single site connector.

2. **Type "DDA" (Domain Defined Attribute)**: These entries refer to the gateways and connectors that are used to send messages to custom recipients. The most common examples are "MS" (Microsoft Mail Connector) and "SMTP" (Internet Mail Service).

3. **Type "X400" (X.400 Originator/Recipient)**: These entries relate to X.400 connections to either other Exchange servers (site X.400 connectors) or to foreign X.400 MTAs. As you can see from the screen shot, three X.400 O/R addresses are specified for two different countries (DK = Denmark, GB = Great Britain).

Each line in the routing table corresponds to a route that the MTA can take to deliver a message.

There is an understandable temptation for each site (or even multiple servers within a site) to install and configure their own set of connectors. This is a mistake. Not only will all the extra connections complicate the routing table it can also lead to messages being routed to places that you didn't really want them to go.

For example, take the situation where sites in Dublin and Denmark both install an Internet Mail connector, configuring each to be able to handle any SMTP type address (the address space for the connector is configured as SMTP:*) with a routing cost of 1. Connector information is part of the configuration data automatically replicated between sites, so shortly after the two connectors are installed and configured in the respective sites every other site in the organization will learn of their existence. The routing table in each site will also be recalculated, and the MTAs on every server will insert an entry in their GWART. Every time that the MTA meets a message addressed to an SMTP destination it consults the GWART to discover that two routes can be taken, each with a similar routing cost. Normally the MTA favors the home connector, but if it is unavailable for any reason the MTA seeks to use alternate routes to get the mail through. An arbitrary decision will be taken to determine which route each message should take. In this case the messages will be rerouted to Denmark to be sent via the Internet Mail Service in that site. The same situation pertains for messages generated in Denmark. Routing via foreign destinations is great for messages interested in tourism, but it's hardly efficient.

The lesson here is simple. Only install the connectors you absolutely need and make sure that the right routing costs are allocated to each connector so that the optimal route is always chosen by the MTA. This is not as easy as it seems, because everyone wants to give the local connector the lowest possible routing cost. You therefore end up with a set of connectors, all with a routing cost of 1. As we've seen above, as long as the connectors are active everything is OK and the messages will be routed via local connectors, but when things go wrong the messages can be routed in "interesting" directions.

7.2.9   Taking control of routing

The situation where a connector in Copenhagen routes messages for Dublin is acceptable in some cases. In companies that have many different connections to the Internet it probably doesn't make a whole heap of difference if a message finds its way via a slightly tortuous route to an eventual destination somewhere in the Internet. There's probably no great difference in the cost of an Internet message dispatched from Dublin to one sent from Copenhagen. And anyway, because routing favors local connectors until problems occur, the default mechanism that implements alternate routing offers significant benefits in terms of speeding the delivery of messages. It is only in situations where you positively want to route messages through a specific connector or wish to prevent messages from remote sites routing through local connectors that problems really arise.

Take the situation of connectors that have definite costs attached to each message. FAX connectors are a good example. You don't want to install a new FAX connector in a site in Australia to suddenly discover that users in sites throughout the world are sending faxes through the connector. Apart from anything else, the costs involved in someone sending a local fax via a remote connector are considerably higher than if they had used a connector in the local site. The solution, available in Exchange V4.0 SP4 and Exchange V5.0, is to hide the existence of connectors from other sites through a mechanism that controls the replication of routing information outside the view of sites that host the connectors. The "cloaking" mechanism stops routing information for connectors appearing in the routing table in the remote sites and so prevents users from sending messages where they shouldn't.

Marking an element in a site's address space for local use only stops it from being replicated outside the site. Local address space entries are unique to a connector, so a separate entry must be created for each connector you wish to restrict.

Figure 7.6
*Adding a
LOCAL address
space to the
Internet Mail
Service*

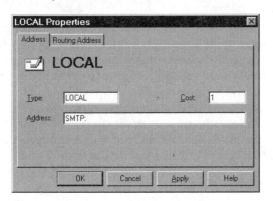

Let's suppose you want to stop other sites using the Internet Mail Service in your site. The default address space is probably something like "SMTP: ", meaning that any SMTP message can be handled by the Internet Mail Service. When you restrict access to the connector you replace the existing address space with one that looks like "LOCAL:SMTP." Amending the existing address space entry can't create the necessary routing instruction for the MTA. You will need to add a new "General" address space entry similar to that shown in Figure 7.6, and then delete the existing SMTP address entry. After these two steps have been taken you should end up with a connector address space similar to that shown in Figure 7.7.

The existence of the LOCAL address space allows the GWART generation code to include the connector in the local site routing table while instructing the mechanism that builds the GWART in other sites to ignore the connector. The other sites will continue to receive information about connectors that you'd like them to know of, such as the one and only SNADS connector in an organization. Only servers running the correct level of code obey the address space restriction. Servers running Exchange V4.0 (pre SP4) or beta versions of Exchange V5.0 will ignore the hurdles now being placed in their way.

Figure 7.7 *The address space for the Internet Mail Service after adjustments have been made*

It is possible for administrators to override local address space entries on other sites. This is useful where you are willing to allow another site in the same country to have access to something like a FAX connector, but you definitely don't want people in foreign sites sending their faxes through your connector.

In this situation you'll need to create specific address spaces for each connector you want to use. For example, if a site in New York wants to use the fax connector in the Boston site, New York must create an address space for the fax connector on whatever connector (site, X.400, or Internet) is used to connect New York to Boston. Confused? Think of this in terms of the GWART (difficult, I know). The GWART has no record of being able to shift faxes from New York to Boston so they can be sent. By adding the address space you give the GWART enough information to route the faxes.

A Microsoft Knowledge Base article (Q161947) covers the topic of controlling address space replication. We're only at the start of our experience with this subject and don't yet know how useful it will be in practice, nor do we know what tricks and techniques can be applied.

7.2.10   The MTACHECK utility

Corrupt data files or messages can cause the MTA to stop processing, or simply refuse to start. The \EXCHSRVR\BIN\MTACHECK utility is provided to help rectify the situation by reviewing the internal structures used by the MTA and make any changes required.

The MTACHECK utility:

- Checks the consistency of the MTA queues.
- Checks the integrity of all of the objects used by the MTA.
- Removes any "orphan" files from the \MTADATA work directory that are no longer required by the MTA.
- Deletes any objects that the MTACHECK utility believes to be corrupt. Hopefully it is the removal of these objects that allows the MTA to restart.

Two command line switches are provided:

- /v instructs MTACHECK to run in verbose mode. Lots of detailed information is output as each object is processed.
- /f allows you to specify a file into which details of all of the actions performed by the utility will be logged.

The normal course is to run MTACHECK only in situations when problems occur with the MTA. You can run MTACHECK at any time, just to see what it does. Before running MTACHECK remember to shut the MTA service down so as to prevent any possible contention between normal processing and the potential fixes made by MTACHECK. If the MTA service is interrupted abnormally as in the case of a power failure or premature system power-down, the MTA queues may be in an inconsistent state. The next time the MTA service is restarted Exchange detects that a problem may exist and verifies the queues, making any repairs that are deemed necessary.

Figure 7.8
Extract from
MTACHECK.TXT

```
Checking queue XAPIWRKQ (id 01000020)
Checking queue OOFINFOQ (id 01000025)
Checking queue REFDATQ (id 01000026)
Checking queue MTAWORKQ (id 0100002B)
```

```
Checking queue /O=DIGITAL EQUIPMENT
CORPORATION/OU=DUBLIN/CN=CONFIGURATION/CN=SERVERS/CN=DBO-
EXCHANGEIST/CN=MICROSOFT DXA (id 010000B8)
```

```
Checking queue /O=DIGITAL EQUIPMENT
CORPORATION/OU=DUBLIN/CN=CONFIGURATION/CN=CONNECTIONS/CN=INTERNET
MAIL SERVICE (DBO-EXCHANGEIST) (id 010000C8)
Checking queue /O=DIGITAL EQUIPMENT
CORPORATION/OU=DUBLIN/CN=CONFIGURATION/CN=CONNECTIONS/CN=INTERNET
MAIL SERVICE (OFFICENT1) (id 010000D9)
```

```
Checking queue /O=DIGITAL EQUIPMENT
CORPORATION/OU=DUBLIN/CN=CONFIGURATION/CN=CONNECTIONS/CN=MS MAIL
CONNECTOR (DBO-EXCHANGEIST) (id 0100003E)
```

```
Starting object integrity checks
   Checking object 03000002 - OK, on queue 01000026
   Checking object 0A000003 - OK, on queue 01000020
   Checking object 0B000004 - OK, on queue 01000020
   Checking object 0B000005 - OK, on queue 01000020
```

```
Object 000000C7 invalid
   - corrupted object file.
   - MTS-ID:        Unavailable
```

```
Object 000000D8 invalid
   - corrupted object file.
   - MTS-ID:        Unavailable
```

```
Starting removal of corrupt objects
Move of .\DB0000C7.DAT successful.
Move of .\DB0000D8.DAT successful.
```

```
Starting garbage collection of orphaned objects
Deleted D:\EXCHSRVR\mtadata\.\DB00002F.DAT successfully.
Deleted D:\EXCHSRVR\mtadata\.\DB000032.DAT successfully.
Deleted D:\EXCHSRVR\mtadata\.\DB000035.DAT successfully.
```

```
Database repaired, some data may have been lost.
- 0 queue(s) required repair out of 8 detected (0%).
- 2 object(s) damaged out of 1230 detected (0%).
```

This process doesn't take very long, except on systems that have many messages waiting in the MTA queues. Each queued message must be verified, and it is conceivable that the MTA service could be unavailable for up to 15 minutes (any longer is a cause for real concern) after the system reboots. Summary information about the actions performed during an MTA check after system restart is recorded in the system event log. Detailed information is available in the file MTACHECK.TXT in the \MTADATA\MTACHECK.OUT directory (see the edited text taken from an actual MTACHECK.TXT in Figure 7.8). Any corrupt files detected during this process are removed from the MTADATA directory to \MTACHECK.OUT.

During the time that the MTA queues are being verified people may still use Exchange to access their mailboxes and send and reply to messages. The unavailability of the MTA will not affect users in the short term as the information store service is enough for people to access mailboxes. Over a longer period the lack of the MTA affects the capability of the messaging service. Users will still be able to send messages to other users whose mailboxes are on the same server (all such messages are handled by the store and not by the MTA), but any messages for remote users will be queued and not processed until the MTA restarts. In the same way, message exchange with remote servers and other mail systems will not operate until the MTA is available.

7.3   General notes on Exchange connectors

All external connectors run as multi-threaded processes on a Windows NT computer. You can decide to run all of the connectors on a single computer within your organization, but you must consider the fact that each connector imposes a certain processing load on the system and attempting to push too much work through a single place may create potential messaging bottlenecks. All of the connectors are registered as entries within the Exchange directory, so once a connector is installed and active it becomes available to any user within the organization. This poses some interesting questions, especially with systems distributed internationally.

Do you, for example, want to have everyone sending messages to external bodies worldwide through a single SMTP or X.400 connector? Given the volume of messages that might be sent to recipients in the Internet this mightn't be a smart idea. Allowing users based in England to send faxes generated by a connector in Germany may not be convenient and might generate higher telecommunications charges. On the other hand, you might decide to take advantage of lower telecommunications charges in a certain country and route all fax traffic out through that country, but would this be legal? Interesting questions, and of course you can configure the different connectors to take account of these issues, but it's amazing how many people never even pause to think.

An implementation plan will ideally clearly identify the set of external communications required by an organization and propose how those connections can be made by Exchange. If you are running an electronic mail system now you'll be able to extract much useful information from whatever connections are already operational, including the volume of messages that are sent and received over a set period. It's better if you have statistics for message traffic over an extended period, ideally taken at a regular interval such as weekly or monthly as these statistics will allow you to see whether volume is growing or declining, and the rate at which the increase or decrease is occurring.

Once you know what connections are needed and the volume that each connection will support (plus a suitable percentage increase to accommodate growth for the first year of operation) you can proceed to plan where the connectors will be installed. Remember to take the network overhead necessary to transport messages to connectors when you look for the correct system to host connectors. The connector software is relatively low-cost so don't try to save too much on expenditure if you're going to impact the service delivered to users.

7.3.1   The bridgehead concept

When you read the Exchange documentation you may come across the term "bridgehead" and wonder what it means. A bridgehead server is a system within a site that is nominated to operate as a point of connectivity between that site and either another site or a foreign mail system. The bridgehead server acts as a target for other sites or gateways to transmit messages to.

For example, if you had a site with three servers and wanted to establish a connection to the Internet it wouldn't make sense to install and configure the IMS on all three servers. Apart from anything else, extra system administration overhead is incurred for each operational IMC. In this situation the best idea is to nominate one of the servers to act as the bridgehead between the site and the Internet and install the IMS on that server. Because of the extra processing performed to send and receive messages to and from another system it is normal to select the system with the best configuration to act as the bridgehead.

7.3.2   Avoiding bottlenecks

Another fact to take into account is that anywhere that connections or gateways exist between one system and another represents a potential bottleneck. Exchange is designed to handle many thousands of messages per hour, but achieving a high rate of throughput relies on optimal transmission paths and a low or nil requirement to convert messages from one format to another. No gateway between systems can be regarded as optimal because electronic mail systems can differ in so many ways, leading to a situation where it is inevitable that some "fix-up" processing has to be performed before a message can be transmitted from or to Exchange. Even the Microsoft Mail connector has to convert messages from MS-Mail format to MAPI and vice versa.

If the network link used by a connector is slow and the message volume passing through the connector is large you run the risk that queues of messages will build up waiting to get through the connector. Installing a heavily used connector on a server that has good network links but is overloaded by other processing is also a good recipe for bottlenecks. Even with properly configured systems fast connections can be overwhelmed by heavy message volume, and a particular danger time is during a migration from one system to another when connections are used to bridge the gap between the old electronic mail system and Exchange. During migration periods you may have to install and operate several different connectors until the bulk of users have moved over to Exchange, at which time the message volume should decrease.

7.4   Configuring and operating a site connector

Before engaging in the discussion as to how to select and configure a connector between two sites in the same Exchange organization it's important to know the type of data that will flow through the connector. It's also good to know which Exchange components are responsible for the generation and transmission of the data.

Figure 7.9
Messages sent between Exchange sites

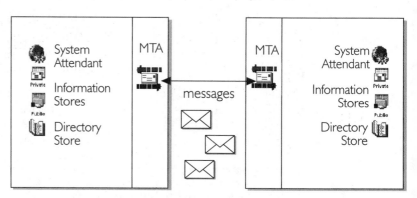

Figure 7.9 illustrates how messages pass between servers over a site connection. As you can see, the MTA in the bridgehead server in each site communicates with its partner MTA to exchange data in the form of messages.

It's easy to see that interpersonal messages flow from the private information store to the MTA for onward transmission. You might also recall that public folder and directory replication is accomplished via messages too. Table 7.2 lists the major types of messages that flow across a link between sites. If you use Directory Synchronization (DX) then messages will also be generated through this service.

Table 7.2   *Messages exchanged between sites*

Type of data	Component generating the messages
Mail messages generated by users	Private Information Store
Replication of changes and additions to objects placed into public folders	Public Information Store
Replication of the public folder hierarchy	Public Information Store
Replication of changes and additions to the Exchange directory store	Exchange Directory Service
Link Monitor test messages	System Attendant (via the Private Information Store)

Note that within a single standalone site composed of a number of different servers the MTA does not handle messages for the directory store. The directory service processes its own messages in this case.

7.4.1   The options to connect sites

The full list of connectors capable of linking sites together has already been discussed. To recall, you can select from the site connector itself, the X400 connector, IMC, and dynamic RAS. Which of these should you use? Table 7.3 lists some common requirements along with an appropriate solution.

Table 7.3   *Selecting a connector to link sites*

Situation	Select
o Very reliable network links between the sites connected by networks capable of supporting RPCs (named pipes, NetBIOS, Windows Sockets)	Site connector
o TCP/IP, TP4 or X.25 connectivity available between bridgehead servers o Requirement to schedule message exchange at particular times o Best ability to utilize low bandwidth o Requirement to restrict message size	X.400 connector or IMC
o Dial-up connectivity when no permanent LAN/WAN connection is available	Dynamic RAS

The standard site connector is generally the fastest in transmitting information, as long as the network link between the servers in each site is capable of handling RPCs in a reliable manner. The connector is relatively simple in comparison to the X.400 connector, so there is less overhead when messages are processed, and the connector performs at anything up to 20% faster than an X.400 or SMTP equivalent, both of which require messages to be converted into a different format before transmission.

The standard site connector is also able to transmit to several servers within a site whereas the X.400 connector is restricted to a single named server. On the other hand, the X.400 or IMS connectors are more resilient when it comes to dealing with network connections that are unreliable from time to time. The X.400 connector is unique in that it is the only connector that supports scheduled connections between sites. The Internet Mail Service is able to support scheduled RAS dial-up connections to services such as those provided by an ISP, and it is possible to backbone sites across the public Internet, but this is not as elegant or as straightforward as the scheduled connections of the X.400 connector. Apart from this aspect of scheduling, because the functionality of the two connectors is so close (apart from delivery and read receipt notifications) selecting the IMS or X.400 to act as connectors linking sites together often comes down to the question of which messaging standard do you prefer?

The dynamic RAS connector comes into its own and beats everything else when a telephone connection is all that's available, and is the most appropriate connection in cases such as small or distant offices or when you don't want to invest in a bespoke network just for messaging. Another example when the RAS connector is valuable is when sophisticated network links are just not available. Microsoft, for example, connects four sites in South America through RAS connectors because they weren't able to install the type of dedicated network links required to support the X.400 or IMS. Available bandwidth is the biggest issue with RAS connectors. It's OK if a site supporting a few messaging users is at the other end of the connection, but problems come into focus if people try and replicate very large documents between public folder replicas. In all instances where RAS connectors are used it's a good idea to keep a constant eye on the queue for connector so that any problems are quickly detected before they result in a large backlog of queued messages.

The initial directory back-fill can also cause problems across a RAS connector. When the new site joins the organization the initial contact is fine, and messages start to flow across the connection. But joining a moderately complex organization can result in having to receive a great deal of directory information containing the GAL and configuration information for all the other sites. If you get in a position where you need to use RAS connectors, consider performing the initial installation at a location where a LAN connection is possible, wait for directory replication to complete the back-fill operation, and then dispatch the computer to its eventual destination.

It is possible to configure multiple connectors for each site. A cost is allocated to each connector to tell Exchange which connector should be used as the default link. Let's assume that you have a site connector and an X.400 connector established to link the Dublin and Belfast sites. The site connector has a cost value of 1 whereas the X.400 connector has a cost of 50. In the normal course of events messages will always be sent via the site connector, but if any problems occur with the site connector messages can be rerouted via X.400. Messages are not rerouted automatically, and messages are not taken off one queue to be dispatched via the connector that is now taking up the load. Everything must be done manually by amending the relative costs attributed to each connector.

If you give the two connectors the same cost Exchange will attempt to balance the load of messages transmitted across each connector. Load balancing through multiple connectors enables a degree of fault tolerance within the messaging network. If one connector fails the other will continue transmitting messages until its companion resumes. A connector can be given a maximum cost of 100, but this has a special meaning in that Exchange will only use it as a very last resort when no other connector is available.

Remember that the replication of organizational information means that sites know about the connections existing between other sites. You may have no control over the connectors established by other system administrators or the cost allocated to these connectors. It's possible to get into strange situations with cost values because they are cumulative. In other words, if messages have to pass through one site to get to another the cost of each link is added to form a cost for the overall route. It may well be that a direct route between two sites is created with a cost of 10, but Exchange "discovers" that it is possible to route messages via an intermediate site using a connector with cost 5 and another (from the intermediate site to the target site) of cost 4, resulting in an overall cost of 9, lower than the direct and preferred route. Clearly this points to a need to understand the connections that exist within an organization and not to introduce new connections without being aware of the potential impact on other sites. Hopefully if you look after the interest of other sites, their administrators will look after yours!

It is possible to attribute different costs to different servers within a site when using the site connector. The normal course of events is to transmit messages to a bridgehead server in each site, but it's also possible to seek to balance the load across multiple servers in the same way that you'd try to balance the connectivity load across multiple connectors.

7.4.2   Making the connection

When a server transfers messages to a remote server in another site, the MTA must bind to the remote MTA using the Exchange service account. It is possible to use different service accounts in both sites, as long as the accounts in each site possesses the necessary permissions to bind to the remote MTA, but it's much easier and convenient to use the same service account in both sites.

As described in Chapter 3, to use a site connector you must establish a Windows NT trust relationship between the communicating domains if the sites being connected reside in different Windows NT domains. The rule here is that the domain for the site being connected to must trust the site making the connection. If different accounts have been set up for Exchange in the two Windows NT domains it is necessary to use the property pages of the site connector to instruct Exchange that a specific service account should be used to connect to the remote site. You'll have to provide a password for the account in most cases.

In effect you're telling the Exchange MTA to connect to the remote site using a different account than that used for normal day to day administrative operations. Think of this as similar functionality to the Connect Network Drive (Connect As) option used by the File Manager when connecting to a file server.

Figure 7.10 illustrates the general properties of a standard RPC-based site connector. In this case we're configuring the connector in the Dublin site to talk to the Belfast site. Note that the server OFFICENT1 is specified as the server to act as a bridgehead for the local site. The Target Servers property page allows you to specify one or more servers to connect to in the remote site.

Configuring a site connector is a relatively straightforward operation that can be accomplished in a few minutes. Once the connector is established it will take a little while for the configuration information for the remote site to be replicated across the link and appear in the organizational tree displayed by the administration utility. As long as the data transmitted by the RPCs can pass without hindrance from one server to another you should see little problem with the site connector.

Figure 7.10
*Configuring a
site connector*

7.5   Exchange Server, X.400 and X.500

Compliance with international messaging standards is a good thing. Without standards it is very difficult to communicate from one messaging system to another, a fact that all too many corporate telecommunications technicians are unpleasantly aware of. It is easy enough to send a text message from one system to another, but sending compound messages, those composed of several different body parts, requires a good deal of understanding on both sides before successful transmission is accomplished.

X.400 and X.500 are two important sets of recommendations for the exchange of electronic mail messages and directory services. The recommendations are defined through the efforts of the CCITT (the International Consultative Committee on Telephony and Telegraphy), a division of the United Nations now called the International Telegraph Union (ITU) and based in Geneva, Switzerland. The CCITT bases its recommendations on the Open Systems Interconnection (OSI) model, taking into account the needs and requirements of many different bodies before the final shape of a standard is issued. Although X.400 and X.500 are sets of recommendations which are only mandatory when organizations decide to make them so, a set of recommendations is often referred to as a "standard."

The primary goal of any standard is to make things easy. Standard screw sizes make screwdrivers easier to manufacture and sell. The X.400 standard seeks to establish ground rules to allow users of different messaging systems, perhaps in the same organization, exchange messages with each other as easily as if they were connected to the same system. Three separate sets of X.400 recommendations have been issued to date in 1984, 1988, and 1992. The recommendations continually evolve to better define the internal structure of an inter-personal message and its components (such as attachments), the basic structure of the message handling system, and how messages are transported from one point to another within the system.

7.5.1   Using X.400 with Exchange

The X.400 connector is the most generic of the range. It can be used to connect Exchange sites together as well as connecting to any other X.400-compliant MTA. The generic nature of the X.400 connector means that it is slower than the standard site connector. Apart from the range of systems it can connect to the X.400 connector delivers a number of significant features that may well be of interest to administrators when deciding what type of site connector should be used. Among these are:

- Message transmission can be set to occur at scheduled times. This optimizes the traffic that goes across potentially expensive network links by ensuring that data is passed in a long continuous stream rather than in small pieces throughout the day.

- A limit on the size of messages accepted by the connector can be set. This stops people sending very large messages and potentially blocking a slow connection to all other traffic.

- Limits can also be set on the set of users authorized to use the connector. Due largely to deployments in corporate messaging environments it is common practice in X.400 implementations not to let everyone communicate with external parties via X.400. Apart from the obvious risk that confidential information is transmitted to unauthorized individuals, restricting the set of users reduces the risk of virus-laden binary files arriving through the mail. Remember that for many years X.400 was the only way to transmit binary information through the mail with some assurance that files could be read by a suitable application when they reached their destination. SMTP/MIME offers this capability too, but MIME has only been readily available in the recent past.

Microsoft Exchange is able to communicate with other X.400-based systems that comply with either the 1984 or 1988 recommendations using a multi-threaded Windows NT service called MSExchangeMTA. The first step in an X.400 implementation is to decide which transport stack is going to be used by the MTA to host the X.400 connector. Connections can be made simultaneously to a number of X.400 MTAs via three different transport stacks:

- TP0 (Transport class 0) over a TCP/IP connection via the RFC1006 specification.

- TP4/CNLP (Transport class 4/Connectionless Network Protocol) to provide a suitable OSI interface across a LAN.

- TP0 over an X.25 connection using an Eicon port adapter on a Windows NT computer.

Figure 7.11
Configuring an MTA stack

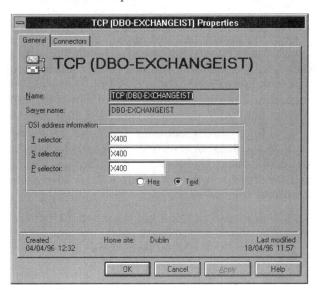

Configuring a new transport stack for the MTA is done with the File.New Other.MTA Transport Stack option from the Administrator program. Once a stack is installed (such as the TCP/IP stack shown being configured in Figure 7.11) we can proceed to get a new connector up and running. Before a connector can be created we need to know something about the capabilities of X.400-based messaging. We also need to understand the different terms used in the X.400 world.

7.5.2 The different X.400 recommendations

Most other X.400-compliant mail systems available today communicate using the 1984 or 1988 recommendations. In general, complying with a later recommendation implies that a greater degree of communication is possible with less effort, especially when dealing with multiple bodyparts, or attachments. The 1984 recommendations, for instance, only distinguish between text and binary bodyparts whereas the 1988 recommendations allow each body part to be allocated its own tag, or indicator of which application should process the body part's content. We'll return to this point later on in this chapter.

Clearly it is best to pass as much explicit information as possible when communicating with other messaging systems, and the 1988 set of recommendations, at this point in time, represents the most complete and pragmatic guideline for inter-system message exchange available today. Before a connection is made to another messaging system it is important for you to know whether it supports the 1984 or 1988 recommendations.

7.5.3   Exchange and the X.500 standard

The X.500 standard sets rules by which mail user agents and other applications are able to inquire for directory information no matter where the directory is located or how it is accessed. In terms of implementation the most common use of a mail directory is to look for the correct mail address to use for a particular person. Validating the addresses for a message doesn't need an X.500 service—the Global Address Book does an effective job for Microsoft Mail users. However, an X.500 directory is not restricted to just storing information about mail addresses; a directory can hold information about any type of data item that an application cares to store (and eventually retrieve). The value, of course, is that once the data is held in an X.500 directory the route to that data is well defined and the data is therefore available to any application that complies with the public X.500 programming interfaces.

The current version of the Exchange server does not comply with the X.500 recommendations. Instead, Microsoft has designed an "X.500-like directory schema" to represent the directory entries for people and routing between servers. This distinction between different types of entries is important. Unlike the classic model of a mail directory, X.500 stores information about people who receive mail and how messages can be routed to other systems. The directory used by Exchange is very similar in many respects to a standard X.500 model but it does not support interfaces such as LDAP (Lightweight Directory Access Protocol) or DAP (Directory Access Protocol) that can be used by external agents to interact with the directory. In addition, Exchange server does not support the XDS (X.500 Directory Services) API. According to position papers published in April 1996[1], Microsoft intends to support these standards in the next release of Exchange. At

[1]   "Microsoft's position on LDAP," dated April 22, 1996.

this time the directory service will be fully X.500-compliant. It is also likely that a future version of Windows NT will include some aspects of a directory service embedded as a standard part of the operating system. Details of this development are unclear at the time of writing.

Address synchronization between Exchange server and other directory sources, such as those maintained by other messaging systems, would be facilitated if Exchange supported the full gambit of interfaces described in the X.500 recommendations. Until the time arrives when Microsoft upgrades Exchange to comply with the full set of protocols defined in the X.500 recommendations it is inevitable that hand-crafted tools will be required to keep Exchange coordinated with other systems.

Exchange is often represented as a strong supporter of the CCITT standards. This position is correct in relation to X.400, but the story is weaker for X.500. However, it is important to draw a clear line between the areas where Exchange fully complies with standards and the places where Microsoft has, for one reason or another, taken a stance that aligns a server component with the appropriate international standard but doesn't quite get there in terms of implementation or interfaces.

7.5.4   The X.400 messaging model

The X.400 standard is based on a store and forward messaging model. A store and forward model means that messages are transferred when links between servers and backbones are available, and when links are not present (for example, because of network failure) messages are held within the system ready to be released when the links are re-established. After a message is sent it flows long the backbone from link to link, much like a telephone connection is made across a series of switches. In both cases the user who originated the transmission is unaware of all the work and links made on their behalf. The system takes care of the internal management and, as far as the user is concerned, they don't have to do anything more after the message enters the system. The store and forward model is robust, proven, and well suited to heavy traffic between multiple distributed sites.

The X.400 recommendations describe a complete messaging system, referred to as a Message Handling System, or MHS. The components of an MHS include:

- The Message Transfer Agent (MTA). Literally, a method to route messages from their submission through user agents to the point of eventual delivery to recipients. A complete MTA is bundled in Exchange, so a single server can act as an MTA.

However, a more practical view of an Exchange implementation would create a single MTA composed of a number of Exchange sites with a number of optional gateways for communication outside the MTA.

- The Message Transfer System (MTS). The set of one or more MTAs that communicate with each other to send and receive messages. Think of a number of Exchange servers located in a set of distributed sites that send messages to each other.

- The Message Stores (MS). In many electronic mail systems the message store is referred to as a "file cabinet," a somewhat more human-friendly term to describe the location where messages are stored in transit between their creation and introduction to an MTA. In an Exchange environment the message store can be thought of as the set of folders used when people generate and send messages. Stores can hold messages and other objects, text or otherwise.

- The User Agents (UA). The client programs used to generate, send, and retrieve messages from an MTA. Think of the set of clients supported by Exchange and you'll know what user agents are. Some user agents operate in a remote manner over dial-up connections.

- The Access Units (AU). Gateways or methods used to communicate with other messaging systems that do not comply with the X.400 recommendations. For example, the Microsoft Mail X.400 gateway.

Figure 7.12 outlines the components of the X.400 model and the protocols (Pn) used to communicate between the different components. We'll return to a variation of this picture shortly to map Exchange on top of the model.

The fundamental principles of an X.400 Message Handling System embody the concept of a global messaging network or global MHS. In other words, nothing is done while implementing an MHS to prevent its expansion to accommodate growth to a stage where the MHS is capable of serving a global audience. The global MHS, while obviously an X.400 messaging network itself at a macro level is comprised of other, smaller X.400 messaging networks underneath.

X.400 is not a new standard that has suddenly descended onto the shoulders of electronic mail administrators. It is well known and understood and has formed part of the electronic mail strategy for many large corporations for the last ten years or so, especially in Europe. However, if you are moving from a PC LAN-based mail system you're probably not too familiar with X.400, as the standard didn't play a big part in LAN implementations, except when used as a connection from the PC mail system to other mail systems. The Microsoft Mail Gateway to X.400 is a good example of one such connection.

Figure 7.12
X.400
reference
model

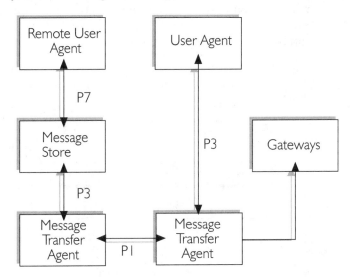

The first set of X.400 recommendations were defined in 1984 and a more functional set arrived in 1988. These dates are important when qualifying compliance. A system complying with the 1988 standard is capable of delivering more functionality than one that is 1984-compliant.

7.5.5   How can Exchange use X.400?

Exchange is able to use X.400 to interface with other mail systems in a number of different ways:

To communicate with other mail systems: This is the most obvious use of X.400. Connections are made between Exchange servers and an X.400 backbone or MTA that acts as a message switch. The X.400 MTA might belong to a public carrier when communication is required with other organizations, or it might be an internal X.400 MTA used to provide a common messaging backbone for all of the mail systems in use within an organization.

To connect two or more Exchange sites together via an X.400 network: Each Exchange site is a separate MTA and the two connect on a peer to peer basis over an X.400 backbone. Messages are sent by each Exchange site to the X.400 MTA that forms the "glue" in the middle. The X.400 MTA, probably provided by a public carrier such as a PTT, takes care of the routing and delivery of the messages to their destination where they are received by another Exchange server for eventual delivery to user mailboxes. This type of set-up could be used to connect lots of different Exchange servers together in a single country without having to go to the trouble of establishing connections from each server to the other. The solution is flexible because a new server can be introduced without affecting other servers.

Figure 7.13
*Exchange server
and X.400*

To link to Microsoft Mail systems via the Microsoft Mail Gateway to X.400: In this scenario an Exchange server and the Microsoft Mail gateway are two entry points to an X.400 MTA, again probably one provided by a public provider. Messages are sent by Exchange to the X.400 MTA and then fetched by the gateway for delivery to the Microsoft Mail users in the normal manner. This is an alternative to a direct connection from the Microsoft Mail clients to the Exchange server, possibly because the Microsoft Mail users are in a location that isn't served by a good or continuous network link.

As illustrated in Figure 7.13, from a purist's perspective Exchange Server does not implement the X.400 reference model, largely because of the use of MAPI as the internal protocol instead of the P3/P7 combination outlined in the model. Implementing the complete reference model would be an interesting exercise, but Exchange is designed to handle many more e-mail connections than X.400. The Exchange MTA and its X.400 connector form a practical and pragmatic real world X.400 implementation that fully interoperates with other X.400 MTAs.

7.5.6   X.400 body parts

Obviously because X.400 is all about standards, an X.400 message is built according to a carefully defined formula. That formula incorporates the concept of header data, including information about the message originator and the recipients the message will eventually be delivered to, and the component body parts, literally the pieces that collectively form the content.

Simple messages have a single body part, sometimes known as the cover memo. Depending on the user agent, cover memos can be created with a simple text editor or a more comprehensive editor. The Windows 95 Exchange client can create cover memos with Word for Windows, for instance, an editor that's slightly more complicated than the Windows Notepad, a good example of a simple text editor.

Compound messages have a set of one or more body parts, or attachments, which follow the cover memo. Each body part is tagged to tell receiving mail systems how to deal with the attachment. For example, if the attachment is an Excel worksheet an indication is given that this is the case, although the tag that's placed on the attachment is up to the originating user agent and there is no general agreement between user agents from different vendors as to the tags that should be used for different types of attachments. Some of the more intelligent user agents available today are equipped with either format detection technology, which allows an attachment to be "sniffed" and identified, often by comparing the first couple of bytes from the attachment with a set of known electronic "signatures." Once the attachment is identified it can be processed by launching the appropriate application or, if an application isn't available, the normal backup method is to call a specialized viewer program that is able to display the content of a file but not edit it.

In addition to the body parts listed below, Exchange also supports Body Part 9 (BP9) to handle embedded or forwarded messages within an X.400 messaging system.

The difference in tagging behavior defined by the various sets of X.400 recommendations (see Table 7.4) is often a cause for confusion when the time comes to connect different systems together. The 1984 recommendations were defined at a stage when PC file formats were not generally used in electronic mail systems, so defining different types of attachments didn't receive much attention. All attachments in a 1984-compliant X.400 system are tagged as binary files, known as body part 14, or BP14. In this scenario it becomes the responsibility of a receiving user agent to interrogate the various binary attachments and decide what format they actually contain. An attachment could be a Word document, or an Excel worksheet, or even a simple text file. In all cases there is no external sign of what's inside.

Table 7.4   *X.400 file tagging mechanisms*

X.400 recommendations	Body part type	File format information passed as
1984	Body Part 14 (BP14)	None. Mail user agents must decide how to process binary body parts which could contain any format type (apart from text).
1988	Body Part 15 (BP15)	X.400 Object Identifier (OID)
1992	File Transfer Body Part (FTBP)	Original file name encapsulated and passed in the attachment attributes.

Figure 7.14
Simplified X.400 message structure

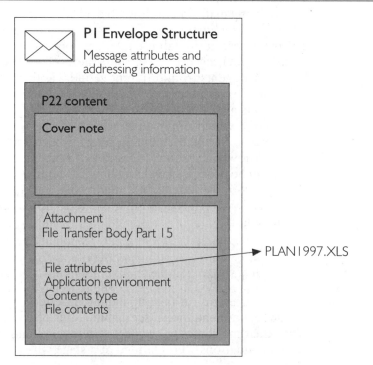

The 1988 recommendations took note of the growing influence of PC systems and the wide variety of file formats in use and expanded the tagging scheme considerably to allow user agents to include format information to be sent along with each body part. 1988 X.400 systems use a tagging scheme referred to as body part 15, or BP15, where information about the file format of attachments is passed as an "object identifier," or X.400 OID.

If a human being looks at an X.400 OID there is little information about file formats immediately obvious. Like many data structures associated with standards, an OID is carefully constructed to accommodate all possible circumstances. The eventual OID is therefore a string containing many different pieces of information, all useful in their own way, but the resulting combination is very un-human friendly. Of more concern to application developers, if applications are to be able to deal with message attachments code must be written to extract the information about format types from the OID. The extraction code is, in itself, not particularly difficult to write nor will it take long to execute when the time comes, but sometimes incorporating a requirement to decipher encoded strings to extract a file format tag seems a bit of an overkill.

The latest version of the X.400 recommendations was established in 1992 at which time another attempt was made to provide format information. Body part 15 encoding has been superseded (in some respects) by the File Transfer Body Part, or FTBP15. Instead of holding format information in an OID the original file name of an attachment is passed as an attribute. This scheme relies on user agents being able to use the file name to locate the correct application whenever the attachment's content needs to be processed and is by no means fool-proof. For example, if I use Lotus Word Pro to create a document called FOO.DOC and attach it to a message, I rely on the mail user agents being used by recipients knowing that FOO.DOC should be processed by Word Pro. If, as in many cases, another application also creates documents with the .DOC file type much potential exists for confusion.

In defense of the FTBP scheme, creating associations between file types and applications is a well known and understood method, and one that has been in use for many years by Windows clients. The most common example is perhaps the Windows File Manager, which creates associations between file types and applications to be able to launch the correct application when a user double-clicks on a file. The direct association between a file type and an application is very simple, a quick and dirty method to get the job done, and as we've seen above, is prone to error. Later versions of Windows, including Windows V3.1 and Windows 95, use a Windows API function called FindExecute to search the system registry to match files up with applications able to process their content. The use of the system registry in a Windows-dominant environment improves matters by largely ensuring that the correct application is located and then launched, provided of course that an appropriate application is installed on the PC.

Microsoft Exchange Server is the first mainline messaging server to use FTBP15 as its baseline for communication with other 1988 X.400 MTAs, a fact that clearly causes some difficulty if any of the other MTAs you want to talk to don't support FTBP15. Encouraged by industry groups like the Electronic Mail Association (EMA), many X.400 vendors are retrofitting FTBP15 support into their 1988 X.400 implementations, but the majority of MTAs have not yet been upgraded. It seems ridiculous to make such a remark about a standard, but until the time arrives where all X.400 MTAs can agree on a common interchange format for multi-bodypart messages, probably FTBP15 in the long term, some degree of confusion and negotiation between MTAs will be required before seamless message exchange is automatic. If possible, try and use FTBP15 as the basis for interpersonal message transmission between Exchange and other X.400 systems.

7.5.7 Encoding schemes

Before messages are introduced into an X.400 system they must be encoded. This is done to ensure that messages are sent in a common internal structure that can be processed globally. The internal structure of messages transmitted within an X.400 network differs according to the set of recommendations supported by the systems making up the network. The lowest common denominator for X.400 systems is a structure known as P2 established as part of the 1984 recommendations. X.400 1988 systems use a more developed internal structure referred to as P22.

The fact that encoding occurs at all and the differences between P2 and P22 are completely hidden from users so you don't normally have to worry about it, except to know that there is an overhead incurred by an Exchange server to encode messages for transmission via an X.400 link. The encoding translates messages from the internal MAPI structures (known as MBDEF, or Message Bodypart Encoding Format) used by Exchange into the format expected by other X.400-compliant systems. For instance, OLE objects inserted into Exchange messages are transformed into X.400-type body parts because there is no guarantee that the receiving system will be able to deal with an OLE object. If the translation wasn't done then objects would arrive as random collections of bytes that don't really make a lot of sense to recipients. Exchange knows which encoding should be done because the content type is defined when an X.400 connection is defined to the system. Clearly it's important to get this right because the two types of X.400 encoding are very different.

As well as the communication load, any Exchange server where an X.400 connector is active incurs all the processing overhead involved in translating messages from Exchange to X.400 structures and vice versa. A heavy load of messages being sent or received to or from an X.400 connection can slow an entire system. Evidence that this is happening can be gained from user feedback or the fact that queues of messages waiting to be sent to X.400 build up. In these circumstances it is best to move the X.400 connector to a more powerful system or to install a dedicated server to take over the load. The same can be said of any Exchange connector, but perhaps the X.400 connector needs to have most attention and monitoring. This is especially true in circumstances where the X.400 connector is used to link Exchange and other legacy messaging systems together. In these situations you should monitor the connector regularly to preserve the quality of service delivered to users, especially during the period where users are migrating from the older system to Exchange.

The work required in translating from MBDEF to the appropriate X.400 content type is only strictly necessary to communicate with other messaging systems. If you're in the situation where you want to use an X.400 network to link different Exchange servers you could instruct the connector to perform no conversion and send MBDEF content directly. This enables faster throughput and imposes lesser demands on the server, but you will run into problems if messages find their way to non-Exchange systems, or if the X.400 network performs format integrity checks as messages are transported across the network. Several public X.400 systems will fail messages containing MBDEF content if they consider the messages to be "invalid" because of their MBDEF content, so always perform some tests before making a final decision.

7.5.8   Interoperability with other X.400 messaging systems

Microsoft has validated the ability of Exchange to exchange messages with other X.400-based systems using a suite of interoperability tests defined by the OSINET (USA) and EUROSINET (Europe) organizations. Table 7.5 lists the most important X.400 systems that Exchange has been tested against. The test suites cover points such as:

- P1 interoperability to test whether the information in message envelopes can be passed between Exchange and other MTAs. The most important information in this context is the MTA name, password (if required), and OSI addressing data.

- P2 and P22 interoperability. P2 defines the content of 1984-type messages and P22 defines the content for 1988-type messages. The test suites see whether Exchange can successfully send and receive messages to and from other MTAs and that recipients (user agents) can successfully view the content of the messages after they arrive. The tests cover BP14, BP15, and FTBP15 as well as text-only body parts.

Table 7.5　*Interoperability with other X.400 MTAs*

Manufacturer	X.400 MTA	X.400 standard
Retix	Open Server	1984
Microsoft	Microsoft Mail X.400 Gateway	1984
Lotus (IBM)	Soft*Switch Central	1984
Digital Equipment Corporation	Message Router X.400 Gateway (MRX)	1984
Isocor	Isoplex 800 MTA	1988
Hewlett-Packard	OpenMail	1988
Lotus/IBM	Message Switch	1988
Control Data Corporation	MailHub	1988
Digital Equipment Corporation	MAILbus 400 MTA	1988
Novell	MAWG X.400 Gateway	1988

Further testing is performed to establish that communication can be achieved using TP0 over X.25 and TCP/IP connections, and TP4 over CLNP links. Finally, tests are performed to verify that Exchange can communicate with public administrative domains operated by PTTs and other public X.400 service providers world-wide. Among the ADMDs tested are:

- AT&T X.400 and X.25 services (USA)
- MCI X.400 and X.25 services (USA)
- SPRINT X.400 and X.25 services (USA)
- Infonet X.400 services (USA)
- Northern Telecom X.400 services (Europe)
- British Telecom X.400 and X.25 services
- NTT X.400 services (Japan)
- Australia Telecom X.400 and X.25 services (Telstra)
- Swedish Telecom (Televerket) X.400 and X.25 services

OSTC (Open Systems Testing Consortium) acts as a single point of contact for many other European PTTs including France, Germany, and Switzerland.

The existence of such a broad range of test suites and results means that there's a good chance that Exchange will be able to successfully interoperate with other X.400 MTAs which don't feature in the list above. After getting over the initial hurdle of getting the two systems to connect to each other the next most likely problem area is successful body part recognition as messages flow from one system to another. It's always likely that simple text messages will get through, but the fun only starts once multi-format attachments come into the picture. A process of trial and error is often required before a consistent and reliable message flow is established.

7.5.9   User Agent format handling

All systems should be able to exchange simple text messages without real difficulty, but the true interoperability test is when compound messages with multiple body parts flow between systems without hindrance and all body parts can be read without difficulty by any user agent. Even after all the issues with body parts are resolved much of the responsibility for interpreting format tags correctly to make sure that the correct applications or viewers are called to process message contents is still devolved to user agents. Some intelligence or auto-format detection functionality is often built into the more feature-rich user agents. Auto-detection is usually carried out by reading a few bytes from the start of a file to see if it matches a known "signature" attributed to a particular file format. Most user agents don't engage in this degree of sophistication and rely on the format tag itself to indicate which application should be called to process message content. This isn't usually a problem when a single integrated messaging system is used because the same format tag can be used everywhere. For example, a format tag of "XLS" always indicates an Excel attachment, while "WK3" might mean a Lotus 1-2-3 spreadsheet. However, it can often be a real issue when heterogeneous systems are operated.

How does the Exchange client handle format tags? The answer lies in the Windows system registry, the common repository on Windows-based systems where information is stored about applications. Details such as the OLE capabilities of an application, or the correct DDE commands to instruct an application to print a file are stored in the registration database, as well as a set of associations to link a format tag, such as XLS, with an application such as Excel. The majority of Windows applications capable of producing files in a specific format now provide details for the registration database and these details are loaded into the database during the installation procedure.

When the Exchange client encounters an attachment the format tag is compared against the registration database and if a match is found the associated application is launched to read or print the content. Problems can arise if the registration database is inaccurate or application details have not been loaded, but this is unlikely to occur. Greater potential for problems arises when multiple applications share the same file extension. Selecting a common set of applications to use across an organization and ensuring that a consistent set of format tags is used everywhere normally eliminates the source of the problem.

7.5.10   Message-encoding schemes used by Exchange

Several different message-encoding schemes have been mentioned to this point. Some belong to X.400 and some do not. Before going any further this is an appropriate point at which to attempt to consolidate our knowledge of where and when Exchange uses the different encoding schemes available to it, outlined in Table 7.6.

Table 7.6   *Message encoding schemes*

Encoding scheme	Where used
MAPI (Microsoft Messaging Application Programming Interface)	Native coding scheme for Exchange message properties such as TO: or CC: recipient lists.
MBDEF (Message Bodypart Encoding Format)	Native coding scheme used to encapsulate body parts as they pass from Exchange server to server.
MIME	Internet format used to encode binary body parts for transmission across an SMTP messaging network.
TNEF (Transport Neutral Encapsulation Format)	Used to package a message's MAPI properties into a binary attachment when a message passes across a non-MAPI backbone en route to another Exchange server.
P2	X.400 coding scheme used for transmission of message contents to 1984-compliant X.400 MTAs.
P22	X.400 coding scheme used for transmission of message contents to 1988-compliant X.400 MTAs.
P1	X.400 coding scheme used for transmission of message envelopes to foreign X.400 MTAs.

7.5.11   The meaning of TNEF

TNEF allows Exchange to preserve extended features such as rich text message content and information about attached or embedded (OLE) objects when messages are sent between Exchange servers across a messaging backbone that doesn't support the transmission of such data.

For example, X.400 envelopes do not normally support information about message formatting as this is usually left to the receiving mail user agent to sort out. The Exchange X.400 connector has a "Remote clients support MAPI" check box on the General properties page. If checked, the X.400 connector will code the extended features into TNEF and include the data as part of the message envelope before a message is sent. This is OK as long as an Exchange client is at the receiving end, because it will be able to make sense of the extended features and it will allow a recipient to see the message content and format exactly as it appeared on the originator's PC. However, if the recipient uses a different user agent that doesn't know how to deal with the extended features it's likely to cause some problems. In these cases it's best to force the X.400 connector to strip off the extended features before sending the message by not checking the box. The most obvious effect of not using TNEF is that rich text memos will be translated into simple text, losing any formatting that may have been used.

7.5.12   Setting up an X.400 connector

We've spent a lot of time on X.400 concepts, let's proceed to use the X.400 connector to do some real work. A certain amount of information needs to be collected before the new X.400 connector can be created. Much of the necessary information can be gained by asking the questions listed in Table 7.7 (see page 432). If you're unsure about the answers to any of these questions you should review the connection with the administrator who looks after the MTA you want to connect to. The Exchange administrator's guide also contains a lot of useful information, particularly in respect to the different settings that can be defined for a connector.

Two separate references to MAPI are made in Table 7.7. First, should MAPI contents be sent to remote clients? If the X.400 connector is configured to pass MAPI message contents for eventual delivery to clients it means that all of the rich text formatting in messages (bold, underline, different colors, and so on) will be retained. Attachments, and icons for those attachments, will be positioned where they were placed in the message. If the remote mail system can't handle MAPI contents the X.400 connector will convert rich text to plain text and

Table 7.7   *Questions to ask when setting up an X.400 connector*

Question/Area of investigation	When connecting is required to another Exchange site	When connecting to a foreign MTA
What is the name of the remote MTA? Does it have a password?	A password is seldom, if ever, required when two sites connect over X.400.	A password should be used when connecting to a foreign MTA.
What MTA transport stack is going to be used?	TP4, TCP/IP, or X.25.	TP4, TCP/IP, or X.25.
Do lines in messages have to be wrapped?	No.	It depends on whether the mail systems behind the X.400 connection are able to handle long lines of unwrapped text.
Will remote clients be able to support MAPI message contents?	Yes.	Unlikely.
When can messages be transferred?	Exchange servers should be able to transfer messages on a demand basis.	Scheduled transfer is often the most appropriate mechanism when connecting to foreign MTAs.
What OSI TSAP, SSAP, and PSAP[1] information is required?	Pass blank values or an agreed value up to 4 characters in each field.	You can decide what Exchange will pass, but have no control over what the incoming MTA will provide.
Will delivery restrictions be enforced?	Unlikely when using X.400 to connect two sites.	Possible to restrict the transfer of messages outside the company, or restrict whom you'll receive messages from.
Degree of X.400 compatibility?	Full 1988.	1984 or 1988.
Send MAPI-encoded messages?	Yes. It's best to use MAPI when connecting two sites together as this avoids any conversion overhead.	No. Foreign MTAs require messages to be presented in P2 or P22 format.
Allow two-way alternate communication?	Yes. Exchange servers are happy to send and receive messages alternatively during one connection.	Perhaps. Some MTAs prefer to send all messages and then receive any messages.
Limit on message size?	Unlikely when connecting two Exchange sites, unless the network link is very slow.	Many companies restrict the size of outgoing messages when sent to external agencies.
X.400 Global Domain Identifier OK?	The default GDI can be used.	May need to restate GDI for the remote MTA.
Connected sites?	Other sites may be reached through this connector.	Not applicable when connecting to a foreign MTA.

(1)   TSAP, SSAP, and PSAP are OSI Transport Service, Session Service, and Presentation Service Access Points representing the different layers in the OSI model that are used by the Exchange X.400 connector.

convert embedded attachments into normal X.400 attachments. The rendering information, used to position an embedded attachment within a message, is also discarded. An extra attachment (the infamous WINMAIL.DAT) is added to the message. This file includes information about the rich text information that has been lost during conversion.

Figure 7.15
General properties for an X.400 site connector

The second point relates to the internal format of the messages passed from one MTA to the other. If you're connecting Exchange sites together you can safely leave the messages in their native format (MDBEF). This avoids any need for the MTA to convert messages and attachments into the X.400 P2 or P22 formats and reduces the demand on system resources.

7.5.13 Connecting two sites with an X.400 connector

The most popular connection (and easiest to set up) is using the TCP/IP stack, so that's what we'll use as an example. The two sites we want to connect are Dublin and Denmark. The sites are in different European countries with a reasonable network link between them. It's a good idea to use an X.400 connector to link sites across wide geographical distances where it is costly or impractical to create the type of high-speed link required by the standard site connector. If there are a number of sites in each country the X.400 connector can be used as the glue in the middle, with site connectors used to link all the sites within each country. The general properties for the connector are shown in Figure 7.15. Note that no password is required for the remote MTA. This is the normal course of events when connecting sites together. The stack defined is TCP/IP as installed on the DBO-EXCHANGEIST server. We can see more information about the stack by clicking on the Stack property page (Figure 7.16). Note the IP address entered for the server we want to talk to. If you refer back to the OSI settings for the TCP/IP stack configuration illustrated in Figure 7.11 you'll see how the outgoing OSI information is determined.

Figure 7.16
Stack properties

Examining Figure 7.16 you'll see that a fixed TCP/IP address is specified for the remote server. This approach is a bad idea in production environments. Using a host name is preferable because it insulates you from any change in the underlying IP address for the remote server. IP addresses have been known to change in the past!

The fields used for the outgoing and incoming OSI information can be entered as text or hex values. Hex values are a throwback to the past, when older X.400 implementations wallowed in configuration information that was very difficult for human beings to understand. Computers certainly understand hex, but I haven't met many humans who can read it fluently. It's best to enter values in text format so that you can see and understand what you've entered, but don't be too quick to write hex off because it can help, sometimes.

There have been situations when, as in Figure 7.16, an agreement was made between two sites to use a string like "X400" as a default value for all the OSI information. Adopting a default string like this is a good idea when the X.400 connector is used internally. You'll probably end up with different OSI information for external connections, but there's no point in making things more complicated than you have to, so pick a default string and use it for all internal X.400 connectors. The default string helps makes connections easy to establish as long as everyone enters the same string. I have known instances where a connection proved remarkably difficult to debug because one site had entered "x400" instead of "X400" in all the OSI fields. A lowercase "x" is very different to an uppercase "X," but a quick glance doesn't always detect the problem, especially when you might be worried about the more esoteric things that can go wrong when setting up X.400 connections. Reverting back to hex revealed the problem, because the exactitude of hex showed up the different values.

Figure 7.17
*X.400
interoperability
options*

The Advanced property page contains all the settings to control the level of interoperability this connector will have with the remote MTA. In the case of two Exchange sites the interoperability, as expected, is extremely high, as shown in Figure 7.17. Refer to the earlier discussions regarding body part types or the Exchange Administrator's manual for the meanings of BP15 and BP14.

Many people have shied away from X.400 because it accumulated a reputation for unfriendliness in the past. It's certainly true that it's all too easy to lose your way if you are forced to resort to poking around under the hood and have to speak in the somewhat convoluted terminology the X.400 recommendations foster. The graphical interface presented by the Exchange administration utility eases the pain somewhat, even if there still are eight property pages to deal with, so the task of setting up an X.400 connector is easier in Exchange than most other messaging systems.

Figure 7.18
Connecting a site using the X.400 connector

The final thing to do to complete connecting a site over the X.400 connector is to define the address space for the site or sites you want to communicate with. A valid X.400 address, or enough of the address to allow Exchange to route messages to addressees in the site, is entered. Figure 7.18 shows that the site "SI.DOM" is connected using an address C=dk;A=dk400;P=Digital, meaning that any message to a person whose X.400 O/R address begins with these attribute values can be routed using this connector. Remember that setting up a connector is only one part of connecting sites. Messages can certainly be routed through the new connector, but users will have to enter in full X.400 addresses to get the messages to their correspondents. A directory replication connector is required to replicate directory information between the remote site and your server. For more details, see the discussion on directory replication connectors in chapter 8.

7.6   The Exchange Internet Mail Service

The Internet Mail Service (IMS) is a connector which enables messages to be sent and received using SMTP (simple mail transfer protocol), the predominant standard for electronic mail within the Internet. There's a fairly subtle renaming exercise in V5.0, where the V4.0 Internet Mail Connector (IMC) becomes a fully-fledged service. One reason for this is the much closer relationship between the IMS and the information store, which is now used for storage of messages as they make their way to and from the Internet. The same mechanism is used by the other connectors that are integrated with the MTA (the site and X.400 connectors) and establishes a point of differentiation between these connectors and others, like the Microsoft Mail, Lotus cc:Mail, or third party SNADS and PROFS connectors, all of which use the file system to hold messages in transit.

Exchange V5.0 implements native Internet protocols like SMTP and MIME within the information store. You might recall the discussion on the IMAIL content and protocol engine in Chapter 2. This facility allows clients to retrieve information in the format they want, and points the way to the future when it is possible that Exchange will use Internet protocols for all storage. Using the information store enables a higher degree of integration, but it certainly didn't help the reliability of some beta versions of Exchange V5.0. With these releases it was fairly common for misformed SMTP messages to cause the IMS to shut down abnormally, with a knock-on effect on the information store that caused it to shut down also. Happily the engineers appear to have sorted these issues out and the Exchange V5.0 IMS is very resiliant.

7.6.1 Internet Standards

Within the Internet world a set of standards for communication have been established through a series of generally agreed upon papers called Request for Comments, or RFCs, generated by the Internet Engineering Task Force (IETF), a volunteer group made up of representatives from major organizations and institutions. The Internet Mail Service supports the RFC 821 and RFC 822 standards that define the SMTP server-to-server protocol and the format of messages sent between servers. As the name implies, SMTP began life as a very simple messaging format, basically marking the lowest common denominator for messages that could be sent between servers manufactured by different software vendors using different operating systems.

The original RFC 822 standard defined in 1982 considered messages that could only contain 7-bit ASCII text characters, and supported lines that could not contain more than 1,000 characters, not to mention a restricted overall message size. All these limitations appeared perfectly acceptable in a world where telex machines still generated the majority of electronic communications. These limitations have long been lifted.

7.6.2   SMTP and MIME

SMTP messages are always transmitted as text. Clearly the restrictions imposed by the original RFC 822 standard could not be maintained in a world where PC formats are now the norm. A new set of features is defined in RFC 1521 and RFC 1522 to allow for an agreed encoding standard for non-text attachments. These standards are referred to as MIME (Multipurpose Internet Mail Extensions), and are supported by the IMC. MIME allows users to send complex objects across an SMTP link up to and including multimedia files. The Internet Mail Service also supports UUENCODE, an earlier encoding scheme for handling non-text attachments, defined in RFC 1154. Messages generated by Exchange are not simple ASCII text as the basic editor produces files in Rich Text Format. Lots of messages include embedded files. One of the functions of the Internet Mail Service is to encode the Rich Text Format memos and any embedded files using MIME before the messages are sent out via SMTP. Upon receipt any foreign messaging system that understands MIME should be able to unpack the MIME-encoded parts and rebuild the message as it was originally sent.

Coding a message's bodyparts according to an established scheme is a great step towards being able to send complex files anywhere throughout the world via SMTP. But the world doesn't use an ASCII character set everywhere; different cultures use different character sets, so international mail servers must be able to support a range of character sets when messages are encoded or decoded. Exchange supports US-ASCII, the Western European ISO 8859-1 set, Scandinavian IA5, and character sets support for Korea, Taiwan, and Japan.

Exchange V5.0 supports RFC 1869 and RFC 1870, also known as ESMTP. The two RFCs describe how SMTP systems communicate to relay information about delivery status and size of messages (DSN and SIZE commands). The DSN command is important, because it addresses a major weakness in SMTP's capabilities, the inability to provide a satisfactory indication that a message has reached its intended destination.

The combination of SMTP and MIME has laid the foundation to allow companies to build messaging backbones comparable to those constructed with X.400 but at lower cost and with less technical effort. The combination has gone from the original proposals to worldwide deployment within the Internet in just a few years.

7.6.3   SMTP conversations

SMTP depends on TCP/IP networks to send and receive messages. The IMS uses TCP/IP to create the connection to the remote mail server, conduct a conversation with the remote server to transmit message header information and contents, and then break off the connection. All SMTP communication generated by the IMS is channeled through TCP port 25, the port number defined in the SMTP standard.

A common set of steps forming a structured conversation between two SMTP systems is used to pass messages between SMTP mail servers. The conversation occurs between one computer acting in the role of the client and another acting as a server. The client initiates and drives the conversation and the server responds to the demands from the client. These steps are illustrated in Figure 7.19 and proceed as follows:

1. The conversation is started by the client though a connection to port 25 on the server.

2. After the network connection is established the client sends an SMTP "Hello" command to the server. The server responds with "OK" to indicate that it is willing to accept an SMTP message. Exchange V5.0 is able to send an "EHLO" command instead of the normal "HELO," indicating that Exchange supports ESTMP.

3. The client proceeds to pass originator information in a "Mail From" command. The server checks the information to ensure that it is willing to accept the message from the originator.

4. The client then sends a list of recipient information in the form of a set of "Rcpt To" commands. Note that only SMTP recipient information is transmitted. Information about non-SMTP recipients will be passed later in the general body of the message.

5. After all the header information is exchanged the client begins the process of sending content. A "Data" command is sent to indicate that the client is ready to begin, followed by an acknowledgment from the server. The data is transmitted in 7-bit ASCII characters, which may include files encoded previously into MIME or UUENCODE format.

6. Once all the content has been sent the client signs off and terminates the connection by sending a "Quit" command. However, if the client has another message to send it can start to send the next message by returning to step 3. This process continues until all messages have been sent.

You can trace a conversation between the IMS and another SMTP server by looking at the log files kept in the \EXCHSRVR\IMCDATA\LOG directory. Indeed, by turning the diagnostic setting to maximum, full and complete transcripts of all the communication between the IMS and other SMTP servers will be captured.

Figure 7.19
*Steps in passing
an SMTP
message*

7.6.4   The Internet Mail Service and SMTP

The Internet Mail Service provides a full-function SMTP service. Transport, message routing, translation, and delivery are all handled by the connector, giving this service a reasonable amount of work to do if a heavy volume of incoming or outgoing SMTP traffic is to be handled. If you expect a heavy volume of messages, perhaps based on the volume seen coming in or going out of a previous messaging system, or because you have decided to operate an SMTP-based corporate messaging backbone, then implementing specific servers to handle the SMTP traffic should be considered. Routing messages out of the system is not a very demanding activity; the majority of the potential system load is generated by the need to convert messages from the internal format used by Exchange into the appropriate SMTP format. Converting large attachments from PC file formats and the message's MAPI properties over to the appropriate MIME encoding is not a simple affair, especially when OLE objects are included.

The process of content conversion from Exchange's internal format can have some unforeseen side effects. One example is the rendering of rich text format content into simple ASCII for messages sent to SMTP recipients that aren't connected to an Exchange server. Any formatting effects inserted by users into messages such as bolding, underlining, italics, different colors, and typefaces are all reduced to simple non-proportional fonts. The advantage here is that the conversion creates content that can be read by almost any messaging system. The disadvantage is that the layout of messages may suffer greatly, leading to a situation where users become dissatisfied with the way the system treats "their" messages.

7.6.5   And if you can't use MIME?

MIME is the de facto standard for bodypart encoding exchanged between e-mail systems across the Internet. However, sometimes it's just not possible to use MIME and another encoding scheme is more appropriate. The most likely situation is that the intended recipient isn't able to handle MIME attachments. The solution is to create a PAB entry for the recipient and use the send options to define exactly how the contents should be encoded.

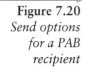

Figure 7.20
*Send options
for a PAB
recipient*

As shown in Figure 7.20, the options available in Exchange V5.0 include plain text (any mail system should be able to read plain text) and HTML. Macintosh mail clients usually understand BINHEX, so that option is available too. The actual encoding is done by the Internet Mail service when the message is taken from the queue and processed for sending.

7.6.6   Using the Internet Mail Service

Exchange is able to use the Internet Mail Service in a number of different ways. These are the three most common options:

- Making a direct connection to another SMTP mail server in the Internet or within a corporate Intranet.

- Using an external SMTP relay host for routing purposes.

- Using an internal SMTP backbone to link Exchange sites together. This option is slightly more complex than the preceding two because it usually involves directory replication in addition to interpersonal messaging. See Chapter 8 for more information on directory synchronization and replication.

In all cases the IMS depends on Windows NT being correctly configured for TCP/IP. Use the Network option from the Windows NT Control Panel to allocate important TCP/IP parameters such as the IP address of the computer and a FQDN (Fully Qualified Domain Name[2]). In fact, the IMS will not start if you don't provide a FQDN. A test is made to see whether the computer's host name can be resolved during IMS initialization, and if an FQDN cannot be resolved the IMS will terminate. A Windows NT error is logged if this happens and you can see details of the error through the Windows NT event. The event viewer is the first place to look if you ever discover problems starting the IMC.

Making a direct connection to the Internet or an Intranet allows Exchange to send messages to any other SMTP server. The basic requirements for such a connection include TCP/IP and a static IP address for the server. The computer's IP address is used in conjunction with your system's host name[3] by other SMTP mail servers to address messages to Exchange users. If you use DHCP to allocate IP addresses you must take out a permanent lease for the IP address allocated to the

---

[2]   An FQDN is basically the domain name containing all the pieces necessary to route data back to a particular computer.

[3]   If the name of the host for the IMC is not the same as the electronic mail domain an entry must be added to the local domain name server (DNS) to map the domain name to the IMC host name.

server and not permit dynamic reallocation as this will prevent incoming messages finding the correct destination.

7.6.7   Notes about Internet Mail Service operation

If a single server equipped with the Internet Mail Service is established to handle all SMTP mail for the organization you should set the routing cost to be 1 in the Address Space properties. You also need to define the set of names that the IMS is able to process. For example, if you put "*.com" into the address space for a system's IMS it means that the connector is able to send messages to any SMTP address ending in ".com," such as my normal address:

```
Tony.Redmond@dbo.mts.dec.com
```

In the example where "*.com" is defined in its address space the IMS will reject any SMTP address ending in any other form. So in this instance if I was to attempt to send to:

```
Tony.Redmond@zyz.net
```

the message would be rejected and returned to me.

If the IMS address space is left blank it indicates that the IMS is able to handle any form of SMTP address, subject always to the ability of the local DNS to resolve the host's address and provide the appropriate TCP/IP address for onward routing.

When SMTP hosts are already active within an enterprise the IMS can connect to them for routing purposes. This is a variation on the theme above where the work is split between Exchange and the SMTP host. Exchange takes care of preparing messages for SMTP transmission (format conversion and so on), while the SMTP relay host actually sends the messages to other systems after they are delivered to the SMTP relay host by Exchange. The only difference between this option and the first is that the Message Delivery property for the connector is set to forward all messages to a single nominated host.

If lots of small messages are dispatched into the Internet this configuration offers a potential performance gain over letting Exchange do its own routing. But if the messages are large and complex then the additional routing cost incurred by Exchange to transmit messages to their final destination will largely be overshadowed by the work necessary to convert them from MAPI to SMTP/MIME.

Many enterprises, most commonly in the United States, already operate SMTP-based corporate messaging backbones to unify disparate electronic mail systems running on different platforms as well as to provide a single point of external contact (an SMTP "smart" host) for the enterprise. To external recipients all the messages coming from the enterprise appear to be generated from a single domain. For example,

    Tony.Redmond@xyz.com

rather than what might be the case where the full routing address required to reach my mailbox is:

    Tony.Redmond@exchange.xyz.com

The SMTP host uses a set of proxy addresses to map the addresses on incoming messages to full routing addresses. The host is regarded as "smart" because it is able to reroute messages using proxies. You define the correct proxy for Exchange by creating an outbound proxy in the IMS Connections property page. The Message Delivery property for the connector is set to forward all messages to the "smart" host.

In all cases, external SMTP addressees can be created as custom recipients in the Exchange directory. Creating a set of custom recipients is a convenience for users, who then don't have to remember to add sometimes complex SMTP addresses to their personal address book (or type the addresses in directly from memory). If you choose to put custom recipients into the directory a certain implied responsibility is assumed to ensure that the recipients' addresses are kept up to date. Keeping internal addresses updated is a task that can be approached with a certain air of confidence (assuming that directories of mail addresses are available from the other SMTP-compliant systems). Keeping external addresses updated is quite another matter because so much is out of your control. With this in mind it's probably best to devolve the responsibility onto users' shoulders and ask them to store any external SMTP addresses they need in their personal address books.

7.6.8   Exchange as a relay host

We've already discussed the use of an external (outside the Exchange organization) host computer to route messages to and from the rest of the SMTP world. At present, those computers tend to be UNIX systems, mostly because of the history of UNIX and its close association with SMTP. However, what steps can you take if Exchange is the only mail system in use within the company, and you don't really want to learn UNIX just to do some routing?

Exchange V5.0 provides the answer. The Internet Mail Service is now able to route messages as they arrive onto a server. Indeed, this function must be set up to allow POP3 clients to send mail to recipients outside the organization. When routing occurs, the Internet Mail Service is able to selectively reroute messages to other SMTP hosts without performing any other processing.

Smart routing is controlled through the routing properties of the Internet Mail Service, as illustrated by Figure 7.22.

Figure 7.22
Setting up a routing table

The screen shot is taken from the server called RUCKS. Two entries are in the routing table. The bottom entry tells the Internet Mail Service that it should handle any mail addressed to a domain called rucks.dbo.dec.com. The top entry is a selective reroute because it causes any mail coming in that's addressed to a domain called

    ist.dbo.dec.com

to be rerouted immediately to the server

    dbo-exchangeist.dbo.dec.com

This is a good example of how the Internet Mail Service can now act as a single point of contact between a company's mail environment and the Internet, a capability that just didn't exist before Exchange V5.0. If the "do not reroute incoming SMTP mail" radio button is clicked the Internet Mail Service will only deliver messages to recipients that can be found in the GAL. Any other message presented to the Internet Mail Service will generate a non-delivery report.

7.6.9   Using the Internet Mail Service instead of a Site Connector

Within an internal TCP/IP network you have a choice as to the connector to use when linking sites together. Site connectors are the optimum choice and should be used whenever possible, but the IMS offers a viable alternative to the normal site connector when the link between sites is often interrupted and prone to failure.

Figure 7.23
Sites connected by the IMC

Site connectors use direct RPC communication to send and receive messages in real time. The data transmitted is in native Exchange format and requires no manipulation when it is received by the target system. Thus, site connectors provide the most efficient use of system resources but they depend on highly available bandwidth (> 64KB).

While not as efficient as the RPC-based site connector because of the requirement to translate messages into SMTP/MIME, the IMS permits store and forward messaging. Messages can be sent to a smart host that collects messages from many different SMTP-based mail systems, and retrieved from the smart host when available. The SMTP version of a site connector still works even if part of the communications path to the other site(s) is unavailable for whatever reason. However, store and forward messaging via SMTP is bought at the price of the overhead required to translate messages into SMTP/MIME, an overhead which may be unacceptable on a heavily loaded system or one that must handle a high volume of messages.

7.6.10 Communicating with the Internet

The ease with which the Exchange IMS facilitates communication with recipients dotted around the Internet is a double-edged sword. On the one hand you get good interoperability and messages flow easily, but on the other, you possibly don't want all the information that might flow to escape outside your enterprise. The IMS includes a number of interesting features that allow system administrators to exercise some control over outbound and incoming connections. These include:

- Stopping out-of-office notifications going out to Internet users. People can use the Out of Office Assistant to create helpful messages for other users to know that they are unavailable and won't be able to process any messages they receive. It's not always a good idea for this information to be broadcast externally. Do you really want people to know when senior management are traveling? You should set up the IMS to prevent these notifications going outside. Use the interoperability dialog (see the Internet Mail property page) for the connector to stop out of office notices and automatic replies going to Internet correspondents.

- The ability to accept or reject connections based on IP addresses. The Internet Mail Service can be configured to only permit messages to be sent to particular hosts, or only accept messages arriving in from others. These restrictions can help you restrict communications to a set of hosts that are deemed essential to the business, or stop unwanted inflows of large quantities of messages from overactive Internet mailing lists, and so on. Stopping unwanted connections also helps to stop potential hackers probing your system for holes by which they can gain unauthorized and unwanted entry.

- You often don't want to give everyone the ability to access the Internet. Why should temporary staff or contractors have the chance and the tools to transmit confidential data (extracted, for instance, from an unguarded public folder) to people outside? Use the Delivery Restriction property page for the IMS to restrict any users you'd prefer not to have free and easy communications. Along the same line, you can restrict the size of messages that either go out to the Internet as well as those that come in. Restricting the size of outgoing messages can stop large chunks of data being transmitted (like strategy documents), and restricting the size of incoming messages can stop a "denial of service" hacker strike, basically an attempt to send a system so much mail that disk space is exhausted and the system has to be taken off the air.

Figure 7.24
Internet interoperability options

These features should be operated in tandem with a well configured and secure firewall. There is no situation when the IMS should be connected directly to other Internet hosts unless you want to create a truly open system (in terms of its ability to be attacked).

7.6.11   Interaction with the Domain Name Server

Another item to consider is how to enter records for Exchange servers into your organization's Domain Name Server. The basic function of DNS is to act as a distributed database that translates host names to and from IP addresses. The contents of the DNS database include entries for specific systems within your own network as well as the points of contact for other organizations. All organizations which connect to the Internet have "bastion hosts," systems which connect to the Internet directly. Another term much used is a "relay host," a system that is able to process or reroute messages for a domain, directing them from the time messages enter a domain down through the internal network to the correct server and recipient.

DIGITAL, for instance, has a couple of systems acting as bastion hosts and relay hosts. Collectively these systems process all messages sent to "dec.com" (the public DIGITAL domain). Addresses on arriving messages are examined by these systems, checked against the DNS database to see whether the addresses are valid, and then routed on their way to the eventual recipients. Large, distributed messaging networks incur a fundamental requirement to ensure that all mail servers are correctly entered into DNS as otherwise there'll be no chance of messages ever being delivered.

A request to PING a named computer, such as System1.xyz.digital.com results in a look-up against DNS to resolve the host name that's provided into its base IP address, unless of course the host name and IP address have been entered in the system's local "hosts" file. Windows NT computers can also resolve host names using WINS or by looking up its local LMHOSTS file.

Apart from the straightforward host name to IP address mapping records, DNS holds information specific to mail servers. These records are "MX" (Mail Exchanger) records, and serve to identify which systems are able to accept mail, or act as "relay hosts," systems that accept incoming messages for a domain and relay them onwards to their final destination.

MX records can also be used to give a different name to a computer being used as a mail server, in effect an alias that the outside world can use to send messages to that computer. You might want to do this if you didn't want the FQDN of your computers published to the Internet. For example, a system called Internet-gateway.xyz.com might have the following records in DNS:

```
Internet-host.xyz.com IN A 16.240.111.111
Internet-host.xyz.com IN MX 10 Internet-host.xyz.com
```

These DNS records associate the IP address 16.240.111.111 with the FQDN of a computer that we'll use to host an IMC. The second DNS record tells us that the system is able to accept mail messages.

The example host name I've chosen to use here may be very accurate in a purely technical sense but "Internet-host@xyz.com" isn't going to win any prizes for brevity. Adding a different MX record to DNS allows us to substitute our longwinded name with a shorter version:

```
Mail.xyz.com IN MX 10 Internet-host.xyz.com
```

Now we've associated the alias mail.xyz.com with the system's FQDN, allowing external correspondents to address mail to people within our organization as:

```
username@mail.xyz.com
```

rather than

```
username@Internet-host.xyz.com
```

Putting both "A" and "MX" records into the DNS database speeds up message delivery by giving the system less work to do to figure out whether a computer is able to accept messages or not.

If an Exchange server is going to accept messages from external Internet systems you'll have to ensure that two records for the Exchange server are entered in your local DNS database. The first maps the host name for the Exchange server with its IP address, the second identifies the Exchange server as a mail system.

When you configure the IMS you can decide to provide it with the IP address for the DNS to query to resolve addresses for messages. This allows the IMS to resolve the IP address itself and send messages on their way without further intervention. However, you might not want to have every Exchange server in an organization generate messages in this manner, preferring instead to route all messages to one or more systems dedicated to the task of external mail connectivity. These systems might, for instance, be fully equipped with a range of gateways to enable messages to be exchanged with a wide range of other messaging systems. They might also serve as the point of connection with an Internet Service Provider (ISP); the company who provides the necessary link between your organization and the rest of the Internet. In this case you can configure the IMS to route all messages to a specific system.

There are many tips, tricks, and techniques that can be applied to DNS and the way external connections are handled. Certainly far too much information to be discussed in any comprehensive manner here. If you're in charge of Internet connectivity make sure you have a firm grasp of the techniques that can be applied. Messaging is a critical part of connectivity, but it's one that needs to be controlled, so make sure your implementation is well planned.

7.6.12   Sending rich text message contents

In an Exchange-pure environment all of the clients connected to the network are able to read rich text format messages. The same is true when an Exchange client sends a rich text message across an SMTP network to another Exchange client. Problems begin to occur once you begin to communicate with other mail systems.

The cover notes (initial body part) of rich text messages sent to external mail systems through the IMS will be translated into plan text. At the same time the IMS will attach a copy of the formatted text as an extra binary attachment. Depending on how the IMS is set up the extra attachment is provided as a UUENCODE file (called WINMAIL.DAT) or a MIME-encoded file with a MIME type of MS-TNEF (see the discussion about TNEF earlier).

Recipients who expect a simple message can be quite confused when they see the extra attachment. There's no indication as to what the attachment might contain. It might be an exciting picture, a financial spreadsheet, a copy of their job plan, or details of an important project. All they see is the attachment. Naturally people are curious and won't just let the matter rest there, so they'll call the help desk and pester them with questions like "What's in the file?," "Why have they sent me something I can't read?," or "What application should I use to see inside the file?" All good questions, but something that the help desk can do without.

If you're in the situation where you expect a lot of mail to go out via the IMS to non-Exchange recipients you can configure whether rich text messages are sent to recipients on a per-domain basis. For instance, if you know that lots of messages go to a domain called xyz.com you can configure the IMS to never send rich text messages to a recipient in that domain. Recipients in users' personal address books[4] or custom recipients in the directory[5] can be configured to always receive messages in rich text format, but if you instruct the IMS to send plain text messages to specific domains the settings in personal address books or the directory are overridden. This step effectively stops Exchange adding the extra attachment and stops users worrying about the contents of the mysterious attachment. Note that if the IMS is used to connect sites together you should always allow rich text messages to flow unimpeded between the sites.

---

[4]   Via the SMTP Address property page for personal address book entries.

[5]   Via the Advanced properties for custom recipients.

7.6.13   Managing the message flow from the Internet

If you haven't been used to communicating via the Internet the amount of message traffic generated once a link is established may come as a shock. As soon as people realize they have been released from the boundaries imposed by the internal e-mail system and can send e-mail to friends, relatives, and other correspondents throughout the world they'll start doing it. Be prepared to see outgoing traffic volumes mount up at a fairly rapid rate.

Letting users subscribe to Internet list servers is a good way to generate lots of incoming messages. Many of the active lists handle well over a hundred messages per day, all of which will be sent to list subscribers unless they have opted to receive a daily digest (a concatenated set of all the submissions to the list server sent as a single message). Exchange V5.0 allows you to redirect mailing list activity towards the new Internet News Service (see next section), but it's unlikely that any such changeover will happen quickly. The sheer number of people who maintain individual subscriptions to news groups and mailing lists is probably the major limiting factor.

If users do subscribe to Internet list servers make sure that you don't allow out of office notification messages being sent through the IMS (the default is to prohibit them). Apart from annoying the other people who subscribe to the list server, out of office messages can often convey business sensitive information to people you wouldn't really wish to share it with. It's OK to compose an out of office message to let fellow workers know that you're off to Australia for two weeks to work on an important deal, but do you really want this information going outside?

Having a single point of contact for Internet mail makes things easier to manage, but it also introduces a potential bottleneck into the messaging system. Any organization generating or receiving more than a thousand SMTP-type messages per day should consider spreading the load by implementing multiple Internet connectors. It is possible to configure multiple connectors so that each handles different domains. In other words, the IMS on one server deals with everything sent to "*.com" and "*.gov" whereas another handles messages sent to "*.edu." Configuring connectors in this manner is really only possible if you have a good idea about the volume of traffic sent to different domains, so an easier solution is to let all connectors process messages to any domain and let the Exchange MTA balance the load across the available connectors.

Some of the heavier messaging sites have found it convenient to dedicate servers purely to Internet mail. In fact, some have gone so far as to dedicate one server to handle outgoing mail and another to handle incoming mail. Dedicated IMS servers don't need a high-end hardware configuration. A system equipped with a 100MHz Pentium, 64MB of memory and at least 2GB disk is a good starting point. Better performance will be gained if the system is equipped with an uprated I/O subsystem, principally by spreading the I/O load generated by the processing of SMTP messages across several disk spindles. Such a system is more than capable of handling the load for most organizations, and if you find that message queues build up you can divide the load across two servers or enhance the hardware configuration. Overall, this is a convenient and practical solution for Internet messaging and avoids the need to run multiple connectors across an organization. Remember though that you need to license all servers to use the IMC.

7.7 The Internet News Service

The Internet News Service, newly introduced in Exchange V5.0, can be closely associated with the Internet Mail Service, if only because the same underlying communications paths support both services. The big difference is that the Internet News Service uses the NNTP protocol to transport its messages while the Internet Mail Service uses SMTP.

Mail protocols do not generally lend themselves to threaded or group discussions. Protocols like SMTP are much more focused on getting messages from one place to another. Each message is treated as a standalone entity, with no real relationship to another message or set of messages. Messages sent to a large number of people are often sent in a scattergun fashion, with copies dispatched to all points of the network. Thus, using messaging as the basis for discussions or structured forums is inefficient and makes ineffective use of scarce network bandwidth. Lotus Notes addresses the issue by keeping all items relating to discussions inside databases, with each discussion being allocated its own database. A similar approach was taken with Digital Equipment Corporation's VAX Notes product, a forerunner of Lotus Notes. Both suffer from the same problem: before you can take part in a discussion, you must be able to access the relevant database.

Usenet, a distributed bulletin board system, is the oldest of the Internet solutions to the problem of how to handle discussions. Newer technologies are becoming available, such as Alta Vista Forum, but for the moment Usenet reigns supreme. Usenet provides a topical hierarchy of threaded discussion newsgroups. Communication between the newsgroups is accomplished using the NNTP protocol, which permits messages to be exchanged over TCP/IP. Public-domain news servers support the majority of the active newsgroups within the Internet, but this situation is changing as Microsoft and other software vendors create commercial newsgroup products. For example, Microsoft has its Internet News Server, in direct competition with similar products like Netscape News Server. And anyone running Exchange V5.0 is now able to use the Exchange Internet News Service to correspond with the many and varied newsgroups scattered around the Internet.

NNTP is designed to hold news articles in a central database (on a server). Subscribers can browse through the contents and select the articles they wish to read, ignoring the rest. Articles can be indexed and cross-referenced for further convenience. In structure and functionality the NNTP protocol is much like SMTP. Commands are available to send messages between the set of NNTP servers that collectively form the Usenet, and other commands are available for servers to query and update each other with details of newly formed newsgroups. The Exchange implementation of NNTP in the Internet News Service positions the public information store as the NNTP database. Public folders act as the repositories for individual newsgroups, and users access information in exactly the same manner as they would other public folders. Figure 7.25 shows a newsfeed being configured. In this case the newsgroups all relate to computer subjects.

Figure 7.25
*Selecting
newsfeeds for
public folders*

Knowing what to do with the Internet News Service is the major issue in corporate deployments. Many companies will simply ignore NNTP completely. Either they have no need for newsgroup functionality or they already have an application in place to provide similar functionality. Indeed, there is some competition within Exchange itself because it is possible to use public folders as the basis of discussions. Public folders are still somewhat Exchange-centric whereas newsgroups are platform-independent, so perhaps the argument for public folders can only be made when everyone (or at least a sizeable majority of the user community) is connected to Exchange.

Some companies will seek to replace individual subscriptions to newsgroups (maintained by users) with a form of "corporate" subscription. In essence this means that a single feed will come into the company from the Internet and the information will then be distributed and accessed through public folders. As noted earlier, I don't think it will be easy to replace individual subscriptions purely because it is nearly impossible to track down all such subscriptions. Where do you start? However, I think the idea of a corporate subscription has great merit because it can act as a catalyst for people to realize the quantity of information available in the Internet. Of course, selecting the right type of newsgroups to feed into public folders is an important part of the catalyst. If rubbish flows into public folders user opinion of the value of newsgroups in general will be pretty low.

NNTP has been around for many years. Its incorporation into Exchange provides more evidence that Exchange is becoming more and more open. Before considering any deployment I suggest that you read the appropriate section in the Exchange documentation set, and consult some of the FAQs covering NNTP and newsgroups that are available on the Web.

7.8 Connecting to Microsoft Mail

The file-based architecture of Microsoft Mail (MS-Mail) is totally unlike the client/server approach taken by Exchange, but the replacement of Microsoft Mail post offices and clients represents one of the clearest initial markets for Exchange to grow and prosper in. Achieving good interoperability between MS-Mail and Exchange is therefore a critical success factor for the new server.

Two separate components are used to bridge the gap between MS-Mail and Exchange. These are:

1. The MS-Mail Connector: used to transport messages between MS-Mail and Exchange.

2. The Directory Synchronization Agent (DXA): used to enable directory information to be exchanged between MS-Mail and Exchange.

Connections between Exchange and other MS-Mail post offices can be established over:

- LAN or WAN
- Asynchronous telephone dial-up
- X.25

Any protocol supported by Windows NT can be used to connect Exchange with other MS-Mail post offices over a LAN or WAN. These protocols include TCP/IP, NETBUI, and Novell's IPX/SPX.

Telephone dial-up connections require modems on the Exchange server and the computers hosting MS-Mail post offices. Dial-up connections are made by the MS-Mail Connector MTA (see next section) in exactly the same way as "normal" MS-Mail MTAs.

X.25 connections can only be made if an X.25 card and X.25 software are installed and configured for Windows NT. As mentioned at the start of this chapter Eicon Technologies is the only vendor currently shipping X.25 cards and software for Windows NT. Windows NT RAS is not used for either asynchronous or X.25 connections between Exchange and MS-Mail post offices.

7.8.1   Components of the Microsoft Mail Connector

The MS-Mail Connector can be further broken down into three separate components:

1. MS-Mail Connector Post Office (sometimes called the "shadow" Post Office). This is a specialized version of a normal MS-Mail Post Office used to manage messages in transit between other MS-Mail Post Offices and the Exchange environment. The Connector Post Office links the Interchange and MTA because both the other components read and write messages in the Connector Post Office. The Connector Post Office shares many of the files with a normal MS-Mail post office, but some important files are missing which means that the Connector Post Office can only be used in its specialized connectivity role.

2. MS-Mail Connector Interchange. This is a Windows NT service with two main functions. First, it accepts messages addressed to MS-Mail recipients from the Exchange MTA and writes them into the Connector Post Office. Second, the Interchange accepts messages from MS-Mail users addressed to Exchange recipients and dispatches them through the Exchange MTA to their final destination. Messages addressed to Exchange recipients are stored in the Connector Post Office until the Connector Interchange is able to deal with them. You'll find a queue for messages sent by Exchange users to MS-Mail recipients among all the others listed when you view MTA queues.

3. MS-Mail Connector MTA. Another Windows NT service that assumes responsibility for transferring messages between other MS-Mail post offices and the Connector post office. In essence, the Connector MTA provides the same functionality as a regular MS-Mail V3.2 MTA[6], except that it is able to route messages to the Connector Post Office for eventual pick-up by the Connector Interchange. Several other differences exist in the Exchange version of the MS-Mail MTA, but these are enhancements rather than omissions. The bottom line is that it is possible to replace standard MS-Mail MTAs with Exchange MS-Mail Connector MTAs.

The route messages take between Exchange and Microsoft Mail users is illustrated in Figure 7.26.

Figure 7.26
How the Microsoft Mail Connector transfers messages

Microsoft Mail Connector

The MS-Mail Connector post office acts as a temporary storage area for messages in transit between MS-Mail and Exchange. Messages vary greatly in size and it's important that enough space is available to allow messages to be processed correctly. The space taken up by messages rolls over as messages come in from the Connector Interchange (from or to Exchange) or the Connector MTA (from or to MS-Mail). Messages are deleted as soon as they've been passed on so the exact amount of space you'll need depends greatly on the volume of mail passing between Exchange and MS-Mail. Just like any other situation

---

[6]   MS-Mail MTAs are available on the OS/2, Windows NT, and MS-DOS platforms.

where disk space is required for temporary storage it is wiser to over allocate than end up in the position where everything grinds to a halt because the disk has filled up. The extra allocation will stand you in good stead during the times when users insist on sending messages with very large attachments, or during situations when (for one reason or another), problems exist in the link between Exchange and MS-Mail and a queue builds up.

Either an NTFS or FAT disk will do but make sure that at least 200MB is available after you install the connector and check progress on a regular basis. Danger signals should go up if less than 100MB is available on the drive.

The MS-Mail Connector post office is a special version of the regular MS-Mail post office and uses the same directory structure on disk. Only one user (ADMIN) is known to the post office and many of the files you'd expect to find in an MS-Mail post office are missing. There are no folders, client message files, group membership files, or Schedule+ files, but none of these are necessary to route messages. The important configuration files—MASTER.GLB, CONTROL.GLB, and NETWORK.GLB—are all in place.

7.8.2   Configuring the Microsoft Mail Connector

Configuring the MS-Mail Connector is relatively straightforward. Some of the more important points to consider are discussed below.

- Maximum message size (General properties). This property establishes the maximum size of messages (including the cover note and any attachments) that can be sent from Exchange to an MS-Mail recipient.

- Primary language for clients (Interchange properties—see Figure 7.27). Exchange is a truly international product, largely because of the Unicode capability of Windows NT, but MS-Mail is not. Different language versions exist for MS-Mail. The default language chosen for this property is that of the Exchange server, but if you communicate with MS-Mail clients that use a different language you may want to change the language to that of the clients. A connector can only be configured to use one language.

- MS-Mail compatibility (Interchange properties). If not checked, Exchange sends embedded OLE objects in messages to MS-Mail clients. The only problem is that MS-Mail won't be able to view or save these objects thus generating a fair amount of frustration among recipients! If checked, Exchange will export embedded objects and add the objects as attachments which can be read by MS-Mail. The only problem is that this increases total message

size, which may be an issue on servers that don't have a lot of
disk space. In these situations you should get some more disk!

■   Network and post office name (Local Post Office properties).
By default this is the name of the Exchange organization (network) and site (post office). Unless really necessary it's best to
leave these values alone as changing their values causes the MS-
Mail for all the mailboxes to be regenerated, causing messages
en route to Exchange to fail (because their destination addresses
have changed since they started out).

In addition MS-Mail connectors support the same concept of routing costs as the SMTP and X.400 connectors. You can have multiple
paths to post offices through different connectors. The cost allocated
to each connector tells Exchange which connector to use to send messages. If the MS-Mail Connector with the lowest cost is unavailable
Exchange will automatically route via the next-lowest connector, and
so on.

Figure 7.27
Configuring the
Microsoft Mail
Connector

Microsoft Mail supports the concept of "downstream" post offices. This means that when the MS-Mail Connector joins an existing
MS-Mail network via another MS-Mail post office (the point of contact between Exchange and MS-Mail) that post office may lead on to
other post offices. Information about downstream post offices accessed through the point of contact is extracted from NETWORK.GLB
data files held on the MS-Mail post office. NETWORK.GLB describes
routing information between different MS-Mail post offices and its

provision during the configuration process reveals the presence of those post offices to Exchange, thus making it possible for Exchange users to send messages to recipients hosted by all MS-Mail post offices in the network. If you like, you can think of the information held in NETWORK.GLB as a primitive forerunner of the routing data for servers and connectors within an organization maintained by the Exchange directory.

It's always possible that you might have a requirement to link two separate MS-Mail networks together. Exchange allows you to create a logical backbone (in effect, Exchange acts as a message switch) between the two networks by configuring an MS-Mail Connector on one server to handle messages coming in from the first MS-Mail network and then by configuring another MS-Mail Connector on another Exchange server to do the same thing for the second MS-Mail network. In this scenario messages flow into the Exchange organization from the two MS-Mail networks and are processed there in exactly the same way as any other messages. They are routed by Exchange from one server to another and can pass in this manner from the first MS-Mail network to the second. Apart from message switching Exchange can also use its directory synchronization capabilities to deliver a unified global address list to each MS-Mail network.

7.8.3   Using Microsoft Mail gateways with Exchange

Because of its popularity and market share there are many gateways available for MS-Mail. These gateways connect MS-Mail to backbones like X.400, SMTP, and e-mail systems like IBM PROFS or Lotus Notes. If you're migrating from MS-Mail and have some gateways in operation you have two choices:

1. Elect to channel messages from MS-Mail to Exchange and on to an Exchange connector. This option depends on a replacement connector being available and configured. It's easy to move in the case of the X.400 or IMC, but maybe not so easy if you have a more esoteric gateway in operation. In this situation you'll need to install the appropriate gateway access component in all the MS-Mail post offices that want to use the Exchange connector and then identify the MS-Mail Connector post office as the post office which provides the gateway to the rest of the MS-Mail network.

2. Continue to use the MS-Mail gateways. The gateways are left in place and operated as before. MS-Mail users continue to send messages via the gateway and you can also opt to make those gateways available to Exchange users. This is done by either installing an MS-Mail V3.* gateway access component in the MS-

Mail Connector post office (to route messages via MS-Mail to the gateway), or to install a gateway against the MS-Mail Connector post office. The latter option allows the MS-Mail Connector post office to send mail directly via the gateway without having to route it via another MS-Mail post office. The list of supported gateway access components includes PROFS, SNADS, FAX, AT&T Easylink, MHS, and M-Bridge (MCI).

Installing a gateway directly into the MS-Mail Connector post office seems a retrograde step. My preference is to opt for an Exchange-pure solution if at all possible. Installing another MS-Mail gateway, even under the guise of Exchange's MS-Mail Connector isn't a strategic step to take if Exchange represents the future cornerstone of your messaging infrastructure, so why take a short-term decision?

7.8.4   The advantages of moving from MS-Mail

Coming to Exchange from MS-Mail it may appear that the world has suddenly become much more complex. The client/server nature of Exchange and the replacement of the file sharing underpinnings of MS-Mail by a transactional database alone are enough reasons to consider that the level of complexity has greatly increased. But in return for the extra complexity Exchange delivers much more client and server-level functionality, integrates with and exploits Windows NT, provides a much nicer directory replication system, and has a highly capable MTA complete with many different connectors. More importantly everything is presented in an integrated and easy to use fashion instead of the somewhat scatter-gun or fragmented approach that's often all too visible in an MS-Mail environment composed of more than one post office.

Is the move worthwhile? Definitely. Should it happen as soon as you can swing Exchange into production to take over from MS-Mail post offices? Without a doubt. Will you gain any added value for the extra investment in time, energy, and money? You'll get a much more scaleable, reliable and robust messaging system—one that's designed to operate as an integrated whole. The case to move from MS-Mail to Exchange is compelling. The good news is that the MS-Mail Connector will help you during the transition, but I wouldn't wait around to enjoy the connector in action for very long. If at all possible get to Exchange as soon as possible and leave MS-Mail to rest in peace.

The Microsoft Exchange Directory Service

8.1   Of directories, Exchange, and Windows NT

The Exchange Directory Service is responsible for managing information held about an enterprise's messaging structure—user mailboxes, servers, distribution lists, and the configuration data used to route messages and map address types. All of this information is kept within a single directory. The directory is relatively sophisticated when compared to other messaging directories, if only for the amount of detailed configuration data held and the way that the data is shared between all of the servers in an organization. Distributing the configuration data in this manner allows a server to view the entire configuration and structure of an organization even when working off-line, disconnected from the network. Of course, it is impossible to change any part of the configuration of a remote server without a network connection, but it is always possible to view the data.

Like other entities within Exchange, all of the items held within the directory are treated and manipulated as objects. An object like a server has properties that define the specific characteristics of the object. Properties also specify the users who are able to manage objects. All management activities on the directory store are carried out through the Exchange administration program.

Today, Windows NT has one directory, and Exchange has another. The connection between the two is limited at present. Exchange stores some NT-related security information in its directory, and each Exchange mailbox has an associated NT user account. The future is different and a close and tight integration will occur between the Exchange and Windows NT directories in NT V5.0 and beyond. The merged directory, for this is what the end result will be, is called the "Active Directory" and will not be the directory we know today. Changes will have to occur to facilitate the requirements of both NT and Exchange and make sure that the resulting single directory is scaleable, secure, robust, and adaptable to all needs.

A close integration between the Exchange and Windows NT directories can be compared to something like the Novell NetWare V4 NDS (Netware Directory Service) in that it accommodates configuration information about computers and users, together with the data relating to messaging. Instead of Windows NT domain controllers to manage security information and hold data about the servers and other computers in the domain we should see a situation similar to the Exchange organization today. The Windows NT configuration will be held in the Active Directory in a manner similar to the Exchange site/server information we have now. In fact, documentation released by Microsoft so far refers to sites and servers in much the same manner as we understand these terms in an Exchange context today. The Active Directory is based on X.500 concepts, so it's not at all surprising to have Exchange and Windows NT coming so close together for directory information and services.

The Active Directory will hold much more than just user information. There are many different types of directories used by Windows NT applications today, and there's a fair chance that a lot of this information, such as WINS, network shares, and so on will end up in the directory. Today's SAM is fixed and cannot be extended to meet specific needs of a company, but the Active Directory is designed to be extendible.

Windows NT V5.0 replaces the current domain controller authentication mechanism in favor of a new scheme based on MIT Kerberos V5 (RFC 1510). Like Exchange advanced security, Windows NT V5.0 supports X.509 public keys, and stores the keys in the Active Directory. The keys are mapped onto user ids by the directory to allow users to authenticate themselves when they connect to a computer. It is conceivable that the same X.509 certificate might be used as the basis for both user authentication and electronic mail encryption.

Complete details of exactly what's going to happen will not become clear until Windows NT V5.0 firms up, probably in late 1997. The initial iteration of the Active Directory will incorporate domain, account, DNS, and WINS information, establishing a base that will be developed later on to incorporate the Exchange directory. "Later on" means a number of software releases, both Windows NT and Exchange. Those releases might be service packs or full software releases. Apart from the vision of achieving a unified directory nothing is settled yet.

The effect of these changes on Exchange and the exact degree of integration that is then possible will emerge at the same time. It is certainly possible that the Active Directory will provide a solution to the problem of inter-organization communications we have today; will allow sites to be split and merged in a reasonably automatic manner; and may even be able to accommodate different Exchange organizations within a single directory structure. All of these operations are required for Windows NT domains today, so the advance in functionality for Exchange organizational management is both logical and inevitable, given that the Active Directory is delivered.

In all this flux around directories and their futures we can be sure of two things. First, an upgrade to Windows NT V5.0 will be required before any use can be made of an extended, expanded, merged directory service. Windows NT V4.0 domains will be able to "see" Windows NT V5.0 domains, and correspond with them, as this is a requirement to facilitate successful corporate migrations towards the new directory. The second truth is that the current releases of Exchange must change to use the new directory. Thus, system administrators must keep a careful eye on this area and make sure that they are ready to upgrade systems to take advantage of the new possibilities, if these are important to an organization.

Functionality such as the ability to merge directories from multiple Exchange organizations to form a unified organization, the ability to move users between containers within a directory, and achievement of full compliance with the X.500 recommendations, may arrive as a result of the new directory service.

The merge between the two directories won't happen overnight. Microsoft has to release Windows NT V5.0 first, and people have to ready their companies to move to V5.0. In anything other than a small network the move will be in the form of a rolling upgrade, so networks will potentially have mixtures of Windows NT V3.51, V4.0, and V5.0 servers all working together. After the upgrade is complete and full Windows NT V5.0-based infrastructure is established the merge with Exchange can be contemplated. Exchange V5.0 won't provide the basis for the merge, nor I think will the next major release because it must be able to run on Windows NT V4.0. In any case, whatever the software release, people are likely to wait until at least one service pack has appeared. No one wants to be the first to try the merge out, so another timelag is created while everyone waits for someone else to bite the bullet. The most likely scenario places the first set of merges in mid to late 1998. That's not too far away—just enough time to complete the planning.

8.1.1   Is the Exchange directory X.500-compliant?

As described earlier in this chapter, X.500 is a set of ITU recommendations describing the interconnection of different information systems or directories. Two sets of X.500 recommendations have been issued to date, in 1988 and 1992. The central X.500 concept is the directory, an information system that holds data about a set of objects of interest. An object of interest is something that somebody might want to consult the directory to discover more information about. Recipients are practical examples of an object of interest. Clients consult the directory to discover information about recipients, such as correct address to use when sending messages to a particular recipient.

X.500 information is collectively stored in a DIB, or Directory Information Base. The DIB provides an interface between the users of the directory and the services that provide and maintain the information within the directory. You can think of objects, such as recipients, being stored as records within the DIB in much the same way as transactional information is written into an accounting database. The DIB imposes certain rules on the objects stored in the directory to ensure that a degree of consistency is maintained. The overall set of rules for the DIB is known as the directory schema. Objects are classified by type, known as object classes. The DIB imposes consistency by only allowing objects to be created according to the rules stated for a particular object class. For example, if you attempt to create a new custom recipient (a new directory object) and the Administration program is not currently positioned in a "Recipients" container (an object class), Exchange signals an error and offers to move into a container that allows custom recipient objects to be created there.

The internal hierarchy and structure of an X.500 directory is determined by the Directory Information Tree (DIT). Beginning from the root, or top of the directory the DIT allows navigation through entries called containers and leaves. The basic difference between a container and a leaf is that a container acts as a repository for leaves and other containers whereas a leaf normally represents an object of interest. Think of the Exchange Administration program. You can see a containers such as "Configuration" and "Recipients." "Configuration" holds other containers such as "Monitors" and "Servers," but the "Recipients" container only holds objects of interest, actual recipients or mailboxes. In this example I am purposely ignoring distribution lists which are stored in "Recipients" and can be regarded as containers, albeit not in the true meaning of the X.500 term.

The directory used within Exchange is based upon the X.500 recommendations, meaning that the directory schema used to represent an Exchange organization within the directory is very similar to the model defined in the X.500 recommendations. Microsoft decided not to implement a true, fully compliant X.500 directory because the Exchange directory is designed to store items not supported by X.500

such as titles, organizational information (manager and reports), and the customizable attributes that a system administrator can define for recipients. Microsoft product briefings have contained hints that support of the X.500 protocols such as DAP and DSP will be forthcoming in future releases of Exchange, probably after the directory service is united with the Windows NT directory. Supporting protocols like DAP will be a welcome advance, as it should enable easier synchronization between Exchange and other X.500-compliant directories.

Figure 8.1
X.500 object classes used in the Exchange directory

Figure 8.1 illustrates how the objects within the Exchange directory are mapped on top of X.500 object classes. Both directory schemes organize objects into a well-defined hierarchical structure, the DIT. The concept of the DIB is also supported, as are container and leaf entries.

The full Exchange directory schema consists of:

- Object classes representing different types of objects such as mailboxes, servers, connectors, monitors, and so on.

- Sets of attributes for each object class. For example, a common name, the name of the object class itself, the distinguished name, the date and time when the object was created.

- Details of the hierarchical structure within the directory. For example, *Organization* ➡ *Site* ➡ *Recipients* ➡ *Mailbox*.

- The consistency rules governing which objects can be added to which containers.

Apart from recipients, the Exchange directory holds entries for the other objects that form Exchange including the System Attendant, the MTA, and the directory itself. Thus, all objects in Exchange are addressable, so you can see how this provides the basis for information to be transmitted between components in the form of specially formulated messages. Directory replication is an excellent example of this concept in action as messages containing the information to be replicated are exchanged between the directory store objects in all the sites within an organization.

The Exchange directory is physically represented by a database (DIR.EDB) which is subject to the same 16GB restriction as the information stores. How many entries can be stored in the directory? Theoretically speaking, according to Microsoft sources, probably more than 10 million. Will a directory ever be constructed to hold such a number of entries? Probably not—and from a practical perspective it's fair to say that the Exchange directory is more than capable of handling the largest corporate directory in use today.

8.1.2   X.500 naming

Within an X.500 DIB each object is uniquely identified by a name called the X.500 Distinguished Name. A distinguished name is constructed from the ordered set of object names representing the path through the DIT that must be taken in order to arrive at a specific object. The set of names within a distinguished name is referred to as relative distinguished names, or RDNs. Each RDN provides the name of a container or leaf entry within the DIT. Within the Exchange directory distinguished names are made up from the name of the organization, the name of the site, the name of the recipients container, and the name of the user's mailbox. Thus, based on the graphical representation of the Exchange DIT shown in Figure 8.2, the different RDNs necessary to form my X.500 distinguished name (and thus locate my mailbox within the directory) are:

```
Organization = Digital Equipment
Site = Dublin
Common Name = Recipients
Common Name = Tony Redmond
```

Amalgamated together in the format used by an X.500 directory the entry becomes:

```
o=Digital Equipment, ou=Dublin, cn=recipients, cn=Tony Redmond
```

In the Exchange directory the last RDN in a distinguished name is normally the mailbox alias. In my case this might be something like "TonyR." If you're getting confused by all these terms you could think of RDNs as simply fields in the database that makes up the Exchange directory. Many fields can be held for each mailbox, custom recipient, or distribution list object. A quick glance at the database schema (we'll find out more about how to work with the schema in a little while) reveals that there are nearly 500 available fields for each object. In passing it is worth noting that Exchange attempts to make effective use of space within the directory; if a field does not hold a value for an object no space is reserved for a value until it is first populated. Thus, the directory does not have a whole mass of blank space in it representing fields that could be filled but aren't.

Figure 8.2
Navigating through the Exchange Directory Information Tree

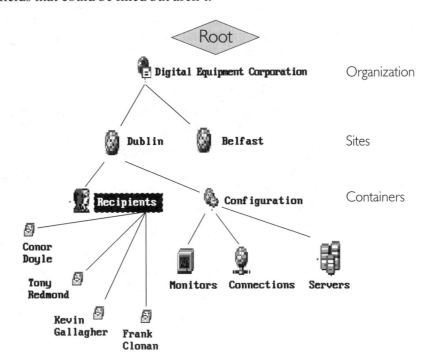

8.1.3   The Ambiguous Name Resolution Process

RDNs are important because they are used when Exchange attempts to check a name presented to it for resolution, normally when a user addresses a mail message. The resolution process is known as ANR, or Ambiguous Name Resolution. In other words, the directory is searched against a number of different fields to find any or all matching addresses. If a number of addresses are found we have an ambiguous name, and the addresses are presented to the user in a dialog for them to make the final selection. Fields such as the first name, surname, display name, and mailbox alias are checked during the ANR process.

An automatic check on addresses is performed when messages are sent, but you can always force a directory look-up through the CTRL/

K shortcut. Being underlined when displayed in message headers indicates addresses that have been resolved.

How do you know which fields are checked during the ANR process? The answer is simple. Each field in the directory can be indexed. Clearly not all fields are indexed as this would mean that the indexes for the directory would potentially be larger than the directory itself, and any time a field was added or updated the directory would have to also update an index, adding an unacceptable overhead to processing. Exchange has a search flags property to indicate which fields are to be searched by the ANR process; the same flags dictate whether the field is indexed or not. Three values can be passed:

1. Do not index this field, and it is not checked during ANR

2. Index the field and so enable fast searching, but do not include the field in the ANR process

3. Index the field and include it in the ANR process.

So now we have our answer. All the fields in the database that have the search flags property set to 2 are automatically checked when a mail address is resolved. By default these fields include the display name, first name, surname, and even office. I have no idea why anyone should want to address mail to someone based on their office code, but the Exchange directory accommodates such weird and wonderful thoughts. You can, if you like, amend the value in this property for any field you like, a subject that we will deal with later on in this chapter.

Obviously the distinguished name is very important to Exchange, in some ways surprisingly so. Let me give you one example. Let's assume you have two sites—London and Chicago—with an Internet Mail Service configured in each site. A user in London creates a message and addresses it by selecting an Internet recipient from the Global Address List, which just happens to come from a custom recipient entry made in Chicago. The message is duly sent. Instead of routing the message via the local Internet Mail Service Exchange examines the address, finds that the distinguished name (from the Global Address List) references the Chicago site, so the message is sent to Chicago for processing by the MTA there. Eventually the message is sent and will be delivered to the right place, but its route via Chicago is curious to say the least.

8.1.4   DUAs and DSAs

Having a directory stuffed full of information isn't very interesting if that information can't be easily and quickly retrieved. In the X.500 world Directory User Agents (DUAs) and Directory Service Agents

(DSAs) accomplish the retrieval of data from the directory. A DUA is responsible for initiating a request for some information from the directory, while a DSA takes charge of responding to any requests that arrive in to the directory. The DSA retrieves the information directly or corresponds with other DSAs (if the directory is distributed throughout a network) to satisfy the request.

Figure 8.3
X.500 DSAs
and DUAs in
Exchange

Figure 8.3 illustrates the Exchange implementation of X.500 DUAs and DSAs. Exchange clients, the Administrator program, or behind-the-scene components such as the MTA, Information Store, or System Attendant initiate requests for directory information. A client might, for instance, request the directory to supply a mail address for a custom recipient. The Administrator program corresponds with the directory when information is added, amended, or deleted about mailboxes or custom recipients. The System Attendant uses the directory to store the certificates used by advanced security, among other things.

In all instances requests for directory information are processed by the Exchange Directory service, which fulfills the role of an X.500 DSA. Because the Exchange Directory is distributed and replicated across all sites in an organization the chaining from one DSA to another to retrieve directory information when required is accomplished in a transparent manner.

8.1.5 Multiple address storage within the directory

Exchange automatically creates a distinguished name within the directory when a new mailbox is created. At the same time a number of proxy addresses may be created, one for each connector that's available for sending messages. For example, if the MS-Mail, X.400, and SMTP connectors are operational, three separate proxy addresses will be created for a new mailbox. Each proxy address represents the address format used by another messaging system to reach an Exchange recipient (via a connector). So the proxy address for MS-Mail is therefore in MS-Mail format and looks and feels just like a regular MS-Mail address when viewed by an MS-Mail user. The same is true for an SMTP or X.400 address, and so on for all the various connectors. In fact, Microsoft requires vendors who sell connectors for Exchange to create well-formed proxy addresses for recipients when connectors are plugged into an Exchange server. Adding a template to the directory proxy table when the new connector is installed does this.

Figure 8.4
Multiple e-mail addresses

It's also possible for the directory to hold multiple addresses of the same type for mailboxes. This is a useful feature when you have modified an X.400 or SMTP addressing scheme, or when users have migrated to Exchange from another system. Let's look at an example to see if it clarifies things. Assume that you have migrated some users from a UNIX system to Exchange. The form of SMTP address used to direct messages to the Internet Mail Service is user@imc.xyz.com. The SMTP address used for the UNIX system was user@mail.xyz.com. Default addresses for the IMS are generated automatically as mailboxes are created, and we can generate new Internet addresses for each mailbox afterwards. New addresses are added through the E-Mail Addresses property page for the mailbox. After you add a new address you'll see that some of the addresses are bolded and some aren't (see Figure

8.4). The bolded addresses are the primary address used by each connector type, in other words, the address that you expect the connector to use most often as well as the reply address that will be placed on ongoing messages.

Having a number of potential mail addresses seems confusing and wasteful but it allows Exchange to meet a goal of the Universal Inbox concept. That is, to allow users to receive messages generated from many different mail systems into a single mailbox. This can only be done by providing a range of mail addresses for correspondents to send mail to. As it happens, Exchange automatically checks the addresses on incoming messages against all possible recipient addresses held in the directory, so messages sent to any valid address actually end up in the same mailbox. Users remain blissfully unaware of the fact that messages have been addressed differently.

8.1.6   Maintaining directory information

The Exchange directory holds much valuable information. Data like this must be carefully protected, but unfortunately Exchange has gone overboard on this point and stops users updating even the most mundane of the information held about them in the directory. There are no client options to allow people to update fields such as their internal telephone number, office location, or other attributes that can hardly be regarded as strategic data. All changes to the directory must therefore be made by administrators, an unwelcome overhead and addition to the list of day-to-day tasks already cluttering busy days.

It is possible to write a client extension to allow users to access and update directory information, and indeed a number of programs like this already circulate among the general Exchange community. All extensions written to date seem to follow the same route—a client MAPI extension (new menu option) to allow users to browse directory information and make changes which are then handed over to a background Windows NT service running on the server. The service takes responsibility for applying the changes to the Exchange directory. Why two steps and not make immediate updates to the directory? Control is one possible response—it is easier to filter entries through a separate process, rejecting the changes or making small alterations before the changes are applied (with an e-mail to the user confirming the update).

8.1.7   X.400 addresses

Confusion often arises between X.400 addresses and X.500 directory entries. At first glance both can appear similar, but they are different. This is especially so within an Exchange environment where the X.500

distinguished name is used primarily to locate recipients or other objects within the directory and an X.400 address is just one of the proxy addresses that may exist for a recipient.

The X.400 recommendations set a standard whereby the electronic mail address for a recipient can be constructed in a perfectly unambiguous manner. This means that the address given to any one person should be built in such a way that it is guaranteed to be unique, and the quest to achieve the level of uniqueness necessary to achieve the goal has arrived at the somewhat strange and unwieldy address format used by X.400 systems today.

An X.400 e-mail address is built up in stages from the country where the MTA is located through the name of the organization responsible for the MTA and down eventually to the personal details of the user who actually composes and sends messages. The full address is referred to as an "O/R address," or "Originator/Recipient address," meaning, in effect, that the address of the originator (sender) can be taken from the message and used to address a response back without interfering with the address in any way. An O/R address is composed of a set of attributes. Each attribute has a value and the collective set of attributes and their values enables a messaging system to deliver messages to a person.

Let's look at how an X.400 O/R address is built up using the following example:

```
C=IE; admd=EIRMAIL400; PRMD=XYZ Corporation; O=RETAIL;
OU1=Sales; CN=Tony Redmond
```

Each of the component parts of an X.400 address has its own special meaning. The first term refers to the country where the recipient is located and each country has its own two-character code as defined in the ISO 3166 standard. In this case the code "IE" refers to Ireland, so according to the standard this recipient must be located somewhere in Ireland. However, this isn't strictly true as some organizations group everyone under a single country code no matter where they are located in order to have a single common entry point into the organization.

The next component refers to the administrative domain (ADMD) while the third refers to the private management domain (PRMD), the two major types of X.400 management domains. An X.400 address must contain one or both domains.

A private administrative domain can be thought of as the collection of electronic mail systems within an organization. Within a single organization that never makes connections to the outside world you would only ever use the private administrative domain. The X.400 addresses created by Exchange use the Exchange organization name as the private administration domain, another good reason for getting the design of your organization, sites, and servers well thought out before you start an implementation.

On the other hand, administrative domains are typically managed by a PTT or other public telecommunications provider (such as those operated by MCI, Telecom Eireann, British Telecom, or AT&T) and serve the function of relaying messages between other management domains. A PTT is often used to connect the administrative domains of organizations working within a single country, and then, on a somewhat higher level, to connect into the domains managed by other PTTs. The collection of administrative domains currently operated throughout the world forms an international message transfer backbone.

The "O" attribute holds the organization name and in the case of the example it's XYZ Corporation. This should be the same top-level name used when Exchange is implemented for your organization. Up to four organizational units (the "OU1" through "OU4" attributes) can be specified to provide further definition. In most cases only a single organizational unit is ever used, and for our purposes we can equate the first organizational unit to a Microsoft Exchange site. The final attribute in the example (CN) defines the "common name," literally the name used to identify a certain recipient within an organization. Many other attributes are available to help identify a recipient including initials and a generation qualifier. If all the attributes are spelled out it's certainly possible to create very long and complex X.400 addresses.

8.1.8 Lightweight Directory Access Protocol (LDAP)

The introduction of lightweight clients in Exchange V5.0 means that the directory had to expand the set of protocols supported for directory access. Exchange and Outlook clients use MAPI to browse the directory and retrieve information, but it is highly unlikely that you'll find a lightweight client that supports MAPI, and certainly not any of the shareware clients.

The University of Michigan in conjunction with the IETF developed LDAP. The current version of the standard protocol is LDAP2, and this is what's been implemented in Exchange. LDAP3, a revision of the standard, is currently being worked on. When it is available LDAP3 will be incorporated into a future version of Exchange. Many other software vendors support LDAP: Netscape uses LDAP in its Directory Server; Novell has announced its intentions to support LDAP as an access point to NetWare Directory Services; DIGITAL has Info-broker software that uses LDAP to communicate with its X.500 directory; and as we'll see later on, Microsoft has plans for LDAP in the Windows NT context as well as Exchange.

Figure 8.5
*LDAP access for
a Web client*

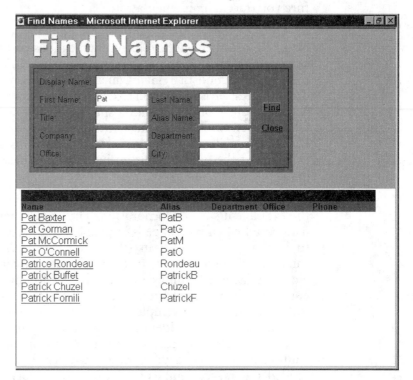

Obviously, because LDAP can communicate with the Exchange directory store, the protocol supports much more than just X.500 directories. As designed, LDAP can communicate with any hierarchical, attribute-based directory. LDAP does, however, assume that the X.500 naming model is used within the directory being accessed. The Exchange directory, based on X.500, is very hierarchical, supports the X.500 naming model, and maintains many different attributes for objects held in the directory, so LDAP and Exchange are a good match.

LDAP is important to lightweight clients, but it's also important in the overall evolution of the Windows NT account database towards the Active Directory, when Exchange and Windows NT will share a common directory. As noted earlier, the Active Directory will store much more than just directory entries, because it will hold domain information; DNS name spaces, and unite many of the different sources of directory information used by Windows NT system components today. As a generalized directory it is logical that the Active Directory

will support LDAP, possibly to allow NT directory entries and configuration information to be managed from a Web browser. If you consider what Microsoft has been able to do to build the Web client with a
mixture of HTML, Java, and ActiveX, it doesn't take a huge leap of the
imagination to envisage Web-based management applications for
Windows NT domains.

Outside of Windows NT and Exchange, Microsoft provides another good example of the power of LDAP in the Internet Address Book
Server (ABS). The ABS is another component of the BackOffice suite,
designed to provide a generalized directory service for applications
like the Commercial Internet System (CIS), previously known as Nor-
mandy. CIS can be used as the basis for many different applications
that need to record information about their users, including on-line
shopping. The ABS is a directory, similar in concept to the Exchange
directory store, and it supports LDAP as a mechanism for applications
to store and fetch entries from the directory.

Figure 8.5 is an excellent example of a client using LDAP to browse
the Exchange directory. In this case it's a Web client, but any LDAP client is able to execute exactly the same type of commands. The functionality enabled by LDAP is minimal, but this is understandable when
you understand that the very reason LDAP evolved in the first place
was to build a streamlined interface to access and update directory information, avoiding the necessity to support a full-function interface
to interrogate X.500 directories. The interface for X.500 is DAP, an
interface not supported by Exchange either due to the use of Microsoft's own interface—MAPI.

When used by Exchange, LDAP is primarily a query interface. In
other words, clients provide some search criteria and LDAP will query
the directory for entries matching those criteria. In the example illustrated by Figure 8.5, the criteria stated are "Find any entries whose
First Name begins with Pat," resulting in 8 entries being returned. Unlike the interface used by Exchange clients to look at the Global Address List there is no opportunity to browse; a query is executed, its results returned, and if you want to look at the directory any further you
must submit another query.

Fetching directory entries through queries is relatively efficient, as
long as the criteria stated in the queries allow a reasonable filter to be
applied to the search. For example, searching any reasonably large directory for a common surname like "Smith" or "Jones" might return
over a hundred entries. Searching the directory for anyone whose surname begins with "M" would probably return even more. All of the
entries must be fetched from the server and stored (in memory) on the

client, leading to potential performance problems if very many entries are requested. It is for this reason that Exchange allows administrators to limit the number of entries returned at one time.

There isn't much else to say about LDAP. The protocol is simple and well defined. The implementation in Exchange is simple and works well. The most important points that can be made are that LDAP is an important protocol for the future, and that its implementation is an excellent example of the ease in which new protocols can be absorbed by the Exchange architecture.

8.1.9   Blocking access to some directory attributes

It's great to be able to share directory information with different clients, but sometimes you don't want everything that's in the directory to appear in open view. Anonymous users, who might well connect to the directory using LDAP, are certainly not candidates to access items like internal telephone numbers, reporting relationships, or even job titles. The DS Site Configuration allows you to determine which attributes are available to different user communites, and even to reduce the amount of traffic generated between sites for directory replication.

Figure 8.6
DS Site
Configuration

Figure 8.6 shows a filter being applied to the attributes replicated between sites. Notice that you can apply similar filters to authenticated requests (clients that have connected to a known mailbox) as well as anonymous requests. The normal situation is to restrict the attributes available to anonymous clients to items like the display name. If you look through the list of attributes you'll see items like "Best friend"

and "Birthday," neither of which are attributes provided with Exchange. These are customized attributes, added on a site basis. We'll discuss how to add customized attributes to the directory later on in this chapter.

Reducing inter-site replication traffic is a useful feature if you operate a site that is primarily used for directory sychronization activity. Feeds from other messaging systems are unlikely to support all the attributes in the Exchange directory. There's no real point in Exchange attempting to replicate blank or missing information after a directory import operation has occurred. Eliminating the missing attributes from the set presented here allows Exchange to replicate on a more efficient basis.

8.2   Directory synchronization and replication

Given that Exchange is a messaging system designed for distributed operation it's critical that the entries for user mailboxes which are stored and managed by the directory service can be quickly and easily synchronized between the different servers in an organization. Exchange automatically synchronizes address information within a site when changes are made to the directory from any server in the site. You don't have to do anything to initiate the process; it occurs automatically once a new server is added to the site.

In Exchange terminology the intra-site directory synchronization process is known as a multi-master full-mesh environment. All of the servers within the site participate and act as masters. A new mailbox or updates to existing mailboxes can be made at any server and the new data will be shared with all the other servers in the site. Data is not sent immediately. It is "bulked up" and replicated at a five-minute interval. A short latency period like this allows for situations when many directory changes are made in quick succession, for example when a large number of new mailboxes are imported from a Windows NT or Novell NetWare user directory. If the latency period did not exist the servers would become very busy communicating between each other to update their directories as each new mailbox was added.

Directory synchronization between sites is performed through a replication scheme similar to that used to distribute the contents of public folders. Because synchronization (or replication) between sites is accomplished by the exchange of specially formatted mail messages, everything depends on an operational mail connector being available between the sites. This is the reason why the directory service in each site is allocated a mail address. In itself the directory service takes no great interest in the underlying details of how its messages are transported between sites. The assumption is made that because a mail connection is available it can be used to transport messages containing directory information from the directory service on one site to its counterpart on another. The MTA, in its turn, regards these messages as any other and does not allocate any great importance to them. If you look at MTA queues you are quite likely to see messages originated from the directory service—notification messages to say that a change has occurred, or data messages containing directory information to be applied to a directory on a remote site.

Once a valid mail connection is available between sites you can configure a directory replication connector. Two approaches can be taken:

1. The connector can be configured on each site. In this case all you need is the ability to send messages to the remote site. This option is very useful when the systems in the remote site are not part of the same Windows NT domain and no trust relationship exists between your domain and the remote domain. The disadvantage is that a certain degree of cooperation and synchronization must take place between the system administrators in the two sites before directory replication works.

2. The connector can be configured in a single operation from either site. This option is only possible within the same domain or when trust relationships exist within the two domains. In addition, the account being used for configuration must possess administrative permissions for the remote site.

Figure 8.7
*Configuring a
directory
replication
connector*

Figure 8.7 illustrates a directory replication connector being configured. In this instance we have elected to configure each site separately.

8.2.1   Transitive connections

Directory information never propagates more than one "hop" (link between two servers) at a time. The connector can be direct, or transitive. In other words, directory replication is possible when two sites are linked by a direct site connector, or when two sites are linked indirectly, with another site in between. Take the example of three sites, Dublin, Belfast, and London. Dublin and Belfast are linked with a direct site connector, and Belfast and London are linked with an X.400 site connector. Dublin and London have no direct connection, but the intermediate link established via Belfast is enough to enable directory replication to proceed. In this instance the messages containing directory information are routed in two "hops"; from Dublin to Belfast and hence to London, and vice versa in the other direction. The important point to understand is that as long as a path exists for messages to travel along, that same path can be used for directory replication. Note that transitive directory replication is configured automatically for standard site connectors, but not for sites connected via the X.400, Internet, or Dynamic RAS connectors. In these instances the sites which "hide" behind the directly connected site must be specified in the Connected Sites property page for the connector.

8.2.2   Replication Bridgeheads

The Directory Replication Bridgehead is a term describing the server within a site that takes charge of managing the synchronization process for a connector between that site and another. There can be multiple replication bridgeheads active in a site, one for each operational site connector. However, a site cannot have two replication bridgeheads configured for any other particular site. This is logical—each site has a directory, and if multiple replication connects were made between one site and another there would be clear potential for synchronized chaos occurring within the directory. Preventing chaos or inconsistency within a distributed enterprise-wide directory is important because you want to encourage users to believe that the directory represents a definitive statement of user mail addresses for the organization. If erroneous or duplicated entries are registered users will lose faith in the directory, which is bad.

Figure 8.8 illustrates the general properties for a directory replication connector. The local bridgehead server for the site is the DBO-EXCHANGEIST server, whereas the bridgehead on the remote site is the TCHOUP1 server. Directory replication is accomplished through a request process. Bridgehead servers generate request messages to the remote sites that they service rather than pushing or force-feeding changes in directory information to remote sites. Thus, the DBO-

EXCHANGEIST server will issue requests to TCHOUP1 whenever it wants to be updated about the directory entries managed in the site where TCHOUP1 is located.

Figure 8.8
Directory
replication
connector

When a directory has changes (additions, deletions, or updates to existing entries) notification messages are generated and sent to all the other servers within a site and to all directory bridgehead servers in other sites, but the actual directory data is not transferred until remote sites request it. In addition to notification messages a scheme of Update Sequence Numbers (USNs) is used to track the status of directory updates between servers. USNs simply track the changes that have been made to a directory on a server, starting from 1. If a server queries another server to discover what its current USN is, and finds that the USN on the remote server is higher than its own, a request to transfer directory updates is immediately initiated.

Replication is performed on an object basis. In other words, if any part of a directory entry (configuration information, mailbox, custom recipient, or distribution list) is changed, complete details of that object are replicated across whatever directory connectors are available. It is not possible, with today's directory, to replicate at the field level. Distribution lists are a special case. When an entry in a distribution list is altered it is not the distribution list object that is replicated. Instead, details of the mailbox or custom recipient object that has been added, deleted, or amended are replicated. The logic behind this scheme is simple. A distribution list can contain many hundreds or even thousands of names, making it a very much bigger object to replicate than the details of individual entries. In most cases, the changes made to distribution lists only affect one or two entries, so this particular replication scheme works very well.

8.2.3   The Knowledge Consistency Checker

With the possibility that servers, sites, and connectors constantly change within an organization it's easy to see how Exchange might lose track of the details of internal messaging structure, leading in turn to problems routing directory updates from site to site. To avoid this problem Exchange uses a component called the Knowledge Consistency Checker (KCC).

The role of the KCC is simple. It must make sense of all the configuration data exchanged between sites to determine what links have been set up between the different sites. Knowing which sites are connected prevents multiple directory replication bridgeheads being created between two sites, avoiding the problems discussed above. The KCC checks configuration information when it is first supplied (when a site is joined to an organization), and continues to review configuration information as it is replicated between sites at regular intervals. If new sites are discovered from configuration information the KCC attempts to figure out how the sites are connected into the organization and whether other sites are connected in via the newly discovered sites. Transitive directory replication, or propagation across multiple links, is enabled through knowledge of these indirectly connected sites.

How do you know that the KCC is active? The only real indicator is when new sites suddenly appear in the administration program. It is the KCC which discovers that the new site is available and then makes that information (about the site, configuration, and recipients containers from the new site) available for display to the administration program. Immediately after a new site is "discovered" its containers appear to be empty, but fairly soon afterwards their contents will be populated via normal directory replication.

The process of populating directory information into newly discovered containers is known as backfill. If containers for a new site are displayed but their contents are not available three hours afterwards (given the standard directory replication schedule) it's a good indication that problems exist in the mail connection between the two sites.

Figure 8.9
*Successful direc-
tory replication
with Belfast,
but not with
Valbonne*

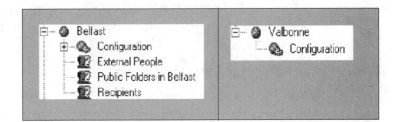

For example, compare the two site views extracted from the administration program in Figure 8.9. The view of the Belfast site is complete, because we can see the different recipient containers within the Belfast configuration. However, the view of the Valbonne site is incomplete because only the configuration container can be seen. In this instance backfill has not occurred and we need to check whether the connector between the two sites is operational.

8.2.4   Successful directory replication

Putting everything together we can see that successful directory replication across multiple sites depends on a number of steps:

1. Synchronization must be active between all servers within a site. This implies that the nominated bridgehead server in each site must know all the servers within its own site. Fortunately the synchronization between the bridgehead server and its peers within a site is totally automatic and requires no human intervention.

2. Sites must be able to communicate together. In other words, a site connector (direct, X.400, or RAS) must be configured and operational to allow configuration data to be exchanged between the different sites.

3. The KCC in each site must be able to create the site and configuration containers for other sites to form an accurate picture of the complete replication environment.

4. Once the configuration containers have been established normal directory replication can proceed to request data from bridgehead replication connectors. The data is populated into the recipient containers for each site. Remember that there can be several recipient containers active for each site. Replication will ensure that the appropriate recipient information is placed into the various recipient containers.

8.2.5   Understanding the replication schedule

Changes and new directory entries are normally replicated every three hours, unless overruled by the schedule property page for a directory replicator. Updating remote sites every three hours may not be satisfactory in the early stages of an Exchange implementation where the directory is likely to be in a state of flux as mailboxes and custom recipients are added at frequent intervals. Later on, when the system has stabilized, updates every three hours are more acceptable because there won't be so much traffic.

Figure 8.10
Directory replication schedule

You should remember that the directory replication schedule is a property that only applies to the connector it is configured for (see Figure 8.10). Take the example of the organization with sites in Dublin, Belfast, and London that we discussed earlier. Directory replication occurs every three hours between Dublin and Belfast, and every three hours between Belfast and London. It doesn't follow that changes made in Dublin will turn up in London three hours afterwards, courtesy of the transitive connection through Belfast. It may well be the case that the replication schedule between Dublin and Belfast is not in line with the schedule between Belfast and London, meaning that it could take, at maximum, six hours to get a changed directory entry from Dublin to London. In one way this is pretty similar to making an airline connection through a hub airport. If you manage to time the connection just right you don't have to wait too long between getting off one plane to getting to your connection, but if anything goes wrong (weather, airport congestion, problems with the aircraft) then you end up waiting around looking at interesting items in an airport. The lesson here is not to assume anything: map how directory replication occurs on top of messaging links and chart out the likely time delays, and then adjust replication schedules as required. Users won't thank you if they send messages to outdated addresses just because the directory wasn't updated in time.

If required, you can force directory replication to occur, but only on a server by server basis. Forced updates are desirable in situations where you have applied many different updates to the directory and now want to have this information distributed throughout the organization. The "Update Now" command button on the General property page for the Directory Service object sets off the process of forced directory updates. As directory propagation only happens one step at a time you may need to initiate several update processes, beginning at the bridgehead server furthest from the server you want to be updated. Think of this process as "pulling" the updated directory information one step at a time, from server to server, through the organization until you reach the point you want the information to reach. The process isn't particularly graceful and it's easy to miss something along the way, so hopefully Microsoft will come up with a better way to start a forced directory update from every site in the organization, perhaps through the equivalent of an "all points bulletin" message sent to all bridgehead servers requesting an immediate update in reply.

8.2.6   The need for synchronization

Synchronization with directory information in other mail systems raises a very important question. What is your strategy for an organization-wide directory?

If you are moving to a homogeneous implementation of Exchange throughout the enterprise then the answer is easy. In these situations the strategy for directory synchronization should be based around the Exchange directory. But if you foresee a heterogeneous messaging environment composed of multiple e-mail systems you also have the option to select a common directory such as X.500 or a directory synchronization product like LinkAge Software's Directory Exchange, a product capable of synchronizing the directories from Exchange, Microsoft Mail, Lotus Notes, Lotus cc:Mail, HP OpenMail, IBM PROFS, and Verimation MEMO among others.

The number of directory synchronization tools available from third parties will inevitably increase as the number of Exchange installations climbs in the corporate world. Synchronization gets more and more important as the size of the user community increases and the number of mail systems involved with the synchronization process grows. Corporate messaging environments usually support many thousands of users and are prone to the operation of many different mail systems, hence the requirement for synchronization.

8.2.7   Synchronization with other Exchange organizations

Exchange does not currently support automated directory replication between different organizations. This would be useful in an environment where a corporation is not able to form an Exchange organization for one reason or another but still wishes to share directory information. Microsoft is aware of a demand for such a feature and it may be supported in a future version, probably after the unification of the Exchange and Windows NT directories has occurred, as explained earlier.

In the meantime, there is a manual workaround to the problem. Exchange offers a feature to export and import directory entries in the form of CSV (comma separated value) data files. Thus it is possible for organizations to export their directory to a file and arrange to swap their exported data with other organizations. Addresses in exported files are treated as custom X.400 or SMTP recipients by the importing organization, so an appropriate connector will also be required to send messages to the recipients after they've been imported. It is convenient to create a new recipients container for imported directory information, clearly separating custom recipients from native Exchange addresses (mailboxes and distribution lists). If you import data from multiple sources you may like to have separate recipients containers for each source. For example, an organization that imports data from PROFS, Lotus Notes, and Internet (sendmail) systems might have a set of containers named as follows:

- Recipients (to hold native Exchange addresses)
- PROFS Recipients
- Lotus Notes Recipients
- Internet Recipients

Apart from anything else, it is convenient for users to be able to select and browse through a specific recipients container if they know that the person they wish to send mail to uses a certain mail system. The extra recipients containers are not created on each server and every site. They are only required on the server used to import directory information from the foreign mail systems.

8.2.8   Synchronization with foreign directories through DXA

Synchronization is also possible with non-Exchange sources through a Windows NT service called the Directory Synchronization Agent (DXA). The service operates in conjunction with the DXA database, built using the same database engine as the information and directory stores. The DXA database is used to track changes that have been made in the Exchange directory between the times when synchronization occurs with foreign directory sources. The database also maintains records of the synchronization operations it has recently performed. Unlike the information store no transactions logs are maintained.

The protocol used by DXA is the well tried and tested mechanism implemented by Microsoft Mail V3.2 directory synchronization. This allows any system that performs directory synchronization with Microsoft Mail to also support Exchange.

Microsoft Mail post offices synchronize the contents of their Global Address List (GAL) through a relatively complex series of events which, in outline:

- Generates directory information from individual post offices
- Collects the directory information from the post offices to a central directory synchronizer
- Merges the directory information into a new GAL
- Distributes the new GAL to the different post offices.

Within this scheme Microsoft Mail post offices act as either a DirSync Server or a DirSync Requestor. The server acts as the central directory synchronizer while the requestors provide directory information and accept the merged GAL back afterwards. Through the DXA Exchange is able to assume either role, but an individual server cannot be configured to act in both roles.

When the Exchange DXA assumes the role of the DirSync Server all the Microsoft Mail post offices must be reconfigured to identify the Exchange MS-Mail Connector post office as the DirSync Server. Only one DXA Server can be configured per site, and it takes charge of propagating the addresses for the MS-Mail users (attached to the post offices it synchronizes) to other Exchange sites via normal directory replication.

When DXA acts as a DirSync Requestor it means that DXA will receive copies of the MS-Mail GAL from another DirSync Server, and then propagate the addresses in the GAL to other Exchange sites. Multiple DirSync Requestors can be active within a site, but this configuration would only be used if there were multiple available sources of MS-

Mail address information. For example, if there were two or more separate MS-Mail networks. In this case you could create a separate DirSync Requester to receive the GAL from the DirSync Server acting in each MS-Mail network.

8.2.9 Synchronization with foreign mail directories using load files

As we've seen, automatic synchronization for Exchange directories is seamless within an Exchange organization, and relatively painless for Microsoft Mail directories or systems that support the Microsoft Mail directory synchronization methodology. Outside of these scenarios the picture isn't so clear and the work required to achieve high fidelity within a synchronized directory is very demanding. In this context, a high-fidelity directory means one that has a low incidence rate of invalid directory entries introduced as a result of synchronization operations. Large corporate directories, those with over 20,000 entries, can expect to have an invalid entry rate of between 2% and 4% at any time, chiefly due to the inevitable number of changes that occur within large corporate entities all the time. Staff turnover and transfers, especially in international organizations, is normally the reason for the largest number of invalid entries. The challenge is to reduce the rate down as low as possible so that the user community is willing to depend on the directory.

Unfortunately the mechanisms available to achieve directory synchronization are limited. If you can't go along the Microsoft Mail/DXA route you're limited to using the administration program to load import files containing directory data. The general approach taken in these instances normally includes:

1. Establish a separate container within the directory to hold the imported entries. All the imported entries become custom recipients within the Exchange directory. It is generally unwise to mix different recipient types within the same directory container whenever synchronization is required. Exchange allows you to create a clear differentiation between recipient types within the directory, and you should use this facility.

2. Extract an export file from all the mail systems that need to be synchronized with Exchange. The format of the import file is defined by Exchange, and the best way to discover what that format should be is to export the entries for some custom recipients from the Exchange directory. You don't need to complete all fields. In general, minimize the number of fields that you synchronize to those that are really essential.

3. Import the export file from the source foreign mail systems into Exchange. The administration program can be used for this purpose. You can either use the Tools.Directory Import option through the normal GUI (Figure 8.11) or run the administration program in batch mode to import the contents of the file. See the notes on page 491 for more information on how to use the administration program as a directory import/export command line utility. Before you attempt any batch runs, make sure that any files you create can be processed using the GUI. This simple step eliminates a lot of common formatting problems with files generated from other messaging systems.

Figure 8.11
Exporting some directory information

4. Create an export file from Exchange to provide to the other mail systems. There's no real point in doing one-way directory synchronization. Exchange will create an export file for you, but you'll probably need to perform some text manipulation on its contents to prepare it for the other mail systems. PERL, a text-manipulation language originally for UNIX and now available for Windows NT, is often used for this purpose. It is highly unlikely that the other mail systems will understand the syntax and format of the export files generated by Exchange!

5. Import the duly amended directory information from Exchange into the directory of the other mail systems. The exact mechanism to perform these operations is highly specific to the individual mail system and cannot be described here. Make sure that the import procedure ignores any directory information that originated from the target mail system, as otherwise you will end up with duplicate addresses in the directory.

The steps outlined above will accomplish a basic synchronization process. Three important decisions must be taken before you can achieve a more refined synchronization process.

Directory Import/Export command line interface

Export

```
ADMIN/E export-file /D=server /N /O=options
```

Import

```
ADMIN/I import-file /D=server /N /O=options
```

In both cases the options file creates a specific context for the import or export operation to proceed. For example, the container to operate against. The server indicates the name of the Exchange server that will either export or import the directory data. The /N switch indicates that you don't want to see a progress bar on-screen. The only mandatory switch is either /E or /I. Usually import or export operations are carried out on the server hosting the relevant directory information.

The first question is how the directory entries should be inserted into Exchange. There is no problem whatsoever inserting a new directory entry. The question is what to do with that entry thereafter. The easiest approach is to delete all entries relating to a specific mail system from Exchange before importing any data. This method avoids the need to worry about making amendments to directory entries that are already in the directory, but it's rather crude and can take longer to process. There are usually relatively few amendments to perform when compared against the requirement to first delete one or two thousand entries followed by the recreation of the same (or more) entries. The directory database will also become a little less efficient with each series of delete/import operations, so you'll need to consider whether the directory should be compacted with the EDBUTIL utility from time to time. Executing amendments to the directory requires a lot more intelligence to be built into the synchronization process. It must be possible, for example, for the synchronization process to be able to first check for an entry before it either amends it with new data or inserts a brand new entry into the directory.

The second issue that must be decided is how often directory synchronization should occur. Generally speaking, during the early stages of an implementation, when it is quite likely that many changes are occurring in the directory as users migrate to Exchange, the need for frequent directory synchronization is more prevalent than when the messaging systems have stabilized (in terms of their user communities). The more frequently synchronization occurs the more up to date the directories (Exchange and the other messaging systems) will be, and the less Non-Delivery Notification messages will be generated to be sent to users (and promptly referred to the help desk). However, it may not be possible to perform directory synchronization very frequently (nightly, for instance) because of other operational requirements such as staff not being available to supervise the procedure.

Most installations find that a weekly synchronization is sufficient, although it is a good idea to allow for special synchronization runs to occur, such as immediately after a workgroup is moved to Exchange. In all cases the procedure to migrate a user to Exchange should incorporate directory updates for both the source and Exchange directory. In terms of Exchange the old custom recipient entry should be removed and replaced with the mailbox entry. The directory for the source mail system should be updated, if possible, with an autoforward or redirect address to force messages sent to the "old" address to be sent on for eventual delivery to the new Exchange mailbox.

Within any typical Exchange organization a network of directory replication connectors distributes directory updates. Any plan for synchronization must consider how long it will take for the newly synchronized updates to be dispatched to all sites within the organization, taking due note of the time delays that may occur due to replication schedules for sites downstream of major hubs (see the discussion about transitive directory connections earlier in the chapter). Ideally synchronization should be performed so that all sites in the organization are fully refreshed with up to date directory information within 6 hours of the new data being imported into the synchronization server. Large directory updates, those involving 20,000 entries or more, can generate a considerable amount of network traffic to fan out the updates to all sites, so make sure that synchronization occurs at a time when the network is not fully occupied with other (more important) work.

The final, but perhaps most strategic decision to make is whether Exchange or another directory should be the focal point for synchronization. I've already made the point that if you are going towards a homogeneous Exchange messaging environment the wisest decision is to base synchronization around the Exchange directory. On the other hand, if there is a continuing requirement to operate multiple systems then Exchange might not be such a good choice, primarily due to the lack of user-friendly or highly functional synchronization utilities

(some might define the situation a little more harshly, and say "non-existent synchronization utilities.)

If you're in the latter situation it's probably best to spend some time looking at what's currently available on the market. Writing your own set of synchronization routines is guaranteed to be a time-consuming and expensive business. One project to create a set of bespoke routines to synchronize directory data from Novell Groupwise, Microsoft Mail, DIGITAL ALL-IN-1, and Exchange took over six months elapsed time to complete. The job could have been done a little quicker, but it would have had a number of rough edges that might have led to invalid addresses creeping into the directory. The resulting synchronization worked automatically with a great deal of success for over 50,000 entries, but it was expensive. Selecting an off-the-shelf package is always going to be cheaper and transfers problems to someone else. Dealing with changes in directory structures in new versions of any of the contributing messaging systems is one obvious example of a problem waiting to happen.

8.2.10   Understanding Directory Import/Export files

As noted earlier, Exchange supports simple text comma separated, or CSV files for directory import and export operations. CSV files use the comma character as a delimiter between each field in a record. The major value of using CSV files is that they can be easily generated and manipulated by many different systems. Each record occupies one line in the file, although the records are often wrapped when viewed in a text editor.

Directory import/export files are divided into two parts. The first record in the file is the header (Figure 8.12) used to define the directory attributes that might be stated for each record thereafter. The attributes are stated in the order they will occur in the other records.

Figure 8.12
Header section for directory import/export file

```
Obj-Class,First Name,Last name,Display Name,Alias Name,Directory
Name,Primary Windows NT Account,Home-Server,E-mail address,
E-mail Addresses,Members,Obj-Container,Hide from AB
```

Note that the header does not have to state all of the attributes that can be held for directory entries. There is certainly a requirement to state enough of the attributes to create a reasonably complete entry in the directory, so some of the attributes, like the directory name and e-mail address, can be regarded as mandatory. All of the records following the header are deemed to contain directory information, a sample of which is shown in Figure 8.13. This record was obtained by exporting details of a recipients container from a server and editing the resulting CSV file to extract details of a custom recipient created using the GUI of the administration program.

```
Remote,Owen,Doyle,Owen Doyle,OwenD, OwenD,,,
SMTP:Owen.Doyle@IRFU.IE,
MS:DIGITALEQU/EXCHANGEIS/OwenD%X400:c=IE;a=eirmail400;p=digital;o=digital;s=Doyle;
g=Owen;ou1=Exchange IST;%SMTP:Owen.Doyle@IRFU.IE,,Internet recipients,
```

Figure 8.13
Import entry for a custom recipient

In addition to its cross-platform support, the CSV file format is understood and supported by many Windows applications, making it possible to use these applications to manipulate or clean up directory information before it is imported into the directory. It is not recommended to manually check files using any application before every import operation. If you find that the directory import files created by your synchronization process are flawed and need attention before they can be given to Exchange you should track down the reason for the problem and fix it.

Figure 8.14
Using Excel to work with directory import information

Using a tool like Excel (see Figure 8.14) to check directory information should really only occur when an unforeseen problem arises. The old adage that rubbish in results in rubbish out is especially true for directory information, and inaccurate directory entries are very irritating (and worse than useless) to users.

Using a sample directory CSV file exported from Exchange is a good starting point, but you don't need to populate all the fields (or, more correctly, directory schema attributes) to create custom recipient entries for mail addresses from other systems. The fields in a header file for a typical import operation are described in Table 8.1.

Table 8.1   *Fields for a directory import file*

Header Field	Use
Obj-Class	Remote (for custom recipient), or Mailbox (for an Exchange recipient).
Mode	The default mode is Add, in which case the column is left blank. Other valid modes are Delete and Modify.
Directory Name	The internal RDN used by the directory to identify the recipient. If omitted the alias name will be used to create a directory name. Normal practice is to make the directory name the same as the alias (which is what Exchange does) or the display name.
Alias Name	The unique nickname or alias for the custom recipient. This is a mandatory value.
Display Name	The display name shown to users in the GAL. This is a mandatory value because there's no point in adding an entry to the directory unless users are able to select it.
E-Mail Address	The mail address to use to route messages to. The e-mail address is prefixed with a known term (like SMTP) indicating the type of address. Naturally, this is also a mandatory value.
Obj-Container	The name of the recipients container to operate on (import/delete/modify). If omitted, the default recipients container is used.

Many more fields can be incorporated into the import file. Once you've included the really essential attributes (detailed above), the only question to be answered is how easy it is for the procedure that generates the import file to generate and output appropriate values for each attribute. Some attributes may not be available or cannot be generated if you're taking data from a human resources database or another messaging directory.

The CSV header therefore looks like this:

```
Obj-Class, Mode, Directory Name, Alias Name, Display Name, E-Mail
Address, Obj-Container
```

And a sample data line for a custom recipient with an SMTP mail address to be inserted into the "Internet Recipients" container is:

```
Remote,, Jim Smith, JimSmith-970601, Jim Smith,
SMTP:Jim.Smith@abc.com, Internet Recipients
```

It's best when unique aliases are created in the directory. If the import files are generated automatically by a program or other procedure it's easy enough to insert logic to generate a unique alias for each entry. In the example shown above the load date (970601 = 1st June 1997) is appended to the display name to create a unique value. Other algorithms may be more appropriate for your company.

Creating entries is the easiest task you have. The CSV header for delete operations is slightly more complicated:

```
Obj-Class, Mode, Directory Name, Alias Name, Obj-Container
```

If passed, the mode command must be stated in the second column. If this is not done the operation will fail. Events that occur during import or export operations are written into the system event log for object MSExchangeDSImp (import) or MSExchangeDSExp (export). For example, if the mode command wasn't in the second column event id 222 is reported. The start and finish of import operations are reported as event ids 31 and 32, while the start and finish of export operations are event ids 36 and 37.

The data lines look like this:

```
Remote, Delete, Jim Smith, JimSmith-970601, Internet Recipients
```

Modifications are accomplished with a similar header file, albeit with fields added for each attribute to be changed. The data lines contain values for each field to be changed or just a comma if the field is to be ignored. For example:

```
Obj-Class, Mode, Directory Name, Alias Name, Display Name, E-
Mail Address, Obj-Container
```

```
Remote, Modify, Jim Smith, JimSmith-970601, Jim (New) Smith,
SMTP:Jim.Smith@xyz.com, Internet Recipients
```

Commands to add, modify, or delete custom recipients can be combined together into a single file. The same header can be used, providing it contains the mode command in the second column. Combining all directory commands into a single file delivers an advantage in that the administration program must only be initialized once. It does make recovery a little more difficult if something goes wrong such as a system crash (unlikely, but possible over the lifetime of a system). In these cases it is easier if the various operations (adds, updates, and deletes) are spread across a set of files, one for each type of operation. Further information about the complete set of valid schema attributes as well as general advice on directory synchronization can be found in the Exchange migration guide, part of the product documentation set.

8.2.11   Batch synchronization procedures

Automating synchronization operations is clearly desirable. No one wants to be tied down to a set of manual procedures, so you should investigate how best to create a batch job to do all the work when the system is quiet (and system administrators asleep). Here's an example of a batch procedure in use within a real production environment:

```
REM Synch.Bat — Synchronize files from X.500 with Exchange
REM First copy the necessary files from the UNIX system
ECHO *** Preparing to synchronize ***
CHDIR C:\EXCHSRVR\SYNCH
DEL *.CSV
ECHO *** Copying commands to delete entries ***
COPY X:EX-DEL.CSV EX-DEL.CSV
ECHO *** Deleting old entries ***
ADMIN/I EX-DEL.CSV
ECHO *** Deletions finished ***
ECHO *** Copying commands to create new entries ***
COPY X:EX-NEW.CSV EX-NEW.CSV
ECHO *** Now processing modifications ***
ADMIN/I EX-NEW.CSV
ECHO *** New entries added to Exchange ***
ECHO *** Copying commands to modify entries ***
COPY X:EX-MOD.CSV EX-MOD.CSV
ADMIN/I EX-MOD.CSV
ECHO *** Modifications complete ***
ECHO *** Please check System Event Log ***
EXIT
```

This procedure assumes that drive X is connected before anything starts. The CSV files are generated from an X.500 directory that serves as a common synchronization point for a number of different messaging systems. Using an X.500 directory is convenient, but it's not important. All that matters is to establish a repository for directory information that can be provided to Exchange. A similar procedure can be used to export information from Exchange before importing details of Exchange mailboxes into the common directory. The export procedure is much easier when all Exchange mailboxes are gathered together into a distinct container, isolated from the entries created by the import operations. If this is not the case then a certain amount of preprocessing will be necessary to eliminate data lines containing information about distribution lists and custom recipients before the export files can be processed by the common directory.

8.2.12 How long will directory synchronization procedures take?

Directory synchronization operations vary greatly. The factors influencing the time required to process import files include:

- **The capability of the server where the import operations are being processed.** The faster the processor, the faster the import operations will happen. High-end processors such as Alpha systems are good choices for directory import servers.

- **The other workload that the server is handling during the import operation.** Clearly the less work the server is doing, the less contention will occur with the import operation. This is the best reason to schedule directory imports for night-time when systems are normally at their quietest.

- **The number of directory entries to process.** The larger the amount, the longer the import will take. Restricting the amount of data to the entries that definitely need to be added, changed, or deleted is a good tactic to adopt. Never include entries that don't have to be processed. If necessary, do some pre-processing to eliminate any entries that shouldn't be included in the import.

- **The number of attributes for each directory entry.** The smaller the number of attributes the quicker each entry is processed. However, this factor has the least impact in the elapsed time for import operations so it is not an excuse or reason not to include attributes such as telephone numbers if you have this data available.

As an indication of directory updates in a real-life situation, Table 8.2 contains details of synchronization operations performed for a large customer that I have worked with.

Table 8.2 *Timings for synchronization operations*

Influencing factor	Details
Import Server	175MHz Pentium Pro, 196MB memory, 2GB system disk, 2GB transaction log, 8GB RAID-5 set for stores (including directory).
Workload	Low (operation occurred at night).
Import data	50,000 entries, each containing 11 attributes. Average entry size 176 bytes, total data to process 8.38MB.
Average import rate	13 entries/second.
Time to process entire file	67 minutes.

Delete and modify operations produce similar results. The results show that synchronization operations are pretty resource intensive. Importing 50,000 entries generates a fair amount of replication load for the organization afterwards, with updates being sent to other sites according to the replication schedule for the import server. All of the other servers in the site where the import server is located should be fully updated between ten and fifteen minutes after the import server processes the last entry. The time taken to ripple the new directory information out throughout the organization greatly depends on the replication topology you have implemented. Considerable delays (more than a couple of hours) may be experienced if a number of transitive connections are used.

8.2.13 Other uses for directory import files

Directory import files are not only used for directory synchronization operations. They can also be used to create a set of new mailboxes for users before a migration begins (in this case, you use "Mailbox" as the object class you wish to create). Manually creating 50 or 100 mailboxes is a boring task, but it's just about bearable if it only needs to be done on an irregular basis. If you're faced with the need to create a thousand mailboxes the task is much more daunting. You can automate mailbox creation for a group of new users by creating a CSV load file with Excel before feeding it into the administration program. Everything, including Windows NT accounts, will be set up for the new users, and all in much less time than you'd be able to create the accounts manually.

The CSV header and the data specified for each entry is slightly more complex than for custom recipients. In this instance you have to specify the name of the Exchange server where the mailbox is to be created as well as the name of the Windows NT account to use. Note the "Hide from AB" attribute. This controls whether or not the new account is shown to other users when they browse the address book. If you're creating a set of new user accounts you may not want to reveal their existence until the new users have received training and are ready to use Exchange. Setting the "Hide from AB" attribute to "N" hides the new account from the GAL. You can modify the directory entry later on and set the switch to "Y" when everything is ready to go.

Let's look at an example of adding a new account:

```
Obj-Class, Mode, Directory Name, Alias Name, Display Name, E-Mail Address,
Obj-Container, Home-Server, Assoc-NT-Account, Hide from AB

Mailbox, Create, Tony Redmond, TonyR, Tony Redmond, SMTP:Tony.Redmond@dbo-ex-
changeist.dbo.dec.com, Recipients, DBO-EXCHANGEIST, OFFICESI\T_Redmond, N
```

Although the data provided is similar, creating mailboxes isn't as straightforward as custom recipients, especially when Windows NT accounts are involved. In fact, an import options file is required to override the default options that the administration program takes when it processes import files. One of the important options we need to use allows us to create new Windows NT accounts. The option file looks like this:

```
[Import]
DirectoryService=
Basepoint=
Container=Recipients
InformationLevel=Minimal
RecipientTemplate=
NTDomain=OFFICESI
OverwriteProperties=No
CreateNTAccounts=Yes
DeleteNTAccounts=No
ApplyNTSecurity=Yes
GeneratePassword=Yes
RawMode=No
CodePage=0
```

The important fields are CreateNTAccounts, ApplyNTSecurity, and GeneratePassword. In the example I create an NT account called T_Redmond in the OFFICESI domain. A password is automatically generated for the new account, with the password set to the same value as the account name. The user will be required to change the password the first time they log-in to the server.

Always import CSV files to create new mailboxes on the server that will host the mailboxes. If you want to create new Windows NT accounts, make sure that the primary domain controller is available (in other words, don't attempt to create new accounts if the server is disconnected from the network or a backup domain controller is all that's available).

In addition to mailboxes and custom recipients, distribution lists can also be created, modified, and deleted through import files. For example, to create a distribution list called Management Team, you might use the following CSV file:

```
Obj-Class, Mode, Directory Name, Members, Obj-Container
Dl, Create, Management Team, Recipients/cn=FrankC%Recipients/
cn=FrankB%Recipients/cn=TonyR, Recipients
```

This file creates the distribution list and populates it with three members. The distribution list must not already exist, and all of the members specified must already exist in the directory in the specified container. I've used the standard "Recipients" container for the example, but you can specify other containers if you need to fetch recipients from them. The directory alias name for recipients is the best way to include them in a distribution list. Exchange only needs a pointer to each member in the distribution list because that's what a distribution list is—a set of pointers to directory entries. Those entries can be mailboxes, custom recipients or other distribution lists. Note the % (percentage sign) used to separate each member in the list.

I've already recommended Excel to you as a good tool for composing CSV files. Distribution lists pose a particular challenge for Excel and other spreadsheets because the possibility arises that we may exceed the maximum limit for a spreadsheet cell. In Excel V7.0 that limit is 255 characters, a value that can easily be encountered with large distribution lists.

To amend the same diustribution list and add a new member we can use the following CSV file:

```
Obj-Class, Mode, Directory Name, Members, Obj-Container
Dl, Modify, Management Team, Recipients/cn=PhilipI, Recipients
```

I don't honestly believe that many people will create distribution lists using import files. The exception is when you need to migrate a mass of distribution lists from another system, where the choice is either to create the lists from scratch or to generate the lists using a program. The latter option is preferable if there are more than 20 or so lists to move. In this case the program (which is not yet written and certainly not available off the shelf) will read list members in the format used by the legacy system and write out an import file in Exchange load format. Remember that all the entries in the list must already exist in the directory before you attempt the import.

8.3   Expanding the set of Address Book Service Providers

X.500 (or other corporate-type) directories don't have to remain hidden from Exchange users. MAPI extensions can be built to make a directory available as another source of address information, along the same lines as the Exchange directory or the Personal Address Book. DIGITAL personnel have always enjoyed a facility called ELF (for Employee Locator Facility) which can be consulted to find out details about other employees—their mail stop, electronic mail address, phone number, and so on. ELF data is stored in an X.500 database distributed across a set of UNIX servers, and the Exchange implementation within DIGITAL uses a MAPI Address Book Service Provider to map ELF as an additional source of directory information for Exchange clients.

Figure 8.15
DIGITAL's
Employee
Locator Facility
accessed by an
Exchange client

Figure 8.15 shows the results gained by consulting ELF to discover the DIGITAL employees with the surname "Redmond." Apart from anything else, making a corporate directory accessible to all users via their mail client helps the client to be accepted quickly. It also leverages the information in the corporate directory and prevents any requirement to rekey information or otherwise transfer entries into another directory.

To complete this discussion on corporate directories I'll take the opportunity to note that DIGITAL offers a number of different synchronization tools that can help to keep DIGITAL DDS (Message Router Distributed Directory Service) and X.500 directories in line with Exchange. If you're moving from a DIGITAL system or simply trying to integrate Exchange into an existing DIGITAL messaging environment you should check out DSU, XDSU, and X.500 synchronizer. DSU and XDSU enable synchronization between DDS and other directories, X.500 and other directories, while the X.500 Synchronizer product links Exchange and AltaVista Directory Service.

In the future, when Exchange offers direct support of external directory access products such as DAP, it may be possible to build a more elegant directory synchronization scheme, possibly using features built into Exchange but more likely through third party add-ons.

In all cases the critical selection factor is which directory service supports the highest degree of automatic synchronization (once everything is set up—it's too much to expect totally automatic directory synchronization) across all potential directory sources. There's no point in performing manual synchronization if you can at all avoid it.

8.4   The Off-line Address Book

The Off-line Address Book is a snapshot of a subset of the Exchange directory that can be downloaded to clients so that they can work when disconnected from the server. When clients are working in off-line mode they perceive no difference between the off-line address book and the directory held on the server; both are used to validate the addresses entered into message headers, and both can be browsed to retrieve information about mailboxes, distribution lists, and custom recipients.

Figure 8.16
*DS Site
Configuration
Object*

Each site nominates one server to create its own Off-line Address Book and determines when it is generated. The DS Site Configuration object (see Figure 8.16) from the site Configuration container is used to determine:

- The name of the server within the site that will generate the Off-line Address Book

- The schedule used to generate the Off-line Address Book

- The containers from the server Address Book that will be included in the Off-line address book.

When the Off-line Address Book is generated it is stored in a hidden folder in the Public Information Store of the server. Clients retrieve the Off-line Address Book with the Tools.Synchronize.Download Address Book option. At this point the data is fetched from the server and downloaded to a set of five .OAB files in the client's Windows directory. The data is highly compressed to limit the time taken to perform the download, and you can speed things up even more if you elect to download the address book without "details information." However, this option is not recommended because, while you'll save a little on disk space, you won't be able to see a lot of valuable information (such as phone numbers) when you browse through the address book. You also won't be able to send encrypted messages because the public keys for Exchange recipients aren't available. Public keys are among the attributes downloaded for mailboxes when detailed information is retrieved together with the bare minimum mail addresses.

How compressed is the data downloaded from the server? Well, Microsoft quotes the example of its own off-line address book that holds 51,000 entries (mailboxes, distribution lists, and some custom recipients). This address book is 6MB when compressed, and 12MB when it is uncompressed on the client to create the .OAB files. Another example is a customer with a 95,000-mailbox directory. The off-line address book in this case is 13MB when compressed and 23MB when uncompressed.

Downloading such a large data file is OK when you're attached to a LAN (although things might get interesting if lots of users tried to download the file at the same time). Even if you have such a large directory there's no requirement to create an off-line address book that contains everything. The DS Site Configuration properties allow you to determine exactly what container from the directory is used to create the off-line address book. In most situations where the GAL is a reasonable size it's best to select the GAL because this means that off-line users will be able to access all the addresses they can when working online. With large directories you might want to select another container, such as the recipients container for the local site. Exchange V4.0 doesn't allow you to select multiple containers for this operation, but this may be possible in a future release.

Most installations schedule the off-line address book for generation at least once a day. I like to schedule generation to occur twice. Once in the morning and once just before close of business each day. That way an up-to-date off-line address book is almost always available, and the generation towards end of day helps people who are packing up ready to go on a road trip because they can always pick up a new copy that includes any directory changes made during the day. Generation does not place much strain on a server, nor does it take very long, so generating the off-line address book twice a day is no big deal. If necessary, you can generate the off-line address book whenever you need by clicking on the "Generate Off-line Address Book Now" command button in the DS Site Configuration object.

8.5 Address Book views

Address Book views are a new concept introduced in Exchange V5.0. Not much experience has yet been gained in their operation and use, so it will be a little time before the full range of techniques available to implementation teams become obvious. In the meantime we can concentrate on a discussion revolving around how Address Book views might be used.

Figure 8.17
Creating a new
Address Book
view

Address Book views attempt to make navigation within large directories easier. A view is a logical grouping of directory entries (mailboxes, custom recipients, distribution lists and even public folders) according to a common set of criteria. For example, a view might incorporate all the entries in the directory that are located in Dublin. Immediately we meet the first issue. Address Book views are only useful if the directory is populated with a reasonable selection of attributes that can be used to create views. If the data held in the directory is minimal, for example, just alias, first name, last name, and display name, then the views that can be created aren't going to be very useful. To create viable views you need first to review and update directory entries with information that could be used to create views, such as the names of cities, countries, departments, offices, or other attributes that make sense within your organization. Processes that feed information into the directory, perhaps as part of directory synchronization with external directories, also need to be reviewed to ensure that any new entries are created with enough information to make address views work properly.

Figure 8.17 shows the grouping properties of an address view. Grouping defines how Exchange orders the directory entries. As you can see, four levels of grouping are supported. In this case the view is being created on the basis of company names, with country names used as a second level grouping. Thus, when the address view is opened we should see directory entries ordered first by company name and then subdivided into countries. Such a view is very appropriate for a company like DIGITAL, which operates in over 80 countries around the world. It possibly wouldn't be appropriate for a company based in a single country, especially if custom recipient entries for external correspondents are also located in the same country. In this instance you'd be better off creating a view based on company and then city. Like sites, geographical terms are a good basis for the creation of views. Countries and cities don't tend to change often whereas other organizational terms, like department names, do.

Figure 8.18
Browsing an Address Book view

The result of the address view ordered by company and then country is shown in Figure 8.18. The screen shot is taken from my group's own production server and illustrates some of the points that I have just made. First, you can see that the view is reasonably effective. The company "Digital Equipment Corporation" is subdivided neatly by country, and expanding the "Belgium" container exposes the entries, all custom recipients in this case, whose directory entry specifies "Belgium" in the country attribute. While the view is reasonably effective we can see a flaw too. Look at the list of company names. There are duplicate entries for "Butterworth Heinemann," one with a hyphen separating the two parts of the company name, and one without. There are two entries for DIGITAL, this time resulting from a mis-spelling of the word "corporation." Without accurate directory information the old adage that rubbish in equals rubbish out will be proved. In this instance the damage is obvious and easily rectified, but this might not be the case always.

Address views are replicated to all sites in the organization. Some agreement or discipline is therefore required among system administrators to assure that everyone works together to create an appropriate set of views. It does not make sense for each site to do their own thing, as all you'll create is a mess.

The results of address views are available to users through the client Address Book. The Show Names From drop-down list (displayed at the right top-hand corner of the window) allows users to select a view to browse for names.

8.6 Directory customization

The Exchange directory is designed for corporate deployments. It would be unreasonable to expect that every company in the world is exactly the same in terms of the information they'd like to hold in a directory, so Exchange allows its directory to be customized to a certain degree in two ways.

First, there are 10 pre-defined custom attributes (or fields) provided for mailbox or custom recipient entries in the directory (no custom attributes are available for distribution lists). The default names for the custom attributes are quite boring—"Custom Attribute 1," "Custom Attribute 2," and so on. But you can easily change the names to whatever you want. For example, you might want to store everyone's car registration number so you can quickly find out who's left their lights on in the car park, or perhaps people's birthdays so you can send them a cheery message on the day in question, or even something boring like their staff numbers. The custom attributes are accessed through the "Custom Attributes" page of the DS Site Configuration object (see Figure 8.19).

Figure 8.19
*DS custom
attributes*

Figure 8.19
*DS custom
attributes*

Changing the name of a custom attribute is one thing. The second customization is used to let people see the newly renamed attributes. Administrators are always able to insert data into the attributes and see what's been put in because the administration program has a "Custom Attributes" page to view mailbox or custom recipient properties. Regular users will be left in the dark unless you customize one of the templates used by Exchange to present attribute information to users, or to allow people to use attributes, for example, to perform a search against the directory. These templates are stored in the Addressing container of a site's Configuration container (see Figure 8.20).

Figure 8.20
*Address
templates*

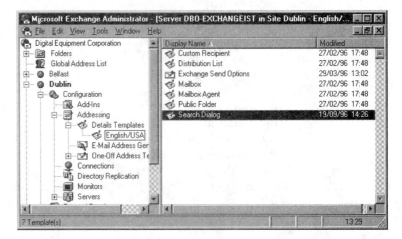

Single-language servers will have templates just for that language while multi-language servers will have templates for all the languages used by clients that connect to that server. Let's assume that we have modified one of the custom attributes to be "Birthday." The following steps would be taken to add this attribute to the set of attributes presented to users when they searched the directory:

1. Open the set of templates for the client language. On US systems this will be English/USA.

2. Click on the "Templates" page. After a brief pause to load in attribute details from the directory schema the set of attributes that users are shown is displayed. Each attribute is defined in terms of its x and y coordinates on a page or set of pages, together with its width and height. All of these definitions are in pixels. Most attributes are 12 pixels high and between 50 and 100 pixels wide. No graphical tool is available to position the new attribute on the page; getting it right is mostly a matter of trial and error.

3. You need to make two additions to the set. One of these is a label, the other the actual "box" that will be used to display the attribute's information.

4. Each page (in the dialog presented to users) must start with a page break. Click on a field below the first page break in the set and then click on the New button. A set of field types will be presented. Select "Label" and enter "Birthday" into the text box. Click on OK to add the new label to the set.

5. Repeat the operation to add the text box to display the attribute information, this time selecting "Edit" from the set of field types. You'll need to spend a little time playing with the X and Y coordinates and the height and width of the fields. As a tip, 10 is the X coordinate that lines up labels on the left-hand side of the screen, and 65 is the corresponding X coordinate to line up the text boxes.

6. When you've entered the two new fields, click on the Test button to view the results. Make whatever changes are required to satisfy yourself as to the appearance of the form until you're happy, then click on OK to save the updated template. Clients will be able to see the updated template immediately, as they will fetch it from the server whenever they attempt to perform a directory search.

Figure 8.21 shows the set of fields for the Search Dialog template together with the set of field types you can add to the dialog. You can see the X and Y coordinates and the width and height settings for all the fields. It's pretty easy to work out how things mesh together to create the screen presented to users, but it would have been much nicer if a more graphical tool was available.

Figure 8.21
*Modifying a
template*

8.6.1   Modifying directory Search Flags

Earlier we discussed Ambiguous Name Resolution (ANR), the process used by Exchange to search the directory to find addresses that match information provided by users. It may be advantageous to alter the directory schema to include our customized field in the ANR process. Each field has a Search Flags property, and the value in this field determines whether the field participates in the ANR process. Normally we can't access or change directory properties through the administration program, but we can through "raw mode," activated by starting AD-MIN.EXE with the /R command line qualifier (Figure 8.22).

Figure 8.22
*Starting
ADMIN.EXE
in raw mode*

When the administration program runs in raw mode you have direct access to the directory schema and properties. Having access is great, but it's also slightly dangerous in so far as it's easy to make mistakes. Normal administration mode attempts to prevent mistakes by presenting directory information through a well-designed user interface. Raw mode circumvents the user interface and therefore avoids its protection.

After starting the administration program in raw mode all of the attributes in the directory can be viewed by selecting View.Raw Directory, an option that's not available in normal mode. At this stage the "Schema" container appears in the left-hand pane and the directory fields are listed in the right hand pane. As you can see from Figure 8.23, the "Birthday" customized field is listed amongst all the others. The raw properties of the attribute are accessed through File.Raw Properties, another option that's only available when working in raw mode.

Figure 8.23
Viewing the directory schema

Move to the Search-Flags attribute by selecting an attribute in the left-hand list box and typing "s". The attribute value should be 0 (zero), meaning that this field does not participate in the ANR process. To allow people to search against birthdays (somewhat weird, but useful to illustrate the point), enter 2 into the edit value field and click on the "Set" button (Figure 8.21). At this stage you'll be warned that messing with directory contents is an activity that shouldn't be undertaken without reference to Microsoft product support. Clicking on OK twice will convince Exchange that you really know what you're doing, and the server will proceed to create an index to use during the ANR process.

Note that any changes you make to the directory are replicated within the site, but no further. This is because the schema is a container within the site container, so its contents are not replicated outside the site. If you want the same changes to be effective at other sites, the changes must be made at a server at those sites.

Figure 8.24
*Amending the
Search-Flags
property*

Testing that the customized fields participate in the ANR process is easy. Select a recipient mailbox, go to the Custom Attributes property page and enter some data into the custom attributes, for example, a birthday of 1 Dec 1961. Create a new message and type the data you just entered into the To: box, and then press CTRL/K. Exchange should take the data and use it to search the directory, returning the name of the recipient whose birthday it is.

8.6.2   Changing display names for LDAP clients

Adding birthday information to the directory is an interesting example of how the directory can be customized, but it doesn't solve any business problems. Changing information provided for LDAP lookups is much more practical.

By default, Exchange provides LDAP clients with the common name attribute any time a client requests information. The common name attribute is normally taken from the directory name, not the display name. However, the directory name differs across recipient types (mailboxes, custom recipients). The directory name is not always what you want displayed, especially if it has been automatically generated through a directory synchronization process, something that often happens when custom recipients are loaded from address information taken from another messaging system.

Exchange allows any directory attribute to be mapped as an LDAP attribute. The normal situation is for the Directory Name attribute to be mapped as "cn", so we need to remap this to point to the Display Name attribute. Do this as follows:

- Start the Exchange Administration program in raw mode.

- Select the Schema container.

- Select the Directory Name object and double click to expose its attributes. Modify the "Description" attribute and change it from the default value ("cn") to something else, such as "ExDirectoryName." Click on OK and confirm that the action should proceed.

- Select the Display Name object and change its "Description" attribute to "cn". Click on OK.

The display name is now mapped to the LDAP common name attribute. Remember that this modification is site-specific and must be made on all sites that provide directory access to LDAP clients.

9

Conducting a Pilot for Exchange Server

9.1 Introduction

Conducting a pilot will be easier for some companies than others, and everyone will find that different aspects of the Exchange server (or clients) and its interoperability with various components of already installed systems have to be covered.

The easiest pilots will be those for sites which already have a Microsoft Mail network up and running. Exchange is the natural and evolutionary path for Microsoft Mail installations and anyone who is operating this mail system should look at Exchange with a very serious eye to a quick introduction to production status. Exchange addresses the majority if not all of the architectural weaknesses of the technology embodied in the Microsoft Mail Post Office and provides a great deal of new functionality at the same time. In addition, Exchange allows you to connect Microsoft Mail clients with the new server fairly easily so users don't have to be retrained when the new server is initially introduced. Finally, the migration wizards that are available for Microsoft Mail are much more developed and functional than the equivalents for any other mail system. The wizards enable Microsoft Mail users to migrate all their messages to Exchange private folders with ease. The fact that the migration wizards for Microsoft Mail are so good isn't altogether surprising but is welcome as it eliminates much of the pain otherwise felt at the user level during any migration process.

Longer and more complex pilots will have to be conducted if you currently operate a non-Microsoft mail system. The degree of complexity will vary considerably and no hard or fast rules can be given yet, but logic indicates that a pilot to assess the technical issues involved in the introduction of Exchange into a Windows-based user community that's already running a LAN-based e-mail system, such as Novell GroupWise or Lotus cc:Mail, might well be easier than the altogether different issues that will come up during an analysis of a similar situation involving a system delivering "more than just mail" already, such as Lotus Notes. In general in these circumstances you won't, for example, have to sort out basic problems like PC networking and connectivity. However, often other non-technical issues like user unwillingness to move to a new system have to be addressed.

9.1.1   What do I want to prove in a pilot?

A pilot implementation of any product seeks to prove that the product is suitable for deployment into a particular production environment. An Exchange pilot is no different. You want to validate many different aspects of your deployment plan to catch and solve any potential problems before they get a chance to occur in production. Among the most important aspects to be validated during the pilot are:

- Windows NT domain design
- Other elements of the Windows NT infrastructure, including items like WINS
- Network capacity and throughput
- Exchange organization design
- Server and client hardware sizing and installation
- The desktop environment, including support for roving and mobile users, if these issues are important to you
- The ease and effectiveness of your migration strategy and the impact on users
- Disaster recovery plans
- Third party software add-ons
- Mobile access

If you accept that the purpose of the pilot is to validate the items listed above it logically follows that the pilot must accurately reflect the production environment that you are attempting to create. In reality this means that the pilot systems must actually be "early deployments," servers that operate under the same Windows NT domain model as intended for the roll-out. The servers should comply with the same organizational model, use the same types of messaging and directory replication connectors, and operate the same software and hardware configurations that you want to use in production. In other words, the pilot is not going to be discarded when it is over. Instead, the pilot systems will evolve into the full-scale deployment and become production servers immediately the pilot period finishes. If you choose to run in any other type of environment you can't be sure that the pilot will accurately validate your design.

Classic pilot systems are usually discarded once the pilot is over, if only to allow the lessons learned from the pilot to be incorporated into a deployment design that is executed from scratch. You can certainly discard the Exchange servers used in a pilot and start over again, but I would only do this if the pilot revealed some fundamental flaws in your design.

9.2 Approaching a pilot

In the world of monolithic, centralized computer applications specifying the boundaries of a pilot was pretty easy. The new mini- or main-frame computer was rolled in, the software was installed, and you connected a number of video terminals to run the application. Between ten and twenty-five terminals were enough to generate a realistic test load for the application's functionality, and you could confidently scale up the results gained from the test to get a good idea of the size of system required to support the eventual user community.

With client/server systems the situation isn't as clear-cut. It is easy to take client software out of the shrink-wrap and install it on individual PCs, then connect the clients to the server to check out the functionality. But this isn't really fulfilling the purpose of the pilot by generating a realistic load to check whether the application will function when it's scaled up. Consider the following questions:

- Are the client platforms used in the pilot representative of the PCs actually used by users? Are the systems covering the range of CPU types and speeds and is the memory configuration the same?

- Are all the client operating systems represented in the pilot—Windows V3, Windows 95, and Windows NT as well as any other non-Windows platforms? In conjunction with this topic I would consider whether you intend to upgrade to a Windows 95 or NT desktop environment in the near future and, if so, what impact this will have on the client configurations under test. How are you going to configure desktop clients so that they can connect to Exchange? Do you have a WINS and DHCP environment to set up?

- What clients are you going to consider for deployment? Are all of these clients going to be adequately tested during the pilot so that a full and fair comparison of the different capabilities can be arrived at? Are you going to use Outlook instead of the standard Exchange client? How will client software be distributed during the pilot and then eventually during the full implementation?

- Are all connectors going to be tested in the pilot? If you plan to use the X.400 connector to connect sites together in production there's little point in using the Internet Mail Service or site connector for this purpose during the pilot. If you plan to use connectors to foreign messaging systems such as PROFS, SNADS, Lotus Notes, or FAX then these should be factored into the pilot too.

- What will you do to satisfy people who use systems like Apple Macintosh, IBM OS/2 or UNIX workstations? There is an Apple Macintosh client for Exchange, but perhaps it's not suitable because you're not running the appropriate hardware or software revisions. The obvious solution is to deploy either POP3 or Web clients for these platforms, but you have to make a choice and test one or both options. Will the POP3 or Web clients be used in other circumstances than non-Wintel platforms?

- Are the network connections between the clients and servers the same as will be used in production? For instance, do you need to check out remote access over an asynchronous telephone connection?

- Is the software installed in the same method as you want to use for full deployment? For example, do you want to test the difference (if any) in start-up time for client software loaded from a network file service and local hard disks?

- Are all third party add-ons going to be tested during the pilot? Backup products such as Cheyenne ArcServe or Seagate's Backup Exec provide significant advantages over the standard Windows NT backup software, but they have to be tested during a pilot in order for you to take maximum advantage of their capabilities when they go into production. For example, you need to ensure that your disaster recovery plan (which, of course, you also have ready to go) incorporates the installation of third party backup software.

- Can the client software be deployed and managed easily? Microsoft's solution is System Management Server (SMS), another part of the Back Office suite, but you may already have another PC management tool in place. How will this work with Exchange?

Another point to consider is the type of personnel taking part in the pilot. To provide an accurate assessment of any application's value in real life it's important that a good cross-section of the user population is included in the pilot. If you have people who have never seen PCs in their lives before then clearly the pilot is going to take a long time before any worthwhile data becomes available. On the other hand, you don't want to staff the pilot with too many technical people because they tend to be either too forgiving or too critical of a product's performance depending on whether they "like" the product. Liking a product often comes down to whether someone approves of the technical nature of the product, the vendor, or any associated reasons that come to hand during coffee room debates!

All of the above points could be made for any PC client/server product. Because Microsoft Exchange is a messaging system there are some other important points that must be considered during a pilot. These include:

- How will the entries for Exchange mailboxes and custom recipients be synchronized with other directory sources? This is only going to be really important if you already have a messaging system in production. If you do, you better make sure that it is possible to achieve an easy synchronization of addresses between Exchange and the other system, using an automated procedure if at all possible. Can the same synchronization procedure handle address information from all the potential sources within your organization? Is the synchronization bi-directional or only one-way?

- How will Exchange send and receive messages to and from any other messaging system that's in place internally or externally? What connectors (SMTP, X.400, etc.) are going to be operational and how will you test the connection between Exchange and other messaging systems? Do you have a full list of all the connections already used by people within your organization? How will you test that multi-bodypart messages are able to flow from one side to the other while preserving their essential attributes?

- Can the content of messages generated and sent by Exchange be read after they have been delivered to people using the other messaging systems in place within your organization? Exchange is able to generate messages in Rich Text Format (RTF) and ASCII. It is indeed wonderful to be able to send your thoughts out to the world in bold red 24 point Arial. There shouldn't be many problems with messages generated in ASCII, but will recipients throughout your organization (and beyond) be able to deal with RTF and Word?

Asking these questions, even if you think you're pretty sure of the answers, is a good way to make sure that all the essential issues are covered during the pilot. Possibly even more important, it's a way to isolate potential costs so that you can factor them into a deployment budget. Software components like directory synchronizers, format converters, and mail gateways are expensive to buy or build. It's important that you uncover all the situations where additional costs might be incurred before Exchange can be put into full production. If you don't you'll find that your deployment schedule and budget will be afflicted by complexities that arise and have to be dealt with when you should really be concentrating on delivery. Good preparation is half the battle in achieving good deployments.

Failure to ask the correct questions both when considering a migration and during a pilot implementation inevitably ends up in an exercise that's a waste of time, energy, and money, and one that will lead to a shoddy deployment that delivers a low level of service to the user community.

9.2.1   The numbers involved in the pilot

Anybody can set up a single Exchange server and connect a few clients to it. A single Exchange server is not an accurate or even useful pilot for a corporate deployment because you're not reflecting the production environment. Here are some guidelines to consider in terms of the number of systems and users that should participate in pilots to validate plans for large corporate deployments.

- **Servers and Sites**: You need to test messaging connectivity and directory/public folder replication. This requires at least three servers, in at least two sites. The sites should be connected using the connectors you intend to use in production. If you only have two sites but intend to use more than one type of connector in production you can configure the different connectors to link the two sites for different periods during the pilot. If the final design calls for sites to be connected across different Windows NT domains then reflect this fact in the pilot and make sure that you test items such as public folder affinity and message tracking.

- **Users and Clients**: You need to place a real load on the servers, and test Exchange across a wide variety of user types and client platforms. Confining the pilot to a group of technical users from the MIS department, all of who run well-configured Windows NT workstations is not a true test if the majority of target users are currently running Microsoft Mail on low-end 80486-class systems. It's best to look for a reasonably large user population (between 50 and 100) spread across several types of people (technical, non-technical) who use the complete range of clients that need to be supported in production. Non-technical users will tell you how much training is really required to help their peers once Exchange is being rolled out to everyone, and the problems they encounter during the pilot will assist the help desk to determine how they can best support the user community.

Engaging in such a comprehensive pilot may seem like a lot of effort, but you should remember two things. First, getting your design for Exchange deployment right is a critical success factor and, to some degree, it's a one-time operation. If you get your design wrong it might mean that you have to re-implement some or all of your deployment. Second, my attitude is that pilot systems are just an early deployment and will not be thrown away after the pilot. Thus, any work that's done to make the pilot a success is even more valuable than it seems at first.

9.3 Training

I don't believe anyone can pick up the documentation set for Exchange and become a trained expert by close study of its contents. It's good to read the documentation, including the release notes, but some degree of formal training should be part of the project plan for any pilot.

Initially you'll want to cover training focused towards system management and administration. Programming, including the whiz-bang aspects of Exchange like electronic folders and MAPI, can be left until the next phase (formal deployment) begins. It's essential to master the basics of any subject, and the basics of Exchange include topics like planning the network, defining how servers are placed into sites, the relationship with the Windows NT security model, and other aspects of system management.

Your pilot shouldn't ignore user training. The people participating in the pilot will need some training, otherwise they won't be able to properly exercise the product's functionality, so make sure that at least one formal training session is made available to pilot users. It's likely that you won't have in-house skills to be able to run this course so you need to contact a local Microsoft qualified training centre (ATEC) and get them involved.

9.3.1 Helping users form good habits

The opportunity to give people good e-mail habits is one major advantage gained through well-planned user training. If people learn how to do things properly right from the start they'll work with the system in an intelligent and constructive manner. Table 9.1 lists ten good user habits that you may want to encourage. Use this table as a base to build on, adding your own ideas to the list.

Table 9.1   *Good user habits to encourage*

1	Make a decision to delete or keep a message as soon as you've read it. If you're keeping the message move it into an appropriate folder.
2	Check the "Empty Deleted Items folder upon exiting" option. This deletes unwanted mail and stops it accumulating in the Deleted Items folder.
3	Don't include the text of original messages in replies as this increases the overall size of messages within the system.
4	Don't include documents in messages unless you really need to. Send pointers to documents (the name of the file in a shared file service, a suitable public folder, or a short-cut to the document) if at all possible.
5	Don't use messaging as a way to broadcast information to people who may not want to receive it. In other words, try and keep the distribution list for messages as short as possible.
6	Don't add graphics to Auto Signature files as this will drive up the overall size of messages and create a demand the network may not be able to handle.
7	Compact personal folder files on a regular basis to reclaim space on your hard disk.
8	Don't leave an unattended PC logged into your Exchange account. Protect your work with a password-protected screen saver or log-out of Exchange if you have to leave your PC alone.
9	If you travel with your computer remember to download the off-line address book before you leave for a trip. This makes sure that any message you create while traveling will be addressed correctly. Remember to synchronize some or all of the folders in your mailbox before you travel as otherwise you won't see up-to-date information when you work off-line.
10	Use the Out of Office Assistant to notify people whenever you won't be able to respond to messages for any reason.

Many installations print up "cheat sheets" for users to publicize hints and tips. Users can keep the cheat sheets beside their PCs and if you take the opportunity to inform people about good working habits among the other hints and tips there's a fair chance that users will actually follow the advice.

During the pilot it's a good idea to check with the people who received training and see whether the training was relevant and helpful. After reviewing feedback from users who have received training you can decide whether or not the same training can be used during the roll-out phase. Bear in mind that off-the-shelf training is often delivered at a lowest common denominator level so the content of the initial course will often need to be adjusted to reflect your organization's computing infrastructure as well as how you intend to use Exchange in day-to-day life. Some people are happy enough to go with standard training, perhaps supplementing the course material with a booklet covering site-specific details while others design and deliver their own tailored training. Cost, as always, has some bearing on the decision, but remember that good training will invariably repay its cost several times over by driving down the number of calls that support personnel have to deal with.

9.3.2 Programmer and administrator training

User training is a critical part of the pilot, but it's a mistake to concentrate totally on this aspect alone. Programmers and system administrators will also need training and this need should be factored into an overall training plan that begins in the pilot stage and continues on through implementation.

Consider the skills necessary in an Exchange environment. In your environment they might include:

- Windows NT server including Apple Macintosh client and networking support (if required).

- Exchange Server and clients

- TPC/IP utilities such as WINS, DHCP, and DNS

- SMTP, X.400, and the site connectors, plus knowledge of any other messaging systems you want to connect to

- Associated technologies such as Windows NT workstation

- Directory synchronization with external directories

- Migration tools and utilities

- Windows 95, Windows V3.11, DOS, UNIX utilities associated with SMTP-based messaging such as sendmail, and Internet firewalls

- Visual Basic, Visual C++, and other development tools used to build or enhance electronic forms applications

- General networking experience

Few people have the ability to master all of these skills, neither time nor the wide experience required to achieve a good understanding of them all. This means that you'll probably need to spread skills across a team of individuals engaged in the pilot or use expertise brought in externally.

Don't forget other associated developments that may be happening at the same time as they may affect your pilot or the implementation by introducing new skills that must be factored into a training plan. For instance, SMS might be used to manage the deployment of

Exchange clients and other desktop applications. Or your company may well have decided to use the Microsoft Internet Explorer (client) and Microsoft Internet Information Server for World Wide Web access and home page management. Who's responsible for these issues?

9.4   Was the pilot successful?

At the end of the exercise all pilots have to come up with some results, the most fundamental of which is an assessment of whether the product under trial is suitable for widespread deployment. Attached to this assessment are many caveats that determine the degree of success the deployment is likely to have. You may find that network links between servers need to be upgraded, that new hardware needs to be installed, client systems need more memory, or even that the whole thing should be put off for six months or so to allow you to sort out some other aspect of the overall infrastructure. You'll definitely need to have carefully built a draft plan for the roll-out in order to gauge whether a roll-out is feasible. The plan should include details of the Exchange sites and servers that are proposed together with details of how the Exchange structure is layered on top of the Windows NT security and network models. Finally, you should have a technical and end-user training plan laid out. All of these conclusions need to be documented and reviewed so that all possible issues are fully covered.

At the end of the day your management are likely to ask a number of basic questions that you'll need to have good answers for. Among the normal questions in this category are:

- How much will the deployment cost in total—software (server and clients), hardware (including upgrades), training, systems management, day-to-day operations, and consultancy?

- How long will the complete roll-out take from beginning to end?

- What benefits will the new messaging environment deliver to the organization (in general) as well as the end-users?

The final question is whether or not it is worthwhile to move from an existing messaging infrastructure to a new one, albeit one as interesting as Microsoft Exchange. That question deserves far more attention than a brief paragraph or two here, so I'll cover it in detail in a separate chapter.

9.5   Summary

Running a pilot is always an interesting and important activity because it's the place where marketing hype is discarded and technical reality comes into focus. A good plan for the pilot that identifies all the important questions for your organization is an essential aid to producing accurate results and eventually a productive long-term implementation. Hopefully this chapter has managed to identify some of the challenges that you're likely to meet along the way if you make the decision to look at Microsoft Exchange Server and its clients.

10

Migrating from Other Messaging Systems

10.1   An end, or a beginning?

Computer applications evolve in either of two ways. One route is to continually update, applying software and hardware upgrades as they become available. The other is to migrate from one system to another. The former is less painful than the latter, but sometimes a migration is deemed to be imperative and so it proceeds. In this chapter we'll look at some of the aspects of messaging systems that migrations bring to the fore, with particular reference to the tasks involved in planning for and then executing a migration of a messaging system to Microsoft Exchange Server.

I hate migrations. It's a fact of life that a large number of Exchange installations will involve a migration in some form or other. Any migration I have ever been involved with has been painful, and many have left a bad taste in my mouth. No migration is or can be seamless and users always experience some impact. So it's important to be sure that a migration is justified, feasible, and the right thing to do. Asking yourself some questions and making sure you have answers, and then analyzing the content of the answers is an excellent way of verifying that a migration is the right thing to do. In my opinion, among the first questions that must be answered in relation to a migration from an existing electronic mail system to Exchange are:

- Why are we considering a migration away from our existing system?

- What benefits are going to be delivered to the user community after the migration is accomplished?

- Can the benefits be quantified in terms of finance or extra functionality that can now be provided to users?

- When do we want the migration to be completed by?

- What data will be involved in the migration?

■ How will the data be migrated?

Different organizations will place varying degrees of importance on the questions listed above, and no doubt everyone has their own specific questions that they'll want to add. I feel it's important to have absolute clarity about all the issues before plunging into a migration so that those involved can justify the time, expense, and other costs to both users and management.

Perhaps another question that should be asked at this time is whether a better and more effective job can be done with the messaging system that you're considering moving from? I have seen many situations where a messaging system is badly managed and doesn't deliver a good level of service to user communities. It may well be the case that replacing the current system with a new system, like Exchange, will draw a line underneath all of the ineffective management that has gone before, but it's more likely that the old bad habits will be transferred from one system to another. Clearly if you're aware of the danger, steps can be taken to ensure that current problems are addressed and eliminated as part of the migration project.

If a mail system is in operation today you should take advantage by extracting various operational statistics to help understand:

■ The volume of messages being processed by the system.

■ The amount of data (messages) being stored in shared system areas and user (or personal) areas.

■ Details of any other application that depends in any way on the messaging system. Workflow systems are obvious examples of systems which often depend on electronic mail, but there can be applications that make sporadic use of electronic mail, possibly to generate warning or other status messages, and you need to know about these.

■ The service levels being delivered to users. For example, how long does it take to transfer a message from one side of the organization to another? How long does it take for a message to arrive within the same physical site?

Migrations are unsuccessful if the new system cannot meet the same service levels as the existing system once the migration process is complete. If the hardware installed cannot cope with the volume of messages, if applications are disabled because they cannot communicate using the messaging system, if user data is lost or otherwise becomes inaccessible, or message delivery times are not improved then you really have to ask why you are even considering a migration in the first place.

10.2   Why migrate at all?

Are you migrating to Microsoft Exchange Server because:

- You think it's a good idea, and anyway, everyone else seems to want to do it.

- Windows NT is the strategic computing platform for your organization, or at least Windows NT is the strategic choice for distributed application servers.

- Microsoft is the preferred software vendor for desktop and other applications.

- Exchange offers a significant increase in the functionality you already enjoy from your existing system.

- Exchange is the natural upgrade path for your existing mail system.

- The operation of an Exchange server will help to achieve a return on the additional investment required to perform the migration.

Not many people will openly agree with the first response listed above. Thinking something is a good idea is not a rational argument to back up a major change in any technical or computing infrastructure. The old adage "There goes the crowd; I must be with them" springs to mind here. Are you proposing to migrate because someone else says that it's a good idea?

I often wonder about the ideas and opinions expressed in the content of reviews written in computer magazines as well as the conclusions reached at the end of product reviews. There's no doubt that many journalists are very competent individuals with a broad range of expertise, but it's difficult to write knowledgeably about a mail system unless you've lived and breathed with the system in an operational environment over a period of time. Running a messaging system for ten or twenty users is easy, running the same software for hundreds of users exposes the weak points as well as the strengths. The lesson here is simple. Never take someone else's opinion as fact. You know your computing environment best so accept input from many sources and then make your own mind up.

10.2.1   Dealing with the existing investment

Many companies find themselves in a situation where they have a huge financial investment in their current mainframe or mini-computer based electronic mail system. The investment is represented by hardware, software licenses, knowledge (programming, administration, and user), data, any associated applications which may use the system in one form or another, the infrastructure put in place to enable the electronic mail system to operate, and whatever connections exist to other messaging systems. Quite a shopping list when the time comes to justify a migration!

If you find yourself in a situation where your company really must continue to leverage off its existing financial investment and can't afford to engage in a total migration the best tactic to adopt is to establish Exchange as the "new" platform. If any opportunity arises to move users off the older system, perhaps as hardware maintenance contracts expire or systems reach their end of life, or new user communities request an electronic mail server they can be attached to an Exchange server. This tactic establishes a situation where two "islands" of electronic messaging exist within the company—the old established system and Exchange. Gradually, over time, the aim is to grow the Exchange island and diminish the other and get to a stage where a total cut-over can be justified.

An approach like this minimizes the additional investment required to introduce Exchange while it maximizes the investment represented by the existing system. It also allows the Exchange implementation to progress at a comfortable, well-controlled pace. On the other hand, you will have to devote a lot of time and attention to ensuring that the best possible connectivity is maintained between the two messaging islands.

Electronic mail is a highly visible application because it affects almost every desktop in a company. Everyone from the Chief Executive Officer down to the newest entrant might well be using e-mail, so when something goes wrong its effects are felt everywhere, including in the job continuation prospects of system administrators. Accordingly it is essential that the migration is done right no matter what tactics need to be adopted in order to achieve eventual success.

10.2.2   Strategic computing platforms

The decision about the strategic computing platform for your organization is often not surrounded in clarity. The larger the organization and the more autonomous the divisions within the organization the harder it is to enforce strategic decisions. In these situations you'll often find tactical compromises being made to facilitate the requirements of specific applications or organizational entities.

Windows NT grows in capability and functionality all the time. The original version (V3.1) was slow, lacked applications, and needed lots of hardware. Even so, V3.1 created a clear differentiation between

Windows, the user-oriented desktop operating system, and a much more robust and interesting high-end server specifically designed for applications. Each release since has added functionality to the point where Windows NT workstation is a more than viable option for deployment as a generalized desktop platform, and Windows NT server is probably the most flexible distributed application server available today. It's important not to engage in too much hype however. Windows NT is good, but there are lots of situations where it would be inappropriate or just plain foolish to even consider NT. The time when Windows NT takes over from mainframes with applications like airline booking systems is probably not yet with us!

If your organization has determined that Windows NT is a strategic computing platform the decision to migrate towards Exchange is easy. But what happens if the strategic platform is UNIX (any variant), or a proprietary operating system such as OpenVMS or IBM MVS? How then does Exchange fit into the overall picture? Can the implementation of an electronic messaging system on Windows NT be represented (and agreed on) as a tactical solution? And how will the Windows NT servers fit into other aspects of the computing infrastructure such as network security or integrated network management?

Even if Windows NT is the nominated choice for a strategic organization-wide computing platform you must ensure that the implementation of Exchange accommodates the Windows NT domain and network infrastructures that might already be in place. Or if you're only starting with Windows NT, as we've mentioned before, the initial implementation of Windows NT must take the requirements of Exchange into account. Remember that it is very difficult to change items such as server and site names once the implementation starts, so it's important to take these factors into account in your migration plan.

If Windows NT is new to your organization a migration is easier because you can plan the introduction of Exchange and Windows NT together as an integrated entity rather than having to retrofit Exchange on top of an existing NT infrastructure. However, the purely practical aspects involved in the introduction of any new computer platform such as physical security, data backups, and communications might well be impacted by the requirements of Exchange. For instance, how will the Exchange data structures be backed up, when will this take place, and will it stop people using the messaging service while backups are made?

The question of Microsoft as the preferred vendor for software applications is linked, in some respects, to the decision about Windows NT. If Windows NT is your strategic computing platform then there are strong and compelling reasons to select other Microsoft applications in the areas they are available. All of the products in the BackOffice and Microsoft Office sets fall into this category.

10.2.3   Will Exchange provide more functionality than my existing system?

Determining whether a move to Exchange will provide more functionality than an existing system depends on:

- The functionality in Exchange that your users will actually use. For example, there's no value at all in replication of public folders if this type of information sharing is not going to be used.

- Whether any commonly used or otherwise desirable features available in the existing system are not available in Exchange. Workflow is one example. The workflow currently available in Exchange is not as good as that available in Lotus Notes, for example, and if many workflow applications are used on a day-to-day basis to solve real business problems you'll have a challenge to move the people who depend on those applications if you can't come up with a replacement, not to mention a method to access old data represented by workflow items that have been processed in the past.

Knowledge of the features the user community deems to be important is essential when you compare one system against another. You might get excited about the prospect of the latest whiz-bang-wallop feature that's only available in a specific product. However, how many people actually use all of the features provided in the products they have today and will your users feel the same way about the features you now propose to introduce? Will the feature make them more productive, assuming they'll ever use it?

The AutoSignature and Inbox Assistant features offered by Exchange clients are two good examples of what I mean. AutoSignature allows users to add a piece of text to messages before they are sent to provide additional information about the originator. In the UNIX messaging world this text is known as a signature. Inbox Assistant can act as a filter against new mail messages as they arrive, taking action for messages that meet preset criteria. For instance, refile all new messages from my manager into the wastebasket, or send anything that references a particular project to another user because they've taken responsibility for that project now.

10.2.4   Following the upgrade paths

Microsoft Mail is the only mail system for which Exchange can reasonably be regarded as the natural or evolutionary upgrade path. Indeed, the primary market for the initial implementations of Exchange is the many thousands of Microsoft Mail post offices running around the world.

So if you're running Microsoft Mail now you have the easiest argument to make for a migration. Exchange servers can be installed to take the place of the Microsoft Mail Post Offices, and the Microsoft Mail clients can be replaced by Exchange clients. Because the two clients come from the same vendor they share many common features, at least on the surface and in terminology, so the visual and immediate impact on day to day use after a switch-over is reasonably limited. Exchange Server includes a migration wizard to help users transfer the contents of their Microsoft Mail file cabinets into Exchange, so most of the important points in relation to a migration can be taken care of in an almost automatic manner. If you're running another mail system the situation is different. No other vendor is going to be happy to see customers migrating away from their software (not to mention hardware), so you can hardly expect to see glowing recommendations for Exchange as the upgrade option of choice. You can also expect to incur more costs during the migration because the movement of user information, messages, and documents is not going to be as automatic or straightforward.

10.2.5 Achieving a return on your investment

Messaging often becomes a mission-critical application. In other words, if messaging is not available to users business suffers. Even after messaging is acknowledged to be a mission-critical application you want to get good value for the investment made to build and operate the messaging environment. If you now propose to migrate from one system to another then ideally the total value gained from the exercise should exceed the costs by a considerable margin.

Determining an accurate total for the costs of migration is not an exact science as there are many factors that will influence the outcome. Migrations tend to be difficult to cost to any exact degree. In fact, migrations are rather like household do-it-yourself exercises in that hidden costs reveal themselves after a start is made on a job. For instance, you decide to change the wallpaper in a room only to find that there are holes behind the existing wallpaper, so you need to fill them in. Once the paper is up it looks good, but the woodwork looks dull and blemished in comparison so you really need to apply a new coat of paint. And if the woodwork is done the ceilings should be done to match. All additional costs.

To avoid unpleasant surprises I think it's a good idea to set down a list of bullet points to cover the major cost headings. Here are some common areas of cost that might be met during a migration:

- Installation and configuration of all the necessary hardware, including upgrades to existing computers.

- Installation and configuration of Windows NT on the hardware according to the domain and security models you have chosen to use.

- Licensing and installation of Exchange on all relevant Windows NT computers and clients on whatever PCs are required.

- Training people to use the client functionality (this is more expensive if you have to support a number of clients), including details about how to get to data that might remain on other systems.

- Migrating user messages and documents from the existing mail system.

- Running a pilot and then proceeding with a roll-out.

Apart from the financial aspects of a migration I think it is also wise to consider the question of the long-term future for your current electronic mail system. Ask the vendor whether plans exist for new versions, when the new versions will be available and what features will be delivered in the new releases. If there is little future in the current mail system then the financial aspects of a proposal to migrate to Exchange may quickly become a moot point. If a migration is going to be required anyway at some point in the future it makes sense to take the pain now to establish a new messaging system and go forward so that maximum benefit can be gained from the new system. On the other hand, if detailed plans exist to develop and enhance your existing electronic mail system the question of how much it will cost to upgrade to new releases should be asked. If you don't have a maintenance or other type of support contract you may have to purchase server and client software again, albeit possibly at a discounted price, but even if the software upgrades are free what other possible costs might be incurred? The points above list some of the areas where costs may arise. It's often a useful exercise to compare the costs of migration against the costs of staying with an existing mail system, as shown in Table 10.1. There are two ways to approach this exercise. First, you can assume that the existing system will stay in place in much the same shape as it is today. Or, more realistically if users are complaining about the features and service provided by the current system, you can factor in the costs to evolve the system so that it provides approximately the same level of functionality as you can expect from Exchange.

Table 10.1 *Comparing the cost of upgrading or migrating*

Potential area of cost	$ cost of migration to Microsoft Exchange	$ cost to evolve existing electronic mail system
Client software.		
Server software.		
Ongoing support costs for client software. For example, the cost to upgrade to new releases of the software or the right to report problems to a support center.		
Ongoing support costs for server software.		
User training. Remember that moving to a new version of any software may impact users and require some degree of retraining.		
Programmer/system manager training.		
Any additional or new hardware costs (memory upgrades, disks, etc.) for user PCs.		
Any additional or new hardware costs for the servers involved in the electronic mail system.		
External consulting or other personnel costs.		
Messaging gateways. Some gateways may only be required during the migration period.		
File format converters or viewers either for PC clients or elsewhere in the network.		
Associated applications (e.g. time management, workflow), both servers and clients. Costs might include rewriting or replacing applications.		
Directory synchronization, both initial costs to implement synchronization plus ongoing costs to ensure that synchronization occurs on a regular and predictable basis.		
Ongoing system management/system administration.		
Operating a user Help Desk.		
Remote access (telephone communications, RAS systems and whatever other infrastructure is required).		
LAN/WAN networks and other communications. For example, will you require new telecommunications links?		
Overall Total Costs	$	$

Listing the potential areas of cost is easy, but putting a real degree of exactitude on these costs is not. Costs are likely to occur over an extended period of time and the amounts involved will differ from site to site. The desired (or required) rate of return on investments will also vary from organization to organization. Technical people might sometimes wish that financial issues would go away but you have to be able to answer the question about how much the whole exercise will cost, and what additional value will be delivered to the organization once the migration is complete. Saying that everything will be better, more up to date, more robust and compliant with standards, messages will be transmitted more securely and faster or that the Exchange architecture is much more impressive than the current system will surely cut no ice with the financial wizards. It's better to come up with some realistic figures for the work, factor them into an operational budget, and seek to justify the expenditure through reasons like:

- Lower cost of ownership (based on deployment on Windows NT systems rather than mini- or mainframe computers) over a reasonable period, say three years.

- Enabling the organization to achieve higher levels of quality through the deployment of work-group applications rather than the purely interpersonal nature of simple electronic mail. Give some examples to illustrate the point such as the use of replicated public folders to automatically distribute up to date marketing information across the enterprise.

- Implementation of other valued-added applications enabled by Exchange that solve business problems. For instance, integrating a voice mail system with Exchange to replace an existing voice mail system that may be standalone and perhaps showing signs of age.

Whatever logic you come up with to justify the decision you must be realistic. Use figures intelligently to show cost benefits and illustrate your points with examples of how new functionality will enable people to work together more effectively. If your logic is not reasonable and cannot be backed up to other peoples' satisfaction the decision to progress with a migration is probably not a good one and you should take another hard look at your situation before going on.

10.3   When will the migration be over?

Migrations, like all other techniques, occupy a spectrum defining the different approaches that can be taken to the actual process. At one end you have the "Big Bang" approach, moving all users as quickly as possible from the old system to the new. Right at the other end of the spectrum is the phased, gentle movement, generally involving the migration of groups of users over an extended period of time.

Few experienced system managers like the risk factor involved in one-shot migrations. The one-shot technique is only ever practiced when the number of users and data involved is small, certainly at levels where people are comfortable that the migration can be carried out in a single day or over a weekend. Extended migration periods can be difficult to manage, and more often than not involve the introduction of potential bottlenecks as messages pass through gateways. Directory synchronization for addressing information is also an issue to be managed during migrations. We'll discuss these points in more detail later on in this chapter.

Most organizations will conduct a pilot for Exchange before engaging in widespread deployment. Even if you have made a strategic decision to use Windows NT and Exchange as your future messaging platform it's still a good idea to run a pilot. To reinforce the advice offered throughout this book, consider these good reasons for including a pilot implementation of Exchange server and clients in your migration plan:

- A pilot allows technical staff to get to know the capabilities and weaknesses of the new server in a real-life environment. You can use this experience to plan for:

  o The hardware configuration for server deployment. Determine how many servers will be required to support the total user population and where those servers will be located, as well as how they will form sites within the Exchange organization. You should make a first pass at allocating users across the servers. You should consider the hardware and software required for client deployments too!

  o The operational rules to be followed by system administrators and operators. For example, when will backups be made and how will the backups be secured?

  o The network links required to connect servers and clients. Do you need to reconfigure any parts of the network?

  o The way Exchange will be installed on top of the Windows NT domain and security models deployed within the organization. If problems are detected the models may need adjustment, work that must be carried out before general deployment of Exchange begins.

  o What third party software will be used in conjunction with Exchange? There is no point on planning to use different backup software, or a fax connector, or a full text retrieval package or virus checker in production if you don't include it in the pilot. The pilot will reveal the good and bad points about the add-on software, allowing you to make a more intelligent decision about its deployment into production environments.

○ The order in which different groups within the organization will be moved to Exchange. In general it's best to plan to move groups that share a high degree of data commonality at one time in order to maximize the usefulness of functionality like public folders and to minimize the message flow outside the Exchange environment. This part of your plan will also help you identify when older systems can be switched off and hardware removed (and hardware and software maintenance contracts for the old systems terminated).

○ Which Exchange servers will act as messaging servers and which will fulfill special roles such as points of connection with foreign messaging systems or public folder servers?

○ Which clients will be used—Exchange, Outlook, Web, POP3?

○ Migration of documents and users. Perhaps some special tools are required to extract, manipulate, and then import data from the system you are migrating from. If so, can these tools be obtained from external agencies or will they have to be written internally?

■ Users need to be trained as they move from the older system to an Exchange client. A training plan should be prepared so that the user community is ready to move. The pilot allows the plan to be developed and verified. The training plan should answer questions like:

○ What training will they receive? Will you provide users with customized quick look-up guides or cheat sheets for items specific to your environment such as electronic forms applications? Are there any good habits (for example, how to effectively use disk space within the private information store) that you want to enforce during training sessions?

○ Do users need to be told how to deal with data migrated from the old system? For example, how to deal with distribution lists that contain a mixture of people using the old system as well as Exchange.

○ Who will deliver the training? Do you have an internal training department that can do the work or will an external training provider come in to deliver courses? How much will the training cost? Do you have a proposal to charge departments for the training their personnel will receive or will the total cost of the training be rolled up into the overall migration plan?

    ○ When is the training available? Make sure that training is synchronized with the movement of users to Exchange. Training people too early is nearly as bad as training them too late.

■ Support must be put in place so it's important to involve those who deliver end-user support in the pilot. Support personnel need training too, and this requirement should be addressed in the overall training plan. Experience gained in the pilot will help you identify exactly what form and content that training should take.

A proper pilot cannot be rushed. There's always a temptation to take a short cut on the basis that the sooner the new system goes into production the better, but this is a short-term view that inevitably leads to tears. The old adage that fools rush in where angels fear to tread comes to mind here.

Several times during 1995 Bill Gates was widely quoted to say that Exchange would not ship until its customers told Microsoft that it was ready (the same was said about Windows 95). Customers in this sense are the technical community, not end-users, and the judgment as to when the software was ready was made in a technical context and not related in any sense to corporate deployments. Make sure you are ready on all fronts by conducting a comprehensive pilot before proceeding with the migration. How long will this take? That depends on your organization, but allow at least two months.

After a good pilot you should have much of the information necessary for the deployment. You won't have everything, and you can expect to encounter unforeseen problems as you proceed, but at least you should be confident enough to plan for a fairly aggressive roll-out schedule. Migrating 50 to 100 users a week is certainly a sustainable rate over a prolonged period of time. Going any faster will place strain on everyone—the implementation team, technical support, help desk, training department, and the users themselves. At 50–100 users per week you'll be able to migrate between 2,500 and 5,000 users in a year while maintaining service levels to users.

10.4 Migrating information

Messaging systems, or rather messaging systems that are not well managed, have a remarkable tendency to accumulate vast quantities of data. Even when systems are managed and the amount of messages users can keep are restricted there will still be a fair amount of data to deal with when migration time comes around.

All messaging systems have some degree of junk mail. By this I mean messages that have no relationship to any business activity. Invitations to lunch, to meet after hours, to engage in a social activity, or just people exchanging views on the major topics of the day all generate message traffic, tying up valuable disk space and possibly even preventing users sending business messages because some system limits are reached. Clearly junk mail should not be migrated and the first step before attempting to perform any migration is to strip any such messages from the system.

Figure 10.1
*The Migration
Wizard*

The largest folder I ever saw in active use in a mail system held 14,000 messages, while the largest file cabinet held 225,000 objects. Migrating message containers that hold such a large volume of documents is clearly a challenge, but maybe you don't have to migrate them at all. Can the older file cabinet system remain in situ for an agreed length of time after users begin to use Exchange as their default messaging system? Can the documents be accessed in a mode that allows users to perform read, fetch, and delete operations, perhaps from a customized version of the application that they were originally created with? If you decide to leave the older system operational, albeit in a read-only mode, it's a good idea to clearly set a date in the future at which time the older system will be disconnected. Turning off a system, albeit it on a clearly advertised date is hard for users as it irrevocably removes their access to documents that may well contain valuable information and this is the point when migration utilities need to be considered.

10.4.1   Migration wizards and other tools

Microsoft has provided a tool called the Migration Wizard to move messages and other information created in foreign messaging systems to Exchange. The Migration Wizard always runs on a Windows NT workstation or server, so the information it processes must be made available to the Wizard. This is done in two ways:

- Direct access (perhaps via a networked drive) to PC files. This is the approach taken when migrating messages from Microsoft Mail and Lotus cc:Mail post offices.

- Stripping information from a messaging system and writing it out into files in a highly structured manner. These files are then moved to the Windows NT system and processed by the Migration Wizard. This is the approach used to migrate host-based electronic mail systems.

The Exchange Migration Wizard is able to migrate messages from the following messaging systems:

- Microsoft Mail
- DIGITAL ALL-IN-1
- IBM PROFS
- Lotus cc:Mail
- Novell Groupwise
- Netscape Collabra
- Verimation MEMO

The Exchange resource kit includes unsupported migration utilities to help migrate users of UNIX systems that use the sendmail utility. Even though they are built around a standard utility, the nature of UNIX means that sendmail-based messaging systems vary greatly in implementation. The sendmail migration utilities might therefore be regarded as a starting point, something that may require additional effort to get right in any particular set of circumstances.

While all migrations eventually use the same Migration Wizard to import data there are fundamental differences between e-mail systems built around PC LAN file-sharing architectures and those that run on mini- or mainframe computers. When dealing with a PC LAN-based mail system, like Microsoft Mail or Lotus cc:Mail, the extract and load operations can sometimes be carried out on the same server, or at least the extract files can be created and immediately accessed by the migration wizard on a network file location that's accessible from the Windows NT computer where Exchange Server is running. This makes the whole process much easier as you don't have to copy files around the network during the transfer. Because data held in host-based systems (PROFS, MEMO, and ALL-IN-1) is not normally directly accessible from Windows NT the basic approach to the task of migration is evolved a little into three phases, illustrated in Figure 10.2.

1. Create the extract files on the host system. Procedures for the supported operating system are provided as part of the Exchange kit and can be used to create the extract files. The procedures are written in languages (interpreted or compiled) appropriate for the operating system. For example, some of the procedures to migrate information from Verimation MEMO systems are written in the JCL (Job Control Language) for IBM MVS mainframes while forms, scripts, and some VMS Macro code are provided for ALL-IN-1 systems.

2. Transfer the extract files to the target Exchange server. Some form of network connection can be used or the information can be transferred using magnetic media.

3. Run the Exchange Migration Wizard.

Figure 10.2
Steps in migrating host-based messages

Apart from the ease of data access (for PC-based migration utilities), the potential volume of data that may need to be migrated often marks another difference between host- and PC-based electronic mail systems. As I've mentioned before, there are known instances of single user accounts storing hundreds of thousands of messages. Of course, such accounts are unusual and the majority of system managers impose strict quotas based on the number of messages a user can store or the amount of disk space they can occupy on the server. Nevertheless, my own personal observation is that users on host-based systems are more prone to the accumulation of old or unwanted messages, what you might call "file cabinet debris," especially if they've been using the host system for years. Clearly steps should be taken to eliminate most of this debris before the migration process begins as otherwise the whole procedure will take much longer and will use more resources than necessary.

10.4.2   Extracting and importing

In simple terms, the Exchange migration wizard works by analyzing the contents of one or more files generated from a source messaging system. Typically three different types of files are extracted from a source system:

- The packing list file. This file contains some information about the data that is being migrated, such as the code page for the character set used to create the contents, plus the names of all the other files associated with the extract.

- Primary intermediate files. These files contain the data necessary to create new Exchange mailboxes or custom recipients. They also contain message headers, entries for the personal address book, and pointers to data used by secondary intermediate files.

- Secondary intermediate files. These files contain the bulk of the data to be imported into Exchange and include message bodies and attachments and any data that can be extracted from an older time management or scheduling system.

Packing list files are usually given a file extension of .PKL. For example, TREDMOND.PKL. Primary intermediate files use a file extension of .PRI while secondary intermediate files use the file extension .SEC. There are no hard and fast rules for naming the files and each source extractor is free to name files whatever way it wishes. The intermediate files must be located in the same directory as the packing list. The Exchange migration wizard is not able to search disks for intermediate files, so if they can't be found in the same directory the import operation will fail.

Figure 10.3
*Selecting an
extract file for
the Migration
Wizard*

The source extract files are formatted according to a set of rules specified by the Exchange developers. Failure to follow the rules when extracting information from a source system will inevitably lead to problems when the time comes for the Exchange migration wizard to process the badly-formatted data. The old rule of "rubbish in leads to rubbish out" is very true in this case.

The basic approach to the migration process for host-based messaging systems is:

- Extract files from the source messaging system
- Run the migration wizard

There can be a period of elapsed time between the two steps, but this is undesirable because the users involved cannot participate in messaging communications until their mailboxes have been transferred to Exchange. An important part of the planning for migration is to establish when mailboxes can be moved with the least impact on users.

For best results the migration wizard should be run on the server where the private information store for the new mailboxes is located. As the import operations require a fairly heavy level of processing it's wise to schedule some time when the server is relatively inactive. Attempting to import thousands of messages for newly migrated mailboxes in the morning when users are arriving and logging in to their mailboxes to read their new mail will not guarantee good system responsiveness.

10.4.3   How long will the wizard take?

Depending on the capacity of the server and its current workload the migration wizard can take some time to import files for a user who's been a prolific generator of messages and documents on their previous system. Rough measurements taken for a range of users migrated from a host-based system show that on a lightly loaded server powered by an Intel 120MHz Pentium CPU the migration wizard processes between 15 and 40 messages per minute. Messages range in size from small 2K files to 2MB or more (including attachments), so clearly the throughput achieved in your environment greatly depends on the average size of message and the capacity of the server to unpack the messages from the source files. Farsighted system administrators include trial imports in the list of tasks for a pilot.

Apart from the length of time taken to import a user's files system administrators should be aware of two other side-effects of the import process. First, importing a large quantity of information from a legacy system can quickly blow any limit that has been set on the space allocated in the private information store for a user's mailbox. The migration wizard ignores space limitations on user mailboxes, the logic apparently being that it's best to get the information into the mailbox and then let the user sort out what they should discard in order to get back under the limit. Second, importing large quantities of information gives the Exchange databases a lot of work to do and generates a significant load on the system, which may impact response times for other users. Before starting any import operation make sure that enough disk space is available to allow the private information store to expand as files as imported. If you're about to import ten users, each of whom has generated source import files amounting to 30MB or so (which isn't really a lot for many heavy mail users), make sure that the disk holding the private information store has 300MB (plus at least a 10% margin for error) available. This is basic system management, but it's amazing how many people forget to look after the simple things and are surprised when things go wrong.

10.4.4   The effect of migrating data on the private information store

To a certain degree, migrated data is like a millstone around the neck of the private information store. There is no guarantee that users will ever review, visit, use, or process the data that the implementation team migrates so carefully on their behalf. Some data will be used, and that data will no doubt prove valuable to the people concerned, but previous experience of migrations indicates that the majority of migrated data will remain largely untouched until users take it upon themselves to clean it all out, probably when they begin to receive warnings that their allocation within the store is about to be exceeded.

Why describe data taken from a previous mail system as a millstone around the neck of the private information store? What harm does it do to migrate data and import it into the private information store? Consider the consequences of migration:

- Unless users delete portions of the migrated data it will not be compacted by the EDBUTIL utility. Thus, the private information store will grow from a base represented by the data that's been imported and will approach the 16GB limit for the store faster than if everyone had started off with an empty mailbox. I know several installations where migrated data occupies 6GB or more in a store, leaving less than 10GB for use to hold new messages.

- The migrated data must be backed up along with the rest of the store. There's no way to say "only backup new stuff" as everything must be written out to tape. The time required to backup the information store is therefore greatly extended, and restore operations (which hopefully will never be necessary) are also complicated by longer restore times.

- Users are affected too. The migrated data occupies their quota within the store, leaving them less to work with. This assumes that you place limits on the amount of space people can occupy within the store.

The top two points are operational considerations that affect day to day server management. The last point only affects users, but it's easy to spend a lot of time cleaning up mailboxes just to get under a user's limit. Inevitably the messages that are cleaned out are never the data that was migrated, perhaps because users don't want to delete items that they brought across from their "old" system.

10.4.5   How long will it take to migrate a user?

Experience of a large number of migration projects involving different mail systems shows that it takes a surprising amount of time to migrate a single user. Consider the tasks that are involved:

1. Creating the new Windows NT account and Exchange mailbox.

2. Adjusting the contents of distribution lists on both the legacy system and Exchange.

3. Extracting data to be migrated from the legacy system.

4. Transferring the data to the Windows NT server where the Migration Wizard will run.

5. Running the Migration Wizard.

6. Checking that data has been loaded correctly into the user's mailbox.

7. Checking that the user profile is correctly configured and that the user can log-in to the mailbox.

8. Setting up an auto-forward or auto-direct on the legacy system so that new messages will be forwarded to Exchange.

9. Disabling the old user account on the legacy system so that the user can't revert back to using the legacy system after their data is migrated.

10. Updating the corporate directories so that the migrated user is correctly identified as an Exchange user.

11. Contacting the user to tell them that their new mailbox is ready to go.

Each step takes its own amount of time and it's difficult to trim it down. Extracting data, transferring it across the network to the new server, and running the migration wizard takes the most time, but even if the amount of migration data is minimized it's hard to get the average time per user under 25–30 minutes. Taking this figure as the basis for calculation, over a sustained period of time a system administrator can probably transfer 16–20 users in a working day. However, the amount of time to process a user is greatly dependent on the volume of data to be processed. For example, large Microsoft Mail MMF files (greater than 100MB) can easily take 30 minutes to process, and it is not unknown to encounter MMF files larger than 400MB. Processing a huge amount of data will extend the time to migrate any user to several hours and extend the overall migration period. For this reason alone it is wise to aggressively encourage users to reduce the amount of data to be migrated. Murphy's Law (the 22nd in the series) states that the users with the largest amount of data occupy the most senior positions within a company, and if this is true in your case you're probably going to have to grin and accept the challenge.

If other steps are included, like having to configure the user PC with a new TCP/IP address, DHCP or WINS information, then the number of users that can be migrated in a single day will drop to between 8–10. Your mileage will vary, but you'll only know exactly how when you begin the actual migration.

Inexperienced or low-level staff cannot carry out all of the tasks listed above. Privileged access is required to the legacy mail system,

Windows NT, and Exchange. A certain knowledge of networking is required, and a fair knowledge of Exchange. Using valuable system administration time to migrate hundreds of users over hundreds of hours of work isn't perhaps the most effective use of your system administrators, so attempts have been made to reduce the average time required to process a single user. Among the most valuable tactics are:

1. Reduce the amount of data to be migrated to nil, or as close as possible to that figure. Encourage users not to take any of their old messages over to Exchange. There is no auto-magic function in the migration tools. Data that is processed by the migration wizard isn't automatically upgraded in the value of its content so that it becomes essential business data once it's imported into Exchange. A non-delivery notification message in one messaging system is the same everywhere, but it still surprises me to find that people are quite content to allow users to move anything they want, including all the junk mail in their old mailboxes, to Exchange. Apart from slowing down the migration process, the old junk reduces the space available in the private information store and increases the time required to make system backups.

2. Provide tools that can be run by users rather than system administrators. If a MAPI service provider exists for the legacy system it can be used to allow users to connect back to the old system from an Exchange client. They can then drag and drop any items they wish to keep over to Exchange. After a specified period of time access to the legacy system should be turned off, so the user has an interest in doing the work themselves before their old account is discarded. Apart from MAPI service providers there are other specialized migration tools that can be controlled by users. A quick scan of the Web to see what's available now would be a good thing to do. Document format conversion is the major issue encountered with these tools. If the legacy system stored items in a particular format then the tool must be able to convert the items to a more suitable format (simple text, RTF, or Word for Windows) as the items are moved to Exchange.

3. Stage PCs and ready a "hot-swap" of the user environment. If you're moving from Windows V3.11 to Windows 95 or Windows NT, upgrading your office application suite, and changing a network protocol in addition to migrating to Exchange, then big benefits can be gained by preparing a PC off-line before swapping it in when the time comes to migrate the user. The configuration can be fully tested before it is presented to the user and should therefore work without any difficulties when installed on the user

desktop. This tactic is particularly useful if you intend upgrading desktop hardware.

Everyone's experience of Exchange migrations is growing all the time. Talk to other system administrators and consultants to see how they have handled the situation, and then make your own decision based on the requirements of your site.

10.4.6 The quality of the migration tools

The quality of the source extractors and their ability to deal with different items of data that may be stored in the repositories on the host systems varies greatly. I don't find this situation to be surprising at all because it is very difficult to build generic extract utilities capable of handling the situation at every installation. In general it seems that if you've restricted your use of the host system to pure messaging you shouldn't have any problems, but if you've built applications on top of the host messaging system then those application objects may not be processed correctly by the source extractors. And of course, even if the source extractor can process the application objects there is still the issue of what should be done with that object after it is imported into Exchange.

The evolution of a host-based system to incorporate PC clients can also cause problems. Host systems accessed through video terminals typically only store simple text messages and attachments, but PC clients introduce PC format objects as attachments to messages or electronic documents stored on the host in preference to a DOS device. PC clients such as TeamLinks (for DIGITAL's ALL-IN-1 or MailWorks servers) leverage the central storage capabilities of a host system and off-load processing to intelligent clients, and have become more and more popular over the last few years. The question that arises when PC clients join the equation is whether the source extractor is able to deal with PC format documents, messages, and attachments, and if they are, will the information written into the files for the migration wizard make any sense after it is imported into Exchange? I have certainly encountered some significant problems with the standard source extractors when they attempt to process PC format files, especially with ALL-IN-1. If you're interested in migrating from ALL-IN-1 be aware that the Macro code provided with Exchange V4.0 to populate the source extract files is only able to run on VAX processors. There are updated modules available with Exchange V5.0 that should be able to run on Alpha.

These issues point to a general need to test the migration utilities in your own environment before making any assumption that just because the utilities come along with Exchange they're going to perform perfectly. My own experience with the migration utilities indicates that problem areas do exist and need to be worked around. Reducing the amount of data to be migrated helps. The less data there is to migrate, the less chance there'll be that problems will be encountered.

10.4.7 Breaking up the migration into achievable steps

It is wise not to attempt to transfer too many users at one time, unless you know that the users have very few messages to move. Some of the migration tools impose a limit, but even if they don't you should think the whole operation through. Breaking up the user population into groups of 50 or 100 creates more extract and move operations, but it also creates a much more manageable situation. For instance, if you attempt to move 500 users at one time:

- Do you have enough disk space for all the temporary files required for extracted data?

- Will you be able to move the volume of data represented by the extract files over to the Exchange computer in a reasonable time?

- Will the Exchange migration wizard be able to import all the data in the extract files in a reasonable time?

- Will your training department be ready to train so many users in a short period of time?

It may be possible that everything can be accomplished in one weekend, but is it the case that everything can be done provided it all goes exactly to plan without any errors creeping in? In other words, do you have any redundancy built into the plan just in case something goes wrong?

Host systems that provide purely messaging functions are easier to migrate than those which take a broader view of office automation. MEMO and PROFS are both good electronic mail systems, and offer some degree of other functionality like scheduling. But neither takes the concept of an electronic file cabinet much further than the level necessary to store and access messages. Systems which enable distributed shared drawers or folders, such as Exchange, are more difficult to migrate because the shared elements of the file cabinet may not have an equivalent in Exchange, or the migration utilities may not be able to process the data stored in these repositories. Further complications arise if the file cabinet is used as a base for applications such as workflow or EDI, especially if users are allowed to mix and match application-specific objects with mail messages and documents within their mailboxes.

All messaging systems differ in one way or another, so it is more than possible that some of the information held about messages by your current mail system may not migrate across to Exchange. The migration wizard is easy to use and provides reasonable functionality, but it doesn't attempt to resolve conflicts between Exchange and the source system. The general rule is that if a reasonable match can be made between Exchange and the other system regarding message attributes the information will move across. Some message attributes are generic and shared across all systems, such as message subject. Others, such as the X.400 concept of a reply-to-list, are more esoteric and will not be migrated.

10.4.8 Getting help on migrations

Lots of people are going to migrate other messaging systems to Exchange. In turn this means that there should be plenty of experience recorded in public forums dedicated to Exchange like those maintained on CompuServe (GO EXCHANGE), the Microsoft Network (MSN), the Exchange web site or, in particular, the Internet Exchange mailing list. It would be unreasonable to expect that the migration utilities will be able to handle 100% of all the different types of messages and other objects held on messaging systems, so you can expect to encounter some problems or adventures along the way. In these situations it can be very profitable to browse through the contents of whatever sources of information are available to you, or to send a message to the Exchange mailing list.[1]

For example, the migration wizard uses the cc:Mail export program to extract information from cc:Mail post offices. There's a known problem with this export program in that it can't deal with any messages for users with account names containing quotes. For example, B O'Brien. When the export program comes to process such a name it notices the blank character between B and O and attempts to apply the export parsing rules which dictate that names containing blanks should be enclosed in quotes. Unfortunately the export program isn't able to handle quotes that already exist within names, and this forces the migration wizard to halt. The solution is to rename the cc:Mail user—easy if you know how. This is a good example of the type of information discussed in the Exchange mailing list, proving the usefulness of external or unofficial channels when problem-solving.

---

[1]   The address of the Internet mailing list for Exchange is given in the appendix at the back of this book.

10.4.9   Migrating without a wizard

It's nice to have some automatic wizards available to migrate data to Exchange, but what happens if you have a mail system that Microsoft don't provide a migration wizard for? The wizards packaged in Exchange are carefully targeted to facilitate migration of the most popular electronic mail systems, but over the last decade almost every computer manufacturer has developed one or more electronic mail systems. For example, DIGITAL's electronic mail systems include ALL-IN-1, MailWorks for OpenVMS and MailWorks for UNIX, not to mention the free VMSmail utility packaged with every OpenVMS computer. A migration wizard is only available for ALL-IN-1, so anyone migrating from one of the other systems is on their own.

What options exist for a do-it-yourself migration? The most obvious answer is to establish a connection via SMTP or X.400 and ask users to mail selected messages and other items of interest to their new account on the target Exchange server. This approach is practical and workable, but only when the quantity of messages involved is fairly limited. Most users rapidly lose patience if they are forced to mail more than a few dozen files, and no one will be happy to be faced with the prospect of having to mail several hundred items before the connection is removed or their old account is deleted. Remember that mailing documents to Exchange is a two-part operation. First the messages have to be created and sent, and then they must be processed when they arrive into Exchange.

Some electronic mail systems have APIs or script languages and these can be used to develop automated procedures to export medium to large quantities of old messages and documents. One way to approach this task is to look at a sample load file generated from one of the source messaging systems supported by the Exchange migration wizard, and then proceed to work out how a similar load file can be created by extracting messages from your mail system. Make sure that all the necessary formatting information is included. There's no good rule to say what formatting information is mandatory and which is optional, so to avoid any messing around it's wise to create a load file that looks exactly the same as one prepared by an "official" extractor. Be prepared to go through a certain amount of trial and error before everything works all the time. Depending on the richness of the source system's APIs and the availability of experienced programmers accustomed to the APIs, expect to devote three to four weeks of hard work to produce a robust source extractor.

If your current electronic mail system runs on a DOS platform it may be enough to just export the messages out to DOS and leave them there, letting users import the files into Exchange as they are required (or missed). Importing files is easy—a simple drag and drop operation from the Windows Explorer or File Manager direct to the folder where the files should go. It's so easy that users may be tempted to drag and drop a little too much information, thus clogging up the information store with data that isn't really valuable any more.

Any do-it-yourself migration procedure will cost time and money. The question has to be asked whether all the energy devoted to migrating old messages could be used in a more productive manner elsewhere, and whether the cost involved in moving old information to Exchange can be justified by the content. Sites that have taken the radical approach to migration, that is to turn off the old system as the new system is turned on, often experience a period of confusion immediately after the change-over. But costs are lower and users quickly get used to the fact that the old messages are no longer available. As with many other aspects of a migration what users demand and how you react to the demands really depends on the situation pertaining within the installation. The golden rule is not to do any more work to migrate information than is strictly and absolutely necessary.

10.4.10   Migrating other data

An existing system may be used for more than just electronic mail or document management. DIGITAL's ALL-IN-1 office system is a good example of a popular office system in use worldwide since 1982. One of the reasons for ALL-IN-1's popularity is its application development capabilities which have allowed many organizations to build reasonably complex data processing applications which can be totally integrated with the electronic mail subsystem. While a migration wizard exists to move documents and messages from ALL-IN-1 file cabinets into Exchange folders, the wizard's magic cannot cope with any application-specific data.

In cases where a messaging system has been used as the basis for applications arrangements will have to be made to migrate the application completely or move the data into a format that is understood by an application available for Windows NT. In the latter case the usual tactic is to try to output the data into a format that's understood by the target application. One instance of where I've been able to do this is with 20/20, a spreadsheet application sold by Access Technology which was quite common in its day, due to its multi-platform nature. 20/20 is able to write information out in WK1 format, and most Windows spreadsheet programs such as Lotus 1-2-3 or Excel are quite happy to import WK1 data.

While it is often possible to output data from an older application in a compatible format the data may not be immediately reachable from Windows NT. This situation usually occurs when the source system is a mini- or mainframe computer. Moving data between computer systems is an area fraught with pitfalls, but there are at least three obvious methods to investigate:

1. Using a common network protocol to transfer data from source to target system. FTP (File Transfer Protocol) is the protocol that offers most potential because it is supported on a very wide range of computer systems, including Windows NT. Be careful to ensure that data originating on systems with different character sets (for example, mainframes running the IBM MVS operating system) is converted before or after the transfer is performed.

2. Moving the migration data to somewhere available to both source and target systems. For example, logical network-based disk drives that can be directly accessed by Windows NT. Novell Net-Ware or DIGITAL PATHWORKS network drives are both good examples of network devices that can be mapped by Windows NT and other computer systems.

3. Using manual transfers via magnetic media. This method relies on a common type of media (disk or tape) being supported by both source and target systems as well as Windows NT having the ability to correctly interpret the data on the media once it is presented for reading.

In all cases don't assume that a method works just because you are able to transfer a small file, or even a selection of small files. Test all methods with real data and try and build an automated procedure to speed up the process. It's common to suddenly discover that the method you've chosen, or the procedure that's been carefully written, works quite happily with small amounts of data but falls over or takes an inordinate amount of time to complete when confronted with the data generated by more prolific users.

10.4.11 Cleaning up after the migration

It's obvious that disk space will be used during the migration process. You can't expect to extract information from the source messaging system to feed into Exchange without occupying some type of transient storage. Make sure that your preparations for the migration take transient disk space requirements into account. It's a good idea to thoroughly analyze the current disk space occupied by user messages and other files due to be moved before the migration process begins, and plan to make the total storage determined by the analysis plus an extra

20% margin for error available during the migration. The margin for error should also take care of the slight additional overhead imposed by the "format wrapper" created around messages by the Exchange migration tools.

Calculating the disk space used by an individual user is pretty easy if the current messaging system delivers separate copies of messages to all users. All you have to do is see how much disk space is allocated to message files in any user's account to know what figure to use for planning purposes. Calculating the requirements when a shared server-based message model (like Exchange) is used is harder unless utilities exist to report how much space a user is responsible for within the shared message store. This figure isn't always easy to get, nor is it obvious as to how you might go about getting it, so you may even end up writing some utilities to analyze data structures and extract the relevant information.

Before the migration process gets under way it's important that you take whatever steps are feasible to reduce the amount of data to be moved. If the source system provides facilities to remove unwanted or obsolete messages and documents from user mailboxes they should be used before any extracts are created. There isn't much point in moving all the contents of users' wastebasket (deleted) folders across into their new Exchange mailboxes, for example.

Depending on the space available on the source system you even may have to install an additional drive to use during the migration period. Of course, if small groups of users are to be moved you'll only have to ensure that the total disk space occupied by these users (plus the safety margin) is available. The disk space used for this activity should be reclaimed as soon as possible after the extracted data has been loaded into Exchange.

Apart from space used for migration purposes, it's also important to recognize that removing user-specific files from the system after a user has been successfully migrated to Exchange can reclaim disk space. You may want to leave a gap of a week or so after a user has been moved before taking the plunge and deleting their files, as you never know when problems might occur and the user has to be moved back to their original system. When the time comes to clean up you'll find that the task is purely manual as there is no functionality to do this included in the migration wizard.

10.5   Maintaining quality of service during the migration period

The migration period imposes stress on all layers within the messaging system. Backbones and connectors have more messages to process; the network is generally handling more data; users are struggling to cope with change brought upon by new applications; help desk staff are running harder to keep up with requests for help from users; and the system designers and implementation team are overseeing the migration process. The strain makes it difficult to maintain the overall quality of the service delivered to users, but keeping quality as high as possible should be a concern for the migration team, if only to avoid the "coffee machine" syndrome.

The coffee machine syndrome describes how easy it is for rumors and misconceptions about any change to arise. People gathering around the coffee machine, or water foundation, to discuss various happenings can quickly decide that a new computer system or application isn't much good, coloring the view of other users including those who have never even used the system! The migration team wants to make the implementation of Exchange a complete success, and the best way to do this and stop rumors spreading is to maintain or increase the level of quality delivered by the messaging service.

In this respect the messaging service is composed of the legacy mail system or systems, backbones and connectors, the corporate directory, and Exchange. It is not just Exchange, but many people make the mistake of concentrating on Exchange to the expense of the other components. Once the migration is complete then absolute concentration can be devoted to the exploitation of Exchange, but until the migration is over we've got to deal with the entire service as a whole.

There are a number of important areas to consider:

- The speed with which messages are delivered throughout the whole system and the degree of fidelity for message contents and attachments.
- The accuracy of the corporate mail directories.
- The satisfaction of users with the migration process.
- Mail-enabled applications.
- Operation of the legacy mail systems.

When two or more messaging systems are joined together it is inevitable that gateways and connectors must be used to achieve the join. Messages can be slowed as they pass through gateways, so the first goal to achieve is to maintain the overall transfer time for messages between different systems. People perceive transfer time differently to the stark technical detail. As long as users are happy that their messages are transported between systems as fast as they were delivered by the legacy system they'll be happy. Fortunately the Exchange connectors are fast and capable of handling a large volume of messages on a daily basis, so providing adequate network links are available, messages should flow at a sufficient speed.

Preserving message contents is a different matter. The gateway should be able to preserve the format of attachments, but this will only be possible if Exchange and the legacy system share a common understanding of message structure and formats. Conversion may be required as messages pass between the systems, and users are usually only satisfied if they don't see extra attachments (such as the infamous WINMAIL.DAT), and are able to work with the contents when they arrive in Exchange, or when an Exchange message arrives back at the legacy system. Remember the 80/20 rule—80% of all messages are typically sent to people you work with, so ease this aspect of migration by migrating complete departments or workgroups at one time. If you split a department between different mail systems you're only creating problems for yourself.

We've already discussed the dissatisfaction that arises when messages are not delivered because mail addresses are incorrect through no fault of the user. If a corporate directory is consulted and a mail address retrieved, and that address proves to be inaccurate, then users have a real and justifiable cause for complaint. Every effort should be made to ensure that the corporate mail directories—those used by the legacy systems as well as Exchange—are up to date. Any large corporate directory (over 20,000 entries) will have some degree of inaccuracy, but over 1% (200 inaccurate entries in the 20,000 entry directory) is unacceptable. Directories with more than 10% inaccurate entries are basically useless and will be an irritation for users. Directory synchronization on a regular basis during the migration period should be built into all migration plans. It is probably too difficult to track down every distribution list and personal address book and try to update the addresses contained within against the corporate directory, so using a redirect or auto-forward feature (if available) on accounts that have been migrated to Exchange is the only practical way to address the issue. Most redirect or auto-forward functions disappear when an account is removed from a system, so it's better to disable user accounts on legacy systems instead of deleting them.

Users believe that all the information they hold on the legacy system is valuable. Their starting point is to require all information to be migrated, but as we've already seen, this approach is impractical. The migration team must therefore convince users that they don't need the old data and will be much better off to start afresh with a new account. This is a difficult proposition to sell, and it requires a certain amount of propaganda to convince people that the pain of moving to Exchange will be repaid by all the great new functionality that's available in Exchange. Addressing the coffee machine syndrome by training people, making them aware of new functionality, and not allowing users to focus on what they might have lost but concentrate on what they've gained is an effective tactic. Back this approach up with a team of super-users, specially trained on the advanced features of Exchange and so able to answer user queries immediately, or debunk incorrect assertions about Exchange and stop rumors before they get going. A supportive and knowledgeable help desk staff to support the help desk is a pre-requisite.

Out of the box Exchange is a messaging system. If the legacy system included some mail enabled applications then the migration project must seek to provide replacement functionality as quickly as possible. If Exchange can't provide the functionality then maybe another application can be used in conjunction with Exchange. For example, if an expense reporting application built around electronic forms is available on the legacy system, maybe an Exchange e-form can do the same job, or if not, perhaps a combination of an Excel template and Exchange messages will do the trick. Migrating people who work together won't address the problem, but it will stop you getting into a situation where people are attempting to use incompatible mail-enabled applications between Exchange and the legacy systems.

A temptation exists for operations staff to concentrate on Exchange once it's put into production. After all, Exchange is the new technology and people want to learn. Concentrating on Exchange can lead to the legacy systems being ignored, so good system management practices are not kept up. System tuning, backups, monitoring, software upgrades, and all the other day-to-day tasks may not be carried out as well as they were done before, inevitably leading to a degradation of service from the legacy system. If this happens the users who remain on the legacy system will not be happy and they will relay the feeling of discontent to their peers. Also, a legacy system that is not maintained will probably affect some of the other aspects of service quality discussed in this section. Inaccurate entries will end up in the corporate directory; the legacy system may become unreliable and suffer system failures; the gateways operating on the legacy system may experience bottlenecks, queues, or failures to the detriment of message transfer times. Users will not understand that these problems are due to mismanagement of the legacy system. They will perceive the problems as being due to the introduction of Exchange—after all, everything worked just fine before the migration project started, didn't it?

The search for quality in all aspects of life is a difficult path to follow. Achieving real levels of quality during a messaging migration project is one of the more difficult things to do, but it can be achieved if real attention is paid to the issue by the migration team.

10.6   Coexisting with other messaging systems

The vast majority of migrations do not happen overnight. In fact, if you are moving from another system supporting thousands of users the migration period is often extended over months or even years. During this time Exchange and its predecessor mail systems will need to coexist and cooperate within a single, logical messaging environment.

It's obvious that the most basic need to coexist can be defined on the level of interpersonal message interchange between the two systems. One of the Exchange connectors or a link to an SMTP or X.400 backbone will probably solve this problem, albeit perhaps after a degree of testing to ensure that all message body parts can be successfully transmitted from one electronic mail system to the other.

After messages, what are the issues that may prove to be of concern during the period of coexistence? Here are a few of the issues I have encountered.

- Directory Synchronization. The Exchange directory is no doubt different to the one used by the existing system. How will the address information contained in the two directories be synchronized so that people are able to address messages to anyone within the organization without having to remember complex address syntaxes?

- Transferring users from Exchange back to the older electronic mail system. During a migration phase the normal operation will be to transfer a user from the older system to Exchange, but there may be instances where someone is transferred from a department that uses Exchange to a department where they don't. In these cases there will be problems extracting user data from Exchange and transferring it to the "old" mail system, mostly because no wizard or "backward migration" tools are probably available (unless you build your own).

- Interchange of scheduling information. Schedule+ provides excellent scheduling functionality in an Exchange environment but it's difficult to schedule meetings and appointments with anyone else, even people using older versions of Schedule+!

- Mail-enabled applications. Workflow applications built on top of the electronic mail system are compromised if everyone who may be part of a document's routing cycle cannot be reached through the electronic mail system. Even if they can be reached with a message, the recipient may not be able to interact with the contents and participate in the workflow.

- Guest users. With a single consistent mail system throughout an organization it's normally possible to access your mail from any workstation, provided that your access can be authenticated from the workstation. If some parts of the organization are still using the old mail system will Exchange users be able to access their mail when they visit? Will users of the older mail system be able to read their mail when they visit a department that uses Exchange?

- Distribution lists. Maintaining the contents of distribution lists so that the addresses contained in the lists are up-to-date, accurate, and don't lead to undelivered messages can be a nightmare. How do you make sure that distribution lists are updated as users migrate from the older system to Exchange? Can the selected techniques cater for personal distribution lists as well as those shared between groups of users or system-wide? Can you apply the same technique to solve the problem posed by mail addresses held in nickname files or personal address books? While you can take some steps to enable local users to continue to use old addresses problems may still arise for external messages delivered from other organizations.

Human beings generally like a settled environment and often resist change. It's fair to assume that greater problems will be encountered at the beginning of the migration when users struggle to cope with new ways to address messages to colleagues, transfer documents from one system to the other, find equivalent options on client menus, or even just cope with the trauma of moving from a different style of computing and user interface to client/server Windows. Help desk and programming staff will experience the same transition pressures but their extra technical knowledge will assist their personal migration, so the overall impact on these people shouldn't be as great. Migrations proceed more smoothly (and usually quicker) when everyone recognizes that problems will occur, and steps are taken to lessen the impact of the problems before users meet them. This is one good reason why a thorough and extensive pilot is essential to pinpoint the specific areas of interoperability which may affect your users most. Knowledge gained through pilots is a great help in achieving non-traumatic migrations.

10.6.1   Operating Mail Gateways

Gateways have been a fact of electronic messaging life since the earliest days of e-mail. Following the same line as operating system development, no great efforts were initially made to ensure that messages could be sent to other systems. Everything was focused on optimizing the messaging design and architecture for the computer and operating system it ran on. Some of the IBM mainframe e-mail systems written in APL, a unique symbol-driven programming language in many respects, provide eloquent examples of the approach taken when developing e-mail.

With a wide range of e-mail systems in production, each having its own idea about how to create and send messages, gateways rapidly became a necessary evil of a messaging administrator's life. Gateways are a necessary evil because they delay messages en route to their final destination and so degrade some of the raison d'être for e-mail, the desire to send information quickly from one person to another. Gateways often impose restrictions on users, for instance limiting their ability to send anything but simple text messages to users contacted via the gateway. Attached or embedded documents are often stripped out as messages transit the gateways, and generally speaking the message that leaves an originator's desk arrives in a fairly bent shape at its final destination. Of course, it's a mistake to blame gateways for all the restrictions. Target e-mail systems mightn't be able to cope with embedded documents or rich text format cover memos, or many of the other advanced features of modern systems. In these cases gateways merely act as a negotiator between different e-mail systems, transforming messages arriving at the gateway into a form that's acceptable to the other systems.

Any medium to large-scale migration usually requires a gateway between the old system and the new, in this case, Exchange. Smaller migrations that can be done in a "big bang" or over a short period of time may remove any need to install and operate a gateway. Once you have to deal with more than a few hundred users the sheer logistics of migration determine that the period of migration extends to such an extent that a gateway is needed to facilitate communication between the two user communities.

Given that one or more gateways are necessary during an extended migration period, it follows that it is sensible to take any necessary steps to ensure that the best possible interoperability for all types of messages is achieved. Important points to consider include:

- Can a common messaging standard be used by the gateway to transfer messages from the older system to Exchange? The two obvious options are SMTP/MIME and X.400.

- What features are supported by the gateway? Is it limited to simple (single-bodypart) messages or can attachments in different file formats be sent through the gateway? Does the gateway preserve attachment information such as file formats and titles? Is the gateway able to handle attachments in a format that it doesn't recognize, for instance, a compressed file produced by the PKZIP application?

- What happens when a message generated by a mail-enabled application arrives at the gateway? Remember that this situation can arise from either direction. In other words, a message can be generated and sent from the older system or an electronic form can be generated and sent by Exchange. The important thing to consider is whether the fact that a message arrives at the gateway influences the immediate and future processing by the mail-enabled application. For example, if the message is part of a workflow cycle that consists of a number of serial steps, each of which involves a message being sent to the next person in the cycle, can the cycle be re-established after the message is sent to a user via the gateway?

If the responses to these questions are largely negative it is time to consider whether another gateway should be used. There is no point in operating a gateway that enables a minimalist degree of interoperability between the two systems because this only leads to additional strain on the help desk staff and system administrators, who get to explain to users the reasons why their messages sometimes don't get through. Buying a cheap gateway with a low level of functionality can be a case of engaging a low up-front cost while incurring higher costs over the lifetime of the gateway.

Sometimes the most demanding users, those who will place most strain on the gateway's capabilities, can be identified before the migration begins, or they become obvious quickly afterwards. If this is the case it's reasonable to concentrate on migrating these people first to avoid the problems they may encounter. For example, if you know that a specific group of people, perhaps spread across several departments, communicates on a regular basis via a workflow application it makes little sense to split them across different migration stages. Move them together instead. This is an example of where it's good to ignore organizational or corporate divisions when considering when users should be moved.

Hopefully a gateway is a transient component in your messaging environment, one that can be discarded once the migration is complete. Of course, larger migrations can take many years to arrive at the last user, so gateways can quickly become a semi-permanent fixture. Even if the gateway is temporary don't take short cuts. Pay attention to gateway details and avoid lots of problems in the future.

10.6.2   Maintaining addressing sources

After gateways electronic directory services and other sources of address information are the most common problem areas that must be addressed during the migration period. People hate receiving non-delivery notifications, and the potential for "bad" electronic mail addresses greatly increases as people are moved to any new messaging system. Exchange is no better or no worse than any other mail system. It offers no panacea for badly addressed messages and during the course of the migration the chances are that you won't be able to avoid some undeliverable messages due to invalid addresses. Over the long term you can take steps to significantly reduce the number of invalid addresses within the system.

Most electronic mail systems in use today have some form of directory service. This may be a simple list of subscribers (mailboxes) or it might be something more complicated, such as an X.500 or similar distributed directory service. In all cases the repository holds information about other users' electronic mail addresses which people can consult when they wish to send messages. Some systems validate all addresses entered in message headers against the directory to ensure that a user cannot attempt to send a message to an undeliverable address. The personal address book is a form of directory service, in this case, a purely personal service totally under the control of an individual user.

When people are migrated from a system to Exchange two basic courses of action in respect to the directory can be taken by a system administrator.

1. The directory entry for the user is removed. This can be frustrating for users who remain on the older system because they will no longer be able to "see" the migrated user in the directory. Also, messages sent to the old address, perhaps those originating from another connected system will be undeliverable unless they can be redirected.

2. The entry for the user is altered so that any new messages addressed to the user are redirected to their new Exchange mailbox. Not all systems support message redirection, and this approach assumes that the system is capable of sending messages

to Exchange, normally via a gateway. A further complication is that redirection may require that the user's old mailbox or account is retained. If this is the case you should disable access to the account so that no one can log into it.

Enabling directory synchronization between Exchange and the old system is a more sophisticated but costly answer. It requires the older system to support the MS-Mail directory synchronization facility or a utility program to provide directory information to Exchange and import directory information originating from Exchange. Despite the almost inevitable costs involved, maintaining a fully synchronized directory is the best solution and will stop users becoming unhappy during the migration process because they can't address messages to their friends, or their friends' messages don't arrive.

One final point. Unless absolutely necessary (for example, if the company changes its name), whatever you do, take steps to maintain the mail addresses that people use for external communications. It is a mistake to force people to publish new mail addresses and will cause discontent. They won't like doing it, mostly because their friends and business contacts already have an e-mail address that's in use today and there is no immediately obvious benefit from a changeover so why do it? There is a relatively high potential for mistakes to be made in the transmission of new mail addresses to external contacts, so further potential exists for confusion to be introduced. The net result is user discontent, something to be avoided at all costs.

Using something like a smart relay host as the external point of contact for your company is generally a better approach to take. Smart relay hosts are able to examine and rewrite mail addresses as messages arrive. Old addresses can be quickly reformatted into new addresses and directed away from legacy systems to arrive to Exchange for eventual delivery to recipients. Using computers like this relieves users of an irritating task and greatly enhances accuracy, thus contributing to the overall stability and reliability of the messaging infrastructure.

Keeping Your Exchange Server Healthy

11.1 Performance Optimizer

To a certain degree Exchange can be said to be self-maintaining. You shouldn't have to continually perform system tuning to make everything run smoothly, but there are going to be times when things go wrong. In this chapter we'll look at some of the utilities that come with Exchange that help system administrators keep servers in shape.

The Exchange Performance Optimizer utility is a somewhat intelligent program designed to analyze the current status of an Exchange server and make changes based on:

- Information about the intended role for the server as input by a system administrator before the analysis begins (Figure 11.1). This allows the utility to consider what changes are required to enable the server to support an increase in the user community or the way the server is used. For example, a change in server workload from "messaging only" to a situation where messaging and public folders are supported.

- The disk hardware available to the system.

- Internal parameters currently in operation and performance data gathered by Exchange as it runs.

One useful, but sometimes overlooked aspect of the Performance Optimizer is its ability to move the work directories for the MTA and Internet Mail Service away from the location where the directories are first installed (on the same disk as the Exchange executables). Any system expecting to deal with a large volume of traffic through the MTA or IMS should move these directories onto a different disk.

Performance Optimizer cannot run with Exchange in an active state. All services must be halted before any analysis can begin. Run the utility early in the morning or late in the evening when users will feel the least impact.

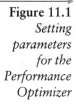

Figure 11.1
*Setting
parameters
for the
Performance
Optimizer*

By default Performance Optimizer reveals little of the internal calculations it makes and offers no opportunities for experienced system
administrators to selectively tune one or more settings before new parameters are created. You can request (or force) Performance Optimizer to show you more options to change by running the program with
the -v option enabled. To do this, select the desktop icon for the "Microsoft Exchange Optimizer" and then change the properties to include the -v parameter. The resulting command line should look something like this:

```
C:\EXCHSRVR\BIN\PERFWIZ.EXE -V
```

Figure 11.2
*Log from
Performance
Optimizer run*

```
---------------------------------------------------------------
Microsoft Exchange Server Performance Optimizer log file
opened.: 2/29/96 - 2:21:34 PM
---------------------------------------------------------------
Detected 1 processor(s)
Detected 134021120 bytes physical memory
Found fixed logical disk C:
Found fixed logical disk D:
Found fixed logical disk E:
Found fixed logical disk F:
Found fixed logical disk G:
Performance Results
(Smaller values better)
```

```
DiskRA(ms)Seq(ms)
----------------------------------------------------------------
C: -- Not Analyzed --
D: 21789  15258
E: 21234  14969
F: 21101  14883
G: -- Not Analyzed --
Microsoft Exchange Server Information store log files was
moved from D:\exchsrvr\MDBDATA to E:\exchsrvr\MDBDATA
Microsoft Exchange Server Message Transfer Agent log files
was moved from D:\EXCHSRVR\mtadata to E:\EXCHSRVR\mtadata
Microsoft Exchange Server Public information store file was
moved from D:\exchsrvr\MDBDATA to F:\exchsrvr\MDBDATA
Microsoft Exchange Server Internet Mail Connector data files
was moved from D:\exchsrvr\imcdata to E:\exchsrvr\imcdata
Set # of information store buffers from 1000 to 12226
Set # of directory buffers from 1000 to 100
Set Minimum # of information store threads from 8 to 3
Set Maximum # of information store threads from 20 to 5
Set # of directory threads from 48 to 50
Set Maximum # of cached categorizations from 20 to 25
Set Maximum # of cached restrictions from 20 to 25
Set # of private information store send threads from 1 to 2
Set # of public information store send threads from 1 to 2
Set # of information store gateway in threads from 1 to 2
Set # of information store gateway out threads from 1 to 2
Set # of information store users from 500 to 25
Set # of XAPI MT threads from 1 to 2
Set # of XAPI MT queue threads from 1 to 2
Set # of dispatcher threads from 1 to 2
Set # of transfer threads from 1 to 2
Set # of kernel threads from 1 to 3
Set # of database data buffers per object from 3 to 6
Set # of RTS threads from 1 to 3
----------------------------------------------------------------
Microsoft Exchange Server Performance Optimizer log file
closed.: 2/29/96 - 2:26:08 PM
```

Each run of the Performance Analyzer creates a log called PERFOPT.LOG in the \WINNT35\SYSTEM32 directory. The log file can be reviewed at leisure after the analyzer has run, and any corrections that seem necessary can be made afterwards. If we look at the sample log illustrated in Figure 11.2 we can see that the Performance

Optimizer took a number of steps to improve the configuration on the target server. These included:

- An analysis of all the logical disks found on the server. The analysis is performed to determine which are the fastest disks on the system. Some disks are discounted because they are FAT drives or don't have enough available space to be useful. Note that the Performance Optimizer cannot detect the difference between multiple partitions on a single physical drive. Each partition is analyzed separately, so this is one reason why you might want to adjust the results of the Performance Optimizer after it is complete. For example, it's always a good idea to separate the information store and its transaction logs by placing them on separate physical drives.

- After the analysis is completed the Performance Optimizer redistributes important Exchange data structures across all available disks. You will be given the option not to move the files according to the recommendations before anything happens.

- Performance Optimizer then proceeds to review a set of internal counters and parameter settings that are maintained by Exchange in order to determine whether any parameters need to be changed to accommodate the workload observed to date on the server.

- After the new parameter values are set all of the Exchange services are restarted.

As a server's workload changes over time for many reasons including increases in user knowledge and the number of users supported by the server this is an important reason why Performance Optimizer should be run on a fairly regular basis.

11.1.1   Memory and RISC systems

Performance Optimizer allows you to limit the amount of memory that the system will allocate to Exchange. The value is used by the Optimizer to compute internal settings such as buffers, and if no value is set the Optimizer will assume that the total system memory is available for Exchange.

RISC systems such as the DIGITAL Alpha processor use executables that are larger than their Intel $x86$ equivalents. This fact means that the paging profile is different on RISC systems than $x86$ systems. The Performance Optimizer provided with Exchange Server V4.0 is tuned for $x86$ systems and you must take this into account when running the Optimizer for RISC systems. This issue may well be resolved in later releases of Exchange.

For example, because the Exchange executables are larger on RISC systems, it is better to have less memory allocated to buffers and more available for the executables as this results in less paging. Some tests performed by DIGITAL for Alpha systems showed that instructing the Performance Optimizer to limit memory usage to 50% of the total available system memory produced good results in all cases. In other words, if your system has 128MB available to it, the Performance Optimizer allocates 64MB to Exchange; if 256MB is available, Exchange gets 128MB, and so on.

All of this goes to show that you can't completely depend on automated tuning devices. Knowledge of the system environment and observation of what's happening on an ongoing basis is essential when the time comes for a system tune-up.

11.1.2   Server monitors

Server monitors are used to determine whether specified Exchange services are operating correctly on target servers. The entire set of core services—System Attendant, Information Store, Directory, Message Transfer Agent as well as any optional connectors can be monitored.

Each server monitor operates on a set of servers that you select from any site in your organization. When you select a server you determine which of the Exchange services you wish to monitor. Each service is detected by sending an "are you there" message over the link to the target service and seeing whether the message arrives.

Monitors can also check the system clock on servers to see whether any inconsistancy exists between the expected and actual time. This is important because a server with an incorrect time can generate message time-stamps that cause concern to users. Receiving a message that appeared to be sent two days ago or a day in the future does not generate a great level of confidence in the messaging system.

Figure 11.3
*Detecting an
inoperative
server with a
monitor*

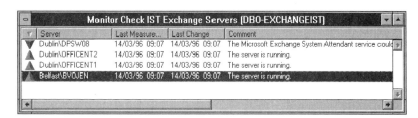

The results of server monitors are recorded in two places—graphically and in a log file. The graphic display (Figure 11.3) shows one line for each server being monitored. The beginning of each line displays an icon to flag the current server status. A red down arrow means trouble. In Figure 11.3 you can see that the DPSW08 server in the Dublin site is flagged because the monitor cannot detect the System Attendant service. Graphical displays are great for indicating a problem, but only if someone is watching the display all the time. Not every installation can afford the luxury of having a system administrator engaged in nothing but monitoring all the time. To make sure that all problems are detected you should:

- Run one or more server monitors all the time to observe the most important servers in each site. The most important service to monitor is the System Attendant, as without it Exchange has no chance of ever working correctly. Servers who host IMS or X.400 connectors on behalf of one or more sites should also be monitored to detect possible blocks in message transmission or reception.

- Review the server monitor log files on a regular basis, if possible once a day but at least once a week. A different log file is created for each monitor. You can find out the name of the server monitor log by viewing the general properties of the monitor.

Creating server monitors and making them active should be one of the first actions you take after deploying Exchange servers into an operational status. Server and link monitors form an important part of a proactive attitude to problem detection that can pay back great benefits from just a little effort put in at the start.

11.1.3   Link monitors

Link monitors operate by sending PING-like messages to all the servers configured in the monitor. Messages are dispatched at regular intervals and calculations are performed to determine the round-trip time between the server where the monitor is running and the servers being monitored. Administrators can configure the frequency and threshold times for messages and the notification list for any alarms generated as a result of a message not being returned or arriving outside the predetermined threshold. The results of the messages being sent to and from the servers are displayed in a separate window within the Exchange Administration utility, as illustrated in Figure 11.4. If a monitor is active when the Administration utility is closed it will be restarted the next time the Administration utility is initialized.

It's a good idea to run a link monitor on all the important sites in your organization from a central server. No human intervention is required as automatic alarms are generated if anything goes wrong. Alarms can be notified by standard Windows NT alerts, which flash a message up onto the server's screen, or by sending a mail message to a designated individual or distribution list. The latter is preferable in most cases, especially when a number of people share the task of managing the Exchange infrastructure.

Figure 11.4
*A link monitor
in operation*

11.2   Message tracking

Users send messages at the drop of a hat, but sometimes those messages don't get through and when this happens it falls on the head of the system administrator to try and find out just what happened to the message. Was it delivered to someone else? Did a gateway reject the message? Maybe the message is stuck somewhere waiting for a connection to be established to a remote system.

The majority of messaging systems allocate a unique identifier to messages as they are generated. Exchange is no different in this respect. Complete identifiers are built for Exchange messages as follows:

1. The country code for the server. For example, "IE" means Ireland.

2. The administrative X.400 domain for the server, if defined.

3. The private X.400 administrative domain. For example, "Digital."

4. A unique identifier built from the name of the server, the date and time when the message was created, and a computer-generated suffix to ensure uniqueness.

The first three parts of the complete message identifier come from the X.400 site address. An example message identifier generated at 2.29 p.m. on 14th March 1996 on the server called DBO-EXCHANGEIST is:

```
C=IE;A= ;P=Digital;L=DBO-EXCHANGE960314142937FA000101
```

You can view the message identifier generated for a message from any Exchange client as follows:

- Select the message.

- Select the File.Properties menu option.

- Select the Message Id page.

A Message Id property page is only shown if the message originated on an Exchange server connected into the same organization. Messages generated by other messaging systems normally bear their own types of message identifiers. Generating unique message identifiers provides the fundamental basis for message tracking but identifiers are of little use in themselves if they are not recorded somewhere as a message makes its way through the different links in the system. Exchange will record the necessary data, but only if it is instructed to do so. To turn message tracking on, select the MTA Site Configuration and check the "Enable Message Tracking" box.

11.2.1   Message tracking logs

After message tracking is enabled Exchange records details of messages as they are processed by the MTA. Details are held in a set of tracking log files stored in the \tracking.log directory on each server. A new tracking log is created at midnight, so each log holds details of all the messages processed in a single day. Tracking logs are named in a YYYYMMDD.LOG format. For example, the tracking log created on 20th April 1996 is called 19960420.LOG.

Tracking logs quickly grow to large sizes on even moderately busy Exchange servers. You might expect to accumulate between 10 to 15MB of log on moderately busy servers dedicated to user mailboxes. A greater volume of data is usually produced on systems with connectors installed. Lower volumes will be seen on public folder servers. An Internet Mail Connector that links Exchange to other messaging systems might generate between 10 and 20MB of logs on a busy day. These values come from real-life experience in organizations that have deployed Exchange to more than 10,000 users. Expect lower volumes of data inside smaller organizations. These volumes are not excessive and do not provide an excuse not to implement message tracking. All production servers should keep message tracking logs. Apart from anything else, the message tracking logs provide the raw data for statistic gathering and reporting programs like Crystal Reports, which is able to export data in a number of different formats appropriate for reporting purposes.

Figure 11.5 is a chart (generated by Excel) of hourly message traffic through one of the largest Exchange servers operated by DIGITAL. The chart clearly illustrates the spread of message traffic over the hours in the day (18 February 1997), peaking at nearly 14,000 message transactions between 4 and 5 o'clock GMT, or between 11 and 12 o'clock in the morning, U.S. Eastern Standard Time. The data used to create the graph comes from the message tracking log for the day. Each message can generate a number of transactions as the server processes it, so the actual number of unique messages handled in any particular hour is less than the numbers in the chart. For example, the 14,000 message transactions were generated by approximately 4,500 messages, still a large number for a server to handle in one hour.

Figure 11.5
A simple chart of the data in the message tracking logs

It is possible to edit or read the contents of tracking logs with a text editor and because the fields in the logs are tab-delimited they can be loaded into a spreadsheet, such as Excel. Once in the editor or spreadsheet the contents of the log reveal the interaction between the MTA and messages, and how messages proceed as they are submitted by users, delivered to other mailboxes, or pass off the system via a site or other connector. Given experience and knowledge of the codes [1] and fields used in tracking logs it is feasible to use the raw logs as the basis for satisfying user requests to discover where messages went. Such an approach might be taken by masochists, but the more sanguine system administrator quickly learns to appreciate the standard "Track Message" option featured on the Tools menu of the Exchange Administration utility.

Figure 11.6 illustrates a sample from a message-tracking log. The sample has been edited slightly to clarify the information contained in the tracking log. In the extract a message is submitted (code 4) to the MTA. The message originates from a user whose local alias or distinguished name is "TONYR" and is addressed to a distribution list called "Exchange IST." The first step the MTA takes is to expand the distribution list (code 26), where it is discovered that a nested distribution list called "IST-Management" is part of the original list. The nested list is then expanded to complete the set of recipient mailboxes where the MTA must deliver the message.

---

[1]   Details of fields and the data they store, and the meanings of the codes used in message tracking logs can be found in chapter 17 of the Exchange Server administration guide.

```
/C=IE;A= ;P=Digital;L=DBO-EXCHANGE960314142937FA00010141996.3.14 14:29:36
/O=DIGITALEQUIPMENT CORPORATION/OU=DUBLIN/CN=CONFIGURATION/CN=SERVERS
/CN=DBO-EXCHANGEIST/CN=MICROSOFT PRIVATE MDB
/O=DIGITAL EQUIPMENT CORPORATION/OU=DUBLIN/CN=RECIPIENTS/CN=TONYR
/O=DIGITAL EQUIPMENT CORPORATION/OU=DUBLIN/CN=RECIPIENTS/CN=ExchangeIST
/C=IE;A= ;P=Digital;L=DBO-EXCHANGE960314142937FA000101261996.3.14 14:29:37
/o=DIGITAL EQUIPMENT CORPORATION/ou=DUBLIN/cn=RECIPIENTS/cn=ExchangeIST
/C=IE;A= ;P=Digital;L=DBO-EXCHANGE960314142937FA000101261996.3.14 14:29:39
/o=Digital Equipment Corporation/ou=Dublin/cn=Recipients/cn=IST-Management
/C=IE;A= ;P=Digital;L=DBO-EXCHANGE960314142937FA00010191996.3.14 14:29:40
/O=Digital Equipment Corporation/OU=Dublin/CN=Recipients/CN=JohnH
/C=IE;A= ;P=Digital;L=DBO-EXCHANGE960314142937FA00010191996.3.14 14:29:40
/O=Digital Equipment Corporation/OU=Dublin/CN=Recipients/CN=PeterM
/C=IE;A= ;P=Digital;L=DBO-EXCHANGE960314142937FA00010191996.3.14 14:29:40
/O=Digital Equipment Corporation/OU=Dublin/CN=Recipients/CN=EricP
/C=IE;A= ;P=Digital;L=DBO-EXCHANGE960314142937FA00010191996.3.14 14:29:40
/O=Digital Equipment Corporation/OU=Dublin/CN=Recipients/CN=JamesR
```

Figure 11.6
Extract (above)
from a message
tracking log

Once all the recipients have been determined the MTA can begin to deliver the message. This occurs in a series of delivery operations (code 9), one for each recipient. The recipient is clearly indicated by recording their directory name in the log. If the message is transferred to another system via a connector the connector's name will be shown in the log. Apart from their obvious use in message tracking exercises there is no formal requirement to keep tracking logs for any length of time. If you find that tracking logs are occupying too much storage you can delete some or all of the logs to free up some space. However, if something with relatively low storage demands is causing disk storage problems perhaps it is a good hint that now is an excellent time to buy another disk?

11.2.2   Using the Track Message command

Browsing through large amounts of tracking log data is an interesting experience once, but not something you want to do every day. The Track Message command provides an easy to use graphical interface to the data contained in message tracking logs and the steps necessary to interpret the data and follow the message from server to server. As an example we'll use the graphical interface to track the message described in the extract from the tracking log shown in Figure 11.6.

Tracking a message is a two-stage process:

1. First, select the message to be tracked.

2. Track the selected message via the "Message Tracking Center."

Selecting a message means that you provide Exchange with search criteria to filter the contents of message tracking logs in order to find messages that meet the stated criteria. You can elect to search the current tracking log (the default option) or search back through as many tracking logs as are available on a server. Searches can also be carried out against tracking logs stored on remote servers, an operation that can be quite slow if the network is occupied or the remote server is busy. Once a message is being tracked the logs on all the servers in the relevant site are automatically searched.

Figure 11.7
Selecting a
message to track

Clearly the better and more focused the search criteria the fewer messages will be discovered and the bigger chance that the messages found will actually be the ones you are interested in. The message we're interested in was sent by Tony Redmond to the Exchange IST distribution list. This information can be entered into the form (see Figure 11.7) as the initial search criteria. We weren't quite sure when the message was sent, so the logs for the last seven days are to be scanned. After the search is executed we find that eight messages meet the criteria. Any of these messages can then be selected for tracking. Once a message is selected we return to the Message Tracking Center where the actual tracking process can begin.

Tracking begins after the "Track" button is pressed and is accomplished by scanning the tracking log files to interpret the actions performed for the message. Each action is then displayed to the screen to allow the system administrator to see exactly how the message was processed. If you look at Figure 11.8 you'll see a graphical view of the conclusions we reached when the extract of the tracking log was analyzed earlier. As you can imagine, it's a lot easier to click a few buttons than it is to delve into the depths of a tracking log. At the bottom part of the routing steps displayed in Figure 11.8 you can just see that several attempts were made to reroute the message to a server called OFFICENT1, the site's bridgehead server for connections to other sites. If you select one of the entries and then click on the Properties button a little more information is revealed (Figure 11.9).

The properties information doesn't tell us that anything has really gone wrong, but the fact that multiple attempts were made to transfer a message indicates that the connection between the server and OFFICENT1 was inoperative at the time. The fact that a number of attempts were made to transfer the message confirms that a problem existed.

Figure 11.10
Properties for a transferred message

Eventually the OFFICENT1 server became available and the message was transferred. Viewing the properties of the transferred message tells us the names of the mailboxes on the remote site or system (Figure 11.10).

At this point in time we might think that all deliveries have been made, but the Message Tracking Center now proceeds to consult the tracking logs on the remote system to see what happened after the message arrived. Details of events are displayed as they are uncovered, and we can see that an internal report was generated after the message was handed over to OFFICENT1 (Figure 11.11). Internal reports usually indicate that the message encountered a problem along its route. In this instance the recipient mailboxes in the remote site couldn't be found, so NDR (non delivery receipt) messages were generated by the MTA to report this fact back to the originator.

Apart from the problem leading to generation of NDRs, the final set of information displayed by the Message Tracking Center shows that tracking could not be performed for recipients whose mailboxes are located on the local server DPSW08 because message tracking has not been enabled on that server.

Figure 11.11
*Problems with a
message on a
remote system*

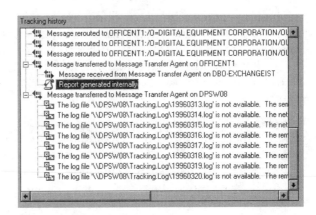

No message tracking system is ever perfect in the eyes of everyone who tries to use it. It's either too simple and doesn't display enough information or too complex and can't be used by normal human beings. The message tracking system in Exchange walks a line down the middle and as such will satisfy the vast majority of system administrators. If you're not happy with the out-of-the-box facilities you can always write your own tracking utility based on the data collected in the message tracking logs.

11.3   The Exchange Load Simulator

We've already discussed how you might approach the selection of hardware for Exchange servers, but how can you be sure that a particular configuration will perform to any given level? Do you depend on figures supplied by hardware vendors, or do you attempt to carry out your own tests, preferably in the same type of environment that you expect a production server to operate in?

Microsoft supplies a tool called LoadSim (Load Simulator) to help assess hardware configurations. You'll find the necessary files in the \SUPPORT\LOADSIM directory of the Exchange CD. Using LoadSim is easy—just double-click on LOADSIM.EXE and you'll be started, but before we do that let's consider what the tool is designed to do and the different steps you have to go through in order to use it properly.

A new version of the load simulator program is packaged with Exchange V5.0. The new version differs in a number of key areas. It is less customizable than LoadSim V4.0, uses a non-text file to hold test results, and does not show any indication of the current score. It's surprising to see Microsoft reducing functionality in such a useful program, but perhaps they have plans for future versions that we don't know of today. LoadSim V4.0 works with Exchange V5.0, as long as you run on Windows NT 3.51. Some of the steps, including User Initialization do not complete successfully on Windows NT V4.0. Load-Sim V5.0 runs with both Exchange V4.0 and V5.0, but only on Windows NT V4.0. The description in the remainder of this section is based on LoadSim V4.0, largely because it is more functional.

In simple terms LoadSim allows you simulate the workload generated by multiple concurrently connected clients. Multi-threaded processes running on one or more computers (Windows NT servers or workstations), each of which has the Exchange client software installed generate the workload. Windows 95 clients can be used to place additional load on the server during the test but Windows 95 doesn't offer the operating system features necessary to support such a simulation. Up to several hundred clients can be simulated from a single computer, meaning that it's easy to conduct your own tests on different hardware configurations. You certainly don't have to create a hugely complex testing laboratory to test hardware with LoadSim.

Figure 11.12
Defining parameters for LoadSim

LoadSim works by generating a number of processes, typically no more than 30. Each process represents a set of clients, each represented by a separate thread within the process. During the simulation the client threads generate MAPI calls to emulate common actions performed by real users. Commands are issued to create and send messages, to add recipients and distribution lists to messages, to read messages that have arrived in user mailboxes, to create appointments with Schedule+, and so on.

11.3.1   Different client mixes

Note that the current load simulation workload is biased towards Exchange clients and does not take Outlook, POP3, or Web clients into account. If you're interested in using these clients you need to adjust the results from the simulation. No good quantative information exists yet to tell us how the results should be adjusted to arrive at accurate determinations. We need to see how these other clients behave in production environments before we can make such determinations, and in any case, client behavior differs radically from company to company, so you will always have to put the results into context. In the interim, let me suggest some adjustments you might like to use as a basepoint.

- If using Outlook clients, reduce the number of supported clients by 10%. The logic here is that Outlook makes more extensive use of Exchange server folders. For example, to store calendar and contact information.

- If using POP3 clients, increase the number of supported clients by 50%. POP3 clients use a much simpler messaging model so they should decrease the load each client imposes on the server. 50% is an arbitrary figure selected to be safe rather than setting an expectation that Exchange server might be able to support twice the number of POP3 clients as it can for Exchange clients. This might well be the case, but I want to see firm evidence first.

- If using Web clients, increase the number of supported clients by 30%. Web clients make less demand on the server than Exchange clients, but have more functionality than POP3 clients.

- If using a mixture of clients, the figure reported by LoadSim can probably be taken as is. The extra load imposed by one client type will offset the advantage gained by using one of the other clients.

Microsoft will release an updated LoadSim test in the future. I expect the simulator to allow you to specify different client mixes at that point.

11.3.2   Load Simulator Test phases

A LoadSim test is broken down into a number of phases:

1. **The topology for the test is defined.** In other words, what elements of an Exchange organization (specifically the servers) will be used to conduct the test. You can define how many accounts for simulated clients will be allocated to each server used for the test. You can also define the type of users profile to use during the test (see Figure 11.12), whether public folders are used, and if so,

how many are stored on each server. If you want the test to include the extra processing required to expand distribution lists you can specify that these should be configured into the test. Distribution list configuration means specifying parameters such as the minimum, maximum, and average number of recipients per list.

2. **Generation of user accounts.** LoadSim uses a specific naming convention for the user mailboxes employed during the simulation. Details of these mailboxes have to be generated into a file suitable for importing into the Exchange directory on the system under test. When the file is imported the mailboxes are created in a new "LoadSim" recipients container. Note that you don't need to create separate Windows NT accounts for each mailbox because the import file grants access to all accounts to the Windows NT "Domain Users" group, enabling any account in the local domain to access all LoadSim mailboxes. If you want to run a test across multiple domains or you have other reasons to force LoadSim to use specific accounts you can edit the import file to specify other account permissions. Three separate import files are created—the directory import (to set up the mailboxes) and separate import files to set X.400 and SMTP addresses for each mailbox. You only need to import the directory import file if you conduct tests within a single Exchange organization (the norm).

3. **User and public folder initialization.** LoadSim needs to place some messages into user mailboxes for use during the simulation. The user initialization (known as the "UserInit" test) phase cycles through all the mailboxes and creates the necessary messages in each one. If you have included public folders in the simulation you should run the public folders initialization test. This step populates public folders with some test data. Before running these tests you can specify various parameters through property pages. For example, what recipients to use.

4. **Execute the load simulation test.** This can only be done properly after all the other steps are complete. You can give a name to each test scenario you create. The scenario defines how long the test should last (it can last forever, meaning that the test can be stopped at any time), the length of a typical user day, whether users should log off at night-time (a test can span several working days) and empty their deleted items folder, and whether clients log-off during the working day. You can even compress the standard length of day from 8 hours to 4 or less, creating an effect of very busy users who place more stress on the system.

All of the information you enter to specify settings for a test (topology, number of users, parameters, etc.) is stored in a file with a .SIM extension. This allows you to repeat tests under the same conditions across multiple LoadSim sessions. The parameter file also allows you to run LoadSim from a command line prompt or from a batch file as follows:

```
C:> LoadSim simulation_file_name test_name /q
```

for example:

```
C:> LoadSim LargeServer.SIM FullTest /q
```

This command instructs LoadSim to recreate the simulation scenario described in the LargeServer.SIM file and then proceed to run the test called FullTest. If the name of a test is not specified LoadSim will open but won't attempt to run a test. The /q parameter instructs LoadSim to terminate after the specified test is complete.

Figure 11.13
*Load Simulation
test in progress*

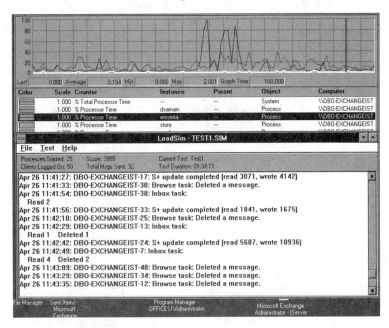

During the test the actions being simulated for clients are echoed to the LoadSim window, allowing you to see exactly what's going on. Figure 11.13 illustrates results being echoed to the LoadSim window with a performance monitor also active (see the discussion later on in this chapter). Running the performance monitor during the simulation allows you to see how different system components respond to the test load. Test results are logged to a file for later analysis. If multiple client computers are used each produces a log file. All of the log files from a test can be merged together at the end in order to create a single file for analysis. You don't have to have a dedicated test system to run Load-Sim. The utility will run happily on any Exchange server. If you decide to run a simulation on a production system be aware of several side effects:

- The test recipients are created in the special LoadSim container.

- Details of the test recipients are automatically added to the global address list.

- The volume of messages created and sent during the test will impact the private and public information stores. PRIV.EDB and PUB.EDB will both expand as all the test messages are created and sent, and a large series of transaction logs are also written. It is possible to exhaust disk space if you're not careful, so make sure that the Performance Optimizer has been run before the test to distribute Exchange files across all available disk spindles. Also check that there's at least 200MB free on the disks where information stores and transaction logs are located.

It's a good idea to take a backup of the information stores before starting the test and compact them afterwards with the EDBUTIL utility. On test systems the ISWIPE utility (provided on the Exchange CD-ROM) can be used to completely erase the contents of the information store. It goes without saying that it's unwise to run ISWIPE without knowing what you're doing.

A test can be stopped at any time or allowed to run through to its designated completion time. If you elect to stop a test the results are only an indication of the events processed up to that time. Not all client processes may have connected, only a subset of message types might have been sent, and perhaps only some of the public folder manipulations may have been carried out. Stopping a test too early leads to unreliable results. You have to let the test run for long enough for the simulation to stabilize and have produced enough results to be meaningful when analyzed. Microsoft's Performance Testing Group runs tests for between six and eight hours when they measure hardware configurations, a good indication of what they feel is an appropriate timespan.

11.3.3   Using the LsLog utility

LsLog, the LoadSim Performance Log Parser, is a command line executable that can be found in the same directory as LoadSim. The major function of this utility is to analyze the log files recorded during a simulation test. The results or answers delivered by LsLog after it has analyzed the logs are 95th percentile [2] results for all of the actions tested during the simulation as well as a weighted average 95th percentile for all actions. The results are reported in milliseconds, so lower values are better because the system has taken less time to respond to a client request to perform an action. If you compare two similar hardware configurations with the same test and one configuration delivers better results than the other it should be a fair indication of which one to use for production purposes. Don't always accept results without question. In a situation where you compare two similar configurations and find one performs significantly better than the other by a wide margin (more than 10%), ask the question whether the two configurations are really so similar. Are the network controllers identical? What disk controllers are used? Is there more memory cache in one system than the other? Because errors can arise during the set-up of test scenarios knowledge of Exchange and PC hardware is invaluable when conducting tests and then interpreting results afterwards. The steps to use LsLog to analyze a performance log file are as follows:

- Merge the performance logs from each computer participating in the test. Ignore this step if only one computer is used.

- Extract a specific time window from the log. This is an optional step as the default is to analyze the entire log. Extracting a time window allows you to focus on a period after the test scenario has stabilized.

- Use the LsLog "answer" option to generate the 95th percentile results for the actions recorded in the performance log. The results are displayed to the screen, but can also be redirected to a file for inclusion in a report or distribution by mail. Figure 11.14 illustrates results achieved from a simulation.

Figure 11.14
Sample results from a simulation run, as reported by LsLog

Category	Weight	Hits	95th Percentile
SEND	1	27	11084
Sub-weight	16	6	48640
Sub-weight	2	1	1863
Sub-weight	5	2	721
Sub-weight	60	15	2914
Sub-weight	4	3	991
READ	10	535	801
REPLY	1	6	1412
REPLY ALL	1	5	2103
FORWARD	1	56	1222

[2]   In other words, 95% of all response times recorded were equal to or below the reported value. 95th percentile measurements are often found in statistical analyses.

```
MOVE            1    104    490
DELETE          2    206    411
SUBMIT          0     94    942
RESOLVE NAME    0     83    560
LOAD IMSG       0     41   1712
DELIVER         0    236    660
Weighted Avg   17   1393   1479
```

Some sample LsLog commands:

```
C:> LsLog Merge System1.Log System2.Log > Systems.Log
C:> LsLog Truncate Systems.Log 2 4 > Test.Log
C:> LsLog Answer Test.Log > Results.Txt
```

These commands merge System1.Log and System2.Log (performance log files from two client computers) to form Systems.Log, which is then stripped of data spanning four hours' testing (for 2 clients). The stripped test log is then analyzed and the test scores written into Results.Txt.

11.3.4   Putting results into context

Even after carrying out a successful test it's important to put the results into a realistic context. For example, you should realize that LoadSim is able to run everything on a single computer. That's fine, but in a production environment clients will connect to servers over the network, so the LoadSim results need to be adjusted because they don't account for any network latency or fallibility. It's important to ensure that the network bandwidth available to servers is sufficient to handle client connections in real life.

The type of messages used during the test is another item to bear in mind. Unless you customize the test by adding a set of messages you have determined to be typical, the set of default messages is quite simple. Some of the default messages contain Word and Excel attachments, and there's even one with an embedded bitmap image. Useful as these messages are they may not reflect the type of messages sent by your users, and they don't test the impact of users sending very large messages or messages with lots of complex attachments. They do, however, deliver a reasonably weighted average of the type of messages seen in general messaging, which is possibly the type of system you'll operate.

LoadSim runs in an artificial environment. That's obvious because real human beings are not producing the load placed on the server under test. Aside from the human factor there's another huge influence that is never seen in a load simulation. No real network activity is ongoing. You might try and create the same type of Exchange organization (sites, connectors, directory replication connectors, and so on) to run the servers in while they are under test, but it is impossible to generate exactly the same stress that will be seen in production. You might well get to a 70% level (my best guess), but it's awfully difficult to move on from this point. There's no way, for instance, to simulate the complex RPC-driven interaction that occurs between servers in a site as they communicate with each other to update the directories and process interpersonal mail. The impact of a fax or other connector is difficult to simulate as well.

Finally, the server should run the same set of applications during the test that you expect to run in production. Executing a test for Exchange only is only useful if you want to compare one hardware configuration against another, as in the case when you might want to compare two Intel Pentium-powered systems from different vendors against each other. Depending on the other components wrapped around the CPU, two systems with apparently the same CPU type and clock speed can differ in real delivered performance by 10% or more.

11.4   Using the Windows NT Performance Monitor

The Windows NT Performance Monitor provides a graphical interface to allow many different aspects of a Windows NT system to be monitored. The utility provides charting, alerting, and reporting capabilities to report live data as it is generated by applications or to capture performance data to log files for later analysis. Performance Monitor depends on applications having probes or points of measurement buried in the code, ready to provide information to the monitor should the need arise.

Windows NT refers to the items being monitored as objects, and objects can be:

- Aspects of the system itself such as memory usage
- An individual process
- A section of shared memory
- A physical device.

In the case of Exchange you'll be interested in monitoring aspects of the many services that collectively deliver functionality to users. Important Exchange objects that can be monitored include those shown in Table 11.1.

Table 11.1 *Important Exchange Services for Performance Monitor*

Service Name	Meaning
MSExchangeDS	The Directory Store
MSExchangeISPriv	The Private Information Store
MSExchangeISPub	The Public Information Store
MSExchangeDX	Directory Synchronization
MSExchangeMTA	The MTA
MSExchangeIMC	The Internet Mail Service

Each object is broken down into "counters." Monitoring tracks the counts of specific events and allows system administrators to report what it's found. Normally reporting is done graphically, as shown in Figure 11.15, perhaps on a dedicated workstation. Any counter supported by the Windows NT Performance Monitor can be exposed to and collected by an SNMP network-based monitoring service (such as HP's OpenView product). You can use the PERF2MIB utility (from the Windows NT Resource Kit) to generate HP OpenView or IBM NetView compatible MIBs (SNMP Management Information Base) from any Performance Monitor counter. The MIBs allow the performance data collected about Exchange to be reported and monitored by these popular SNMP management tools. It's worth noting here that the version of PERF2MIB in the Windows NT V4.0 Resource Kit is a huge improvement over its V3.51 counterpart. Apart from some bugs being eliminated, PERF2MIB works almost all the time now.

Figure 11.15
"Server Health"
Performance
Monitor

When you start a Performance Monitor session you must tell it what objects and counters you're interested in. This process involves selecting from a list of available objects and counters and adding them to the "workspace," a description of the current monitoring environment.

When you're happy with a set of parameters that record whatever data you need to log, the whole scenario can be saved in the form of a workspace file. When you install Exchange onto a Windows NT computer a number of prepackaged performance monitor workspaces are installed into the \EXCHSRVR\BIN directory. The set of workspaces is divided between five that are useful on all servers and three specifically for servers running the IMC.

Because the performance monitor scenarios have been developed as Exchange evolved through the different stages in the product's development process, they therefore capture the most important statistics based on knowledge of server and system behavior. The workspaces describe scenarios that are very usable and useful in their own right and provide an excellent starting point for system administrators who wish to develop performance monitor workspaces tailored to fit their own server environment.

For example, EXHEALTH.PMW holds the parameters for the "Server Health" workspace illustrated in Figure 11.15. To make things easier for system administrators, pointers to each workspace are created as icons in the Exchange Server program group. A full list of the prepackaged workspaces is shown in Table 11.2.

Table 11.2 *Pre-Packaged Performance Monitor workspaces*

Packaged Performance Monitor workspace	Important statistics tracked in workspace
Server Health	Overall % processor time; % processor used by directory store; % processor used by MTA; % processor used by information store; system paging.
Server Load	Rate messages are delivered to recipients; rate messages are submitted by clients; number of connections to other MTAs; address book activity.
Server History (since server was last stated)	Total messages delivered and submitted to users; total messages sent by MTA; total recipients for messages; number of users connected to the server; length of work queues (messages waiting to be processed by the MTA); system paging.
Server Users	Number of users currently connected to the information store.
Server Queues	Number of items in the MTA work queue; number of items in the send and receive queues for the private and public information stores.

Table 11.2 *Pre-Packaged Performance Monitor workspaces (continued)*

Packaged Performance Monitor workspace	Important statistics tracked in workspace
IMCTraffic	Number of inbound and outbound connections to other SMTP hosts; number of messages awaiting conversion to and from SMTP/MIME format.
IMCStatistics (since server was last started)	Total number of messages delivered to the Internet Mail Service and the total number of messages sent out to the Internet.
IMCQueues	Number of messages coming in from the Internet; number of messages going out to the Internet; number of messages waiting final delivery to recipients.

In cases where message submission and delivery activity is being tracked it is normal to collect separate figures for the private and public information store. Private information store activity relates to interpersonal messaging, that is, messages generated and sent between people. Public information store activity relates to messages and other documents posted to public folders. On most servers it would be safe to expect that the private information store gets more work to do than the public, the exception being those servers dedicated to public folder storage.

Which of the pre-packaged workspaces are most useful? It all depends on the workload of your servers, but my favorites are:

- Server Health
- Server History
- IMCTraffic

All servers should have some indication that the system is running smoothly. I find the "Server Health" workspace provides a good overall picture of what's going on at any particular point in time.

Figure 11.15 is a good example of the active workspace. You can see that there is a lot of activity in one of the counters because its line is at the top of the chart at the left-hand side (most recent figures). It's not obvious from the screen shot (because the different colors used for the counters are not reproduced), but the very active counter is system paging, expressed as paging operations per second. The other lines, including that for the MTA counter (shown as the white line), display a fair amount of activity, so clearly this computer is doing a reasonable amount of work. If system paging exhibited the same rate of activity during normal daily operations a system administrator would be worried because it's delivering a strong indication that the computer is overloaded. In this instance there's a reasonable explanation: the screen shot was taken shortly after the computer was rebooted, and all the system services, including the Exchange services, had just been restarted. Just listen to the disk activity after a system is rebooted and you'll immediately realize that a great deal of work is done in this period, as reflected in the results charted by the counters in the "System Health" workspace.

As to my other favorites, I like running "Server History" from time to time just to see what workload the computer has processed since it was last restarted. The figures reported in this chart vary greatly and depend on the number of days since the last reboot. However, a browse through the different counters sometimes provokes questions that should be answered. For example, is there any reason why the computer has processed a larger number of messages than normal?

Systems running the Internet Mail Service, especially those that connect internal messaging networks to the big (sometimes bad) world of the Internet, need careful monitoring if reliable message delivery times are to be guaranteed to users. The "IMCTraffic" workspace captures and displays details of all the most important IMCcounters.

Feel free to disagree with my opinions. Play around with the prepackaged workspaces and make changes if you like, but don't add too many counters to any workspace as the chart will become very cluttered and difficult to interpret. The important thing is to ensure that monitoring is a part of day-to-day system administration and not just an activity that's engaged in whenever problems appear on the horizon.

11.5 Logging and viewing Windows NT events

Windows NT logs a great deal of information about different events that occur during applications and system processing. Event information is initially logged internally, and can be written to a file if required for later analysis, or to be used as evidence relating to a problem. The Windows NT Event Viewer (Figure 11.16) allows you to view event logs on any server you have access to. On any moderately large server many events are generated each day, so filters can be applied if you know you're looking for a particular problem. For example, you could apply a filter to view only events relating to the MTA.

Exchange uses the Windows NT Event log to record information specific to the processing performed by Exchange components such as the MTA, Key Management Server, or Internet Mail Service (to name but a few). All Exchange events are deemed to be "application" events rather than system or other events. The Exchange Resource Kit contains a number of tools to help you filter and store event information related to Exchange.

Figure 11.16
Windows NT Event Viewer

You can influence the amount of information logged through the diagnostics property of these components, but be aware that it is all too easy to generate vast amounts of data if you enable maximum event logging. Few people have the patience and knowledge to be able to make very much sense of the huge quantity of events logged at full flow by the Exchange MTA (Figure 11.17).

Figure 11.17
Turning on diagnostics

The quantity of data produced when full diagnostic logging is enabled has the capacity to exhaust the space reserved for the Event Log after a couple of minutes on any reasonably sized server. You will be forced to clear the log and save existing data to a file if you want to continue to record information. For these reasons it's best to leave diagnostic logging at minimal levels in day-to-day operation and reserve full diagnostic levels for the times when it's justified, for instance, when requested by a support center to help track down the root cause of a problem.

Even when minimal diagnostics are enabled the Event log should be browsed on a daily basis to ensure that problems aren't being recorded and then missed. Any event associated with Exchange that is not information status (shown as an "i" surrounded by a blue circle) must be investigated and the reason why the event was logged determined to your satisfaction. Failure to do this might lead to a situation where a small problem develops into something that's rather more serious.

Event logs should also be checked immediately after a system has been restarted. This step is to ensure that all the Exchange services have started correctly.

11.6   The Exchange Resource Kit

All large and complex applications generate spin-offs; small pieces of code (sometimes large pieces of code) that are useful add-ons to standard functionality, or documents which explain finer or less obvious parts of the product. Sometimes the spin-offs are written by engineers to help test functionality or find bugs during the development process, sometimes they're written by people who aren't part of the main development project but are knowledgeable about the product. The Exchange developers have created a collection of useful tools and documents available to you as the "Exchange Resource Kit." The latest version of the Resource Kit can be found in the Exchange section on Microsoft's TechNet CD[3] (from May 1996 onwards) or it can be downloaded from Microsoft's Web site[4].

New versions of the Resource Kit will appear over time, certainly to correspond with new versions of Exchange, so there is a brand new Resource Kit now available for Exchange V5.0. Because of this you should check the Web for new versions on a regular basis.

It's fair to assume that the code and documents provided in the Resource Kit haven't gone through the same quality assurance process

---

[3]   See the Technical Resource CD-ROM Components section.

[4]   See http://www.microsoft.com/Exchange/freesoft.htm for kit information. A table of contents for the Resource Kit can be found at http://www.microsoft.com/Exchange/techcd.htm. Note that the Exchange Resource Kit is approx 30MB (as of May 1996) and will therefore take a long time to download, even over a relatively fast connection. A TechNet subscription looks like a good value if you want access to "free" software like this.

imposed on the regular product. If you elect to follow the suggestions in non-approved documents or use code that hasn't been through a full quality assurance process you have to live with any of the consequences arising from those actions. Any of the code from the kit I have used appears to be of high quality and is reluctant to fall over, but I can imagine situations where personnel in support centers might be less than happy to deal with installations using what they perceive to be "non-standard" code.

The Exchange modeling tool (see page 134) is also part of the Exchange Resource Kit. Currently, all tools are provided for Intel systems only, but versions for other hardware platforms can be expected to ship over time. The tools are only available in English, a fact that shouldn't cause too many problems because the majority of non-US system administrators have been forced to learn English and work with system management utilities through English due to the volume of software originating from the US or UK.

Figure 11.18
Message store
analyzer

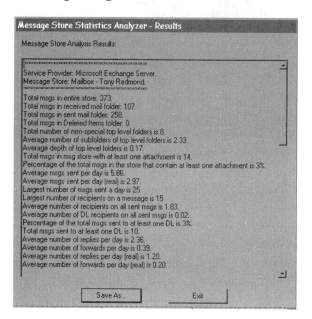

The majority of the extensions packaged in the Resource Kit are directed at system administrators. The usefulness of these tools will depend on the situation in your own company. STORSTAT, the Message store statistics analyzer (see Figure 11.18) is of interest if you want to know what's really contained in a user's mailboxes, but you're probably not likely to use the analyzer on a regular basis. On the other hand the mailbox cleanup agent is an automated version of the standard "Clean Mailbox" administrator program option and is of interest to anyone who wants to keep a tight rein on the number of messages people keep in their mailboxes. Instead of having to manually select the user mailboxes to clean, the mailbox cleanup agent allows cleanups to occur in the background. You can determine which mailboxes are to be cleaned, the folders to be examined, and the criteria on which to select messages for deletion and the frequency of clean up operations. Having such a tool at your disposal is a great help in the continuing battle to keep control of information store resources.

Anyone engaged in the often onerous task of setting up and maintaining directory synchronization between Exchange and other messaging systems will be glad of the tools that graphically aid to create directory header files or help convert Exchange source information to the format demanded by other systems. The best example in this respect is Exchange to Microsoft Mail.

Figure 11.19
Exchange client for Windows 95 with the preview pane extension

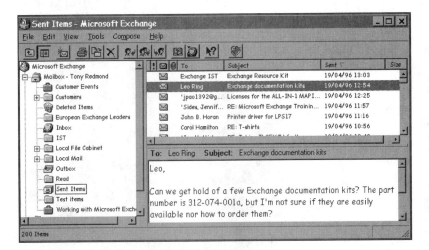

Other items in the Resource Kit are of interest from a user perspective and can be used on a daily basis. The preview pane extension allows the first couple of lines from a message to be displayed in a separate pane within the client window, as illustrated in Figure 11.19. Unfortunately this useful tool is only available for 32-bit clients (Windows 95 and Windows NT). Out of the box the Outlook client supports different views of message content. One of the standard views is able to display the first couple of lines of a message. This isn't quite the same as the preview pane, so Microsoft has released a separate preview pane extension for Outlook, which is available for download from the Microsoft Web site [5].

---

[5]   See http://www.microsoft.com/OfficeFreeStuff/Outlook/ (link valid as of April 1997).

12

Bringing It All Together—How to Proceed

12.1 Things you'll enjoy about Exchange Server

These are the best things I've enjoyed when working with Exchange. Selecting aspects of a product that are pleasing is a very personal activity, so feel free to disagree . . . The points are not listed in any order of importance because they're all important.

- **MAPI.** The power and flexibility of the Messaging Application Program Interface can be seen in Microsoft's own clients as well as the MAPI service providers appearing from other vendors.

- **Exchange clients** are easy and powerful to use, even if they require fairly substantial hardware resources for truly satisfactory performance. Microsoft has followed their own user interface standards to good effect. Outlook is an interesting alternative to the standard client and is the right choice for 32-bit desktops. The Web client is a splendid example of excellence in user interface design for Web applications, although its splendor has to be paid for by network bandwidth.

- **Single point of administration.** Maybe it's missing some features that I'd like to see included, but the Exchange Administration program is the most integrated messaging administration utility I've ever encountered to date.

- **The transactional nature of the information store** is a huge advance on Microsoft's previous file sharing architecture. It's also at the center of Exchange's ability to scale up for corporate implementations. The single-file-entity nature of databases poses challenges of its own, but good planning minimizes these while optimizing the store's capabilities.

- **The Exchange MTA** almost manages to bring plug and play capabilities to the e-mail world. It also coordinates connectors for different messaging systems in a very nice manner.

- **The Exchange connectors** are generally reliable, robust, and extremely fast. The Internet Mail service deserves special mention.

- **The Exchange Resource Kit** is a mine of useful information. It's backed up by TechNet. Together a lot of knowledge and useful tools on Exchange, Windows NT, and other products is available for those who care to search it out.

- **Advanced security** delivers encryption and digital signatures for those who really need them. You have to invest time and energy to deploy advanced security, but once it's implemented advanced security delivers what it promises.

- **Integration between a messaging system and its host operating system** has moved to a new level with Exchange. Account management, performance monitor, event logging, backup, and all the other points of integration make Windows NT and Exchange work together in a great combination act.

- **The Load Simulation utility** is something every messaging system should provide. Being able to conduct your own automated benchmarks is great!

12.2   Some things that aren't so good

Nothing in life is ever perfect, and Exchange certainly doesn't attain that unreachable standard (despite the best efforts of Microsoft's undoubted marketing muscle). I have my own black list of pitfalls and imperfections. I imagine that Microsoft will address many of these as new versions of Exchange are rolled out over the next few years. At least, I hope they will. In the meantime you can avoid these areas of difficulty!

- **Directory synchronization** is the black hole of Exchange because lots of system administrators will spend many aimless hours wandering around unless they run a pure Exchange environment or only ever have to synchronize with Microsoft Mail. Moving away from the antiquated scheme used to synchronize the Microsoft Mail global address list to support a standard (and API) for directory synchronization is an essential step for the future. Directory synchronization should occupy many hours of Exchange administrators' time and be a happy hunting ground for third party tools.

- **The migration source extractors** vary in quality. I wonder how some managed to get through Microsoft's normally excellent QA cycle. They are certainly nowhere near the same level of quality achieved elsewhere in Exchange.

- **Inter-site mailbox transfers** are a complex manual process. Why can't it be as easy as moving a mailbox within a site?

- **Inter-organization communications** (aside from messaging) doesn't appear to have been considered necessary. But people will move between operating companies within a group, or from an organizational unit in one country to another where each country wants to do its own thing. In short, it's not always going to be possible to go with a single organizational unit so it would be nice to be able to have items like advanced security, scheduling, user mailbox moves, and public folder replication supported on an inter-organization basis.

- **Conflict handling** for updates applied to multiple copies of a document in a replicated public folder is not neat. Surely it should be possible to lock a document for exclusive write access without having to set permissions on the entire folder each time?

- **Backups are great, but restores aren't.** Accidents will happen and restores will be necessary. Restoring a user mailbox without having to restore the entire information store would save a lot of time and money. In fact, needing to restore the entire information store when problems arise is going to cause a lot of system managers sleepless nights. Be sure you have a "hot-box" server waiting to swap in to replace failed hardware, and practice restore. All Exchange implementations need a well thought-out disaster recovery plan, just in case.

- **The integration and dependency with Windows NT is a double edged sword** because it's all too easy to mess up an Exchange implementation by not paying enough attention to the underlying Windows NT infrastructure. Microsoft can't do much about this point, but I make it yet again in the hope that a loud and clear message goes out—get Windows NT right first before trying to do anything with Exchange. As we go towards Windows NT V5.0 the importance of getting NT right before starting with Exchange increases.

- **There is a lack of enterprise-wide monitoring and management tools** so knowing exactly what's happening on your Exchange servers is quite difficult. Capturing information like statistics (number of messages in the store, who owns them, number of messages sent in a period) or configuration data (human-friendly routing tables, details of connectors and other setup data) is too hard for a system aspiring to be a true enterprise solution. It is also far too difficult to split sites up, or merge them together.

- **Network planning for Exchange requires too many finger in the air type guesses.** The amount of network traffic within a site is unpredictable, especially when there are more than 10 servers. Communication between sites can be controlled, but only if you go to the trouble of setting schedules for public folder content and directory replication.

12.3   10 essential points to get right when implementing Exchange

Distilling the content of this book into a single page is not easy, but lots of people demand a road-map to follow when planning the implementation of Microsoft Exchange Server. With this request in mind I have created my own "Top-10" issues to consider and decide upon before an implementation begins.

Table 12.1 *10 Essential points*

	Issue	See Chapter(s):
1	Design the Windows NT infrastructure.	3
2	Plan how Windows NT will be layered onto the internal network.	3
3	Chart out the Exchange organization in terms of the sites and servers. Determine how the sites will communicate in terms of message flow, public folders, and all aspects of replication.	3
4	Determine what platforms are to be used for both servers and clients. Will you use Windows 95 or NT on the desktop? Also, what hardware configurations will be used for both clients and servers?	4
5	Design the naming conventions for use within the Exchange organization—sites, servers, and mailboxes.	3, 6
6	Determine where the points of external communications will lie and what connectors (SMTP, X.400, Microsoft Mail, others) will be used to connect Exchange with other mail systems. Also, do you need to create a corporate mail directory by synchronizing with other mail directories?	3, 7, 8
7	Look at how public folders can be used to address business needs and requirements within your enterprise. What folders are needed? Where will they be located? Who will control their content? Will electronic forms be required?	5
8	Consider how the Windows NT computers will be managed. What system administration policies will be implemented to cover important topics such as backups?	5
9	If you are migrating from another electronic mail system what plan are you going to follow to migrate users and their data to Exchange?	10
10	Create a training plan that accommodates the needs of users, programmers, and system administrators so that the true power of Microsoft Exchange Server can be unleashed.	9

These issues are not presented in order of importance. However, it's obvious that the first three issues should be tackled before anything else. While I encourage you to conduct a pilot so that you gain valuable experience with Exchange, experience that will enable you to build a better plan afterwards, it is critical to have a clear and well thought-through plan before you commence a full implementation. Experience is a hard master, but it tells that taking short cuts just to get a system into operation can have disastrous consequences afterwards!

12.4   The Exchange manager's toolkit

Managing any computer system is a challenge. Having the right set of tools at hand makes everything go a lot more smoothly. Table 12.2 is my list of the items I think should be in the Exchange manager's toolkit.

Table 12.2 *An Exchange manager's toolkit*

Item	Reason
Windows NT Resource Kit	The kit contains many interesting and useful tools to help keep Windows NT systems running smoothly.
Exchange Resource Kit	Less interesting than the Windows NT resource kit, but still valuable!
Site Disaster Recovery Kit	When things go wrong you'll need your kit. It should include Windows NT repair disks, software distribution CDs (including all service packs), valid backups, documentation on the system configuration, and a cool head.
Subscription to TechNet	The CDs hold an unbelievable amount of information (but be sure to put the ideas in context for your own company), including the Knowledge Base. When things go wrong the Knowledge Base is the first port of call.
Third party products	Windows NT and Exchange system administration tools are OK, but there are some gaps, like enforcing disk quotas for users. Third party products, including backup utilities, full text retrieval systems, and virus checkers help move the system from a 95% solution towards a 100% fit.
Performance Monitor, Link and Server Monitors	Something to keep running so you know when problems arise before your users point this salient fact out to you!
Event Viewer	Check this every day!
Training vouchers	Keep on being trained! Go to the Exchange Deployment Conference and keep up to date with new versions of Windows NT and Exchange. Lots is happening at a bewildering pace.

Acronyms

The language of electronic messaging technology is full of acronyms. This appendix describes many of the acronyms used in a Microsoft Exchange environment.

BDC: Backup domain controller. A Windows NT server allocated the task of acting as a backup to the Primary Domain Controller (PDC) in case a problem arises with the PDC.

CA: Certification Authority. The Key Management Server is the Exchange component which acts as a certification authority to control X.509 security certificates.

CAST: A proprietary encryption algorithm developed by Northern Telecom.

CCITT: In English, the International Consultative Committee on Telephony and Telegraphy, a body concerned with the formulation and definition of standards for electronic communications. The CCITT is a sub-delegation of the International Telegraph Union (ITU).

DDA: Domain Defined Attribute. A DDA can be encapsulated in an X.400 O/R address to allow routing to occur through an X.400 network to a gateway which takes the DDA and uses it to deliver the message to its final recipient. In such cases the DDA holds the recipient's address in the format used by the mail system serviced by the gateway.

DES: Data Encryption Standard. An encryption algorithm developed by the US National Bureau of Standards.

DHCP: Dynamic Host Control Program.

DIB: X.500 Directory Information Base.

DIT: X.500 Directory Information Tree.

DMD: Directory Management Domain. The collection of DUAs and DSAs within an X500 directory. In an Exchange organization the DMD is represented by the set of directory services run in all sites.

DN: X.500 Distinguished Name composed of a set of RDNs.

DNS: Domain Name Service. The part of TCP/IP networks that contains and provides information about networked computer systems, basically by looking up computer names and providing the IP addresses for those that can be resolved.

DSA: Directory Service Agent. An X.500 concept of a computer process responsible for handling directory queries initiated by a DUA. The DSA will either satisfy the request itself or consult with another DSA.

DUA: Directory User Agent. An X.500 concept of a computer process that makes queries against an X.500 directory on behalf of a user.

DXA: Directory Synchronization Agent. The Exchange component responsible for synchronizing the contents of MS-Mail Global Address Lists and the Exchange directory.

FQDN: Fully Qualified Domain Name. An Internet (or Intranet) name for a computer which contains all the necessary pieces to allow data to be routed back to the computer.

GAL: Global Address List.

GWART: Gateway Address Routing Table. The internal routing table used by the Exchange MTA to determine how messages can be routed through all the connectors and gateways operating within an organization.

HTML: Hypertext Mark-Up Language. A standardized set of mark-up codes used to format pages for display by a World-Wide Web browser such as Netscape.

HTTP: Hypertext Transport Protocol. The protocol used to communicate between Web browsers and servers.

IMAP: Internet Mail Access Protocol.

ISP: Internet Service Provider. A company which provides Internet connectivity to other companies or individuals.

ISO: International Organization for Standardization.

ITU: International Telegraph Union.

KCC: Knowledge Consistency Checker. An Exchange component responsible for tracking the various links and connections that exist between different sites.

KMS: Key Management Server.

LDAP: Lightweight Directory Access Protocol. A protocol used by clients to access X.500-based directory services.

MAPI: Microsoft's Messaging Application Programming Interface.

MIB: Management Information Base for SNMP systems.

MTA: Message Transfer Agent.

MX: Mail Exchanger. A type of record stored in DNS databases.

NDR: Non Delivery Report. A special form of message sent back to users if a message they send can't be delivered.

NNTP: Net News Transfer Protocol.

PDC: Primary Domain Controller. The Windows NT server that validates all authentication and security requests within a domain. The PDC also maintains the definitive copy of the security database for the domain.

RAID: Redundant Array of Inexpensive Disks.

RAS: Remote Access Server. The component of Windows NT that permits dial-in or asynchronous connections to be made between a client and a Windows NT computer.

RDN: Relative Distinguished Name. A name used to navigate within the Exchange directory.

RFC: Request for Comment. An Internet standard.

RSA: A public key encryption standard developed by Ron Rivest, Adi Shamir, and Leonard Adleman at the Massachusetts Institute of Technology in 1977.

SMTP: Simple Mail Transport Protocol. SMTP is the de facto standard for electronic mail within the Internet.

SNMP: Simple Network Management Protocol. A protocol allowing applications and other components to be managed across a distributed network.

SPI: Service Provider Interface.

WINS: Windows Internet Name Service.

X.400: The international standard for electronic mail interchange.

X.500: The international standard for electronic directory services.

XAPI: X/Open Application Programming Interface.

XDS: X/Open Directory Services.

Useful Points of Reference

World Wide Web sites

Much useful information about Microsoft Exchange server or associated products is available from World Wide Web sites. These include:

`http://www.microsoft.com/exchange/`	General information about Microsoft Exchange server
`http://www.exchangecenter.com`	The Exchange Center (run by Microsoft)
`http://www.microsoft.com/backoffice/`	General information about Microsoft BackOffice and Windows NT
`http://www.microsoft.com/exchange/workflow.htm`	Exchange and Workflow
`http://www.microsoft.com/win32dev/mapi`	Information about MAPI
`http://www.microsoft.com/technet/boes/bo/mailexch/exch/tools/appfarm/appfarm1.htm`	Exchange "Application Farm"
`http://www.microsoft.com/Exchange/freesoft.htm`	Exchange Resource Kit
`http://www.microsoft.com/TechNet`	Microsoft TechNet information, including subscriptions
`http://www.digital.com/`	Home page for Digital Equipment Corporation
`http://altavista.digital.com/`	Alta Vista Search Engine
`http://www.anjura.com/exchfaq/`	Exchange Server Frequently Asked Questions (FAQ)
`http://www.slipstick.com/exchange/index.htm`	Slipstick Systems Microsoft Exchange center (lots of interesting information)

Internet Mailing List for Exchange

The Internet Mailing List for Microsoft Exchange is available by sending an electronic mail message to:

msexchange-request@insite.co.uk

The word "SUBSCRIBE" should appear in the body of the message. Do not include any other text. Leave the subject line blank.

File name index

File type index

Main index

A

Related Digital Press Titles

The SQL Server Handbook
A Guide to Microsoft Database Computing

Ken England

1995   480pp   1-55558-152-8   pb   DEC Part No: EY-T818E-DP $36.95

Migrating to the Intranet and Microsoft Exchange

Randall J. Covill

1997   250pp   1-55558-172-2   pb   DEC Part No: EY-V420E-DP $29.95

TCP/IP Explained

Philip Miller

1997   450pp   1-55558-166-8   pb   DEC Part No: EY-V416E-DP $39.95

Local Area Networks, 2ed
An Introduction to the Technology

John McNamara

1996   200pp   1-55558-149-8   pb   DEC Part No: EY-T854E-DP $39.95

Strategic IS/IT Planning

Ed Tozer

1995   530pp   0-7506-9666-4   pb   DEC Part No: EY-T887E-DP $51.95

Detailed information on these and all other Digital Press titles may be found in the Digital Press Catalog (Item #400). To request a copy, call 1-800-366-2665. You can also visit our web site at: http://www.bh.com/digitalpress

These books are available from all good bookstores or in case of difficulty call: 1-800-366-2665 in the U.S. or +44-1865-310366 in Europe.

E-Mail Mailing List

An e-mail mailing list giving information on latest releases, special promotions/ offers and other news relating to Digital Press titles is available. To subscribe, send an e-mail message to majordomo@world.std.com. Include in message body (not in subject line) subscribe digital-press